KING AND COUNTRY

ENGLAND AND WALES IN
THE FIFTEENTH CENTURY

RALPH A. GRIFFITHS

THE HAMBLEDON PRESS
LONDON   AND   RIO GRANDE

Published by The Hambledon Press, 1991

102 Gloucester Avenue, London NW1 8HX (U.K.)

P.O. Box 162, Rio Grande, Ohio 45672 (U.S.A.)

ISBN 1 85285 018 3

British Library Cataloguing-in-Publication Data

Griffiths, Ralph A. (Ralph Alan), *1937-*
    King and country: England and Wales in the fifteenth century.
    1. England. Monarchy. Relations with local communities, 1400-1500.
    I. Title
    354.4203'12

Library of Congress Cataloging-in-Publication Data

Griffiths, Ralph Alan
    King and country: England and Wales in the fifteenth century/
    Ralph A. Griffiths.
    Selection of essays and papers, published variously in Wales,
    England, France, and North America between 1964 and 1990.
    — Introd.
    Includes bibliographical references and index.
    1. Great Britain – History – Lancaster and York, 1399-1485.
    2. England – Civilization – Medieval period, 1066-1485.
    3. Wales – History – To 1536.
    I. Title.
DA245.G85   1991
942.04 – dc20   91-11235 CIP

Printed on acid-free paper and bound in Great Britain
by Bookcraft Ltd., Midsomer Norton

Contents

Acknowledgements

The articles and essays collected here first appeared in the following publications and are reprinted by the kind permission of the original publishers.

1 *Kings and Nobles in the Later Middle Ages*, ed. Ralph A. Griffiths and James Sherborne (Alan Sutton, Gloucester, 1986), pp. 15-46.
2 *Princes, Patronage and the Nobility: The Court at the Beginning of the Modern Age*, ed. Adolf von Birke (Oxford University Press for the German Historical Institute, 1990).
3 *Aspects of Late Medieval Government and Society*, ed. J.G. Rowe (Toronto University Press, 1986), pp. 83-105.
4 *Fifteenth-Century England, 1399-1509*, ed. S.B. Chrimes, C.D. Ross and R.A. Griffiths (Manchester University Press, 1972), pp. 145-72.
5 *Patronage, Pedigree and Power in Later Medieval England*, ed. C.D. Ross (Alan Sutton, Gloucester, 1979), pp. 13-36.
6 *Law Quarterly Review*, XCIII (1977), 248-58.
7 *Huntington Library Quarterly*, 49 (1986), 197-218.
8 *Transactions of the Royal Historical Society*, 5th Series, XXX (1980), 109-30.
9 *British Government and Administration: Studies presented to S.B. Chrimes*, ed. H. Hearder and H.R. Loyn (University of Wales Press, Cardiff, 1974), pp. 69-86.
10 *Transactions of the Bristol and Gloucestershire Archaeological Society*, LXXXIII (1964), 70-77.
11 *National Library of Wales Journal*, XIII (1964), 256-68.
12 *Welsh History Review*, II (1965), 213-31.
13 *Annales de Bretagne et de l'Ouest*, LXXXVI (1979), 399-403 (translated into English).
14 *Transactions of the Hampshire Field Club and Archaeological Society*, XXXIII (1977), 89-93.
15 *Bulletin of the John Rylands Library*, LI (1969), 381-99.
16 *Huntington Library Quarterly*, XLII (1979), 181-91.
17 *Welsh History Review*, VIII (1976), 14-25.
18 *Journal of Medieval History*, I (1975), 187-209.
19 *English Historical Review*, XCIX (1984), 67-82.
20 *Speculum*, XLIII (1968), 589-632.
21 *Midland History*, V (1980), 1-19.

FOR MY MOTHER
MARION LOVIN GRIFFITHS

Introduction

This selection of essays and papers, published variously in Wales, England, France and North America between 1964 and 1990, deals with the fifteenth century. It explores themes in the history of England, Wales and, to some extent, the dominions of the English crown beyond. Such a triple perspective can be instructive for the historian of England as well as for historians of Wales and of the king's lands overseas. Crown, court and capital were the fulcrum of political, administrative and social developments throughout the English realm and its associated dominions, as is illustrated here by the experience of Yorkshire and the north, and the principality and marches of Wales. Regional and more local relationships among magnates and gentry and their tenantry, among townsmen and religious and secular clergy, are of comparable significance in a polity which had strong and intricate links between capital and country, crown and localities, realm and dominions, court, castle, manor and town house. The following chapters draw on evidence from West Wales and the marches, the midlands and Yorkshire, as well as from public and private bureaucracies in order to demonstrate these features. Fifteenth-century kings had substantial responsibilities beyond the borders of the realm, in dominions as large as Ireland and Gascony, and as small as the Channel Islands and the Isle of Man. These responsibilities were reflected in developing attitudes in England to subjects, aliens and denizens, and at the same time they helped to crystallize concepts of Englishness and foreignness.

All of these developments had their particular bearing on the dynastic disputes of the century, and the drift towards civil war in the 1450s. The problems of rulership, personal relations, and the pursuit of power that were posed had significant effects on ways of government, communication between crown and people, on family ties and individual loyalties that reveal the fifteenth to be a peculiarly fascinating century, rather than the depressingly confused period which some earlier writers have described.

In reprinting these essays and papers, opportunity has been taken to correct minor errors and misprints, and to provide cross-references. One paper (Chapter 13) has been translated into English. A bibliographical note has been added at the end of several of the chapters to indicate relevant publications which have appeared more recently. Otherwise, the essays and papers re-appear virtually unaltered.

University College of Swansea

Abbreviations

CP	Calendar of Patent Rolls
Croyland	Ingulph's Chronicle of the Abbey of Croyland, ed. H.T. Riley London, 1854)
EHD	English Historical Documents, IV (1327-1485), ed. A.R. Myers (London, 1969)
EHL	C.L. Kingsford, English Historical Literature in the Fifteenth Century (Oxford, 1913)
EHR	English Historical Review
LQR	Law Quarterly Review
P and P	Past and Present
PPC	Proceedings and Ordinances of the Privy Council of England, ed. N.H. Nicolas (7 vols., London, 1834-37)

1

The Crown and the Royal Family in Later Medieval England

The stability, strength and effectiveness of English kingship before the Glorious Revolution of 1688 depended, first and foremost, on the character, ability and experience of individual English monarchs. And in the later middle ages, England's was an exclusively male kingship, since there was no queen regnant between the ill-starred Matilda in the mid-twelfth century and 'Bloody Mary' Tudor in the mid-sixteenth. Secondly, this kingship depended on the attitudes and ambitions of the English nobility, and on the sense of responsibility they showed towards interests other than their own – what, by the thirteenth century, they themselves articulated as 'the community of the realm'.[1] It depended, too, on the royal family or kinsfolk – those whom contemporaries identified as having 'blood royal' flowing in their veins. This third prop of kingship, though less prominent and less significant than the other two, came to enjoy in the later middle ages a self-conscious identity that made the king's kinsmen widely regarded as a distinct 'estate' within the English ruling establishment. In the fourteenth and fifteenth centuries, these members of the blood royal became more important than ever before, in almost every facet of public life: social, dynastic and military, political and governmental. And yet, unlike the kinsfolk of Anglo-Saxon kings, 'the royals' of late-medieval England have attracted only a modest amount of attention in their own right.[2]

From the king's point of view, his kinsmen were well placed to provide a dependable corps of leaders within the nobility at large. It may be considered the good fortune of Henry V to have had the support and companionship, at home and abroad, of his brothers Thomas, John and Humphrey for much of his reign. From the nobility's standpoint, the royal kin formed a privileged circle which others could aspire to join through friendship or marriage or both, and which offered opportunities for increased influence, wealth and standing in the realm.

---

1. For a recent comment, in the context of 'The Prehistory of Parliament', see J.C. Holt in *The English Parliament in the Middle Ages*, ed. R.G. Davies and J.H. Denton (Manchester, 1981), pp. 25–26.
2. Anne Crawford, 'The King's Burden? – the consequences of royal marriage in fifteenth-century England', in *Patronage, the Crown and the Provinces in Later Medieval England*, ed. R.A. Griffiths (Gloucester, 1981), pp. 33–56, is confined to the queens of England. Cf. Pauline Stafford, 'Sons and mothers in family politics in the early middle ages', *Studies in church history*, I, ed. Derek Baker (1978), pp. 79–100, and 'The King's wife in Wessex, 800–1066', *P. and P.*, XCIX (1981), 3–27, whose comments embrace the royal children too. There are some brief, interesting remarks on the significance of royal offspring in K.B. McFarlane, *The Nobility of Later Medieval England* (Oxford, 1973), pp. 156–58.

For example, William, Lord Willoughby (d. 1409), who seems to have had a close personal relationship with Henry IV, was allowed to marry, as his second wife, the wealthy heiress, Joan Holand, daughter of the earl of Kent and widow of the king's uncle, Edmund, duke of York. Willoughby became a valued, loyal and intimate member of the court circle.[3] Potentially, therefore, the king's relatives were a vital link between crown and nobility, a link that was capable of forging particularly close relationships between the monarch and his greater nobility. Equally, in some circumstances – and Charles Ross has graphically described those of Yorkist England – the blood royal could turn into a quagmire that might overwhelm the kingship itself or indeed, as in 1483–85, lead to the actual extinction of the ruling dynasty. If only Edward IV and his brothers George and Richard 'had been able to live without dissension', lamented the continuator of the Croyland chronicle, their talents could have been placed unitedly at the service of their family and the crown.[4]

It is well known that during the fourteenth and early-fifteenth centuries the ranks of the English nobility were gradually differentiated, became more distinct and ultimately were institutionalised in the context of a parliamentary 'House of Lords'. It was admittedly still possible during Henry VI's minority for knights and esquires among the young king's councillors to be decribed as 'lords of the council', but the upper reaches of society were now more closely defined and refined as a group, with a special status and special titles as barons or better.[5] By the mid-fifteenth century these so-called magnates had become the English peerage, with a right to receive a summons to attend parliament, and that in turn institutionalised their status and role. By 1500 there were no more than sixty of these magnates in England.[6]

At the same time, and for allied reasons, the king's kinsmen were more highly esteemed and consciously identified, even though – or perhaps because – the blood royal was now more difficult to define. It was more difficult to do so at this juncture partly for accidental reasons: first, the propensity of Edward III and Queen Philippa to produce lusty sons (seven of them, five of whom survived to manhood and married); secondly, the extraordinary marriage of Edward III's eldest son, the Black Prince, with a widow, Joan of Kent, whose two sons (the Holands) by her first husband were treated by their half-brother, Richard II, as members of the royal family; and, thirdly, the practice of granting titles to noblemen who were not the king's relatives, something which Edward II revived when he created his friend, Peter Gavaston, earl of Cornwall in 1307.[7]

---

3. CP, XII (2), 661–63; for a comment on Willoughby, see A.L. Brown, 'The Reign of Henry IV', in *Fifteenth-century England, 1399–1509*, ed. S.B. Chrimes, C.D. Ross and R.A. Griffiths (Manchester, 1972), p. 12.
4. *Croyland*, p. 470. See Charles Ross, *Edward IV* (1974), and *Richard III* (1981).
5. E.g., PPC, III, 158 n. 2 (William Alyngton, esquire, July 1424), 163 (Thomas Chaucer, esquire, November 1424). See especially T.B. Pugh, 'The magnates, knights and gentry', in Chrimes, Ross and Griffiths, op. cit., pp. 86–128, and K.B. McFarlane, op. cit., pp. 1–18, 122–125, for the general development.
6. M.L. Bush, *The English Aristocracy: a Comparative Approach* (Manchester, 1984), pp. 19, 37.
7. See J.E. Powell and K. Wallis, *The House of Lords in the Middle Ages* (1968), p. 264: 'the first man outside the royal family to be created an earl since Hubert de Burgh was made earl of Kent in 1227'. No English king (or his heir) had married a widowed mother since the mid-twelfth century; whenever it did occur, it almost always caused political or dynastic trouble.

Accidental or not, during the ensuing century the immediate kinsmen of kings, those with royal blood, were increasingly designated as such and were regularly distinguished from the rest of the nobility by all sorts and conditions of people.

Take, first, the populace. In stark contrast to the peasants' clamour in 1381 against Richard II's uncle, John of Gaunt, and other ministers, John Cade's rebels in 1450 pleaded with Henry VI 'to take about his noble person his trew blode of his ryall realme, that is to say, the hyghe and myghty prynce the Duke of Yorke [who was Henry's second cousin] . . . Also to take about his person the myghte prynce, the Duke of Exeter, the Duke of Bokyngham, the Duke of Norffolke, . . .' These latter dukes were not described as '*hyghe* and myghty' but, like York, they were the king's cousins; each of them was either a grandson or (like Henry VI himself) a great-grandson of Edward III.[8]

Earlier in 1450, and higher in the social scale, the commons in parliament tried to impeach Henry VI's chief minister, the duke of Suffolk. Though the commons themselves were not quite so explicit, it was widely believed in the city of London that he had had a hand in the 'dethe of that nobylle prynce the Duke of Glouceter', and that he and his henchmen had plotted the destruction 'of our excellent prince ye Duke of Glowcetter, the whiche is to myche to reherse, . . . Also the Duke of Exeter, and our holy fader the Cardenall of Wynchester, the nobill princes the Duke of Somersett, the Duke of Warrewike, deliuered and distroyed by the same meanys.' All were kinsmen of the king.[9] When the commons assembled for the next parliament in November 1450, they doubtless had some at least of these charges in mind when they accused Suffolk formally of the 'fynall destruction, of the most noble, vaillant true Prince, youre right Obeissant Uncle the Duke of Gloucestre, whom God pardon, and of the abreggyng of the dayes of other Princes of youre blode', and 'estraunged from youre good grace, favour and conceyte, full grete Lordes to you right nygh'.[10] Here the commons presumably had in mind the mysterious death of the king's second cousin, John Beaufort, duke of Somerset, in 1444, and the sudden death of his fourth cousin, Henry Beauchamp, duke of Warwick in 1445. The circumstances surrounding the demise of both – Somerset allegedly by suicide and Warwick suddenly at the age of twenty-one – would have been sufficient to arouse suspicion and give rise to gossip, implicating the unpopular Suffolk by the way. On the other hand, to father on him the death of John Holand, duke of Exeter, and Suffolk's own patron, Cardinal Beaufort, was absurd; the simple fact that so many deaths occurred in or shortly before 1447 was enough to fuel speculation.

As might be expected, the nobility were even more sensitive to the position of the royal kin by the fifteenth century. The lesser among them prided themselves on their loyal service to the 'true Lordes of youre noble blode', as did Thomas, Lord Lumley in his petition to Edward IV in 1461.[11] Disputes over precedence often quoted in evidence nearness to the royal stock and entitlement to bear the

---

8. *Three Fifteenth-century Chronicles*, ed. James Gairdner (Camden Soc., 1880), p. 97, from memoranda in the hand of John Stowe. Details of these and other descents are in CP, passim.
9. *The Historical Collections of a Citizen of London*, ed. James Gairdner (Camden Soc., 1876), p. 189 ('Gregory's chronicle'); EHL, p. 361 ('Collection of a Yorkist partisan').
10. *Rot. Parl.*, V, 226.
11. Ibid., V, 486. Lumley was petitioning for the restoration of his title.

royal arms; thus did the earl of Norfolk's attorney in 1425 when, in his master's dispute with the earl of Warwick, he asserted that Norfolk 'was descended of ye Blode Riall from Thomas of Brotherton, sone to Kyng Edward ye Firste, and bare the Armes of yis Lond'.[12] Noblemen, too, took to commissioning illuminated royal pedigrees on to which their own lineages could be grafted (as did another of Henry VI's cousins, Henry Percy, earl of Northumberland).[13] Royal kinsmen in the fifteenth century were even prepared to use their special blood as a standard of revolt against a king's minister or even against a king who was seemingly betraying the blood royal. In 1440 Humphrey, duke of Gloucester, at that time the heir presumptive of his nephew, Henry VI, hit out at Cardinal Beaufort, who dominated the king's counsels and had 'enstraunged me your soole uncle, my cosyn off Yorke, my cosyn of Huntyngdon, and many other lordis of your kynne, to haue any knowlege of any gret mater'.[14] A generation later, in 1469, George, duke of Clarence and Richard Neville, earl of Warwick pointedly reminded Edward IV himself that those conspicuous failures as king, Edward II, Richard II and Henry VI, had 'estraingid the gret lordis of thayre blood from thaire secrete Councelle, And not avised by them; And takyng abowte them other not of thaire blood, and enclynyng only to theire counselle, rule and advise, the wheche persones take not respect ne consideracion to the wele of the seid princes, ne to the comonwele of this lond . . .' Edward IV, in their view, was allowing himself to be led in the same direction by unworthy advisers, who 'have causyd oure said sovereyn lord to estrainge his goode grace from the Councelle of the nobile and trewe lordis of his blood'.[15] In the eyes of Clarence and Warwick – admittedly self-interested eyes – the welfare of the blood royal was equated with the welfare of the king and the entire realm.

Even the most formal and authoritative source of opinion drew a clear distinction between the blood royal and the rest of the English peerage. When Henry VI's occupancy of the throne was challenged by his second cousin, Richard, duke of York, in the autumn of 1460, the king's justices – who were admittedly nervous about expressing any opinion on the challenge – declared that 'they durst not enter into eny communication thereof, for it perteyned to the Lordes of the Kyngs blode, and th'apparage [peerage] of this his lond, to have communication and medle in such maters'.[16]

These people who portrayed the king's kinsmen as a distinct and superior élite did so for personal, sectional or political reasons; yet during the fifteenth century the practice was common and well before 1500 it had entered the canon of English constitutional custom. Given the nature of a hierarchical society, we can be certain that it echoed what kings and their kinsmen articulated themselves. The proliferation of noble styles and titles in fourteenth- and

12. Ibid., IV, 267.
13. Bodl., Marshall MS. 135 (c. 1427–41). For other likely examples of noble-sponsored pedigrees, incorporating the genealogies of the Beaufort, Stafford and Holand kinsmen of Henry VI, see R.A. Griffiths, 'The Sense of Dynasty in the Reign of Henry VI', in *Patronage, Pedigree and Power in Later Medieval England*, ed. Charles Ross (Gloucester, 1979), pp. 24–25 and references cited p. 34. **See below p. 94 and n. 40.**
14. Richard Arnold, *The Customs of London* (1811), p. 280.
15. *A Chronicle of the First Thirteen Years of the Reign of King Edward the Fourth*, ed. J.O. Halliwell (Camden Soc., 1839), pp. 47, 50.
16. *Rot. Parl.*, V, 376.

early-fifteenth-century England served to emphasise the special status of the blood royal. Claiming to be king of France, where the 'princes of the fleur-de-lys' were already a discrete company, Edward III took a significant step towards an English royal identity for the blood royal when, in 1337, he created his eldest son the first duke in English history.[17] During the next sixty years, 12 other dukes and 1 duchess were created: 4 were the sons of kings, 2 the grandchildren of kings, 2 were the half-brothers of kings, and all had a fair amount of royal blood in their veins. Even by the time of Henry VIII's death in 1547, almost all the 52 dukedoms created in England had been for the benefit of the royal family – and that was no accident. Moreover, 3 of the 6 noblemen granted the even newer title, derived from France, of marquess after 1385 were closely related to English kings.[18] Thus, the diversification of the peerage and the invention of its two senior titles were primarily designed to highlight the blood royal.

The precision given to the crime of treason did so too and at roughly the same time. Edward III's statute of 1352, which defined the basis of the legal concept of treason for long after, specifically protected the king, his queen, his eldest son and heir, his eldest daughter and the wife of his eldest son. Case law extended the scope of his statute to cover Richard II's uncles (Edward III's other surviving sons) in 1394 and Henry V's brothers in 1414 – in other words, all the sons of a king who were then living. And in 1536 Henry VIII declared that even a king's sisters, aunts and nieces merited special protection under the law of treason.[19] Violation of the blood royal was evidently regarded as of a different order to assaults on any other subject.

The signs and tokens of royalty represented social and political realities in an age before the imperatives of democracy turned them into the picturesque and the frankly bizarre. In the chivalric age, the fashion for arms, the 'ensigns of nobility', was a matter of sufficient substance for the crown to attempt to control the granting and use of arms by the fifteenth century.[20] Already the special place of at least the king's male kinsmen had been acknowledged when Edward III allowed all his sons to bear the new royal arms of France and England quarterly, differenced only by an emblem or a label surrounding or superimposed on the king's arms.[21] Richard II went further to elevate the royal stock in the public consciousness, applying a mind that was fascinated with heraldry and kingly dignity, and besotted with things French. In the 1390s he allowed the male descendants of Edward I, his own half-brothers, the Holands, and the illegitimate children, the Beauforts, of his uncle, John of Gaunt, to use the king's distinctive arms, impaled as they were with the alleged arms of Edward the Confessor from about 1394. And when he legitimated the bastard Beaufort children in 1397, Richard referred to them as 'our most dear kinsmen . . .

17. For France, see P.S. Lewis, *Later Medieval France* (1968), pp. 187ff.
18. They are conveniently listed in CP, V, appendix H; VIII, appendix A. For some comment, see J.T. Rosenthal, *Nobles and the Noble Life, 1295–1500* (1976), p. 32.
19. *Statutes*, I, 319–20 (1352); *Rot. Parl.*, III, 316 (1394); *CPR, 1413-16,* p. 162 (1414); D.L. Keir, *The Constitutional History of Modern Britain, 1485–1951* (5th ed., 1953), pp. 105–6.
20. Anthony Wagner, *Heralds of England* (1967), pp. 48ff; Richard Marks and Ann Payne, *British Heraldry* (1978), p. 13. The crown sought this power from 1417 onwards.
21. Rodney Dennys, *Heraldry and the Heralds* (1982), pp. 108–11. See Newberry Library (Chicago), Case MS. F. 0745. 1915, an illustrated book of armorial bearings of kings and noble families that was compiled in 1572 by Robert Cook, Clarence king of arms.

sprung from royal stock'.[22] Like many of Richard's actions, these were both novel and imaginative, designed to enhance his own majesty by honouring the blood royal in a peerage whose function he saw as shedding lustre on the crown itself. When his uncles, Edmund of Langley and Thomas of Woodstock, were created dukes in 1385, Richard declared 'that the more we bestow honours on wise and honourable men, the more our crown is adorned with gems and precious stones'.[23] He believed, too, that to legitimise the Beauforts would enhance the 'reverence of the very excellent person of the king . . . and of his blood' and the 'honour of his blood'. In his vivid account of the 'Merciless Parliament' of 1388, during which Richard confronted his noble critics, Thomas Favent revealed the king's developing attitude toward the peculiar qualities and special honour inherent in the blood royal. When his uncle, Thomas of Woodstock, stood before him to deny any treason, the chancellor declared thus on Richard's behalf: 'Lord Duke, you have sprung from such a worthy royal stock, and you are so near us in a collateral line, that you cannot be suspected of devising such things'.[24]

Under Henry VI and the Lancastrians, heraldry continued to mirror the special quality of the blood royal, and Cade's rebels in 1450 believed that Henry VI would be 'ye Richest Kyng cristen' if he drew his royal cousins about him.[25] Even Edmund and Jasper Tudor, who had no English blood whatever in their veins, but who were recognised as Henry VI's uterine brothers when they were created earls of Richmond and Pembroke, respectively, in 1452, adopted the royal arms differenced only by a border. They might not be of the blood royal of England, strictly speaking, but they were regarded as members of the royal family and therefore entitled to bear the king's arms.[26] The Yorkists went further still, for it cannot reasonably be doubted that when, in 1474, Henry Stafford, duke of Buckingham, was allowed by the king's heralds to use the royal arms of his ancestor, Edward III's son, Thomas of Woodstock, King Edward IV had authorised it.[27]

The formal style used by some of the closest royal kinsmen in the fifteenth century reflected the same reality. Self-conscious awareness of his position led Humphrey, duke of Gloucester, to style himself in his formal letters and on his

22. Dennys, op. cit., ch. 11. The Holand brothers bore Edward I's royal arms as sons of Joan of Kent, daughter of Edward's younger son (Newberry Library, Case MS. F. 0745. 1915). For the Beauforts, see *EHD*, IV, 169, translated from *Rot. Parl.*, III, 343.

23. Anthony Tuck, *Richard II and the English Nobility* (1973), p. 84, quoting *Reports from the Lords Committees touching the dignity of a peer of the realm* (5 vols., 1829), V, 64–65.

24. 'Historia sive narracio de modo et forma mirabilis parliamenti per Thomam Favent clericum indictata', ed. M. McKisack, in *Camden Miscellany*, XIV (Camden Soc., 1926), pp. 14–15, as translated in *EHD*, IV, 162.

25. *EHL*, p. 361.

26. Dennys, op. cit., p. 118, with illustrations of the new arms borne by Edmund and Jasper on p. 119. For Earl Jasper's arms, with its border of martlets, see his seals as described and illustrated in R.S. Thomas 'The Political Career, Estates and "Connection" of Jasper Tudor, Earl of Pembroke and Duke of Bedford (d. 1495)' (unpublished University of Wales, Swansea, Ph.D. thesis, 1971), pp. 474ff.

27. Wagner, op. cit., p. 69; Dennys, op. cit., p. 110, where the record of the chapter meeting of the Office of Arms on 18 February 1474 is quoted.

seal as 'son, brother and uncle of kings' after 1422.[28] And this pretentious style was copied by Henry VI's half-brother, Jasper Tudor, who described himself as 'the high and mighty prince, Jasper, brother and uncle of kings, duke of Bedford and earl of Pembroke', following the accession of Henry Tudor in 1485.[29] To trumpet one royal relationship is understandable; two or three exhibits the pride of a peacock.

That these distinctions were a relatively recent development in the early fifteenth century is perhaps indicated by John Russell's description of how to organise a noble household, in his 'Book of Nurture' that was based on his experience of serving Humphrey of Gloucester, 'a prince full royal'. Though Russell acknowleged that royal blood ranked higher in status and regard than land and livelihood, he was puzzled by lords of royal blood who could be poorer than other lords, and by ladies of royal blood who married non-nobles and yet kept their rank.[30]

This consciousness of, and sensitivity towards, the blood royal was sharpened by the rapid succession to the English throne of three cadet branches of the Plantagenets between 1399 and 1485, and it was illustrated by the names chosen by these dynasties for the sons and daughters of their kings. Of the Yorkists' eleven legitimate children, only two bore a name favoured by the Lancastrians, and that was the name of King Edward the Confessor whom all medieval kings had venerated since Henry III's day.[31] Likewise, Henry Tudor looked to his own antecedents when choosing names for his sons: Arthur, Henry and Edmund. And although three of his daughters had names borne by Yorkist aunts (Margaret, Katherine and Mary), they also commemorated three ladies of the Lancastrian past (including Henry's mother and grandmother).[32] A sense of familiarity, in the strict sense of the term, was present in earlier centuries, but in the fifteenth dynastic developments made it all the stronger. It was the Baltic blood of Stuart and especially Hanoverian kings that lowered commemorative royal nomenclature to the absurd, so that Charles Philip Arthur George had so many names that his bride got them in the wrong order when they took their

28. Cf. *EHD*, IV, 893, where the style is echoed in the University of Oxford's acknowledgement of Duke Humphrey's donation of books in 1439. Before the death of Henry V, his seal referred to him as 'son and brother of kings' (K.H. Vickers, *Humphrey, duke of Gloucester* [1907], p. 455), and he seems to have remained content to use seals bearing this style for a few years after the accession of his nephew, Henry VI: W. de Gray Birch, *Catalogue of Seals in the Department of Manuscripts in the British Museum* (6 vols., 1887–1900), II, 157–58 (1424, 1426).

29. R.S. Thomas, thesis cited, p. 250; and see *Archaeologia*, XVIII (1817), 439–42 and plate XXIX. Cf. the style used by Edward IV's brother, Richard, duke of Gloucester, during the few weeks of Edward V's reign in 1483, 'brother and uncle of kings': *York Civic Records*, I, ed. A. Raine (Yorks. Archaeological Soc., 1939), 73, 75.

30. *The Babees Book*, ed. F.J. Furnivall (Early English Text Soc., old series, XXXII, 1868), p. 190, summarised and modernised in *EHD*, IV, 1167.

31. Edward was the name given to Edward IV's eldest son and to Richard III's son.

32. Henry's sons commemorated the mythical Arthur of British tradition, Henry VI, the half-uncle whom Henry Tudor venerated, and Edmund Tudor, the king's own father. His daughters were probably named after his mother, Margaret Beaufort, his grandmother, Katherine of Valois, and the ancestress of the Lancastrians, Mary Bohun, first wife of the first Lancastrian king. For a comment on 'The Blessings of Ancestry' enjoyed by Henry VII, see R.A. Griffiths and R.S. Thomas, *The Making of the Tudor Dynasty* (Gloucester, 1985), ch. 13.

marriage vows in 1981.[33]

Some of the reasons for the emergence of the royal family as a distinct and distinctive element in the English polity have already been mentioned in passing. The compelling desire to emulate, rival and ultimately to surpass the French monarchy created the conviction in English kings from Richard II, and especially Henry V, onwards that they were the 'Most Christian' kings on earth and their subjects the chosen of God.[34] To be supported by a blood royal bearing novel titles of superior honour lent added distinction to the monarch himself.

Moreover, from the end of the thirteenth century, English kings ruled dominions and provinces beyond the borders of the realm, and yet whose common bond was the king's lordship. In an age when London and Westminster were developing as the settled capital of the kingdom and the permanent headquarters of royal government, these territorial conquests and acquisitions placed greater strain on the structures and practices of a personal monarchy. Problems of administrative supervision and of asserting the royal presence could be partly solved by the use of an acknowledged and respected royal family. Apart from Richard II, no medieval English king himself visited Ireland after 1210; Edward I was the last king-duke to visit Gascony; few monarchs could spend much time in Wales or on the wearisome task of subduing the Scots; and only Edward III and Henry V were prepared to commit themelves to lengthy stays in France. Instead, Edward III's son Lionel was the first royal lieutenant of Ireland when he was appointed in 1361, and he was created England's second duke to underline the significance of his mission.[35] Jasper Tudor, newly created duke of Bedford, itself a royal title last borne by Henry IV's second son John, was Henry VII's lieutenant there from 1486. Edward III's eldest, the Black Prince, became the royal lieutenant in Gascony and so did his younger brother, John of Gaunt; and of the six royal lieutenants there in the fifteenth century, five were close relatives of kings.[36] As for Wales, more than half of the country was the patrimony of the prince of Wales who, after 1301, was the king's eldest son and heir. The fact that few princes of Wales reached manhood as princes emphasises that it was their royal status, rather than their individual capabilities, that commended them as nominal rulers of the king's Welsh principality.[37] In Northern France, too, the blood royal was frequently preferred when the king could not cross the channel himself to visit his conquered dominions: Edward III's son, John of Gaunt; John, duke of Bedford, during the minority of his

33. James I and his wife, Anne of Denmark, were the first English monarchs to give their offspring a double-barrelled name; to have several Christian names in the royal family was common from George I onwards.
34. See J.W. McKenna, 'How God became an Englishman', in *Tudor Rule and Revolution*, ed. D.J. Guth and J.W. McKenna (Cambridge, 1982), pp. 25–43, for full references from Henry V's reign onwards. But an even earlier reference to 'Most Christian King' is in Longleat MS. 38 (*Tractatus de sanguine Christi precioso*), which was probably dedicated to Richard II by William Sudbury. I owe this reference to Ms. M.L. Kekewich and Emden, *Oxford*, III, 1813.
35. Powell and Wallis, op. cit., p. 363.
36. CP, II, 73; M.G.A. Vale, *English Gascony, 1399–1453* (Oxford, 1970), p. 246.
37. J.G. Edwards, *The Principality of Wales, 1267–1967* (Caerns. Hist. Soc., 1969), p. 29.

nephew, Henry VI; and Richard, duke of York and Edmund Beaufort, duke of Somerset, later on.[38] Even within the realm, the late-medieval kings who adopted something akin to French methods of apanage government looked to their sons and kinsmen as their agents: the prince of Wales and the dukes of Lancaster in the fourteenth century; Richard, duke of Gloucester under Edward IV, and the duke of Buckingham under Richard III.[39] To convey the royal will and substitute for the royal presence when the king's responsibilities were now so broad, the royal family was considered best.

Then, too, the constitutional uncertainties and dynastic rivalries of the fifteenth century helped to give the blood royal a high profile. Henry IV publicly contrived to claim Richard II's crown in 1399 'be right lyne of the Blode comyng fro the gude lorde Kyng Henry therde, and thorghe yat ryght yat God of his grace hath sent me'.[40] A few years later, Henry twice declared in parliament how the crown should pass to his eldest son and his heirs – in short, to the royal blood of Lancaster.[41] When this blood ran dangerously thin after the death, without legitimate heirs, of Henry V's three younger brothers, the sole surviving direct male descendant of Henry IV, his grandson Henry VI, took steps to emphasise the dignity of his remaining royal kinsmen, widening the circle of the blood royal to include even his Tudor half-brothers.[42]

For the blood royal had its uses, especially in a turbulent age. English noblemen had often married royal princesses in the past, and Edward I's marital arrangements on behalf of his daughters brought political and material benefits to the crown at home.[43] Both Edward IV and Henry VII were behaving traditionally when they arranged royal marriages, though in Edward's case he used his wife's children by her first marriage, and Henry Tudor used, not his own daughters, but those of Edward IV to the same end: social and dynastic control and domestic stability. Not one of Edward's daughters was married by the time their father died in April 1483. Mary and Margaret were already dead, and Bridget was eventually placed in a nunnery. But Henry VII arranged that Cecily should marry his uncle, John, Viscount Welles, in 1487 or 1488; Anne married Thomas Howard, earl of Surrey, in 1495; and in the same year Sir William Courtenay, later earl of Devon, wedded Katherine of York.[44]

The diplomatic value of royal marriages was equally well recognised, and no reigning king of medieval England married English until Edward IV and Henry VII did so. Yet, as Henry VI's marriage to Margaret of Anjou in 1445 showed, the results were not always worthwhile. By contrast, Edward IV's marriage to a widowed Englishwoman, Elizabeth Woodville, enabled him to use his wife's numerous children and relatives in an attempt, mainly by means of the marriage bond, to consolidate his control over important segments of the English

38. R.A. Griffiths, *The Reign of King Henry VI* (1981), ch. 9, 17, 18.
39. Bush, *English Aristocracy*, pp. 93–94.
40. *Rot. Parl.*, III, 423.
41. Griffiths, 'Sense of Dynasty', p. 15. See below, p. 85.
42. Ibid., pp. 19–23. See below, pp. 89-92.
43. K.B. McFarlane, 'Had Edward I a "policy" towards the earls?', *History*, L (1965), 145–59, reprinted in his *Nobility of Later Medieval England*, pp. 248-67.
44. S.B. Chrimes, *Henry VII* (London, 1972), p. 35 n.2. For the general point, see Bush, *English Aristocracy*, p.101.

aristocracy.[45] If he did not put his own children to work in this direction or in foreign diplomacy, it was mainly because they were too young, though there is a suspicion that he was too interested in the financial haggling associated with diplomatic match-making to reap the wider political rewards before he died.[46] As for Henry VII, whose children were scarcely older, he was much more successful in finalising foreign marriages for his children; whilst his sisters-in-law, Edward IV's girls, were propelled into carefully considered marriages at home.[47]

For these and doubtless other reasons, in the later middle ages more sub-stantial significance was attached to the blood royal than ever before, distinguishing those who had it from those who did not, raising the status of the royal kin within the nobility and emphasing their value to the king and kingdom. In 1483, parliament acknowledged this special breed when, for the first time, it banned the wearing of cloth of gold and purple silk except by the king and his queen, the king's mother, his children, and his brothers and sisters.[48] Later that same year, ironically, Richard III reviled the Yorkist royal family and did his best to destroy it. On 10 June 1483, he denounced the queen and 'hir blode adherentts and affinitie' for plotting the destruction of himself, the duke of Buckingham 'and the old royall blode of this realme'. Then, a week or so later, after his claim to the throne had been publicised, Richard impugned the legitimacy of his own brother, Edward IV, and his young nephews, Edward V and Richard, duke of York.[49] Soon afterwards he also stigmatised Henry Tudor's royal blood as bastard.[50] Arguably it was these affronts to royalty that demolished Richard's own reputation and alienated his subjects. The circumstances that had defined and elevated the blood royal, by the end of the fifteenth century had all but destroyed it: three branches of the Plantagenets had perished in the Wars of the Roses. The *coup de grâce* was delivered in the sixteenth century by the chronic infertility of the Tudors.

45.   Ross, *Edward IV*, ch. 5; Michael Hicks, 'The changing role of the Wydevilles in Yorkist politics to 1483', in *Patronage, Pedigree and Power*, pp. 60–86, though both writers concentrate on their subsequent malign influence on Yorkist politics.
46.   Ross, *Edward IV*, pp. 245–49.
47.   Chrimes, *Henry VII*, pp. 35 no. 2, 67 n.3, and ch. 15.
48.   *Statutes*, II, 468.
49.   *York Civic Records*, I, 73–74; Mancini, p. 91. See Ross, *Richard III*, pp. 88–91, for a full discussion of Richard's denigration of his own blood relatives.
50.   *The Paston Letters*, ed. James Gairdner (6 vols., 1904), VI, 81–84 (the proclamation of 23 June 1485).

2

The King's Court During the Wars of the Roses:
Continuities in an Age of Discontinuities

The monarchy and regal politics in England have never ceased to capture the attention of late medieval and early modern historians. In 1953 K.B. McFarlane voiced his irritation at what he described as the over-whelmingly 'royalist' interpretation of medieval English history by writers whom he called 'King's Friends'. Indeed, at that particular moment, he feared lest this devotion to the kingly office should result in these writers and their unwary readers 'slipping into totalitarianism'.[1] Such sentiments had special meaning for McFarlane and his audience in the immediate post-war years, although several of his pupils have voiced them approvingly since. On the other hand, it has always been recognised (not least by McFarlane himself) that, for good or ill, public policy in late medieval and early modern England was devised, and the personal fortunes of individuals best advanced, by kings and those around kings. And McFarlane and others inspired by his work have placed their favoured concept of 'patronage', including the links between king and subject, in the forefront of late medieval historical study. At the beginning of his biography of Edward IV, Charles Ross announced that:

> The ways and means of gaining and keeping power are central themes of this study. For the same reason, Edward's relations with the English nobility, and especially his use of patronage, occupy a prominent place . . .[2]

Early modern historians, in their pursuit of similar interests, have lavished much attention on what they describe as 'the court', wherein the patronage nexus was at its most effective.[3] By contrast, apart from a few

---

[1] K.B. McFarlane, *The Nobility of Later Medieval England* (Oxford, 1973), p. 2, expressed at the beginning of his Ford Lectures, delivered in the University of Oxford in 1953.

[2] Charles Ross, *Edward IV* (London, 1974), p. xi. See also his *Richard III* (London, 1981), in which he confessed (p. xi) to an 'emphatic concentration on the problems of how to gain, and even more of how to keep power in late-medieval England, and on the inevitable centre of these operations, his use of patronage . . .' Charles Ross is unusual among McFarlane's pupils in indulging in royal biography, and with conspicuous success.

[3] For example, D. Rubini, *Court and Country, 1688-1702* (London, 1967); P. Zagorin, *The Court and the Country* (London, 1969); A.H. Smith, *County and Court* (London, 1974); J.R. Jones, *Country and Court* (London, 1978); Robert Ashton, *The City and the Court, 1603-1643* (London, 1979); even, somewhat incongruously, Roy Sherwood, *The Court of Oliver Cromwell* (London, 1977).

Victorian forays into what was dubbed 'court life' during the early Plantagenet period in the second half of the twelfth century – one thinks of scholars like R.W. Eyton (1815-81) and Hubert Hall (1857-1944), who were familiar with the records of English government as well as with contemporary commentaries by Peter of Blois, John of Salisbury, Walter Map and Gerald of Wales[4] – medievalists have preferred to enter 'the household' rather than 'the court', and to anatomize the household's functions and functionaries.

Late-medieval historians during the past half-century have taken their cue from T.F. Tout's influential, if modestly entitled, *Chapters in the Administrative History of Medieval England*, and from his charting of the processes whereby the king's *curia* – his 'court', no less – gradually shifted routine administrative tasks to a number of institutionalised departments, yet always retaining general oversight and the making of policy in the hands of the king and those about him. Tout seldom described this regal environment as 'the court', and late medieval historians have since been content to examine its institutional and administrative engine, the king's household.[5] Part of the explanation for late medievalists' coyness lies, perhaps, in the regrettable fact that Tout's great study, whose final two volumes were published posthumously in 1930 and 1933, concluded with the deposition of Richard II in 1399. Since 1933, the 'no-man's land' between 1399 and 1485 (or even 1509) has been occupied, with increasing confidence, by medievalists more frequently than by early modernists, but neither 'the court' nor 'the household' of Lancastrian and Yorkist kings has been authoritatively examined in its entirety; indeed, 'the court' has been barely identified with any precision.[6]

Quite recently, two Tudor historians – David Loades and David Starkey, the latter aided and abetted by D.A.L. Morgan – have boldly elbowed their way into the fifteenth century and planted the banner of 'the Tudor court' firmly in the decades immediately following 1450, claiming by the way that a new kind of court emerged in Edward IV's reign which blossomed into the phenomenon familiar to sixteenth-century historians.[7]

[4] R.W. Eyton, *Court, Household and Itinerary of King Henry II* (London, 1878; repr. Hildesheim and New York, 1974); Hubert Hall, *Court Life under the Plantagenets* (London, 1890; repr. London, 1899).

[5] T.F. Tout, *Chapters in the Administrative History of Medieval England* (6 vols., Manchester, 1920-33). The modest number of references to the court in the Index (sixth) volume is instructive.

[6] A.R. Myers (ed.), *The Household of Edward IV: the Black Book and the Ordinances of 1478* (Manchester, 1959), is primarily an edition of mid-fifteenth-century ordinances for the household. The standard biography of Henry VII (London, 1972) was written by the eminent medieval historian, S.B. Chrimes.

[7] David Loades, *The Tudor Court* (London, 1986); David Starkey (ed.), *The English Court from the Wars of the Roses to the Civil War* (London, 1987), with D.A.L. Morgan's excellent essay, 'The House of Policy: The Political Role of the late Plantagenet Household', as ch. 2.

This hypothesis was perhaps heralded by remarks made by C.A.J. Armstrong and Neville Williams in 1977. The latter credited Edward IV with 'innovations in palace ceremonial' which Henry VII continued, and the former noted (as others had before him) the significance of King Edward's visit to the Burgundian court during his exile in January 1471 and the copy of certain household ordinances which Richard Whetehill, one of Edward's servants at Calais, obtained in 1474 from Olivier de la Marche, chamberlain of Charles the Rash, duke of Burgundy.[8] The literary, artistic and chivalric contacts between the English and Burgundian courts during Edward IV's reign have been eloquently described, but it is quite another matter – one for which evidence is lacking – to claim that the Yorkist court was in some fundamental way transformed in the Burgundian court's image.[9]

At the same time, but more cautiously, and not always consciously, Chris Given-Wilson's recent work on the royal household between 1360 and 1413 has begun to identify the court and its courtiers, as well as the household and its officialdom.[10] All these are very recent historiographical developments, and yet, of course, late medieval historians have long referred to the English court in the fifteenth century as often as they have referred to the royal household. They have, indeed, used the words interchangeably as if the court was the household, and the household was the court. Contemporaries thought otherwise.

I suspect that the fifteenth-century court has been conjured before our mind's eye (including my own) largely by Hollywood, and Hollywood ultimately raised most of its images from the Gothic Revival – from, for example, the splendid series of eight pictures illustrating the life of Edward III which were commissioned by George III for the King's Audience Chamber at Windsor Castle and painted in 1787-89 by Benjamin West (1738-1820), an expatriate American who was first taught to paint by a Cherokee Indian; or else from the vaults of historical pictures submitted in competition for the decoration of the new Houses of

---

[8] C.A.J. Armstrong, 'The Golden Age of Burgundy' (ch. 3) and Neville Williams, 'The Tudors' (ch. 7), in A.G. Dickens (ed.), *The Courts of Europe: Politics, Patronage and Royalty, 1400-1800* (London, 1977). The hypothesis may have a more venerable lineage reaching back to J.R. Green's concept of a 'New Monarchy' inaugurated by Edward IV and continued by Henry VII, which was popularized in *A Short History of the English People*, first published in London in 1874 and reprinted many times thereafter.

[9] Myers (*Household of Edward IV*, pp. 4, 33) hesitated to draw such an implication, and David Loades (*Tudor Court*, pp. 18-19) specifically eschewed any such. For a review of courtly contacts, see C.A.J. Armstrong, 'L'Echange culturel entre les cours d'Angleterre et de Bourgogne à l'époque de Charles le Téméraire', in idem, *England, France and Burgundy in the Fifteenth Century* (London, 1983), ch. 15 (first published 1970).

[10] Chris Given-Wilson, *The Royal Household and the King's Affinity: Service, Politics and Finance in England, 1360-1413* (New Haven and London, 1986). Professor Loades equates the court with the household: *Tudor Court*, pp. 10-13, 38ff.

Parliament following the destructive fire of 1834.[11] In its turn, the Gothic Revival in art was partly influenced by those richly illuminated pictures of Henry VI and Edward IV and their queens being presented, in the presence of clusters of noble and other figures, with the books in which these illuminations appear. Witness the portrayal of a public scene in a royal palace in 1445, when John Talbot, earl of Shrewsbury presented Margaret of Anjou with a book of romances, in the presence of her husband, Henry VI, and his courtiers, who included the chamberlain with his staff of office, the queen's ladies and various noblemen. Or witness the scene set in a more private royal room, where Anthony Woodville, Earl Rivers, presented to his brother-in-law, Edward IV, a book which Rivers had translated from French and which William Caxton published in 1477 as *Dictes and Sayings of the Philosophers*; the presentation took place in the presence of the queen, Prince Edward, a monk, a judge, a noble and several other on-lookers who represented a larger group hovering just outside the open door.[12] The striking, stylised court scenes in Laurence Olivier's films of Shakespeare's *Richard III* and *Henry V* spring readily to mind – especially the latter (1944), whose closing scene of peace and concord at the marriage of Henry V and Katherine of Valois was inspired by such brilliantly colourful illuminations as those in the earl of Shrewbury's book, compiled almost exactly 500 years before (1445) as a gift for the next French bride of an English king, on the occasion of her marriage to Henry VI.

The trouble is that the fifteenth-century historian has nothing comparable with (for example) Walter Map's observations – at once humorous and ironic – on the twelfth-century court in his *Courtiers' Trifles*.[13] The writings of Sir John Fortescue are mainly concerned with the institutional mechanisms of Lancastrian and Yorkist government and with the common law, and they generally lack informality and observations of human behaviour. Nor do we have a chronicle written, like Westminster Abbey's chronicle of Richard II's reign, close to the heart of regal affairs – certainly none composed near Windsor Castle.[14] The author of the Crowland Chronicle of the 1470s and 1480s is still not

[11] For West, see *D.N.B.*, *s.n.*, and Helmut von Erffa and Allen Staley, *The Paintings of Benjamin West* (New Haven and London, 1986); and for Parliament, Kenneth Clark, *The Gothic Revival* (3rd ed., London, 1962; repr. London, 1975), ch. VI. See, in general, Mark Girouard, *The Return to Camelot* (London, 1981).

[12] British Library, Royal MS. 15 E VI; Lambeth Palace Library, MS. 265 f. VI. These pictures have been reproduced many times: for example, respectively and in colour, John Cannon and Ralph Griffiths, *The Oxford Illustrated History of the British Monarchy* (Oxford, 1988), p. 237; Hubert Cole, *The Wars of the Roses* (London, 1973), p. 121.

[13] M.R. James (ed.), *Walter Map: De Nugis Curialium: Courtiers' Trifles*, revised by C.N.L. Brooke and R.A.B. Mynors (Oxford, 1983).

[14] L.C. Hector and B.F. Harvey (eds.), *The Westminster Chronicle, 1381-1394* (Oxford, 1982).

known for certain, and he may have purposely concealed almost as much as he gave away in dangerous and unpredictable times.[15]

In marked contrast, a good deal of the routine administrative archive of the king's household has survived from the fifteenth century, most notably the financial accounts of the treasurer and controller of the household, supplemented by those of the keeper of the Great Wardrobe outside, but associated with, the household.[16] Yet these accounts are both narrow in scope and specific in purpose; they are the records of accountants, rather than descriptions of offices and analyses by informed observers. They record the expenditure and disposal of the income of the household: in short, the regular financial management of the organisational structures of the king and his entourage. Similarly, the several household ordinances which survive from this period outline the allowances and fees payable to officers of the king's household; they are less often concerned with detailing the duties which these officers performed about the court.[17] However, they record fees paid to ushers who take lords and ladies to their chambers in the king's house or palace, and they note the fees paid to esquires of the household who 'help occupy the court and accompany strangers' there, and help to entertain lords in their chambers 'within courte' (as Edward IV's ordinances put it).[18]

The household was the institution which to a degree organised the court, but the court had no organisational aspect of its own and accordingly produced no administrative archive of its own. For this reason, it has proved easier to describe the household and understand its workings than to comprehend the fifteenth-century court. However, between the lines of household accounts and ordinances, the foot-prints of the court can be detected; and from time to time they betray the presence of the encompassing court by their references to traditional rules and customs 'of the court' ('the good, old, sad, worshupfull, and profitables rulez of the court used before tym'), usually dating back no further than the reign of Edward III.[19]

Foot-prints become substance in those rare documents which describe individual departments of the household. There survives such a

[15] Nicholas Pronay and John Cox (eds.), *The Crowland Chronicle Continuations, 1459-1486* (London, 1986). For comment on the authorship, see Ross, *Richard III*, pp. xliii-xlvi, and Daniel Williams, 'The Crowland Chronicle, 616-1500', in idem (ed.), *England in the Fifteenth Century* (Woodbridge, Suffolk, 1987), pp. 371-90.

[16] The surviving accounts are briefly noted by D.A.L. Morgan in Starkey, *English Court*, pp. 30-31.

[17] Ibid., pp. 27-30, with detailed commentary in Myers, *Household of Edward IV, passim*.

[18] *A Collection of Ordinances and Regulations for the Government of the Royal Household* (London, 1790), p. 115 (1493); Myers, *Household of Edward IV*, p. 129 (1478).

[19] For the 'old rule of courte' (1445), see Myers, *Household of Edward IV*, p. 63; and for references in Edward IV's 'Black Book' to earlier ordinances, including those of Edward III, ibid. pp. 84, 90, 133, 182; and for the phrase quoted in the text, ibid., p. 147.

description of the Royal Chapel, and there may once have been others in existence. To have an account of the Royal Chapel is particularly fortunate because the dean of the Chapel and his staff held the key to most of the ceremonies in which the king and his entourage participated; if entered in a king's diary, these ceremonies would have claimed a substantial part of his year. This is surely the reason why, in 1449, Count Alvaro Vaz d'Almada asked for an authoritative account of Henry VI's Royal Chapel, rather than of any other department related to the court, for presentation to his master, King Alfonso V of Portugal.[20] The count visited England in the summer of 1445: he was elected to the Order of the Garter on 11 July and was formally installed as a knight on 16 August.[21] Whenever the request for the account was made, during Count Alvaro's visit or after he had returned to Portugal, it was William Say, dean of the Royal Chapel from February 1449 and a king's chaplain since 1446, who authorised its compilation in the spring of 1449.[22]

A number of royal ceremonies were special and highly formal, the dean of the Royal Chapel acting as their impresario. His authority extended *infra curiam Regis*, and he had direct access to the king as well as to the king's chamberlain.[23] Among the ceremonies for which he was responsible were the funerals of kings and their consorts, the coronations of kings and queens, the baptism of their sons and daughters, the churching of queens as they recovered from childbirth, and the Garter celebrations. Other ceremonies took place more frequently and were more common sights at court: royal crown-wearings, which were held six or more times a year; ennoblements of peers which usually took place in royal residences rather than in parliament from the reign of Henry VI to that of Henry VIII; anniversaries of coronations; and royal observance of the year's religious festivals. And someone had to organise the plays and dramas at court, the tournaments, and the marriages of royal kinsfolk, nobles of the court and their children, as well as the banquets held by the king or queen or both, with dancing, singing, gift-and-honours-giving, in the presence of privileged English and other observers.[24]

This constant round of ceremonies and events required advice and regulations which, when they survive, reveal the fifteenth-century court to

---

[20] Walter Ullmann (ed.), *Liber Regie Capelle* (Henry Bradshaw Soc., XCII, London, 1961). For the suggestion that rules and regulations for other departments may have existed, ibid., p. 5.

[21] G.F. Belz, *Memorials of the Most Noble Order of the Garter* (London, 1841), p. clx.

[22] R.A. Griffiths, *The Reign of King Henry VI* (London, 1981), p. 304. For details of Say's career, see A.B. Emden, *A Biographical Register of the University of Oxford to A.D. 1500* (3 vols., Oxford, 1957-59), III, 1649-50.

[23] Ullman, *Liber*, pp. 56-57.

[24] Ibid., *passim*; M. Letts (ed.), *The Travels of Leo of Rozmital* (Hakluyt Soc., 2nd ser., CVIII, Cambridge, 1957), pp. 45, 47-48, 53, 63; Anthony Wagner and J.C. Sainty, 'The Origin of the Introduction of Peers in the House of Lords', *Archaeologia*, CI (1967), 122-24.

have been a ceremonious and deferential society. Their careful and precise stress on status and precedence underlines the formality of many such occasions and the central role of the nobility, both spiritual and temporal, in them. These records of precedence and ceremony, it might be thought, reflect the very essence of the court as a series of occasions, a noble environment of considerable formality, over which the king presided.[25]

There are, too, the impressions left by several people who attended these ceremonies, or who were present at court at other times. These informal accounts were penned by foreigners and Englishmen alike, and they offer *vignettes* of the court's day from the inside. Of the foreigners who attended the English court, were admitted to the hall (*in aulam*), and waited on the king, several were granted a personal interview with His Majesty. Three Prussian envoys were invited in May 1386 to Windsor Castle where, they reported, the king and his lords were taking part in wedding festivities and the Garter celebrations.[26] French envoys in July 1445 were struck by the richness and formality of Henry VI's court at Westminster (though the king himself later relaxed), and also by the array of noblemen about him. Substantial bodies of bishops, magnates, knights and esquires were assigned (presumably by the king) to conduct the envoys from place to place through the streets of the capital and by water to Westminster, where:

> . . . they found the king upon a high stool, without a bed stretched over it, of blue tapestry, diapered, of the livery of the late king, that is to say, Pods, and his motto 'Jamais', of gold, and a backpiece of tapestry representing some ladies who present to a lord the arms of France; and the whole was of gold, very rich, and a high chair under the said back-piece; and he himself was clothed in a rich robe down to the ground, of red cloth of gold.[27]

Jörg von Ehingen, a German nobleman, could compare his impressions of Henry's court in 1458 with those he formed during his tour of other

---

[25] On precedence, see Myers, *Household of Edward IV*, p. 32 n. 5 (rules of precedence *c.* 1467); *Collection of Ordinances and Regulations*, pp. 109-33 (1493).

[26] G. von der Ropp (ed.) *Hanserecesse*, vol. 1, part 3, no. 198 (a reference I owe to Mr. T.H. Lloyd).

[27] James Stevenson (ed.), *Letters and Papers illustrative of the Wars of the English in France during the Reign of Henry the Sixth, King of England*, vol. 1 (Rolls Ser., 1861), pp. 87-148, 153-59, with the quotation p. 103. These are the envoys' own accounts of their reception in London, Westminster and Fulham; at first they greeted the king on their knees, but later had less formal conversations in the king's presence. Cf. the reception of Louis of Bruges, lord of Gruthuyse, at Windsor Castle in 1472: 'The Record of Bluemantle Pursuivant' in C.L. Kingsford (ed.), *English Historical Literature in the Fifteenth Century* (Oxford, 1913; repr. New York, 1962), pp. 385-88, where nobles of the 'kinges owne courte' were among the reception party.

European courts, including that of Scotland.[28] The companions of the
queen of Bohemia's brother, Leo of Rozmital, who visited England in
1466, were quite bowled over by the opulence, regal splendour and noble
company characteristic of Edward IV's court more than four years before
he visited Burgundy; they witnessed some of the very ceremonies –
notably, the churching of Queen Elizabeth after the birth of her first-born
in February 1466 – whose organisation was the responsibility of the dean
of the Royal Chapel, as outlined in the account given to the Portuguese in
1449. The Bohemian delegation noted admiringly that Edward:

> has the most splendid court that could be found in all Christendom. Some days
> later he invited my lord Leo and his honourable company and provided a most
> splendid banquet with fifty dishes according to their custom. Then the King
> admitted my lord and his attendants to his fellowship.[29]

Things seemed hardly different to the Venetian envoy and his servant in
the winter of 1496-97, except that the suspicious personality of Henry
Tudor contrasted with that of the rumbustious Edward IV. Indeed, it was
observed that Henry, though inclined to be personally frugal, 'does not
change any of the ancient usages of England at his court, keeping a
sumptuous table'.[30]

Dominic Mancini, the Italian who spent almost a year in England in
1482-83, did not stir from London and Westminster, and he seems to have
had an entrée to the court, perhaps facilitated by influential Italians
already living in London. At any rate, he saw (or learned) a good deal
besides the jovial openness and magnificence of Edward IV's court; he
recognised that the king himself 'contrived many performances of actors
amidst royal splendour, so as to mitigate or disguise this sorrow' (of the
news of the Franco-Burgundian treaty sealed at Arras in December 1482).
Mancini was also made aware of the intrigues and aristocratic factions
'who were the very powerful at court' (*in regiam, in aulam*, even *in regiam
aulam*) during the king's later years. Whereas Richard, duke of Gloucester
was rarely present at court (*in regiam*) after the execution of his brother
George, duke of Clarence, the queen (said Mancini):

[28] M. Letts (ed.), *The Diary of Jörg van Ehingen* (London, 1929), pp. 39-40. Von
Ehingen's impression of Henry's court was so little different from that of other royal
'courts', where he was usually shown honour in 'hunting, dancing and feasting', that he
wrote little about it, save that he met King Henry, who gave him his Order; this may refer
to the Lancastrian SS collar rather than the Garter, since there is no record that he was
admitted to the Order of the Garter. See Belz, *Memorials of the Garter*, pp. clxi-clxii.

[29] Letts, *Leo of Rozmital*, with the quotation (from Gabriel Tetzel's report) at p. 45. The
visitors noted how lords and ladies, as well as servants, knelt before the king and his queen.

[30] C.A. Sneyd (ed.), *A Relation, or rather a True Account, of the Island of England . . . about the
year 1500* (Camden Soc., 1847), with the quotation at p. 46.

ennobled many of her family. Besides she attracted to her party many strangers and introduced them to court [*in regiam aulam*], so that they alone should manage the public and private businesses of the crown, surround the king, and have clients, give or sell offices, and finally rule the very king himself.[31]

These interstices of formal court life – the flattery and faction, both personal and political, that were the darker side of a world of ceremony and deference – tend to dominate the impressions which Englishmen have left of the court. Such observers were perhaps less surprised and overwhelmed by the splendour of it all and most of them, in truth, were not honoured guests at court, as the foreign commentators generally were. One of the heralds who helped to ensure that ceremonies went as planned wrote an elaborate account of ceremonial at 'the king's own court' in 1471-72: how the king 'kept his estate' at crown-wearings, religious festivals, the Garter ceremony and at the banquets.[32] Of the royal councillors, Sir John Fortescue has left but few words about the court, but these are at least concrete and direct:

I praise highly the magnificence and grandeur of the king's house [*domus*], for within it is the supreme academy for the nobles of the realm, and a school of vigour, probity and manners by which the realm is honoured and will flourish,. . .[33]

The same may be said of the author of the Crowland Chronicle. Casting his mind back to Edward IV's court which he knew well, he commented that 'you might have seen a royal court such as befitted a mighty kingdom, filled with riches and men from almost every nation and (surpassing all else) with the handsome and most delightful children' of the queen.[34] He had witnessed crown-wearings and religious festivals at court; but he was, even more intimately than Mancini, alive to its seamier side as well. He was familiar with 'the royal familiarity' (or circles). Of the time when the king quarrelled with his brother, the duke of Clarence, he recalled:

---

[31] C.A.J. Armstrong (ed.), *The Usurpation of Richard The Third, by Dominic Mancini* (2nd ed., Oxford, 1969), with the quotations at pp. 59, 65. For other hints of the relationship between the court, the great hall and the chambers of the king and queen, see Ullman, *Liber*, pp. 67-72 (1449).

[32] 'Bluemantle Pursuivant', pp. 379-88. At Westminster, the White hall was most commonly the location of these events.

[33] *Sir John Fortescue: De Laudibus Legum Angliae*, ed. and transl. by S.B. Chrimes (Cambridge, 1942), p. 111.

[34] *Crowland Chronicle Continuations*, with the quotation at p. 149.

You might have seen (as such men are found in the courts of all princes) sycophants running to and from the one side and the other carrying the words of both brothers backwards and forwards even if they had been spoken in the most secret chamber.[35]

To the inquisitive outsider, the court seemed an inexhaustible storehouse of gossip about the great and the noble. Robert Fabyan, the prominent London draper and city politician who seems to have been the author of the so-called 'Great Chronicle of London', had a good ear for rumours about the court and an eye for the humorous and ironic. He recalled an incident 'In the Court' in 1469 which illustrates both the entertainments and the political intrigue at Edward IV's court. On a hot, dry summer's day, a jester well known at the court for the titillating undertones of his capers, entered the king's chamber. He was dressed in a short coat cut at the bottom in points, and he wore a pair of boots long enough to be tied to the points; in his hand he carried a pike. When Edward enquired why he was wearing such long boots and holding a pike, the jester replied with a veiled but scathing comment on the queen's father, Earl Rivers, and the influence which he and his family enjoyed in the kingdom. It was a jibe which would have been savoured by a number of those present:

I have passyd thorwth many Cuntrees of your Realm, and In placys that I have passid the Ryvers been soo hieh that I coude hardly scape thorw theym, But as I was fayn to serch the depth wyth this long staff.[36]

Edward knew what he meant but took it in good part. Yet within a few months the realm had fallen into civil war, with dissident Yorkists who resented the prominence of Earl Rivers and his relatives sinking their differences with the exiled Lancastrians.

Long ears, honied tongues and capacious pockets were needed by those who, like the Paston family from the provinces, hoped to advance their personal causes by visiting the court or ingratiating themselves with members of the king's household. A piece of fifteenth-century doggerel nicely illustrates the popular contemporary view of the court as a place of social advancement:

> Man vpon mold, whatsoever thou be,
> I warn vtterly thou getyst no degre,
> Ne no worshyp abyd with the,
> but thou haue the peny redy to tak to.

---

[35] Ibid., pp. 147, 145. For Richard III's crown-wearing at Christmas in the great hall, ibid., p. 173.

[36] A.H. Thomas and I.D. Thornley (eds.), *The Great Chronicle of London* (London, 1938), p. 208.

If thou be a yeman, a gentyllman wold be,
Into sum lordes cort than put thou the;
Lok thou haue spendyng larg and plente,
And alwey the peny redy to tak to.

If thou be a squyre, and wold be a knyght,
And darest no in armur put the in fyght,
Than to the kynges cort hy the full tyght,
And lok thou haue the peny redy to tak to. . . .[37]

Margaret Paston was proud of her eldest son John and urged him in May 1478 that he 'may do as meche wyth the Kyng as ony knyght that ys longyng to the Corte'; she further exhorted him to continue his efforts there to 'mary rygth nygth of the Qwenys blood'.[38] Much of the political news which the Pastons relayed home to East Anglia must surely have come from chatting at court. These and other comments enable us to penetrate the 'busy' word of personal relationships, politicking and patronage which represent the penumbra, the informal underside, sometimes sordid and venal, of the king's court.[39] In its darker corners – so it seemed even to the king's officials – were 'the rascals and hangars uppon thys court', whom it was desirable to expel.[40]

What these differing sources reveal is that the court was something more than the household. The so-called 'Black Book' compiled early in the 1470s 'diffined throughely this royal court to stond after thies apoyntmentz that folowe after, of all the intermixtious peysed by wysedom, profyte, and by reason, answering to euery astate and degree,. . .'[41] This too is clear: court politics and their impact on the realm at large were more than the life of the royal household and its staff and their relations with the king and his subjects. Apart from the servants and officials of the household and the sworn councillors on whom the king relied, and their entourages, 'the intermixtious' at the court included numbers of English nobles and bishops who, along with the king and his family, more than any other social group set its tone. These were the people who made ceremonies ceremonious ; they were the 'nobles of the kinges owne courte', male and female.[42] They included the households of the queen and (if any) of the king's young sons and daughters, of the king's

[37] R.H. Robbins (ed.), *Secular Lyrics of the XIVth and XVth Centuries* (2nd ed., Oxford, 1955), pp. xxvii, 55-56, from Bodleian Library MS. Eng.e.1 (*c.* 1480).

[38] Norman Davis (ed.), *Paston Letters and Papers of the Fifteenth Century*, part I (Oxford, 1971), p. 381.

[39] Helen Miller, *Henry VIII and the English Nobility* (Oxford, 1986), p. 79.

[40] Myers, *Household of Edward IV*, p. 162 (1471-72).

[41] Ibid., p. 47.

[42] 'Bluemantle Pursuivant', p. 387, a common enough phrase. For the ranks of noblemen 'in the court', see Myers, *Household of Edward IV*, pp. 94-104, 197 (1471-72).

brothers and his mother. The description of Henry VI's Royal Chapel distinguished lords from the rest of the court, and household officials from others of the court.[43] And when the Bohemian envoys were taken into the queen's apartments in 1466, they saw dukes dancing there.[44] Some of the nobility had been familiar with the court since their youth, for wards of the king resided at court, were brought up there with members of the royal family, and were educated in what amounted to a royal school of noble virtues and accomplishments.[45]

Strangers were constantly at court, too. If their presence was approved, they required lodging and meals according to their estate and degree, for court rules observed the social niceties and distinctions.[46] A report of the arrival of the king of Armenia in England in 1385 suggests that he was received at Eltham by the court:

> . . . he received a courteous welcome from him [Richard II] and was enriched by a quantity of truly splendid gifts and presents not only from the king but from the king and the nobles who were there.[47]

Among more frequent visitors were foreign envoys, most of whom were invited by the king 'to lie within the courte'. They had their own chambers and attendants, provided by the officials of the household.[48] Their initial reception was highly formal, arranged no doubt by those who organized court ceremonies. And, of course, there were the lowlier visitors to the court: the plaintiffs to whom Edward IV in particular was ready to lend 'a willing ear'; the parasites and hangers-on whom the household officials tried to remove; the sycophants who thrived in an atmosphere of intrigue and gossip; and the plain curious, before whom Edward loved to disport himself:

> . . . even the least notable. Frequently [Edward IV] called to his side complete strangers, when he thought they had come with the intention of addressing or beholding him more closely. He was wont to show himself to those who wished to watch him, and he seized any opportunity that the occasion offered of revealing his fine stature more protractedly and more evidently to on-lookers.[49]

[43] E.g., Ullmann, *Liber*, pp. 63, 56, 61-62. For royal kinsfolk and envoys at court, see also *Collection of Ordinances and Regulations*, pp. 117-18 (1493); Myers, *Household of Edward IV*, p. 92 (1471-72); Sneyd, *Italian Relation*, p. 46 (1496-97).

[44] Letts, *Travels of Leo of Rozmital*, p. 47.

[45] Above p. 19. For a comment, see Griffiths, *Reign of Henry VI*, p. 54, and, over a longer time-span, Nicholas Orme, *From Childhood to Chivalry* (London, 1984), pp. 48-55.

[46] Myers, *Household of Edward IV*, pp. 63 (1445), 87, 90 (1471-72), 214, 216 (1478).

[47] Hector and Harvey, *Westminster Chronicle*, pp. 154-55. The king 'held his court at Windsor' in February 1386, the Armenian king still in his company: ibid., pp. 158-59.

[48] *Collection of Ordinances and Regulations*, p. 118 (1493); Myers, *Household of Edward IV*, p. 229 (*temp.* Henry VII).

[49] *Mancini*, p. 65, a lengthy illustration of how easy of access Edward IV was at court.

There is even a suggestion in the reign of Henry VII that the court opened at eight o'clock in the morning, as did certain contemporary Italian courts.[50]

Like any large, varied and fluid society, the court was sometimes a scene of disorder and law-breaking. The jurisdiction of the judicial officers of the household, the so-called sovereigns, extended to all cases of debt and contempt, and to breaches of the peace (except homicide) commited within 'the verge' of the king's residence, and it encompassed members of households other than the king's and the entourages of visitors such as the chancellor and the chief justices.[51]

Those who knew the court, whether they were observers from outside or, more especially, those who fully understood its formal and declaratory role from the inside, described it variously as 'royal', 'splendid', 'noble', 'honourable' and 'famous', and the king and queen at its centre as worthy of 'courtly' and 'extraordinary' reverence. In the 'magnificence and state' of the royal palace, 'days of estate' were held, and 'costly apartments' were to be found; there, too, 'silent spectacle' was staged, and 'sumptuous table' or 'splendid banquet' provided, all 'amidst royal splendour'.[52] Gavin Douglas captured exactly the ethos of the neighbouring Scottish court when he described 'The Palice of Honour' (1500-1): Honour was the monarch, inhabiting an allegorical palace in whose presence chamber he held the court.[53] There were more down-to-earth descriptions of what went on less formally at court, on the more personal level of politics, competition and intrigue, even faction. In the 1530s it seemed a 'quesy' world, 'unstable', 'busy', 'a wily world' – descriptions of a kind which are commonly used of any hub of political power and which were certainly used of the English king's court in Walter Map's day and by several chroniclers in the centuries that followed.[54]

But it is the regal, noble and chivalric adjectives which best convey the

[50] *Collection of Ordinances and Regulations,* p. 109. A gentleman usher was required to be present 'within the court' each day by 8 o'clock in the morning. For the phrase 'within the kinges yates', see Myers, *Household of Edward IV,* pp. 220-21 (1478); cf. ibid., p. 105 (1471-72).

[51] W.R. Jones, 'The Court of the Verge: the Jurisdiction of the Steward and Marshal of the Household in Later-Medieval England', *Journal of British Studies,* X, no. 1 (1970), 1-29. For the sovereigns 'of thys most hygh court temporall', who had the power to exclude persons (even those stricken with leprosy or pestilence) 'out of courte', see Myers, *Household of Edward IV,* pp. 124, 163, 216. By the early fourteenth century, their jurisdiction extended up to twelve miles from the king's presence.

[52] For such descriptions, see ibid., pp. 92, 101. 120, 144, 151-52, 168, and the contemporary sources above.

[53] Priscilla Bawautt, *Gavin Douglas* (Edinburgh, 1976), ch. 3; for a comment, see Mervyn James, *Society, Politics and Custom* (Cambridge, 1986), pp. 310ff. For reference to 'the honour of thys court' in Edward IV's reign, see Myers, *Household of Edward IV,* pp. 92, 152.

[54] Miller, *Henry VIII and the English Nobility,* p. 79; Dickens, *Courts of Europe,* ch. 1, 2.

ethos of the late medieval court and reflect the ideas to which it aspired in the service of the king and his kingdom. This ethos and these ideals were those which fourteenth- and fifteenth-century English kings sought to project visually by magnificence and ceremony designed to impress and impose the king's majesty and power on subject and visitor alike, partly (it must be said) in imitation of French example. In this the nobility, especially its higher ranks, played a crucial part. The appearance of an institutionalised body of peers by the beginning of the fifteenth century, assembled in an exclusive house of peers; the creation of new ranks of nobility from the late fourteenth century, and the careful application of rules of precedence; and the emergence of the royal family as a distinct estate among the nobles during the latter part of the fourteenth and in the fifteenth centuries – all had a powerful impact on the court, just as (in Richard II's view) ennoblement and the elevation of the king's kinsmen shed lustre on the crown itself.[55] Thus, the meaning of the fifteenth-century court was imparted to it pre-eminently by the king, his kinsfolk and his nobility. John Blount, Lord Mountjoy, in the last days of his mortal illness in October 1485, might counsell his sons 'never to take the state of Baron upon them if they may leye it from nor to desire to be grete about princes, for it is daungeros'.[56] But it was nevertheless the nobility who helped to set the tone of the king's court, in both its formal and informal aspects: 'certain people, certain behaviour, certain attitudes', as Sir Geoffrey Elton put it.[57] And this suggests, in turn, that we should look to Richard II's reign, perhaps even to Edward III's, for major new departures in the court's evolution.

The business of the court was the business of the king, and the nobility was central to it. Moreover, the formal and public and the informal and private aspects of court life were closely entwined. This can be illustrated, from among court ceremonies, by a study of court marriages; the implications of such marriages were carefully gauged behind the scenes. The Westminster chronicler, who was well informed about Richard II's court, knew that Richard at his own expense organized the marriage of several companions of his beloved queen, Anne of Bohemia, to men of rank whom he favoured.[58] We know even more about one court marriage

[55] For the developments noted in this paragraph, see R.A. Griffiths, 'The Crown and the Royal Family in Later Medieval England', in idem and James Sherborne (eds.), *Kings and Nobles in the Later Middle Ages: A Tribute to Charles Ross* (Gloucester, 1986), pp. 15-26 (reprinted above pp. 1-10). For the treatment of visitors to the court 'after their astate', see Myers, *Household of Edward IV*, p. 101 (1471-72); and for noble disputes over precedence earlier in the century, Griffiths, *Reign of Henry VI*, pp. 80-81, 353, 358-59.

[56] Public Record Office, PCC, 27 Legge, quoted in G.E. Cokayne, *The Complete Peerage* . . . (12 vols. in 13, London, 1910-59), IX, 338n.f.

[57] G.R. Elton, 'Tudor Government: the Points of Contact. III. The Court', *Transactions of the Royal Historical Society*, 5th Series, XXVI (1976), 211.

[58] Hector and Harvey, *Westminster Chronicle*, pp. 160-61.

of great diplomatic significance: that of Henry VI's aunt, Joan Beaufort, to the captive Scots king, James I, who had spent eighteen years in and out of the English court prior to his release in 1424. The marriage took place at the Church of St. Mary Overy, now Southwark Cathedral, and its preparation and the wooing are immortalised in James's own words, in his poem, 'The Kingis Quair'.[59]

Thirty years later, the sojourn of Henry VI, his queen and his loyalist circle in the English Midlands between 1456 and 1460, on the threshold of civil war, allows us to see the court in high relief, settled in or around the loyal provincial towns and castles of Coventry, Kenilworth and Leicester. Not only did Henry rely on his court for administrative and military commanders at a time of growing tension, but its claustrophobic noble atmosphere is vividly conveyed by a series of aristocratic marriages that were evidently arranged at court in these years. Queen Margaret and Humphrey Stafford, duke of Buckingham, the most senior magnate loyal to the king and himself a descendant of Edward III, figured prominently in the arrangements; and three of the marriages were recorded in the episcopal register of the compliant bishop of Coventry and Lichfield, Reginald Boulers.[60]

The queen, Margaret of Anjou, had the most intimate interest in the wedding in 1456 of her kinswoman, Marie, daughter of Charles, count of Maine, to Thomas Courtenay, the son and heir of the earl of Devon. That this was a court-contracted marriage is suggested by the fact that Marie's wedding gown was supplied in September 1456 by the king's Great Wardrobe.[61] The earl of Devon was anxious to ingratiate himself with the Lancastrian régime for reasons that concerned his power in Devon. From the court's point of view, the marriage brought the earl into the royal circle and an outlying part of the realm under Lancastrian control. The ceremony, arranged by the queen and held at Coventry in the presence of the court, and presumably conducted by the loyal Bishop Boulers, had a political importance that transcended the personal and family links forged at the altar.

The second notable marriage of 1457 to be arranged at court was that between the king's cousin, Margaret Beaufort, countess of Richmond, and her third husband, Henry Stafford, second son of the duke of Buckingham. This additional bond among the king's blood relatives buttressed the Lancastrian régime and the royal family at a time when the survival of the dynasty rested on the young shoulders of Prince Edward, the only son and heir of King Henry VI and Queen Margaret. The arrangements for this marriage are recorded in the register of Bishop

[59] E.W.M. Balfour-Melville, *James I, King of Scots* (London, 1936), ch. II-V.
[60] Lichfield Record Office, B/A/1/11.
[61] P.R.O., E101/410/19; Bodleian Library, MS. ch. England 30 (the king's signed warrant sent from Lichfield on 9 September 1456).

Boulers, and papal letters of dispensation were evidently requested by the court and delivered to the bishop at his Warwickshire palace of Beaudesert in the vicinity of the court.[62]

Two further Stafford marriages – between the duke of Buckingham's daughter and the earl of Shrewsbury's heir, and between the duke's younger son and the daughter of his landowning neighbour, Henry Green, esquire – took place on the same day in July 1458 in the chapel of Buckingham's castle at Maxstoke in Warwickshire. Once again, the dependable bishop of Coventry and Lichfield was involved and there can be little doubt that these matches too were arranged within the aristocratic circle at the Lancastrian court resident in the Midlands.[63] It is, indeed, a striking fact that no aristocratic marriages of comparable significance took place outside the court circle in these crucial years before the onset of civil war. Most – if not all – of those that did take place were probably discussed at court among magnates – Staffords, Courtenays, Beauforts, Talbots, Berkeleys, Butlers, Greys and Percies – who were loyal to the house of Lancaster and prominent at King Henry's court.[64]

In the next decade, Edward IV's marriage in 1464 to the English-born widow, Elizabeth Woodville, was the prelude to another series of court marriages. They involved the new queen's numerous relatives in an expansion of the Yorkist royal family that bound several aristocratic families to the king and the new Yorkist dynasty. By 1467 seven such ceremonies had taken place between Woodvilles and the noble houses of Buckingham, Exeter, Norfolk, Arundel, Essex, Kent and Herbert.[65] In some cases, the king personally played a part, offering bribes to reluctant fathers. Other matches were arranged 'at the instance of our Souereyn Lord the king and his pleasure' or by the queen herself. Almost all of them took place at court, in one or other of the royal palaces – as Sir John Paston's correspondent suggested in a letter sent from the capital in February 1466.[66] Marital policy had helped to make Edward's court a

---

[62] Lichfield R.O., B/A/1/11 f. 87*v*.

[63] Ibid., f. 93*v*.; Griffiths, *Reign of Henry VI*, pp. 803, 841 n.181.

[64] For detailed background to the marriages and the wider role of the court in these years, see ibid., pp. 797-804.

[65] These marriages have provoked much discussion: Ross, *Edward IV*, pp. 92-94; J.R. Lander, *Crown and Nobility, 1450-1509* (London, 1976), pp. 110-14 (first published in 1963); M.A. Hicks, 'The Changing Role of the Wydevilles in Yorkist Politics to 1483', in Charles Ross (ed.), *Patronage, Pedigree and Power in Later Medieval England* (Gloucester, 1979), pp. 66-70; T.B. Pugh, 'The Magnates, Knights and Gentry', in S.B. Chrimes, C.D. Ross and R.A. Griffiths (eds.), *Fifteenth-Century England, 1399-1509* (Manchester, 1972), pp. 87-93, 111-12. According to *Mancini*, p. 75, the duke of Buckingham was forced to marry the queen's sister, Catherine Woodville, when he was in the king's wardship.

[66] Norman Davis (ed.), *Paston Letters and Papers of the Fifteenth Century*, part II (Oxford, 1976), p. 375 (following the marriage of the earl of Arundel's son to Margaret Woodville). Lord Herbert married Mary Woodville at Windsor Castle in January 1467 (C.L. Scofield, *The Life and Reign of Edward the Fourth* [2 vols., London, 1923], I, 397n.); and Buckingham

court of patronage and profit, 'the stock exchange of the day'.[67] And Edwardian court matrimony lay even closer to the regal heart of the court than did Henry VI's, but for that very reason it was also more divisive as it gradually helped to alienate those who resented the consolidation of a royal faction.

When it came to his own children, Edward IV behaved traditionally, after the manner of Henry IV and Edward III, preferring diplomatic matches with foreign royalty. So did Henry VII. But not one of Edward's children was in fact married when the king died in April 1483. Mary and Margaret were already dead, Edward and Richard soon disappeared, and Bridget was shunted into a nunnery by Henry VII. It was Henry who arranged court marriages for the rest. Under his direction, Cecily married Viscount Welles, Henry's own uncle, as part of a bargain struck at court. In 1495 Anne married Thomas, Lord Howard, later earl of Surrey, and the wedding of Catherine and Sir William Courtenay, later the earl of Devon, took place at Greenwich Palace.[68] These court festivities had carefully calculated political and dynastic purposes, formulated by the king himself.

The consequences of politicized matrimony were not universally approved. One of the Woodville matches – that between Sir John Woodville and Catherine Neville, dowager duchess of Norfolk, in January 1465 – was stigmatized as *maritagium diabolicum* by one observer because she was a three-times widow in her middle sixties while he was only twenty.[69] A misalliance arranged at Henry VII's court – that of William de la Pole, a younger brother of Edmund, earl of Suffolk, with the twice-widowed (and therefore wealthy) Catherine Stourton – appears to have caused even a visiting Italian's eyebrows to rise in the winter of 1496-97:

> I saw, one day that I was with your Magnificence [his Venetian master] at court, a very handsome young man of about 18 years of age, the brother of the Duke of Suffolk, who, as I understand, had been left very poor. . .; this youth . . . was ogled by a widow of fifty, with a fortune . . . of 50,000 crowns; and this old woman knew how to play her cards so well, that he was content to become

---

was married to Catherine Woodville at Greenwich. See Hicks, 'Changing Role of the Wydevilles', pp. 67-70.

[67] Lander, *Crown and Nobility*, p. 108.

[68] E.B. Fryde, D.E. Greenway, S. Porter and I. Roy (eds.), *Handbook of British Chronology* (3rd ed., London, 1986), pp. 41-42. For Edward IV's abortive marriage negotiations abroad on behalf of his children, see Ross, *Edward IV*, pp. 230, 233, 245-56, 284. Only his second son, Richard, duke of York, had been provided with a bride in the person of Anne, heiress of the vast Mowbray inheritance of the dukes of Norfolk. This was a court marriage celebrated in St. Stephen's Chapel, Westminster, in 1478, but Anne died less than four years later at Greenwich: ibid., p. 148.

[69] Lander, *Crown and Nobility*, pp. 110-11, quoting the chronicle attributed to William Worcester.

her husband, and patiently to waste the flower of his beauty with her, hoping soon to enjoy her great wealth with some handsome young lady.[70]

The de la Poles were Yorkist siblings on whose activities Henry Tudor kept a watchful eye, especially after the eldest of them, John, earl of Lincoln, led the rebels at the battle of Stoke in 1487. Edmund de la Pole seems to have spent most of his time at the Tudor court, even after he succeeded to the dukedom of Suffolk in 1491 at the age of twenty. And so, it seems, did his young brothers, William and Richard. King Henry's suspicion of this family could not prevent Edmund and Richard from fleeing the country in 1501 and plotting abroad; William was arrested and put in the Tower. Thus, William de la Pole's marriage in 1496 can hardly have been contracted without the king's approval, especially since Catherine Stourton was a wealthy widow, the disposal of whose estates and income was a matter of some public importance.[71]

More deeply shocking to English court-watchers in the months before the death of Richard III's sickly wife, Anne, in March 1485 was the rumour that Richard was scheming to marry his niece, Elizabeth of York. Looking back on the Christmas festivities at court in 1484, the Crowland chronicler noted ominously that:

> too much attention was paid to singing and dancing and to vain exchanges of clothing between Queen Anne and Lady Elizabeth . . . who were alike in complexion and figure. The people spoke against this and the magnates and prelates were greatly astonished . . .

When the queen died two and a half months later, the cavorting at court seemed, in retrospect, to have sinister implications, at least for one spectator.[72]

Such ceremonies are more than what they seem, and their back-stage arrangements are as much the reality of court life as what went on before the foot-lights. That may be less true of the funerals of kings, which

[70] Sneyd, *Italian Relation*, pp. 27-28 (for the quotation, though the editor wrongly supposed it referred to William's younger brother, Richard de la Pole).

[71] *Complete Peerage*, XII, part I, 450-54, Appendix I (for the de la Poles); A.B. Emden, *A Biographical Register of the University of Cambridge to 1500* (Cambridge, 1963), p. 181 (William de la Pole). For Catherine Stourton's second marriage to Henry, Lord Grey of Codnor, who died in 1496, see *Complete Peerage*, VI, 131-32. Her first husband, Sir William Berkeley of Beverston (Glos.), died in 1485: A.F. Sutton and P.W. Hammond (eds.), *The Coronation of Richard III: The Extant Documents* (Gloucester, 1983), p. 312. For marriages at Henry VII's court in 1494-95, see S. Bentley (ed.), *Excerpta Historica, or Illustrations of English History* (London, 1831), pp. 98, 101.

[72] *Crowland Chronicle Continuations*, p. 175; Ross, *Richard III*, pp. 145-46. The comment on the clothes of the queen and Elizabeth of York may have something to do with Richard's attempt to win the trust of the princess and her mother, Queen Elizabeth, at a time when Henry Tudor was known to be planning invasion and a marriage with Elizabeth of York.

marked the dissolution of the court and usually attracted all among the prominent of the realm who were able to attend. We cannot say the same or different about the funerals of queens in the fifteenth century, either because, like Joan of Navarre or Katherine of Valois, they were living in seclusion and out of favour when they died, or else, like Margaret of Anjou, they died abroad forgotten.[73] But one interment in the century does indeed reveal the complex character of the court at formal play: this was the re-burial in 1476 of Edward IV's father, Richard, duke of York, who had been killed in battle all of sixteen years before. He and his second son, Edmund, earl of Rutland, fell at Wakefield on 30 December 1460 and were buried in Pontefract Priory in Yorkshire.[74]

In July 1476 Edward IV and his court travelled north to re-inter the two bodies at Fotheringhay in Northamptonshire, whose collegiate church was patronised by the house of York. The event was organised by the master of ceremonies of the fifteenth-century English court, the dean of the Royal Chapel, William Dudley.[75] The Yorkist court was in attendance almost to a man. The cortège was accompanied the seventy miles from Pontefract by a group of nobles and bishops headed by Richard, duke of Gloucester, and the king's recent nominee to the archbishopric of York, Lawrence Booth. It was met at Fotheringhay by King Edward and Queen Elizabeth, by George, duke of Clarence and the king's two eldest children, his daughters Elizabeth and Mary; by the nobles who were married to the king's sister and to the queen's sisters, by the queen's brother, Earl Rivers, and the marquess of Dorset, her son by her first husband – in other words, by almost all the adult senior magnates in England – and by half a dozen other lords and faithful friends who were members of one or other of the royal households. Present also were two envoys from King Louis XI of France, and one each from Denmark and Portugal.[76] The duke of York's personal accoutrements were brought into Fotheringhay Church, including his old charger ridden by the duke's former retainer, Lord Ferrers. The noble, chivalric and courtly character of this occasion is unmistakeable.

To judge by the 20,000 dinners ordered for the company, and paid for by the cofferer of the royal household, it was a court enlarged by numerous hangers-on and invaded by the general public. It was an assembly of the court for formal ceremony, diplomatic exchange and political demonstration, for this macabre occasion, and the slow perambulation

---

[73] Griffiths, *Reign of Henry VI*, pp. 61-63, 892.

[74] Ross, *Edward IV*, pp. 30, 271.

[75] Scofield, *Life and Reign of Edward IV*, II, 167-70, based on B.L., Harleian MS. 48 f. 78-91, a contemporary description. For William Dudley, see Emden, *University of Oxford*, I, 599-600.

[76] C.L. Scofield (*Life and Reign of Edward IV*, II, 169) erroneously says that two Danish ambassadors were present.

through the English countryside, celebrated and publicised the restored Yorkist monarchy, seemingly stable after the return of Edward IV from exile in 1471, and underpinned by a network of loyalties focussed on the houses of York and Woodville, and constructed at court. This network included almost all the aristocracy who then mattered in the land.

Among the continuities of court life from one dynasty to the next, there were bound to be discontinuities, especially during the Wars of the Roses and the aftermath of persistent foreign war. Above all, courts changed their complexion and their tone because they were a collection of individuals gathered in a regal environment largely created by the personality, abilities and health of the king and the character of his family, as well as by courtly custom and tradition. In the last weeks of the tempestuous year 1450, during which the critics of Henry VI's rule were crowding in upon him, Parliament presented the king with a hostile petition. The parliamentary commons demanded that he remove from his presence twenty-nine named individuals who were regarded as exerting undesirable influence on him. Twenty of the twenty-nine were either officers of Henry's household or in receipt of fees from his household. The others were closely associated with his régime in England and Lancastrian France, and intimates of either the king or his queen. What they all had in common in 1450 was their place at court. Henry VI responded to the demand with a stubbornness that enabled him to retain:

> certein persones which shall be right fewe in nombre, the which have be accustomed contynuelly to waite uppon his persone, and knowen howe and in what wise they shall mowe beste serve hym to his pleasure. . . . the remnaunte shall absente theym frome his high presence and from his court for the space of an hoole yere,. . .[77]

Richard II, much earlier in his reign, had precipitated an even greater crisis at his court when he allowed a dangerous chasm to open between a section of his nobility and his personal entourage, with the result that in the winter of 1387-88 the opposing nobles insisted on pruning not only the number of officials in his household but also 'those who stood about the king, considering whether or not they deserved to remain with the king'. A substantial number were forthwith expelled 'from the court' (*curia*) on 1 January 1388:

> These were illustrious names in the chivalry of the day, men of repute who were distinguished by many virtues. There were also three ladies who abjured

---

[77] *Rotuli Parliamentorum* (6 vols., London 1767; Index volume, 1832), V, 216-17, reprinted in S.B. Chrimes and A.L. Brown (eds.), *Select Documents of English Constitutional History, 1307-1485* (London, 1961), pp. 292-94. For detailed comment, see Griffiths, *Reign of Henry VI*, pp. 308-10.

the royal court at this time:. . . On 2 January they removed from the court all
the king's familiars (*familiares*) and especially those who had been closest to the
king,. . .[78]

Even more dramatic dissolutions of the court occurred between 1399
and 1485, and with unprecedented frequency at each dynastic change. In
the confusing circumstances of 1469-71, kings and courts appeared to
scuttle away with the speed and ignominy of the Bourbons leaving the
Tuileries in 1815. Dominic Mancini observed a not altogether different
situation in 1483: the former intimates of the late king, Edward IV,
meeting in one another's houses, the entourage of the boy-king, Edward
V, gradually barred from his presence, and Richard, duke of Gloucester
entertaining in his own house a growing number of well-wishers and
attendants. Courts were dissolving while others were in the making.[79]
During the minority of Henry VI, the central, essential element of a court
was missing, except on the most formal of occasions, and during Henry's
incapacitating illness the court was rudderless until it was taken in hand
by Queen Margaret.[80]

Such circumstances as these influenced the way in which the court
acted as a forum in which government was supervised and royal
relationships with, and management of, the nobility were maintained.
The four adult monarchs between 1437 and 1509 were as different from
one another as chalk is from cheese, and their personalities had a powerful
effect on the inner workings and outward appearance of their courts.[81]
Few kings failed to dominate their household establishment or to use it to
advance their interests in the realm; the wider court was often less
amenable. The mature Henry VI's court successfully sustained a
Lancastrian establishment, including a large section of the nobility, for
more than a decade after 1437. But it failed to contain and resolve dissent
and dissatisfaction, and when the king himself became a cipher, the court
grew too exclusive and ingrown and relations between crown and nobility
were fatally damaged.[82]

Edward IV was just as ready as Henry VI to give a ready ear to any who
approached him, but unlike Henry he was not a generous man and was as

---

[78] Hector and Harvey, *Westminster Chronicle*, pp. 228-33. Occasionally a slightly more
precise translation of the Latin has been preferred.

[79] *Mancini*, pp. 91, 93, 95.

[80] Above p. 25. There are indications that the house of Humphrey, duke of Gloucester,
perhaps also of Cardinal Beaufort, was the focus of political life and patronage when
Henry VI was a child: Griffiths, *Reign of Henry VI*, p. 31.

[81] For the differences between Edward IV and Henry VII, as reflected in their courts,
see above p. 18.

[82] R.A. Griffiths, 'The Sense of Dynasty in the Reign of Henry VI', in Ross, *Patronage,
Pedigree and Power*, pp. 18-23 (with further examples of court marriages). See below pp.
88-92.

likely to excuse complaints as to remedy them. He was easy of access, even
to non-nobles, and more than once could be seen putting a friendly arm
round someone who seemed in awe of him and had come to observe or
plead with him. He would talk even to complete strangers and was eager
to parade his physique to onlookers.[83] And for all his informality of
bearing, he loved ceremonial. Yet, Edward was not successful in using his
court to manage his nobility, as the consequences of his marriage and his
early death demonstrate. As for Richard III, he had little opportunity to
create a stable court, not least because he spent so little time at
Westminster.[84] The most fascinating question of all is whether or not
Henry Tudor successfully restored royal control over government and
nobility by developing his court along lines mainly laid down in the
fourteenth century, emphasising its public formality, the place of a loyal
royal family in it, and strict management of the nobility through it. Henry
laid great stress on ceremonial and public display, and his reticent,
withdrawn and suspicious nature, which made him an observer at court
entertainments rather than a participant – unlike Edward IV and Henry
VIII – may have been an advantage.[85]

Having said that, however, the historian of the fifteenth-century
English court can still feel a great deal of sympathy with Walter Map, who
strove to understand the chameleon-like and ultimately elusive character
of the court of his day in the late twelfth century:

> . . . in the court I exist and of the court I speak, but what the court is, God
> knows, I know not. I do know however that the court is not time; but temporal
> it is, changeable and various, space-bound and wandering, never continuing
> in one state. When I leave it, I know it perfectly: when I come back to it I find
> nothing or but little of what I left there. . . . The court is the same, its members
> are changed . . . today we are one number, tomorrow we shall be a different
> one: yet the court is not changed; it remains always the same . . . a hundred-
> handed giant,. . . a hydra of many heads,. . . the court is constant only in
> inconstancy.

And as for the king in this whirlpool of personal relationships:

> The king in his court is like a husband who is the last to learn of the
> unfaithfulness of his wife.

In these respects, if not in others, things seem not to have changed much
since the 1180s.[86]

[83] *Mancini*, p. 65; above p. 22.

[84] Ross, *Richard III*, ch. 4; Rhoda Edwards, *The Itinerary of King Richard III, 1483-1485*
(London, 1983).

[85] Chrimes, *Henry VII*, pp. 298ff.; Starkey, *English Court*, pp. 76-77.

[86] James, *De Nugis Curialium*, pp. 3, 511. This satire is thought to have been written
between 1181 and 1193: ibid., pp. xxix-xxx.

3

The English Realm and Dominions and the King's Subjects in the Later Middle Ages

Historians have said and written much about the powers and responsibilities of English kings in the later Middle Ages and how well or how badly these powers were exercised and the responsibilities discharged. Rather less has been said about the bounds within which these powers and responsibilities operated: the geographical bounds, as defined by the territorial frontiers of the king's realm and the several dominions over which he ruled from the end of the thirteenth century onwards; the bounds of law which the king was brought to acknowledge and the multiplicity of laws that existed in his dominions; and the personal bounds, the identity of those peoples or subjects over whom he ruled and who owed him allegiance and obligations in return.

It is commonly claimed that between the fall of Rome and the sixteenth century men did not define the frontiers of their lordships and kingdoms with precision, as traceable or measurable lines. And yet, Scottish land grants reveal that by 1200 the notion of a geographical kingdom of Scotland, a precise territory ruled by the Scots king, was firmly embedded in men's minds. It is noteworthy that the only area of the Anglo-Scottish borderland still in dispute in the later Middle Ages was a comparatively small stretch of territory specifically designated 'The Debateable Land,' to distinguish it from the rest of the frontier, which presumably was not debatable.[1] Likewise, thirteenth-century men were well aware of where the western English counties ended and the largely autonomous marcher lordships of Wales began; they knew — and declared in court and to commissions of enquiry from Edward I's reign onwards — what was 'within the county' and what was without it.[2] Hardening claims to territorial jurisdiction inevitably led to the delineation of 'metes' and 'bounds,' even to the 'beating' of bounds, a medieval habit eccentric English

1 G.W.S. Barrow *The Anglo-Norman Era in Scottish History* (Oxford 1980) 152–6; W.M. MacKenzie 'The Debateable Land' *Scottish Historical Review* 30 (1951) 109–25, with a map on 112

2 R.R. Davies *Lordship and Society in the March of Wales, 1282–1400* (Oxford 1978) ch II ('The March')

clergy and their flocks follow even today.[3]

As to law, English kings acknowledged – albeit reluctantly at times – that a multiplicity and diversity of laws need not fundamentally detract from the authority of their lordship, and in the formative centuries of the evolution of the common law it was formally conceded from time to time that customary, provincial, and local laws could satisfactorily combine or coexist with English law in several parts of the king's realm and dominions. Even Edward I, the most persistent and prolific of English lawgivers, accepted this in his so-called 'statute of Wales' in 1284, and his successors hesitated on more than one occasion to accede to Irish and Welsh requests that English common law should replace indigenous custom.[4] According to an Irish petition of about 1331, 'Since the conquest there have been two kinds of people in Ireland and there still are – the English and the Irish – and amongst them three kinds of law have been used, each of which conflicts with the others – common law, Irish law and marcher law ...' The petitioners added that 'it seems to us that where there is diversity of law the people cannot be of one law or one community.'[5] But this was a conclusion of the mayors, bailiffs, and communities of the Anglicized towns of Ireland, such as Dublin, Waterford, Cork, and Wexford, and although the ideal of one and the same law for all within the king's Irish lordship was endorsed soon afterwards, on 3 March 1331, it was never a practical proposition throughout Ireland, and native Irish law survived in predominantly Gaelic areas. Likewise, Edward I willed 'that the Welsh have process of law for those things which they have in Wales according to the laws of Wales,' despite his and his advisers' doubts about the quality of Welsh law and the preference of some Welshmen for English common law.[6] Summoned to the court of King's Bench in 1331, a certain Hywel ap Gruffydd

---

3 For example, *Calender of Inquisitions Miscellaneous* I 387 (North Cardiganshire 1284); *Rotuli parliamentorum* 6 vols, ed J. Strachey et al (London 1767–83) (hereinafter *RP*) I 434 (1325); G.C. Homans, *English Villagers of the Thirteenth Century* (Cambridge Mass 1942) 368

4 *The Statutes of Wales*, ed I. Bowen (London 1908) 2–27; *Select Cases Concerning the Law Merchant, 1239–1633*, ed H. Hall III (Selden Society 49, 1932) 141 (for Edward I's acknowledgment of Welsh law in 1279); *Select Cases in the Exchequer Chamber before all the Justices of England, 1377–1461*, ed M. Hemmant (Selden Society 51, 1933) 81–3 (for Sir John Fortescue's comments in of abrogating Scotland's laws and customs at the time of the attempted conquest (*RP* I 268).

5 Quoted in G.J. Hand 'English Law in Ireland, 1172–1351' *Northern Ireland Legal Quarterly* 23 (1972) 413.

6 J.B. Smith 'Crown and Community in the Principality of North Wales in the Reign of Henry Tudor' *Welsh History Review* 3 (1966–7) 146–9 (noting the rejection of Welsh petitions for English law and practices on several occasions in

claimed that he was born in Wales which was outside the realm of England, and that his case should therefore be tried by the laws and customs of Wales and not by the common law of England.[7] Surprisingly successful was the submission made on behalf of John Kynaston, who was accused in 1402 of riding with the Welsh rebel leader, Owain Glyndŵr; it was argued that even acts of treason committed in Wales, beyond the western border of Shropshire, should not be tried by English law in an English county.[8] Thus it was that in 1406 the laws and customs of Ireland and Wales – and of the English dominions of Calais and Gascony too – were confirmed by King Henry IV, and no amount of advocacy could induce late-medieval English kings to eradicate them.[9] This multiplicity of laws made for complication in governing England and its dominions, but it in no way lessened the king's lordship over his subjects ('subditi') or his claim to their allegiance.

Those who were subject to English kings formed a complex series of interlocking and interrelated communities, between them enjoying several systems of law, acknowledging different traditions and bodies of custom, and speaking a number of languages; but they also had a common identity that derived from their history, status, and treatment as the king's subjects. Few attempts have been made to identify exactly who were the subjects of the late-medieval English kings, or what made a non-subject or alien in the English realm and dominions. One reason for this neglect is the difficulty of defining precisely such contemporary concepts as 'gens', 'patria,' and 'natio'; another is that the entire matter bears on those most mistrusted of medieval themes, nationality and the idea of the nation. Alice Beardwood noted some of the implications in her seminal studies of alien merchants in England.[10] But the study of the king's subjects and the aliens within his realm and dominions has another, broader and equally significant, dimension.

the first half of the fourteenth century); B. Murphy 'The Status of the Native Irish after 1331' *Irish Jurist* ns 2 (1967), 116–28; J.F. Lydon, *Ireland in the Later Middle Ages* (Dublin 1973) 44–5, 73

7 *Select Cases in the Court of King's Bench, Edward III*, ed G.O. Sayles v (Selden Society 76, 1957) 58–63

8 *Select Cases in the Court of King's Bench under Richard II, Henry IV and Henry V*, ed G.O. Sayles (Selden Society 88, 1971), 116ff

9 RP III 586. For Calais's judicial autonomy, see ibidem II 359; III 67–8; IV 194; and for Richard II's refusal to modify Calais custom, III 67.

10 *Alien Merchants in England, 1350–1377* (Cambridge, Mass 1931); 'Mercantile Antecedents of the English Naturalization Laws' *Medievalia et humanistica* 16 (1964) 64–76. For general discussions, see H.S.Q. Henriques *The Law of Aliens and Naturalization* (London 1906); W.S. Holdsworth *A History of English Law* 7th ed, 16 vols (London 1956–66), especially IX 72–104; F. Pollock and F.W. Maitland *The History of English Law before the Time of Edward I* 2nd ed 2 vols (Cambridge 1911) I 458–67.

To distinguish the English subject and to see reflected in him a national identity cannot but be an anachronism in the century and a half following the Norman conquest, when England was ruled by Norman dukes and Angevin counts, when many landowners held estates on both sides of the English Channel, and others did so in England and Scotland. But such perceptions become possible during the latter part of the twelfth century, and especially after Normandy was lost to the French in 1204 and formally surrendered to them by the Treaty of Paris in 1259: the English landowning nobility was then required to declare where its prime allegiance lay. Such perceptions are possible, too, with the growing self-consciousness of the Scottish kingdom and the hardening distinction between the jurisdictions of the English and Scots kings during the twelfth and thirteenth centuries.[11] Moreover, the dominance of Flemings and then of Italians in English overseas trade in the thirteenth century heightened Englishmen's awareness of aliens who were beyond the king's allegiance – and fostered resentment of their commercial success.[12] But as perceptions of the subject and the alien sharpened in these directions, they were blurred in another.

Well before the end of the thirteenth century, English kings had acquired dominions beyond the frontiers of their realm, a situation that was bound to raise the question of the status of the inhabitants of these dominions, both within the dominions themselves and within the English realm. In short, to what extent were their inhabitants the king's subjects? With minor exceptions, none of these dominions was incorporated in the kingdom, thereby giving to their inhabitants an unequivocal status as English subjects; rather than part of the realm of England, they could be described as 'parcels' of the English crown.[13] More usually, they were annexed and united to the kingdom of England, though the king was not king of them. This was the situation in Ireland, where since King John's reign the king had been lord; and in Wales, which was declared in 1284 to be 'annexed and united to the crown'; and also in Calais, which was acquired in 1347 after a long siege and whose ecclesiastical government was transferred from the jurisdiction of the diocese of Thérouanne in Artois to that of the archbishop of Canterbury in 1379.[14] The Isle of Man, where English rule was unequivocally established only in 1333, following

---

11 Holdsworth *English Law* IX 73–4

12 T.H. Lloyd *Alien Merchants in England in the High Middle Ages* (Brighton and New York 1982) especially ch 2

13 For the use of 'parcel' in relation to Ireland, see *RP* III 231 (1388).

14 J.F. Lydon *The Lordship of Ireland* (Dublin 1972) ch III; J.B. Smith 'The Legal Position of Wales in the Middle Ages' in *Law-Making and Law-Makers in British History*, ed A. Harding (London 1980) 21–53; P.T.J. Morgan 'The Government of Calais, 1485–1558' (D Phil thesis University of Oxford 1966) 10–11 (I am grateful to Dr Morgan for allowing me extended consultation of his thesis).

centuries of independence under, first, Scandinavian dominance and then, after 1266, Scottish overlordship, had its own peculiarities as an acknowledged 'kingdom.' Though a possession of Edward III and his successors as kings of England, in April 1406 it was granted in perpetuity to the Cheshire and Lancashire landowner Sir John Stanley and his heirs. On several occasions in the years that followed, legal opinion asserted that Man was 'no part of the Realm of England, though in homage and subjection to it'; and as late as 1505 the second Stanley earl of Derby prided himself as being *Rex Manniae et Insularum*, like his predecessors.[15]

English claims to superior lordship over Scotland, trumpeted from Edward I's reign onwards, were rather different. Although in 1363 Edward III was prepared to renounce this claim to superior lordship and return the enthronement stone of Scone to the Scots from Westminster Abbey, whence it had been taken by Edward I, this was only on condition (ultimately unfulfilled) that he be acknowledged as heir to the Scottish crown itself. As it was, there were echoes beyond the Middle Ages of an English overlordship that was dated to the legendary days of Brutus. When King James IV broke the truce and invaded England in 1496, he was severely chided in the English parliament, 'for as myche as he ought of dutie to be Homyger; and holde of You, Sovereign Lorde, his said Realme, as his Progenytours have done before.'[16] In Gascony the English king was lord and duke of Aquitaine, sure enough, but in the view of all but the English his overlord remained the Valois monarch, for the Treaty of Brétigny in 1360 had never been implemented and full sovereignty over Gascony was therefore never conceded to Edward III. Indeed, the duchy's position seemed unclear from that date until the final expulsion of the English in 1453. In the meantime, Gascon merchants were almost always taxed as foreigners in England: when a number of them, who had migrated to England and married and settled there, petitioned parliament in 1411 to be regarded as the king's liegemen and not as aliens, Henry IV proved sympathetic but advised them to seek letters of denizenship like other aliens.[17] Finally, the

---

15 *RP* I 168 (king of Man, 1304), 284 (kingdom of Man, 1312); III 380 (*hors du Roialme*). For a discussion, see B. Coward *The Stanleys: Lords Stanley and Earls of Derby, 1385–1672* (Chetham Society Manchester 1983), 99–102, 179. The privileges of the 'kings' of Man are more usefully compared with those of the Welsh marcher lords (ibidem 101) than with the ducal liberties of Lancashire and Cornwall and the episcopal liberties of Durham.

16 *RP* I 106–7, 225; II 442; III 150; and for the 1496 declaration, VI 513.

17 M.G.A. Vale *English Gascony, 1399–1453* (Oxford 1970) ch I; N.S.B. Gras *The Early English Customs System* (Cambridge Mass 1918) 346ff; *RP* III 656 (1411), with a discussion on this point in Beardwood 'Mercantile Antecedents' 67–8. Compare *Calendar of Patent Rolls, 1388–92* (hereinafter *CPR 23*); *1396–99* 248; *1399–1401* 236 (letters of denizenship for Gascons); but there is no record of a Gascon seeking denizenship thereafter.

Channel Islands of Guernsey and Jersey are a yet different case. Remnant of the duchy of Normandy lost in 1204, within sight of Normandy, and with a close affinity with its coast, they were ruled by the king as duke of Normandy. The islanders' ambivalent psychology is reflected in two expressions of sentiment in the mid-sixteenth century: the Jersey men declared that they would 'rather die English than live French,' while Guernsey's cannier inhabitants stated that they 'wish to be friends of all rather than subjects of any'! But all could claim with justice (as they did in the fourteenth century) that 'the Isles were anciently a part of the Duchy of Normandy and the Islanders still hold of the king as their duke, and ... in the Islands, they hold and observe, and have always observed, the custom of Normandy ... with certain other customs used in the Islands time out of mind.' Even today the islanders are not represented in the British parliament and Queen Elizabeth II sports in the islands the title 'duke of Normandy.'[18]

Complex, complicated, even confused, therefore, was the king's relationship with the inhabitants of the various dominions he had acquired by the later Middle Ages, though he could legitimately claim that they were all his subjects and – even the Scots – that they all owed allegiance to him; but not everywhere were these claims identical or enforceable. The situation is graphically illustrated by the fortunes of a Welsh harpist's son living in Ireland in 1333, long after Wales' annexation by the crown; his right to plead in the Anglicized courts of Ireland was upheld because 'his grandfather was born in Wales and he is a Welshman and of Welsh lineage.' This Welshman, therefore, enjoyed the rights and privileges of a king's subject and in a territory that was not his own and where many of the Irish themselves were not so privileged.[19] Yet whenever he returned home to Wales, there were some courts from which he was barred and certain places – especially towns and boroughs – in which he could not reside.

Such uncertainties of status were made more uncertain by that unimplemented Treaty of Brétigny. Apart from Gascony, the treaty also ceded Calais and Guisnes to England in full sovereignty, annexing them to the realm; but after Henry VI became, in the eyes of Englishmen and Anglophile French, King Henry II of France in 1422, there were some who claimed that Calais and its march were part of his French realm and their inhabitants justiciable

---

18 A.J. Eagleston *The Channel Islands under Tudor Government, 1485–1642* (Cambridge 1949) 6, 159; J. Le Patourel *The Medieval Administration of the Channel Islands, 1199–1399* (Oxford 1937) 109–10

19 Quoted by R. Frame 'The Immediate Effect and Interpretation of the 1331 Ordinance *una et eadem lex*: Some New Evidence' *Irish Jurist* 7 (1972), 109–14. The defendant was Richard, son of Robert le Crouther (Welsh 'crwth,' harp; 'crythwr,' harpist).

in his parlement of Paris, not at Westminster.[20] Then again, in 1385 Richard II ceded his lordship of Ireland to his favourite, Robert de Vere, Earl of Oxford, retaining only the position of superior overlord. For a very brief period (until de Vere's disgrace in 1388), the king's Irish subjects became the immediate subjects of an English magnate, rather as Manxmen were subjects of the Stanleys after 1406 and as the inhabitants of Welsh marcher lordships had been subjects of individual marcher lords for long past.[21] As for merchants of the Channel Islands, they were at first treated as foreigners when it came to paying the special customs duties imposed on aliens in England after 1303, though repeated objections during the fourteenth century culminated in a recognition in 1394 that they should henceforward be regarded as 'reputed citizens' of England.[22] Moreover, the migration of Welsh, Irish, Gascons, Channel Islanders, even Scots, to England, as merchants, clerics, students, and mere drifters, raised further delicate questions about their status. In the process of grappling with these complexities, the nature of the king's subjects and their relationship with the king was gradually defined more carefully.

The emergence of a well-defined and widely accepted notion of the subject was bound, therefore, to be a slow process bestrewn with obstacles. It might be thought that the distinction between those who were born within the king's realm or dominions and those who were not would be simple by comparison. Yet 'alien friends' were often distinguished from 'alien enemies,' particularly after the resumption of hostilities against France and Scotland at the end of the thirteenth century. Friendly aliens were predominantly those merchants whose role in England was economically and financially crucial, if not always welcomed; others included the entourages of royal brides and the foreign servants of English noblemen.[23] By the fourteenth century, such friendly aliens were buying and owning houses and enjoying legal rights as private persons, at least before the king's council and the court of chancery; and the Italians

---

20 See *RP* III 170, for the Commons' hope in the 1380s that Calais was not held of the French king. Prior to 1422, Calais burgesses were regarded as denizens of England (*CPR 1408–13* 389 [1412]), though James Knyght, a citizen and brewer of London who had been born in Calais of an English-born father and a Flemish mother, thought it advisable to purchase letters of denizenship on 3 January 1415: *CPR, 1413–16* 288. Compare *Calendar of Close Rolls, 1389–96* (hereinafter *CCR*), 447.

21 *CCR, 1389–96* 447. Richard II's advisers were even accused of persuading the king to make de Vere king of Ireland: *RP* III 209, 231.

22 Le Patourel, *Channel Islands* 118–19. But see a suggestion that they were regarded as aliens in Cornwall in 1410: *CCR, 1409–13* 43.

23 *CCR, 1381–85* 64–5; *1399–1404* 170. For a friendly alien friar minor, born in Portugal, who was exempted in 1373 from Edward III's order expelling alien friars, see *CCR, 1369–74* 517.

and Germans among them received charters of privileges from Edward III. As aliens, they could not normally inherit land in England or pass it to their heirs, but with permission they might become citizens and aldermen of London, members of London gilds, and they might even purchase royal letters that would make them securely denizens of the realm.[24] The foreign-born wives of Englishmen – the friendliest of all – encountered difficulties when claiming dower rights after their husbands' death. These difficulties were eventually removed by parliament in 1420, and nineteen years later alien women who had married either Englishmen or Welshmen were declared exempt from the taxes on aliens. Such legislation was often prompted by lobbying on behalf of particular groups or individuals: certainly the Portuguese-born Beatrice, dowager-countess of Arundel, availed herself of the provisions of the 1420 act immediately it was passed, and Henry V's land settlement in Normandy promoted marriages between English subjects and foreign-born women whose long-term interests their husbands might well have wished to protect.[25] Among the most friendly of aliens after 1422 were the subjects of Henry VI as king of France. A few of these were made denizens, and in July 1428 it was declared the king's intention that Flemings should be treated as the king's French subjects and allowed to trade freely in his two realms.[26]

Alien enemies were uniformly and specifically denied these privileges. Natives of a country at war with the king of England were liable to arrest and forfeiture, or at the very least to expulsion from the realm unless a safe-conduct had been purchased, or they were in effect prisoners of war. After all, they might, like the inmates of alien priories, contribute money to an enemy; or, like certain alien friars at Oxford, or the Breton servants of Henry IV's queen, Joan of Navarre, dowager-duchess of Brittany, send intelligence to the French.[27] Following Edward III's death, the Commons in Richard II's first parliament in 1377 successfully urged that all alien enemies, lay and clerical alike, should leave the realm. Only the priors of religious houses,

---

24 *CCR, 1377–81* 363 (alien webbers of London); *1381–85* 138; *The Eyre of London, 14 Edward II, A.D. 1321,* ed H.M. Cam I (Selden Society 85, 1968) ccxxvii–xi; *Select Cases in Chancery, A.D. 1364–1471,* ed W.P. Baildon (Selden Society 10, 1896) xlii; *Select Cases before the King's Council, 1243–1482* ed I.S. Leadam and J.F. Baldwin (Selden Society 35, 1918) xxvii. See also Beardwood *Alien Merchants* ch 8 and Appendix G; Beardwood 'Mercantile Antecedents' 68–9; S. Thrupp *The Merchant Class of Medieval London* (Ann Arbor 1962) 50–1, 219–22.

25 *RP* IV 128, 130; V 6. The act of 1439 was confirmed in 1442: ibidem 39.

26 R.A. Griffiths *The Reign of King Henry VI* (London and Berkeley 1981) 168–9

27 *CCR, 1405–9* 122, 130–1, 138–9 (the Bretons); *1419–22* 129 (alien religious); *RP* II 162, 297, 367, 373; III 22, 64, 529, 569, 571–2, 578; IV 5, 13, 79, 306. See *CCR, 1369–74* 517, for the alleged alien friar-spies at Oxford 1373; and compare *CCR, 1374–77* 43–4, 139; *1385–89* 519.

beneficed clergy, and those with offices guaranteed for life were exempt from this Draconian measure. Spying on behalf of the French by alien enemies in Northamptonshire, activities that were investigated by the government in October 1385, was the kind of revelation that led Richard's parliament a few weeks later to confirm the stern action of 1377.[28] Not for nothing had chancery clerks scratched 'Do not show to aliens' on state papers at the beginning of the Hundred Years War.[29]

The status of all these aliens was directly connected with their place of birth and domicile. By the end of the thirteenth century, those who were born abroad were attracting increasing suspicion. Accordingly, in 1295 Elys Daubeney secured letters patent from Edward I conferring on him the status of an 'Anglicus purus' and granting him access to courts in England as if he were an Englishman, despite the fact that he had been born overseas.[30] In the mid-fifteenth century, the lawyer Thomas Littleton tersely defined the alien thus: 'Alien is he which is born out of the allegiance of our lord the king' (not, be it noted, merely outside the realm of England).[31] Intimately related to birth was allegiance: place of birth and allegiance together identified the king's subjects, even in those cases where the parents were foreign-born or owed allegiance to a foreign potentate. This, incidentally, meant that the assimilation of aliens into English society was a relatively rapid process. And it was implicit, too, that an English-born subject did not divest himself of his status if he simply left the king's realm or dominions to live abroad: the bond of allegiance was unaffected thereby.[32] What is more doubtful is that a change of allegiance by simply swearing a new oath could decisively affect the status of an alien; it certainly did not turn him into a subject of the English king.

Several factors combined in the late-fourteenth and fifteenth centuries to hasten the process of definition, thereby preparing the ground for early-Tudor rationalization. The Gaelic Irish cultural resurgence from the thirteenth century onwards accentuated problems stemming from the fact that the English conquest of Ireland was incomplete. This resurgence was likened by one excitable contemporary to a 'woman who has risen again from the horrors of

---

28 CPR, *1385-9*, 88. It seemed reasonably safe in June 1391 to exempt an old Norman nun, who had spent twenty-nine years in the priory at Kilburn and was ignorant of the legislation, from the statute's penalties – provided she behaved herself! CPR, *1388–92* 432.

29 G.P. Cuttino 'The Causes of the Hundred Years' War' *Speculum* 31 (1956) 472, quoting Public Record Office (hereinafter PRO) c47/30/2/21.

30 *RP* I 135, with a comment by Beardwood 'Mercantile Antecedents' 66

31 Quoted by F. Bacon in *The Works of Francis Bacon* ed. J. Spedding et al 8 vols (London 1862) VII 665.

32 CCR, *1369–74* 136. For a comment on the indissoluble nature of subjecthood, see Holdsworth *English Law* IX 78.

reproach.'[33] The colonial settlement around Dublin and a few other towns and ports contracted, and the loyalty of the Anglicized lordships was eroded. Beyond lay the Gaelic countryside, largely unconquered still, with a population that did not acknowledge the English king as their lord and who in turn were scarcely regarded by him as his subjects. Despite Edward III's decision to offer English law to colonists and loyal Irishmen in 1331, the common law operated in progressively fewer and fewer areas, and the Gaelic Irish were described as unfree villeins or 'hibernici.' To one chronicler writing in 1341, it seemed that 'the land of Ireland was on the point of separation from the lands of the king of England.'[34] This posed a threat to the English régime in Ireland and to the coasts of England and Wales; it also altered the attitude of the government to Irishmen in Ireland and to those Irishmen who migrated to England.

After 1366 and the statute of Kilkenny, only Englishmen born in England or in Ireland were regarded as the king's true subjects, and efforts were made, by means of language, marriage, and distinctive dress, to insulate them from the Gaelic Irish.[35] Intermarriage was hedged about with obstacles; from 1447 'wild Irish' could be arrested and ransomed on the grounds that they sported a fortnight's growth of moustache, Irish style; and Irish thieves could be summarily executed after 1465, unless they were accompanied by a loyal subject or dressed English style. Limerick in 1414 debarred Irishmen from civic office and apprenticeships; and it is small wonder that an Irishman living in Waterford at about the same time should have changed his name to conceal his Irish birth.[36] Even the merchants of Dublin were subjected to hostile prejudice. In 1372 they were driven to complain that customs collectors there were treating them as if they were aliens, and it required an order from the king to confirm that they were indeed inhabitants of one of his dominions and therefore should be regarded as native merchants.[37]

The personal and social distress which such treatment caused is illustrated by the fortunes of a fourteen-year-old Irish boy, Robert Sygyn, who had been brought to England by Sir William Windsor about 1370 and had spent the next forty years in Yorkshire, where he acquired a messuage and ten acres of

33 Lydon Lordship of Ireland 152
34 Murphy 'Status of the Native Irish after 1331' 116–28; K. Nicholls, Gaelic and Gaelicised Ireland in the Middle Ages (Dublin 1972) 17–20, 47; Lydon Ireland in the Later Middle Ages 75 for the quotation.
35 A.J. Otway-Ruthven A History of Medieval Ireland (London 1968) 290ff
36 F. Plowden An Historical Review of the State of Ireland 2 vols in 3 (London 1803) I 39–40; Murphy 'Status of the Native Irish after 1331' 124–6. It is significant that under Henry IV and Henry V more grants of English law to native Irish were made annually than in any other reign in the later Middle Ages; compare the evidence of grants of denizenship, below pp 96–8.
37 CCR, 1369–74 406

land. Expulsion orders led to the seizure of his property until Henry IV showed compassion and in April 1410 allowed him to continue living in the realm and to enjoy his lands and goods. Another Irishman, William Saundre, who was a burgess and freeman of Dartmouth in Devon, where he had lived for more than fifteen years, was treated as an alien by the customs collectors of London. In February 1384, he secured a declaration that, 'being born in Ireland under the king's allegiance and held among [the burgesses of Dartmouth] and elsewhere in the king's realm and dominions, [he was] a native and no alien but the king's English liegeman.'[38]

After the unsuccessful efforts of Richard II to reassert royal authority in Ireland, Lancastrian governments treated most of the Irish as second-class subjects. They were frequently required to leave England and return home, not least because they were believed to be the cause of disturbances in Bristol, London, and the university towns. Only those already well settled with inheritances or relatives in England, or who were members of the commercial, legal, or religious professions, were exempt from the repeated attempts by parliament, especially in the first third of the fifteenth century, to expel Irishmen from the realm. Those who remained were subjected to sanctions and constraints to ensure their peacefulness.[39] This was less than subjects merited, but it expressed the government's dilemma as to how Irishmen should be treated when their country was imperfectly subdued and they themselves were uncertain in their allegiance to the king. In other words, it raised the question of their nationhood and their rights as subjects.

The vexed question of errant subjects acquired a new dimension after the Great Schism in the church began in 1378. Inevitably, the unsubdued Gaelic community in Ireland gave its allegiance to the antipope at Avignon.[40] Moreover, the Channel Islands were still part of the Norman diocese of Coutances; attempts to correct this anomaly (by transferring the islands to an English see) had failed. The schism precipitated a decision on the matter, for the bishop of Coutances supported the antipope, but the Norman affinities of the islanders ensured that it was not to an English diocese that they were to be attached, but rather to the Romanist see of Nantes in 1398.[41] The numerous alien priories in England and Wales were an even more serious problem during the schism, because almost all of them belonged to French mother houses and the relationship was far from being a merely formal one. The priories' wealth and their payments to mother houses abroad were countered by confiscation; the related problem of their allegiance was more intractable and was resolved either by the expulsion of the monks from the realm or by collective charters

---

38 CPR, 1408–13 186; CCR, 1381–85 432–3
39 RP IV 13 (1413), 198, 254 (1423); VI 192(1477). See A. Cosgrove *Later Medieval Ireland, 1370–1541* (Dublin 1981) 18–19, 33–5.
40 E. Perroy *L'Angleterre et le grand schisme d'occident* (Paris 1933) 96–103
41 Ibidem 106–9; Le Patourel *Channel Islands* 34

of denizenship.[42] A number of Welshmen, too, declared for the Avignon pope after the outbreak of Owain Glyndŵr's rebellion in 1400. Owain could thereby obtain papal encouragement for his foundation of two universities in Wales after the Scottish example.[43] For several decades, then, the divisions of Christendom ranged subject against subject within England and its dominions.

The Welsh revolt was one of the most potent factors focusing attention on the question of status, if for no other reason than that for a century Wales had been fully conquered and, as the harpist's son in Ireland discovered in 1333, its inhabitants were treated as the king's subjects, even outside their own land. The rebellion led to several restrictions on Welshmen both inside and outside Wales. Legislation in 1401 imposed disabilities which prevented Welshmen from buying property not only in Welsh boroughs but in English ones too; and they – and indeed Englishmen who married Welsh – could not hold office legally in Wales. Although these restrictions were largely ignored almost before the ink on the parliament roll was dry, they could occasionally be implemented with devastating consequences and undoubtedly conferred on Welshmen less than the status of subjects.[44] These new statutes buttressed local regulations under which some Welshmen already laboured in Welsh towns and which made them in certain circumstances seem foreigners in their own land.[45]

The financial straits of fifteenth-century kings also had an impact on the relationship between subjects and aliens. Foreign merchants had paid special higher customs rates in England since the promulgation of the Carta Mercatoria in 1303.[46] It was too much to expect that they would not be exploited further during the lengthy French war, and the government periodically imposed special taxes on all aliens. But precisely who were the aliens? In answering that question, royal officials came closer to defining who was the subject. So desperate for money was Henry vi's government that at first Irishmen and Channel Islanders were subject to the new aliens' tax in 1440, but by 1443 their status at the king's subjects was acknowledged and they were henceforward exempt from the novel imposts; the only concession to

42 M.D. Knowles *The Religious Orders in England* ii (Cambridge 1957) 161–5. For Henry iv's sensitivity to sympathizers with the Avignon pope in his own court and household, see *RP* iii 527 (1404).

43 R.A. Griffiths 'The Glyn Dŵr Rebellion in North Wales through the Eyes of an Englishman' *Bulletin of the Board of Celtic Studies* 22 (1967) 159

44 For the harsh treatment of Sir John Scudamore as late as 1433, see R.A. Griffiths *The Principality of Wales in the Later Middle Ages* I: *South Wales, 1277–1536* (Cardiff 1972) 140–1

45 R.A. Griffiths 'Wales and the March' *Fifteenth-Century England, 1399–1509: Studies in Politics and Society*, ed S.B. Chrimes, C.D. Ross, and R.A. Griffiths (Manchester 1972), ch 7. See below ch. 4.

46 Beardwood 'Mercantile Antecedents' 66; Lloyd *Alien Merchants*, ch 2

desperate financial need affected subjects by creation as opposed to birth, that is, the denizens.[47] In 1453 they were placed in a middle category and that, incidentally, help to clarify yet further the status and nature of both alien and subject.[48] By the 1480s, English administrators were adopting a constitutionally logical attitude to the inhabitants of the king's dominions in relation to the taxation of aliens. In 1482 and again in 1487, the inhabitants of Ireland and Wales, Calais, and the Channel Islands, were treated just like native-born Englishmen; so too were those born in Gascony and Normandy who had chosen to live under the king's allegiance after the loss of the English lands in France.[49]

The Hundred Years War had taken many Englishmen to campaign abroad for substantial periods. They were frequently accompanied by their wives and their children born abroad, particularly outside permanently held English territory, raised the question of whose subjects were they. Parliament was forced to discuss the matter in 1343 and 1351, spurred on by the birth of the king's sons on the continent as well as the offspring of English noblemen. On 2 March 1343 Edward III returned to England after spending much of the preceding five years campaigning from the Low Countries against his adversary and rival, King Philip VI of France. Large numbers of his subjects, both noble and commoner, had travelled with him abroad, and some of his magnates were accompanied by their wives and households. A number of these wives gave birth to children, whose parents were therefore undeniably English but whose own place of birth was outside the realm and the king's dominions, and beyond King Edward's allegiance. Their parents were conscious that some uncertainty might arise in the future as to whether such children born overseas could be regarded as the king's subjects in the fullest sense of the word; in particular, a question mark might be placed over their ability to inherit property and goods in England. On 24 February 1343, a week or so before his return, Edward summoned a parliament to meet at Westminster; it assembled less than eight weeks after his disembarkation, on 28 April. The doubts and potential difficulties connected with subject-status had already been discussed by certain of the nobility, the Commons, and a number of lawyers, perhaps at one of the earlier parliaments held during the campaigning seasons between 1338 and 1342, or else immediately prior to the new assembly. It had then been established that English common law was unclear on these issues and hence that discussion was necessary in the parliamentary session of May 1343.[50]

47 Griffiths *King Henry* VI 555–9; *RP* V 38. In 1449 those who were exempt from the aliens' tax included those born in England, Ireland, Wales, Normandy, Gascony, the Channel Islands, and any other place under the king's obedience: ibidem 144.

48 *RP* V 230; VI 239, 269, 335, 508

49 Ibidem VI 197–8, 401–2

50 Ibidem II 139

The matter was more than a private one, to be pursued by several military commanders whose wives had given birth in France or Flanders, for Queen Philippa herself had been delivered of two sons while she was abroad with the king: Lionel at Antwerp on 29 November 1338, and John at St Bavon's Abbey in Ghent in March 1340. To regularize the position of these two infants was important and fairly urgent, for the king's eldest son, Edward, was still quite young (having been born in 1330) and his second son, William (born in 1336), had died in infancy. In these circumstances, it was the archbishop of Canterbury, John Stratford, who, despite his opposition to Edward on other matters relating to the management of the war, placed the issue of the king's offspring before the spiritual and temporal lords in parliament, presumably on the king's instructions. Each lord present was asked his opinion and all, according to the official parliamentary record, replied that there was no doubt but that any of the king's children born overseas had the same inheritance rights as those born in England itself. But it might well have been appreciated that an authoritative declaration of the law on this point was desirable, because only three of the ten English monarchs since 1066 – Henry III, Edward I, and Edward III – had been the eldest-born son of a king, and therefore the possibility of either Lionel of Antwerp or John of Ghent succeeding to the throne was far from remote. Moreover, all five monarchs since 1189 had been born in England – or, as in Edward II's case, in a principality of Wales that was united and annexed to the English realm. On the other hand, the situation as it affected the royal children did not require a new law in 1343, merely a clarification of existing law, for of the five English monarchs between 1066 and 1189, four had been born in France (Henry I was the exception) and could be regarded as providing sufficient warrant for the lords to confirm in 1343 that birth overseas did not prejudice the rights in England of any royal offspring.

The spiritual and temporal lords and the lawyers in parliament proceeded with greater caution when the wider implications of the matter were considered. It was realized that doubts might be expressed in the future about the comparable rights of children born overseas to any of the king's subjects on campaign. Accordingly, it was agreed that careful thought was required before a law to cover this eventuality was introduced. In the presence of Edward III and the Lords and Commons, it was unanimously acknowledged that the inheritance rights of the king's children were unquestionable, regardless of where they were born, and it was further agreed that the children of those in the king's service should also have their rights of inheritance safeguarded, no matter where these children were born. But because further advice and deliberation were thought desirable in order to devise a law to guarantee these rights, and because parliament came to an end on or about 20 May, after sitting for less than a month, the introduction of an appropriate statute was deferred until the next parliament. In the meantime, the king's justices and others were charged by King Edward and the Lords to ponder the matter further. Thus was the matter left in a period of truce – undetermined but with a clear appreciation that Edward III's campaigns in France posed important questions relating to the nature of the subject and to the current assumption that only those born within the realm were fully the king's subjects.

Despite the intention of 1343, eight years and seven parliaments passed before the matter was discussed again, at least as far as the official record indicates. Then, early in 1351, two years and more after the arrival of the Black Death in England and France, and with military operations continuing in northern France, Brittany, and Gascony, the unfinished business of 1343 was placed on the parliamentary agenda once more.[51]

By the time parliament met on 9 February 1351, more children had been born to the wives of English commanders serving abroad, and it is likely that a group of such influential men secured the king's attention in the assembly. To judge by the statute that resulted, the interests of three children in particular were pressed during the discussions. The first was Henry, the eleven-year-old son and heir of John, Lord Beaumont, who had died in 1342. Henry was born in Brabant in 1340 while his mother, Eleanor, daughter of Henry, earl of Lancaster, was attending Queen Philippa; after her husband's death, Eleanor married Richard, earl of Arundel, a prominent magnate and, along with Eleanor's brother, who was created duke of Lancaster in this same parliament, a powerful advocate of young Henry Beaumont's interests as the heir to a major English inheritance.[52] The second child to be mentioned in the statute of 1351 was Elizabeth, who was the daughter – probably the eldest child – of Guy de Brian, a loyal soldier who fought in Scotland, Flanders, and France, and who was summoned to parliament from 1350 onwards.[53] And the third was Giles, the son and heir of Sir Ralph Daubeney, who had served in the Crécy–Calais campaign of 1346–7.[54]

The king was said to have in mind other children who had been born overseas of English parents. Indeed, the new duke of Lancaster might well have mentioned the birth of his own daughter, Maud, in the Low Countries in 1341; she would very shortly marry, in 1352 in the king's own chapel,

---

51 Ibidem 231; *Statutes of the Realm* 11 vols (1810–28) I 310. What the precise impact of the Black Death was on the English landowning class is still an open question. K.B. McFarlane's inclination to play it down was supported by his study of the extinction of noble houses, but the threat which the plague posed to inheritances, especially in the event of recurrent attacks, was a real one. The statute of 1351 relating to the status of children born overseas of English parents referred specifically to the plague as one reason for its introduction at this juncture: *The Nobility of Later Medieval England* (Oxford 1973) 168–71.

52 G.E. Cokayne *The Complete Peerage of England, Scotland, Ireland, Great Britain and the United Kingdom ...* 12 vols (London 1910–59) II 61

53 Ibidem II 361–2

54 Ibidem IV 96–7

William v, duke of Bavaria, count of Holland and Zeeland, a valued English ally, and any lingering doubts about Maud's inheritance rights would need to be removed forthwith.[55] Arundel too, may have had a more immediate interest in the new legislation, aside from its effect on his step-son, Henry Beaumont. His own son and heir was born in 1346, possibly in France where the earl was a member of the expedition which fought at Crécy and laid siege to Calais.[56] In order to remove all doubt about the ability of such children to inherit in England, in 1351 the king instructed the lords, prelates, and others of his council, assembled in parliament, to resolve the issue. They were unanimous in reaffirming existing law in respect of the children of kings, not simply of Edward iii's offspring, and this was approved by king, Lords, and Commons. They were also unanimous in declaring that other children born during Edward's reign beyond the king's allegiance of the realm of England should have full rights of inheritance in England. This secured the interests of those on whose behalf the petitioners of 1343 and 1351 had acted. And it was added that all children born in the future outside the king's allegiance, but whose parents were subjects of the king of England, should be enabled to succeed to their inheritances within the king's allegiance.[57]

This statute seemed to deal with all eventualities. But by 1368, when Calais and Guisnes had been captured and garrisoned and were being colonized, and when considerable numbers of English, Welsh, and other subjects of the king were settling in Calais and its march, Gascony and Poitou, even in Brittany, further unease was expressed about the implications of overseas settlement. A new petition was accordingly presented by the Commons in the parliament which opened on 1 May 1368. This sought an undertaking that children born in these overseas lordships should have their inheritance rights in England safeguarded. Admittedly, such English settlements in France had not received specific mention in 1351: how could they? But seventeen years later, parliament considered that an amendment to accommodate this precise point was unnecessary and the king simply required that common law and existing statutes should be observed. Not even the birth of the Black Prince's second son, Richard (later King Richard ii), in Bordeaux on or about 6 January 1367 was regarded as meriting an amendment to the statute of 1351.[58]

---

55 Ibidem vii 410

56 Ibidem i 243–4

57 The only limitation in the statute referred to the mothers of such children who had gone overseas without the permission of their husband; in those cases where it was alleged that a child was illegitimate, the bishop of the diocese where the claim was made must testify to the bastardy in the king's court, as would have been the case for those born in England itself.

58 RP iii 297; *Statutes of the Realm* i 389. English settlers in northern France in the reigns of Henry v and Henry vi were covered by the same statute; see C.T. Allmand 'The Lancastrian Land Settlement in Normandy, 1417–1450' *Economic*

Henry v's conquests in northern France did not of themselves pose a new problem of allegiance: the French realm which his son acquired in 1422 was in every sense a separate kingdom. The most that was conceded to Henry vi's French subjects when they were in England was a special protection and ease of movement.[59] But the loss of all but Calais a generation later, by 1453, did raise the problem of the status of those Gascons, Normans, and Picards whose English allegiance spelled danger or even disaster for them under Charles vii and who therefore retired to England for safety. Many of these refugees bought letters of denizenship from the king; on other occasions, a general statement that they should be treated as Englishmen sufficed.[60] But whatever the solution to their predicament, it underlined the need for a clearer declaration of what constituted alien and subject status.

These questions and their related difficulties arose most acutely in the period 1380–1460. Letters of denizenship were granted in increased numbers, especially during the Lancastrian period, thereby underlining the differences between subjects and aliens, and between subjects of the English realm and those of the king's dominions. Their very frequency delineated the nature and scope of denizenship and pointed the way towards more consistent and precise solutions to the complex questions of status. That this was still a relatively novel procedure is indicated by the variable terms in which these letters were couched during the 1380s, although some standardization was soon achieved.[61]

The majority of those who in the period 1377–1422 sought and obtained letters patent of denizenship appear to have been long-time residents in England. Henry Shafot, a Flemish merchant, claimed in his petition, which was granted on 4 November 1390, that he had lived in England since infancy and intended to remain there for the rest of his life. Ernest de Ruden, a German merchant who was made a denizen on 16 January 1399, stated that he had lived in the city of Lincoln since the age of ten, while Warimbald Harlam, a goldsmith born in Holland (perhaps at Haarlem), had lived in the city of York for twenty-four years before his petition was granted on 18 February 1403.[62]

History Review 2nd ser 21 (1968) 461–79; C.T. Allmand *Lancastrian Normandy, 1415–1450* (Oxford 1983) ch iii

59 Griffiths, *King Henry vi* 167–71, 551–61, for an analysis of English attitudes to aliens generally in Henry vi's reign.

60 Ibidem 551–3

61 Compare CPR, *1381–85* 413 (February 1384); *1385–89* 518 (January 1388); *1388–92* 23 (March 1389), 361 (December 1377). For the antecedents of letters of denizenship in a commercial context, designed to release recipients from higher customs duties, see Beardwood 'Mercantile Antecedents' 69–71. The following comments are based on a study of the grants enrolled on the chancery and parliament rolls.

62 CPR, *1388–92* 318; *1396–99* 463; *1401–5* 204; CCR, *1399–1402* 286. Many other examples could be cited.

These foreigners now sensed the wisdom of seeking the king's full and permanent protection.

Some, like the German merchant Hermann Steyford, who obtained his letters on 6 December 1390, had married English women; Steyford was then living with his children in Boston (Lincolnshire) and fully intended staying there until his death.[63] A number had acquired houses, burgages, and property in English towns without a specific licence and now sought to make their titles unassailable. Witness Peter Busseby, a Breton who, when he did homage to Henry IV at Leicester in September 1405, had been living in the realm for more than forty years and had acquired two messuages in Derby which he planned to pass to his heirs in due course; his letters of denizenship were granted on 26 January 1406 in return for a £2 fine.[64] Others, like the alien goldsmith Albert de Albernaco, who was enfranchised on 16 July 1406 after spending twenty-two years in London, were already enjoying the freedom of the city.[65] And yet others had shown by their personal or other services to the king that they deserved to be regarded as if they were the king's subjects born in England. Louis Decouchez, Henry IV's physician, became a denizen on 28 March 1405, and a husband and wife, both Breton-born, who were in Henry's and Queen Joan's personal service, became denizens in 1411–12.[66]

To qualify for denizenship, a considerable number of grantees had already sworn homage and pledged their allegiance to the king, as did the Scotsman Thomas Broune before he was formally admitted 'to the king's allegiance and obedience' on 28 October 1408.[67] A few had even been paying taxes in England, as had Henry Wyman, a German who was already a citizen of York, and a contributor to tenths, fifteenths, and other taxes, when he was made a denizen on 26 January 1388.[68] But weighing heavily with the government, too, was the fine which most of these aliens were required to pay for the privileges they sought. The size of this fine varied widely, doubtless according to means: a Brabanter paid as little as £1 in April 1416, but an Italian merchant from Lucca, Bartholomew Bosan, found £50 in December 1391 for the privilege of being regarded 'as one of the king's true subjects born in England.'[69]

Denizenship soon embraced a standard package of privileges and obligations which delineated in precise terms the difference between an alien and a king's

63 CPR, *1388–92* 367

64 Compare CPR, *1388–92* 407 (a Picard in Dartmouth); *1405–8* 204 (a German in London).

65 CPR, *1403–6* 207

66 CPR, *1405–8* 22; *1408–13* 368, 392 (John and Joan Perian, whose heirs were also enfranchised)

67 CPR, *1408–13* 40

68 CPR, *1385–89* 518

69 CPR, *1416–22* 2; *1391–96* 9 (Bosan's fine was the highest recorded before 1422). These fines were in addition to the administrative costs of securing such letters: Beardwood 'Mercantile Antecedents' 73–4.

subject. Three issues in particular were crucial to the distinction: the capacity to buy, own, and sell land in England (though not to inherit it); the ability to sue and plead personally in the king's courts: and, for merchants, the freedom to trade as an English subject, paying customs duties as a native merchant and no longer as an alien. As early as 12 December 1377, John Moner, who was born in France, was licensed to acquire, hold, and dispose of land in England, and he was enabled to sue for debt in the king's courts as if he were a subject.[70] Adam Hill, a Scots chaplain, was licensed on 28 February 1384 to continue living in the realm until he died.[71] The Luccese merchant Bartholomew Bosan enjoyed even wider judicial rights than Moner after 20 December 1391: he could pursue and plead all kinds of actions, real and personal, in the king's courts.[72] The financial implications of such privileges were made clear in January 1388 in the grant to Henry Wyman, a German citizen of York, who was henceforward exempt from the higher customs duties imposed on alien merchants; and in June 1393, in the grant to Godfrey van Upstall, a Brabanter who was required to contribute to local and royal taxes as the corollary of his denizenship.[73] Thus, by the end of Richard II's reign, these were the rights and obligations that merited an alien petitioner's treatment and status as a denizen.[74]

Most of these grants were made to individual merchants, craftsmen, and tradesmen, to enable them to continue their life and work in England. Between 1409 and his death in 1413, Henry IV enfranchised an increasing number of aliens, several of whom were in his own or his Breton queen's service. In the latter part of his reign, too, the grants were frequently extended to include the heirs of new-made denizens. Although the common law conferred on all born within the realm the status of a king's subject, this did not apply to denizens' offspring born overseas before the grant of denizenship was made.[75] In a period when patriotic sentiment in England was growing sharper, not only did larger numbers of resident aliens seek letters of denizenship, but so too did more recent settlers who strove to safeguard their families in their

---

70 *Calendar of Fine Rolls, 1377–83* 47; *CPR, 1388–92* 361. He complained in 1390 that customs collectors at the ports were still treating him as an alien; hence on 28 October his status as a denizen was confirmed (on payment of a ten mark fine). For the distinction between subject and denizen, especially in the realm of public law, see Holdsworth *English Law* IX 76 and n 5.

71 *CPR, 1381–85* 413. He had sworn homage and fealty, and was accordingly admitted to the king's allegiance.

72 *CPR, 1391–96* 9

73 *CPR, 1385–89* 518; *1391–96* 285 (van Upstall also paid £5 to the hanaper). For local criticism in Grimsby of alien residents who refused to become burgesses and shoulder the obligations of a burgess, see *CCR, 1381–85* 338–9 (1383).

74 See the grants of 1397 in *CPR, 1396–99* 84, 176, 201.

75 *CPR, 1408–13* 26, 157, 368, 392, 460. This may be a reflection of Henry IV's extensive personal and diplomatic links abroad. For an isolated grant to heirs in

new environment. Such grants remained common throughout the fifteenth
century, and by Henry VIII's reign separate rolls recording them were being
compiled. The earliest of these to survive is now fragmentary and dates from
1540–1, though it is likely that others once existed from earlier years in
Henry's reign.[76]

The early Tudor monarchs sought to rationalize developments relating to
status that had been quickened by events in the fourteenth and fifteenth
centuries. Their task was made easier by the loss of all the king's French lands,
except Calais, by 1453. Henry VII attempted to transfer the Channel Islands
from the diocese of Coutances to the diocese of Salisbury in 1496 and then,
in 1499, to Winchester, though his efforts did not commend themselves to
all the islanders.[77] In Wales, English law had gradually advanced, and many
landowners found ways of circumventing the provisions of Henry IV's statutes.
Eventually, Henry VII gave charters conferring English law and rights on
remaining Welsh communities and abrogating the penal legislation that was
now a century old.[78] Henry VIII, who was apprehensive about his Reformation
changes, 'incorporated' as well as 'united and annexed' Wales with England
and created shires throughout the land. He also incorporated Calais in 1536
as 'one of the most pryncypall tresours of the realm.'[79] In distant Ireland his
solution was different but with the same effect: he exchanged the title of 'lord'
for that of 'king' in 1541, affirming the Irish to be his 'true subjects, obedient
to his laws, forsaking Irish laws, habits and customs.'[80]

A sense of 'imperial' unity was already present in the king's claim to the
allegiance of all who were born within his dominions, and there had long been
in existence institutions that afforded common treatment to all his subjects.
Parliament (though the commons' representation was confined to England)

   April 1400, see Reynald Greyle, a Genoese merchant, his son Alaonus and
   his heirs, CPR, *1399–1401* 255.

76 PRO c67/72 (a denizen roll for 32 Henry VIII, signed by the king himself), 77 (a
   similar roll of grants, all made by letters patent on 11 July 1541 and usually
   in return for half a mark each). See *Letters of Denization and Acts of Naturalization for Aliens in England, 1509–1603* ed W. Page (Huguenot Society of
   London 8 1893) i; T. Wyatt 'Aliens in England before the Huguenots' *Proceedings of the Huguenot Society of London* 19, 1 (1953–4) 74–94.

77 Eagleston *Channel Islands under Tudor Government* 49

78 Smith 'Crown and Community in North Wales' 157–71; see in general Griffiths
   'Wales and the March' 145–72. See below ch. 4.

79 Smith 'Legal Position of Wales' 22; *Statutes of the Realm* III 632–50; Morgan
   'Government of Calais' 48, 103ff. There had, in fact, been enquiries by Henry
   VII into Calais' government: ibidem 12, 46–7, 114–15.

80 *A New History of Ireland*, ed T.W. Moody, F.X. Martin, and F.J. Byrne III
   (Oxford 1976) 46–7; B. Bradshaw *The Irish Constitutional Revolution of the
   Sixteenth Century* (Cambridge 1979) 117–18, 160–1, 231–4

was a forum in which the affairs of all the dominions were discussed, and whose legislation was, in part at least, universally applicable.[81] From its earliest days, receivers and triers dealt with parliamentary petitions from Wales, Ireland, the Channel Islands, Gascony, and Scotland.[82] On rare occasions, MPs were summoned from the dominions: from Scotland by Edward I, from Wales twice by Edward II, from Ireland by Edward III (abortive, as it turned out), and from Calais by Henry VIII.[83] Regional custom may have made the common-law courts inappropriate for the hearing of appeals from these dominions, and when Irish, Welsh, or Channel Islands cases came before the court of King's Bench there was sometimes uncertainty as to whether they had any business being there.[84] But with the prerogative courts it was a different matter. In the first statute of Westminster in 1275, Edward I declared it to be his obligation to offer justice to all his subjects, and to his council came cases from Ireland; the chancellor in the fifteenth century judged suits from Wales, Ireland, the Channel Islands, and Calais; and parliament frequently dealt with business relating to the dominions.[85] The basis of a definition of status was there; the early Tudors had only to build on it.

81 Thus, although it was said in 1523 that 'a general Act of Parliament does not extend to the Isle of Man,' the English parliament was fully capable of legislating specifically for the island: Coward *Stanleys* 49, 101, 181. See also E. Coke *The Fourth Part of the Institutes of the Laws of England Concerning the Jurisdiction of the Courts* (London 1644) 283–5 (Man), 286–7 (Channel Islands); G.J. Hand *English Law in Ireland, 1290–1334* (Cambridge 1967) 161 (Ireland); Smith 'Legal Position of Wales' 45; even *RP* III 337, for the Scots in 1397.

82 *RP* passim. Provision was even made for Flemish petitions in 1343 and for those of Brittany in 1344 and 1351. It is of interest to note that the parliament roll recorded two groups of receivers and triers of petitions: up to 1355, one for England and the other for Ireland, Wales, Scotland, Gascony, the Isles 'and all other foreign lands and (all other foreign lands and) places'; thereafter, one for England, Ireland, Wales, and Scotland, and the other for Gascony 'and other lands overseas and the Isles.'

83 Ibidem I 160, 177; Morgan 'Government of Calais' 106; Lydon *Lordship of Ireland* 226–7

84 *RP* IV 361; Sayles *King's Bench, Richard II, Henry IV and Henry V*, 116ff; Sayles *King's Bench, Edward III* v 58–63; Smith 'Legal Position of Wales' 24–5, 34, 37; Le Patourel *Channel Islands* 111–13

85 Such cases were usually heard in the absence of judgment or because of erroneous judgment: *RP* III 68; v 149 (Calais); IV 361 (Ireland): Hall *Law Merchant* III 141; Leadam and Baldwin *King's Council* xxvii, 85–6. In relation to the Welsh march, see Davies *Lordship and Society in the March of Wales* 251–4, and Smith 'Legal Position of Wales' 24ff (who has noted that when Cardinal Wolsey was chancellor, 1515–29, he heard as many as eighty-two cases from Wales and others from Ireland, Calais, and the Channel Islands); for Ireland, Hand 'English Law in Ireland' 393–422.

[A number of recent works bear on these issues, particularly from the Irish standpoint: James Lydon (ed.), *England and Ireland in the Later Middle Ages* (Dublin, 1981); idem, 'The Middle Nation' in idem (ed.), *The English in Medieval Ireland* (Dublin, 1984); and Art Cosgrove (ed.), *A New History of Ireland*, II. *Medieval Ireland, 1169-1534* (Oxford, 1987). See also, for a somewhat earlier perspective, R.R. Davies (ed.), *The British Isles, 1100-1500* (Edinburgh, 1988).]

4

Wales and the Marches in the Fifteenth Century

In the mid-1430s that early essay on 'strategic studies' *The Libelle of Englyshe Polycye* summed up what many Englishmen felt about Wales:

> Beware of Walys, Criste Ihesu mutt us kepe,
> That it make not oure childes childe to wepe,
> Ne us also, if so it go his waye
> By unwarenesse; sethen that many a day
> Men have be ferde of here rebellione
> By grete tokenes and ostentacione.[1]

The great majority of contemporary Englishmen regarded Wales with fear and suspicion. Most English historians have been content to disregard her. Stubbs did not even deign to mention Wales in the third volume of his monumental *History*, while for Professor Du Boulay relations between Englishmen and Welshmen in the later Middle Ages rarely rose above a crude and mutual contempt. Few Welshmen nowadays would wish to echo G. M. Trevelyan's flattering list of priorities: 'The Wars of the Roses [he declared] were to a large extent a quarrel between Welsh Marcher Lords, who were also great English nobles, closely related to the English throne.'[2] Nevertheless, if Yorkshire and the north were to demand recognition of their uniqueness in this period, then Wales (to put it ungrammatically) was even more unique. It certainly demanded special treatment from the English State. Looked at more broadly, Wales displays many of the pressures to which English kings responded in formulating their policy, and also some of the assumptions underlying their attitude to regional problems.

The term 'Wales and the Marches' in the fifteenth century had an air of vagueness about it even thicker than that surrounding until recently the term 'Wales and Monmouthshire' in the twentieth

1 *The Libelle of Englyshe Polycye*, ed. Sir George Warner (1926), 40.
2 F. R. H. DuBoulay, *An Age of Ambition* (1970), 25–6; G. M. Trevelyan, *History of England* (third edition, 1945), 259.

century. The 'Principality of Wales and the Marches' would have been more precise and certainly more comprehensible to modern readers of, for example, the Parliament rolls. To the west of the English shires lay two distinct forms of government still full of meaning in the fifteenth century: the shires of the principality of Wales and Flint, and the Welsh Marches or marcher lordships.[3] Contemporaries appreciated the difference, and it received careful acknowledgement from the Crown. The principality shires, organised in two groups centred on Carmarthen and Caernarvon, with Flint attached by history and convenience to Chester, were vested in the king and his heirs as kings of England. They were governed directly by the king or prince through his appointees, headed both in the south and north by a justiciar and chamberlain, but they stood quite separate geographically and constitutionally from the shires of England.[4] The marcher lordships, on the other hand, were quite different in their origin and development. Ultimately held of the Crown, into whose hands on occasion they fell by escheat, forfeiture or wardship, they were franchises of the most independent kind. Every function of government in each lordship was the sole responsibility of its marcher lord: his courts had power of life and death over his tenants, he could impose his own taxes, royal officials from neighbouring English or Welsh shires had no authority there, and even bishops with letters of excommunication in their pocket sought the support of the lord's secular arm (and not the king's).[5] This was the public framework within which Welshmen lived and English marcher lords and kings ruled in later medieval Wales.

The maintenance of public order in the shires and lordships of Wales depended on the vigour of the Crown and marcher lords and on the responsibility of the local population. Furthermore, Edward I had specifically declared it to be the Crown's sovereign responsibility to guarantee justice to every subject. The effort to achieve order and justice against almost insurmountable odds by these means was the continuing theme of fifteenth-century Wales. I have therefore

3 W. Rees, *An Historical Atlas of Wales* (second edition, 1959), plate 53.

4 W. H. Waters, *The Edwardian Settlement of North Wales in its Administrative and Legal Aspects, 1284–1343* (1935); J. G. Edwards, 'The early counties of Carmarthen and Cardigan', *E.H.R.*, xxi (1916), 90–8; Ralph A. Griffiths, 'Royal government in the southern counties of the principality of Wales, 1422–85', unpublished Ph.D. thesis, University of Bristol (1962).

5 J. G. Edwards, 'The Normans and the Welsh March', *Proc. Brit. Acad.*, xlii (1956), 155–77; *The Marcher Lordships of South Wales, 1415–1536*, ed. T. B. Pugh (1963), 4; F. D. Logan, *Excommunication and the Secular Arm in Mediaeval England* (1968), 114–15; R. R. Davies, 'The law of the March', *Welsh History Review*, v, No. 1 (1970), 9–15.

adopted it as the theme of this paper.

The Crown's response to the rebellion of Owain Glyndŵr, which broke out in 1400, reveals how carefully those features of Welsh government already mentioned were respected, and yet also how Wales's relationship to the English State could be modified in the interests of order. In Parliament on 15 October 1399 Henry IV invested his eldest son and heir with the estate, honour and dignity of Prince of Wales. The king put a circlet on his head, a gold ring on his finger, a rod of gold in his hand; he kissed him on the cheek, handed him his charter and young Henry became thus Prince of Wales. The income of the principality and the reality of government were transferred some weeks later, on 8 November.[6] Such was the uncertainty of 1399, and such perhaps the exclusively seignorial experience of the new king, that Henry IV was not prepared to delegate complete control over the principality (nor indeed over Chester) to his son. Rather was a community of government forged between king and prince which did not give to Prince Henry the freedom enjoyed by the Black Prince. On 20 October 1399 the king had appointed Hotspur justiciar of north Wales and Chester for life, and ten days later William Beauchamp, lord of Abergavenny, became justiciar of south Wales also for life. Six months later, on 24 April 1400, it was again Henry IV who nominated Hotspur to be constable of Chester, Flint, Conway and Caernarvon castles and sheriff of Flint, again during his lifetime.[7]

The Glyndŵr rebellion may have fortified the king's inclination to supervise his son's principality; indeed, it was vital that he should do so if a unified command were to be created and financed to crush the rebels. It was in this spirit that Henry IV's government often paid for the safe keeping of the principality's castles early in the revolt, and despatched ordinances before April 1401 to Hotspur as justiciar of north Wales and Chester.[8] At first this exercise in joint government gave rise to friction. There is no more telling instance of this than the Conway incident of 1401, when the agreement concluded by Prince Henry and Hotspur with the Welsh captors of Conway Castle was angrily repudiated by the king. Henry IV reminded his son that it had been *his* officers who had lost the fortress and *his* financial responsibility to regain it—although the

6 *R.P.*, iii, 426; *C.P.R., 1399–1401*, 61. Cf. J. G. Edwards, *The Principality of Wales 1267–1967* (1969), especially 16–20.

7 *C.P.R., 1399–1401*, 37, 33, 28.

8 *P.O.P.C.*, ii, 264; i, 148–50 and *passim*; *Issues of the Exchequer, Henry III–Henry VI*, ed. F. Devon (Record Commission, 1837), 299; *Anglo–Norman Letters and Petitions*, ed. M. D. Legge (Anglo–Norman Texts, iii, 1941), 301–2.

royal treasury would inevitably have to foot part of the bill.[9] Only gradually did the prince shoulder responsibility for more than the routine business of governing his shires; but from 1405 onwards his father rarely assigned money for operations in the principality and hardly ever made internal appointments there.[10]

To gear the marcher lordships for the suppression of rebellion was a more difficult task. It was too dangerous to override marcher privileges after the manner of Edward I and Hugh Despenser; in any case, it was not in the nature of a man who until recently had himself been a great magnate and powerful marcher lord.[11] Even under the strain of rebellion, Henry time and again confined himself to urging the marcher lords to visit their lordships and garrison their castles.[12] Too often their assistance fell short of expectation, as the petitions presented in Parliament made clear, and, no doubt urged on by the Commons in the Parliaments of 1401 and 1402, the king resorted to more radical measures from November 1401. Henry then appointed lieutenants for north and south Wales, both distinguished magnates, to co-ordinate civil and military rule temporarily in the principality and in the Marches. Thomas Percy, earl of Worcester, was the first, appointed for south Wales in November 1401 after the king had returned from a chastening expedition to Wales. Percy's nephew, Hotspur, joined him on 31 March 1402 as lieutenant of north Wales. They did not supersede shire and seignorial custom, but they could organise the military campaign and punish or pardon the rebels.[13]

This royal intervention was justified by rebellion and treasonable war against the king. Only he could pardon high treason and, according to the statute of 1352, receive the forfeitures of the convicted, whether they were tenants of the king himself or of any other lord. Henry IV continually exercised this prerogative as sovereign in the principality and in the Marches, either directly or through

9 P.O.P.C., I, 145; *Royal and Historical Letters during the Reign of Henry IV*, ed. F. C. Hingeston (Rolls Series, 1860), I, 69–72.

10 E.g. *Issues of the Exchequer*, 314; C.P.R., *1405–08*, 359; *Royal and Historical Letters*, II, 15–17, 22–4.

11 Henry, as the husband of Mary Bohun and the heir to the duchy of Lancaster, was lord of the marcher lordships of Brecon, Kidwelly, Monmouth and the Three Castles in 1399: R. Somerville, *History of the Duchy of Lancaster, 1265–1603*, I (1953), 639–54; R. R. Davies, 'The Bohun and Lancaster lordships in Wales in the fourteenth and fifteenth centuries', unpublished D.Phil. thesis, University of Oxford (1965).

12 E.g., R.P., III, 476 (1401), 612 (1407), 624 (1409–10); S.R., II, 129 (1401).

13 P.O.P.C., I, 173–76; C.P.R., *1401–5*, 53; J. E. Lloyd, *Owen Glendower* (1931), 43–4

the lieutenants of north and south Wales.[14] When Prince Henry became royal lieutenant in January 1406 there existed throughout Wales a measure of unity similar to that achieved by the later prince's Council in the Marches, though in the lordships at least it scarcely extended beyond the temporary needs of a military campaign. His commission was renewed on several occasions and he was still the king's lieutenant in September 1411.[15]

Two pressure groups existed which urged more radical measures to crush Glyndŵr and contain future Welsh uprisings: they were the border English shires and the Commons in Parliament. The border communities were convinced that they were witnessing an upheaval as serious as the Edwardian conquest, to which episode they resorted in the search for precedent in dealing with the troublesome Welsh.[16] The number of petitions presented in Parliament on their behalf betray an extreme apprehension of their Welsh neighbours, even xenophobia; this is likely to have given to the border representatives coherence and persistence as a lobby in a Parliament exasperated with marcher particularism during a war which the Commons partly had to finance.[17] Costs sharpened their minds and their tongues. The parliamentary experience of men such as Sir Ralph Stafford (M.P. for Worcestershire in 1383, 1384 and 1401), Sir Thomas Fitz Nicol (M.P. for Gloucestershire in six Parliaments before he sat in 1401 and 1402), and Roger Thornes and Thomas Pryde (who between them represented Shrewsbury on six occasions before they did so together in 1401 and 1402) must have been invaluable in discussing the border's problems.[18] Henry IV, however, resisted most of such demands in 1401 and 1402 as went beyond precautions for the present and the enforcement of established and reasonable custom: he parried the more extreme or far-reaching of them with 'the king wishes to preserve his right' or 'let this petition be committed to the Council'. Thus, if he was prepared in 1401 to agree

---

14 *S.R.*, I, 320; *C.P.R. 1399–1401*, 396, 451–2; *ibid., 1401–05*, 299.

15 *C.P.R., 1405–08*, 156, 169, 215, 445; *ibid., 1408–13*, 202, 306. The king's personal influence in the Marches was considerably enhanced by the unprecedented number of marcher lords who were under age after 1405 and thus came into Henry's custody.

16 *R.P.*, III, 457, 476, 509.

17 *Ibid.*, III, 439, 472–3, 474, 476, 615, 663–4; IV, 52. For the Commons' contribution to financing the war, see *ibid.*, III, 547, 580, 609, 624, and T. Kido, 'English government finance, 1399–1413', unpublished Ph.D. thesis, University of London (1965), 177–86.

18 W. R. Williams, *The Parliamentary History of the County of Worcester* (1897), 21, 24; *id., The Parliamentary History of the County of Gloucester* (1898), 27, 31; E. Edwards, *Parliamentary Elections of the Borough of Shrewsbury* (1859), 7.

by statute that no Welshman should purchase land in England or in the Welsh plantation towns (presumably of Edwardian foundation), in 1402 he declined to interfere with local privileges by prohibiting all Welshmen from trading elsewhere in Wales than in the market towns. Moreover, when he agreed to a petition that no Welshman be an officer in Wales or a councillor of an English lord there, he inserted an important, open-ended reservation that excluded bishops and all loyal lieges from the measure.[19]

If the Crown was not prepared to impose major modifications on the political structure of Wales in an emergency like this, it certainly did not do so after Glyndŵr had withdrawn into obscurity. Henry V was as careful of marcher susceptibilities as his father, but his experience of Welshmen, his statesmanship and, soon after, his need for a tranquil Wales which would pay subsidies and array its men for the French war, dictated a policy combining conciliation and firmness.[20] Whole communities of Welshmen purchased collective pardons during the next four years, albeit with hefty fines: 1,600 marks was imposed on those of Caernarvonshire, Merioneth and Anglesey in November 1413.[21] A certain degree of economic recovery and social stability was induced by royal ordinance when the earls of March and Arundel, the lords of Powys and the chamberlain of south Wales were ordered to return to the principality shires in north Wales tenants who had fled from Anglesey, Caernarvonshire and Merioneth; the king in 1413 even assigned £200 to be spent on cows and sheep for the re-stocking of the Caernarvonshire and Merioneth countryside.[22] Furthermore, corruption and oppression by the king's own servants in the principality were swiftly investigated, and in July 1413 the earl of Arundel headed a commission in north Wales to enquire into treasons and riots committed by royal officials; it was as a result of this investigation that Thomas Barneby, chamberlain of north Wales, was removed from office in the following March.[23] Even the Welsh law of inheritance was

19 *R.P.*, III, 476, 508–9; *S.R.*, II, 129, 141. A comparison of the petitions relating to Wales presented in the Parliaments of 1401 and 1402 with the resultant statutes is instructive.

20 *R.P.*, IV, 10–11 (1413); *S.R.*, II, 171–2.

21 Ralph A. Griffiths, 'The Glyndŵr rebellion in north Wales through the eyes of an Englishman', *Bull. Board of Celtic Studies*, XXII (1966–68), 152; *C.P.R., 1413–16*, 137, 195; W. T. Waugh, *The Reign of Henry V*, I (1914), 108.

22 *P.O.P.C.*, II, 231 (2 May 1417); Griffiths, 'The Glyndŵr rebellion', 152. For Henry V's sensitivity to hardship in south Wales, see R. R. Davies, 'Baronial accounts, incomes, and arrears in the later Middle Ages', *Ec.H.R.*, second series, XXI (1968), 224.

23 Griffiths, 'The Glyndŵr rebellion', 151–2; *C.P.R., 1413–16*, 114.

guaranteed in the royal territories, while in north Wales debts to the Crown incurred before 5 November 1411 were cancelled and everyone restored to the lands they had held before the revolt broke out.[24]

But Henry V could also be firm. He guarded against further insurrection, especially in north Wales, where the poor and inaccessible county of Merioneth was seen as the key to future peace in the region.[25] He also enlisted the aid of the great lords to ensure order in the Marches, and lordships in his own hand were circumspectly disposed of, frequently to members of his own family.[26] It was a notable achievement: no large-scale rising occurred even when the fugitive Sir John Oldcastle proposed a Celtic alliance in 1417, and many Welshmen fought for their king in France.[27] War taxes were paid even in north and west Wales, whilst in the duchy of Lancaster lordships the degree of recovery was such that local officials were eventually able to realise 98·8 per cent of the potential revenue for the years 1411–17.[28] The king's policy in Wales had been eminently successful, and the brevity of his reign scarcely allowed time for its more oppressive features to ripen into protest.[29]

After the rebellion neither the Crown nor the marcher lords were capable of displaying the vigour they had shown during it; and as time passed the local population exercised less and less responsibility. The Welsh squirearchy, brothers-in-arms of the gentry and knights of England, were the leaders of local society, the moulders of opinion, patrons of the Welsh Church and Welsh culture, and, in a society bereft of a substantial mercantile community, also the main repository of landed wealth. Above all, they

---

24 Griffiths, 'The Glyndŵr rebellion', 153, 166–7; *R.P.*, IV, 90–1; *C.P.R., 1413–16*, 380, 405.

25 In May 1417 Henry ordered sheriffs to be resident in Anglesey, Caernarvonshire and Merioneth, and that castle constables should be equally conscientious and of English birth. J. B. Smith, 'The last phase of the Glyndwr rebellion', *Bull. Board of Celtic Studies*, XXII (1966–68), 253–4; *P.O.P.C.*, II, 231–2.

26 *C.P.R., 1413–16*, 347; *ibid.*, 170, 192, 229, 306–7, 395; P.R.O., Ministers' Accounts, 1165/11 m. 1; 1165/12 m. 3*d*; 1166/1 m. 1; 1166/2 m. 1; 1222/10 m. 4.

27 Smith, 'The last phase of the Glyndŵr rebellion', 254–5; H. T. Evans, *Wales and the Wars of the Roses* (1915), 43–6, 63–4; Waugh, *Henry V*, I, 113–14; A. D. Carr, 'Welshmen and the Hundred Years' War', *Welsh History Review*, IV, No. 1 (1968), 35–41. For negotiations to reconcile Maredudd, son of Owain Glyndŵr, see Lloyd, *Owen Glendower*, 143–4, and Smith, 'The last phase of the Glyndŵr rebellion', 255–6.

28 P.R.O., Ministers' Accounts, 1216/3 m. 2; 1223/1 m. 1; Davies, 'Baronial accounts', 226–7; Pugh, *Marcher Lordships of South Wales*, 42, 148.

29 I am grateful to Mr T. B. Pugh for a timely reminder on this point.

provided political leadership as public servants of the Crown and the marcher lords.[30] They were a gregarious and enterprising body of men, whose unusually durable ties of kinship enabled them to play a crucial part in fifteenth-century politics. They had held the key both to the temporary success of Glyndŵr and, after they had deserted him, to the ultimate failure of his enterprise.[31] For all the repressive instincts of Henry IV's early Parliaments, the Crown needed these squires to administer its estates, collect its revenue and preserve the peace. As Welshmen, they were excluded from the most prestigious positions in the principality; thus, between 1400 and 1461 no Welshman born of Welsh parents was appointed to the post of justiciar or chamberlain of south Wales. But men such as Gruffydd ap Nicholas in Carmarthenshire and William ap Gwilym ap Gruffydd in Caernarvonshire deputised so regularly for the English officials that this was a hollow restriction. The former was deputy justiciar of south Wales by August 1437 and again between 1447 and 1456 in the inevitable absence of magnate justiciars like Lord Audley, Humphrey of Gloucester and Sir John Beauchamp of Powick; Gruffydd extended his service by acting as deputy chamberlain for Sir Edward Stradling, Lord Sudeley and Lord Audley. At the other end of Wales, William ap Gwilym's achievement was only a whit less noteworthy, for he had become deputy chamberlain of North Wales by 1457.[32] Both men took the precaution of securing by letters of denizenship ultimate legal protection against the largely moribund legislation of Henry IV, for the abrupt end to the career of Sir John Scudamore, Glyndŵr's son-in-law, only a few years earlier had indicated that what lay dormant on the statute book could, if desired, be roused to endanger an official position.[33]

The Welsh squire may have been even more vital to the marcher

30 For a study of this important class in one area, see Ralph A. Griffiths, 'Gentlemen and rebels in later mediaeval Cardiganshire', *Ceredigion, Journal of the Cardiganshire Antiquarian Society*, v (1965), 143–67.

31 R. R. Davies, 'Owain Glyn Dŵr and the Welsh squirearchy', *Transactions of the Honourable Society of Cymmrodorion* (1968), 150–69; Griffiths, 'Gentlemen and rebels', 153–8.

32 Ralph A. Griffiths, 'Gruffydd ap Nicholas and the rise of the House of Dinefwr', *National Library of Wales Journal*, XIII (1964), 256–68; id., 'Gruffydd ap Nicholas and the fall of the House of Lancaster', *Welsh History Review*, II (1965), 213–31; J. R. Jones, 'The development of the Penrhyn estate up to 1431', unpublished M.A. thesis, University of Wales, Bangor (1955), ch. IV.

33 *R.P.*, IV, 440. Gruffydd ap Nicholas's letters of denizenship probably date from March 1437, whereas William ap Gwilym secured his in two stages: on 26 November 1439 and 24 January 1443. P.R.O., Ancient Petitions 130/6464–5; *R.P.*, v, 16, 45, 104; Griffiths, 'Gruffydd ap Nicholas and the rise of the House of Dinefwr', 258; *C.P.R., 1436–41*, 416; *ibid., 1441–46*, 164. Below p. 190.

lords than he was to the Crown. The vast complexes of estates in England, Wales and overseas of, for example, Duke Richard of York, Richard Neville, earl of Warwick, and Duke Humphrey of Buckingham were staffed from a much smaller pool of retainers, servants and councillors than that available to the king. The local man was consequently enlisted as steward and receiver, and not simply as an effective deputy paying lip-service to the harsh enactments of Henry IV's early Parliaments; like William ap Thomas and his son William Herbert in Usk, Glamorgan and Monmouth, he often enjoyed seignorial power by default of the lord himself.[34] Such a man was capable of providing peaceful and efficient government, but equally his selfishness and neglect could create resentment among his less powerful neighbours and promote anarchy in his locality.

The greatest opportunity for the Welsh and English squirearchy in Wales came during Henry VI's reign—even for erstwhile rebels. For several reasons, central control over Wales was weaker then than at any time since the Edwardian conquest. Already in the late fourteenth century, some marcher houses were losing their direct interest in Wales, and this continued to be so in the early fifteenth century. The Bohun inheritance was divided, and the Mortimers' attention was diverted elsewhere, especially to Ireland before the turn of the century.[35] The Despenser, Mortimer and Stafford families were blighted by minorities: for forty-one of the sixty-five years between 1349 and 1414 the head of the Despenser family was a minor; for thirty-four years in the period 1382–1432 most of the Mortimer properties were in youthful hands, and Humphrey, earl of Stafford and lord of Newport, was under age from 1403 to 1423.[36] Some inheritances, like the duchy of Lancaster lordships, the Mortimer estates, the county of Pembroke and the lordship of Glamorgan, were incorporated into such large landed complexes

34 *Dictionary of Welsh Biography*, 101, 354; Evans, *Wales and the Wars of the Roses, passim*; D. H. Thomas, 'The Herberts of Raglan as supporters of the House of York in the second half of the fifteenth century', unpublished M.A. thesis, University of Wales, Cardiff (1967), chs. I–VI; Somerville, *op. cit.*, 650.

35 G. A. Holmes, *The Estates of the Higher Nobility in Fourteenth-century England* (1957), 18–19, 24–5; A. J. Otway-Ruthven, *A History of Medi-aeval Ireland* (1968), 13–38, 362–3.

36 *The Glamorgan County History: Medieval Glamorgan* ed. T. B. Pugh (Cardiff, 1971), 182; *C.P.*, IV, 273–82; VIII, 448–53; D. H. Owen, 'The lordship of Denbigh, 1282–1425', unpublished Ph.D. thesis, University of Wales, Aberystwyth (1967), 82ff; Pugh, *Marcher Lordships of South Wales* 151–2.

that their lord could devote only a fraction of his time to the Welsh properties and their officials. Aristocratic households could be remarkably sophisticated and organised, but an older organisation may have undertaken additional commitments less easily than a newer one, and, as the case of William, Lord Herbert shows, a frequently resident magnate probably supervised his estates more effectively than an habitual absentee.[37] Moreover, the Crown's territories in Wales after 1399 were so large and so widespread that to supervise effectively the duchy of Lancaster, the principality, and lordships in royal hands, each with its own customs and traditions, was a heavy burden for a monarchy increasingly racked by faction and ultimately overwhelmed by civil war. In 1461 the earldom of March was added.[38] Nor could the problem be eased by transferring at least the principality and Chester to a capable young prince: between 1413 and 1509 there was a prince for only thirty-seven years and at no time was he an adult.[39]

There was, then, a certain inevitability about Wales's detachment from its rulers in the fifteenth century. This was accentuated by the fear of Wales which many Englishmen felt after the revolt and which the *Libelle of Englyshe Polycye* expressed.[40] In addition, Wales's principal attraction for its lords—its revenue—had become much attenuated of late. Lords such as the king, the duke of Lancaster and the earl of March found it difficult to maintain their Welsh income in the late fourteenth century; after the rebellion their fortunes were in marked decline. In Glamorgan, for example, the lord's revenue never recovered from the experience of the revolt; in Denbigh the yields of the late fourteenth century had been possible only with considerable strain and by judicial pressure which could not be sustained after Glyndŵr's rebellion; in the southern counties of the principality the extraordinary subsidies that Richard II had demanded in the 1380s and 1390s could not safely be emulated by Henry VI, whose income there declined sharply.[41] The same story can be told of the earl of Shrewsbury's border manor

37 *Ibid.*, 180.

38 For the declining efficiency of government in the southern counties of the principality under Henry VI and in the duchy of Lancaster, see Griffiths, 'Royal government in the southern counties of the principality', ch. xi; Somerville, *op. cit.*, i, 190–8; Davies, 'Baronial accounts', 228. See also Pugh, *Marcher Lordships of South Wales*, 9–10, 21.

39 Edwards, *Principality of Wales*, 29.

40 As in the excerpt which opened this paper.

41 Pugh, *Medieval Glamorgan*, 185, 202; Holmes, *Estates of the Higher Nobility*, 97–101; Owens, 'The lordship of Denbigh', 202; Griffiths, 'Royal government in the southern counties of the principality', chs. viii, ix; P.R.O., Ministers' Accounts, 1306/4 m. 3; 1210/5 m. 1d; 1222/6 m. 6d.

of Blackmere (Salop), where 'the whole history of the estate in the late Middle Ages is dominated by one event: the sacking of Whitchurch and the surrounding country by the Welsh rebels in 1404'.[42] Increasingly, lords resorted to financial expedients, exploiting their precious judicial privileges, but no longer could this be done without concessions to the Welsh population. This explains why most marcher lords followed the Crown's rapidly established practice in Carmarthenshire and Cardiganshire of frequently allowing the annual great sessions or sessions in eyre in each lordship to be prematurely suspended—even completely terminated—in return for a substantial grant from the community.[43] The principle of a subsidy from the great sessions of these two counties was firmly established during the reign of Henry IV, when a concession of such magnitude had to be offered to the local population if a substantial grant were to be extracted from them. It was not without the occasional precedent elsewhere before 1399, but now it became a habit difficult to break. During the period 1422–85 only twelve of the fifty-two Carmarthenshire sessions for which some sort of record survives ran their proper course and were not prematurely dissolved in return for a 'general fine'. During these decades 'dissolution of the sessions' spread like a contagion to almost every marcher lordship in south and central Wales, and to Denbigh at least in the north.[44] As a fund-raising device it was immediately profitable, but its impact on government in the widest sense was ultimately disastrous. Justice was too often subordinated to financial gain, and seignorial and royal authority to local squirearchical power. Its damaging effects could, perhaps, be obviated by a resident lord or a conscientious official, but both were rare phenomena. As it was, Richard of York rarely visited his Welsh estates other than at times of personal crisis; Richard Neville's and Duke Richard of Gloucester's interests were remote from Glamorgan, and at Pembroke Humphrey of Gloucester

---

42 A. J. Pollard, 'The family of Talbot, Lords Talbot and earls of Shrewsbury in the fifteenth century', unpublished Ph.D. thesis, University of Bristol (1968), 359 and table facing 388.

43 T. B. Pugh and W. R. B. Robinson, 'Sessions in eyre in a marcher lordship: a dispute between the earl of Worcester and his tenants of Gower and Kilvey in 1524', *South Wales and Monmouth Record Society*, IV (1957), 113; Pugh, *Marcher Lordships of South Wales*, 36–43; Griffiths, 'Royal government in the southern counties of the principality', 50–67.

44 Pugh, *Marcher Lordships of South Wales*, 17–20, 37–40; P.R.O., Ministers' Accounts, 1222/12 m. 2; 1222/14 m. 2; Griffiths, 'Royal government in the southern counties of the principality', 649–58. The phenomenon cannot be detected in the principality's sessions in north Wales.

must have been little more than a tourist.[45] It is difficult to prove that the preoccupations of marcher lords were greater in the fifteenth century than in the fourteenth. But it is incontrovertible that the small number of aristocratic families which dominated Wales made it impossible for lords to give personal attention to their estates. Nor, one suspects, was this peculiar to Wales.

The result of royal and seignorial withdrawal, judicial paralysis and squirearchical power was to intensify the disorder for which Wales had long been a by-word. Lawlessness is impossible to quantify in an age which was not statistically minded, and it is therefore difficult to speak comparatively about it. However, its prevalence is indicated by the steps taken by the Crown to curb it in its own territories in Wales, by the appeals to the king's Council from both royal and seignorial lordships, and by the complaints of the border shires in Parliament. Underlying Welsh disorder in the fifteenth century was, first, the deep resentment of the conqueror which Glyndŵr had recently brought to the surface once more. The aftermath of revolt was keenly and bitterly felt by loyalists in the border English shires as well as in Wales itself.[46] In an age of absentee lordship, it was directed especially at the plantation towns and their privileged burgesses—still very largely of English extraction in the northern shires and maintaining their 'colonist' mentality to the end of the century: it was their protests in 1445 which temporarily brought to an end the granting of letters of denizenship.[47] The bitterness was directed also at the inhabitants of the neighbouring English shires, who were subjected to acts of revenge after the revolt—raiding, cattle rustling and holding to ransom.[48] Second, marcher privilege had always been a source of potential injustice and disorder. Distress taken indiscriminately by aggrieved tenants outside their lordship in retaliation for destructive acts within it, the opportunity for criminals to escape their just deserts by disclaimer into another lordship, and the localised hostilities which periodically engulfed any frontier community—these exasperations contributed to the mass violence of later medieval

45 J. T. Rosenthal, 'The estates and finances of Richard, duke of York (1415–60)', *Studies in Medieval and Renaissance History*, II, ed. W. M. Bowsky (1965), 197–200; Pugh, *Medieval Glamorgan*, 201.

46 *R.P.*, IV, 10–11 (1413), 52 (1414), 329 (1427); V, 104 (1445); *S.R.*, II, 171–2, 188–9.

47 *R.P.*, V, 104, 138–9; J. B. Smith, 'Crown and community in the principality of north Wales in the reign of Henry VII', *Welsh History Review*, III, No. 2 (1966), 156, 170–1. There seem to have been no such grants during the remainder of Henry VI's reign.

48 *R.P.*, IV, 52 (1414); V, 53–4 (1442), 104 (1445), 151 (1449); *S.R.*, II, 188–9, 317–18, 331, 351.

Wales.[49]

A diversity of laws need be no more conducive to disorder than a uniform, centralised system such as the common law of England provided. Moreover, in Wales means existed to control turbulence without involving the sovereignty of the Crown: 'love days', 'parliament days', 'days of redress', or 'days of the March' were proclaimed at traditional meeting places on the border between adjacent jurisdictions for the purpose of composing their differences, while virtual extradition treaties were periodically concluded by neighbouring marcher lords and their officers.[50] But too often they could be subverted by kinship loyalties, negligent officers and lack of forceful direction. The Severn Valley was especially turbulent, with the Welsh from nearby lordships descending on its river traffic, killing, destroying, and blackmailing traders who frequented the wealthy commercial centres as far south as Bristol.[51] Nor were the royal territories more orderly. Carmarthenshire and Cardiganshire were falling more and more out of the control of the central government between 1430 and 1455. In 1435 one complainant to the king's Council claimed that he dare not 'suy the Com[on]e lawe' out of fear of violence because Morgan ap Dafydd Fychan, recently a royal official in Carmarthenshire, 'drawyth un to hym utlaws and diverse mysrewlede men the whech obey not zour lawe ther nethyr zowyr officers'. Even a wayward deputy justiciar was singled out for dismissal in 1436. Moreover, Gruffydd ap Nicholas, for all his willingness to curb lawlessness in others, forged a career for himself in west Wales which cut through the restraints of royal authority as cleanly as a knife through butter.[52] In the north of Wales that termagant among Welsh shires, Merioneth, had become ungoverned and ungovernable by the 1450s: it was noted in July 1452 and August 1453 that the county had persistently failed to produce rents and hold audits and sessions since 1449, while for years its tenantry had been a plague on the neighbouring lordships of Powys and

49 *R.P.*, III, 615 (1407), 663–4 (1411); V, 137 (1447), 154–5 (1449), 200 (1449–50); *S.R.*, II, 159–60, 356; Pugh, *Marcher Lordships of South Wales*, 13, 15 (1415).

50 Davies, 'The law of the March', 29–30; J. B. Smith, 'Cydfodau o'r bymthegfed ganrif', *Bull. Board of Celtic Studies*, XXI (1964–66), 309–24, whose conclusions are expressed in English in *id.*, 'The regulation of the frontier of Meirionnydd in the fifteenth century', *Journal of the Merioneth Historical and Record Society*, V (1965–68), 105–11.

51 *R.P.*, IV, 332–3 (1427), 351 (1429), 379 (1431); *S.R.*, II, 265–6.

52 P.R.O., Exchequer, T.R., Council and Privy Seal, 55/40; 56/29; Ministers' Accounts, 1166/11 m. 7*d*; 1166/12 m. 3*d*; 1167/3 m. 6*d*; 1167/2 m. 8; 1167/5 m. 1; Griffiths, 'Gruffydd ap Nicholas and the fall of the House of Lancaster'. See below ch. 12.

Mawddwy.[53] To judge by the exasperation expressed in Parliament
and by the commissions issued by the government, the 1420s, '30s
and '40s saw public order in Wales deteriorate alarmingly. Existing
agencies for its preservation were now woefully inadequate: the
links in what Professor Glanmor Williams has described as 'the
chain of command' in government had become perilously weak.
A petition presented to the Commons in Parliament in 1449 could
maintain that even in the royal territories the population 'dayly
habundeth and encreseth in misgovernaunce'.[54]

Various remedies were devised by the late Lancastrian, Yorkist
and early Tudor governments to replace outmoded and unworkable
procedures. In the first place, the Crown was the only superior
authority which could re-establish order and stability in Wales. Its
responsibility to do so had been clearly enunciated by Edward I,
and where treasonable activity was involved it could even override
the protection ordinarily afforded by seignorial custom. King
Henry IV's intervention had been in such an emergency, prompted
by what he regarded as Glyndŵr's treason. Thus most of the commissions of oyer and terminer which Henry V and Henry VI sent
into the principality and Marches carried the same justification in
law: the breathless catalogue of 'felonies, misprisions, oppressions,
extortions, conspiracies, confederacies, maintenances, champerties,
concealments, ambidexterities, falsities, contempts and deceptions,
and other trespasses, offences and negligences' was prefaced by
'treasons, insurrection and rebellions'.[55] But such intervention was
now less effective against an increasingly autonomous Welsh squirearchy. The colourful story of Gruffydd ap Nicholas's cavalier treatment of a royal commissioner, who was plied with drink, robbed
of his commission, and despatched home in Gruffydd's livery, may
be apochryphal in detail but it is redolent of the true state of mid-
fifteenth-century Wales. It was a society coming adrift from its
former loyalties.[56]

Second, Edward I had guaranteed to every subject the right of

53 *C.P.R., 1446–52*, 581; *ibid, 1452–61*, 124; P.R.O., Exchequer, T.R.,
Council and Privy Seal, 52/55 (10 July 1430); 78/1–3, 94 (26 November 1448);
Smith, 'The regulation of the frontier', 106–10.

54 *R.P.*, v, 154–5; *C.P.R. 1416–61, passim.*

55 *C.P.R. 1441–46*, 106. See also *ibid., 1413–16*, 114, 179; *ibid., 1416–22*,
76, 270; *ibid., 1422–29*, 218, 362; *ibid., 1429–36*, 130, 200; *ibid., 1436–41*,
452; *ibid.,1446–52*, 585; *ibid., 1452–61*, 120, 444, 564–5.

56 Griffiths, 'Gruffydd ap Nicholas and the rise of the House of Dinefwr',
261–2. See below p. 195.

appeal to the king.[57] During Henry VI's reign the normal means of securing justice by common law or marcher custom were so paralysed that complaints were received by the Council and Parliament from humble subjects in the royal shires and occasionally the Marches. In reply to the harrowing petition presented in the 1439 Parliament on behalf of Margaret Malefant, who was kidnapped in the lordship of Gower and taken into Glamorgan, the king agreed that the kidnappers should be arraigned before King's Bench, provided the rights of the marcher lords were safeguarded.[58] But when the local agencies of law enforcement had to be relied upon, even the Council and Parliament fulminated in vain.[59]

Third, King Edward had outlined his responsibility to intervene in private warfare between Welsh lords or lordships by his treatment of the earls of Hereford and Gloucester.[60] It is true that the fifteenth century did not witness the worst excesses of violence between marcher lords of a century earlier, but there were many occasions when communities of a shire or lordship descended on a neighbouring lordship to wage localised war. The growing ineffectiveness of the customary march days and mutual agreements to curb these outrages was evident in the 1430s and '40s, when the Crown had to command their use by royal and seignorial officials. In October 1442 the marcher lords were firmly ordered by the king and his Council to meet together and agree on a remedy for the disturbances that were prevalent in Wales; and in a particular case, in 1448, several marcher lords (or their officers) and the king's justiciar and chamberlain of north Wales were required by Henry VI to stop the wholesale theft that inflamed the borders of Merioneth, Caernarvon,

57 'And this is to be intended in all Places where the King's Writ lieth. And if that be done in the Marches of Wales, or in any other Place, where the King's Writs be not current, the King, which is Sovereign Lord overall, shall do Right there unto such as will complain.' *S.R.*, i, 31 (Statute of Westminster, 1275); T. F. T. Plucknett, *Legislation of Edward I* (1949), 30.

58 *R.P.*, v, 14–16. For petitions to the Council, see Griffiths, 'Gruffydd ap Nicholas and the rise of the House of Dinefwr', 260–1, and above, p. 67 (from the principality); P.R.O., Exchequer, T.R., Council and Privy Seal, 44/38 (Llanstephan, 1424); 59/20 (Traean, 1438); 72 (Denbigh, 1444).

59 Griffiths, 'Gruffydd ap Nicholas and the fall of the House of Lancaster', 220–4. Abuse of official position was a frequent source of complaint in the mid-fifteenth century. P.R.O., Exchequer, T.R., Council and Privy Seal, 59/20 (Traean, 1438); 59/71 (Cardiganshire, 1439); 63/66 (Kidwelly, 1440); *R.P.*, v, 366–67 (royal counties of Wales, Chester and Flint). See below pp. 208-12.

60 H. M. Cam, 'The decline and fall of English feudalism', in *Liberties and Communities in Medieval England* (1963), 207; J. E. Morris, *The Welsh Wars of Edward I* (1901), 220–38.

Powys and Mawddwy.[61] On occasion, the traditional means of settling local disputes were even adopted in desperation on the initiative of the communities themselves to deal reciprocally with criminals and stolen property.[62]

These were the avenues open to a king who wished to deal with Wales as a whole. If they were paved with good intentions, they were also pitted with local custom and privilege. Only the most courageous of kings would launch a frontal attack on these. When the Commons petitioned that the border J.P.s be empowered to try Welshmen from adjacent lordships, Henry VI temporised, put his faith in marcher custom and issued cloudy statements. The most that could be achieved was that in 1442 the J.P.s were allowed to try Welsh raiders provided an appeal to the marcher lords had been made and failed—but these lords should receive any forfeitures that might result and the statute was to last for only six years.[63] Even in the king's own lands the government was reluctant to tamper with age-old custom. Instead, officers were ordered to their posts and lords to their lordships, futile steps in an age of persistently absentee officials and preoccupied lords. Small wonder that by September 1453 negligent officers and extortionate officials had become the subject of an enquiry in the three northern shires of the principality.[64] Under Henry VI the aim was to tighten up the existing machinery for law enforcement. Only reluctantly did the king and the marcher lords accept the need for a more radical solution imposed by the Crown's sovereign power.

Collective action by the king and marcher lords, with the advice of prominent local gentry ('six, five or four at least of the notablest of their lordships'), was proposed by the Crown in 1437–38 and 1442–43 to re-establish what it described as 'the good governance of Wales'.[65] The degree of co-operation achieved during the rebellion may have been in the proposers' mind, and the warnings of the *Libelle of Englyshe Polycye* may have influenced the government in this as in several other instances. Moreover, Henry VI's own

61 *P.O.P.C.*, v, 211; P.R.O., Exchequer, T.R., Council and Privy Seal, 78/1, 2, 3, 94; Smith, 'The regulation of the frontier', 109. See also *R.P.*, v, 137 (1447), 154–5 (1449), 200 (1449–50).

62 National Library of Wales, Kentchurch Court MS 1027 (29 November 1451, involving Hay, Clifford and Elfael.)

63 *R.P.*, IV, 329, 332–3 (1427), 351 (1429), 379 (1431); v, 53–4 (1442); *S.R.*, II, 265–6, 317–18.

64 *P.O.P.C.*, v, 3 (1436); VI, 60 (1447); P.R.O., Exchequer, T.R., Council and Privy Seal, 41/110 (1423); 78/237 (*c.* 1436–38); *C.P.R., 1452–61*, 173.

65 *P.O.P.C.*, v, 82, 95, 211, 213, 215; Evans, *Wales and the Wars of the Roses*, 36.

initiative may perhaps be seen in the threat made in October 1442 that he himself would act in the Marches if the lords failed to do so: it has the ring of a personal ultimatum about it.[66] But so long as exhortation was supported by conservative methods and the local officialdom, there could be little improvement. There was none as aristocratic faction and civil war overwhelmed the provinces: York replaced Somerset, and Jasper Tudor replaced York in the principality shires; in 1453 Warwick fought Somerset in Glamorgan; Sir William Herbert and Sir Walter Devereux, tenants and probably councillors of York, captured Edmund, earl of Richmond, in west Wales in August 1456; and Jasper Tudor strove thereafter to rally much of Wales to the house of Lancaster.[67] Moreover, the bewildering changes of lordship in Wales, intensified by the political tergiversations of the 1450s, and the bloody battles in which Welshmen were involved sapped the strength of men's loyalty to their absent lords.[68] Such ties were fast becoming an irrelevance: the squirearchy's personal instinct for power transcended responsibility to a lord.

Duke Richard of York, during his two protectorates, may have wished to remedy the worst excesses of misgovernment in Wales and the chronic weakness of the Crown's authority there. Certainly his several manifestos evinced a concern for effective government and the reformation of justice. But these months were so full of personal problems and political difficulties for the duke that in Wales no headway was made in the principality—let alone in marcher lordships other than his own. One enthusiastic writer said of York during his first protectorate that 'for one whole year he governed the entire realm of England well and nobly, and miraculously pacified all rebels and malefactors . . .' In Parliament in July 1455, shortly after his victory at St Albans, a committee consisting of marcher lords (*Domini Marchearum*) and the Crown's legal advisers was set up to investigate means of establishing 'restful and sad rule in Wales'. Yet in his dealings with the lawless gentry of west Wales the duke showed how futile a distant government's efforts

66 G. A. Holmes, 'The *Libel of English Policy*', E.H.R., LXXVI (1961), 193–216; P.O.P.C., v, 211 ('or elles ye Kyng lateth hem wite that he wol ordeine a remedy').

67 C.P.R., 1452–61, 245, 340; R. L. Storey, *The End of the House of Lancaster* (1966), 135, 239–40, 179–80; Griffiths, 'Gruffydd ap Nicholas and the fall of the House of Lancaster', 225–8; Evans, *Wales and the Wars of the Roses*, 75ff; R. S. Thomas, 'The political career, estates and "connection" of Jasper Tudor, earl of Pembroke and duke of Bedford (d. 1495)', unpublished Ph.D. thesis, University of Wales, Swansea (1971), ch. iv. Below pp. 213-16.

68 Glamorgan and Pembroke passed in turn to half a dozen different families between 1400 and 1485.

could be.[69]

This pattern of intermittent discussion about ensuring public order in Wales was overtaken by the civil war and its aftermath. Edward IV's most urgent need in 1461 was not for experiment which might antagonise his aristocratic allies but for a strong regime that would re-establish order and loyalty in a traditional setting. This was provided by William Herbert, the son of Sir William ap Thomas, 'the Blue Knight of Gwent', and Gwladys Ddu, daughter of the famous Welsh commander, Dafydd Gam, who was killed in Henry V's service at Agincourt. With such an upbringing, it is hardly surprising that Herbert came to inspire devotion from Welsh propagandists, while around him were grouped both family and friends who were enlisted in Edward IV's service as a core of loyal officers.[70] In nine months between May 1461 and February 1462 Herbert gathered into his and his relatives' hands the southern counties of the principality and practically all the southern marcher lordships apart from Glamorgan, Abergavenny and the earldom of March.[71] By 1468 there were few areas in Wales as a whole (Glamorgan is again the principal exception) of which he was not either lord, custodian or principal official. One Welsh poet fittingly described him as 'King Edward's master-lock'.[72] It was far from the king's mind to modify drastically marcher custom and privilege, for he actually created two new independent lordships for Herbert himself: Crickhowell and Tretower were detached from the earldom of March in June 1463 and erected into a fully-fledged marcher lordship, and so was Raglan (formerly part of the lordship of Usk) in March 1465.[73] Rather was Herbert's position akin to that of Henry IV's lieutenants, although his personal control over all the lordships which came into the king's hands was unique. But elsewhere in the Marches and the border English shires he only headed com-

69 *The Paston Letters*, ed. J. Gairdner (1904), I, 97–8; II, 177–8; Trinity College, Dublin, MS E.5.10, *f*. 187 (translated); Griffiths, 'Gruffydd ap Nicholas and the fall of the House of Lancaster', 218–24; *R.P.*, v, 279–80.Below ch.12.

70 *Dictionary of Welsh Biography*, 354; Thomas, 'The Herberts of Raglan', ch. VIII; Evans, *Wales and the Wars of the Roses, passim*; *Mynegai i Farddoniaeth y Llawysgrifau*, ed. E. J. L. Jones and H. Lewis (1928), 130, 143, 205, 208, 243.

71 *C.P.R., 1461–67*, 7, 13, 30, 34, 43, 114, 119; Somerville, *op. cit.*, 644–5, 648. Thomas Vaughan, Herbert's uterine brother, became receiver of Brecon, Hay and Huntington during a minority in August 1461: *ibid.*, 43; *Dictionary of Welsh Biography*, 996–7.

72 *Gwaith Lewis Glyn Cothi*, ed. J. Jones and W. Davies (1837), 64; *Gwaith Lewis Glyn Cothi*, ed. E. D. Jones (1953), 4; *C.P.R., 1461–67*, 271, 352, 526–7, 533; *ibid.*, *1467–77*, 22, 25, 62, 41, 154, 163.

73 *C.P.R., 1461–67*, 268, 425–6.

missions of traditional scope encompassing treason, rebellion or counterfeit money, all of which violated the Crown's sovereignty.[74]

The death of Herbert in 1469 created a vacuum which not even Duke Richard of Gloucester could fill, with the result that 'the outrageous demeanyng of Walsshmen' continued. Although Gloucester became justiciar of north and south Wales, and chief steward, approver and surveyor of the principality of Wales and earldom of March in 1469–70, his authority was not revived after the readeption of Henry VI.[75] During the 1470s, therefore, Edward IV was driven to attempt a more constructive solution to the problem of order which would bring the king's sovereignty more to the fore. But it took time. Created Prince of Wales in June 1471, Edward of Westminster did not secure full control over his inheritance until November 1472, when the income of the principality and of Chester was made over to him.[76] During the next four years a Council managed his affairs for him very much as Councils had done for princes in the past. In the meantime, conditions in Wales were made perfectly plain to the king by Parliament in 1472 and 1473. Once more the men from the border English shires were feeling the brunt of the disorder—or so it was claimed on their behalf by the Commons.[77] Responding to their plight, Edward conferred with the marcher lords in 1473, and at Shrewsbury in June he concluded agreements with them.[78] These indentures codified current customary and statutory methods of preserving public order in the marcher lordships and border shires, and the king sealed them as earl of March and not as sovereign. The familiar expedients of a conscientious and resident officialdom, and a satisfactory relationship between neighbouring lordships, were the basis of these agreements.[79] As in the past, the king's Council was made available only as an appeal court or to settle disputes between marcher lords. In its details, this was a conservative code which rationalised and publicised existing procedures; even the placing of the chief officers of each lordship, both royal and seignorial, under a financial surety

74 E.g., *ibid., 1461–67*, 38, 280; *1467–77*, 54, 57, 58, 102; *S.R.*, I, 320.

75 *R.P.*, VI, 8–9; *C.P.R., 1467–77*, 179–80, 185, 275.

76 *C.P.R.,1467–77*, 283, 361.

77 *R.P.*, VI, 8–9, 159–60.

78 While in the border country, he referred certain cases to King's Bench because local jurors were afraid to speak out. *R.P.*, VI, 159–60; C.L. Scofield, *The Life and Reign of Edward the Fourth*, II (1923), 60.

79 P.R.O., Exchequer, Augmentations, Miscellaneous Books, 40/75 (3 June 1473). The 'olde composicion betwene the lordshipps of Glamorgan, Neuporte and Brekenok' was still in force at the end of the century, although even in 1476 it was difficult to produce in the court of one lordship offenders who lived elsewhere. Pugh, *Marcher Lordships of South Wales*, 23–6, 32–3, 256, 272.

to observe its provisions was not a novelty.[80] But at last the king had advanced from mere exhortation to securing from the marcher lords a promise to fulfil ancient responsibilities. The absence of any method of correcting a lord who failed to do so was now that much more obvious. This is just what the prince's Council could provide.

According to Dominic Mancini, Prince Edward in Wales 'devoted himself to horses and dogs and other youthful exercises to invigorate his body'.[81] His affairs were managed by an impressive body of prominent advisers. Even before he undertook full responsibility for the government of his possessions, Queen Elizabeth and her brother, Lord Rivers, the king's brothers, the dukes of Clarence and Gloucester, the archbishop of Canterbury and ten other persons had been nominated in July 1471 to administer the principality and his other properties for him until he reached the age of fourteen. On 20 February 1473 this group was increased in size from fifteen to twenty-five and specifically entrusted with full powers of government in Prince Edward's name; in the following winter it was strengthened by a small household of permanent and influential councillors appointed during pleasure.[82] About the same time they received authority to deal with disturbances in Herefordshire and Shropshire, and in February 1474 the prince and his Council were provided with assistance from the border population to arrest some felons who had fled into Wales; but these were commissions designed for a specific purpose.[83] It was not until the early months of 1476 that more thoroughgoing measures were being discussed which would give continuity to the Crown's supervisory power in Wales, the marcher lordships and the border shires. The prince's Council would be its instrument in an act of governmental devolution which was by no means unique in Yorkist England.

On 2 January 1476 the prince was given a commission of oyer and terminer throughout Wales and the neighbouring English shires of Gloucester, Hereford, Worcester and Salop; in March he, or certain of his councillors, was instructed to enquire about franchises in the

---

80 In a Welsh context the bond or recognisance haᶜ been employed after Glyndŵr's rebellion to ensure that officials discharged their responsibilities properly (Davies, 'The Bohun and Lancaster lordships', ch. v, quoting P.R.O., Duchy of Lancaster, 41/9/8 m. 5; 42/16, ff. 16v, 74v; 25/3489). For the similar use of sureties or pledges for the receiver of Brecon in 1451 and for even minor officials in the principality shires from 1454, see Pugh, *Marcher Lordships of South Wales*, 246 n. 2; N.L.W., Badminton manorial records, 1561; P.R.O., Ministers' accounts, 1168/8–9; 1169/1.

81 *The Usurpation of Richard III*, ed. C. A. Armstrong (second edition, 1969), 71.

82 *C.P.R., 1467–77*, 283, 366, 401, 414, 417.

83 *R.P.*, VI, 160–1; *C.P.R., 1467–77*, 429 (26 February 1474).

Marches and the border shires which were suitable for resumption by the Crown, and about criminals who escaped justice in the same area.[84] Moreover, the importance which the king attached to his son's Council is indicated by the conference he arranged at Ludlow in March 1476 between it and the marcher lords to discuss the punishment of crime in Wales and the Marches. One probable outcome was the commission issued on 29 December to the prince during pleasure to appoint judicial commissions in Wales, the marcher lordships and the four border shires, to array men if necessary to punish criminals, and to enquire into negligent officials. This was a notable accession of authority outside the principality and royal lordships, and evidently the basis on which the prince's Council in 1478 issued ordinances for future peace in Shrewsbury 'and for good Rule to be kepte [amongst] thofficers' there.[85] The Crown's responsibility as sovereign in Wales and the border country was being delegated semi-permanently to the prince's Council settled in the Marches at Ludlow. It was doubtless part of the design that the earldom of March was gradually transferred to the prince's hands, as also was the county of Pembroke in 1479 'for the reformation of the wele publique, restfull governaunce and mynystration of Justice in the said parties of South Wales'.[86] There now existed in Wales an authority which had complete powers of government in the principality, the earldom of March and other royal lordships, together with a supervisory jurisdiction in the English shires and private marcher lordships when justice should falter or officials were negligent. The prince's Council even entertained, probably *ad hoc* and for reasons of sheer convenience, a few complaints ordinarily heard by the king and his Council at Westminster. Twice in 1480–82 appeals were made to Prince Edward at Ludlow by men from Coventry, a city well outside the territorial scope of his earlier commission but one which had a long connection with the princes of Wales. On each occasion the prince acted in his father's name and with his authority, while in June 1481 Edward IV specifically asked his son to assume the task of raising men from Coventry for the projected Scottish campaign. The king was delegating his sovereignty to young Edward's councillors for specific purposes and for reasons of convenience in a city which had a

84 C. A. J. Skeel, *The Council in the Marches of Wales* (1904), 26–7; *C.P.R., 1467–77*, 574–605. Worcestershire was omitted from the latter commission.

85 *C.P.R., 1467–77*, 574; *1477–85*, 5; Skeel, *op. cit.*, 21–2, 27; Williams, *Council in the Marches*, 9.

86 The earldom was tranferred piecemeal between 1477 and 1483 (*C.P.R., 1477–85*, 59–60, 94, 339). Pembroke was exchanged with William Herbert, earl of Huntingdon, as from 25 March 1479 (*R.P.*, VI, 202–4).

special attachment to the king's heir. The commissions of 1476 in
no way provided the authority under which the prince and his
advisers intervened in Coventry.[87]

In May 1483, barely three weeks after Edward V left Ludlow as
king, Protector Gloucester at one stroke tried to perpetuate at least
the concept of delegated prerogative.[88] He assigned to his ally,
Duke Henry of Buckingham, for life the government of all the
royal lands in Wales: he became justiciar and chamberlain of north
and south Wales, steward and receiver of Pembroke, and either
custodian or principal officer of all the king's lordships throughout
the length and breadth of Wales. To this was added

the oversight of oure [i.e. the king's] subgettes now being or herafter to be
in Southwales, Northwales and in the merches of Wales and in the countees
of Salop, Hereford, Somerset, Dorset, and Wiltshire, and also power and
auctorite by his discrecion in oure name for oure defence and the defence of
oure realme and for the defence and keping of oure peaxe of and in the said
parties to assemble oure said subgettes defencibly arreied and them conveie or
sende to suche place or places and fro tyme to tyme as shalbe thought to the
same duc expedient and necessarie in thet behalve . . .[89]

This 'oversight' was equivalent in nature to that exercised by the
prince's Council before 1483, but territorially it was much wider.
That it reposed in the hands of one man was probably due to the
delicate political position of the Protector. Buckingham combined
the personal ascendancy of Herbert with the judicial and administrative authority of the late Council. But he enjoyed them for only five
months, for on 15 October the duke was proclaimed a rebel and less
than three weeks later he was executed.[90]

The problems which faced the first Tudor king in Wales were
the same as those which had confronted the last of the Plantagenets.
Neither the use of the so-called dragon banner of Cadwaladr nor the

---

87 *The Coventry Leet Book*, ed. M. D. Harris, II (Early English Text
Society, 1908), 432–42, 474–7, 484–510; T. F. Tout, *Chapters in the Admini-
strative History of Medieval England*, IV (1928), 319 n. 2. Professor
A. R. Myers brought this matter to my attention. For a similar connection
with Coventry of Prince Edward (*c.* 1479–80), Prince Arthur and Prince
Henry (*post* 1504, not 1502), see M. D. Harris, 'Unpublished documents
relating to town life in Coventry', *T.R.H.S.*, fourth series, III (1920), 104–6;
H.M.C., fifteenth report, appendix, part x, 147.

88 The new king left Ludlow about 24 April 1483: E. F. Jacob, *The
Fifteenth Century* (1961), 611.

89 *C.P.R., 1477–85*, 349, 356, 361; *Grants of Edward V*, ed. J. G. Nichols
(Camden Society, 1854), 33. On that day, 16 May, Buckingham became steward
and receiver of the Welsh lordships of the duchy of Lancaster, and constable
of their castles: *ibid.*, 32; Somerville, *op. cit.*, 640–2, 648.

90 Jacob, *Fifteenth Century*, 625–6.

king's Welsh harp and part-Welsh ancestry could alleviate them.[91] Jasper Tudor doubtless inspired admiration for his tenacity over twenty-five years if for nothing else. Since 1461 he had first plotted and campaigned in the interest of Henry VI, and then advised and protected in exile his young nephew, Henry Tudor.[92] But in Wales conditions had not fundamentally changed: Brecon castle was attacked and ransacked by rebels in 1486, and twelve years later there was insurrection in Merioneth.[93] The new government's response followed essentially the lines laid down by Edward IV.

In order to reactivate the Crown's authority in Wales, on 11 March 1486 Henry VII empowered his uncle Jasper, during pleasure and in terms identical with those of 1476, to oversee the workings of justice in Wales, the Marches and the three English shires of Hereford, Gloucester and Worcester, to array men to provide assistance if necessary, and to keep watch on the abuse of office.[94] The code of public behaviour of which Jasper was now the guardian was that contained in Edward IV's indentures. But Henry did not give his uncle the breadth of responsibility for the internal administration of Wales's shires and lordships which Buckingham had enjoyed. It is true that Jasper, now duke of Bedford, was the most powerful personage in the south of Wales: he had Caldicot, Pembroke, Cilgerran, Llanstephan and other lordships in the south-west returned to him, and he received the lordships of Glamorgan, Haverford and Abergavenny *in tail male* by grants issued in March 1486 and March 1488. Moreover, by virtue of his marriage to Katherine Woodville, the duke of Buckingham's wealthy widow, he controlled Newport, and by May 1491 seems to have been in possession of Builth as well.[95] Elsewhere in Wales, most notably in

---

91 C. Morris, *The Tudors* (1955), 60–1. The symbolic propaganda which Henry VII directed at Welsh hearts, if not Welsh heads, has been coldly and sceptically analysed by S. Anglo, 'The *British History* in early Tudor propaganda', *Bulletin of the John Rylands Library*, xliv (1961–62), 17–48, and in *Spectacle, Pageantry and Early Tudor Policy* (1969), 16, 44–5.

92 These were often the qualities for which Jasper had been praised in verse before 1485.

93 Smith, 'Crown and community', 166–7; Pugh, *Marcher Lordships of South Wales*, 242 and n. 2; P.R.O., King's Bench, Ancient Indictments, 957/8; B.M., Egerton roll 2192 m. 2*d*, 5. (I am grateful to Dr R. S. Thomas for drawing my attention to these documents.)

94 *C.P.R.*, *1485–94*, 84. Already on 18 February Jasper had headed a commission of oyer and terminer in the Welsh lordships of the earldom of March, while as justiciar of south Wales he had been exercising the king's authority in Carmarthenshire and Cardiganshire since 13 December 1485: *ibid.*, 47, 85–6.

95 *R.P.*, vi, 278–9; *C.P.R.*, *1485–94*, 64, 220, 345; Pugh, *Marcher Lordships of South Wales*, 241.

the earldom of March and the principality, authority was diffused.[96] Indeed, the co-ordination of royal administration was achieved gradually during the reign by the king himself, not by Duke Jasper or by Prince Arthur's Council.

By 1485 the majority of marcher lordships belonged to the king, and others came his way by death or forfeiture. The administrative separateness of the earldom of March was duly abolished as from 2 February 1489, so that thenceforward every kind of grant from the earldom's estates would pass under the great seal of England 'as it is used in all othir thinges concernyng the Crowne by the Cours of the comen Lawe'.[97] Stewards of Welsh lordships who had been appointed by Edward IV or Richard III were removed in Parliament in 1487, and in the later years of the reign charters of liberties to the northern lordships ensured uniformity of law, particularly of the common law relating to property, and guaranteed uniformity of privilege and opportunity throughout the royal territories by the annulment of Henry IV's penal legislation.[98] Yet, apart from Duke Jasper, no one was allowed to enjoy hereditary possession of any of the lordships in the king's hands. Viscount Welles, who was given the lordships of Usk and Caerleon for life in August 1490, was Henry's own uncle, whereas Prince Arthur, his son, held the lordships of the earldom of March from November 1493 during the king's pleasure.[99] Once his immense debt to Uncle Jasper had been paid, Henry VII, probably for financial reasons, was reluctant to delegate his powers of government completely and permanently.

After the creation of Arthur as Prince of Wales in November 1489 his Council exercised this authority, although Jasper seems to have hung on to his position as the prince's alternate.[100] The means of ensuring peace and good government were still those of Edward IV's indentures. These were now supplemented to emphasise the crucial importance of the steward, and they were used more extensively by Henry VII than hitherto. It is likely that by 1491 not only had the marcher lords been made party to them, but so also had the

---

96 E.g. *C.P.R., 1485–94*, 5, 10, 24, 55, 65, 88, 299, 316, 365.

97 *S.R.*, II, 538–9 (1489); C. A. J. Skeel, 'Wales under Henry VII', in *Tudor Studies presented to A. F. Pollard*, ed. R. W. Seton-Watson (1924), 3.

98 *R.P.*, VI, 403; *C.P.R., 1494–1509*, 434, 464–5, 471, 523, 534–5, 586–7; Smith, 'Crown and community', 145–71. Dr R. R. Davies pertinently quotes the Welsh poet Sion Tudur's comment that Henry VII was 'the one who set us free': 'The twilight of Welsh law, 1284–1536', *History* LI (1966), 153 and n. 60.

99 *C.P.R., 1485–94*, 316, 453.

100 For the appearance of the prince's Council as early as the end of 1489, and its activities in the principality shires of north Wales during 1489–91, see Smith, 'Crown and community', 160–1.

stewards of every royal lordship in Wales; and they were concluded with Henry as king. As far as a written and sealed undertaking with a financial penalty clause could do so, the Crown had established a machinery for order and justice in Wales. The prince's Council, or Jasper Tudor in its absence, was specifically required to superintend its working.[101] A wide-ranging commission on the Yorkist model was issued to Arthur and Jasper on 20 March 1493 to superintend the execution of justice throughout Wales and the shires of Salop, Worcester, Hereford and Gloucester; at the same time Arthur received military powers to facilitate law enforcement and he was authorised to replace unsatisfactory officials. This was the authority under which the prince and his Council acted in 1494 to stop a dispute between the Worcestershire towns of Bewdley and Kidderminster and to insist that differences between them in the future should be referred to Arthur and his councillors; the commission also enabled the prince to urge Shrewsbury's bailiffs to remedy a complaint received from the local Dominican priory.[102] Again, as in 1476, Arthur was to enquire into further private franchises in the Marches which deserved to be resumed by the Crown and thereby be put under uniform administration.[103]

The cardinal weakness of Prince Edward's Council as a political and judicial instrument had been its dependence on the existence of a prince. This defect was finally removed in 1502, when Prince Arthur's Council remained in being until the creation of his brother as prince two years later restored its customary form. Arthur died on 2 April, but on 18 June the Council 'within the principality of Wales', under the presidency of Bishop William Smyth of Lincoln, was given the now familiar commissions of oyer and terminer and of array in north and south Wales, Chester, the Marches and the

---

101 P.R.O., Exchequer, Augmentations, Miscellanea, 15/37 (with Jasper Tudor, 1 March 1490); Cardiff Free Library MS 5.7, ff. 78–9 (with the earl of Huntingdon (d. 1490)), 80 (the steward of Usk, June 1488); Pugh, *Marcher Lordships of South Wales*, 29–30, 257–8, 279–81 (the steward of Clifford, Winforton and Glasbury, March 1490). The existence of a book of recognisances at Newport, which recorded bonds between the duke of Buckingham and some of his prominent tenants, indicates that an indenture was concluded with the duke too. *Ibid.*, 244–6. For a glimpse of Prince Arthur's Council dealing in traditional fashion with disputes involving Buckingham's lordships, see *ibid.*, 257–8, 272, 274–5.

102 Williams, *Council in the Marches*, 10; Skeel, *op. cit.*, 29, 30; *C.P.R., 1485–94*, 438–9, 441.

103 *C.P.R., 1485–94*, 439. For the more general encroachment on franchises under Henry VII, see Cam, *Liberties and Communities*, 214–19, and I. D. Thornley, 'The destruction of sanctuary', in *Tudor Studies*, ed. Seton-Watson, 182–207.

four border shires.[104] As at periods in the past when there was no
Prince of Wales, from the beginning of 1503 most of the revenue of
the principality was taken to the king at Westminster, but 'his
commissioners in the parts of the March of Wales' stayed on at
Ludlow or Bewdley to exercise other aspects of his sovereignty.[105]
The machinery at their disposal was now a generation old. There
was nothing novel in the recommendation of these commissioners
that 'all lordes marcheres be bowndon by indentures to the kynge's
grace for the good rule and ordre of the lordschippes, accordyng to
the good and laudable usage and customes ther'; the result, in the
case of Edward, duke of Buckingham, at least, was the renewal in
1504 of the 'olde indenture' with the king.[106] The royal prerogative
was now permanently delegated to ensure law and order throughout
Wales and the English border land, and to bind all lords and major
officers formally to discharge their obligations. It was a job still only
partly done by 1509.[107]

The fifteenth century in Wales had seen a struggle to preserve
peace, stability and justice. They were imperilled by social and
political changes. On the one hand, the feudal position and political
power of the aristocracy were decaying to the point where they
increased the disorder common to many a frontier or marchland.
On the other hand, the rising Welsh squirearchy was eager to
shoulder the responsibilities of government and political leadership.
To enable these developments to take place peacefully, the Crown
needed to realise its sovereignty in Wales more consistently than
hitherto. It did so not by revolution but by hesitant and often
painful steps in an effort to marry the traditional privileges of
English and Welsh lords in Wales with effective royal supervision.
It was truly a long struggle, and the imperfections in the achievement were to provide much of the justification for the momentous
changes of the 1530s.

104 *C.P.R. 1494–1509*, 295. Williams, *Council in the Marches*, 10, gives the
composition of this Council.

105 Smith, 'Crown and community', 167–8.

106 Pugh, *Marcher Lordships of South Wales*, 29–30; T. B. Pugh, 'The
"Indenture for the Marches" between Henry VII and Edward Stafford
(1477–1521), Duke of Buckingham', *E.H.R.*, LXXI (1956), 436–41.

107 Williams, *Council in the Marches*, 10–11; Skeel, *op. cit.*, 31–7. For its
continuation under Henry VIII, see P. R. Roberts, 'The "Acts of Union" and
the Tudor settlement of Wales', unpublished Ph.D. thesis, University of Cambridge (1966); Pugh, *Medieval Glamorgan*, ch. XII, section 2.

[Further details on the role of Henry IV and Prince Henry during the Glyndŵr rebellion are in W.R.M. Griffiths, 'Prince Henry, Wales and the Royal Exchequer, 1400-13', *Bulletin of the Board of Celtic Studies*, XXXII (1985), 202-15, and his 'Prince Henry and Wales, 1400-1408', in Michael Hicks (ed.), *Profit, Piety and the Professions in Later Medieval England* (Gloucester, 1990), ch. 4, as well as in T.B. Pugh, *Henry V and the Southampton Plot of 1415* (Southampton, 1988), ch. II; whilst Edward Powell, *Kingship, Law and Society: Criminal Justice in the Reign of Henry V* (Oxford, 1989), esp. ch. 8, assesses Henry V's settlement of Wales after the rebellion. The government and governors of parts of Wales have been explored by Ralph A. Griffiths, *The Principality of Wales in the Later Middle Ages*, vol. I. *South Wales, 1277-1536* (Cardiff, 1972), A.C. Reeves, *The Lordship of Newport, 1317-1536* (Ann Arbor, 1979), and A.D. Carr, *Medieval Anglesey* (Llangefni, 1983). Valuable material on Yorkist rule is in D.E. Lowe, 'The Council of the Prince of Wales and the Decline of the Herbert family during the reign of Edward IV', *Bulletin of the Board of Celtic Studies*, XXVII (1977-78), 278-96, and 'Patronage and politics: Edward IV, the Wydevills and the Council of the Prince of Wales, 1471-83', ibid., XXIX (1980-82), 545-73. For Henry VII, see Glanmor Williams, *Henry Tudor and Wales* (Cardiff, 1985). Recent more general works on the fifteenth century are Ralph A. Griffiths and Roger S. Thomas, *The Making of the Tudor Dynasty* (Gloucester, 1985), R.R. Davies, *Conquest, Coexistence and Change: Wales, 1063-1415* (Oxford, 1987), esp. ch. 17, and Glanmor Williams, *Recovery, Reorientation and Reformation: Wales, c. 1415-1642* (Oxford, 1987), part 1.]

5

The Sense of Dynasty in the Reign of Henry VI

The importance of dynastic title and royal pedigree in the later years of Henry VI's reign is expressed unequivocally by the early-Tudor chronicler, Polydore Vergil, in his *English History*. Richard, duke of York (he wrote under the year 1452)

> aspired to the soveraintie, trusting to that title, whereby, as we have before described in the life of king Richard the second, thinheritance of the kingdome was to descend unto the house of Yorke . . .

And later in his chronicle he referred to the year 1455,

> . . . when those two, that is to say, king Henry, who derived his pedigree from the house of Lancaster, and Richard duke of Yorke, who conveied himselfe by his mothers side from Lyonnell, sonne to Edwarde the Thirde, contended mutually for the kingdome . . . But the source of all this stirre rose (as we have before shewed) from Richard duke of Yorke; for he had conceaved an outrageous lust of principalitie, and never ceassed to devise with himselfe howe and by what meanes he might compasse it; . . .[1]

In brief, Polydore Vergil's judgement (and in this he was followed closely by Edward Hall and other sixteenth-century writers, Richard Grafton among them) was that Richard of York had coveted the kingdom of England since at least the early-1450s, resting his title on descent from Edward III's second surviving son, Lionel of Clarence.[2]

In striking contrast are the opinions of two twentieth-century historians, writing quite recently about the same question. According to Mortimer Levine,

---

[1] Sir H. Ellis (ed.), *Three Books of Polydore Vergil's English History* (Camden Soc., XXIX, 1844), pp. 86, 93-94. The quotations are from a translation, made towards the end of Henry VIII's reign, of Vergil's Latin chronicle.

[2] E. Hall, *The Union of the Two Noble Families of Lancaster and York* (London, 1550; repr. 1970), f. 80*v*; R. Grafton, *A Chronicle at Large* . . . (London, 1569; repr. 1809), p. 646. A son William, born in 1336, died in childhood; Lionel was born in 1338.

> The Wars of the Roses did not originate out of any dynastic rivalry . . .
> Whatever the secret ambition of Richard of York, . . . no dynastic issue was
> involved at St. Albans [1455].

And even more recently, Charles Ross has concluded:

> The dynastic issue was not clearly raised until the return of Duke Richard of
> York from Ireland in the autumn of 1460.[3]

To put it equally shortly, Professors Levine and Ross are at one in denying
that the dynastic issue had any significant part to play in precipitating
civil strife in England during the 1450s. In other respects, however, their
views diverge a mite. According to Professor Ross, the dynastic issue was
'not clearly raised' before 1460, though he does not deny that it may have
been present, lurking in some men's minds. Professor Levine, more firmly,
doubts that the issue was at all relevant to the early violence and battles of
the 'Wars of the Roses' before 1455, though even he does not dispute that
the matter could have occupied Richard of York's own mind.

The certainty of Polydore Vergil presumably arose from his
determination to demonstrate that Henry VII and his Tudor successors
united the two ultimately warring houses of Lancaster and York; in the
process he simplified the issues prominent in the early stages of the civil
wars so that the struggle to which they gave rise appeared to be a contest
between Lancaster, who was determined to keep the throne, and York,
who was bent on seizing it. The dynastic issue was reduced in Vergil's
mind to an uncomplicated rivalry between the two. It is this simplification
that is the historical distortion, not the chronicler's assertion that the
dynastic issue was prominent well before 1460.

The views of Professors Levine and Ross probably arise from their
conviction that we should shed the supposedly propagandist veil cast by
Tudor historians about the origins of the 'Wars of the Roses', and
accordingly relegate the dynastic issue (amongst other things) to a more
discreet corner of the picture. That, too, distorts a true appreciation of
late-Lancastrian politics. This paper attempts to re-assess the place of this
dynastic issue in Henry VI's reign and, thereby, its relevance to the
forthcoming civil war. The issue should be placed in a perspective rather
different from that adopted by Polydore Vergil, Mortimer Levine and
Charles Ross, both extending the chronological basis of the discussion
(i.e., both before and after 1450), and by raising it beyond the confines of
what all three writers believed they were observing, namely, a simple and
direct confrontation, sooner or later, between Henry VI and Richard of
York. In this connection it is worth re-examining contemporaries'

---

[3] M. Levine, *Tudor Dynastic Problems, 1460-1571* (London, 1973), p. 15; C. Ross, *The Wars
of the Roses* (London, 1976), p. 43.

conscious awareness of the importance of royal lineage and of the need to maintain and protect it, both for reasons of stability and because God-given qualities ought of themselves to be preserved – until, of course, events showed that what God had given he could also take away.[4] How conscious of lineage were contemporaries; how pre-occupied were they with dynasty; how strong a sense of dynasty had they? It may be suggested that the king and his ministers, the nobility, and even lesser folk, were far more conscious than is usually recognised of this wider 'sense of dynasty', and that it is this awareness which accounts for many of their political actions after Henry VI came of age in 1436-37. If this is so, then the dynastic issue should be brought back to the centre of the stage whenever the origins of the 'Wars of the Roses' are portrayed.

The dynastic stability, strength and cohesion of the house of Lancaster were a matter of permanent concern to many after 1399. It is worth recalling that, even in 1461, the Lancastrians had occupied the English throne for a shorter period of time (sixty-two years) than other Western dynasties had theirs since the twelfth century – in Aragon and Castile, France and Scotland, as well as England herself.

The succession to the English throne had been formally vested in the house of Lancaster by Henry IV's declaration of February 1404, as amended by statute two years later.[5] The crown would henceforth pass to the king's eldest son, Prince Henry, and to his heirs general; should they fail, then it would go to each of Henry IV's other sons in turn and their respective heirs general. The Lancastrian succession to the French throne was acknowledged by King Charles VI in the treaty of Troyes in May 1420.[6] It was vested in Henry V as Charles's adopted son and his heirs, that is, in the same line as the English throne, though Henry V's brothers and their heirs were not specifically mentioned in the treaty. The Lancastrian family met the dynastic challenge quite adequately at first: Henry V had a son, though he succeeded to both thrones at the dangerously early age of nine or ten months; and Henry VI himself had a son, though of course he, Prince Edward, had no opportunity of succeeding to either.

---

[4]This point is well made by J.R. Lander, *Conflict and Stability in Fifteenth-Century England* (3rd. ed., London, 1977), pp. 12, 184.

[5] *Rotuli Parliamentorum* (6 vols., London, 1767), III, 525, 574-76; 7 Henry IV *c.* 2 in *Statutes of the Realm*, II (Record commission, 1806), 151, and reprinted in S.B. Chrimes and A.L. Brown (eds.), *Select Documents of English Constitutional History, 1307-1485* (London, 1961), pp. 225-26. This line of succession seems to have been explicitly accepted even earlier, at councils held shortly before Christmas 1403.

[6] T. Rymer (ed.), *Foedera, Conventiones, Literae . . .* (The Hague, 1739-45), IV, iii, 179-80, partially reprinted in modernised English in A.R. Myers (ed.), *English Historical Documents*, IV, *1307-1485* (London, 1969), pp. 225-26. Significantly, the succession to the French throne was not restricted in the treaty to the heirs of Henry V's body.

Nevertheless, the Lancastrian succession to the English and French thrones was acutely vulnerable throughout almost the entire life of the dynasty. In the first place, it was a usurping dynasty, which inevitably meant that it would have its rivals: whether actual rebels who would attempt to overturn the usurpers (and there were plenty of those up to 1415), or potential challengers (most notably the line of Lionel of Clarence, which was senior in one important respect to that of Henry IV's own father, John of Gaunt).[7] Thus, an unequivocal and assured line of succession beyond the immediate heir was unusually vital to the Lancastrians, especially if the next heir or the king himself was a child (which was the situation after 1421).

No serious dynastic problem arose during Henry V's reign, even though he did not marry until 1420, when he was thirty-three (which was rather old by contemporary standard).[8] He had three apparently healthy brothers, Thomas, John and Humphrey, and then a son in 1421 when the king himself was still only thirty-four. After Henry V's unexpected death in 1422, leaving a nine-month-old heir, the dynastic importance of Henry's surviving brothers, John and Humphrey, became suddenly more immediate, though the succession to both thrones was not in dispute. The position of these brothers would be vitally significant if the child-king died before reaching adulthood, or before he married, or before he produced children. They were important in practical terms in ensuring the stability of the Lancastrian regime during the inevitably long minority ahead, when the government must needs be entrusted to others in place of the king. And they were important, too, in the task of maintaining the French inheritance of the young king, and completing its conquest; during Henry VI's minority these tasks had perforce to be someone else's practical responsibility.

The fate of Henry VI's three uncles demonstrates how vulnerable, dynastically speaking, the house of Lancaster was in reality. The eldest, Thomas, duke of Clarence, was killed at the battle of Baugé in March 1421 in the course of one of those reckless sorties for which he was renowned; although he had married, he left no legitimate or illegitimate heir.[9] The second brother, John, duke of Bedford, married Anne, sister of the duke of Burgundy, in 1423, but he left no legitimate heir either. He had, it is true, an illegitimate daughter Marie and a bastard son Richard; but although the son was legitimated in 1434, when it was doubtless evident that John

---

[7] Lionel's descendants were the heirs general (as opposed to the heirs male) of Edward III.

[8] No English monarch had married so late in life since Richard I (in 1191) and none would do so again until Mary Tudor (1554).

[9] G.E. Cokayne, *The Complete Peerage*, ed. V. Gibbs et al. (12 vols. in 13, London, 1910-59), III, 258-60. For his illegitimate son, John, see S. Lee (ed.), *The Dictionary of National Biography* (63 vols., London, 1885-1900), LVI, 159.

was unlikely to father any more children, Richard strangely enjoyed no significance dynastically or personally as his father's heir.[10] Duke John's sense of dynasty goes some way towards explaining his rapid marriage in April 1433 after Anne of Burgundy died. The wedding to Jacquetta of Luxembourg was arranged within three months and in such haste that he was prepared to brave the angry disapproval of his brother-in-law, the duke of Burgundy, and manfully overcome his undoubted grief. When John died in September 1435 he still had no legitimate heir.[11] And the king was still unmarried and had no children of his own.

The third uncle, Humphrey, duke of Gloucester, married Jacqueline of Hainault early in 1423; then, in 1428, he discarded her in favour of Eleanor Cobham, an English lady who was one of Jacqueline's ladies-in-waiting and had been the duke's mistress for some time past. Despite his somewhat eccentric marital record, Humphrey had no legitimate heir – only an illegitimate daughter whose name, Antigone, he culled from classical reading, and a bastard son Arthur who owed his name to mediaeval romance.[12] Thus, after 1422, the heir to the English throne had been John of Lancaster and his heirs general, followed by Humphrey and his heirs general. By 1435 the dynastic prospect had deteriorated alarmingly: John was dead and had left no legitimate heir; Henry VI, at the age of fourteen, was unmarried and childless; and even Duke Humphrey, now aged forty-four, had little likelihood of fathering the legitimate heir that had hitherto eluded him and his two wives – and this contemporaries realised when, from 1440 onwards, steps were taken formally to arrange the disposal of his property in the event of his death.[13]

The personality and political attitudes of Humphrey and his second wife, Eleanor, intensified contemporaries' concern for the succession, even while Humphrey still lived. It was fully apparent after 1435 that should Henry VI die, Humphrey would succeed to both thrones and Eleanor Cobham would become queen (for no previous English king had not made his wife queen). But (and this intensified the current concern) there was no further heir of the immediate Lancastrian family available and no likelihood of one in the direct line until Henry VI married. Then, too, Humphrey had acquired a formidable list of enemies over the past twenty years. For these two reasons, therefore, the prospect of Humphrey

---

[10] E.C. Williams, *My Lord of Bedford* (London, 1963), pp. 247, 275; *Complete Peerage*, II, 70-72. His first wife seems to have died in childbed.

[11] Williams, *Bedford*, pp. 222-24. There were also pressing diplomatic reasons for the Luxembourg match.

[12] K.H. Vickers, *Humphrey, Duke of Gloucester* (London, 1907), pp. 127-28, 165, 205 (though the exact date of neither marriage is known). For his children, see ibid., pp. 335-36; and for his books, ibid., pp. 426-38, and *Duke Humfrey and English Humanism in the Fifteenth Century: catalogue of an exhibition . . .* (Oxford, 1970).

[13] E.g., *Calendar of Patent Rolls, 1436-41*, pp. 401, 444. These steps were taken even before Humphrey was humiliated by the trial of his wife in July 1441 (for which see below no. 14).

succeeding the young Henry VI probably played a decisive part in the scandal that enveloped his wife in 1441. Eleanor Cobham's eagerness to engage in astrology and magic, partly to discover whether the Gloucesters would ever reach the throne, partly even to hasten their sitting on it, seems to have been skilfully exploited by the duke's enemies. Humphrey was seriously discredited (though he remained the Lancastrian heir), his wife was exiled and (what is more to the dynastic point) their marriage was annulled so that she should never be queen nor produce a king.[14] The scandal of 1441 highlighted the fragile dynastic hold which the Lancastrians had on the English (let alone the French) throne, regardless of whether Humphrey himself was personally acceptable or not in certain influential quarters.

In these circumstances there was an imperative need to fortify the Lancastrian house dynastically. Accordingly, discussions were soon being held to arrange a marriage for the young king – first in 1438 when Henry VI was seventeen, but especially after Humphrey had lost much of his political influence by the beginning of 1440. Eventually, an agreement was reached with the French in 1444 that he should marry Margaret of Anjou. It was demonstrably a slow process, either because suitable brides were in short supply in western Europe, or, more likely, because conflicting political counsels at home postponed a final decision.[15] Even with Henry married or about to be married, it was almost as urgent to fortify the dynasty less directly, though up to the point where the next heir could be indicated. This was a sensitive and delicate matter in view of the existence of a potential challenger of distinguished lineage, York, and the imprecision of the rules then governing the inheritance of the crown; certainly, there was no unequivocal law of succession to guide the thoughts of contemporaries beyond Henry VI and Duke Humphrey.[16]

Urgency was made more urgent by the surprising fertility of Richard of York and his stout-bodied wife, Cecily Neville. Starting with a daughter, Anne, in 1439 and a son, Henry, in 1441, in the thirteen years between 1439 and 1452 they produced eight sons and three daughters – not to

---

[14] R.A. Griffiths, 'The trial of Eleanor Cobham: an episode in the fall of Duke Humphrey of Gloucester', *Bulletin of the John Rylands Library*, LI (1969), 381-99 (p. 394 for the annulment); see below ch. 15 (esp. p. 246).

[15] M.E. Christie, *Henry VI* (London, 1922), pp. 135-36; J. Ferguson, *English Diplomacy, 1422-1461* (Oxford, 1972), pp. 26-27, 114-15. Moreover, changed circumstances abroad, over which the English government had no control, played a part in frustrating the German and Armagnac negotiations of 1438 and 1442 respectively.

[16] S.B. Chrimes, *English Constitutional Ideas in the Fifteenth Century* (Cambridge, 1936), pp. 9-13, 62-64.

speak of an after-thought, Ursula, in 1455.[17] A comparison with this prolific progeny would underline the extreme poverty of the Lancastrian family and increase the dynastic threat from Lionel of Clarence's line.

It was natural that Henry VI and his advisers should turn cautiously, yet unmistakably, to the wider royal family of Lancastrian blood in order to secure dynastic support. The possibilities on the male side were reasonably encouraging. The Beauforts had been born illegitimately to John of Gaunt, Henry IV's father, and John, Henry and Thomas were therefore Henry IV's half-brothers and Joan Beaufort his half-sister. They had been legitimated in 1397 but specifically debarred from the royal succession in February 1407, after Henry IV in parliament had vested the crown in his squad of sons – of whom there then seemed an adequate supply. There was room for doubt about the validity of this act of exclusion, and it may even have been regretted by Henry VI in later years; there was also the possibility that it could be overturned by the letters patent which had established it, though that would admittedly have been provocative.[18] Among the Beauforts, the family's senior heir was Margaret, the daughter born in May 1443 to John, duke of Somerset, who himself died one year later.[19]

Secondly, the Holands were descended from Henry IV's full sister, Elizabeth, whose family in Henry VI's reign was represented by John Holand, duke of Exeter, until his death in August 1447, and then by his son Henry, who was seventeen when his father died.[20] In addition there may be added the Staffords, who, although not of the Lancastrian family itself, were descended from John of Gaunt's youngest brother, Thomas of Woodstock. Earls of Stafford since 1351, in 1444 Humphrey Stafford became duke of Buckingham.[21] To regard Lionel of Clarence's descendants, now represented by Richard of York, in the same light would have been to admit implicitly that Duke Richard had a better claim than the Lancastrians themselves to the English throne. It would have been tantamount to proclaiming themselves usurpers.

There are indeed indications that in the 1440s Henry VI and his advisers chose to ignore the duke of York as a possible heir to the throne.

---

[17] C.L. Scofield, *The Life and Reign of Edward the Fourth* (2 vols., London, 1923), I, 1-3. It is not without significance that in 1441 Richard and Cecily gave their first-born son a name favoured above all others by the house of Lancaster (but not by the Mortimers or Nevilles) since the thirteenth century.

[18] *C.P.R., 1396-99*, p. 86 (fully printed in *Foedera*, III, iv, 126); *C.P.R. 1405-8*, p. 284. See the comment in J.L. Kirby, *Henry IV of England* (London, 1970), pp. 209-10. The words *excepta dignitate regali* were squeezed between the lines of the 1407 confirmation of the act of legitimation of 1397.

[19] *Complete Peerage*, XII, i, 48.

[20] Ibid., V, 211-12.

[21] C. Rawcliffe, *The Staffords, Earls of Stafford and Dukes of Buckingham, 1394-1521* (Cambridge, 1978); below p.90.

Instead, they seem to have espoused the Beaufort, Holand and Stafford families. Without openly preferring one, Henry advanced all three, though ultimately with perhaps some preference for the Beauforts. After all, Henry Beaufort, the cardinal-bishop of Winchester, still had formidable influence at court and in the council in the early 1440s, and his protégé, Suffolk, enjoyed the same later in the decade.[22] Marriages and noble creations were the two principal means employed by the king to achieve his design – and both lay at the heart of any sense of dynasty.

On 28 August 1443 the king's cousin, John Beaufort, earl of Somerset and grandson of John of Gaunt, was created duke, with precedence above the duke of Norfolk, in acknowledgement of his blood relationship to Henry VI.[23] A few months later, in January 1444, John Holand, earl of Huntingdon, was created duke of Exeter specifically (as the patent has it) because of his proximity of blood to the king; at the same time, he was given precedence over all other dukes save York.[24] (In August 1447, John was succeeded by his son, Henry Holand.) In September 1444 Humphrey Stafford was created a duke, only a few months after John Beaufort, duke of Somerset, died, leaving a one-year-old heiress. In May 1447 the new duke of Buckingham was given precedence over all who might in the future be created dukes, unless they were of the king's own blood; and this occurred only three months after the death of the king's heir, Humphrey of Gloucester. Buckingham, incidentally, was already married to Anne, the daughter of Joan Beaufort and the earl of Westmorland.[25] Humphrey Stafford, then, was created duke and given this special precedence specifically because he was close in blood to the king, and these steps were taken immediately after the impoverishment of the Lancastrian house by sudden death.

In March 1448 Edmund Beaufort was created duke of Somerset; he was the younger brother of the late duke and had already, during 1442-43, been raised in quick succession to the dignities of earl and marquess of Dorset; he was also, of course, uncle of the senior Beaufort heir, the five-year-old Margaret (I).[26] It is not without significance that Edmund's own daughter, also called Margaret (II), had married none other than the

---

[22] C.L. Kingsford, *Prejudice and Promise in Fifteenth Century England* (London, 1925), pp. 153ff.

[23] N.H. Nicolas (ed.), *Proceedings and Ordinances of the Privy Council of England*, V (Record commission, 1835), 252-53; *Complete Peerage*, XII, i, 47. The decision to create him duke had been taken as early as 30 March 1443.

[24] *Reports from the Lords Committees touching the Dignity of a Peer of the Realm*, V (London, 1829), 241-42, 248; *Complete Peerage*, V, 208.

[25] Ibid., II, 388-89; *Dignity Reports*, V, 243, 257-58.

[26] Ibid., pp. 238, 240-41, 258-59; *Complete Peerage*, XII, i, 50-51. Henceforward, the daughter of John, duke of Somerset will be referred to as Margaret Beaufort (I), and Duke Edmund's as Margaret Beaufort (II).

duke of Buckingham's son and heir in 1444.[27] When she was barely seven years old, the Beaufort heiress, Margaret (I), was married to John de la Pole, son and heir of the king's chief minister, Suffolk, early in 1450. Some at the time detected dynastic significance in this match as a possible route by which the de la Poles might reach the throne.[28] That suspicion in itself reflects the dynastic importance which contemporaries were coming to attach to the Beaufort family among the Lancastrian relatives.

Margaret Beaufort (I) was a much-married lady. Her marriage to John de la Pole was annulled in February 1453 and soon after March 1453 she married the king's eldest half-brother, Edmund Tudor, who had been raised to the peerage in the previous November as earl of Richmond, one of the late duke of Bedford's titles.[29] Though Edmund could not conceivably have had a claim to the throne himself, this marriage would undoubtedly fortify the royal family and give it greater cohesion. Indeed, this may have been the very reason for the annulment of the de la Pole match. The apparent proof of this particular pudding, of course, lies in the accession of Henry VII, the son of Edmund and Margaret. Perhaps, as S.B. Chrimes speculated, this eventuality was perceived as a possibility by the childless Henry VI at the time the marriage was arranged; after all, in March 1453 it is just possible that it was not yet apparent that Queen Margaret was pregnant for the first time in her eight years of married life.[30] One may wonder, further, whether there is not an echo of this perception of Henry VI's in Shakespeare's *Henry VI*, Part Three, act IV, in the scene, there dated to 1471, in which the king is made to meet the young Henry Tudor and predict his accession to the throne:

> Come hither, England's hope.
> If secret powers
> Suggest but truth to my divining thoughts,
> This pretty lad will prove our country's bliss.
> His looks are full of peaceful majesty,
> His head by nature framed to wear a crown,
> His hand to wield a sceptre, and himself
> Likely in time to bless a regal throne.

[27] Ibid., II, 389; Rawcliffe, *Staffords*, p. 21 n. 45.

[28] R.A. Griffiths, 'Duke Richard of York's intentions in 1450 and the origins of the Wars of the Roses', *Journal of Mediaeval History*, I (1975), 193-94; *Complete Peerage*, XII, i, 449-50. See below ch. pp. 284-5.

[29] The marriage had certainly taken place before 1455: *Complete Peerage*, X, 826. The royal earldom conferred on Edmund Tudor is significant, especially in view of the simultaneous elevation of his younger brother, Jasper, to the earldom of Pembroke, one of Humphrey of Gloucester's titles. R.S. Thomas, 'The political career, estates and "connection" of Jasper Tudor, earl of Pembroke and duke of Bedford (d. 1495)' (unpublished University of Wales Ph.D. thesis, 1971), pp. 32-36, establishes beyond doubt that both earls were created on 6 November 1452.

[30] S.B. Chrimes, *Henry VII* (London, 1972), p. 13. Prince Edward was born on 13 October 1453. There is no record of an earlier miscarriage by Queen Margaret.

Edmund Tudor died in November 1456. Margaret Beaufort (I)'s third (though by no means her last) marriage reflects how her dynastic attractions continued into the late-1450s. By 1459 she had married Henry Stafford, the second son of Humphrey, duke of Buckingham. This was a seemingly obscure union, but it should be remembered that Henry Stafford's elder brother, the earl of Stafford, had recently died in 1458, and that the new heir to the dukedom, the late earl's son, was still only eight and the old duke in his late-fifties.[31] The two family links between the Beauforts and the Staffords helped to buttress the Lancastrian dynasty, ensured unmistakably that the Staffords would resist the pretensions of the duke of York, and pointed towards Beaufort blood as perhaps the best possible means of fortifying the Lancastrian line. May not this conclusion be echoed, not in *Henry VI*, Part One, act II (the scene in the Temple Garden where red and white roses are plucked by opposing factions), but rather in Part One, act IV, where King Henry is portrayed choosing the red rose in preference to the white, for a red rose is likely to have been a Beaufort emblem by this time?[32] If this is so, and if contemporaries' dynastic preoccupation was as strong as it appears, then one may restore some sense of contemporary reality to the concept of 'The Wars of the Roses', of which Professor Chrimes has sought to deprive it.[33]

Before examining the duke of York's reaction to these Lancastrian designs, it is worth considering a few indirect reflections of the importance which King Henry attached to his dynasty's lineal security.

During 1445-46 negotiations were underway between York and King Charles VII of France for the marriage of York's three-year-old son, Edward, to a French princess. Charles offered his fourth daughter, Madeleine (who was all of one and a half), even though his second daughter, Jeanne, was still unmarried. Understandably, York preferred

---

[31] Thomas, 'Jasper Tudor', p. 141; Rawcliffe, *Staffords*, p. 21 n.45.

[32] For the association of a red rose with the Beauforts as descendants of the house of Lancaster, see J.R. Planche, 'On the badges of the house of Lancaster', *Journal of the British Archaeological Association*, VI (1851), 378-83; B. Seward, *The Symbolic Rose* (New York, 1960), p. 56 n.2. A red rose also appears at the head of a pedigree of Henry VI originally composed *c*. 1429-38: A. Wall (ed.), *Handbook to the Maude Roll* (Auckland, N.Z., 1919). A rose (but not the double Tudor rose) also figures on Margaret Beaufort's tomb in Westminster Abbey: R.F. Scott, 'On the contracts for the tomb of Lady Margaret Beaufort', *Archaeologia*, LXVI (1914-15), facing p. 365.

[33] S.B. Chrimes, *Lancastrians, Yorkists and Henry VII* (2nd. ed., London, 1966), pp. xii-xiv. See Ross, *Wars of the Roses*, pp. 12-15, for a less sceptical view of the implications of the roses symbol.

Jeanne's hand, as he explained in a letter to the French king in June 1445. The environment in which the negotiations were taking place changed dramatically when the Dauphin Louis's wife, Margaret of Scotland, died in August 1445.[34] By December, York had withdrawn his request for Jeanne's hand and had accepted Madeleine's. But he was too late. The French king's concern was now focussed on his still childless and recently widowered eldest son and heir, Louis, and nothing further is heard of the proposed Yorkist match. Rather did Charles VII's eyes light on one of the duke of Buckingham's daughters (and his two eldest daughters were still unbetrothed in 1445) as perhaps as close and suitable a link as was possible with a Lancastrian royal family which Margaret of Anjou had recently joined.[35] The creation of Buckingham as a duke little more than a year earlier may have been read as a dynastic signal by Charles VII in 1445. This may, indeed, be the reason why the negotiations with York were broken off, rather than because, after two years of open discussion, Henry VI intervened to prevent a Valois marriage with the house of York (which was Miss Scofield's view).[36] A Stafford match would have seemed the best possibility to Charles VII in 1445: Margaret Beaufort (I) was barely three years old, and the daughter of Edmund Beaufort, the new earl of Somerset, was already married to Buckingham's own son and heir. Charles VII's plan eventually fell through only because the Dauphin had other ideas – much to his father's annoyance.

The second indirect piece of evidence is provided by the researches of T.B. Pugh.[37] He has noted that the largest sum by far known to have been paid by a nobleman in late-mediaeval England to purchase a husband for his daughter was the 6,500 marks which York agreed to pay as dowry in August 1445. The contract allowed his eldest daughter, Anne, to marry the son and heir of John Holand, who had been created duke of Exeter the previous year. Aside from the Beauforts, the Holands were Henry VI's nearest male kinsmen in England, and the fat price may have been dictated (as Mr. Pugh has suggested) by the prospect of a Holand succeeding to the throne of England.[38]

[34] J. Stevenson (ed.), *Letters and Papers illustrative of the Wars of the English in France* (2 vols. in 3, Rolls Series, 1861-64), I, 79-86, 160-63, 168-70; *Catalogue of . . . the well-known Collection of . . . the late W. Westley Manning, esq.* (Sotheby & Co., 24-25 January 1955), p. 45, which is also noticed (but misdated to 1456) in *Historical Manuscripts Commission*, Report IX, part 2 (1884), p. 410.

[35] Rawcliffe, *Staffords*, p. 21; G. du Fresne de Beaucourt, *Histoire de Charles VII* (6 vols., Paris, 1881-91), V, 135-37.

[36] Scofield, *Edward the Fourth*, I, 9-11.

[37] T.B. Pugh, 'The magnates, knights and gentry', in S.B. Chrimes, C.D. Ross and R.A. Griffiths (eds.), *Fifteenth-Century England: Studies in Politics and Society, 1399-1509* (Manchester, 1972), p. 118 n.11.

[38] The marriage is not inconsistent with York's concern for the dynastic rights of his own line.

A third indication arises from the greater appreciation of the parlous dynastic situation of the Lancastrian royal family after the duke of Bedford died in 1435 – perhaps even as soon as it became apparent that he was unlikely to sire legitimate children. This appreciation was certainly strong by 1440, when it was clear that none could be expected from Duke Humphrey either. The consequent need to buttress the Lancastrian line dynastically is accordingly reflected in the buoyant business of pedigree production. Pedigrees from Adam and Eve or Noah especially proliferated during Henry VI's reign, and not solely to stress the king's unique dual descent in the royal lines of England and France.[39] Some of these seem to have been manufactured for domestic dynastic purposes, though they are sometimes difficult to date. There are several still surviving today from the 1430s or '40s which pointedly exclude all reference to the line of Lionel of Clarence, and at least one incorporates the Staffords and the Beauforts, as well as the Holands, and can be dated precisely to 1444.[40]

There is no reason to doubt that Richard of York's sense of dynasty was as strongly developed as the king's, and he could be relied on to react in a predictable fashion once he became aware of the Lancastrian manoeuvres. There is ample testimony that he was so aware by 1450. By that year, there was a welter of suspicion, rumour and accusation abroad that the king should be deposed in York's favour, and some of the evidence at least implicated his servants and councillors.[41] Even if these were not coherent treason plots or formal counter-claims directed at the Lancastrian house, they graphically reflect the uncertainty that existed about the succession to the throne, the confusion that reigned about whose was the better and more senior descent, and the nervous appreciation by some of Lancastrian intentions to secure the present dynasty. Others were also aware of the significance of events, for Cade's rebels, in their demand that the king should recall the greater nobility to his counsels, placed special emphasis on York's 'trew blode of [the] realme'.[42]

When the duke returned to England from Ireland in September 1450, he professed himself to be concerned about the possibility of his own

---

[39] Among many that may be cited, see Bodleian Library, Magdalen Latin MS. 248 (from Adam); B.L., Additional MS. 18,002 (from Noah).

[40] E.g., ibid. (dateable to 1438-41); Bodleian Library, Marshall MS. 135 (c. 1427-41); Bodleian roll 10 (c. 1427-41); Wall, *Handbook to the Maude Roll* (from Noah, c. 1429-38). B.L., Add. MS. 27,342 can be dated between May and September 1444. Many of these genealogies and pedigrees were later amended to include York's descent.

[41] Griffiths, *Journal of Mediaeval History*, I (1975), 191-94; below pp. 280-6.

[42] From John Stowe's memoranda in J. Gairdner (ed.), *Three Fifteenth-Century Chronicles* (Camden Soc., new series, XXVIII, 1880), p. 94, partially reprinted in modernised English in B. Wilkinson, *Constitutional History of England in the Fifteenth Century (1399-1485)* (London, 1964), p. 84, and Myers, *E.H.D.*, IV, 267.

attainder, whereby his blood would be corrupted and his lineage dishonoured – which at a stroke would have undermined his dynastic pretensions and that, surely, was a likely step for the Lancastrians to take?[43] In this context, it is easy to appreciate why, when Thomas Yonge, the M.P. for Bristol and one of York's councillors, proposed in the 1451 parliament that the duke should be formally declared heir apparent to the Lancastrian throne, the outspoken member was treated harshly and peremptorily.[44]

The onset of Henry VI's serious illness in August 1453 gave the question of an heir greater immediacy and to the antagonisms it had already aroused greater bitterness.[45] The birth of a son, Prince Edward, in October 1453 might ordinarily be expected to have taken the heat out of the dynastic discussion. But, coinciding as it did with the king's illness, it simply thrust to the fore the question of who should govern the realm during the king's incapacity while his heir was a minor – or, if the king should die, during the inevitable, long minority. In these changed circumstances, dynastic security became of over-riding importance. Whatever provisions were made for the realm's governance, they were almost bound to have implications for the succession.

Queen Margaret of Anjou's wish was that she should become regent, and that would certainly have averted a crisis in government. But such a French fashion had been unacceptable in the past, and the memory of 1422 was still green in England.[46] Rather was a protectorate preferred, with England ruled by a protector and defender of the realm, aided by a council. In 1422, the next heir to the throne, John of Bedford, had been nominated as protector, unless he were in France in which case the second acknowledged heir, Duke Humphrey, should serve. They had been designated by Henry V to have charge of both realms, and no one challenged their prominence as the baby king's successive heirs. The

---

[43] See York's first letter to Henry VI, in Griffiths, *Journal of Mediaeval History*, I(1975), 203; below pp. 299-300.

[44] Latin annals in Stevenson, *Letters and Papers*, II, ii, [770], translated in Wilkinson, *Constitutional History*, p. 114; *Rot. Parl.*, V, 137. Yonge was sent to the Tower and Parliament dissolved towards the end of May 1451. See J.C. Wedgwood, *History of Parliament: Biographies of the Members of the Common House, 1439-1509* (London, 1936), pp. 981-82; idem, ibid., *Register* (London, 1938), p. 147. That part of 'Gregory's Chronicle' which is considered to have been composed about 1451 refers interestingly to York as 'Rycharde Plantagent' under the year 1448-49: J. Gairdner (ed.)., *The Historical Collections of a Citizen of London in the Fifteenth Century* (Camden Soc., new series, XVII, 1876), p. 189; C.L. Kingsford, *English Historical Literature in the Fifteenth Century* (Oxford, 1913), pp. 96-98; J.A.F. Thomson, 'The continuation of "Gregory's Chronicle" – a possible author?' *The British Museum Quarterly*, XXXVI (1971-72), 92-93.

[45] R.L. Storey, *The End of the House of Lancaster* (London, 1966), p. 136.

[46] J. Gairdner (ed.), *The Paston Letters* (6 vols., London, 1904), II, 297; J.S. Roskell, 'The office and dignity of protector of England', *English Historical Review*, LXVIII (1953), 205ff.

argument in 1422 had rather revolved around their powers in England, nothing more.[47] Nor is it irrelevant to note what happened thirty years later in 1483. On that occasion, Edward IV supposedly nominated his adult heir (that is, after the two young princes who found themselves in the Tower), Richard of Gloucester, as protector and defender of the realm, and he was accepted as such.[48]

Thus, the choice of protector in 1453-54 would be of the utmost significance, not only in assigning the practical powers of government, but as an indication of who the ultimate Lancastrian heir should be in circumstances where it was unclear who he was by right. This explains the lengthy and bitter argument that took place in the winter of 1453-54, contrasted with the smoother passage of events in 1422 and 1483, and the vigour of the queen in forwarding her own demand for the regency. It explains, too, Richard of York's devotion to the memory of Duke Humphrey and his part in the campaign to rehabilitate his reputation.[49] It accounts equally for the imprisonment of Edmund Beaufort, duke of Somerset, late in 1453.[50] And it has some bearing on the rising of the Holand duke of Exeter in the north of England round about Christmas 1453, with its indications that, with so much at stake dynastically, he at least felt that the protectorate should be his.[51]

The similarity between the situation in 1453-54 and that of 1422 is, in fact, only superficial and does not extend beyond the need felt on both occasions to provide effective government. In 1453-54 the king was alive and adult, though incapacitated; England was therefore faced with the possibility of a helpless monarch (or, if he should die, a child king) under the influence of the queen. There is also a sharp contrast to be drawn between the personality of the two queens: between Katherine of Valois, who was a passive figure in English politics, and Margaret of Anjou, a

[47] Ibid.; S.B. Chrimes, 'The pretensions of the duke of Gloucester in 1422', ibid., XLV (1930), 101-3.

[48] Ellis, *Polydore Vergil*, p. 173; J. Gairdner (ed.), *Memorials of King Henry the Seventh* (Rolls Series, 1858), p. 28 (Bernard André's chronicle); J. Gairdner, *History of the Life and Reign of Richard the Third* (2nd. ed., London, 1898), pp. 44, 55. Notice, too, that according to Edward Hall, it was recommended in Parliament on 31 October 1460 that York should be proclaimed heir apparent and protector at one and the same time: Hall, *Union of Lancaster and York*, f. 98, reprinted from the 1809 edition in Chrimes and Brown, *Select Documents*, pp. 318-19.

[49] *Rot. Parl.*, V, 335 (1455); J.S. Davies (ed.), *An English Chronicle* . . . (Camden Soc., LXIV, 1856), p. 88 (1460).

[50] *P.L.*, II, 290-92; Storey, *End of Lancaster*, p. 138.

[51] R.A. Griffiths, 'Local rivalries and national politics: the Percies, the Nevilles and the duke of Exeter, 1452-1455', *Speculum* XLIII (1968), 606ff; below pp. 338ff.

more combative individual.[52] But above all, the experience of the previous decade made the conditions of the 1450s markedly different from those of the 1420s. The attempts to sustain a Lancastrian house, dynastically vulnerable in an uncertain legal situation, had made York's future highly problematical. Hence, perhaps, the rumours that were disseminated at this time that Prince Edward was not, in fact, King Henry's son.[53] It should be said that there is no evidence that Edward of Lancaster was regarded by anyone in authority – least of all by the delighted king – as other than Henry VI's own offspring.[54] But the rumours may well express the disappointment (even the fear) felt by some at this decisive reinforcement of the Lancastrian line.

After the question of regency had been disposed of, York was appointed protector in March 1454 in preference to both Somerset and Exeter. The decision was taken by the lords present as a body, partly on the basis of who was most competent. By 1454 there was considerable resentment at the advancement of the Beauforts in terms of their power, wealth and influence. There were also serious doubts about their past record, particularly in France.[55] They had been, moreover, too closely associated with the reprehensible actions of Suffolk and others, while Exeter was known to be a violent man of limited intelligence ('fierce and cruel', as one contemporary described him).[56]

The choice of York would also have the critical advantage of averting a yet starker polarisation of faction and the further victimisation of his line. Unity, not division; efficiency, not inefficiency and corruption; sound reputation, not failure – these were the considerations that weighed with the lords. And credit must go to them as a body for their choice; it postponed a violent clash. But the implications of the protectorate were potentially just as disastrous.

York may be pardoned for thinking (or choosing to think) that his nomination as protector was a sign of aristocratic favour towards the dynastic possibilities of his line. This belief may have led him incidentally to appeal to James II of Scotland for aid in winning the English crown (or

---

[52] There is no satisfactory biography of either queen, but see R.A. Griffiths, 'Queen Katherine of Valois and a missing statute of the realm', *The Law Quarterly Review*, XCIII (1977), 248-58, and J.J. Bagley, *Margaret of Anjou, Queen of England* (London, n.d. [1948]). See below ch. 6.

[53] Davies, *English Chronicle*, p. 79.

[54] *P.L.*, III, 13 (9 January 1455).

[55] The hostility to Duke Edmund was expressed most pointedly by York in 1452 and by the duke of Norfolk in 1453: Sir H. Ellis (ed.), *Original Letters illustrative of English History*, series I, i (1825), 11-13; *P.L.*, II, 290-92. But it was evidently much more widely felt: Storey, *End of Lancaster*, pp. 137-38.

[56] See the assessment in Griffiths, *Speculum*, XLIII (1968), 628; below p. 360.

so King James said).[57] A second implication arises out of his dismissal from the protectorship in February 1456. The long-term prospect was thenceforward one of a king increasingly incapable of exerting authority himself and dominated by his queen, or of the minority of a Lancastrian prince guided by his strong-willed mother. Thus, after York surrendered the protectorship, there would be slim chance of his ever again being a peaceful choice as protector or, therefore, as England's heir. The comparison with 1483 is striking.[58] The surprising thing is that civil war did not come sooner than 1459.

The fighting at Blore Heath and Ludford Bridge in the autumn of 1459 put the final stop to York's hope of a renewed protectorate and, thereby, of the ultimate accession of his line to the English throne as the acknowledged heirs of Lancaster. Unless he were prepared to accept this situation, his only alternative was to take the throne for himself – almost as an act of self-protection and to do justice to his lineage. This raises the question of the motives of the duke of York and his closest supporters in the months prior to the invasions from Calais and Ireland in 1460.

On 16 March 1460 Warwick and York conferred in Ireland about how best the return to England should be contrived.[59] One may safely assume that they discussed when and how it should happen, and what would follow it. The best available opinion at present is that the actions of Warwick, Salisbury and the earl of March were the previously agreed plan – largely, perhaps, because it actually happened, and also because they appear to have been dismayed when York attempted to do something different.[60] But an alternative scenario can be presented. The meeting in Ireland on 16 March 1460 almost certainly agreed plans for the invasion of England, with the Yorkist lords in Calais bearing the main burden of

---

[57] Stevenson, *Letters and Papers*, I, 324-25 (before 28 June 1456); for a comment, see R. Nicholson, *Scotland: the Later Middle Ages* (Edinburgh, 1974), p. 394. About this time (*c.* 1455-58), genealogies displaying York's descent from Lionel of Clarence began to appear, incorporating emphasis on the death of the royalist earl of Northumberland and the duke of Somerset at St. Albans (1455); York's circle may have encouraged their dissemination. See, e.g., B.L., Harleian roll T. 12; All Souls College, Oxford, MS. 40; Queen's College, Oxford, MS. 168. (These references were made available to me by Dr. A. Allan.)

[58] P.M. Kendall, *Richard III* (London, 1955), pp. 153ff. It was Richard of Gloucester's awareness of the implications of a régime in which the young Edward V would be dominated by the queen and her Woodville relatives that convinced him that he should seize the throne.

[59] Scofield, *Edward the Fourth*, I, 59. A.H. Thomas and I.D. Thornley (eds.), *The Great Chronicle of London* (London, 1936), p. 192, says that Warwick met York 'to have his Counsayll how they shulde Entir in to this land'; compare W. and E.L.C.P. Hardy (eds.), *Recueil des Croniques et Anchiennes Istories . . . par Jehan de Waurin*, V (Rolls Series, 1891), 287.

[60] For an account of the events of July-October 1460, based on contemporary chronicles, see J.R. Lander, *The Wars of the Roses* (London, 1965), pp. 102-15. Compare Storey, *End of Lancaster*, p. 188.

responsibility – and with good reason. Invasion from there was geographically and logistically easier than from distant Ireland; there were indications of support from Kent, Surrey and Sussex; and Calais was much nearer the capital which the Lancastrians had deserted and whose sympathy the Yorkists regarded as crucial. It was perhaps of decisive importance that there was a force of men available in the fortress-town.[61] By contrast, the journey from Ireland was longer and hazardous at the best of times; by 1460, the Lancastrians had established a formidable centre of power in the midlands. York, moreover, had no experienced army of any size with him in Ireland that could be easily transported to the mainland. In any case, the distance from London and from sympathetic opinion in the south-east was a major discouragement, while York's personal estates were scattered and not necessarily reliable for his present purpose.[62] Thus, the Yorkist lords landed from Calais in the south-east of England on 26 June.

York followed them at an interval, after the next stage in the invasion had been achieved; he landed near Chester round about 8 September.[63] By then news of the achievement of this next stage had presumably reached him – it certainly had time to do so. But what he heard may not have been entirely in accord with the original plan. After two or three days in London, the Yorkist lords had marched northwards against the king. For the first time (apart from St. Albans in 1455), Henry was involved in an overt military engagement: in 1459 it was the queen who precipitated the skirmish at Blore Heath, and at Ludford the Yorkist forces had fallen back before the king himself. Now a battle was actually fought (and presumably anticipated), and the death of the king must have been acknowledged as at least a possibility. At Northampton on 10 July, the Lancastrians were defeated and the duke of Buckingham was killed, Henry VI was captured, but the queen and the prince were safely in the north.[64] Was this eventuality foreseen as a possibility on 16 March? It could hardly have been planned that way.

The discussions between Warwick and York in Ireland may also have envisaged an early meeting of Parliament to deal with the situation, and one was summoned only a fortnight after the earl of Warwick returned to London with the captive Henry VI.[65] It was to assemble at Westminster

---

[61] For the importance of Calais in these years, see G.L. Harriss, 'The struggle for Calais: an aspect of the rivalry between Lancaster and York', *English Historical Review*, LXXV (1960), 30-53.

[62] J.T. Rosenthal, 'The estates and finances of Richard, duke of York (1411-1460)', in W.M. Bowsky (ed.), *Studies in Mediaeval and Renaissance History*, II (1965), 194-96.

[63] Scofield, *Edward the Fourth*, I, 101.

[64] Ibid., pp. 76-89.

[65] F.M. Powicke and E.B. Fryde (eds.), *Handbook of British Chronology* (2nd. ed., London, 1961), p. 532.

on 7 October, and York's landing in Wales was well timed for it. One wonders what was its purpose. Was it, in fact, to arrange the deposition of Henry VI after the example of 1399? Certainly no one mentioned the possiblity of nominating York as a protector before he arrived in the capital. Was it also its purpose, in accordance with the plan of 16 March, to acclaim York as king by true dynastic right, for, as York reminded the lords in Parliament, 'though right rest for a time and be put in silence, yet it does not rot nor shall it perish'.[66] All one can say in this connection is that immediately after York landed near Chester on or about 8 September, he acted as rightful king; he progressed in a leisurely and dignified manner through the English shires bordering Wales; he disdained the use of Henry's regnal year from 13 September at the latest; he used Lionel of Clarence's arms and a banner with the royal arms of England; and he had his sword held upright before him.[67] It would be a logical conclusion of this behaviour for him to walk into the Parliament chamber on 10 October and expect acclamation.[68] The circumstances in which Richard of York had found himself in the autumn of 1460 may not have been quite those that were anticipated when the plans were laid in Ireland. Unforeseen obstacles had been placed in his path. For one thing, King Henry was still alive, and accordingly anyone claiming the throne and demanding acclamation would be taking awesome steps. Secondly, the freedom of the queen and the prince was an insurmountable hindrance to any seizure of the throne. The deposition of the king and the disinheriting of his son could hardly be made effective so long as Queen Margaret was at liberty with Prince Edward. If eventually the example of the treaty of Troyes (1420) was followed in order to reach a compromise between York and Henry VI – whereby the latter would remain king until his death, though his son and heir would be disinherited – one lesson of the arrangement made at Troyes was just as obvious. So long as the Dauphin had remained at large, his ultimate recovery of his rights and realm was a possibility – in his case triumphantly realised in 1450.[69]

For these reasons, the Yorkist lords drew back from the consequences of the battle of Northampton, leaving York, who had openly declared his hand, utterly exposed. Merely to capture the king can hardly have been the plan in 1460, if only because it had not worked in 1455; it would certainly not work so long as the queen and the prince were free. Despite the embarrassment which even York's closest associates showed in Parliament on 10 October, and despite the strenuous efforts after the

[66] *Rot. Parl.*, V, 378, reprinted in modernised English in Myers, *E.H.D.*, IV, 418.

[67] K.B. McFarlane, 'The Wars of the Roses', *Proceedings of the British Academy*, L (1964), 92 and n.1, 2; *Great Chronicle of London*, p. 192.

[68] H.T. Riley (ed.), *Registrum Abbatiae Johannis Whethamstede*, I (Rolls Series, 1872), 376-78, translated in Myers, *E.H.D.*, IV, 283-84; Waurin, *Croniques*, V, 310-18.

[69] Myers, *E.H.D.*, IV, 415-19. For the Treaty of Troyes, see above p. 00.

battle to make Henry's household thoroughly Yorkist in its personnel, it is difficult to conclude other than that the original plan had been to depose (even to kill) King Henry VI.[70] It is small wonder that Richard of York refused to greet the king, installed himself in the royal palace, and insisted that the crown was his.

[70] According to Davies, *English Chronicle*, p. 100, he had already arranged that his coronation should take place on 1 November. Many of Henry's household servants were swiftly replaced with dependable Yorkists after the battle of Northampton; they were led by Sir William Scull, treasurer of the household: Powicke and Fryde, *Handbook of British Chronology*, p. 79.

6

Queen Katherine of Valois and
a Missing Statute of the Realm

THE archives of the borough of Leicester contain a collection of statutes of the realm which includes a " lost " statute.[1] This statute relates to the marriage of dowager-queens of England and its text has been lost sight of since the seventeenth century—so completely, in fact, that most historians and legal commentators have subsequently doubted whether it ever existed.[2] The collection, in a small bound volume, consists of the text of statutes culminating in chapter 17 of the Parliament of 1429–30 (8 Henry 6). It is written in a hand of the mid-fifteenth century and may reasonably be supposed to have been compiled not long after that Parliament was dissolved on February 23, 1430, and before the statutes of its successor (meeting between January 12 and March 20, 1431) were received at Leicester. Such collections formed a common genre in their day, and a borough like Leicester would find it undeniably useful to have close at hand a record of parliamentary statutes which might have some bearing on the conduct of the town's government.[3] The mislaid statute appears in the Leicester collection as chapter 7 of the Parliament which met at Westminster between October 13, 1427, and March 25, 1428 (6 Henry 6).[4]

When this Parliament assembled, two queens of England were alive and resident in England, the widows respectively of Henry IV and Henry V. Joan of Navarre, who was born about 1370, had

---

[1] This collection is now deposited with the Leicestershire Museums, Art Galleries and Records Service, B.R.II/3/3, which I was able to consult in the course of work supported by a grant from the Twenty-Seven Foundation. The statute is printed below, pp. 112-13.

[2] The most recent unsuccessful pursuit of the statute was conducted by R. S. Thomas, " The political career, estates and ' connection ' of Jasper Tudor, Earl of Pembroke and Duke of Bedford (d. 1495) " (unpublished University of Wales Ph.D. thesis, 1971), pp. 14–17. Among the legal commentators, see W. S. Holdsworth, *A History of English Law* (1938), Vol. X, p. 448, n. 10; and T. Artemus Jones, *Without My Wig* (1944), Chap. III, whose views are reiterated in " Owen Tudor's Marriage " (1944), XI, *Bulletin of the Board of Celtic Studies*, 102–109. The statute does not appear in *Statutes of the Realm* (11 vols., Record Commission, 1810–28), Vol. II (6 Henry 6), or in *Rotuli Parliamentorum* (6 vols., 1767), Vol. IV (6 Henry 6).

[3] For the dispatch of statutes to counties, courts, municipalities and elsewhere, see S. B. Chrimes, *English Constitutional Ideas in the Fifteenth Century* (1936), p. 230. A number of collections including Henry VI's statutes survive: *ibid.* p. 230, n. 1; *Historical Manuscripts Commission Reports*, I, 49, 61; VI, 300; IX, 360; *Statutes of the Realm*, I, appendix C; below n. 28.

[4] On the statute roll (*Statutes of the Realm*, Vol. II, p. 238), the record of this Parliament ends with c. 6, which is also the sixth statute copied into the Leicester volume. The only other collections that are known to include this statute are slightly later in date than the Leicester volume and of unknown provenance. In British Museum, Royal MS. 19 A XIV f. 235r, which ends with the Parliament of May–June 1432, the statute is c. 5, and c. 6 of the statute roll is omitted; B.M., Stowe MS. 389 f. 79r, ending with the Parliament of July–December 1433, places the statute (as c. 6) before the final statute on the statute roll (c. 7).

married the first Lancastrian monarch in 1403 after burying her first husband, John IV, duke of Brittany, in 1399. It is doubtful if a statute concerned with the future marriage of a dowager-queen of England had Joan in mind. Henry V's queen, Katherine of Valois, had married the victor of Agincourt in 1420 when she was barely 19 years of age. In 1427 she was a widow of 26. Her remarriage was a distinct possibility and a statute governing this eventuality would be of special interest to the inhabitants of Leicester, for the castle, town and honour of Leicester had been transferred from the duchy of Lancaster to Queen Katherine in 1422 as part of her substantial dower.[5] It is not difficult, therefore, to explain the presence of this statute in Leicester's collection.

As well as its interest for the biographer of Queen Katherine, the statute has a wider political and constitutional significance. It provides a comment on the stability of English government during the minority of the Queen's son, Henry VI, and it constitutes a significant step towards a definition by legislative enactment of the position of the king's consort in England. It also has a bearing on the question of whether Katherine of Valois was in fact married to Owen Tudor, the grandfather of King Henry VII, and whether, therefore, the Tudor monarchs sprang from a legitimate union or not.

After the shattering experience of losing her young husband, to whom she had been married for only two years, Katherine was much occupied after 1422 with the upbringing of her baby son, Henry of Windsor; he had succeeded not only to the English throne but also, after Charles VI's death on October 21, 1422, to that of France in accordance with the terms of the treaty of Troyes (1420). The young mother spent a good deal of her time with her son and accompanied him during most of his ceremonial appearances in the 1420s in London and the south-east of England. When he was taken to the Parliaments that met regularly after his accession, she was there with him.[6] On more private occasions before 1427, Katherine took young Henry to her manor at Waltham or her castle at Hertford as readily as she herself resided at Windsor.[7] So much was to be expected of a mother.

Katherine's position as a dowager-queen, on the other hand, presented the King's Council and the Protector of the realm, Humphrey, Duke of Gloucester, with potential problems of considerable magni-

---

[5] *Rot. Parl.*, Vol. IV, pp. 183–189; *Calendar of the Patent Rolls, 1422–29*, p. 17.

[6] *The Brut, or the Chronicles of England*, Part II (Early English Text Society, F. W. D. Brie, ed., 1908), p. 452 (1423); *The Chronicles of London* (C. L. Kingsford, ed., 1905), p. 285 (1425); M. E. Christie, *Henry VI* (1922), p. 375 (1426); Public Record Office (henceforward P.R.O.), Exchequer, E.R., Warrants for Issues (E 404), 42/306 (1426).

[7] Kingsford, *op. cit.*, pp. 281, 285; P.R.O., E 404/44/334; 42/306.

tude. She was young and had a vitality that caused one chronicler to assert that she was " unable fully to curb her carnal passions "; and she continued to reside in England (there was little point in her returning to the France of her brother, Charles VII, whom the English refused to recognise as rightful king of France).[8] The place of queens in medieval English history is a little-studied subject, although it is one of considerable significance, not least because many of them were foreigners with strong links overseas and an understandable predilection for attracting their fellow countrymen to their adopted realm. Such factors could affect policy at home and abroad, arouse suspicion and even, as in Henry III's reign, generate public outcry. So much had been encountered before in post-Norman England. But Katherine of Valois's evident wish to marry again—and to do so in England—was a novel element. Neither of the two queens of England who had outlived their royal husbands and married a second time had stayed in England: Isabella of Angoulême, the second wife of King John (d. 1216), left England in 1217 and stayed abroad after she married her former lover, Hugh de Lusignan; whilst Isabella of France, Richard II's queen, was only 10 when her husband was dethroned in 1399 and soon afterwards returned to France, where she married Charles of Angoulême, later Duke of Orleans.[9]

The question of Queen Katherine's remarriage acted as a focus for the concern felt about her position after 1422. The two most powerful men in the realm during the protectorate (1422–29) were the Protector himself, Duke Humphrey, who, after John, Duke of Bedford and Regent of English France, was the next heir to the throne; and Humphrey's uncle, Henry Beaufort, Bishop of Winchester and a leading figure on the King's Council. They rarely saw eye to eye on political matters and the Queen's remarriage seems to have been yet another cause of friction between them. It is impossible to be certain of Katherine's attitude to these two men, but there are a few indications that she was more attracted to the side of Beaufort than to that of Humphrey. The Bishop spent Christmas 1430 with the Queen at her manor of Waltham, and one contemporary chronicler suggests a strong attachment between Katherine and Beaufort's nephew, Edmund Beaufort, Count of Mortain; sometime in the 1420s there were rumours that the couple would marry.[10] The only other indication of the Queen's relations

---

[8] See *Incerti Scriptoris Chronicon Angliae de regnis . . . Henrici IV, Henrici V et Henrici VI* (J. A. Giles, ed., 1848), Part IV, p. 17, for the comment on Katherine's nature.

[9] *Dictionary of National Biography*, Vol. XXIX, 63, 68.

[10] John Amundesham's chronicle in *Annales monasterii S. Albani, 1421–40* (H. T. Riley, ed., 2 vols., 1870–71), Vol. I, p. 56; Giles, *op. cit.*, p. 17.

with Gloucester and Beaufort comes much later, soon after Queen Katherine's death on January 3, 1437. At that time, Duke Humphrey began to hound the husband she had secretly married in the meanwhile, the Welshman Owen Tudor. He was pursued across England, imprisoned in Newgate jail and had his possessions confiscated.[11] He was eventually rescued from further persecution by his indulgent step-son, the King himself, who had taken him into his household by 1444.[12]

A proposed marriage between Queen Katherine and Edmund Beaufort could not fail to cause considerable fluttering in the political dovecotes. Not even Queen Isabella had contemplated marrying her paramour, Roger Mortimer, after Edward II's murder in 1327, and no dowager-queen of England since the reign of Stephen had married one of her late husband's subjects (even if Edmund Beaufort was related to the Lancastrians on the distaff side). Duke Humphrey, it may safely be presumed, took most unkindly to the plan, as one contemporary chronicler records.[13] In fact, the hostility to the proposal from the Protector and a number of other lords of the Council may have prompted a request from the Commons in the Parliament of 1426 that recent refusals by chancellors of England to license Katherine's remarriage should cease.[14] The request was coldly received by the Council; perhaps even the Beauforts were embarrassed at such a direct demand from the Commons in a Parliament which was meeting at the Queen's own borough of Leicester. The Commons seem to have appreciated the delicate nature of their unprecedented request, which was incorporated within another petition that had no obvious connection with royal marriages. This latter petition expressed dissatisfaction with the Chancellor's recent reluctance to authorise the alienation of lands held in chief of the King. This alleged inflexibility seemed comparable with that which Katherine was suffering. Hence, the Commons asked that the Chancellor be instructed to license such alienations in the future, as he had done in the past, and to treat the prospective marriages of dowager-queens in the same way. If the Commons at Leicester believed that they could proceed successfully on behalf of the Queen by means of such an unobtrusive subterfuge, they were

---

[11] *Proceedings and Ordinances of the Privy Council of England* (N. H. Nicolas, ed., 7 vols., 1834–37), Vol. V, pp. 46–50. The episode is most recently and fully described in Thomas, " Jasper Tudor," pp. 21–27.

[12] *Ibid.* pp. 27–28. Yet Katherine nominated both Gloucester and Henry Beaufort as supervisors of her will: *Rot. Parl.*, Vol. V, pp. 505–506.

[13] Giles, *op. cit.* p. 17.

[14] *Rot. Parl.*, Vol. IV, pp. 306–307. Curiously enough, Bishop Beaufort was the current chancellor (1424–26) and had also occupied the office in 1413–17; Bishop Thomas Langley of Durham was chancellor during 1417–24. *Handbook of British Chronology* (F. M. Powicke and E. B. Fryde, eds., 2nd ed., 1961), p. 85.

mistaken. Their skilful drafting did not deceive the King's advisers.[15] The Duke of Bedford, who was well disposed towards Bishop Beaufort in his quarrel with Gloucester and who presided at this Parliament, equally found the proposal relating to dowager-queens unacceptable. The entire petition was rejected—the clauses relating both to alienations and marriages. The King would be advised, was the reply.

It was the Common's petition of 1426 which caused a statute to be introduced in the following Parliament of 1427–28.[16] The Queen's association with Edmund Beaufort was doubtless in the forefront of the Council's mind, although Katherine's flirtation with the more obscure Welsh squire may have already begun. Historians have failed to discover the date of Owen's and Katherine's marriage, and for this they can hardly be blamed, for it was evidently contracted in secret and did not become common knowledge until after the Queen's death in 1437. It is generally assumed that they married about 1428–29, and the fact that they had four children—three sons and a daughter—would certainly indicate a date prior to 1433. If the queen was ill for some considerable time before she died, an even earlier date is likely.[17] At any rate, the possibility of the Queen establishing a relationship with yet another suitor would reinforce the Council's inclination to promote a statute in the Parliament of 1427–28 to regulate the marriage of dowager-queens of England. The question of alienation of lands was also raised anew in this Parliament, but that petition was now shorn of its intrusive detail. That being so, the Council found nothing objectionable in it and the Chancellor was empowered to license such enfeoffments as in the past until the King should decide otherwise.[18]

Those who formulated the statute relating to the marriage of dowager-queens were clear about the problems such marriages posed. These included the implications that might flow from a new husband whose social status was inferior to that of his wife. Its terms, therefore, expressed fears for the disparagement of the Queen, whose honour (as well as that of the Crown itself) needed to be safeguarded. Secondly, although it was provided that he who married a dowager-queen without the King's permission should suffer forfeiture of his

---

[15] Because of its hybrid nature, the part of this petition relating to dowager-queens has been overlooked by historians and legal commentators alike. It is printed below as Appendix I, with the phrases specifically concerned with dowager-queens italicised.

[16] Printed below as Appendix II.

[17] Thomas, " Jasper Tudor," pp. 10–13, 19. The queen does appear, by her own testimony in her will, to have been seriously ill for a long time before she died: *ibid.* p. 13, n. 4.

[18] *Rot. Parl.*, Vol. IV, pp. 329. The differences in wording between the two petitions on the subject of alienating land are of no substantive significance.

lands and other possessions during his lifetime, this relatively mild punishment reflected an awareness that there might be children of an illicit marriage who would in some sense be members of the royal family and merit treatment as such—as, indeed, Jasper and Edmund Tudor, the sons of Katherine and Owen, were accorded by Henry VI later on. Certainly, there was no question of regarding such a union as treasonable or rendering it null and void.[19] Behind the statute's provisions lay a further apprehension that a new husband might endeavour to play a part in English politics. Consequently, it was declared that permission to marry should be given by the King only when he had reached years of discretion (*esteantz dez anz de discrecion*). If duly observed, this clause would effectively delay Queen Katherine's remarriage for some years yet, for in 1427 Henry VI was barely six years old; and for the time being, there would be no step-father available to influence the impressionable boy-king. This provision was presumably the principal reason for Katherine's marrying Owen in secrecy and the justification for the Welshman's arrest after the Queen's demise in 1437.[20]

From the autumn of 1427 onwards, additional constraints were placed on Queen Katherine's freedom of action. During the following three years (and possibly longer) she and her *familia* were accommodated within the king's own household, where she would be under more vigilant control by councillors and household servants alike. Her receiver-general paid £7 a day to the treasurer of Henry's household to meet the additional expense involved.[21] She may also have travelled with King Henry to France in April 1430, for it was later recorded that while she was at Rouen the Queen gave her son a precious jewel, which he later, in December 1434, presented to the Duchess of York.[22] Mother and son cannot have been together in the Norman capital at any other time.

Such careful cosseting of the Queen did not insulate her from the attentions of Owen Tudor. Their marriage was evidently contracted in defiance of the statute of 1427–28, although while Katherine lived there is no contemporary evidence that any attempt

---

[19] The chronicler, Giles, *op. cit.* p. 17, erred in stating that execution as a traitor would accompany forfeiture.

[20] This was the opinion of the Tudor chronicler, Edward Hall, who mentioned the statute " made in the .vi. yere of this kyng ": *The Union of the Two Noble and Illustrious Families of Lancaster and York* (H. Ellis, ed., 1809), p. 185; Thomas, " Jasper Tudor," p. 15, n. 2. In Giles, *op. cit.* p. 17, it is claimed that Katherine married Owen because he had few possessions to forfeit under the terms of a decree of the Council, and that she did so in secrecy in order to protect his life. Neither reason is likely to be entirely sound.

[21] P.R.O., Exchequer, Various Accounts (E 101), 408/6; 9 m. 2. She was evidently still in her son's household on February 14, 1431, and perhaps even on May 24, 1431: Nicolas, *op. cit.* Vol. IV, p. 77; P.R.O., E 101/408/9 m. 2.

[22] P.R.O., Exchequer, Council and Privy Seal (E 28), 57/96.

was made to punish either her or Owen. Once Katherine was dead, vigorous action was taken against the widower in accordance (wrote Edward Hall, the Tudor chronicler) with the terms of the statute. Owen's possessions, amounting to £137 in value, were seized and he himself imprisoned for a time. Nothing more serious had been decreed by the statute and indeed within a few years Owen was released; he secured a pardon from his step-son and entered his household as an honoured relative.[23]

The statute was probably known to the chronicler who, writing in the late 1450s, recorded that the Council refused to allow anyone to marry Queen Katherine whilst the king was young, and decreed forfeiture and a traitor's death for whoever did so.[24] In view of the vague language employed in identifying the authority for this ban, and the chronicler's introduction of the death penalty as a sanction, it cannot be concluded with certainty that he was aware of the statute of 6 Henry 6, but there is a strong probability that he knew of its existence and purport.

In the next century, the existence of the statute was known to Edward Hall and the Elizabethan chroniclers who followed him. Hall recorded that Owen Tudor was arrested because, " contrary to the statute made in the .vi. yere of this kyng, he presumptuously had maried the Quene, without the kynges especiall assent, and agrement, . . ."; it was a succinct interpretation of the statute's substance.[25] Early in the seventeenth century it was seen by Sir Edward Coke, as is evident from his paraphrasing of certain passages from it: " no man should contract with, or marry himself to any Queen of England, without the special licence or assent of the King, on pain to lose all his goods and lands." Sir William Blackstone 100 years later was fully prepared to accept Coke's authority for the statute's existence, though he had to admit that " the statute be not in print " and he may not have been able to examine its contents himself.[26] The reason for the statute's later disappearance from view and its omission from the Chancery's statute roll is uncertain. It may be that as soon as Katherine's marriage to Owen became known to the Council (and such an event, still less her pregnancies,

[23] Above n. 20; Thomas, " Jasper Tudor," pp. 24–28. Aside from Owen's treatment in 1437 precisely in accordance with the statute, there are other indications that contemporaries regarded Owen and the queen as validly married: see *ibid.* p. 11.
[24] Giles, *op. cit.* p. 17.   [25] Hall, *op. cit.* p. 185.
[26] Edward Coke, *The Second Part of the Institutes of the Laws of England* (6th ed., 1681), p. 18; *The Third Part of the Institutes of the Laws of England* (5th ed., 1671), pp. 34–35, 51, where Coke claims that the " bill " or " act " was on the parliament roll in his day but was not in print anywhere; William Blackstone, *Commentaries on the Laws of England* (4 vols., 15th ed., 1809), Vol. I, p. 223. Blackstone did employ the phrase *pro dignitate regali*, and although this does not appear in the French version of the statute as recorded in the Leicester collection, it may have appeared in a Latin version which Blackstone may have seen.

could hardly be kept secret), the need for the statute evaporated. This had, perhaps, happened by the time that Parliament met on May 12, 1432, when (or soon afterwards) Owen publicly and formally received letters of denizenship to protect him from the consequences of Henry IV's legislation against Welshmen.[27] If the statute roll and the parliament roll relating to the assembly of 1427–28 were compiled some little time after the Parliament itself had ended, then its exclusion may be explained in this way.[28] Alternatively, when the king came to play an active part in government in 1436–37, it might be expected that he would resent the presence on the statute or parliament roll of an act that was implicitly directed at his mother. Suggestions that it was removed even later from the statute roll, whose numbering was thereupon altered—perhaps by the Tudors, who would be equally sensitive about their forebear's marriage—have been dismissed after careful scrutiny of the statute roll itself; no such alterations have been detected.[29] Nevertheless, the statute was publicised at the time and circulated in the realm, including at Leicester, where it was evidently regarded as sufficiently relevant to the municipality for it to be included in about 1430–31 in its collection of statutes. (Leicester's inhabitants, of course, were less likely to be acquainted with Katherine's remarriage and probably shared the ignorance displayed by the chroniclers of the day.) Whatever the reason for the fate of this statute, it is one of the very few cases—probably the only one at present known to historians—of a fifteenth-century statute that does not appear on the official statute roll.[30]

---

[27] *Rot. Parl.*, Vol. IV, p. 415. Was this the occasion when Katherine presented Owen's pedigree before the lords in Parliament, " the which thing was then approbate and taken for excuse of her marriage," as John Leland claimed in the early 16th century? *The Itinerary of John Leland* (L. T. Smith, ed., 6 vols., 1906–10), Vol. I, pp. 307–308; and Thomas, " Jasper Tudor," p. 18 and n. 2, who is inclined to accept the authenticity of this declaration.

[28] For the Council's role in selecting statutes for publication and record, see Chrimes, *op. cit.* p. 228. H. L. Gray deduced that the statute roll in Henry VI's reign was, in fact, " a tardily-made copy of the statutes of several parliaments written some time after the latest of them " (*The Influence of the Commons on Early Legislation* (1933), p. 397). The parliament roll may have been compiled at no earlier a stage (*ibid.* pp. 402–404). This hypothesis is strengthened by the absence of the statute from at least four other contemporary collections of statutes, compiled later in the reign: P.R.O., Exchequer, K.R., Misc. Books 10 (*c.* 1460), and Trinity College, Dublin, MS. 610 (ending at 23 Henry 6 and examined for me by Mr. W. O'Sullivan); B.M., Stowe MS. 387 (ending with the Parliament of October-December 1435) and 388 (ending with the Parliament of 1442); and by its inclusion in the two earlier ones (above, n. 4).

[29] T. Artemus Jones, *Without My Wig*, pp. 28–32, criticising Nicolas, *op. cit.*, Vol. V, p. xvii, who suggested the mutilation of the statute roll.

[30] See Professor Chrimes's view, *op. cit.* p. 239, that " it seems safe to hold that no statute was passed in the 15th century which was not enrolled on the statute roll (up to 1490) "; and again (*ibid.* p. 239, n. 5) that " there can be little doubt that acts intended to be statutes were enrolled on the statute roll throughout the 15th century up to 1490." *Cf.* H. G. Richardson and G. O. Sayles, " The Early Statutes " (1934) 50 L.Q.R. 215–216 who mention the heresy statute of 1406 as an omission.

Not only is this statute not enrolled on the statute roll, but it has not been repealed either. The next occasion when a dowager-queen remarried after a king's death occurred in strikingly similar circumstances. Sometime in May 1547, within a few months of Henry VIII's death, Queen Katherine Parr married Thomas, Lord Seymour of Sudeley. They dreaded to reveal the fact to the Protector of England, Lord Seymour's elder brother, the Duke of Somerset, or to the Council of the young monarch, Edward VI. The political dangers inherent in the match were apparent to the couple as well as to the Council when it learned of it. Whether or not the precedent of Katherine of Valois and the statute of 1427–28 was fully appreciated in the sixteenth century is unknown, but certainly Katherine Parr perceived the best (if not the right) course to adopt: she urged Lord Seymour to secure the approval of the young King (the " Kynge's Letters in yowre favour ") and the support of the more prominent councillors.[31] Moreover, despite Somerset's anger at the match, there was as little to be done about it after the event in 1547 as there was on the earlier occasion. In both cases, the Council eventually acquiesced in the *fait accompli*.[32]

No comparable situation has arisen since the sixteenth century to pose problems similar to those of the 1420s and 1540s, and hence there has been no interest shown by lawyers or historians in the statutory provision made in 1427–28. Yet, the Marriage Act of 1772 has not entirely superseded it. At George III's insistence, it was enacted in 1772—and the statute is valid today—that all descendants of George II required the king's consent before they could marry, with the exception of the issue of English princesses married into foreign families.[33] It made no provision for dowager-queens of England who were not descendants of George II but who wished to marry after their royal husband's death. This eventuality has not arisen since 1547 to tax legal memory and historical investigators.

---

[31] *Original Letters Illustrative of English History*, Ser. 1 (H. Ellis, ed., 3 vols., 1824), Vol. II, p. 152.

[32] It is true that the charges of treason brought against Lord Seymour in 1549 included at least one arising from his marriage to Katherine Parr; yet it was not the fact of the marriage that was thought to constitute treason, but rather the undue influence he had supposedly exerted on the King and Council to induce them to acquiesce in it. There was mentioned, too, the danger posed by the early birth of a child to Seymour and Katherine which could have been regarded by some as the old King's offspring. This entire matter is treated by W. K. Jordan, *Edward VI: The Young King* (1968), pp. 368–371; for the treason charges, see *Acts of the Privy Council of England, 1547–50*, p. 252.

[33] Holdsworth, *op. cit.* Vol. X, p. 447. The principle of the statute was ameliorated in certain of its details.

APPENDIX I

Rot.Parl., *IV*, 306–307

Item, priount les Communes d'icest present Parlement, que come il ad este use de long temps, que le Chaunceller d'Engleterre pur le temps esteant and usee, par vertue de son Office, de grauntier licence a toutz personnes, q'ount tenuz Seignuries, Chastielx, Manoirs, Terres ou Tenementz, ou ascune parcelle d'icelles, des Rois d'Engleterre en chief, de aliener lour ditz Tenures pur resonable fyn, accorde par entre le dit Chaunceller pur le temps esteant, et la partie pursuant pur icell, *sibien come grauntier as vidues du Roi, counge de eux marier a lour volunte, pur antiell fyne come purroit entre eux estre accorde*; tanque ore tarde que les Chauncellers d'Engleterre pur le temps esteantz, lour ount absteignez de graunter tielx licences, a graunde dammage et perde du Roi, et en arerissement des executions des voluntes des tieux Tenantz, *et encountre bone agrement de tieux mariages a fairz, a displeiser de Dieu*; de grauntier par auctorite d'icest present Parlement, que le Chaunceller d'Engle-terre pur le temps esteaunt, eit poiar de faire et face autielx Fynes en tieux cases, come ad este use en temps de les tres nobles Rois E. le tierce, R. le secound, et H. le Quarte. Et que semblablement le dit Chaunceller, purra faire et face Fynes, et grauntier Pardon pur alienations, perquisitions *et mariages* faitz devaunt ses heurs, et a fairz en temps a venir, sanz licence; alienations faitz et affairz au mort mayn forsprisez.

Le Roi s'advisera.

(The passages relating specifically to the marriage of a dowager-queen are in italics.)

APPENDIX II

Leicestershire Museums, Art Galleries and Records Service,

B.R. II/3/3

vii. Item ordine est et estabbliez par auctorite de cest parlement pur la saluacion del honour dez tresnoblez estates dez Roynes Dengleterre que nulle home de quiconque estate ou condicion qil soit ne fait contract dez espouselx ou matrimonie de soy marie a Royne Dengleterre saunz especialle licence et assent du Roi mesmes celuy esteantz dez anz de discrecion et celuy qui ferra le contrarie et ent soit duement convict forface pur terme de sa vie toutz sez terres et tenementz si bien ceux que sount ou serrount en ses mayns propres come ceux que sount ou serrount es mayns dautres a sone oeps et auxi toutz sez biens et chateux en qi mayns qils soient consideres que par la desparagement du Royne lestate et honour du Roi serroient tresgraundement emblemes et donera le greindre comfort et ensample as autres dames dastate queux sont de sanke roialle pur lour le (*interlineated*) pluis ligerement desparager etc.

(The text of the statute as given in the two other known contemporary collections, B.M., Royal MS. 19 A XIV, and Stowe MS. 389, contains no significant variations from the Leicester version.)

[Two subsequent comments are by Geoffrey Hand, 'The King's widow and the King's widows', *Law Quarterly Review*, 93 (1977), 506-7, and G.O. Sayles, 'The Royal Marriages Act, 1428', ibid., 94 (1978), 188-92 (which translates the parliamentary bill on which the statute was based). For more context, see R.A. Griffiths and R.S. Thomas, *The Making of the Tudor Dynasty* (Gloucester, 1985), and G.L. Harriss, *Cardinal Beaufort* (Oxford, 1988), ch. 9.]

7

Henry Tudor: The Training of a King

British schoolchildren are taught that Bosworth Field is one of the decisive battles of British history. In the sixteenth century its significance seemed as great as that of the battle of Hastings, and within a generation of 1815 it was being compared with the battle of Waterloo as an epoch-making encounter.[1] Although scholars by their nature are skeptical of such claims, it is still popularly believed that the battle of Bosworth on 22 August 1485 rang down the curtain on the tired old Middle Ages and opened a spanking new play that took as its themes the power, the Protestantism, and the overseas expansion of the glorious Tudor dynasty.

The contemporary audience in 1485 had no awareness of all this nor, naturally enough, did it see things quite as later generations have done. To most contemporaries the outcome of the battle is likely to have been unexpected, indeed astonishing, and to many the role of Henry Tudor in it doubtless seemed quite incongruous. After all, this was the first battle fought in England since 1066 in which the anointed king—who was widely acknowledged as king and on whom therefore, according to popular conviction and regnal theory, God had smiled—had been defeated and slain, even though he had worn his crown to battle and had stood beneath his unfurled banner.[2] Not since Harold Godwinson died at Hastings had the God of battles changed his mind so devastatingly, even though in August 1485 Richard III had been on the throne of England three times as long as had Harold in October 1066.

---

1. Michael Bennett, *The Battle of Bosworth* (Gloucester, 1985), has an interesting ch. 8 entitled "1485 in English history."

2. The action of the battle is currently the subject of lively debate. C. D. Ross, *Richard III* (London, 1981), ch. 11, provides the best of the commonly-accepted

Secondly, the Almighty's new instrument, Henry Tudor, won his battle with an army that was partly French, at a time when France was still England's most hated adversary. Henry's new subjects, for their part, were not so easily persuaded or deceived into changing the attitudes of centuries. When an epidemic of sweating sickness broke out in England some months later, Henry's French contingents were roundly blamed for bringing it to England:

> which Englishmen got by sleeping and debauching with the Bretons and the French women coming over the sea with the king, amongst whom there were many diseased people, so the English called this disease in English "the French pox."[3]

Incongruous, too (and thirdly), was the fact that Henry seems to have had about one thousand Scotsmen in his army, at a time when Scotland was second only to France on the list of England's enemies. Truer to form, and a better indication of Englishmen's attitudes toward the Scots, is the story of the behavior and treatment of a Highlander, Macgregor by name, who was in King Richard's camp on the eve of Bosworth. He was reported by a later Scots chronicler to be a servant of the bishop of Dunkeld, who happened to be visiting the English court as an envoy when Henry landed in Pembrokeshire on 7 August 1485. When the bishop saw that a battle was likely, he hurriedly left the court. Macgregor tried to make off with Richard's crown before he too departed, but he was apprehended; he confessed and yet was

accounts; but Bennett, *Battle of Bosworth*, ch. 6, has some novel reconstructions, and C. F. Richmond, "The battle of Bosworth," *History Today*, 35 (1985): 17-22, has put the cat among the pigeons by plausibly re-siting much of the action. But there is no dispute about the regal appearance of Richard III as he advanced to battle: see J. A. Buchon (ed.), *Chroniques de Jean Molinet* (Paris, 1828), 2:409; A. E. Goodman and Angus MacKay, "A Castilian report on English affairs, 1486," *English Hist. Rev.*, 88 (1973): 92-99; Polydore Vergil, *Three Books of English History*, ed. Henry Ellis (Camden Society, old series, 29, 1844), 225-226.

3. National Library of Wales MS. 3054D f. 347b (Elis Gruffudd's chronicle, translated by my colleague, Dr. P. T. J. Morgan). The large French contingent is established by R. A. Griffiths and R. S. Thomas, *The Making of the Tudor Dynasty* (Gloucester, 1985), 129, from A. Spont, "La marine française sous le règne de Charles VIII," *Revue des questions historiques*, nouvelle série, 11 (1894): 387-454; *Chroniques de Jean Molinet*, 406-407. For a discussion of the sweating sickness, see Lorraine Attreed, "Beggarly Bretons and Faynte-harted Frenchmen: Age- and class-specific mortality during London's sweating sickness of 1485," *The Ricardian*, 4 (1977): 2-16.

released because (it was reported) the English could not stop laughing at his name. That was the vintage English attitude to the Scots in the later fifteenth century.[4]

More incongruous still, as far as contemporaries were concerned, was the fact that Henry Tudor won his crown on his way from Wales, with considerable help from Welsh landowners and their men. Henry rewarded a number of these, including Dafydd ab Ieuan, who had offered the pretender shelter during his march through Cardiganshire. In the nineteenth century, it was believed in Wales that Dafydd's daughter had also welcomed Henry, a courtesy of which she was supposedly reminded nine months later. This landowner's reward after Bosworth was a fine drinking-horn decorated with authentic Tudor badges; a drawing of it was made in 1684. Dafydd's ultimate heir is the present Earl Cawdor, who admits that the horn now in Cawdor castle, in Scotland, is probably an early-nineteenth-century replica of the original that may have been destroyed in a fire on the family's Carmarthenshire estates two hundred years ago.[5] However well founded this particular tradition is, no-one had ever claimed and won the English crown coming from Wales, and Henry's venture was only two generations after the great Welsh uprising of Owain Glyndŵr (1400-1415). Moreover, when considerable numbers of Welshmen flocked to London after 1485, and Henry made modest grants of privileges in north and north-east Wales later in his reign, there were many protests from suspicious or jealous Englishmen.[6]

4. Robert Lindesay of Pittscottie, *The Historie and Cronicles of Scotland* (Scottish Hist. Soc., 1899-1911), 1:192-193 (written in 1576-1579). For Henry's recruits from the French king's Scots guard, see Griffiths and Thomas, *Making of the Tudor Dynasty*, 130-131; Norman Macdougall, *James III: A Political Study* (Edinburgh, 1982), 215-216. Welsh personal names were regarded with equal levity by fifteenth-century Englishmen: see James Gairdner (ed.), *The Paston Letters* (6 vols., London, 1904), 3:118-119 (1457).

5. For the traditions, see Griffiths and Thomas, *Making of the Tudor Dynasty*, 144-145; S. R. Meyrick, *The History and Antiquities of the County of Cardigan* (London, 1808), 164-165; Lewis Dwnn, *Heraldic Visitations of Wales*, ed. S. R. Meyrick (2 vols., Llandovery, 1846), 1:80. I am grateful to Earl Cawdor for information about the horn in his possession, which is illustrated in Dwnn, *Heraldic Visitations*, vol. 1, frontispiece. For the 1684 drawing, see Thomas Dineley, *The Official Progress of the First Duke of Beaufort* (London, 1684), 225.

6. Although Glanmor Williams, "The Welsh in Tudor England," in his *Religion, Language and Nationality in Wales* (Cardiff, 1979), ch. 8, discusses the absorption of Welsh men and women in English society, J. B. Smith, "Crown and community in the principality of north Wales in the reign of Henry Tudor," *Welsh Hist. Rev.*, 3 (1966), notes the hostility to Henry's charters of liberties. For English

In short, the battle of Bosworth was won by Henry Tudor against the odds and the expectations of most people at the time; and his associations and attitudes in 1485 seemed a most unpromising preparation for the kingship of England. Among themes that are crucial to an understanding of the nature of Henry's training for kingship, and of his subsequent behavior as king, one is the extent of his Welshness; yet, if he is to be regarded as a Welshman, it is as a Welshman largely by adoption. Another is the fortuitous element in his career and the extent to which his early life was shaped by others; indeed, it can be argued that he secured the throne mainly by accident. And a third theme is this: if Henry VII proved to be an effective king (which is increasingly the conclusion of present-day historians), to judge by his training it was little short of a miracle.

By birth, Henry Tudor was one-quarter Welsh, one-quarter French, and half English. Yet it is his Welsh blood that identified him to contemporaries immediately after 1485 and to posterity since then. He and his descendants are known by his great-great-grandfather's Welsh Christian name of Tudur (which was Anglicized in the fifteenth century as Tudor).[7] But if he is to be regarded as England's first Welsh monarch, it is as a Welshman by adoption.

Henry's Welsh forebears had no royal or princely blood in their veins on the male side and very little on the female side; but his family first came to prominence in the service of the most constructive and ambitious of Welsh princely houses.[8] This prominence was achieved in the first half of the thirteenth century, when Henry's ancestors became the most influential and respected of Welsh families in north Wales. There they served three princes of Gwynedd in succession as indispensable councillors, diplomats, and soldiers, at a time when these princes were creating a powerful fledgling state in the mountain fastnesses of Snowdonia. Had it been Merovingian Europe, they might well have been called "may-

---

fears of Wales and Welshmen earlier in the fifteenth century, see R. A. Griffiths, "Wales and the Marches," in S. B. Chrimes, C. D. Ross, and R. A. Griffiths (eds.), *Fifteenth-Century England, 1399-1509* (Manchester, 1972), 145; above, p. 55.

7. In patronymic style, Henry VII was Henry ab Edmund ab Owain ap Maredudd ap Tudur: see Griffiths and Thomas, *Making of the Tudor Dynasty*, 16, 30.

8. It is true that Henry's most distinguished ancestor in the thirteenth century, Ednyfed Fychan, had married a daughter of the Lord Rhys (d. 1197), ruler of south-west Wales. But that is the extent of Henry's Welsh princely blood. Griffiths and Thomas, *Making of the Tudor Dynasty*, 7.

ors of the palace." In return, these great servants of princes acquired property, power, and repute. Their ancestral home lay near Abergele, in modern Denbighshire, close to the north coast of Wales. Among their rewards were properties in Anglesey and Caernarfonshire which included the townships of Penmynydd and Trecastell, with which the family has been popularly associated ever since. Their dominant place in Welsh society was reflected in the poems and eulogies written in their honor.[9]

Nonetheless, they periodically faced personal and family crises during the thirteenth century. There were occasions when these kinsfolk were pulled by conflicting loyalties, as between the princes of Gwynedd and the more distant kings of England; indeed, a few members of the family preferred an attachment to the king when personal or family interests took precedence over loyalty to their immediate masters and fellow-countrymen. This instinct for survival was sharpened at the time of Edward I's final conquest of north Wales (1282-1283). On that occasion, the entire family deserted the cause of the last prince of Gwynedd, Llywelyn ap Gruffydd, and thereby assured themselves of a bright future as important, prosperous landowners in a conquered and increasingly Anglicized country. "No Welshman dare indict them," declared the burgesses of Caernarfon, no doubt proudly since many of these burgesses were of English descent.[10]

Members of this family even entered the personal service of English kings, most notably the household of Richard II a century later. Two of them joined Richard's second expedition to Ireland in 1398-1399.[11] This royal connection, as well as the distant call of Welsh patriotism and kinship ties in north Wales, explains why most adult male members of the family supported Owain

---

9. The most recent accounts of Henry Tudor's forebears in thirteenth-century Gwynedd are in David Stephenson, *The Governance of Gwynedd* (Cardiff, 1984), and A. D. Carr, *Medieval Anglesey* (Llangefni, 1982). The papers of Glyn Roberts, who first investigated the family in authoritative detail, are collected in his *Aspects of Welsh History* (Cardiff, 1969).

10. J. G. Edwards (ed.), *Calendar of Ancient Correspondence Concerning Wales* (Cardiff, 1935), 231 (1345).

11. For the service of five brothers to Richard II in north Wales, and for the more personal link between two of them, Rhys and Gwilym ap Tudur, and King Richard by 1398, see Griffiths and Thomas, *Making of the Tudor Dynasty*, 19. If the references in the royal archives to Ralph "Tudor" (or "Teudre," "Tewder," or "Teuder") refer to Rhys, then he was a yeoman of the Crown by 1394 and yeoman of the chamber in 1396-1398: *Calendar of the Patent Rolls, 1391-96*, 392, 722; Public Record Office, E403/562 (9 December 1398), a reference I owe to Dr. James Gillespie.

Glyndŵr when he rebelled in 1400 against Henry IV, who had deposed Richard II in the previous year. But in contrast to the family's circumspect choice of allegiance in 1282, this association with Glyndŵr spelled utter disaster for the family. After the collapse of the rebellion, their influence in north Wales was destroyed.[12] Thus, the immediate forebears of Henry Tudor emerged from the rebellion defeated and dispossessed. Even Welsh poets, who as the preservers of folk memory forgot hardly anything or anybody, neglected them for the next forty years.[13] The Welsh heritage of Henry Tudor had been shunted into a *cul-de-sac*.

The youngest of the family to survive the rebellion, Maredudd, fled with his young son, Owen. And it was Owen who was to set the family on an entirely different course, one that was largely unconnected with Wales but which eventually gave the family, by chance and sheer effrontery, a unique place in the annals of the British monarchy. It is worth stressing, however, that Owen's personal links with Wales were tenuous, and as a young man he struck no chord in Welshmen—and did not do so until the last years of his life.[14]

In the meantime, life had its compensations for Owen. He attracted and married the dowager-queen of England, Katherine of Valois, princess of France and widow of the great Henry V. Their children, therefore, were half Welsh and half French. Where and how this unlikely pair met is not certainly known, though several delightful stories became current in the sixteenth century, especially in Wales and France. One claimed that the encounter took place at a ball, where Owen was so unsteady on his feet that he fell into the queen's lap. Another places it on a river bank, when Owen and his friends were bathing, with the queen and her ladies secretly observing them. The most plausible explanation is that they met in the household of either Henry V or his queen; several young Welshmen gravitated to the royal service

12. The standard work on Glyndŵr's rebellion is still J. E. Lloyd, *Owen Glendower* (Oxford, 1931).

13. A possible exception may be Ieuan Gethin ab Ieuan ap Lleision, who wrote a poem in praise of Owen Tudor, Henry VII's grandfather, at the time of his imprisonment in 1437, but even this may have been composed later on, when interest in the family revived. See *Dictionary of Welsh Biography Down to 1940* (London, 1959), 412.

14. The best accounts of Owen are in R. S. Thomas, "The political influence, estates and 'connection' of Jasper Tudor, earl of Pembroke and duke of Bedford (d. 1495)" (University of Wales [Swansea] Ph.D. Thesis, 1971), ch. 1, and in Griffiths and Thomas, *Making of the Tudor Dynasty*, ch. 3.

when the doors of opportunity were temporarily closed in post-Glyndŵr Wales.[15] The first moves are likely to have been made by the queen, and one contemporary chronicler openly commented that as a twenty-one-year-old widow, Katherine "was unable fully to curb her carnal passions."[16] After their marriage round about 1430, they lived relatively quietly just outside London, and Owen ap Maredudd ap Tudur adopted the English-style surname of Tudor—most likely quite fortuitously as a result of habitual use by English friends and acquaintances who would have found the patronymic curious and cumbersome. Owen, therefore, acquired his grandfather's name, rather than his father's, as a surname, and by a hair's breadth England avoided a royal dynasty of Meredudds instead of Tudors.[17]

This seemingly ill-matched couple had four children that we know of: a daughter who died young, and three sons, Edmund, Jasper, and Owen. The Christian names of the boys reflect the English, French, and Welsh connections of their parents, with the English to the fore. This Franco-Welsh family's future was evidently seen first and foremost in an English context.

It was in the next generation that Henry VII's family acquired its English blood. King Henry VI treated his stepfather, Owen Tudor, and his half-brothers well. The two eldest were made earls and were given precedence over all other earls in the realm. Yet Henry gave Jasper the earldom of Pembroke in November 1452 not because he was of Welsh descent but because, like the earldom of Richmond which was given to Edmund at the same time, it was a royal earldom most recently held by one of King Henry's dead uncles.[18] The Tudors, then, were regarded as English noblemen, standard-bearers of the royal house of Lancaster

15. Griffiths and Thomas, *Making of the Tudor Dynasty*, 30-31. The earliest known reference to Owen as a servant in Queen Katherine's chamber is in John Rylands Library, Latin MS.113 (a chronicle roll of ca. 1484).

16. J. A. Giles (ed.), *Incerti scriptoris chronicon Angliae . . .* (London, 1848), part 4, 17. For this extraordinary marriage, see R. A. Griffiths, "Queen Katherine of Valois and a missing statute of the realm," *Law Quarterly Review*, 93 (1977): 248-258. See above ch. 6.

17. The entire subject of Welsh names has recently been illuminated by T. J. and P. T. J. Morgan, *Welsh Surnames* (Cardiff, 1985).

18. For the ennoblement of both brothers in November 1452, see Thomas, thesis cited, ch.2. Of Henry VII's uncles, John, Duke of Bedford (d. 1435) had held the earldom of Richmond, and Humphrey, Duke of Gloucester (d. 1447) had held the earldom of Pembroke.

at a time in Henry VI's reign when the royal family was perilously small.[19]

Edmund Tudor was also provided with a wife soon afterwards (certainly by 1455), though Jasper had to wait another thirty years for his bride, largely because he was a penniless exile or a fugitive between 1461 and 1485. Edmund married Margaret Beaufort, only child of John Beaufort, duke of Somerset (d. 1444) and arguably England's richest heiress in the 1450s. Her family was descended from Edward III, though the line was tarnished by illegitimacy because Katherine Swynford had given birth to John Beaufort, earl of Somerset (d. 1410) before her marriage to John of Gaunt, Edward III's third son. The Beaufort family had been declared legitimate by two kings, Richard II and Henry IV, though on each occasion a proviso was inserted in the declaration to the effect that no member of the family should succeed to the throne of England. Needless to say, it was uncertain by the fifteenth century whether such a royal declaration could in fact determine the succession, and no number of public statements could alter the fact of bastard birth. These two question marks hung over the Beaufort family—and over Margaret Beaufort in particular as the potential transmitter of a claim to the crown of England. Yet, if Henry Tudor, the son of Edmund and Margaret, had any English blood in his veins, or any claim to the English throne, it came with all its imperfections from Margaret Beaufort, his mother.[20]

Forty years after the Glyndŵr rebellion, the Tudors (and we may now properly refer to them as such) had become related to the royal house of England as a result of the marriage of Owen and Katherine. By the marriage of Edmund and Margaret Beaufort their son acquired sufficient Plantagenet blood eventually to seek the throne with a plausible claim. The family of Welsh landowners in thirteenth-century Gwynedd had returned to prominence, but on a different, entirely English, stage.

As far as the Welsh reputation of this family is concerned, that had grown cold since Glyndŵr's day. It was now to be rekindled fortuitously as a result of the Wars of the Roses between

---

19. See R. A. Griffiths, "The sense of dynasty in the reign of Henry VI," in C. D. Ross (ed.), *Patronage, Pedigree and Power in Later Medieval England* (Gloucester, 1979), 13-36. See above ch. 5.

20. Although there is a revival of scholarly interest in Margaret Beaufort, at present we have to rely on the classic biography of C. H. Cooper, *Memoir of Margaret, Countess of Richmond and Derby* (Cambridge, 1874). For sound comment on the succession in the fifteenth century, see S. B. Chrimes, *English Constitutional Ideas in the Fifteenth Century* (Cambridge, 1936), 32-34.

the houses of Lancaster and York, and it happened in south Wales. There, affection sprouted for the two young earls of Richmond and Pembroke, and for their father Owen, and for Edmund's son, Henry; it was an affection that would be sustained in the hearts of some Welshmen for long after, and which Henry Tudor exploited enthusiastically at the time of his invasion in 1485 and for two decades thereafter.

Possibly because of his Welsh blood—it was certainly not because of his title or his prior knowledge of Wales—Edmund Tudor was given the task of consolidating Lancastrian power in south and west Wales after the battle of St. Albans (May 1455) had brought England to the brink of civil war. He discharged his duty with vigor and considerable success. Edmund took his wife with him to Pembrokeshire and there their son, Henry, was conceived. But before his birth in Pembroke Castle on 28 January 1457, his father had died at Carmarthen on 1 November 1456. He was buried there in the great Greyfriars church, though his tomb-chest was removed to St. David's Cathedral after the Reformation.[21]

Edmund was replaced as the king's lieutenant in south Wales by his younger brother, Jasper Tudor, Earl of Pembroke. The tragedy of Edmund's early death (he was still in his mid-twenties) and Jasper's arrival and energetic campaign focused attention in Wales on the Tudor family once again: as the first Welshmen to enter the English peerage, as representatives of the Lancastrian monarchy, and as blood relatives of King Henry VI. They were regarded as the most distinguished and loyal Welshmen of their generation. According to one Carmarthenshire poet of the day, Lewis Glyn Cothi, Edmund was "brother of King Henry, nephew of the Dauphin [King Charles VII of France] and son of Owen"— and in that order.[22] When Owen Tudor was captured in battle by the Yorkists and executed in 1461, poets from all parts of Wales lamented his death as the father of the two young noblemen who were half-brothers of the king.[23]

The Tudors had rekindled their family's reputation in Wales,

---

21. For Edmund's and Jasper's role, see Thomas, thesis cited, ch. 4, supplemented by Griffiths and Thomas, *Making of the Tudor Dynasty*, ch. 4. The political background is fully discussed in R. A. Griffiths, *The Reign of King Henry VI* (London and California, 1981), chs. 22-24.

22. E. D. Jones (ed.), *Lewys Glyn Cothi (Detholiad)* (Cardiff, 1984), 11.

23. For a poignant contemporary account of Owen's death, see James Gairdner (ed.), *The Historical Collections of a Citizen of London* (Camden Society, new series, 17, 1876): 211.

but it was a reputation as staunch defenders of the English royal house of Lancaster. They had salvaged the reputation that had all but disintegrated earlier in the century. In this context, therefore, Henry Tudor may be regarded as a Welshman by adoption through the agency of fifteenth-century English politics. Nevertheless, it was this Welshness which he later exploited for its venerable associations with an ancient British past and with the legendary figure of King Arthur.[24]

When Edmund and Jasper Tudor were ennobled in 1452, they were formally recognized as the king's uterine brothers, but there was no question, either then or later, of them being considered as possible heirs to the English throne. After all, they had no English blood whatever in their veins. Edmund's only son, Henry, had such blood but it was marred by illegitimacy. At best, therefore, he was the heir to the Lancastrian earldom of Richmond and, in Wales, a focus of a revived tradition of popular affection as the scion of a newly-emergent distinguished Welsh family loyal to the English crown.

After the deposition of Henry VI in 1461, and the accession of the first Yorkist monarch, Edward IV, the careers of Jasper Tudor and his young nephew seemed blighted. Henry was brought up in obscurity by a Yorkist retainer, William, Lord Herbert, probably at Raglan Castle in Gwent. His uncle Jasper lived the life of a fugitive and international agent, working for the house of Lancaster, to which he remained steadfastly loyal. Welsh poets looked on him as an intrepid Welsh hero, keeping the Lancastrian banner flying in adversity.[25]

Jasper's success was quite limited before 1470, when Henry VI was briefly restored to his throne. For Henry Tudor this political revolution has been made to seem most significant, largely because of the story, popularized in the sixteenth century, that he met the restored Henry VI, who prophesied that one day the boy would be king. But this extraordinary tale was first told in Henry VII's reign, when every measure was being taken to legitimize Henry's seizure of the crown at Bosworth and when steps were being taken to show that his step-uncle, Henry VI, had been in truth a saintly man and fully capable of prophecy. In 1470 it is

---

24. Sydney Anglo, "The *British History* in early Tudor propaganda," *Bulletin of the John Rylands Library*, 44 (1961-1962): 17-48, and his *Spectacle, Pageantry and Early Tudor Policy* (London, 1969).

25. Griffiths and Thomas, *Making of the Tudor Dynasty*, ch. 5.

almost certain that uncle and nephew did indeed meet when Henry was taken from Raglan to London; this meeting may have been a sufficient basis on which the later fable could be grafted.[26]

In reality, when Henry VI and his only son and heir were put to death in 1471, no one mentioned Henry Tudor as a possible Lancastrian claimant. Whatever claim reposed in his family, strictly speaking it was his mother, not he, who could forward it. What was more significant for Henry in these years—and he was fourteen in 1471—was the beginning of that intimate relationship with his uncle Jasper that would last to the end of Jasper's life a quarter of a century later in 1495. For the moment, these two Lancastrian earls fled the country. Henry never saw his mother again until after Bosworth, but she persistently sought a reconciliation with Edward IV so that her son could return and live the life of an English nobleman—nothing more.[27]

Henry spent the next fourteen years in France, as long a period as he had spent in Wales and at a more impressionable age. International relations between England, France, and Brittany directed his life from 1471 until 1485, as well as events beyond his control in England. In short, Henry Tudor became the plaything of circumstance. During these years, he was protected by the duke of Brittany and sought after by four kings, Edward IV and Richard III of England, Louis XI and Charles VIII of France. He became a pawn in their mutual relations and negotiations, as each sought to gain advantage over the others. In the meantime, Henry and his uncle Jasper spent their time in various fortresses in southern Brittany or else at the ducal court at Nantes. Yet Henry was not regarded as a potential claimant to the throne of England, but rather as a possible focus for English dissidents who could be exploited by French and Breton rulers.[28]

---

26. For the likelihood of a meeting between Henry VI and Henry Tudor, see the forthcoming paper of Michael Jones, "Richard III and Lady Margaret Beaufort: a re-assessment" (and I am grateful to Dr. Jones for allowing me to read it prior to publication); for the first notices of the prophecy, Bernard André, *Vita Henrici VII*, ed. James Gairdner (Rolls Series, 1858), 14; and Polydore Vergil, *Three Books*, 135.

27. *Calendar of Papal Registers: Papal Letters*, 14 (1484-1492): 14-26, which merits careful study for its indications of proposals for a marriage between Henry Tudor and Edward IV's daughter, Elizabeth, before 1485. See also Jones, "Richard III and Lady Margaret Beaufort," (forthcoming).

28. For their residence in France, see Griffiths and Thomas, *Making of the Tudor Dynasty*, chs. 7-9, and A. V. Antonovics, "Henry VII, king of England 'by the grace of Charles VIII of France'," in R. A. Griffiths and James Sherborne (eds.), *Kings and Nobles in the Later Middle Ages* (Gloucester, 1986), ch. 9. The older J.

In England, his mother, Margaret Beaufort, worked steadily for his return, even discussing a marriage for her son with one of Edward IV's daughters. If, in Wales, certain of the poets yearned for his return, it was as a Welshman of famous family rather than as a hammer of the English or a possible English king or a fulfiller of ancient prophecies to the effect that one day a descendant of the ancient British would expel the English from British soil.[29]

All this changed dramatically in 1483, and for reasons that were once again beyond Henry's control. The seizure of power by Richard III and his removal (and rumored murder) of the young king, Edward V, and his brother (the ill-fated "Princes in the Tower") gave Henry Tudor a startlingly new significance, and to some it converted him at last into a potential claimant to the throne.[30] But it did not convince all, for the duke of Buckingham, Henry Stafford, seems to have regarded himself as a better prospect than Richard; hence he rebelled in October 1483. Henry Tudor found himself drawn into a series of conspiracies of independent origins and aims, though co-ordinated after a fashion in the early autumn of 1483. The one element which all the conspirators had in common was their antipathy toward Richard III.[31]

The collapse of Buckingham's rebellion in October 1483 made it inevitable that all dissidents would look to Henry as the only surviving plausible alternative to Richard III, even though Henry's own naval effort to coincide with Buckingham's rising had to be aborted. Thereafter, Henry was in the forefront of the plots against the king, and several hundred sympathizers flocked to him in Brittany.[32] Their manifesto was the solemn agreement

Allanic, *Le prisonnier de la Tour d'Elven, ou la jeunesse du roy Henri VII d'Angleterre* (Vannes, 1909), is too often neglected. It can now be supplemented by Henri Marsille, *Vannes au moyen âge* (Bulletin de la société polymathique du Morbihan, Vannes, no. 109, 1982).

29. This whole subject is elegantly illuminated by Glanmor Williams, *Harri Tudur a Chymru: Henry Tudor and Wales* (Cardiff, 1985).

30. The rumors of the murders in the Tower, which were current in the summer of 1483, would have been enough to alienate many Yorkists: Dominic Mancini, *The Usurpation of Richard III*, ed. C. A. J. Armstrong (Oxford, 1969), 92-93.

31. These conspiracies are fully analyzed in Griffiths and Thomas, *Making of the Tudor Dynasty*, ch. 8.

32. More than a quarter of them can be identified from the rewards they received from Henry VII: *Calendar of the Patent Rolls, 1485-1509*; James Gairdner (ed.), *Letters and Papers Illustrative of the Reigns of Richard III and Henry VII* (2 vols., Rolls Series, 1861-1863); William Campbell (ed.), *Materials for a History of the Reign of Henry VII* (2 vols., Rolls Series, 1873-1877). On several occasions, French

reached in Rennes cathedral, in Brittany, at Christmas 1483, whereby Henry undertook to marry Elizabeth of York, Edward IV's eldest daughter, when opportunity allowed; those present took an oath to him as if he were already king.[33] Henry Tudor had now clearly emerged, by a series of unforeseen events during 1483, as the best available claimant to kingship and the most promising unifier of faction in England. Yet, these events had been beyond his manipulation and control, and contrary to the initial inclinations of his mother.

In order to assert his claim, it was necessary for Henry to make the next move; but once again the decision was forced on him by others. Henry headed an exiled community, most of whom lived at Vannes in southern Brittany. They seem to have been mainly young and inexperienced, with several able people among them. They were a financial burden on Francis II, Duke of Brittany, and the burden became heavier when Duke Francis organized a second naval expedition on Henry's behalf in May 1484. It never set sail. The caution that was later to be a byword of Henry's rule as king may have been instilled in him by the failure of the expedition to coincide with Buckingham's rebellion some months earlier.[34] He continued to receive secret encouragement from England and pleas to return, and contact was established with sympathizers or potential sympathizers in both England and Wales, including Rhys ap Thomas in Carmarthenshire, and his stepfather Thomas, Lord Stanley, in Lancashire, Cheshire, and north Wales.[35]

But it was Richard III's energetic efforts to dislodge Henry Tudor from Brittany and lay hands on him that forced Henry's hand. After months of diplomatic and other activity in the first half of

and Breton sources note that between 400 and 450 exiles were with Henry by 1484-1485: A. Bernier (ed.), *Procès-verbaux des séances du conseil de régeance du roi Charles VIII* (Paris, 1836), 148 (up to ca. 400); Archives départementales de Loire Atlantique, Nantes, E212/17 f. 15r (411), a reference I owe to Dr. M. C. E. Jones.

33. For English and Breton sources for this important ceremony, see Polydore Vergil, *Three Books*, 203, and A. Bouchart, *Les grandes croniques de Bretaigne*, ed. Henri Le Meignen (Nantes, 1886), 230. There is no reason to doubt that it took place.

34. For this second, abortive expedition, see Griffiths and Thomas, *Making of the Tudor Dynasty*, 105.

35. The hints of such contacts are too numerous to disregard: for example, Polydore Vergil, *Three Books*, 191, 194, 197-198, 203, 206, 209, 212; "The song of the Lady Bessy," in *Percy Society Publications*, 20 (1847): 1-42; *Chroniques de Jean Molinet*, 2:406.

1484, Richard at last persuaded the Breton government to hand him over. What Edward IV had sought and failed to achieve, Richard III now attained. This is the explanation for the flight of Henry into France by the beginning of October 1484.[36] If Henry was to become king of England, it would now have to be "by the grace of King Charles VIII of France." Charles (or rather his elder sister Anne, the regent) was willing to support an expedition against England for his own purposes, to forestall an Anglo-Burgundian attack on France. Once again, therefore, Henry was a political pawn, though admittedly one who, by 1484, had a far greater dynastic significance that could be exploited. Henry had survived for fourteen years by courtesy of Francis II of Brittany; he was now to be given the chance to be king, not by the old duke whom Henry seems to have respected as if in place of the father he never knew, but by the young king of France whom he had never met until October 1484.[37] But it had been events at the English court in 1483 that had made his prospects brighter and more immediate.

Henry adopted the style and title of king in November 1484. It was the one significant initiative that he himself took and it was an imaginative one. No previous pretender to the English crown had ever dared to assume such a status before he had actually laid hands on the crown.[38] Charles VIII provided financial and naval support, allowed Henry to recruit mercenaries in Normandy, gave him part of his Scots guard, and allowed troops from the French base at Pont de l'Arche in the Seine valley to join him. There were also the exiles from England, most of whom had followed Henry from Brittany, and some students from Paris seem to have been attracted to his enterprise. All told, Henry may have assembled an army as large as 4,000 men by the time he set sail from Honfleur, at the mouth of the river Seine, on 1 August 1485.[39] The wind was fair and southerly.

36. Griffiths and Thomas, *Making of the Tudor Dynasty*, 109-112. The date of Henry's flight is established by the despatch of the governor of the Limousin and the *bailli* of Touraine on 11 October 1484 to welcome Henry Tudor, who had recently left Brittany: *Procès-verbaux*, 128. See also Antonovics, "Henry VII. . . .", 173.

37. For the personal relations between Henry and Duke Francis II, see Denys Hay (ed.), *The Anglica Historia of Polydore Vergil, A.D. 1485-1537* (Camden Society, 1950), 29-31.

38. For a discussion of this significant matter, see Griffiths and Thomas, *Making of the Tudor Dynasty*, 120-121, 124-126.

39. This is considerably more than the 2,000 men who are usually considered to have accompanied him.

Yet, Richard III had set the pace over the past year, and Charles VIII had made the venture possible. Henry had formulated some careful and imaginative plans. The most important decision ahead was probably the responsibility of Henry himself—or perhaps of his uncle Jasper—namely, to make for south-west Wales rather than for the English coast. The fiasco of 1483, when Henry had tried to land in Dorset, may well have deterred him from making for the same general area in 1485. Jasper's knowledge of south Wales, though rather dated, is likely to have been a significant factor in suggesting a landing in Pembrokeshire. Above all, south-west Wales could hardly be farther from Richard's long arm; there Henry had expectations of help from Rhys ap Thomas and Sir Walter Herbert of Raglan, his boyhood companion, and contact could be made with the Stanley family in north-east Wales and Cheshire. Accordingly, Henry Tudor landed on 7 August 1485 at Mill Bay, close to the entrance of Milford Sound. He knelt and quoted from the Psalms, "Judge me, O Lord, and fight my cause." He then kissed the soil of Pembrokeshire, made the sign of the Cross, and enjoined all to follow him in the name of the Lord and St. George, the popular patron saint of England and, especially, of the house of Lancaster. St. David's name does not seem to have passed his lips.[40]

Henry had good reason for landing on the northern shore of Milford Sound, rather than on its southern shore. There were fewer castles in north Pembrokeshire, and his army would have a better opportunity of breaking out to north or east than if it were confined to the relatively narrow peninsula of south Pembrokeshire. Moreover, much of the coastline of south Wales, and its lordships and castles, was in the hands of Richard III's agents, for we should not underestimate the king's astute appreciation of political geography.[41] Henry, therefore, was wise to strike northwards from Mill Bay and Haverfordwest, rather than follow the old Roman road eastwards through Carmarthen (where his father lay buried) and Brecon. In any case, it soon became apparent that some of the most influential people with whom he had been in communication were less reliable and more cautious than the reports reaching France had indicated. Rhys ap Thomas and Sir Walter Herbert were slow to join him, notwithstanding the efforts

40. A. H. Thomas and I. D. Thornley (eds.), *The Great Chronicle of London* (London, 1935), 237; Robert Fabyan, *The New Chronicles of England and France*, ed. Henry Ellis (London, 1811), 672.

41. This becomes clear from an analysis of his appointments in Rosemary Horrox and Peter Hammond (eds.), *British Museum, Harleian Manuscript 433* (4 vols., Gloucester, 1979-1983).

of Rhys' seventeenth-century biographer to persuade his readers otherwise.[42] Henry instead put his faith in the western and northern counties of the principality of Wales which had accepted Yorkist rule after 1461 with reluctance, and in the county of Cheshire, where the Stanleys were dominant.[43] To these areas and to at least some of the marcher lordships he sent personal letters soon after landing. Two of these letters, couched in the regal style, have survived. They are the only ones that are known to have been composed by the king in the weeks when he was on the hoof, though we may safely assume that he sent others. These letters—one original, the other a sixteenth-century copy— reveal the grounds of his enterprise: his royal pretension, his rightful claim to the throne usurped by Richard, and the "crusading" element implicit in the faith which he put in the Lord in a righteous cause. His appeal to the inhabitants of both the English realm and the principality counties of Wales is unmistakable.

The letter sent to a Welsh landowner of south Caernarfonshire, John ap Maredudd, survives in a fascinating history of his family written by a descendant, Sir John Wynn (d. 1627).

> Right trustie and welbeloved, wee greet yow well, and where it is soe that throughe the helpe of almightye god the assistaunce of our lovinge frendes and true subjects, and the great confidence that we have to the nobles and comons of this our principalitye of wales, we be entred into the same,[44] purposinge by the helpe above rehearsed in all hast possible to descend into our realme of England not onely for the adepcion [i.e. recovery] of the crowne unto us of right appertayninge, but also for thoppression of that odious tirant Richard late duke of Glocester, usurper of our said righte and moreover to reduce as well our said realme of England into his [i.e. its] auncient estate honor and prosperitye, as this our said principalitye of wales, and the people of the same to their erst [i.e. original] libertyes, deliveringe them of such miserable servitudes as they have pyteously longe stand in.

42. For this fascinating biography that badly needs re-editing, see *Cambrian Register*, 1 (1796): 49ff.

43. For the residual Lancastrian sympathies of the principality counties of Carmarthenshire and Cardiganshire, see R. A. Griffiths, "Royal government in the southern counties of the principality of Wales, 1422-1485" (University of Bristol Ph.D. thesis, 1962), esp. ch. 11.

44. I.e., he had recently crossed the river Teifi from the marcher lordships to the south into the royal county of Cardiganshire in the principality of Wales.

We desire and praye yow and upon your legeaunce straictly
chardge and comaund yow that imediately upon the sight
hereof with all such power as ye maye make defencibly ar-
rayed for the warr ye addresse yow towards us without
any taryinge upon the waye, unto such tyme as ye be with
us wheresoever we shalbe to our ayde for the effect above
rehersed wherein ye shall cause us in tyme to come to be
your singuler good lord and that ye fayle not hereof as ye
will avoyde our greevous displeasure and answer unto at
your perill. Yeven under our signet at our[45]

When Henry reached the northern extremity of Cardiganshire
and prepared to turn eastwards, close to the southern border of
the principality county of Merioneth, and thence into the large
marcher lordship of Powis, he sent a letter to Sir Roger Kynaston,
who was constable of Harlech Castle, sheriff of Merionethshire,
and temporarily in charge of the estates of John Grey, Lord Powis.

H   By the kyng
Trusty and welbeloved we grete you wele. And forsomuch
as we be credebely enformied and acertaynd that our trusty
and welbeloved cosin the lord Powys hath in tyme past be
of that mynde and disposicion that at this our commyng in
to thies parties he hade fully concluded and determined to
have doo us service. And nowe we undrestond that he ys
absent and ye have the Rule of his lands and folkis we will
and pray you and uppon your allegiance straictly charge
and commaund you that in all hast possible ye assemble
his said folkis and servaunts and with them so assembled
and defensibly arrayd for the werre ye comme to us for
our ayde and assistence in this our entreprise for the Recovere
of the coronne of our Royaume of England to us of Right
apperteynyng. And that this be not feyled as ye will that
we be your good lord in tyme to comme and avoyd our
grevost displaysir and answer to us at your perill. Yeven
undre our signet be side our towne of Machen lloyd the
.xiiij. day of August.[46]

---

45. John Ballinger (ed.), *The History of the Gwydir Family, as Written by Sir John Wynn of Gwydir* (Cardiff, 1927), 28.

46. This letter, dated at Machynlleth, contains no promises to the inhabitants of any part of Wales. It is printed, with a facsimile, by George Grazebrook in *Miscellanea genealogica et heraldica*, 4th series, 5 (1914): 30-39; but I have been unable to locate the present whereabouts of the original.

Henry and his advisers were well justified in following the
northern route through western and central Wales. They made
steady progress at a moderate pace across difficult country, covering the ninety-two miles from Mill Bay to Machynlleth on the
west coast in seven days. Then the army struck out across mid-
Wales towards Welshpool. They had been joined by numbers
of supporters by the time they reached Shrewsbury and the English border.[47] The motives of those who joined Henry en route,
when he was merely a pretender leading a largely foreign army,
are not easy to gauge. It may be doubted that anyone, even the
most backwoods Welshman, saw in Henry, Earl of Richmond,
a scourge of the English: he was a strange candidate for that
role. Others may have been swept off their feet in the heat of
the moment. Others were doubtless flattered by him, especially
when he was on their doorstep and required entertaining. Yet
others would have found it difficult to refuse him aid on the
spot. And many are likely to have rejoiced at the return of two
pre-eminent Welsh nobles, who had recently been re-adopted
by the poets and their patrons. Such opinions and reactions may
have been skillfully mobilized by Henry's messengers during 1483-
1485 in his dynastic cause, for in reality he was the heir of the
house of Lancaster and represented that part of the house of
York that disowned Richard III. If Henry and his actions were
placed by himself or by others in the context of ancient British
prophecies, it was as a means of propaganda in his royal cause—
and was vigorously developed only after 1485.[48]

Even so, until battle was joined it would be wrong to assume
that Henry Tudor's enterprise was overwhelmingly successful
or that victory was a foregone conclusion. However, on Long
Mountain, east of Welshpool, Rhys ap Thomas at last came in,
with up to 2,000 men.[49]

On 22 August one more fortuitous event determined Henry's
future. Richard III's personal, courageous charge on the battlefield

47. For the most recent detailed reconstruction of the march, see Griffiths and
Thomas, *Making of the Tudor Dynasty*, ch. 10, which establishes a slower progress
through Wales than is customarily accepted.

48. Poetry is the only substantial body of evidence available for Welsh opinion,
but it is tortuous to use, not least because the circumstances and date of composition are rarely known. But for an interesting attempt to edge our knowledge
forward in this matter, see G. A. Williams, "The bardic road to Bosworth: a
Welsh view of Henry Tudor," *Transactions of the Honourable Society of Cymmrodorion*,
1986, pp. 7-31.

49. Rhys' seventeenth-century biography needs to be used with great caution
at this juncture. See Griffiths and Thomas, *Making of the Tudor Dynasty*, 148.

decided the issue. Several in Henry's entourage were killed, his dragon standard was overthrown and its standard-bearer slain, and the pretender himself came close to being cut down. Had it not been for the intervention of Sir William Stanley, Richard might have won the day. As it was, the king was hacked to death, his crown was knocked from his head, his helmet smashed into his skull, and his body was beaten lifeless.[50] This single act ended the battle which a moment before was far from decided. Henry was acclaimed king on an adjacent hill.

This brought to an end a year and more of events which had shaped Henry's future from the outside, with only modest help from Henry himself. Certain plans and strategic decisions had been taken by him and his advisers, and not the least of them was the imaginative declaration in 1484 that he was already king; the march, too, seems to have been his own work. But even the final and decisive encounter was fortuitous. He had become king indeed, but only by an accident.

It is a sobering exercise to examine Henry Tudor's preparation for kingship. At twenty-eight, he was one of the least experienced of English kings since the Norman Conquest, at least in the wiles of kingship. He knew little at first-hand about his realm, having spent only a few months in London and the Thames Valley in 1470. He knew even less about the life of a king and the responsibilities of kingship; and he had had negligible training in ruling. These were most unpromising qualifications for a new king of England. On the other hand, his early life had left its mark on Henry, and commentators since 1485 have felt able to assess its meaning. We may well imagine that his precarious existence almost since birth had developed in him qualities of persistence and determination, astuteness and resourcefulness, which made him undaunted and unafraid in adversity. A steely nerve is one abiding quality that his biographer, S. B. Chrimes, detected in the new king.[51]

He had shown himself capable of decisive reactions, yet he had also learned the value of cautious, careful, and detailed planning in order to avoid needless risks, and such qualities as these stood him in good stead in 1485. Henry had come to appreciate,

---

50. On Richard's critical charge, the sources are unanimous: Ross, *Richard III*, ch. 11.

51. S. B. Chrimes, *Henry VII* (London, 1972), 298-322, is a wise assessment of the king.

too, the vital importance of having adequate resources at his
disposal in order to avoid the dangers inherent in dependence
on others. This enabled him to attract men to his side and to
retain their loyalty.

Inevitably, in view of his upbringing, a number of his later
attitudes were quite un-English. He was ignorant of, or at least
unsympathetic toward, the prejudices and attitudes of Englishmen toward other peoples, especially the Scots whom he, as a
later-medieval king of England, should have mistrusted, and the
French whom he was supposed to detest. Yet both formed the
core of his army in 1485. Indeed, Henry Tudor was an unrepentant
Francophile.[52] He liked to speak French and he employed foreign
servants to whom he was generous. He was even thought by
some observers to prefer the habits and methods of government
which he had witnessed at the Breton and French courts. Moreover, his interest in religion and his ideas about the projection
of Christian kingship were possibly somewhat different from those
of his predecessors and may have been learnt abroad.[53] These
attitudes placed Henry in a dilemma after 1485, when he tried
to translate them into a foreign policy that encompassed both
France and Brittany, the refuges of his exile. He was fortunate
in the circumstances in which he found himself at the outset of
his reign, for he was able, with some skill, to reach a placid
understanding with both countries. But these happy circumstances did not last for more than three or four years. He then
discovered that personal experience and inclinations were no
sound foundation for a foreign policy that was practicable in
the longer term and acceptable to most of his new subjects. Yet,
Henry VII never lost his affection for Brittany: the Renaissance
frieze that decorated his new chapel at Westminster Abbey and
the medallions on his tomb incorporated Breton saints, and he
continued to make gifts to Vannes cathedral, where he had wor-
shipped in the 1470s, until the later years of his life.[54]

As to Henry's advisers, he knew very few Englishmen in 1485,
apart from those who had been in exile with him or with whom

---

52. *Calendar of State Papers, Spanish*, I: 178 (1498); Hay, *Anglica Historia*, 29ff,
145.

53. A. E. Goodman, "Henry VII and Christian renewal," *Studies in Church Hist.*,
17 (1981): 115-125. In this connection, it is worth considering the foreign designs
for Henry's tomb, and the role of Guido Mazzoni and Pietro Torrigiano: Timothy
Verdon, *The Art of Guido Mazzoni* (New York and London, 1978), esp. 34-38,
134-141.

54. See Griffiths and Thomas, *Making of the Tudor Dynasty*, 172-173; Allanic, *Le
prisonnier . . . .*, 38, 63; Marsille, *Vannes au moyen âge*, 115.

he had corresponded. Even his stepfather, Lord Stanley, admitted that he did not come to know Henry well until after the battle of Bosworth.[55] Those who were in his confidence were mostly young and inexperienced. As king, his ministers and the senior members of his household were drawn mainly (though not exclusively) from among these people, especially the able clerics who had also been in exile.[56] He may have been instructed by his uncle Jasper as to what was wrong with the state of England, culled from Jasper's recollections of the 1450s and 1460s; and in Brittany and France he would have been able to observe at close quarters the impact of a powerful nobility on ducal and kingly authority.[57] These were lessons of the first importance about the nature of provincial rule and the dangers posed by factious noblemen.

Above all else, Henry's greatest weakness was his questionable claim to the crown, the very foundation of his kingship. This claim was certainly weaker than that of Henry II, Henry IV, and Edward IV when they seized the crown, though unlike Richard III he did not clamber over the innocent bodies of children to mount the throne. What brought Henry victory was not an incontestable claim, but a series of accidents and deaths engineered by others.

Henry had very few relatives with him abroad, or waiting for him in England, to give substance to his pretence to legitimacy; not even his mother had made much of her royal blood during the Yorkist era. Few kings had had so few and moth-eaten relatives at their accession. Henry, however, may not have regarded this as an unrelieved disadvantage; indeed, he turned it into a virtue.

On the other hand, he made the most of those of his relatives who were dead, drawing attention to their Lancastrian blood through his mother, and stressing the plausible link of his part-

---

55. *Calendar of Papal Letters, 1484-92*, 14-26, reviewed by K. B. McFarlane (*English Historical Review*, 78 [1963]: 771-772), who clouded the issue by maintaining that Stanley stated that he did not know Henry at all until two days after the battle—a misconception frequently repeated.

56. For example, Richard Fox and John Morton.

57. The noble intrigues at the two courts are well brought out by B. A. Pocquet de Haut-Jussé, *Francois II, duc de Bretagne et l'Angleterre* (Paris, 1929); J. L. A. Calmette and G. Périnelle, *Louis XI et l'Angleterre* (Paris, 1930); P. Pélicier, *Essai sur le gouvernement de la dame de Beaujeu, 1483-1491* (Chartres, 1882); Y. Labande-Mailfert, *Charles VIII et son milieu* (Paris, 1975). For a general account in English, see R. B. Wernham, *Before the Armada* (London, 1966).

Welsh father with ancient British kings (including Arthur).[58] In both cases he was on shaky ground, but his efforts were unremitting, persuasive, and extraordinarily successful. Within a century of Bosworth, Henry was viewed as the reincarnation of biblical heroes: as Moses, a second Solomon, and as the new King David who had liberated the Welsh just as the Jews had been freed from Babylon. By others he came to be regarded as preparing the way for the union of three kingdoms under his great-grandson, James VI and I.[59] Perhaps it was easy to pull the wool over foreigners' eyes. An Italian visitor in 1498 could conclude, after talking about the Welsh and their relations with the English over the centuries:

> They may now, however, be said to have recovered their former independence, for the most wise and fortunate Henry the 7th is a Welshman.[60]

But among Englishmen, too, Henry and his successors soon came to be adopted as the heirs of Lancaster and the Tudors as a Welsh dynasty.

In 1485 some thought that Henry VII was inexperienced and had a shallow mind.[61] He was certainly the former and poorly trained for kingship. But anyone who could adapt so skillfully and successfully to novel circumstances and forces, and at the same time keep his head; anyone who at one and the same time could overcome his own ignorance and inject an element of careful, imaginative planning and propaganda into his enterprise and his reign; anyone who came to command such approbation in both England and Wales (or perhaps duped both) must have been a truly remarkable man as well as a very lucky one.

[M.K. Jones's article cited n. 26 and 27 subsequently appeared in P.W. Hammond (ed.), *Richard III: Loyalty, Lordship and Law* (London, 1986). Significant aspects of the eventful years 1483-85 are treated by C.S.L. Davies, 'Bishop John Morton, the Holy See and the accession of Henry VII', *English Historical Rev.*, CII (1987), 2-30; M.K. Jones, 'Sir William Stanley of Holt: politics and family allegiance in the late fifteenth century', *Welsh History Rev.*, 14 (1988), 1-22; and Rosemary Horrox, *Richard III: a study of service* (Cambridge, 1989).]

58. See Griffiths and Thomas, *Making of the Tudor Dynasty*, ch. 13; Anglo, works cited in n.24.

59. Williams, *Henry Tudor and Wales*, 93ff.

60. C. A. Sneyd, *A Relation, or rather a True Account of the Island of England* (Camden Society, 1st series, 37, 1847), 19.

61. National Library of Wales MS. 3054D f.345a (Elis Gruffudd's chronicle).

8

Public and Private Bureaucracies in England and Wales in the Fifteenth Century*

IT is just fifty years since Thomas Frederick Tout died on 23 October 1929. Apart from a few formative years at St. David's College, Lampeter, Tout spent the whole of his academic career in Manchester. It was there that in 1908 he read and reviewed Eugène Déprez's *Etudes de diplomatique anglaise* and soon afterwards conceived the monumental work of a lifetime, modestly entitled *Chapters in the administrative history of Mediaeval England*.[1] This six-volume work describes the organization of the household of England's medieval kings between the Norman conquest and the revolution of 1399, and the way in which the great administrative departments of state sprang from it. Beginning as a study of the king's personal chamber and wardrobe, it blossomed into a study, first, of the principal and less personal offices of the chancery, the exchequer and the privy seal—their growing complexity and bureaucratization, their increasing professionalism and specialization, and their eventual permanent settlement in or near London— and, second, of the way in which these offices affected, and were affected by, the relationship between individual kings and their subjects. The focus of Tout's work was the court and the central government, institutions and administration.[2]

It is too readily forgotten, however, that Tout had a profound appreciation of the humanity of his subject. He believed, rightly, that a familiarity with the structure of the administrative machine was essential to a proper understanding of its working and a full appreciation of those who worked it. But towards the end of his life, he made clear where the emphasis should lie: 'To understand that machine properly one has to learn something about the men engaged in

---

* I owe several items of information quoted in this paper to the kindness of Dr. R. W. Dunning and Dr. R. S. Thomas.

[1] For the impression which Déprez's work (published in Paris in 1908) made on Tout, see J. Tait's obituary notice in *Eng. Hist. Rev.*, xlv (1930), 82; Tout reviewed it in *ibid.*, xxiii (1908), 556–9.

[2] *Chapters* was published by Manchester University Press, in whose foundation Tout was centrally involved, between 1920 and 1933. For a statement of its developing purpose, see *Chapters*, I, pp. 4–6, and III, pp. vi–vii.

working that machine.'[3] He had always been conscious of the crucial importance of what he described as the medieval civil service. After all, at Lampeter he had instructed in political administration those students who (like himself initially) wished to enter the British civil service, and one of his celebrated lectures, in 1915, discussed the forebears of those black-coated, tall-hatted gentlemen—and these were days prior to the introduction of the bowler hat—who paraded west London and Westminster, and 'are seen every morning flocking to the government offices in Western London at hours varying inversely with their dignity'.[4] In the two years before his death, Tout returned to the people who staffed his central administrative machine, their more private accomplishments, their personal foibles, their flesh and bones.[5] Sir Maurice Powicke later judged his historical attitudes well:

> 'He was concerned to understand the methods of mediaeval government, and to adjust the generalizations of the constitutional historian to the salutary experience of men, great men and little men, ministers of state and clerks, living their lives of routine among associations now long forgotten.'[6]

It would be equally unjust to think that Tout had little awareness of those private organizations and bureaucracies that flourished beyond the capital under the direction of secular lords, abbots, priors and bishops, even city fathers. He recognized the importance of the links that existed between the institutions of the king and the state and those of his aristocratic subjects, though his *Chapters* rarely looked beyond the temporary administrative organizations of the royal family—and then, appropriately enough, he delegated his own relatives to study them: the household and estate organizations of the queens of England and of the Black Prince.[7] The latter's brother, John of Gaunt, was on the work-sheet of the Tout circle, but it was left

[3] 'Literature and learning in the English civil service in the fourteenth century', *Speculum*, iv (1929), 366.

[4] D. T. W. Price, *A history of St. David's University College, Lampeter*, I (Cardiff, 1977), p. 202; T. F. Tout, 'The English civil service in the fourteenth century', *Bull. John Rylands Library*, iii (1916–17), 185–214, reprinted and elaborated in *The collected papers of Thomas Frederick Tout*, III (Manchester, 1934), pp. 191–221 (with the playful quotation on p. 185).

[5] See the list of his later writings compiled by his widow (*History*, xiv (1929–30), 323–4).

[6] Obituary in *Proc. British Academy*, xv (1929), 517.

[7] *Chapters*, III, pp. 187–201. For the queens, see H. Johnstone, *ibid.*, v, pp. 231–89; 'The queen's exchequer under the three Edwards', *Historical essays in honour of James Tait*, ed. J. G. Edwards *et al.* (Manchester, 1933), pp. 145–53; and *The English government at work, 1327–1336*, ed. W. H. Dunham *et al.*, I (Cambridge, Mass., 1940), pp. 250–99. For the Black Prince, see M. Sharp, *Chapters*, v, pp. 289–440, and 'The administrative chancery of the Black Prince before 1362', *Essays in mediaeval history presented to Thomas Frederick Tout*, ed. A. G. Little *et al.* (Manchester, 1925), pp. 321–33.

to Sir Robert Somerville to complete that particular task much later.[8] Meanwhile, if seignorial administration in the later middle ages was illuminated at all it was as a by-product of a newer tradition of historical investigation—that of aristocratic society and politics—centred at Oxford, guided by K. B. McFarlane and heralded by N. Denholm-Young's 'sociological and administrative history' (as he described it in 1937), entitled *Seignorial administration in England*.[9]

Unfortunately, few have ventured to adapt Tout's approach to the fifteenth century in any systematic way, and one has no alternative but to agree with Professor Chrimes's conclusion in 1952 that 'the difficulties of viewing English administrative history in the fifteenth century [and here he was talking of the central executive] still remain formidable.'[10] The King's household and the departments of state lack their historian and therefore an essential preliminary to a full examination of those who made the machinery work is not available.[11] Some attention has been paid to diocesan administration and episcopal households, and one must be grateful to the upheaval of the Dissolution for the albeit small number of authoritative monastic histories that have been written.[12] Even less has been achieved on the urban front, largely because it is rare for English towns outside London to have preserved at all carefully their administrative records for this period.[13] To comment on the nature of public and private bureaucracies in fifteenth-century England and Wales may seem foolhardy;

[8] *Chapters*, III, p. v; V, pp. v–vi; R. Somerville, *The history of the duchy of Lancaster*, I (London, 1953).

[9] N. Denholm-Young, *Seignorial administration in England* (Oxford, 1937), with the quotation taken from the preface. See the posthumously published essays of K. B. McFarlane, *The nobility of later medieval England* (Oxford, 1973).

[10] S. B. Chrimes, *Introduction to the administrative history of mediaeval England* (Oxford, 1952), p. 241. For the changing emphasis in fifteenth-century historiography, see De Lloyd J. Guth, 'Fifteenth-century England: recent scholarship and future directions', *British Studies Monitor*, vii (2) (1977), 3–50.

[11] Some corners of the subject have been illuminated by A. J. Otway-Ruthven, *The king's secretary and the signet office of the XV century* (Cambridge, 1939); A. L. Brown, *The early history of the clerkship of the council* (Glasgow, 1969), and 'The privy seal clerks in the early fifteenth century', *The study of mediaeval records: essays in honour of Kathleen Major*, ed. D. A. Bullough et al. (Oxford, 1971), pp. 260–81; M. Hastings, *The court of common pleas in fifteenth-century England* (Ithaca, N.Y., 1947); M. Blatcher, *The court of king's bench, 1450–1550* (London, 1978).

[12] See R. L. Storey, *Diocesan administration in the fifteenth century* (2nd edn., York, 1972); and, for some examples, R. W. Dunning, 'The households of the bishops of Bath and Wells in the later middle ages', *Proc. Somerset Arch. and Nat. Hist. Soc.*, cx (1966), 24–39, and R. B. Dobson, *Durham Priory, 1400–1450* (Cambridge, 1973).

[13] Good series of records survive, for example, for Shrewsbury (now being studied by Mr. D. R. Walker) and Exeter (deposited in the Devon Record Office). See the forthcoming paper by R. M. Horrox, 'Urban patronage in the fifteenth century' (which also uses the archives of Beverley and Hull), which the author allowed me to read in typescript. See *Patronage, crown and provinces*, pp. 145–66.

it is certainly hazardous. But nothing attracts scholarly attention more than a well-extended and defenceless neck, and many a fruitful investigation has begun where blood has spilled. Accordingly, at this stage, a number of significant themes may be identified: phenomena which Tout and others noticed in earlier centuries can be reported from the fifteenth, whilst other features of the bureaucratic world acquire a significance for the first time in this period. One can, therefore, go some way towards answering the most fundamental questions that any age asks of its bureaucracy: what is its quality and how strong is the control exerted by it and by its masters?

The remarks in this paper are directed towards the bureaucrats, rather than the organizations with which they worked. Some might question whether bureaucrats existed at all in the fifteenth century. The word has an impeccable pedigree extending to the later middle ages when French administrative offices dealing with finance, law and management were centred about tables covered with an official cloth or *burel*, just when contemporary English clerks were huddled round green exchequer cloths at Westminster and in private, provincial exchequers, chanceries or treasuries, whether they were located in baronial fortresses like Brecon, royal castles like Carmarthen, monasteries like Durham or cathedrals like Wells.[14] The *burel* or *bureau* and the exchequer quickly became the administrative office itself. The usage in France thereafter remained steady until, in the eighteenth century, those who staffed the offices became known as bureaucracy and, soon afterwards, as bureaucrats.[15] Before that, the English language had adopted the former term, admittedly pejoratively and perhaps as a result of the greater prominence accorded to French methods of government, or rather misgovernment, at the time of the French revolution.[16] It must be a source of satisfaction to President Giscard d'Estaing, who worries about such matters, to know that the English-speaking world now talks of bureaucrats rather than 'exchequerites'.

---

[14] *Trésor de la langue française*, IV, *sub* 'bureau', quoting the royal household accounts for 1316. For Brecon's exchequer, see Staffordshire Record Office, D 641/1/5/2; for Carmarthen's chancery, exchequer and green cloth, R. A. Griffiths, *The Principality of Wales in the later middle ages, I: South Wales, 1277–1536* (Cardiff, 1972), pp. 37–40; for Durham's organization, Dobson, *Durham Priory*; for the exchequer at Christ Church, Canterbury, D. Knowles, *The religious orders in England*, II (Cambridge, 1957), ch. XXV; and for the administration of Bath and Wells, R. W. Dunning, 'The administration of the diocese of Bath and Wells, 1401–1491' (unpublished University of Bristol Ph.D. thesis, 1963).

[15] *Trésor de la langue française*, *sub* 'bureau'. See also R. Cotgrave, *Dictionarie of the French and English tongues* (1611, reprinted 1968 and based on a sixteenth-century compilation), *sub* 'bureau'; *Dictionnaire de la langue française*, I (edns. of 1882 and 1953), *sub* 'bureau'; *Dictionnaire de la langue française du seizième siècle*, II, *sub* 'bureau'.

[16] *A new English dictionary*, I (1888), *sub* 'bureau'.

Others may doubt whether these bureaucrats were an identifiable section of society. Despite uncertainties and difficulties in individual cases, it is possible to identify the man (never, so far as I know, a woman) who brought to a fifteenth-century organization the professionalism born of special training.[17] Take John Sedley, an exchequer clerk since 1488 and a royal auditor from 1492, who entered the Middle Temple in 1503 to complement his considerable experience with a professional training which kept him in office almost until his death thirty years later.[18] One can identify, too, the man who devoted a larger part of his time and career to the paper- and parchment-work of administration than to any other single activity. One thinks of William Botiller, whose financial skills were used by all three Lancastrian kings and several marcher lords throughout south Wales at a time of particular difficulty following the Glyndŵr rebellion; in the circumstances, he worked few miracles with the disorganized resources of the Welsh lordships, but by his training and long, continuous experience he comes close to the modern conception of the working, white-collar man.[19]

Bureaucrats were specially engaged, judged, and frequently promoted. Nicholas Dixon was taken on as a young clerk in the upper exchequer in 1402; he became a senior clerk in 1413, clerk of the great pipe roll in 1414, deputy-treasurer of England in 1421 and then, after twenty-one years of (so far as I know) exemplary service, baron of the exchequer two years later. He could scarcely go higher.[20] Many of these bureaucrats felt themselves to be well suited to the administrative niche they occupied, managing other people's affairs. When John Throgmorton looked back on his life, after a generation of continuous service in the exchequer and almost as long in the employ of the Beauchamp earls of Warwick, not to speak of more temporary associations with four other west Midlands lords, he spoke philosophically of how

---

[17] On the other hand, women were often landowners in their own right and very occasionally occupied lowly administrative positions for brief periods (for example, Kent County Archives Office, U71/M49, for Juliana Bromlegh, beadle of Orlestone in 1421-2).

[18] *Calendar of ancient deeds*, I, p. 453; *Cal. Pat. Rolls, 1485-94*, p. 407; *Middle Temple records*, ed. C. T. Martin, I (London, 1904), p. 5; P.R.O., E.159/307, Michaelmas, m.46. He died in 1532 (P.R.O., P.C.C. 20 Thower).

[19] R. A. Griffiths, 'William Botiller: a fifteenth-century civil servant', *Trans. Bristol and Glos. Arch. Soc.*, lxxxiii (1964), 70-7. For his record as chamberlain of south Wales, see Griffiths, 'Royal government in the southern counties of the principality of Wales, 1422-85' (unpublished University of Bristol Ph.D. thesis, 1962), VIII. Below, ch. 10.

[20] J. L. Kirby, 'The issues of the Lancastrian exchequer and Lord Cromwell's estimates of 1433', *Bull. Inst. Hist. Res.*, xxiv (1951), 131-4; *Proceedings and ordinances of the privy council of England*, ed. N. H. Nicolas (7 vols., London, 1834-7), III, p. 22.

'I have been all the days of my life in my country's service in the
world as the world asketh'.[21]

The breadth of Throgmorton's service reminds us that the late-
medieval bureaucrat was not in his office or on its business from 9
a.m. to 5 p.m., day in and day out. The vacations at Westminster
were so long as to appear paradisaical, and while a skeleton staff kept
the chancery and the exchequer open, colleagues were pursuing professional and private interests elsewhere.[22] Moreover, the bureaucrat
on a mission from Chester to London, or from Westminster to south
Wales, was making a very leisurely tour indeed by modern standards.
William Troutbeck, chamberlain of Chester, was on the road for four
months each year in the 1420s, travelling to and from London to
report on the affairs of the palatinate;[23] and John Brown, the duke of
Norfolk's auditor and much else besides, rode from Gower to Shropshire, and on to the duke's estates in Warwickshire, Leicestershire,
Derbyshire and Cambridgeshire in 1445 in between working at the
exchequer and the royal household.[24] In short, they had ample opportunity for other activities and additional employment; and the fifteenth-century bureaucrat was approached by individuals and institutions which sought to enlist his expertise. Richard Verney, an officer
of Richard Beauchamp, earl of Warwick, after his patron's death in
1439 passed into the service of Lady Grey, the duke of Buckingham,
Lord Ferrers, Lord Beauchamp and Lord Sudeley within the space
of the next ten years.[25] And to take another example, quite at random:
George Heton, who began his administrative career as a clerk in
Henry VI's kitchen, moved into the duchy of Lancaster's service, and
then into the exchequer; he attracted the attention of the archbishop

[21] J. C. Wedgwood, *History of parliament: Biographies of the members of the commons house,
1439–1509* (London, 1936), pp. 851–2 (quoting from his will, P.R.O., P.C.C. 31 Luffenham); J. S. Roskell, *The commons in the Parliament of 1422* (Manchester, 1954), pp. 224–
5. For his connection with Lord Ferrers of Chartley, Lord Sudeley, the bishop of Worcester and the abbot of Evesham, see M. Carpenter, 'Political society in Warwickshire,
c. 1401–72' (unpublished University of Cambridge Ph.D. thesis, 1976), p. 106; Wedgwood, *History of Parliament, Biographies*, p. 852; Roskell, *Parliament of 1422*, p. 225; Hereford and Worcester Record Office, 705/175/92475.
[22] For vacations at Westminster, see Tout, *Chapters*, II, pp. 97–8; *Proceedings of the
Privy Council*, VI, p. 297.
[23] P.R.O., E.101/620/24 (1426–30).
[24] Hereford Record Office, B63/5 dorse. See also Wedgwood, *History of Parliament,
Biographies*, p. 120. He had been in the royal household and exchequer since Henry
V's day (*Cal. Pat. Rolls, 1416–22*, pp. 63, 105; *ibid., 1441–46*, p. 344).
[25] Carpenter, 'Political society in Warwickshire', pp. 104, 106, 108; Shakespeare
Birthplace Trust, Willoughby MS. 642a. For John Verney's Beauchamp service, see
C. D. Ross, *The estates and finances of Richard Beauchamp, earl of Warwick* (Dugdale Soc.,
1956), p. 8.

of Canterbury, for whom he acted as an auditor, and also of the abbot of Cirencester, whose bailiff he became.[26]

Some of the most successful and ambitious bureaucrats considerably enlarged their political and economic horizons, even to the point of deserting their professional calling: some were elected to parliament by constituencies that sought their advocacy, and this was probably why Totnes and then Bridgwater persuaded William Hody, a local lawyer and later chief baron of the exchequer, to represent them in Edward IV's parliaments.[27] Men of the calibre and ambition of Adam Moleyns went further. A University-educated clerk in the privy seal office, his golden opportunities came when he was clerk of Henry VI's council; he soon became a councillor himself, commended himself to the powerful earl of Suffolk as a diplomat and administrator, and eventually by 1449–50, when he occupied the see of Chichester, was one of the most hated men in England.[28] Others built upon their position to promote the private interests of themselves, their family and friends. John Brown, for example, combined a career in the royal household with prominent service in the king's exchequer; he was able to accumulate sufficient wealth eventually to rebuild his house in his home shire of Warwick.[29]

The geographical parameters of a bureaucrat's existence are not easily defined. He was not necessarily trapped, like Thomas Hoccleve seems to have been to judge by his poetic lamentations, by the routine of a journey from lodgings in London to an office in Westminster, or by the location of his lord's estates, or by the confines of the city he served.[30] He had family ties and provincial loyalties, he had clients and patrons scattered in some cases over a wide area, and he might reasonably hope for a country estate of his own and one not necessarily situated near his ancestral heath. John Walsh, for instance, a longserving auditor of the duchy of Lancaster and in Wales, was employed by the abbot of Westminster as his steward in Surrey, and although he seems to have hailed from Worcestershire, he lived for almost thirty years of his life at Cheshunt in Hertfordshire before his death there in 1464.[31] When the city of Coventry asked one of its own

[26] F. R. H. Du Boulay, *The lordship of Canterbury* (London, 1960), pp. 274–5; Somerville, *Duchy of Lancaster*, I, pp. 411, 625.

[27] Wedgwood, *History of Parliament, Biographies*, p. 461.

[28] A. B. Emden, *A biographical register of the University of Oxford to A.D. 1500* [*B.R.U.O.*], II (Oxford, 1958), pp. 1289–91; R. L. Storey, *The end of the house of Lancaster* (London, 1966), pp. 41, 52, 62.

[29] Above, p. 142; *V.C.H., Warwicks.*, IV (London, 1947), pp. 13, 16–17.

[30] See *Hoccleve's works*, ed. F. J. Furnivall and I. Gollancz (Early English Text Soc., I–III, 1892–7), and A. C. Reeves, 'Thomas Hoccleve, bureaucrat', *Medievalia et Humanistica*, new ser., v (1974), 201–14.

[31] Somerville, *Duchy of Lancaster*, I, pp. 439–40, 445n; *Cal. Pat. Rolls, 1429–36*, p. 453; Westminster Abbey MS. 27,489, m.2; P.R.O., P.C.C. 6 Godyn.

sons, Thomas Kebell, a trained lawyer, to become one of its legal counsel, his service with several magnates and with the duchy of Lancaster and the crown at Westminster led him to reply:

'... if I be sergeaunt I thynke I couth not be with you at thassises tyme. Parauentur I shulde be Justice of assise in som other contrey ... And onlesse than I may haue liberte to duell out of the Citie, ant to be absent at thassises tyme, yf nede be, I can nott occupie that office.'[32]

That was not good enough for Coventry, much as they valued Kebell's expertise, and instead they looked elsewhere. The historian, in other words, needs to be fleet of foot in pursuing the bureaucrat: at his office, yes, but also at home; one has to enquire into his education and training, his early patrons and supplementary employment; one has to follow him across the kingdom—sometimes beyond it—and up the ladder of promotion; and one has to take note of activities in which he engaged precisely because he had become someone's capable administrator, but which might ultimately take him outside the bureaucrat's world. He is a recognizable bird, but a ubiquitous one not easily trapped.

To pin-point precisely the social origins of fifteenth-century bureaucrats would require an extensive prosopographical study well beyond the customary resources of mere mortal historians; but I doubt if its general conclusions would depart much from the statement that bureaucrats were drawn from every class in society—even the lowest and including the aristocracy. To some extent this is demonstrated by a study of their education and training. Grammar schools were evidently being founded in late-medieval England with quickening momentum. Before 1500 even the small borough of Caernarvon could support a school to which the grandfather of the gentleman-historian, Sir John Wynn, was sent.[33] The size of the educated and literate community increased rapidly, especially the lay part of it. Even unfreemen (the so-called *nativi*) were sending their sons to school, usually with, but sometimes without, their lord's permission. John Hody, who grew up to be an ecclesiastical bureaucrat in and around Somerset, went to a small chantry school at

---

[32] For Kebell, see E. W. Ives, 'Promotion in the legal profession of Yorkist and early Tudor England', *Law Quarterly Review*, lxxv (1959), 348–63 (with the passage quoted on p. 358 from *The Coventry leet book*, ed. M. D. Harriss, II (Early English Text Soc., 1908), p. 527).

[33] N. Orme, *English schools in the middle ages* (London, 1973), and *Education in the west of England, 1066–1548* (Exeter, 1976); J. H. Moran, *Education and learning in the city of York, 1300–1600* (York, 1979); *The history of the Gwydir family*, ed. J. Ballinger (Cardiff, 1927), p. 50.

Woolavington in Somerset with the blessing of his father's master, Lord Audley.[34]

Clerks from obscure and well-to-do families alike studied at the Universities, and a number of them—even the sons of noblemen—became clerical bureaucrats of distinction and in more than one diocese. After graduating, John Hody attracted first the attention of the bishop of Norwich in 1408, possibly while he was still at Oxford, but he soon returned to the west country whence he came, to hold a number of the highest administrative (as opposed to spiritual) posts in the sees of Worcester and Bath and Wells.[35] An increasing number of clerics, like Hody, were studying civil or canon law, and the new colleges produced more and more law-trained clerks who were available for ecclesiastical and secular employment: in the crown's service their grasp of an international code of law made them well suited to diplomacy and the admiralty courts, though dioceses and monasteries engaged them too.[36] The archbishop of Canterbury's provincial court hired a brilliant group of such lawyers early in the fifteenth century, including two Welshmen, Philip Morgan, later bishop of Worcester, and Henry Ware; they found it easy to practise in the king's admiralty courts in London and provided Henry V with an outstanding corps of diplomats when they were most needed.[37] But from the middle of the century onwards, the tendency to appoint laymen and non-University-trained bureaucrats gathered strength on monastic estates as in the English dioceses.[38]

Fifteenth-century bureaucrats were literate men; they could handle sheaves of parchment and paper, compile bundles of accounts and memoranda, give receipts now that wooden tallies were disappearing from many organizations, affix seals to a variety of instruments, and they could do all these things in French, English and Latin.[39] An increasing proportion of them in both public and private

---

[34] H. C. Maxwell-Lyte, 'The Hody family', *Somerset and Dorset notes and queries*, xviii (1925), 127. For the fining of a *nativus* who sent his son to a grammar school without permission, see Gloucestershire Record Office, D621/M10, m.1d (1437–8); and for the subject in general, Orme, *English schools*, pp. 50–2.

[35] Emden, *B.R.U.O.*, II, pp. 941–2; Dunning, 'Administration of Bath and Wells', p. 379.

[36] Storey, *Diocesan administration*, pp. 14–17.

[37] Emden, *B.R.U.O.*, II, pp. 1312–13; III (1959), p. 1985. For Morgan, see most recently M.-L. Bull, 'Philip Morgan (d. 1435): Ecclesiastic and statesman' (unpublished University of Wales M.A. dissertation, 1976).

[38] *E.g.*, Dobson, *Durham Priory*, ch. 4; Du Boulay, *Lordship of Canterbury*, pp. 249, 260–3; Knowles, *Religious orders*, II, 284–5, 312.

[39] For the disappearance of tallies as receipts, see Denholm-Young, *Seignorial administration*, p. 21 and n. 8; and for the use of bills, even by tradesmen, *The Stonor letters and papers*, ed. C. L. Kingsford (Camden Third Series, 1919), pp. 90–1 (1479).

organizations were laymen, even in monasteries, cathedrals and episcopal households. The last clerical registrar at Canterbury died in
1474, but estate officials had generally been laymen in most dioceses
for some years already—a phenomenon which was to have some bearing on the willingness of English society to tolerate the dismember-
ment of the church by Henry VIII.[40]

Further education was available to the layman, especially in those
estate management techniques that were highly prized by landlords
and institutions. Practical training in administration for literate
laymen had been common since the thirteenth century, and boys were
regularly engaged as junior clerks in the chancery and exchequer at
Westminster, where they learned through apprenticeship and frequently gained promotion to senior posts.[41] In fact, promotion in the
bureaucracy of the central government—perhaps less so in smaller,
local bureaucracies—was usually from within, and one can appreciate
that office tradition, knowledge of precedent and forms, proven competence in literary composition and appropriate elements of the law
were valued qualities. When the privy seal office decided in 1483 to
look outside to recruit to one of its senior clerkships, the protests from
the under-clerks were sufficient to cause Richard III to insist that
a cleric who had earned the job by years of good service should get
it.[42] These bureaucrats learned as they worked, modelling themselves
on their seniors, studying when they could—by joining an inn like
John Sedley or by borrowing books from a colleague as did one wardrobe clerk who had to pay a fine of one goose per week when it was
not returned.[43] Those beginning their administrative careers in private employment had similar training, though the circle in which
it was provided was inevitably smaller. What is significant about the
petition of Cardinal Wolsey's nephew for a post is less that he had
acquired a knowledge of the law at Gray's Inn, but rather that his
father and his employer, the late duchess of Norfolk, had trained him

[40] Storey, *Diocesan administration*, p. 33; Du Boulay, *Lordship of Canterbury*, pp. 260–
76; Dobson, *Durham Priory*, p. 125. For the trend towards laicization in the chancery's
service by Richard II's reign, see H. C. Maxwell-Lyte, *Historical notes on the use of the
great seal of England* (London, 1926), pp. 2–3; T. F. Tout, 'The household of the chancery and its disintegration', *Essays in history presented to R. L. Poole*, ed. H. W. C. Davies
(Oxford, 1927), pp. 82–3; A. F. Pollard, 'The clerk of the crown', *Eng. Hist. Rev.*, lvii
(1942), 314; Pollard, 'Fifteenth-century clerks of parliament', *Bull. Inst. Hist. Res.*, xv
(1937–8), 139; Pollard 'The mediaeval underclerks of parliament', *Bull. Inst. Hist. Res.*,
xvi (1938–9), 70–1.

[41] B. Wilkinson, *The chancery under Edward III* (Manchester, 1929), chs. IV, VI; Tout,
'The household of the chancery', pp. 73 ff.

[42] Maxwell-Lyte, *Great seal*, p. 34.

[43] Above, p. 141; T. F. Tout, 'The human side of mediaeval records', *T.R. Hist. S.*,
4th ser., 11 (1928), 6.

in secretarial duties, accounting and auditing.[44] The archbishop of Canterbury's administration could similarly train a lowly young clerk of account so that in time he became receiver of a group of archiepiscopal manors.[45]

More formal vocational training in what may be called business studies was available for concentrated periods of cramming at Oxford and, rather later, at a few other centres—probably more than we realize.[46] At Oxford, which has never ceased to attract the penumbra of educational institutions, independent teachers were prepared from the early thirteenth century to instruct would-be bureaucrats and others in a range of subjects: the use of legal terms, the drawing-up of household accounts, the holding of courts, the writing of charters, deeds, writs and accounts—in other words, most of the arts of an estate or household official. Some teachers wrote and had copied their own text-books, and advertised their wares to young men in lords' households or clerks working on landowners' estates.[47] Such schools may have been declining in importance in the fifteenth century, as the emergent inns of chancery and of court in London attracted their potential clients, but they had certainly not disappeared.

It is easier to visualize the role of these inns in training the late-medieval lawyer, though some features of their early history are still obscure.[48] Buildings housing would-be lawyers met their practical needs at Westminster. A household or inn for chancery clerks had provided accommodation and company in the suburbs of London by Edward I's reign, though in the late fourteenth century their sense of community was weaker—perhaps as a result of the intrusion of laymen into the royal bureaucracy—and these inns were appropriated instead by the apprentice-lawyers.[49] In the fifteenth century, the inns of both chancery and court belonged to the common lawyers, those of chancery perhaps tending to attract students who did not envisage a full-time legal career at Westminster. Sir Robert Plumpton sent his young kinsman, Edward, to a chancery inn, Furnival's, for legal training in the late fifteenth century with the intention of

---

[44] E. W. Ives, 'The common lawyers in pre-Reformation England', *T.R. Hist. S.*, 5th ser., 18 (1968), 152, quoting P.R.O., S.P. 1/10, fos. 50–2.

[45] Du Boulay, *Lordship of Canterbury*, pp. 273–5.

[46] Orme, *English schools*, pp. 75–9; *Walter of Henley and other treatises on estate management and accounting*, ed. D. Oschinsky (Oxford, 1971); P. D. A. Harvey, 'Agricultural treatises and manorial accounting in mediaeval England', *Agric. Hist. Rev.*, xx (1972), 170–82.

[47] H. G. Richardson, 'An Oxford teacher of the fifteenth century', *Bull. John Rylands Library*, xxiii (1939), 436–57, and 'Business training in mediaeval Oxford', *American Hist. Rev.*, xlvi (1940–1), 259–80.

[48] *Cf.* R. Roxburgh, *The origins of Lincoln's Inn* (Cambridge, 1963).

[49] Tout, 'The household of the chancery', pp. 46–85.

employing him as a business adviser and secretary thereafter.[50] This mushrooming of the inns reflected the greater importance attached to a knowledge of the law in all business dealings in the later middle ages, whether it be in the households of the great or in the offices of the crown.

Yet, there was no real substitute for a practical training in administration, even when the rudiments of the law, accounting and charter-writing could be obtained at school or at the inns. What could be picked up in the family home was just as valuable. It is not fortuitous that families of bureaucrats, engaged over several generations, often by the same institution or magnate house, are commonly encountered in the fifteenth century. Not only might a father be able to gain an entrée for a son or a brother in the organization he himself served, but he could also provide an introduction to the necessary skills. The Hodies of Somerset, bureaucrats of the Luttrells and other landowners in the south-west, are matched by the Hugfords of Worcestershire, who were pre-eminently servants of the earls of Warwick, and by the Appletons of Kent, who for three generations were auditors at the royal exchequer.[51] The warning in Walter of Henley's classic thirteenth-century treatise on estate management (which was still read two hundred years later) was salutary:

'If youe bee to choose a bayly or a servaunt choose hym not by parentage nor comlynesse nor otherwise, unlesse [it went on to add] he bee of good reaporte and be loyalle and well advised and can skylle of husbandrye.'[52]

A family immersed in administrative service could provide the loyalty and transmit the expertise that Walter rated so highly.

Large numbers of business manuals and dissertations were in circulation from the mid-thirteenth century onwards. If the copying of them tended to slacken in the fifteenth century, this may have had as much to do with well-established traditions of estate management and the widespread availability of these manuals as with any declining interest in what they had to say. When the first generation of Hody bureaucrats joined the Luttrell service at Dunster in the early fifteenth century, they would have found one in the castle's archives. Some

[50] S. M. Walker, 'The Plumpton correspondence: an historical and social survey' (unpublished University of Leeds M.A. thesis, 1962), pp. 138–9.

[51] For some of the Hody family, see Wedgwood, *History of Parliament, Biographies*, pp. 460–1; *D.N.B.*, XXVII, p. 78; Maxwell-Lyte, 'The Hody family', 127–9; for Hugfords, Ross, *Estates and finances of Richard Beauchamp*, p. 8; Wedgwood, *History of Parliament, Biographies*, pp. 478–80; Carpenter, 'Political society in Warwickshire', pp. 102, 112–13, 117; and for Appletons, see their wills, P.R.O., P.C.C. 7 Rous, 48 Marche, 17 Luffenham. *Cf.* Pollard, 'Clerk of the crown', 312, 324.

[52] *Walter of Henley*, p. 317.

were sufficiently useful to be among the first printed books to be published towards the end of the century. These manuals discussed accounting, court practice and estate management in general.[53] Formularies were equally common-place, providing exemplars for young bureaucrats and reference works for their seniors; in the privy seal office, the poet-clerk Thomas Hoccleve spent many hours compiling a formulary of royal letters for all occasions, and most private and local exchequers and chanceries contained similar volumes for the practising bureaucrat.[54] Specimen accounts for receivers and bailiffs, specimen writs and letters, compilations of legal texts and statutes were well-thumbed handbooks.

By such practical means, the apprentice-bureaucrats were introduced to their craft. Though their formal education might vary considerably and their careers be spent in differing traditions, they were schooled in the same principles of administration—secretarial, financial and with a strong injection of law. One may perhaps distinguish the bureaucrat who specialized in accounting and auditing from his colleague who did not, but in the fifteenth century it is too early to separate one kind of education and training in bureaucracy from another.

Recruitment to public and private bureaucracies is an unusually fascinating subject, not least because it raises questions of contemporary morality relating to talent, opportunity and influence, questions which not even the democratic age has satisfactorily resolved. Medieval historians delight in recording the story of an obscure family or an unprivileged individual who grasped the opportunities of a fluid society to climb to respectability, prosperity, even to national prominence.[55] Ability and competence were undeniably desirable qualities, as Walter of Henley had stressed in the thirteenth century. Richard Lussher, a Devon man who secured the relatively minor local post of feodary of the duchy of Lancaster estates in the south-west, by sheer good work (we may presume) commended himself to senior duchy officials and became the first of several generations of Lusshers to serve in the crown's bureaucracy.[56] Yet incompetence and bungling all too rarely prejudiced job-security (if one may use the phrase) and often

---

[53] *Ibid.*, pp. 10–50, with the Dunster manuscript (B.L., Egerton MS. 3724) described on pp. 21–2. For supplementary comment, see Harvey, 'Agricultural treatises', 170–82, with additional manuscripts noted on pp. 178–9.

[54] Brown, 'Privy seal clerks', 260 ff. (with Hoccleve's formulary in B.L., Add. MS. 24,062); Griffiths, *Principality of Wales*, p. 61; W. A. Pantin, 'English monastic letter-books', *Essays to Tait*, pp. 201–22.

[55] *E.g.*, E. L. G. Stones, 'Sir Geoffrey le Scrope (*c.* 1285–1340), chief justice of the king's bench', *Eng. Hist. Rev.*, lxix (1954), 1–17.

[56] Somerville, *Duchy of Lancaster*, I, pp. 445, 634; *Cal. Pat. Rolls.*, *1446–52*, p. 245. For his service in Wales see, for example, P.R.O., S.C.6/1225/3, m.6; /4, m.6; /5, m.8.

had their rewards rather than their deserts. William Soulby was a singularly unfortunate man to be dismissed from his post as bailiff and coroner of the Yorkshire town of Beverley by Archbishop Kemp in 1435; he was merely negligent or corrupt.[57]

Patronage, influence and 'connection' were much more potent factors in securing employment and promotion. We have already had occasion to acknowledge the advantages which a family introduction and sponsorship could confer on an aspiring bureaucrat.[58] Once launched on a career, the opportunity to move from one organization to another depended heavily on continued patronage. A successful term in a Westminster office might lead to employment by a private individual or an institution. Most obviously the crown's legal officers were well placed to give advice, show good will, or even connive at illegality—and sometimes on a permanent retainer from a lord or an abbot or a city. The services of Sir John Hody, serjeant-at-law and eventually chief justice of king's bench, were enlisted by the earl of Devon, Lord Hungerford and the earl of Stafford.[59]

Other bureaucrats cut their teeth on the administrative problems of a private landowner, entering the service of the crown later. Royal councillors and ministers found it easy to recommend their protégés and servants. For example, until 1483 the earls of Warwick had a traditional right to nominate one of the two chamberlains of the exchequer, and more often than not they appointed an experienced bureaucrat from their own household or estates—someone like John Throgmorton who, before becoming chamberlain in 1419, had been in Richard Beauchamp's service and indeed remained in it throughout the earl's life.[60]

Bureaucrats, like their masters, risked all during political revolution, but for the servant of the successful the opportunities were golden. Twice in the fifteenth century, in 1399 (if one may appropriate an extra year) and 1461, did a leading magnate ascend the throne unexpectedly and in such circumstances of distrust and inexperience that he inevitably continued to rely on loyal, professional administrators from his own private bureaucracy. That Henry of Lancaster in-

---

[57] Borthwick Institute, York, Register of John Kemp, fo. 179v, quoted in M. Witchell, 'John Kemp (d. 1454): an ecclesiastic as statesman' (unpublished University of Wales M.A. thesis, 1979), p. 260, n. 35.

[58] Above, p. 148.

[59] E. Foss, *A biographical register of the judges of England* (London, 1870), pp. 348–9; *D.N.B.*, XXVII, p. 78; Devon Record Office, CR 621; Wiltshire County Record Office, 490/1480; C. Rawcliffe, *The Staffords, earls of Stafford and dukes of Buckingham, 1394–1521* (Cambridge, 1978), p. 220.

[60] Ross, 'Estates and finances of Richard Beauchamp', p. 11, n. 3; Wedgwood, *History of Parliament, Biographies*, pp. 851–2; Roskell, *Parliament of 1422*, pp. 224–5; above, p. 141.

troduced numerous servants from his duchy to the government of the realm is well known. The process was repeated in 1461 when the duke of York's heir became King Edward IV. John Harper, who had been employed by Edward's father and his ally, Warwick the Kingmaker, before 1461, found large opportunities in the royal service opening before him like an oyster after 1461. That the same did not happen in 1485 is simply explained: Henry Tudor had spent his adult years either on the run or abroad or in protective custody, and as a result had gathered about him no professional bureaucracy of any size that was devoted to his personal service.[61]

By contrast, the collapse or extinction of a magnate house brought to the crown's notice seignorial administrators who needed a patron. John Gunter, for instance, had become well nigh indispensable to the Stafford dukes of Buckingham; but he passed easily into the king's service when Duke Henry was executed in 1483, leaving a young boy as his heir.[62]

The way in which a bureaucrat actually brought his talents to the attention of an employer is usually concealed. Manuals enjoined caution on the landowner and the existence of schools and inns is testimony to the importance of good training. Some ambitious young men were prepared to trumpet their own virtues in the direction of an employer. In 1462, John Russe appealed to his patron, John Paston:

'... plese it youre good maistirshyp to wete that it is seyd here that my Lord Wurcestre is lyk to be Tresorer, with whom I truste ye stonde right wel in conseit, ... Wherfor I becke youre maistirshyp that if my seid lord haue the seid office that it lyke you to desyre the nomynacion of on of the officez eythyr of the countroller ore serchorshyp of Jernemuth for a servaunt of yowrez, and I shuld so gyde me in the office as I trust shuld be most profit to my seyd lord. And if youre maistirshyp lyked to gete graunt thereof, that than it plesyd you to lycence on of youre servauntez to take out the patent of the seyd office, and if it cost v or vi or viij marke I shal trewly contente it ageyn; and yeerly as longe as I myght haue

---

[61] A. L. Brown, 'The reign of Henry IV: the establishment of the Lancastrian régime', *Fifteenth-century England, 1399–1509*, ed. S. B. Chrimes *et al.* (Manchester, 1972), pp. 14 ff; D. A. L. Morgan, 'The king's affinity in the polity of Yorkist England', *T.R. Hist. S.*, 5th ser., 23 (1973), 1–25; S. B. Chrimes, *Henry VII* (London, 1972), ch. 1. For Harper, see *Cal. Pat. Rolls, 1452–61*, pp. 49, 570; *ibid., 1461–67*, p. 91; *Cal. Close Rolls, 1454–61*, p. 56.

[62] *The marcher lordships of south Wales, 1415–1536*, ed. T. B. Pugh (Cardiff, 1963), pp. 84–5, 290; Rawcliffe, *Staffords*, pp. 59, 128, 199, 226, 242; P.R.O., P.S.O. 2/1 (24–25 September 1485).

the officez, or ony of hem, I shal geue to my maister youre sone
v marke toward an haukeney.'[63]

Russe at least had the grace to apologize for his effrontery. And well
he might, for his petitioning came close to bribery, and that was something not universally acceptable in the fifteenth century. When
Richard III insisted on the internal promotion of a long-serving
clerk in the privy seal office, he disapproved of the contender partly
because he had flouted the 'old rule and due order by means of giving
great gifts and by other sinister and ungodly ways'.[64]

References and recommendations from influential personages
played a crucial role in communication between an employer and
prospective employee. In this connection, one may quote a letter by
a younger John Paston addressed to Lord Hastings in 1476. To an
audience used to reading and writing references, seeking recommendations and arranging interviews, it should sound familiar:

'... please it your good lordshepp to have knowlage that, accordyng to your commandement, jn my wey homeward I remembred
me of a persone whyche to my thynkyng is meetly to be clerk of
your kechyn, whyche persone is now in seruyse wyth Master Fitzwater, and was befor that wyth Whethyll at Gwynes and purveyor
for hys house, ... Thys man is meane of stature, yonge j-nough,
well wittyd, well manerd, goodly yong man on horse and foote.
He is well spokyn jn Inglyshe, metly well in Frenshe, and verry
parfite in Flemyshe. He can wryght and reed.... And when I had
shewyd hym myn jntent he was agreable and verry glad if that it
myght please your lordshepp to accept hym in-to your servyse, ...
Wherfor I advysed hym to be redy wyth-in xiiij dayes of Marche
at the ferthest, that if it pleasyd your lordsheppe to accept hym
or to haue a syght of hym be-for your departyng to Caleys, that
ther shold be no slaughthe in hym. He desyred me to meve Master
Fitzwater to be good mastyr to hym in thys belhalve, and so I dyd;
and he was verry glad and agreable ther-to, seying if hys sone had
ben of age, and all the seruauntis he hathe myght be in eny wyse
acceptabell to your lordshepp, that they all, and hym-silff in lyek
wyse, shall be at your comandment whyll he leveth.'

At the same time, Paston recommended to Hastings another young
man who was then in the duchess of Norfolk's service. Of both, he
concluded,

'I trust that your lordshepe shall lyek bothe ther persones and ther
condicyons, and as for ther trowthes, if it may please your good

---

[63] *The Paston letters and papers*, ed. N. Davis, pt. II (Oxford, 1976), p. 276. For Russe,
see *ibid.*, p. 103; Wedgwood, *History of Parliament, Biographies*, pp. 730–1.
[64] Maxwell-Lyte, *Great seal*, p. 34; above, p. 146.

lordshepe to accept my poore woord wyth thers, I wyll depose largely for that ...'[65] .

The enthusiasm with which FitzWater greeted Paston's proposal may betray an eagerness to be rid of his servant (who incidentally went out of his way to tell Paston that his first employer had been very reluctant to let him go). But what strikes one about this recommendation is the thoroughness with which the considerable qualities of the officer concerned are itemized, the care taken to secure the agreement of present employers, and the importance attached to referees and interviews.

Of his own attitudes to work, employer and colleagues, the fifteenth-century bureaucrat has left precious little record. Unlike Chaucer, who rarely gave anything away in his writings about his private life as a bureaucrat, Thomas Hoccleve, a more minor literary figure, is quite informative. English bureaucracies, unlike those of contemporary Italian cities, did not consciously seek out the exceptionally learned or the culturally cultivated for employment as administrators. Consequently, Hoccleve's picture of the frustrations of the office, the earthy diversions of a bureaucrat, relations with colleagues, and the deadly routine of clerking (which may have been responsible for his nervous breakdown), is all the more valuable.[66] Rare, too, are the doodles of bureaucrats in their idle, yet imaginative, moments. Aside from monkeys, angels and flowers (which may perhaps reflect something or somebody), one has a more direct significance. It was dexterously woven into the capital S of the word *Summa* by a minor accountant in Berkshire in 1444 as he totalled the financial charge laid against him. With arrears mounting and difficulties increasing, he wrote laconically *Res nequid hec esse nil pervenit absque labore*—and broke off his account.[67]

The one consolation of the depressed or frustrated bureaucrat in a large institution was that he and his colleagues were all in the same boat. Some may have been more ambitious than others, some more successful or better patronized or luckier than others; but they were all colleagues together and valued one another's company. Not only did they belong to an identifiable occupational group, but those who worked together cultivated mutual interests beyond the office: they were often friends, sometimes neighbours and business partners who

---

[65] *Paston letters*, ed. Davis, pt. I (Oxford, 1971), pp. 600–1; Richard Whetehill was controller of Calais from 2 December 1460 (*Cal. Close Rolls, 1454–61*, p. 472). For a similar commendation see Dobson, *Durham Priory*, p. 129.

[66] J. Mitchell, *Thomas Hoccleve* (Urbana, Ill., 1968), ch. 1; Reeves, 'Thomas Hoccleve', 201–14.

[67] Berkshire Record Office, D/Ec/M97. For doodles, see Tout, 'Human side of medieval records', p. 6.

recognized the expertise of each other just as they valued their own. In the king's exchequer (though seignorial organizations could furnish examples too), their camaraderie can be observed from several angles. Royal auditors spent much time in one another's company, travelling the country for weeks on end. Roger Appleton and Richard Bedford spent sixty-three days in one another's pocket early in 1424, journeying to Carmarthen and Cardigan on the king's business; in the course of such travels, they got to know each other well.[68] When wills were drawn up they frequently called on one another to act as executor or supervisor. Richard Lussher, an exchequer auditor, drew up his in 1502, and John Gunter, a colleague, was named as executor: Lussher came from Devon and Gunter from Surrey, but they worked together at Westminster and in September 1485 had been sent to south Wales on a tour of duty.[69] When business transactions were concluded—enfeoffments of property arranged, sales of land negotiated—colleagues were frequently among the witnesses, feoffees and agents. Roger Appleton, whose family was well ensconced in the exchequer's auditing department, had close business ties with several other auditors, though as the behaviour of Walter Gorfen, another crown and duchy of Lancaster auditor, demonstrates, certain colleagues were unscrupulous enough to betray the trust placed in them and frustrate the arrangements to which they were a party. What is remarkable about Gorfen is that his expertise continued to be relied upon by his workmates.[70]

Even closer associations were formed at work and privately. At the exchequer, several of the auditors were thrown together in what appears to have been a small and rudimentary Welsh office, employing over a long period the same bureaucrats who specialized in the affairs of the royal counties of north and south Wales, Chester and Flint, as well as whatever marcher lordships fell into the king's hands; even dioceses on the border were entrusted during episcopal vacancies to these same men. Roger Appleton served on this Welsh circuit for nineteen years, Richard Bedford for fifteen; they would have spent a good deal of time at Westminster preparing for, and assessing, their regular visits to Wales, which themselves took weeks to conclude.[71] A degree of specialization of this kind followed the Glyndŵr rebellion, when a premium was placed on experience and detailed knowledge

[68] P.R.O., S.C.6/1160/12. For their appointment, see *Cal. Pat. Rolls, 1422–29*, p. 54.

[69] P.R.O., P.C.C. 18 Holgrave. For Lussher and Gunter, see above, pp. 149, 151; for their service together in Wales, P.R.O., P.S.O. 2/1.

[70] *Cal. Fine Rolls, 1413–22*, p. 432; *ibid., 1422–30*, pp. 22, 190; *ibid., 1429–35*, p. 236; *Cal. Close Rolls, 1422–29*, p. 458 (Appleton); P.R.O., C.1/26/251; 19/10, 188; C.81/1376/5 (Gorfen).

[71] *Cal. Pat. Rolls, 1413–16*, pp. 247, 338; *ibid., 1422–29*, p. 54; *ibid., 1429–36*, pp. 189, 254; P.R.O., S.C.6/1167/4, m.4 (Appleton); 1160/12; 1167/7, m.9 (Bedford).

by a government that was striving to bring the country back to peace, stability and profitability. John Geryn, in the same group, remembered his only visit as an auditor to Chester in 1429, for in his will he bequeathed money to the city and to one of its priests, who had presumably helped him in some way or offered him comfort.[72]

The social dimension of this royal bureaucratic community is best observed in the home counties, though one may recall that most lords, bishops and abbots also had their London headquarters where their officials spent some time. The laicization of English bureaucracy was proceeding apace, with the result that the customary bestowal of benefices as a reward became singularly inappropriate. An administrator's collection of benefices, many of them without cure of souls, might be scattered widely throughout the realm and would rarely be visited by their incumbent. Richard Caudray, Henry V's secretary and a particularly inventive clerk of the council, had a clutch of them—and he was by no means an exceptionally well-endowed pluralist.[73] The lay bureaucrat, on the other hand, required different treatment, not least because he was likely to acquire a layman's commitments associated with family pride, providing for sons and daughters, and willing property. The benefice, therefore, was replaced as patronage and reward by the lease, the sale, investment and chicanery; his administrative experience taught him the virtues of a compact property and the means he could adopt, with the aid of friends and colleagues, to obtain it. It was this laicization of bureaucracy, not exclusively in the crown's service, that aided the drift to the south-east that is a feature of the capital's growth. Resentment at its progress is likely to have been one factor behind John Cade's rising in 1450.

After a lifetime's employment in the king's exchequer, several of its bureaucrats preferred to spend their declining years in or near London, and be buried there. Thomas Gevendale never forgot his origins near Ripon in Yorkshire, but he wanted to be buried at St. Bartholomew's hospital, Smithfield, not too far from the office where he had worked as clerk of the parcels and an auditor at the exchequer.[74] One other example will illustrate this feature as well as the close personal relationships created between professional colleagues. Nicholas Dixon, an exchequer clerk of the old style from Lincolnshire, rose to become baron of the exchequer in 1423 and was rewarded in the

---

[72] *Cal. Pat. Rolls, 1422–29*, p. 459; *ibid., 1429–36*, pp. 70, 189; P.R.O., P.C.C. 25 Luffenham.

[73] Brown, *Clerkship of the council*, pp. 20–8; A. B. Emden, *A biographical register of the University of Cambridge to 1500* (Cambridge, 1963), pp. 126–7.

[74] London, Guildhall Record Office, Register V, fos. 166v–167 (1455).

traditional manner; among numerous benefices that came his way was the rectory of Cheshunt in Hertfordshire, where he rebuilt the parish church and may have built the manor house—at least it dates from this period.[75] In the following decades, so many younger exchequer bureaucrats were drawn to Cheshunt that one cannot but conclude that they were attracted by the example, patronage or personality of Dixon himself. John Fray, a fellow baron at the exchequer, and John Walsh, an exchequer auditor by 1432, acquired property there. In the church, where Dixon's brass may still be seen, there is an inscription to the wife of John Luthington, a crown and duchy of Lancaster auditor at about the same time, not to speak of a brass of the wife of John Parr, who may be identified with the household official of the Yorkist kings.[76] Cheshunt had become a rural retreat for hardworking royal clerks who rated professional comradeship highly and who benefited from personal associations formed at the office.

A highly trained profession, many of whose members served church and state, crown and subject, city and estate, and travelled extensively from county to county and from capital to province, was a powerful force in society and politics. Its activities must surely have softened animosities, promoted co-operation and understanding among neighbours, and brought disputes closer to solution. One hears much of the disruptive and violent implications of indentured retinues, but the wages, fees and annuities paid to clerks and administrators had a significant countervailing effect. As receivers, counsellors, auditors and stewards, they sat on a lord's council and advised a city's aldermen, and it would make no sense at all if they, who took fees from several lords, were not encouraged by their wide connections to compose seignorial quarrels rather than contest them.[77] It requires much more investigaton to be certain, but one's impression is that arbitrations between disputants, usually concerning land or rights, were more in evidence in the fifteenth century, though they were known before. Common-law procedures creaked ever more slowly

[75] Above, p.141; Kirby, 'Issues of the Lancastrian exchequer', 131-4; *V.C.H., Herts.*, III (London, 1912), pp. 441 ff.

[76] *V.C.H., Herts.*, III, pp. 454-5. See Foss, *Register of judges*, p. 282 (for Fray); above, p. 143; Somerville, *Duchy of Lancaster*, I, pp. 439-40, 445n (Walsh), and pp. 435-6 (Luthington); P.R.O., E.404/73/3/24, 46; 76/1/1 (Parr). See the 'court of good company', a kind of bureaucrats' dining club over which Henry Somer, chancellor of the exchequer, presided on 1 May 1410 (*Hoccleve's Works*, I, pp. 64-6).

[77] For seignorial councils, see Denholm-Young, *Seignorial administration*, pp. 25-31, and, most recently, C. Rawcliffe, 'Baronial councils in the later middle ages', *Patronage, pedigree and power in later mediaeval England*, ed. C. D. Ross (Gloucester, 1979), pp. 87-108.

and extra-curial devices of this sort had the merits of speed, reliability and mutual acceptance. Those who negotiated them, and sometimes acted as arbitrators, were the councillors of each side or mutually acceptable outsiders proposed by opposing councils.[78] One feels rather more certain that arbitrations were arranged increasingly frequently to avert or terminate violent clashes; by mid-century a standardized form of agreement had evolved for use by panels of arbitrators in several parts of the country, with a tariff of compensation reminiscent of the Anglo-Saxon blood-feud.[79] Even more common, especially in minor disputes, was the so-called 'love-day', arranged and attended by officials and councillors at pre-arranged locations acceptable to both parties. Anyone who talked or wrote about or organized these *dies amoris* was half-way towards settling potentially dangerous quarrels; and in the forefront was the bureaucrat.[80] It is worth noticing in this connection that when public order in the provinces collapsed in the mid-fifteenth century, some of the most notorious violence was precipitated not by the earl of Northumberland and the earl of Salisbury, or by the earl of Devon and Lord Bonville, who had experienced bureaucracies to advise and restrain them, but by their reckless younger sons, who appear to have acted with considerable independence.[81]

An aristocratic council, like the crown's bureaucracy, was ultimately answerable to its master. Ever alert and suspicious of officials, Walter of Henley had advised his reader to

'Looke upon your things often and cause theim to be looked upon and then suche as serve you will so muche the rather eschewe to doe evell and wille endevoure to doe the better.'[82]

But such control depended squarely on a lord's personality. Richard of York, father of King Edward IV, deferred to his councillors to an extent commented on by contemporaries.[83] Sir James Ormond, later

---

[78] E.g., *Cal. Close Rolls, 1447–54*, p. 502; *ibid., 1454–61*, p. 431; Shakespeare Birthplace Trust, DR 98/497a (1446). The entire matter of arbitration needs fuller investigation.

[79] E.g., Derbyshire Record Office, 410 M/Box 14/488 (1446); Box 1/432 (1455).

[80] E.g., Leicestershire Record Office, 26/D 53/2328 (1454–5); Somerset Record Office, DD/L Box 1/17/3 (1422), and (for *dies concordie*) DD/CC/110739/15 (1439–40). For this subject, see J. W. Bennett, 'The mediaeval loveday', *Speculum*, xxxiii (1958), 351–70, and, in relation to the Welsh march, R. R. Davies, *Lordship and society in the march of Wales, 1282–1400* (Oxford, 1978), pp. 245–8.

[81] R. A. Griffiths, 'Local rivalries and national politics: the Percies, the Nevilles and the duke of Exeter, 1452–55', *Speculum*, xliii (1968), 589–632; Storey, *End of Lancaster*, ch. XIII. See below ch. 20.

[82] *Walter of Henley*, p. 343.

[83] E.g., C. L. Kingsford, *English historical literature in the fifteenth century* (Oxford, 1913), pp. 339, 341; *Proceedings of the Privy Council*, V, p. 288; *The Paston letters*, ed. J. Gairdner (6 vols., London, 1904), III, pp. 25, 27.

earl of Wiltshire, was far less docile in 1444, when two of his officials were sharply upbraided:

> '... for as mekyll as I have grete a doo in this contrey that ye make ordienaunce for as much money as ye may gete and that ye sende it to me by the berer of this seid lettre and that he be no taried therfore in no wyse. ... And I late you well wyte that I am not well pleased with you that ye kepe no better youre dayes of peyement but I wole that ye amende it heraftre as ye wole have my lordshyp.'

Perhaps Ormond would have been better taking a leaf from York's book, for he got himself into such situations that he had to flee from every battle in which he fought.[84]

The ultimate sanction of sacking was available, though all too rarely used. It seems, indeed, as if many bureaucrats were retained for life or at least for very long periods. In the case of the crown, the misfortunes of the Lancastrians and the ensuing civil war fatally weakened its hold over its servants. The long minority of Henry VI, during which the lords ruled collectively, introduced competing systems of patronate and pressure that had not been quite so obvious before. Offices were appropriated for political purposes, and yet when Henry VI came of age in 1437 his innate generosity and inexperience allowed many offices to be granted for life, in survivorship or even on a hereditary basis—and at a time of increasing lay involvement in the bureaucratic service. As a result, the crown's control of its own officialdom slackened, its provincial authority was weakened and its efficiency undermined.[85] The chronology of these developments and any measure of recovery from them has not yet been established. But it would certainly need exceptional resolution on the crown's part to tighten its grasp when the venality of lay office-holding was working powerfully against it. Well might one of Queen Elizabeth I's subjects lament nostalgically:

> 'I would the Lord Keeper weare a bishop (not that I think justice ill ministered but I would have the cleargie in honor); I would a bishop were Master of the Rolls; I would all the vj. clarkes of the Chauncerie weare priestes.'[86]

[84] Northamptonshire Record Office, Finch-Hatton MS. 454. See Storey, *End of Lancaster*, p. 91.

[85] *E.g.*, R. A. Griffiths, 'Patronage, politics and the principality of Wales, 1413–61', *British government and administration: studies presented to S. B. Chrimes*, ed. H. Hearder and H. R. Loyn (Cardiff, 1974), pp. 68–86. See below ch. 9.

[86] *H.M.C.*, *Salisbury manuscripts*, pt. II (London, 1888), p. 63 (1573), partially quoted in Tout, 'The household of the chancery', p. 83.

Additional Note to Chapter 8

[Organs of late medieval English government have recently been discussed by A.L. Brown, *The Governance of Late Medieval England, 1272-1461* (London, 1989), esp. ch. 3 ('The Westminster Offices'), and Edward Powell, *Kingship, Law and Society: Criminal Justice in the Reign of Henry V* (Oxford, 1989). On bureaucracy, see R.L. Storey, 'Gentlemen-Bureaucrats', in C.H. Clough (ed.), *Profession, Vocation and Culture in Later Medieval England* (Liverpool, 1982), pp. 90-109, and C.W. Smith, 'A conflict of interest? Chancery clerks in private service', in Joel Rosenthal and Colin Richmond (eds.), *People, Politics and Community in the Later Middle Ages* (Gloucester, 1987), pp. 176-92.]

9

Patronage, Politics and the Principality of Wales, 1413-1461

Iɴ the pre-democratic age, patronage—of offices, pensions, and property—was the surest support of power. Kings, governments, bishops, nobles, and gentlemen employed it to reward good service and ensure future loyalty; aristocrat and yeoman alike sought it to attain personal wealth, political power, or social position. Throughout western Europe the prerogative of patronage was inseparably united with the obligation to govern. The circumspect exercise of patronage would ensure orderly government in the state and provide sufficient opportunity to obviate tensions in society. Dangers and resentments would occur if patronage were imprudent or ineffectual, as those could testify who witnessed the disasters of King John's reign in England or the conflicts in France while Charles VI was insane. Lancastrian England and Wales amply illustrate the potentialities and pitfalls of patronage.

Within the limits imposed on him by wisdom, advice, and importuning, the king dispensed the greatest patronage. This power was implicitly reserved by Henry IV when he asserted that he was 'in as great a royal liberty' as his predecessors. It was inherited by Henry V in 1413, and when Henry VI began his personal rule, he announced in November 1437 that this same power was his 'for to do and dispose for hem as hym good semeth'. It remained intact when the king was too young or too ill to exercise it personally, and then arrangements were made for others to do so for him.[1]

Throughout England, Wales, and territories overseas, the Lancastrian kings disposed of hundreds of offices, considerable quantities of cash augmented by tallies and bills of assignment on future revenue, and a replenishable stock of demesnes, escheats, forfeitures, and wardships. In England this patronage was often shared with, and therefore limited by, several of their subjects; in Welsh marcher lordships that were not their own, these kings had few rights at all. But in the palatinates of Chester and Lancaster, in the duchy of Cornwall, and the principality of Wales, the Lancastrians were exclusive, direct lords. There, their patronage was rarely curtailed, and

---

[1] *Select Documents of English Constitutional History, 1307–1485*, ed. S. B. Chrimes and A. L. Brown, London, 1961, 199, 235, 251–2, 275–6, 299–302. I am grateful to Dr. C. D. Ross for his valuable comments on an earlier draft of this article.

hence the impact of their appointments and grants on government, society, and the practice of kingship can be clearly observed.

In the principality shires of Wales (Anglesey, Caernarvon, and Merioneth in the north, Cardigan and Carmarthen in the south), the king had an extensive repertoire of offices, rights, and resources by means of which the principality was governed. To keep gifts and government in perspective was the art of kingship. The greater offices conferred influence and political or military power, although their obligations were real and often heavy enough. The justiciars of north and south Wales were the king's vicegerents; limited patronage was delegated to them, for they could appoint lesser officers in the commotes of each shire and lease Crown lands.[2] Especially did they enjoy personal patronage in nominating lieutenants or deputies to act in their absence—friends, associates, or retainers whom they could trust. John and Henry Wogan, Pembrokeshire esquires of Edward, duke of York, deputized for the duke as justiciar of south Wales (1407–16); and Sir Thomas Stanley, controller of the king's Household, was made deputy-justiciar by William, earl of Suffolk, who was steward of the Household and, in 1440, justiciar of north Wales. The justiciar's responsibilities were onerous, especially at times of political turmoil. Sir Thomas Stanley was said to have resigned from the northern justiciarship in October 1450 because he was 'occupied in divers business whereby he has no leisure to exercise his office';[3] whereas lack of confidence in William, Lord Abergavenny, the justiciar who faced Glyndŵr's threat to south Wales, led to his dismissal in August 1401.

Principality finance was managed at Caernarvon and Carmarthen by two chamberlains, who also kept the king's great seals of north and south Wales, the very instrument of patronage; when leases were sealed, and fees and wages authorized, their advice was naturally sought. Most chamberlains employed a deputy, to whom they extended their own patronage. Sir Geoffrey Radclyff had an entrée to north Wales's government through the good offices of his kinsman, Sir John Radclyff (chamberlain in 1434–7),[4] whilst William Burghill, who was employed by Sir Edward Stradling in south Wales in 1430–5, had worked with Sir Edward some years earlier. A chamberlain's opportunities for enrichment were even greater. Thomas Barneby, chamberlain of north Wales (1406–14) during the Glyndŵr revolt, feathered his nest by embezzlement and extortion; the reckoning was correspondingly severe, for

---

[2] For a full discussion of this and other aspects of principality government mentioned in this article, see W. H. Waters, *The Edwardian Settlement of North Wales in its Administrative and Legal Aspects, 1284–1343*, Cardiff, 1935; R. A. Griffiths, *The Principality of Wales in the Later Middle Ages*, i: *South Wales, 1277–1536*, Cardiff, 1972.

[3] *C.P.R. 1446–52*, 403. Full references to officers of the principality in south Wales mentioned in this article, together with biographical details, are to be found in Griffiths, *Principality of Wales*. Appointments to office in north Wales are recorded in *C.P.R.*, unless otherwise stated.

[4] P.R.O., Special Collections, Ministers' Accounts (henceforward Min. Acc.), 1216/4 m. 9.

Barneby was sacked in March 1414 after Henry V had inquired into the activities of royal officers in north Wales.

Military power was concentrated in a small group of castle-constables, whose duty was to protect the castles at Beaumaris, Conway, Caernarvon, and Harlech, Aberystwyth, Cardigan, and Carmarthen. After the rebellion, they commanded enlarged garrisons which put at their disposal a small, but permanent, core of fighting men maintained at the royal expense.[5] These constables, too, employed trustworthy lieutenants, although the shock of Glyndŵr's rising led to subsequent injunctions that they themselves should be resident, or at least visit their castles regularly.[6] John Stanley installed his relative, Rowland Stanley, in Caernarvon castle in 1437–8;[7] another deputy-constable, Gruffydd Dwnn at Carmarthen in 1431–2, was not only a colleague of the constable, Sir John Scudamore, in the administration of Kidwelly, but also his son-in-law.

Despite the similarities between north and south Wales at the apex of government, there were considerable differences at the secondary level. The statute of Rhuddlan had outlined the sheriff's judicial, executive, and financial responsibilities in the three northern shires, but the slow evolution of royal administration in the south dispersed these responsibilities among a sheriff, a steward, and two bailiffs itinerant in Carmarthenshire and Cardiganshire. Hence, the northern sheriffs were more prominent than any one of the southern officers; but in both areas unfulfilled obligations could jeopardize a career, as James Butler, earl of Ormond, and his deputy-sheriff in Carmarthenshire discovered in 1442–3, when they were imprisoned for allowing a detainee to escape.

These major offices combined obligations which were at times heavy, and a discretionary patronage that enabled friends, relatives, or servants to enjoy some of the perquisites and reciprocate their patron's favour. Another significant attraction of office-holding was the annual fee; Sir John Radclyff was specifically appointed chamberlain of north Wales in February 1434 so that the Crown could help discharge its enormous debt to him of more than £7,000.[8] If a friend could be found to deputize, or if obligations could be discharged lightly, these Welsh offices would be worthwhile catches.

On a smaller scale, commote offices were granted as gifts or farmed for an annual sum to men who made what they could from the customary fees; such offices had few—if any—duties attached to them. There were a surprising number in the principality, partly because Edward I retained certain Welsh elements of local government while at the same time creating new offices on the English pattern. His

---

[5] P.R.O. Min. Acc. 1288/2; 1223/8 m. 5; B.M. (Add. Ch.) 26597 m. 3.

[6] *P.P.C.*, ed. N. H. Nicolas (7 vols., Record Commission, 1834–7), v. 3 (1436); vi. 60 (1447), 302–4 (1460); P.R.O. Exchequer, T.R. Council and Privy Seal, 78/ 237 and 238 (27 February 1436, misdated to 1449).

[7] B.M., Add. Ch. 26597 m. 5.

[8] *P.P.C.* iv. 199–200; *C.P.R., 1429–36*, 269–70, 338. Radclyff was also allowed to keep the north Wales revenue until the debt was discharged.

conquest, therefore, had a legacy of over-administration which eventually made several offices well-nigh superfluous and irrelevant to current needs; there was no reason to cavil when they were held by deputy. The customary fees that ensured their survival provided patronage for the king and a modest profit for those whom he patronized. In south Wales, the archaic office of *rhaglaw* or constable had a monetary

FEES OF MAJOR OFFICERS[9]

Office	Annual fee £ s. d.	Other payments £ s. d.
Justiciar, north	66 13 4	
south	40	66 13 4–133 6 8*
Chamberlain, north	20	
south	20	
Constable, Carmarthen	20	
Cardigan	40	
Aberystwyth	town's income	91 5 0†
Beaumaris	40	127 15 0
Conway	40	109 10 0
Caernarvon	40	167 5 10
Harlech	26 13 4	146 0 0
Sheriff, Anglesey	20	
Caernarvon	20	
Merioneth	20	

* A 'regard' payable after the Glyndŵr revolt at a variable rate: Griffiths, *Principality of Wales*, p. 33.

† This and the following four sums were maximum payments to support castle-garrisons under the Lancastrians: Min. Acc. 1223/5 m. 8; 1216/7 m. 4, 5, 6, 7; 1216/8 m. 4, 5.

value that ensured its continuance. The constableships of Caeo and Mallaen (Carms.) had once reimbursed a farmer who paid £12 per annum for them, though by 1451 £6 was a more realistic figure.[10] This was the order of profit anticipated by William Catton, Henry IV's servant who acquired both offices for life in September 1408. The *rhaglaw* and woodward in north Wales had a similar history, and in the fifteenth century their offices were granted to royal servants, most of whom remained strangers to Snowdonia: two grooms of Henry VI's larder, John Martin and William Bangore, shared the *rhaglaw*'s office in Ystummaner (Caerns.) from February 1433 with a reasonable expectation of 42s. a year; William Randolf, another royal servant, received the woodwardship of Is Conwy, Uwch Conwy, and Eifionydd (Caerns.) for life in 1438 in the hope that it would realize £8 per annum. The *amobr* fine paid throughout Wales when a woman lost her virginity in marriage (or less happy

9 P.R.O. Min. Acc. 1216/7 m. 3–8; 1223/8 m. 3–5.   10 Ibid. 1168/7 m. 5.

circumstances) was still imposed in the fifteenth century. In south Wales, *amobr* fines were extended at £7. 6s. 8d. per annum when their farmer, John Wodehouse, Henry V's dependable servant, died in 1431; but they were a wasting asset, for by 1450 their value was thought to have slumped to £3. 10s. 0d.[11] Offices such as these were desirable perquisites for yeomen, gentlemen, and esquires, to whom a few pounds from several of them could make the difference between poverty and comfort. None was a juicy plum, but several plucked together could content a royal servant, despite complaints of extortion and difficulties of collection which some officers experienced in post-Glyndŵr Wales.[12]

The remaining local offices still had essential functions in the fifteenth century, though their fees were modest at best. They were therefore pre-eminently the preserve of Welshmen, whose local standing was enhanced by becoming, for example, bailiff itinerant of Carmarthen. But those who served as commote beadle or reeve in south Wales and as *rhingyll* in the north did so reluctantly, for the small fees were poor compensation for the duties assigned them; hence, they occasionally had to be nominated to office by the justiciar or chamberlain—even offered a wage later in the fifteenth century. Such officers hardly thought of themselves as benefiting from royal patronage, but more likely as tenants discharging a tiresome obligation.

The Crown had few substantial demesnes to dispose of in Wales. Gerardston, near Cardigan, was one, and the hamlets of Maenorsilian, Talsarn, and Trefilan (Cards.) another. Rhys ap Thomas ap Dafydd, a king's esquire, secured both, Gerardston to the value of £6, and the three hamlets were farmed for £7. 0s. 4d. annually. Yet they need not have been jealously fought over, for Gerardston was never worth more than £5 and the hamlets' farm was soon lowered to £6. 3s. 4d. The decay of Dinefwr and Dryslwyn castles (Carms.) put these royal estates, too, on the market: John Perrot, a Pembrokeshire esquire, acquired Dinefwr for twenty years in 1433 for a £5 farm, and John Wodehouse was granted Dryslwyn in 1409 for £10 per annum. The manor of Aber (Caerns.) was similarly available, and in 1437 John Fray, a baron of the Exchequer, acquired it for life believing it to be worth 40 marks, although his predecessor had complained that its income never reached that level. Escheats and wardships were equally modest in a principality that had few large landowners and where Welsh inheritance customs retained their vitality and, indeed, were confirmed by Henry V even for former rebels and their sons![13] As the Glyndŵr revolt receded into the past, forfeitures, too, occurred less frequently. Here, the patronage nexus had less scope. Nevertheless, the Clements' Cardiganshire estates, as an example, were worth bestowing on Edmund Beaufort and Gruffydd ap Nicholas in 1437 at £40 per annum during the heir's minority.

[11] Ibid. 1161/5 m. 2; 1167/5 m. 3d; 1168/7 m. 4; 1162/7m. 4d; *C.P.R., 1429–36*, 253 (for north Wales).
[12] P.R.O. Exchequer, T.R. Council and Privy Seal, 47/40; 68/47; 73/2; 78/53. Leases of mills and woods, advowry fines in north Wales, and the income from the ferries between Anglesey and the mainland, were also part of the royal patronage: *C.P.R., 1422–9*, 48; ibid. *1436–41*, 63, 117; P.R.O. Min. Acc. 1305/5 m. 1.
[13] *Rot. Parl.* (6 vols., 1767), iv. 90–1; *C.P.R., 1413–16*, 380, 405; ibid *1436–41*, 50, 69.

Finally, the king had substantial sums of cash at his disposal once the expenses of Welsh government had been met. In 1433 the treasurer of England estimated them at £470. 5s. 4½d. in south Wales (in addition to £212. 13s. 4d. already spent on annuities) and £590. 18s. 4d. in the north. This was no wild—if a pessimistic—guess: at the end of the year 1435–6, £664. 6s. 11½d. (in addition to £376. 7s. 2½d. paid to annuitants) remained in south Wales and for the eighteen months up to Michaelmas 1438 £912 in the north. During Henry VI's minority a good deal of this cash was expended on annuities, sometimes in Wales itself, like the 5 marks from Bala which Thomas Sandeway, Prince Henry's servant, received for life in 1411. The payment of other annuities at Westminster was anticipated by bills of assignment when the chamberlains were thought to have money available. Richard Beauchamp, earl of Warwick, had assignments on south Wales worth £837. 7s. 3½d. in the summer of 1437 alone, though by April 1440 only £140 had been honoured.[14]

These grants of offices, lands, and cash brought the principality within the Court-centred scheme of patronage. Just and efficient government might be eroded if this patronage were dominated by courtly motives. The limitations on Lancastrian patronage were hardly likely to maintain a balance between the desire to reward and the obligation to govern. The grant of Merioneth to Henry V's widow between 1422 and 1437 merely restricted the extent of her son's patronage. The conferment of the entire principality on Prince Edward in 1457 placed all offices, estates, and pensions at the disposal of his Council. More fundamental were the limitations imposed by the Glyndŵr revolt, whose legacy of suspicion led to the careful control of patronage in the English interest. Responding to the Commons' petition, parliament in 1401–2 ordained that no Welshman should be appointed to office in Wales in his own right or as a deputy; even when the king exempted bishops and 'bons et loialx liges', this statute (extended to include Englishmen married to a relative of Glyndŵr or an active rebel, and upheld in 1410) was a major restriction on royal patronage. Sir Ralph Botiller was reminded in 1436 that his deputies as constable of Conway castle should be Englishmen.[15] More striking is the way in which Edmund Beaufort used this legislation to victimize Sir John Scudamore, the husband of Glyndŵr's daughter Alice; after a generation of loyal service in south Wales and elsewhere, in 1433 he was deprived of office for reasons far removed from the legislators' purpose.

The Crown's disposal of property was also curtailed by statute. After 1401 no Welshman should purchase land in the English boroughs in Wales or have burgages and liberties there; in the following year this was even applied to English burgesses who had married Welsh. It was presumably under this enactment that Madog ap Llygaid duon ('the black-eyed') was deprived in 1407 of ten acres given him in the franchise of Beaumaris. Parliament's concern for security produced the further declaration that castles, defensible buildings, and walled towns should be in non-

---

[14] *C.P.R., 1422–9*, 49; *P.P.C.* v. 32–3; P.R.O. Exchequer, E.R. Receipt Roll, 752.
[15] *Rot. Parl.* iii. 457, 509, 624; *Statutes of the Realm* (henceforward *S.R.*) (11 vols., Record Commission, 1810–28), ii. 141; *C.P.R., 1399–1401*, 469; *P.P.C.* i. 148–50; *C.P.R., 1429–36*, 590.

Welsh hands (bishops and lords only being excepted).[16] These statutory restraints on patronage profoundly affected for a time relations between government and governed, the opportunities open to Welshmen, and the effectiveness of local government in fifteenth-century Wales. Their severity was tempered in practice by a blind eye or by letters of denizenship, but their existence made the discharge of the king's responsibilities as patron even more complex than they already were.

Bribes and *douceurs*, inducements and importunings—all played a part in fifteenth-century patronage. By their nature they were commonly offered on the backstairs or by word of mouth, and are rarely documented. Men frequently and openly petitioned the king (or the king and Council) for a specific reward for services rendered, as did John Claiton, a page of Henry VI's cellar, in 1445. Some requests did not elicit quite the response the petitioner anticipated, which may explain why John Hampton was appointed sheriff of Merioneth in 1433 'until he be provided with some other office not requiring personal residence'.[17] But more sinister was the intrusion of a person confident of royal patronage into a life-grant enjoyed preferably by an older man, whose expected early demise would put the office or gift at the survivor's disposal. This was probably why Roger Norreys was associated with Rhys ap Thomas ap Dafydd, an active figure from about 1390, in the stewardships of Cardiganshire and Cantrefmawr in 1438; but patron and client had not bargained with Rhys himself, who was still alive at 'a great age' in 1446. Other grants in survivorship were willingly approved by the incumbent—even perhaps made at his suggestion. In December 1443 the earl of Suffolk took the unusual step of formally associating with him Sir Thomas Stanley, his colleague in the king's Household, as justiciar of north Wales and Chester. It was a device that also made possible the continuance of an office in the same family: John Stanley, the king's esquire, surrendered the constableship of Caernarvon castle in 1441 so that he and his son could be installed in survivorship. One can only speculate at the pressure which James Grisacre, yeoman of the Chamber, brought to bear on two other Household servants in 1435 for them to surrender offices in Ardudwy (Merioneth) which he promptly occupied. Equally concealed are Sir John Bolde's thoughts as he gave his consent to the surrender of the constableship of Conway castle in 1436 so that Sir Ralph Botiller could have it. Such pressures may have been most compelling in the king's Household itself, for it is striking that Suffolk, Henry VI's favourite and justiciar of north Wales, was steward of the Household when several Household servants secured Crown patronage in Wales by successful petition or mutual agreement. Confusion may have been one corollary, for John Water, a Chamber groom, acquired several minor Caernarvonshire offices in 1438 'provided always that the said offices are not already granted'.[18] Another was the needless dissipation of the Crown's financial resources, which was later corrected by

---

[16] *Rot. Parl.* iii. 476, 508–9; *S.R.* ii. 129, 140–1; P.R.O. Min. Acc. 1152/9 m. 8; *C.C.R., 1399–1402*, 328.
[17] P.R.O. Exchequer, T.R., Council and Privy Seal, 75/52; *C.P.R., 1429–36*, 266.
[18] Ibid., *1436–41*, 194. For the Council's concern for this and similar inefficiencies by about 1444, see Chrimes and Brown, op. cit., 277–9.

the insertion in patents of a clause that enabled a higher bidder to secure the grant. As offices, lands, and pensions were disposed of by such leverage hundreds of miles away at Westminster or Eltham, considerations of ability, experience, and merit were in danger of being shouldered aside.

Henry V's policy in Wales was statesmanlike and his patronage carefully considered. His father interfered incessantly during the early years of the Glyndŵr revolt, but by 1405 young Henry was making his own appointments and saw no need to change them in 1413. Continuity of government under Henry as prince and king was natural. The military crisis still cast its shadow over the highest offices: Edward, duke of York, justiciar of south Wales since 1407, and Gilbert, Lord Talbot, northern justiciar since September 1406, were successful soldier-magnates with estates in or near Wales. But by 1416 the king was laying greater stress on order and reconciliation, and in the south he turned to the Devon lawyer, Robert Hill, to deal with the post-war tangle of accusations, dispossessions, and treasons. In June 1421 he was replaced by one of Henry's most dependable administrators, John Merbury, a self-made Herefordshire esquire who was deputy-justiciar in 1411–13 and chamberlain from 1400. The financial recovery achieved by Merbury and William Botiller, his successor as chamberlain in 1421, owed much to their experience and lack of preoccupation elsewhere. Thomas Walton, a young Cambridge don who was prebendary of St. John's, Chester, from 1410, became chamberlain of north Wales in 1414 and restored the north's finances with equal effect. These men displayed that intense loyalty, efficiency, and dedication that Henry V could inspire. If Henry made a mistake, it was in appointing the resourceful but unprincipled clerk, Thomas Barneby, who was Walton's predecessor, but the speed with which the investigation of his corruption led to dismissal in March 1414 underlines Henry's concern for responsible government.[19] Justiciars and chamberlains such as these attracted equally capable deputies. Three notable lawyers were commissioned—Sir William Hankeford (1413) and John Russell (1413, 1416–17) in the south, Hugh Huls in the north (1413)—but especially were they assisted by loyal, experienced administrators from Wales or the border shires. Men like Sir John St. John from Herefordshire, Thomas Walter of Carmarthen, and Merbury himself acted for Duke Edward, while Thomas Walter and Henry Slack (who doubtless knew Merbury as a fellow Herefordshire gentleman) served as deputy-chamberlain in the south; the Cheshireman, Richard Bolde, was deputy-justiciar of north Wales in 1422. If the king was careful to abide by the legislation of 1401–2, he was wise enough to enlist men who were knowledgeable of Wales and Welshmen.[20]

   19 R. A. Griffiths, 'Wales and the Marches', in *Fifteenth-Century England*, ed. S. B. Chrimes, C. D. Ross, and R. A. Griffiths, Manchester, 1972, 146–7; P.R.O. Min. Acc. 1216/2 m. 5; 1216/3 m. 3; A. B. Emden, *A Biographical Register of the University of Cambridge to 1500*, Cambridge, 1963, 615; R. A. Griffiths, 'The Glyndŵr Rebellion in North Wales through the eyes of an Englishman', *Bulletin Board of Celtic Studies* xxii, part iii, 1967, 151–68. See above pp. 56-7.
   20 P.R.O. Exchequer, E. R., Warrants for Issues, 29/112; Min. Acc. 1153/1 m. 1d; E. Foss, *A Biographical*

As prince, Henry had staffed the most important southern castles with constables from Herefordshire who knew one another and the chamberlain, John Merbury: Sir John Scudamore at Carmarthen, Andrew Lynne and John Burghope at Cardigan, and Richard Oldcastle at Aberystwyth. Of all the English shires, this county had easiest access to west Wales; moreover, part of it lay with Carmarthenshire and Cardiganshire in the diocese of St. David's, and a substantial Welsh-speaking population lived in its attractive vales. Appropriate to a military establishment in the aftermath of fierce rebellion, at least four of these constables were soldiers (Scudamore, Lynne, Burghope, and Sir John Griffith), and two others had military inclinations that took them to France soon after appointment. But above all, they were devoted to the house of Lancaster and especially (since five were already his retainers or servants) to Henry himself. They formed a coterie of tried and trusted soldiers who knew something of Wales and had much else in common.

Such ties were weaker among the northern constables, for the dubious loyalty of Cheshire in the recent past probably restrained Henry from choosing his constables exclusively in this, the nearest recruiting ground. However, four of them hailed from Lancashire, Staffordshire, Cheshire, and Salop,[21] and the same dependence on Henry as his esquires or bachelors is as evident here as in the south: Sir William Newport at Beaumaris and Sir John Bolde at Conway had fought with him in Wales, while he employed John Norreys simultaneously as a transport expert and as constable of Conway castle. The only Welshman appointed was Sir John Griffith, to Aberystwyth in 1422, but his estates in midland and northern England were more important to him than those in Cardiganshire, and his English forebears allowed him to slip past parliament's legislation.[22]

The qualities Henry sought in his sheriffs of north Wales were no different, though their social origins less exalted. Three of Anglesey's sheriffs, Ralph de Barton, Richard atte Wode, and John Walsh, came from Cheshire, the latter brought to the principality by Lord Talbot, whom he had served before; another, Roger Strangeways, lived in Lancashire.[23] Others had seen military service in north Wales, and, like Barton, were vitally concerned in Henry's French enterprises. The trained administrator acquainted with Wales was therefore at a premium, but the personal connection

Dictionary of the Judges of England, 1066–1870, London, 1870, 358. Huls was also from Cheshire: G. Ormerod, *The History of the County Palatine and City of Chester*, 3 vols., London, 1875–82, iii. 464.

[21] J. H. Wylie and W. T. Waugh, *The Reign of Henry the Fifth*, 3 vols., C.U.P., 1914–29, i. 336, 456 n. 4; ii. 308; *C.P.R., 1422–9*, 15, 56; P.R.O. Exchequer, T.R., Council and Privy Seal, 31/91; *C.P.R., 1416–22*, 46; B.M., Add. Ch. 26597 m. 3, 4; *Reports of the Deputy Keeper of the Public Records*, xxxvii, part 2 (1876), 636–7; R. Somerville, *History of the Duchy of Lancaster*, London, 1953, 462.

[22] Griffiths, 'The Glyndŵr Rebellion in North Wales', loc. cit. 157; J. H. Wylie, *History of England under Henry the Fourth*, 4 vols., London, 1884–98, i. 147, 243, 247, 431; ii. 19; iv. 243, 245; *C.P.R., 1399–1401*, 338; ibid. *1413–16*, 160, 413.

[23] P.R.O. Min. Acc. 1305/5 m. 1; 1152/7 m. 8, 9, 10d; *C.C.R., 1405–9*, 253; Ormerod, op. cit. ii. 749; D.K.R. xxxvii, part 2 (1876), 808, 809, 759–60; A. J. Pollard, 'The Family of Talbot, Lords Talbot and Earls of Shrewsbury in the fifteenth century' (unpublished University of Bristol Ph.D. thesis, 1968), 25 n. 1.

with Henry was equally strong: two sheriffs were his esquires, and Hugh Huls, sheriff of Caernarvonshire in 1411–13, was a royal justice.[24] Needless to say, no Welshman could safely be entrusted with a northern shrievalty, but in the south Rhys ap Thomas ap Dafydd, the loyal Cardiganshire esquire, was made denizen and sheriff of Carmarthenshire in 1413—and steward of Cantrefmawr and Cardiganshire soon afterwards. Rhys's experience in government and as a soldier, and his devotion to Henry IV and Henry V place him alongside other royal servants in Wales. The same can be said of Thomas Walter, royal attorney in south Wales in 1411–36, and a deputy-chamberlain and deputy-justiciar; he was an Anglo-Welsh lawyer from the borough of Carmarthen who was proud of his English loyalty.

Henry did not deny the native Welshmen access to his patronage, but common security dictated that only minor offices be offered them. When William Stalworth and John Vernon, yeomen of the Chamber, became woodward of Penllyn and Tal-y-bont (Merioneth) in 1418, they joined a fraternity of commote officers who were almost exclusively Welsh (some of them, indeed, former rebels); if Henry had not been at Bayeux when he issued the appointment, he might not have made this exception.[25]

The king, however, dug deep into his Welsh coffers for annuities for his personal servants. This was less likely to outrage Welsh opinion than if they had mono- polized the influential, archaic, and profitable offices. South Wales supported more annuities than the north, perhaps because its involvement in the revolt was less deep- rooted and its recovery quicker. Even before 1413 Henry had granted £245 worth of annuities there to nine persons, one of whom, Henry's companion-in-arms, Richard Beauchamp, earl of Warwick, received 200 marks. Although he added another six, in 1422 only seven (worth £217 per annum) were still payable. Most annuitants were Henry's personal servants and three (including Warwick) were retained by him for life. It is significant that three were also Herefordshire esquires, who could seek assistance from friends in the administration to collect their cash; Nicholas Merbury, a £20-annuitant since 1408, was the chamberlain's brother. The only Welshman on the list was the ubiquitous Rhys ap Thomas ap Dafydd, whose favours were un- rivalled among Welshmen of his day.[26]

The pattern was similar in north Wales. In 1413 three annuities (worth £23. 6s. 8d.) had already been granted, and King Henry issued a further nine, totalling £152, especially to Household servants and esquires; the largest (£100 from Twrcelyn commote) was received by Sir William Harington, knight of the Garter, Henry's

[24] P.R.O. Exchequer, K.R. Sheriffs' Accounts, 57/28 m. 1; Min. Acc. 1175/10 m. 5; 1203/6 m. 2; E. Breese, *Kalendars of Gwynedd*, London, 1873, 69; *D.K.R.* xxxvii, part 2 (1876), 647; Wylie and Waugh, op. cit. i. 109, n. 4, 456, n. 4; P.R.O. Exchequer, E.R. Warrants for Issues, 39/57; 40/172; *C.P.R.*, 1422–9, 53; Ormerod, op. cit. ii. 749.

[25] *D.K.R.* xli (1880), 700; P.R.O. Min. Acc. 1305/5 m. 1.

[26] R. A. Griffiths, 'Royal Government in the Southern Counties of the Principality of Wales, 1422– 1485' (unpublished University of Bristol Ph.D. thesis, 1962), 385; P.R.O. Min. Acc. 1222/14 m. 5, 6; 1223/5 m. 9; *C.P.R.*, 1413–16, 42, 99, 164; *C.C.R.*, 1405–9, 45; Griffiths, *Principality of Wales*, 132, 249.

standard-bearer and a commander in France. Several others were in recognition of war service in Wales or France, but not one annuitant was a Welshman.[27] Under Henry V there is less evidence of the northern Welsh being willing to collaborate with the government—and therefore attracting royal favour—than those from the south.

At first, the Minority Council did not alter radically the distribution of royal patronage at its temporary disposal. But as the years passed a shift of emphasis occurred which throws light on the relationship between Englishman and Welshman, on the Council and, as the king grew older, on the Household. Henry V's sudden death at an unusually early age after a brief reign left a mere baby to succeed him barely six years after Glyndŵr had disappeared. These facts made the Council cautious, and in the principality it looked to two prominent aristocrats to head the government. Thomas Beaufort, duke of Exeter and justiciar of north Wales from February 1423, was the late king's uncle; he was one of the two dukes on the Council and had taken charge of the baby king. Thomas had had a distinguished military career in Wales and France, and was justiciar of Chester from 1420. The Council chose a younger man for the south, Lord Audley: although his experience was limited, as a marcher lord he had a personal interest in south Wales. These two men represent a return to the type of justiciar appointed by Prince Henry. Exeter's death in December 1426, when the rift between his brother, Bishop Beaufort, and Duke Humphrey of Gloucester was widening, produced a stop-gap appointment in the person of James Strangeways, Henry V's serjeant-at-law and a royal justice who had been deputy-justiciar in 1413–14. When the bishop left England in March 1427, Humphrey took steps which in May secured for himself the justiciarship of north Wales and Chester. Conciliar politics had invaded provincial government by means of royal patronage.

James Audley was encouraged to be a conscientious justiciar by his possession of estates in south Wales. He used a deputy infrequently, and then usually Staffordshire men whom he, as a Staffordshire magnate, would know and trust. William Legh acted for him on several occasions, and when Audley went to France in 1430–1 a panel of lieutenants was formally constituted: Sir Richard Vernon, Thomas Mollesley, and Legh were from Staffordshire; Sir Edward Stradling was chamberlain of south Wales, and Sir John Scudamore was so experienced that he could hardly be excluded. As a group, these deputies were connected with one another, while Vernon and Stradling were associated with the Beauforts; furthermore, Legh, Vernon, Scudamore, and Mollesley served the Stafford family, of whom the earl was married to Bishop Beaufort's 'niece'. One of Gloucester's lieutenants in the north was William

---

[27] *C.P.R., 1422–9*, 49, 57, 61, 88; ibid., *1413–16*, 106, 108, 143, 169, 184; ibid., *1416–22*, 60; ibid., *1436–41*, 163, 482–3; *Rot. Parl.* iv. 184; P.R.O. Min. Acc. 1152/7 m. 3d, 7d; Exchequer, E.R. Warrants for Issues, 22/256; 31/326.

Burley, a Shropshire lawyer who was sufficiently trusted by Humphrey to be nominated by him as deputy-justiciar in north Wales and Chester. For all this suspicion of conciliar connection, these deputy-justiciars were skilled administrators.[28] The remaining lieutenant in south Wales was Dafydd ap Thomas, whose Lancastrian loyalties earned him letters of denizenship in 1427, but who so allowed personal ambition to triumph over loyalty that he was dismissed for partiality in 1436.

Rank and connection appealed just as forcibly to the Council in its choice of chamberlains. The Anglo-Welsh landowner Sir Edward Stradling became chamberlain of south Wales in 1423; if he could justifiably claim that there was 'noo chamberlein there this hundred wyntres that maad bettre levee of moneye due', his marriage to Bishop Beaufort's 'niece' is equally significant. In the north, Richard Walkestede, the Oxfordshire knight appointed chamberlain that same year, had appropriate experience as constable of Beaumaris castle, clerk of the market in Henry V's Household, and as a military administrator in France. If Stradling had the Beauforts' endorsement, Walkestede was likely to receive that of the martial Gloucester and Bedford. Walkestede's successor in 1434, Sir John Radclyff, was from the same mould. A soldier-administrator in Gascony from 1419, Radclyff was of Cheshire origin and served in France under Bedford, who was in England when he was appointed chamberlain.[29] Political sponsorship now ranked with merit as a prerequisite for the chamberlainship.

The choice of deputy-chamberlains, however, continued to respond to the chamberlain's own wishes. Thomas Dawkinson (Walkestede's deputy, and escheator of Caernarvonshire and Merioneth in 1417-8, and sheriff of Merioneth in 1430-2) and John Foxwyst (Radclyff's lieutenant) were Cheshiremen, while Sir Geoffrey de Radclyff was one of Sir John's kinsmen.[30] In breaching the legislation of 1401-2, Sir Edward Stradling stood alone. Although he relied on William Burghill, a Herefordshire gentleman with whom he had served elsewhere and who had been deputy-constable of Cardigan castle, and on the Kidwelly burgess, Thomas Castell, he also employed two Welshmen. One, Gruffydd ap Dafydd ap Thomas, was the son of the denizen whom Henry V had found reliable. The other, Gruffydd ap Nicholas, owed less to his family than to his extraordinary ability and powerful instinct for self-preservation and self-advancement. Thus, although political motives unconnected with Wales were increasingly directing patronage in the principality, the door was

[28] J. S. Roskell, 'William Burley of Broncroft, speaker for the Commons in 1437 and 1445-6', *Trans. Shropshire Archaeological and Natural History Soc.* lvi, 1960, 263-72; B.M., Add. Ch. 26597 m. 4.

[29] R. A. Griffiths, 'The Rise of the Stradlings of St. Donat's', *Morgannwg, Trans. Glamorgan Local History Soc.* vii, 1963, 22-6; *C.P.R., 1416-22*, 65; M. D. Lobel, 'The History of Dean and Chalford', *Oxfordshire Record Soc. Publications*, xvii, 1935, 58-9, 114 and n.; *D.K.R.* xli, 1880, 716, 718, 753; xlii, 1881, 358, 390, 397, 406-7, 425-8, 433, 438, 447, 450; M. G. A. Vale, *English Gascony, 1399-1453*, Oxford, 1970, 86, 96, 97-8, 102, 103, 105, 245-7; Wylie and Waugh, op. cit. iii. 73, 313; *D.K.R.* xxxvii, part 2 (1876), 603-6; P.R.O. Exchequer, E.R., Warrants for Issues, 45/140, 156.

[30] B.M., Add. Ch. 26597 m. 2; P.R.O. Min. Acc. 1216/3 m. 1; 1216/4 m. 6, 9; *D.K.R.* xxxvi (1875), 140; xxxvii, part 2 (1876), pp. 120, 183, 496; Vale, op. cit. 98; P.R.O. Exchequer, K. R. Sheriffs' Accounts, 57/28 m. 1; Breese, op. cit. 69; Ormerod, op. cit. iii. 668.

opening for Welshmen of a new generation to achieve power as lieutenants of the greater officers.

The constraints felt by Henry V in the choice of constables for the royal fortresses still operated after 1422, and none of the experienced soldiers appointed by him was replaced. At Caernarvon Thomas Barneby died in harness in 1427, and so did Sir John Bolde at Conway in 1436; others lasted even longer. However, the Council's two appointments in north Wales are significant. At Caernarvon John Stanley, Henry V's Cheshire esquire, had been sheriff of Anglesey since 1425, and his advancement enhanced the Stanley tradition of service in north Wales and Cheshire. The appointment of the war captain Sir Ralph Botiller to Conway in June 1436 was a striking political nomination without the guarantee of merit which residence or experience in Wales could give; he spent most of his time in the king's company and the need for deputy-constables was acknowledged in his patent—provided they were English.[31] Continuity was equally apparent in the south. Christopher Standish at Dinefwr was the first to be replaced in 1425 by his soldier-son, Sir Roland, one of Bedford's retinue. The lieutenant-constables, too, are predictable. At Cardigan, John Burghope relied on two Herefordshire men with whom he was doubtless acquainted, William Burghill (1426–43) and Hugh Eyton (1428–9); whereas Scudamore at Carmarthen looked to his son-in-law, Gruffydd Dwnn, for assistance. On the other hand, at Dinefwr, where the Standishs were unlikely to attend to their duties in person, two Welshmen nosed their way into positions of authority: in 1428–9 Rhys ap Gwilym ap Philip, a Carmarthenshire gentleman from Kidwelly, and in 1429 the forceful Gruffydd ap Nicholas. The vindictiveness of Henry IV's Parliaments was evaporating even with regard to the royal castles.

More disturbing were the political purposes to which patronage was put towards the end of the minority. Despite Scudamore's record, in August 1433 Edmund Beaufort destroyed his career by recalling that provision of 1402 which made ineligible for office in Wales any Englishman married to a relative of Glyndŵr. He used the statute for partisan motives, for Beaufort was anxious to counter Scudamore's claim to those of Glyndŵr's estates granted to John Beaufort in 1400. Two years later, Edmund succeeded Sir John Griffith as constable of Aberystwyth castle, and south Wales's most important fortresses were thereby placed at the disposal of the Beaufort faction. The northern shrievalties were open to political pressure too. When it needed to replace Henry V's appointees, the Council continued to enlist experienced men of modest fortune preferably near at hand in Cheshire. But John Stanley (sheriff of Anglesey from 1425 and of Merioneth in 1433) and John Hampton of Staffordshire (sheriff in Merioneth from 1433) were also Household men of long standing.[32]

[31] Griffiths, 'The Glyndŵr Rebellion in North Wales', loc. cit. 157, n. 4; P.R.O. Min. Acc. 1216/4 m. 8; 1216/7 m. 5; B. Coward, 'The Stanley Family, *c.* 1385–*c.* 1651: A Study of the Origins, Power and Wealth of a Landowning Family' (unpublished University of Sheffield Ph.D. thesis, 1968); Breese, op. cit. 35; *Complete Peerage*, xii, part i, 419–21.

[32] *D.K.R.* xxxvii, part 2 (1876), 343, 571; Breese, op. cit. 35; J. C. Wedgwood, *History of Parliament, Biographies of Members of the Commons House, 1439–1509*, London, 1936, 415–17, 797–9.

This feature is graphically illustrated lower down the official scale. Whereas Henry V was reluctant to assign the near-sinecure offices to carpet-baggers, the Council began to insinuate Household servants into them. The courtly influence of William, earl of Suffolk, may have been partly responsible, for he was steward of the Household by 1433 and this pattern of patronage persisted until he retired in 1447. Of the eight non-Welshmen to become *rhingyll, amobr* collector, or woodward in north Wales during 1422–36, six were yeomen or grooms of the Household, Thomas Bateman was cofferer of Queen Katherine's household, and another was clerk of the privy seal; almost all had served either Henry IV or Henry V. Furthermore, these grants were concentrated between February 1432 and February 1435, at the beginning of Suffolk's regime as steward. In south Wales Household intrusion into the commote constableships occurred earlier, during Prince Henry's time, but it was never as extensive as in the north.

The Council was at least inhibited from granting life annuities during the minority, and in Wales it did not add to those issued by Henry V. However, it was determined to exploit Wales's income by using bills of assignment to satisfy Exchequer annuitants. Those who, accordingly, collected their annuities from the chamberlains were quite different from those to whom Henry V had granted annuities in Wales. Foremost among members of the royal family who were promised (and were largely paid) large quantities of cash in this way were Margaret, widow of Henry V's brother, Duke Thomas of Lancaster (£1,739), the Queen Dowager Katherine (£1,627), and even Henry IV's widow, Joan of Navarre (£417), who had lived under a cloud for some years after 1419; Gloucester was assigned £910, Bedford £767, and John, earl of Somerset £500. The Council was especially generous after Gloucester's victory over Beaufort in 1426, and again after the duke renewed his attack on the cardinal in 1431. Thus, from the beginning the aristocratic Council looked after its own. In the early 1430s, it also granted profitable offices to Household servants, probably at the prompting of Suffolk in the king's Household, although such men received no life annuities in Wales. After 1433 larger sums even than those assigned to the greater aristocracy were diverted from Wales to the royal Household, where the earl stood ready to supervise their expenditure. 'Where money was so acutely short, political power was used to secure preference for its disbursement . . .'; the same could be said of profitable Welsh offices—and even before Henry VI came of age.[33] Single-faction government was in the making.

Henry VI played an active part in government from the autumn of 1436, though Earl William of Suffolk continued to direct his patronage just as the duke of Bucking-

[33] G. L. Harriss, 'The Finance of the Royal Household, 1437–1460' (unpublished University of Oxford D.Phil. thesis, 1952), 2; Griffiths, 'Royal Government in the Southern Counties', op. cit. 391–6; P.R.O. Exchequer, E.R. Receipt Rolls, 703–48 *passim*. See also B. P. Wolffe, *The Royal Demesne in English History*, London, 1971, 87–8.

ham, as Lord Steward, did that of Charles I. The king's personal intervention did mean that grants hitherto made during pleasure were increasingly conferred for life; even some that pre-dated 1436 became life tenancies and a few were extended to the recipient's heir. This made the king's patronage less flexible and, as farms could not be increased or entry fines imposed, and as entrenched officers were tempted to abuse their position, the Crown was steadily impoverished.[34] Such ill-judged developments had disastrous consequences for government in Wales.

By June 1438 Suffolk had replaced Audley as justiciar of south Wales, and soon afterwards he transferred to the north, where patronage was greater and many of his Household subordinates were already installed. Duke Humphrey moved to Carmarthen as justiciar in February 1440 ostensibly to 'ease the great debates' there. This change was probably the earl's idea; it was unlikely to be Gloucester's, for at that moment he was lambasting Cardinal Beaufort and confessing by the way that he no longer had the king's confidence. The chamberlainships had already been recast. Within the space of a month, Sir Ralph Botiller was appointed to south Wales and Sir William Beauchamp, the king's carver, to the north. When the latter was replaced in 1439 by the controller of the Household, Sir Thomas Stanley, Suffolk's influence increased, and in 1443 he went so far as to associate Stanley with him as joint-justiciar of north Wales and Chester in survivorship—a unique step in fifteenth-century Wales.[35]

This change of gear after 1436 was more marked and more rapid in north Wales than in the south, and signalled a veritable Household invasion. The occasional life grant began to be issued in April 1437; with the formal reappointment of Henry's Council in November this turned into a flood. Minor offices, perquisites, and estates, as well as influential positions, were disposed of: twenty-three of the thirty-seven northern grants recorded on the patent roll between 1436 and 1461 were made during 1437–40; in the south, seventeen out of thirty-two were so recorded. Half of these forty patents were for life. Henry VI in his Household was indubitably affixing the seal—in many cases his signet—and within months of grasping his prerogative, he had given away (often for life) a third of the Welsh offices, in north Wales more than half. Most of these appointments were of Household servants: twenty-seven of the thirty-seven made in north Wales during Henry's mature years, sixteen of them during 1437–9; the comparable figure for the south is at least ten out of thirty-two appointments, eight in 1437–40. All minor officers appointed in the north were Household men, except John Fray, a baron of the Exchequer.[36]

[34] Ibid. 88, 108; P.R.O. Exchequer, T.R., Council and Privy Seal, 58; *C.P.R.*, *1429–36*, 188, 513; ibid., *1436–41*, 20, 50, 78, 171; *Rot. Parl.* v. 366–7.

[35] *English Historical Documents*, vol. v: *1327–1485*, ed. A. R. Myers, London, 1969, 254–6. Stanley also secured, in 1443, the marcher lordships of Mold and Hawarden in fee tail: J. S. Roskell, *The Knights of the Shire for the County Palatine of Lancaster, 1377–1460* (Chetham Soc., new series, xcvi, 1937), 162–72.

[36] P.R.O. Privy Seal Office, Warrants, 1/7/372. For the increased size of the Household itself by 1445, see A. R. Myers, *The Household of Edward IV*, Manchester, 1959, 8–9; and for the disposal of the Crown lands generally, Wolffe, op. cit. 106, 108–10.

Suffolk's acquisition of the northern justiciarship is, therefore, readily explicable: it enabled him after 1440 to extend protection to his Household subordinates there, and in this he was assisted by the Lancashire knight, Sir Thomas Stanley. There was less patronage available in south Wales, where Suffolk encountered Herefordshire men, some of whom were retainers of Duke Richard of York. Moreover, since 1433 Edmund Beaufort had held the two most important castles there, and there was no need to challenge his influence. But when Gloucester died in 1447, the coping-stone was placed on this Household edifice by the nomination as his successor of Sir John Beauchamp of Powick, treasurer of England three years later and steward of the Household after that. A battery of similar appointments to the castle-constableships and shrievalties ensured that by 1450 the northern principality especially was a Household preserve—and with a distinctly Cheshire flavour. Notable were Sir Ralph Botiller, constable of Conway castle until 1461 and Suffolk's successor as steward of the Household, and John Stanley, usher of the Chamber and Sir Thomas's kinsman. John's earlier appointments as constable of Caernarvon castle and sheriff of Anglesey were extended for life in 1437, and he had other positions there besides. The escheatorships were also fair game, and one new escheator, Ralph Legh, a king's esquire from Cheshire and serjeant of the catery, was later on to exploit another office for profit.[37] Equally blatant was the intrusion of Household men into offices rarely occupied by absentee non-specialists in the past. The most unlikely individuals took charge of the king's works and artillery after 1437: grooms of the cellar and pages of the kitchen incongruously became armourers, master carpenters, and masons. Scarcely an influential or profitable office was not reserved for a Household servant at some time during Suffolk's regime as steward, and a few that had long been forgotten were revived to furnish financial reward for a favoured servant. The distinction between effective and archaic offices was gradually blurred—with fatal consequences for Anglo-Welsh relations and royal authority: '. . . yf hit were yt the kyng hade .ij. gode shirreffs a bidyng apon thair offys in Caern'schir' and Anglesey . . .', lamented one clerk![38]

Suffolk's patronage in Wales was unrivalled and the protection he could offer to fellow Household officers was powerful indeed. Yet, when Duke Humphrey castigated Cardinal Beaufort and Archbishop Kemp in 1440 for their monopoly of government, he did not link Suffolk's name with theirs. Indeed, the earl's dominance in the Council seems to have become irresistible only from 1441, when Gloucester's duchess was publicly disgraced. One can readily believe in King Henry's 'ready accessibility and uncontrolled largesse', but the installation of so many personal servants in the principality may reflect more forethought than 'inanity' on the king's

[37] Wedgwood, op. cit. 797–9; P.R.O. Exchequer, T.R. Council and Privy Seal, 72/7; 763/3; *C.F.R., 1430–7*, 314; Breese, op. cit. 35; Min. Acc. 1216/7 m. 9; *The Paston Letters*, ed. J. Gairdner (6 vols. 1904), iii. 142; *D.K.R.* xxxvii, part 2 (1876), 451; Ormerod, op. cit. i. 69; iii. 765.

[38] P.R.O. Exchequer, T.R., Council and Privy Seal, 76/19, 69/68; *D.K.R.* xxxvii, part 2 (1876), 602–3; P.R.O. Exchequer, E.R., Warrants for Issues, 58/104, 110–11; Min. Acc. 1216/7 m. 7.

part. Resumption was the only means of challenging this Household ascendancy, but most Household servants with patronage in Wales successfully petitioned for exemption in 1449–51, and the parliament of 1453 confirmed this.[39] The one instrument capable of restoring the balance between patronage and the needs of government, between those inside and those outside the Household, was seriously blunted. However salutary the effect of resumption on the Crown's finances, it did not fundamentally alter Crown patronage in Wales. Rather was the whole structure jeopardized by Suffolk's fall, for far fewer appointments of this sort were made thereafter. But when Richard of York landed in 1450 the Household servants among the officers of north Wales were still there to bar his path.

During the next ten years patronage in north and south Wales followed divergent courses, partly because Edmund Beaufort, the king's new favourite, retained his strategic power in the south, and partly because the Herefordshire remnant there was linked with the duke of York. The rivalry between these two dukes, each with a foothold in south Wales, enmeshed the patronage of the southern principality in national politics before 1455. When Beaufort was killed, York seized his offices, whereas the latter's men, Sir Walter and Hugh Scull, already occupied Cardigan castle and the stewardships of Cardigan and Carmarthen. James Ormond, once York's annuitant but by 1455 a devoted royalist, was sheriff of Cardigan and Carmarthen. This projection of national rivalries on to a provincial screen opened the way for Welshmen like Gruffydd ap Nicholas and his sons to win a prominent place in local government and society.

This solvent was absent from the north. After Suffolk's assassination, Sir Thomas Stanley lost the justiciarship and the chamberlainship, and several household men associated with north Wales were named in the Commons' attack on the Court in the winter of 1450. By July 1452, however, Stanley was back in the saddle and stayed there until 1461; having survived the acts of Resumption, Household influence in north Wales re-emerged as strong as ever. So did the Stanley family and its Cheshire connection. Several Household servants were appointed to major and minor office during Somerset's ascendancy, though instructively not one was patronized by Protector York, to whom unwise patronage and resumption were important concerns.

The Stanleys were a serious obstacle to outstanding Welshmen in north Wales acquiring political power in the way that Gruffydd ap Nicholas did in the south. Despite Sir Thomas's place at Court (and he was Henry's chamberlain during 1455–9), his estates in the north-west sustained his interest in Lancashire, Cheshire, the marches, and the principality. His Cheshire kinsman, John Stanley, buttressed his authority in the region. Few Welshmen of the calibre of William ap Gruffydd ap Gwilym (Stanley's deputy-chamberlain by 1453) were able consistently to fill the

---

[39] Wolffe, op. cit. 120, 124, 127–8, 132, n. 30; *Rot. Parl.* v. 186–99, 267–8; P.R.O. Min. Acc. 1216/8; 1217/1; *C.P.R., 1446–52*, 470; Griffiths, *Principality of Wales*, 218, 252, 539; Griffiths, 'Royal Government in the Southern Counties', op. cit. 412–17.

higher posts in the northern principality, whereas Gruffydd ap Nicholas was regularly deputy-justiciar and deputy-chamberlain of south Wales in the 1440s and 1450s.[40]

Lancastrian patronage had a fundamental effect on Welsh society and government, and on relations between Wales and the Crown. In the south its subjection to national considerations made the Welsh indulgent towards a government that allowed them to benefit from the absence of Beaufort, York, and Jasper Tudor, although the mutual political hostilities of these aristocrats undermined public order. In the north (and to some extent in the south) Henry VI and Suffolk employed patronage after the fashion of Richard II to create an exclusive citadel of Household power which would incorporate Cheshire, Lancashire, and, eventually, the queen's midland estates. Sir Thomas Stanley was its focus, with benefit to himself but restricted opportunities for Welshmen. In the process, effective government was paralysed and political stability eroded, especially in Merioneth, as English and Welsh officials were inadequately supervised. Henry VI had none of the perseverance and shrewdness required to provide a remedy. The prince's Council, under Queen Margaret's guidance, exhibited signs of reasserting superior control, but it could hardly have been aware of the fundamental problem when it retained Stanley and Beauchamp of Powick as justiciars and appointed a Household magnate, Lord Dudley, as chamberlain of north Wales in 1459.[41]

In these circumstances, it is remarkable that there was no recurrence of the bloody resentment which similarly insensitive rule had helped to generate in 1400; now Welshmen had sufficient autonomy for them to tolerate a Lancastrian regime which practised little of the judicial and financial oppression of which Richard II was capable. The principality did not itself rebel during the 'Wars of the Roses', and at times Gruffydd ap Nicholas threw his weight behind Henry VI; but Edward IV had great difficulty in subduing the principality after a generation of carelessness and neglect.

[40] J. R. Jones, 'The Development of the Penrhyn Estate up to 1431' (unpublished University of Wales M.A. thesis, 1955), chs. iv, vi; P.R.O. Min. Acc. 1217/2 m. 1.

[41] Ibid. 1217/3 m. 1, 2, 4–7; Griffiths, 'Wales and the Marches', loc. cit. 154–5; *Rot. Parl.* v. 366–7. See above pp. 66-8.

10

William Botiller: A Fifteenth-Century Civil Servant

IN 1405 a young servant of the prince of Wales stepped ashore in the sheltered anchorage below Cardigan castle, from a ship which was bringing urgently needed ordnance for Andrew Lynne, the deputy-constable of the castle. William Botiller, for that was his name, found himself thrust into the exciting atmosphere of nervous tension which gripped the inhabitants and garrison of Cardigan. For the little town was the last English outpost in a county overwhelmed by the enthusiasm of the Welsh under their leader, Owain Glyn Dŵr, and as the ship skirted the South Wales coast, perhaps out of Bristol, a weather-eye had to be kept open for the French fleet, reported to be in those waters after the rebels' alliance with France in July 1404.[1]

The Welsh, with their curious tongue, were no strangers to William, for he had been sent by Prince Henry on two earlier missions into Wales. In the early summer of 1403 he was detailed by his master to report on the garrison of Sir Richard d'Aston, steward of Denbigh, and this was very likely the first important mission that William had undertaken in his whole life.[2] Within a week or two he was off again, in charge of a supply train sent from Shropshire to Harlech and Aberystwyth castles, which were under close siege by the Welsh. He travelled overland on horseback, clambering over the mountains and wending his way through the winding valleys of mid-Wales, until twelve days had passed before he returned to the English border, having lost his horse on the way.[3] Moreover, William was a Gloucester-shire man in the days when there was no doubt about the affinities of nearby Gwent. His home remained in the county throughout his life, at Corse near the northern border, and Welshmen must have been a

[1] Public Record Office, Ministers Accounts 1222/12 m.2; J. E. Lloyd, *Owen Glendower* (Oxford, 1931), pp. 83–5, 91, 101–3.
[2] J. H. Wylie, *History of England under Henry IV*, IV (4 vols., London, 1884–98), pp. 243, 254, n. 4; P.R.O., Exchequer, K.R., Various Accounts, 404/24 f.11r.
[3] Wylie, op. cit., IV, p. 245; P.R.O., Exchequer, K.R., Various Accounts, 404/24 f.12r; Lloyd, op. cit., p. 61. Probably as a clerk of the prince of Wales, William collected £33 6s 8d from the abbot of St Augustine's, Bristol in September 1403 and delivered it to the keeper of Prince Henry's 'secret treasure'. P.R.O., Exchequer, K.R., Various Accounts, 405/1.

familiar sight to him, either trading at the local markets, or sailing down the Severn, or raiding the prosperous farms of the valley.[1]

His family origins, however, are difficult to unravel. Although there is no obvious connection with the Botillers of Sudeley, a statue of Sir Thomas le Boteler (or Botiller) of Sudeley (*d.* 1398) stands in the church at Upton-on-Severn in Worcestershire, a few miles from Corse.[2] John de Sudeley, the last male representative of his line, had died in 1367, leaving as his heir Thomas, the son of his sister and William le Boteler of Wem in north Shropshire. This was apparently the Botelers' earliest connection with Gloucestershire, and when Thomas came of age Sudeley was his.[3] He married his wife, perhaps a daughter of Sir John Beauchamp of Powick, in 1385, and between then and Sir Thomas' death in 1398 his sons were born: John, the eldest, who was dead by 1410; William, who died a knight in 1417; and the long-lived Sir Ralph, who survived until 1473. All, in turn, succeeded their father as lord of Sudeley.[4] The career of William Botiller must be isolated from that of Sir William Botiller of Sudeley (and, for that matter, from that of Sir William Butler of Warrington, Lancashire), although this is to be done rather by intuition than with certainty. The Lancashire Butler, a knight since 1399, died of dysentery at the siege of Harfleur in 1415, whilst Sir William of Sudeley (*d.* 1417) was probably too young in 1403 to be entrusted with vital missions in hostile country.[5] Nevertheless, a connection between the Gloucestershire Botillers and William Botiller, the prince of Wales' minion, seems to be indicated, and the best possibility lies in an illegitimate union, the historian's refuge for uncertain births. Sir Thomas le Boteler, born about 1354, was getting on in years for a mediaeval man when he married in 1385. William, who was still alive in the 1450s, must have been near 20 at least when he set off for Harlech and Aberystwyth in 1403, so that to claim him as the fruit of a youthful indiscretion of Sir Thomas is not entirely beyond belief.[6] As such he would need a greater degree of conscientious enterprise to make his way in the world than was required of the legitimate sons of a landed gentleman. William soon found his niche in the ranks of the administrators of the Crown, and it is hardly

[1] *Calendar of Close Rolls, 1435–41*, p. 132; *Calendar of Patent Rolls, 1436–41*, p. 373; ibid., *1446–52*, p. 14.
[2] *Trans. BGAS*, vii (1882–3), p. 304. I am indebted for the information about Upton-on-Severn to Mr Irvine Gray, Records Officer for Gloucestershire.
[3] G.E.C., *Complete Peerage*, xii (13 vols., London, 1910–40), pt. i, pp. 417–18; W. Dugdale, *The Baronage of England*, i (2 vols., London, 1675–6), p. 596.
[4] *Complete Peerage*, xii, pt. i, pp. 418–19. There may have been another son, Thomas. L. T. Smith (ed.), *The Itinerary of John Leland*, ii (5 vols., London, 1907–10), pp. 54–5.
[5] J. H. Wylie and W. T. Waugh, *The Reign of Henry V*, ii (3 vols., Cambridge, 1914–29), p. 46; *Complete Peerage*, xii, pt. i, p. 419.
[6] For later connections with Sir Ralph Botiller, Lord Sudeley, see below pp. 184, 185.

surprising that the royal marcher lordships in South Wales should claim his services.

His first appointment came on 10 May 1409 as receiver of the lordships of Brecon and Hay, which had been inherited in 1384 from the Bohun lords by Henry, earl of Derby, later to be King Henry IV. Brecon must have been a second home to William, providing a sheet-anchor during those years up to 1424 when he migrated from lordship to lordship in South Wales. He was still in office on 4 June 1412 and about to renew his contact with the Welsh rebels, for he and the steward of Brecon were then commissioned to treat with Owain Glyn Dŵr for the ransom of a local gentleman, David Gam.[1] To date, his record was evidently eminently satisfactory, and full use was made of his services in the duchy of Lancaster. On 24 March 1411 he became receiver of Monmouth and the three associated lordships of Skenfrith, Grosmont and Whitecastle, as well as of the duchy manors in Gloucestershire and Herefordshire; but on 10 April 1413, less than a month after the death of his patron, Henry IV, the appointment was terminated. In the meanwhile, he had probably been among the squires who accompanied the king's son, Duke Thomas of Clarence, on his expedition to France in 1412. Suitably mounted and equipped, and promised 1s 6d a day as his wages, William sailed from Southampton in August, and after an unpleasant few days caused by adverse winds, the troops disembarked in Normandy.[2] His absence from Monmouth may account for his replacement as receiver, a post requiring constant vigilance, although William was back at Brecon before the year was out as porter of the castle for life and, by 16 February 1414, as receiver.[3]

The accession of a new king in no way stunted his career, for it had been in Henry V's service, when he was prince of Wales, that those first perilous journeys to Wales had been made. Thus, when the chamberlain of South Wales, John Merbury, was detailed to raise men-at-arms and archers for the French war in 1415, it was William Botiller who was entrusted in June with £435 to take to Merbury at Hereford for their wages. He had already conveyed gold and silver for some of the 300 men who, under the command of the earl of Arundel, were considered sufficient to defend Wales while the king was away. This was his small contribution towards the campaign that culminated in the great battle of Agincourt on 25 October.[4] During the latter part

[1] R. Somerville, *History of the Duchy of Lancaster*, I (London, 1953), pp. 67–8, 647; T. Rymer (ed.), *Foedera, conventiones, literae. . . .*, VIII (20 vols., London, 1704–35), p. 753. [2] Wylie, op. cit., IV, pp. 73–7.
[3] Somerville, op. cit., pp. 647, 650; P.R.O., Duchy of Lancaster, Miscellaneous Books, 17 f.77ʳ.
[4] P.R.O., Min. Acc. 1222/14 m. 7–8; Exchequer, L.T.R., Memoranda Roll, 198, Brevia retornabilia, michaelmas, m.15d; Wylie and Waugh, op. cit., I, p. 114, n. 2, p. 456 and n. 4; J. E. Lloyd (ed.), *A History of Carmarthenshire*, I (2 vols., Cardiff, 1935–9), pp. 255–6.

of the reign, William retained his old post of receiver of Brecon, combining with it the receiverships of Hay and Cantref Selyf.[1] By this time his talents as an administrator had attracted wider interest, for in March 1415 he was appointed one of the justices to preside at the forthcoming sessions in the lordship of Chepstow, part of the estates of John Mowbray, earl of Nottingham. Although a number of their own councillors were usually nominated to perform such duties, the marcher lords also called upon the services of certain gentlemen of ability who could supplement with their local knowledge the more impersonal and professional experience of the lords' household servants. This was William's task at Chepstow in 1415. Although the sessions lasted only three days, the justices were hard at work before 6 o'clock on the morning of the first day, 6 May.[2]

Just over a year before his death, on 10 June 1421, Henry V transferred this loyal servant from the Welsh estates of his duchy of Lancaster to the southern counties of the principality of Wales, which had been conquered for the Crown by his ancestor, Edward I. William served as chamberlain of Carmarthenshire and Cardiganshire, an office identical with that of the more familiar receiver in the marcher lordships, during the following three years, with his headquarters at Carmarthen castle. There, in a white-washed Exchequer chamber, staffed with its own clerks and housing the bulk of the records of this part of the principality, he presided over the finances of the two counties. Times were calmer now, for the Welsh rebellion had been over in this locality for a dozen years and the royal administration was almost back to normal. Still, hostility and devastation had left their scars, most graphically on the financial accounts of the chamberlain and his subordinates. It was a herculean task for anyone to bring anything more than order to the situation, and it had to wait for William's successor as chamberlain, Sir Edward Stradling of St Donat's castle, to increase the revenue markedly.[3] While he lived in that part of the country, William was employed in neighbouring lordships under the king's control: in October 1421 he sat on a commission into piracy in the lordship of Haverford, and a few months later, in February 1422, performed a similar task in Kidwelly.[4] Meanwhile, when the king surrendered Brecon to the countess of Stafford in May 1421, the nearby

---

[1] Somerville, op. cit., p. 647.
[2] T. B. Pugh, *The Marcher Lordships of South Wales, 1415–1536* (Cardiff, 1963), pp. 8, 10, 49–50, 56, 64. For a similar use of both local and household men at the duke of Buckingham's sessions at Brecon in 1503, ibid., pp. 118, 287–99.
[3] *Calendar of Fine Rolls, 1413–22*, p. 390; Ralph Griffiths, 'The Rise of the Stradlings of St Donat's', *Morgannwg*, VII (1963), p. 23.
[4] *C.P.R., 1416–22*, p. 418; P.R.O., Duchy of Lancaster, Misc. Books, 17 f.244r.

castle and town of Bronllys, the manor of Alexanderston, the lordship of Cantref Selyf and part of that of Pencelli became disputed territory between the parties. William and John Merbury of Herefordshire, as receiver and steward of Brecon, were thereupon granted custody of them on 9 July 1421 for two years; when no settlement materialized this was extended for a further three years in May 1423, although in fact they were both replaced by Sir Edward Stradling on 8 November 1424.[1]

Yet another royal demise, that of Henry V in 1422, had therefore hardly affected William's fortunes, and his appointment as chamberlain of South Wales was renewed by the Council of the infant Henry VI on 30 September 1422.[2] Although his successor was appointed on 4 December 1423, William continued in office until 12 February, and after barely three months' rest he was despatched to the lordship of Monmouth on 27 May. Inevitably by this time, his job was that of receiver, and although it might be objected that the short terms he had hitherto served indicated a doubtful ability or choleric disposition, the government was obviously loath to dispense with his services. He remained at Monmouth until 20 February 1428, and soon after his appointment was rewarded for his faithful service with a life-maintenance in St Peter's abbey, Gloucester, on 16 November 1424.[3] By then too William had been brought more closely into the governing circle of the Crown by becoming a king's serjeant, and he retained this position well into old age.[4]

Shortly afterwards William was recommended to the earl of Warwick, just as he had attracted the attention of the earl of Nottingham in 1415. As a result, by Michaelmas 1425 he had become Warwick's receiver of his lordship of Glamorgan and constable of Cardiff castle, offices he occupied for almost as long as his stay at Brecon. For eleven years, while William passed into middle age, he remained at Cardiff, a headquarters which must have stirred his memories of Carmarthen, where the duties were identical financially, though now he was also constable of the castle, as were all the receivers.[5] During these years, Glamorgan seems to have absorbed a great deal of William's time and energy, for only once is he detected engaged in

---

[1] Somerville, op. cit., pp. 179–82; *C.F.R., 1413–22*, p. 400; N. H. Nicolas (ed.), *Proceedings and Ordinances of the Privy Council of England*, II (7 vols., London, 1834–7), p. 294; *C.F.R., 1422–30*, p. 33; P.R.O., Min. Acc. 1157/5 m.8. At this time Merbury was also William's colleague as justiciar of South Wales, *C.P.R., 1416–22*, p. 368; *C.P.R., 1422–9*, p. 3.

[2] *Proc. P.C.*, III, p. 4; *C.P.R., 1422–9*, p. 3.

[3] P.R.O., Min. Acc. 1223/5 m.6; Somerville, op. cit., p. 650; *C.Cl.R., 1422–9*, p. 194.

[4] Ibid.; *C.P.R., 1446–52*, p. 470; P.R.O., Duchy of Lancaster, Misc. Books, 18 f.141r.

[5] National Library of Wales, Bute Ms. 93/142 m.2; 88/G m.2; G. T. Clark (ed.) *Cartae et alia munimenta . . . de Glamorgancia*, IV (6 vols., Cardiff, 1910), p. 1548; *C.P.R., 1446–52*, p. 14; Pugh, op. cit., p. 289.

extra-mural business. This was in May 1435 when he joined Sir
Edward Stradling and Gruffydd Dwnn on an enquiry in the lordship
of Kidwelly, part of the duchy of Lancaster estates he had served so
ubiquitously in the past.[1]

On his retirement from Glamorgan at Michaelmas 1436, William
returned to the king's service. Finance was still his strong-point and
by 13 July 1437 he was acting as deputy-chamberlain of South Wales
in the absence of Sir Ralph Botiller, who had more pressing duties at
Westminster and who may have left South Wales in all confidence to
William as his half-brother.[2] Even when a new chamberlain, Lord
Audley, was appointed in 1439, he may have seized the opportunity to
retain a well-tried deputy, long versed in the running of the Exchequers
of Carmarthen and Cardigan. At any rate, William Botiller emerges
briefly as deputy-chamberlain again in February and July 1440.
He had by this time acquired a house in Fleet Street, where he could
keep his ear to the winds in that power-house of promotion, London.[3]
It served him well. His suggested half-brother, Sir Ralph Botiller, had
become chief butler of the royal Household in January 1435, and two
years later William was one of his subordinates as yeoman of the
buttery or the 'pycherhous'.[4] On 8 March 1437 he was granted, as a
well-earned reward, the virtually duty-less office of rhaglaw of the
commote of Talybolion in Anglesey with its fees, as well as the profits
of the amobr, paid by tenants when their daughters married.[5] Moreover, he had returned to the receivership of the disputed Breconshire
lands of the duchy of Lancaster by 21 December 1439, when he was
replaced, and on 12 July following William became receiver and
chancellor, financial officer and secretary, of the lordship of Kidwelly.[6]
Already, from 3 July 1437 to 7 February 1438, he had been receiver of
the lordship of Laugharne in Carmarthenshire, while it was temporarily
in the king's hands.[7]

As the fifth decade of the 15th century opened, William had spent
a generation in the service of the Crown, and a good number of years as
an officer of two marcher lords. He was one among the hundreds of

---

[1] P.R.O., Duchy of Lancaster, Misc. Books, 18 f.34ʳ.
[2] *C.Cl.R., 1435–41*, p. 132.
[3] P.R.O., Exchequer, L.T.R., Memoranda Roll, 212, recorda, easter, m.7d; Duchy of Lancaster,
Misc. Books, 18 f.141ʳ.
[4] *Complete Peerage*, XII, pt. i, p. 420; *C.P.R., 1436–41*, pp. 64, 280. The identification of William
Botiller with the Household officer of the same name is based on the statement in 1451 that the latter
had served Henry V and Henry VI for over thirty-five years. Below p. 185.
[5] *C.P.R., 1436–41*, p. 64.
[6] *C.F.R., 1437–45*, p. 123; Somerville, op. cit., p. 642. Stradling was still steward and receiver of
Cantref Selyf at the end of 1428. P.R.O., Min. Acc. 1157/7 m.5.
[7] P.R.O., Min. Acc. 1167/6 m.14.

civil servants who made royal and seignorial government work. Apparently educated and evidently highly-trained, by continuous employment he came near in the middle ages to the modern conception of the working man; if William Botiller did not arrive at his Exchequer at 9 and leave at 5 o'clock, at least he never experienced unemployment. Even at the ripe age of more than 60, not only was he at the head of the administration of Kidwelly, but in July 1444 he was nominated to preside over the sessions at Monmouth and Ogmore.[1] William, it might be thought with confidence, could look forward to a retirement in comfort and rewards in abundance. Yet, life had one last, cruel blow to inflict. He had never been an outstandingly efficient financier, working no miracles with the depleted resources of the Welsh lordships, but he had equally never been outstandingly inefficient or oppressive. He was highly valued by Henry VI and his advisers, for, although he had debts outstanding from the last reign, these were all pardoned and dismissed on 5 July 1437 and again on 8 May 1444.[2] Early in the new year, however, there were complaints about his behaviour as receiver and chancellor of Kidwelly and on 11 March 1445 he was suspended from office. He vainly tried to vindicate himself, pleading for an investigation into his actions, and an inquiry was held in August.[3] In no way had he acted improperly, but William Botiller was never again appointed to office. It is not difficult to imagine the impact on him of dismissal after 50 years spent in public administration; already well past 60, the interests of a lifetime had been shattered. His personal life too was at this time blighted by tragedy. While paying a visit to St Albans in 1445 from lands which William had been granted in Hertfordshire, his wife, Rose, was wrongfully arrested and imprisoned. Although his appeals to the chancellor may have secured her release, she only survived a few more years. By September 1450 she was dead and William sold some of his Hertfordshire lands to a London fishmonger.[4] But the king was not without compassion, nor, one imagines, Sir Ralph Botiller without influence. His life-grant of certain profits and fees from Anglesey was renewed for the last time on 18 August 1451 in return for, so the record goes, 'good service to Henry V and the king by the space of thirty-five years and more and in consideration of his age'.[5]

---

[1] Somerville, op. cit., p. 642.
[2] P.R.O., Exchequer, K.R., Memoranda Roll, 220, brevia directa, easter, m.7d.
[3] Somerville, op. cit., p. 642.
[4] P.R.O., Early Chancery Proceedings, 1/15/250, 13/156; *C.Cl.R.*, *1447–54*, pp. 232–3 (William Botiller, the Household servant).
[5] *C.P.R.*, *1446–52*, p. 470. For Sir Ralph's important place in the government as chief butler (1435–58), king's chamberlain (1441–6), treasurer of England (1443–6) and steward of the Household (1447–57), *Complete Peerage*, XII, pt. i, p. 420; F. M. Powicke and E. B. Fryde (eds.), *Handbook of British Chronology* (London, 1961), pp. 76, 102.

Devoted to the king in life, William was eventually to prove himself loyal unto death. Although now too old for local administrative duties, he was still maintained in the royal Household in November 1454, and when Henry VI set out to hold a Council meeting at Leicester in May 1455, William Botiller went with him.[1] But already the duke of York and his supporters were moving south, intent on confronting the king and his detested adviser, the duke of Somerset. The two forces clashed in the streets of St Albans on 22 May; King Henry received a wound in the neck, and when the fracas ceased William Botiller, well into the evening of his life at more than 70 years of age, lay dead.[2]

---

[1] *Proc. P.C.*, VI, p. 230.

[2] C. A. J. Armstrong, 'Politics and the battle of St Albans, 1455', *Bulletin of the Institute of Historical Research*, XXXIII (1960), p. 71 and n.16. On 11 February 1444, when William was receiver and chancellor of Kidwelly, his son John was leased certain lands in the lordship, and 'John Botyllar of Cors' was alive on 3 March 1455. P.R.O., Duchy of Lancaster, Ministers' Accounts, 574/9077 m.2; *Trans. BGAS*, LXXIII (1954), p. 236.

11

Gruffydd ap Nicholas and the Rise of the House of Dinefwr

AT last a phenomenon of outstanding importance in the history of later mediaeval Wales is receiving its merited attention: the rise of native gentry families. Some of the greater houses of sixteenth and seventeenth century North Wales have recently had their origins probed and examined, among them the Maurices of Clenennau, the Wynns of Gwydir, the Griffiths of Penrhyn, the Glyns of Glynllifon and, above all, the Tudors of Penmynydd.[1] By comparison, the stories of equally successful families in South Wales are still largely untold, partly, it must be admitted, because the surviving materials are much less rich.[2] The emergence of the Herberts of Raglan and the Vaughans of Breconshire dearly needs investigation, and so does that of the Dinefwr family, which produced, in Sir Rhys ap Thomas (d. 1525), the doyen among Henry Tudor's Welsh supporters, and, in Sir Rhys ap Gruffydd (d. 1531), a notable traitor to Henry VIII. For this West Wales house, it is possible to trace in shadowy form some of its later mediaeval representatives, culminating in the towering figure of Gruffydd ap Nicholas.

Gruffydd's was a reputable line, several members of which had already served in the administration of the lordship of Kidwelly. With monumental energy, Lewis Dwnn, the Elizabethan antiquary, constructed the pedigrees of many a Welsh gentry family, and his efforts on behalf of that of Gruffydd ap Nicholas have proved so conscientious and accurate as to earn respect for his statement that the family descended ultimately from Goronwy ab Einion, ancient lord of Iscennen and Kidwelly.[3] Gruffydd's grandfather, Philip ap Elidir Ddu, known to posterity as a knight of the Holy Sepulchre, had been one of the attorneys deputed by Sir Gilbert Talbot in 1362 to deliver Carreg Cennen castle and the commote of Iscennen to John of Gaunt, duke of Lancaster; by 1386 he had entered the duke's service, for in 1386–7 he received £50 from him and 100 marks in the following year, payments which must reflect

[1] T. Jones Pierce (ed.), *Clenennau Letters and Papers* (National Library of Wales Journal, supplement, series IV, part 1, 1947), i. viii–xii; G. Roberts, 'Wynn Family, of Gwydir, Caerns.', in J. E. Lloyd and R. T. Jenkins (eds.), *The Dictionary of Welsh Biography down to 1940* (Oxford, 1959), 1097–8; idem, 'Griffith of Penrhyn (Caerns.)', ibid., 1123–6; idem, 'The Glynnes and the Wynns of Glynllifon', *Transactions of the Caernarvonshire Historical Society*, ix (1948), 25–40; idem, 'Wyrion Eden',

Transactions of the Anglesey Antiquarian Society, *1951*, 34–72.

[2] One exception is the Kemeys family of Wentllwg, whose fortunes in the fifteenth century have been chronicled by T. B. Pugh, *The Marcher Lordships of South Wales, 1415–1536* (Cardiff, 1963), 291–3.

[3] S. R. Meyrick (ed.), *Lewys Dwnn's Heraldic Visitations of Wales* (2 vols., Llandovery, 1846), i. 210.

Philip's retention for an important, possibly military, purpose.[4] Of Gruffydd's father, Nicholas ap Philip, there is little trace, for he may have died quite young, shortly before Gruffydd ap Nicholas was born. He lived at Cryg, 'a simple howse' in the Carmarthenshire parish of Llandeilo, in which Dinefwr castle and the town of Newton were also situated.[5] But the family's settlement there probably dates only from Nicholas' marriage to Jennet, daughter of Gruffydd ap Llywelyn Foethus, an experienced officer in the adjacent commote of Maenordeilo in the mid-fourteenth century.[6] More tangible is the career of Nicholas' brother, Gwilym ap Philip ab Elidir, who sat on an enquiry at Carmarthen into the tenure of the lordship of Llandovery on 6 September 1391, whilst in 1408–9 he collected a general fine in Iscennen.[7] He may even have been the William ap Philip who was receiver of Kidwelly in 1387–8 and again by February 1400.[8]

Gruffydd ap Nicholas himself was conceivably born in the last decade of the fourteenth century, for there is apparently no record of him before the reign of Henry V. Philip, John and David Nicholas of Newton were possibly his brothers; John was perhaps still alive in 1459.[9] Too young himself to have been faced with the dilemma of choosing sides during the Glyn Dŵr revolt, Gruffydd's father was probably already dead when the rebellion burst upon history. But, from what little is known of Uncle Gwilym, it is possible that the family stood among those who opposed the self-styled prince of Wales, or at least quickly deserted him.[10] At first, the activities of Gruffydd ap Nicholas were confined to Kidwelly, where they hardly distinguish him from other young gentlemen-administrators. In 1415 he and his cousin, Rhys ap Gwilym ap Philip, were collecting fines from the sale of escheated lands in Iscennen, and on 12 June 1418 he became forester of Cefngorath in the commote of Carnwyllion.[11] Administrative usefulness was further

[4] *Calendar of Close Rolls, 1360–4*, 418; Public Record Office, Duchy of Lancaster, Rentals and Surveys, 15/1 m.3; /2 m.2. I owe these references to Mr. R. R. Davies.

[5] *Dict. Welsh Biog.*, 313; F. Jones, 'Sir Rhys ap Thomas', *The Transactions of the Carmarthenshire Antiquarian Society and Field Club*, xxix (1939), 30, quoting National Library of Wales MS. 1602 D.f. 205 (circa 1609–30).

[6] For example, Gruffydd was constable of Maenordeilo as early as 1355–6 and, as Gruffydd ap Llywelyn Vaughan, beadle of Maenordeilo as late as 1382–3 (P.R.O., Min. Acc. 1158/6 m. 2d; 1164/7 m.4). His son, Rhys, was beadle of Maenordeilo in 1383–4 and beadle of Catheiniog as late as 1400 (ibid., 1221/15 m.1; 1165/10 m.2).

[7] P.R.O., Chancery, Miscellaneous Inquisitions, 249/8; Min. Acc. 1166/11 m. 13.

[8] P.R.O., Duchy of Lancaster, Rentals and Surveys, 15/2 m.2; R. Somerville, *History of the Duchy of Lancaster* (London, 1953), i. 641.

[9] Philip and John appear in deeds dated at Newton in 1419 and 1420, whilst Goronwy ap David ap Nicholas figures in another drawn up there on 20 June 1467. It is significant that all three documents are still among the archives of Gruffydd's descendant, Lord Dynevor (N.L.W., Dynevor Deeds, 276–7, 279). A John Nicholas lived at Kidwelly in 1458–9 (P.R.O., Duchy of Lancaster, Min. Acc. 574/9082 m.1d).

[10] Above p.188; G. Roberts, 'Wales and England: Antipathy and Sympathy, 1282–1485', *The Welsh History Review*, i (1960–3), 394.

[11] P.R.O., Min. Acc. 1166/11 m.13; Duchy of Lancaster, Miscellaneous Books, 17 f. 55r.

reflected in the increased responsibilities he shouldered soon after Henry VI's accession in 1422. In November 1424 he was appointed bailiff itinerant of Kidwelly and deputy in Carnwyllion to the steward, Sir John Scudamore; on 1 June 1425 he was commissioned to hold the king's sessions at Kidwelly and perhaps elsewhere in the duchy of Lancaster estates in South Wales.[12] It was about this time that Gruffydd ventured across the Tywi into the royal county of Carmarthenshire and the ancestral home of his mother's family, for in 1425 he became approver of the royal demesnes at Dinefwr and, a year later, sheriff of the county. Thenceforward, administrative authority came thick and fast, although Gruffydd was never employed in the commotes where he was a tenant. In September 1429 he secured the escheatorship of Carmarthenshire for three years, and in 1428-9 deputised for Rowland Standissh, the Lancashire gentleman who was constable of Dinefwr castle.[13] He was associated in this last with his cousin Rhys, Uncle Gwilym's son, who followed in Gruffydd's footsteps in these years.[14]

Hand in hand with expanding administrative authority went a material position which yearly grew stronger. In Kidwelly a number of leases of land and profits came his way: at the end of 1416 Gruffydd secured the agistment profits from a park near the hamlet of Maerdref, close to Carreg Cennen castle, and from 1424 he leased certain demesnes at Llanelly.[15] The demesne hamlet of Maerdref was granted to him in its entirety in 1429 for the next twelve years, but his crowning achievement was the trust placed in him by the king and Sir John Scudamore, steward of Kidwelly, who in February 1433 made him his deputy with power to appoint local officials. He virtually monopolised the chief offices of the lordship, except that of receiver, for on the same day he became sheriff and bailiff itinerant.[16] In Carmarthenshire his future seemed equally assured, for in May 1429 he was described as a free tenant of Maenordeilo and Catheiniog as well as of the town of Dryslwyn.[17] In 1435-6 he acquired five acres at the demesne manor of Llan-llwch, near Carmarthen, and was evidently sufficiently influential to be granted

---

[12] P.R.O., Duchy of Lancaster, Misc. Books, 18 f. 259r, 198v.

[13] P.R.O., Exchequer, L.T.R., Foreign Enrolled Accounts, 64 F. 8 Henry VI G.; Min. Acc. 1288/2; 1167/2 m.4; /3 m.4d; /4 m.4d. Standissh was constable from 6 December 1425 to 7 June 1438. ibid., 1223/8 m.4; *Calendar of the Patent Rolls, 1436-41*, 177.

[14] Although he lived in the commote of Perfedd, part of the lordship of Llandovery, Rhys seems to have migrated from Iscennen, possibly after February 1419, when the receiver and steward of Kidwelly were ordered to seize his possessions after the murder of Ieuan ap Gruffydd Moel, beadle of Iscennen. In 1424-5 he appears as

the farmer of Newton, but in November 1427 he could still become the royal attorney at Kidwelly. P.R.O., Min. Acc. 1168/3 m.10; 1167/1 m.7d; Duchy of Lancaster, Misc. Books, 17 f. 145r; 18 f. 199v.

[15] P.R.O., Duchy of Lancaster, Min. Acc. 573/9066 m.5, 8.

[16] Somerville, op. cit., 639; P.R.O., Duchy of Lancaster, Min. Acc. 573/9067 m.5d; Misc. Books, 18 f. 14v. He also leased the profits from pannage and the sale of honey and wax in Cefngorath forest for twelve years from Michaelmas 1433. ibid., Min. Acc. 573/9067 m.4.

[17] P.R.O., Min. Acc. 1167/1 m.8.

the marriage of Philip, son and heir of John Clement, lately lord of Penardd and Geneu'r Glyn in Cardiganshire.[18] Although this was soon revoked, Philip's death brought to Gruffydd and Edmund Beaufort, count of Mortain, custody of two-thirds of the Clement lands from 21 January 1437 to 28 February 1439.[19]

No longer a young man, but an experienced and intelligent administrator eager for still greater achievement, Gruffydd ap Nicholas saw the value of patronage in contemporary society. The connection with Edmund Beaufort was a strong one in these years, and in August 1433 Gruffydd was retained as his deputy when the count became steward of Kidwelly.[20] Moreover, with Beaufort's uncle, the cardinal-bishop of Winchester, one of the principal protagonists for supremacy in the king's Council, powerful patronage may have prompted the official acknowledgement of Gruffydd's local influence and administrative ability which came when the government allowed his petition for denizenship, probably on 2 March 1437.[21] Already, in May 1434, the dean and chapter of the New College of Newark, Leicester, whose patron was the queen-dowager, had leased the churches of Llandyfaelog and Pembrey in Kidwelly, with their property, to Gruffydd, John Perot, Richard Newton, a royal sergeant-at-law, and Robert Andrew, another lawyer and royal administrator.[22] In the principality, his greatest success came just as he entered middle-age; on 2 August 1437 he presided over the petty sessions at Carmarthen in place of the justiciar, Lord Audley.[23] Indeed, Gruffydd's growth in official stature could not have been better timed, for at this stage William de la Pole, earl of Suffolk, became justiciar (the early summer of 1438), and first Sir Ralph Botiller (14 March 1437) and then James, Lord Audley (11 February 1438) became chamberlain of South Wales.[24] Until the end of Henry VI's reign, baronial figures monopolised both offices and their continuous absence from South Wales made the use of deputies unavoidable.[25] By making himself

---

[18] ibid., 1167/5 m.8; 1223/10 m.3.

[19] ibid., 1161/8 m.9d. The heir was William, brother of Philip Clement.

[20] Somerville, op. cit., 639.

[21] P.R.O., Ancient Petitions, 130/6464–5; *Rotuli Parliamentorum* (6 vols., Record Commission, 1767), v. 104.

[22] British Museum, Additional MS. 65791. The only known impression of Gruffydd ap Nicholas' seal is appended to this document; it is small, in red wax, and carries what seems to be a helmet surmounted by a standing bird. For Robert Andrew, see J. S. Roskell, *The Commons in the Parliament of 1422* (Manchester, 1954), 147. Llandyfaelog and Pembrey had been granted to Newark by Henry, duke of Lancaster in March 1356, when the hospital was converted into a college. A. H. Thompson, *The History of the Hospital and the New College of the Annunciation of St. Mary in The Newarke, Leicester* (Leicester, 1937), 29–32.

[23] P.R.O., Min. Acc. 1167/6 m. 9d. Audley was justiciar of South Wales from 17 Nov. 1423 until about June 1438. *C.P.R., 1422–9*, 139; N. H. Nicolas (ed.), *Proceedings and Ordinances of the Privy Council of England* (7 vols., Record Commission, 1834–7), iii. 123.

[24] P.R.O., Min. Acc. 1167/8 m.3; /6 m. 1; 1223/10 m. 1; *C.P.R., 1436–41*, 236.

[25] For example, in January 1439 Gruffydd, perhaps as deputy-justiciar, and the acting-chamberlain, William Botiller, held an enquiry at Cardigan into the liability of the abbey of Strata Florida to contribute to a general fine. P.R.O., Exchequer, L.T.R., Memoranda Roll, 204, States and Views of accounts, Michaelmas, m. 14 (2).

indispensable to the government, Gruffydd could almost choose his own reward, and at Michaelmas 1439 he secured the castle, town and demesnes of Dinefwr on an unusually long lease of 60 years, in conjunction with his son, John, and John Perot, possibly his brother-in-law by this time.[26] It was an acquisition of cardinal importance to his family.

Despite the gulf of animosity that separated the Beauforts and Humphrey, duke of Gloucester in the king's counsels, it was the latter's appointment as justiciar in 1440 that was to present Gruffydd ap Nicholas with his greatest opportunities.[27] Towards the end of 1443 he was acting as deputy-chamberlain for Audley and soon afterwards was Gloucester's lieutenant as justiciar.[28] Although Duke Humphrey was more active in South Wales than his predecessor, both he and Audley spent most of their time in England. An efficient and formidable officer was therefore needed to take their place, and in Gruffydd ap Nicholas they found him. He owed his position in the principality ultimately to Humphrey but continued to administer Kidwelly for Edmund Beaufort in the early 1440s.[29] The dependence on, and perhaps affection for, Humphrey was displayed in Gruffydd's presence in the duke's retinue on the fateful journey to the parliament at Bury St. Edmunds in February 1447.

Gloucester arrived at the town on 18 February, having travelled from Devizes in Wiltshire and halting at his manor of Greenwich before the last stage of the journey by way of Lavenham. In a company which one chronicler has estimated at 80, and of whom 42 have been identified, there were at least 26 men from Wales and the marches.[30] Although the rumour that Gloucester was planning rebellion from the safety of Wales was largely a device by Suffolk to strike his enemy entirely from all position of influence, the composition of the retinue would seem to indicate that Gloucester was in Wales when he was summoned to the Bury Parliament. Gruffydd ap Nicholas was prominent among them and was sent to the court of King's Bench when the company was 'arrested, and divided and putte in to the Toure, and in to other strong Castels and places in Inglond'.[31] But the death of Gloucester on 23 February and Gruffydd's despatch to Westminster hardly affected

[26] P.R.O., Min. Acc. 1167/5 m. 8d; /8 m.7; *Dict. Welsh Biog.*, 313.

[27] Gloucester was justiciar from 19 February 1440 until his death in 1447. *C.P.R., 1436–41*, 376.

[28] P.R.O., Min. Acc. 1168/3 m. 10d; /4 m. 1.

[29] Gruffydd was acting for Gloucester and Audley in 1444, 1445 and 1446 (ibid., 1168/4 m. 13–15; /5 m.2; / 6 m.1; 1162/3 m.6; /4 m.6), and for Beaufort in 1441 and 1443 at least (Somerville, op. cit., 639).

[30] J. Gairdner (ed.), *Three Fifteenth-Century*

Chronicles (Camden Series, 1880), 150; J. S. Davies (ed.), *An English Chronicle* (Camden Series, 1856), 116; *C.P.R., 1446–52*, 74; H. Ellis (ed.), *Original Letters illustrative of English History* (second series, London, 1827), i. 108–9; C. L. Kingsford, *English Historical Literature in the Fifteenth Century* (Oxford, 1913), 363–4.

[31] C. L. Kingsford, 'An Historical Collection of the Fifteenth Century', *The English Historical Review*, xxix (1914), 513.

his career, and he was soon back in West Wales to resume his climb
to an unassailable position in the administration. He took the place
of the new justiciar, John, Lord Beauchamp of Powick, at the great
sessions just as he had taken his predecessor's.[32] He even presided over
a meeting of the justiciar's tourn at Carmarthen on 27 February 1449,
and it was probably he who regularly held the petty sessions and county
courts every month at Carmarthen and Cardigan when the records
uninformatively state that the 'locumtenens justiciarii' was present.[33]
By the late 1440s he had virtually supreme control over the government
of the principality in South Wales, accounting in his own name to the
Exchequer for its revenue, implementing the acts of Resumption of
1450–1, holding the highest courts of justice and supervising castle-
building and repairs.[34] He communicated directly with the Council
at Westminster and advised on the issue of commissions to preserve
the peace in Carmarthenshire and Cardiganshire.[35] With Edmund
Beaufort as steward of Kidwelly in these years, Gruffydd's position
must have been hardly less impregnable there. His control over Iscennen
within the lordship was such that he was able to force the inhabitants
'to take justice at Cairmardine and nat at Kidwelly', whilst the king
addressed him as 'right trusty and well beloved friend.'[36]

Meanwhile, Gruffydd's material position grew ever stronger. In
1445, when parliament strongly opposed the granting of Englishmen's
rights to Welshmen, Gruffydd was excepted because of the privilege
of denizenship he had obtained in 1437. Already a burgess of Carmarthen,
in the same year he secured the lease of three mills at the town in
perpetuity, and with Thomas Rede, another burgess, farmed another
on a 40–year lease from 1446.[37] The entire town of Carmarthen was
leased to Gruffydd, Rede and Lewis ap Rhys Gethyn on 6 October
1449 for 20 years at £20 per annum. Potentially more profitable was
the apparently insignificant grant of the profits from forfeitures in
Carmarthenshire made to the trio for 20 years on the same day, for
Gruffydd was already escheator of Carmarthenshire (and therefore
responsible for implementing forfeitures) and was capable of creating
out of this new opportunity a weapon of self-aggrandizement.[38] Gruffydd
also laid hands on the lordship of Narberth when, on 13 May 1449,
Richard, duke of York granted it to him and the bishop of St. David's,

[32] At Carmarthen in 1447, 1449–53 and 1456
(P.R.O., Min Acc. 1306/7 m.1; 1223/11 m.1;
1168/7 m.10, 1d; 1224/1 m.1; 1168/8 m.2); at
Cardigan in 1449–50 and 1452–3 (ibid., 1162/5
m.6; /6 m.6; 1224/1 m.2).

[33] ibid., 1162/5 m.8; 1224/1 m.3.

[34] ibid., 1223/12; 1306/7 m.9; 1224/4 m.8.

[35] ibid., 1306/7 m.9; 1224/4 m.9.

[36] L. T. Smith (ed.), *John Leland's Itinerary in*
Wales (London, 1906), 60; P.R.O., Duchy of
Lancaster, Miscellaneous Books, 18 f. 146r.

[37] P.R.O., Min. Acc. 1168/7 m.1; /8 m.1; /9 m.1;
Rot. Parl., v. 104; above p. 190.

[38] P.R.O., Min. Acc. 1168/8 m.1, 11. Gruffydd
was escheator of Carmarthenshire in 1449–50,
1451–2 and 1454–5 at least. ibid., 1223/11 m.1;
1168/7 m.11; N.L.W., Badminton Manorial
Records, 1561 m.11.

probably as feoffees, whilst on 18 April 1451 he succeeded in intruding himself into an earlier grant of the lordships of Cilgerran, Emlyn Is Cuch and Duffryn Bryan to Gruffydd ap David ap Thomas and William John.[39] With Gruffydd's character and ambition he must soon have dominated the partnership. His dominion even intruded into the ecclesiastical sphere, for the temporalities of the diocese of St. David's were committed to his care by the ever-absent bishop, John de la Bere (1447–60).[40]

In Cardiganshire, too, Gruffydd was not slow to augment his possessions, both in Cardigan itself, where he leased the lands and tenements of John Dyer on 13 October 1441, and also by acquiring two-thirds of the Clement lands once more in July 1443.[41] But far more spectacular and far more steadfastly resisted, was the attempt he made in 1439 to establish his eldest son in a position of influence in the county. Thomas ap Gruffydd was accompanied by a considerable body of men, including Einion ab Iankyn and Gruffydd ap David ap Thomas, the latter a former royal official in Carmarthenshire.[42] Disorder broke out between them and a rival group led by John ap Rhys and Maredudd ab Owain, the latter once a rebel, formerly sheriff and escheator of Cardiganshire and a substantial landowner in four commotes.[43] It is significant that neither of the opposition leaders survived the tussle with Thomas, whereas he and at least one of his supporters, Einion ab Iankyn, reached the peak of their careers after 1439.[44] Maredudd and John appealed to the king's Council, for Gruffydd ap Nicholas was by this time in a position to block all attempts at redress in West Wales itself.[45] As a result, Thomas ap Gruffydd ap Nicholas, his father and his

---

[39] N.L.W., Slebech Papers, 341 (a later copy); *C.P.R., 1446–52*, 234–5; *Calendar of the Fine Rolls, 1445–52*, 183, 197.

[40] E. Yardley, *Menevia Sacra* (Cambrian Archaeological Association, supplementary volume, 1927), ed. F. Green, 74–5; J. A. Giles (ed.), *Incerti Scriptoris Chronicon Angliae . . .* (London, 1848), 35, notices that de la Bere 'nec curam aut patriam curae in vita sua satagit visitare'. Compare G. Williams, *The Welsh Church from Conquest to Reformation* (Cardiff, 1962), 305–6.

[41] P.R.O., Min. Acc. 1161/10 m.6d; 1162/1 m. 11d; Privy Seal Office, 1/18/946. William Clement died on 20 July, leaving his young daughter, Matilda, as the heiress. It is only in 1461 that her husband, John Wogan, is noticed as lord of Penardd and Geneu'r Glyn for the first time. ibid., Min. Acc. 1224/6 m.9.

[42] Gruffydd had been beadle of Caerwedros in 1424–5, of Emlyn Uwch Cuch in 1424–6, of Mabelfyw in 1431–3, of Widigada in 1433–5, of Elfed in 1436–7 and pencais of Widigada and Elfed in 1433–5; Gruffydd ap Nicholas stood surety for him in February 1433 and he

returned the compliment in 1439 and 1441. P.R.O., Min. Acc. 1161/1 m.3d; /10 m.6d; 1166/13 m.7; 1167/6 m.3; /8 m.7; 1223/8 m. 1; /9 m.1, 4; *C.F.R., 1430–7, 135*.

[43] Maredudd had supported Owain Glyn Dŵr and was one of the hostages surrendered from Aberystwyth castle in 1407 at the time of the agreement between the defenders and Prince Henry; he had probably been released by 1409, became bailiff itinerant of Llanbadarn in 1416–8, sheriff of Cardiganshire in 1424, reeve of Geneu'r Glyn and Mefenydd in 1423–5 and escheator of Cardiganshire in 1437–8; in 1429–30 he held 32 messuages and lands in Geneu'r Glyn worth £4; six messuages and lands in Perfedd worth 20s., seven messuages and lands in Creuddyn worth 20s., and 20 messuages and lands in Mefenydd worth 40s. T. Rymer (ed.), *Foedera, conventiones, literae . . .* (10 vols., The Hague, 1745), iv. 120; P.R.O., Min. Acc. 1222/10 m.2; 1160/7 m.4d; 1223/5 m.8; 1161/1 m.1d, 3d; /8 m.9d; /3 m.6.

[44] Thomas was escheator of Cardiganshire from 1428 to 1450, except in 1442–3 (P.R.O., Min. Acc. 1161/8 m.9d; /10 m.7d; 1162/2 m.10;

accomplices were summoned to appear before the Council at Westminster on 14 June 1439. It is doubtful if any of them heeded the order and Gruffydd himself pleaded that 'your besecher was so sike that he might nat wolle ride ne goo'. He even challenged the right of the Crown to summon to London anyone indicted of offences in Carmarthenshire and Cardiganshire, objecting 'that they have a Justice and Chamberleyne and Chauncerie with fulle power for to trie and determine alle manere maters doon there.'[46] Gruffydd, of course, was perfectly willing to appear locally, his illness notwithstanding, for his own influence could be relied upon to remove any embarrassment. The Crown conceded the point; Sir William ap Thomas of Raglan was sent to enquire into the whole business at Carmarthen and Thomas ap Gruffydd ap Nicholas agreed to submit to the justice's ruling.[47] This was in fact playing into the hands of Gruffydd ap Nicholas, who was probably acting as deputy-chamberlain at the time and therefore responsible for taking 'sufficeant suertes for to ansuere atte ye nexte grete Sessions.' The case was postponed until the next sessions, when both sides were required to produce 'suche strangers that both parties broght with hem,' so that the charges might be fully investigated and 'ye right of ye grounde and of ye principalite . . ., be saved.'

In the midst of the confusion of 1439, Einion ab Iankyn (ap Rhys) took advantage of his favourable position and powerful patrons to perpetrate his own act of lawlessness in Cardiganshire. Richard Hore, parson of Llandyssul, claimed that Einion, one of his parishioners, acting on his father's orders, had taken possession of the church, counterfeited the incumbent's seal and thereby obtained revenue amounting to £89. The local officers had already been ordered to arrest him on pain of forfeiting £400, but no action had been taken.[48] On the contrary, the officers had abetted him, for Iankyn ap Rhys had himself been escheator of Cardiganshire in 1424–35, beadle of Gwynionydd Uwch Cerdyn in 1431–4 and would be beadle and reeve of Perfedd in 1441–2; moreover, Thomas ap Gruffydd ap Nicholas, Einion's protector, was obviously winning the battle for supremacy in the county.[49] Both Einion and his father were ordered to appear before the Council, but by July 1440 they had not done so. Although the justiciar of South Wales or his

/3 m.10; /4 m.10; 1306/7 m.6; 1162/6 m.10) and attorney of the reeve of Aberystwyth in 1438–9 (ibid.,1161/8 m.9). Einion became beadle of Mabudryd in 1449–54 and of Gwynionydd Uwch Cerdyn in 1452–3, and escheator of Carmarthenshire in 1452–3 (P.R.O., Min. Acc. 1223/11 m.1; 1224/1 m. 1; N.L.W., Badminton Manorial Records, 1561 m.6). It is hoped to deal with the rift between Gruffydd ap Nicholas and Gruffydd ap David ap Thomas elsewhere. See below, ch. 12.

45 P.R.O., Exchequer, T. R., Council and Privy Seal, 70.

46 ibid.

47 The sessions met on 7 September 1439. P.R.O., Min. Acc. 1167/7 m.1.

48 P.R.O., Exchequer, T.R., Council and Privy Seal, 63/27.

49 ibid., Min. Acc. 1223/6 m.5; 1161/7 m.7; /4 m.5; /6 m.5; 1161/10 m.3. Gruffydd ap Nicholas married Einion's sister. *Dict. Welsh Biog.*, 313.

deputy was then ordered to arrest the son, the real instigator, his father, escaped even this.[50]

There is no indication either of any immediate action being taken against the henchmen of Gruffydd ap Nicholas and his son, but Gruffydd's anonymous biographer tells a story which, though uncorroborated elsewhere and 'sweetened in the relation' by Bishop Andrewes of Winchester (1618–26), is distinctly credible in the light of what is known of Gruffydd and the rapid weakening of royal government in South Wales in the 1440s.[51] It has been attributed to 1441, when Stephen Gruffydd was mayor of Carmarthen, and indeed the only occasion on which Stephen seems to have filled the office of mayor-escheator of the town was 1440–1.[52] As a result of Gruffydd's refusal to put a stop to the general lawlessness of the area—and this may very likely refer to the events of 1439—a commission headed by Sir Robert Whitney was apparently sent to West Wales, Gruffydd himself travelling to Llandovery to meet them.[53] Relations were amicable at this stage, and on the journey to Abermarlais, Newton and Carmarthen, Gruffydd took the opportunity to present his sons to Whitney rather pointedly surrounded by their armed retainers. The inference was inescapable, but nevertheless at Carmarthen the mayor and bailiffs were instructed to assist the commissioners in arresting Gruffydd. Seated at supper the same night, the visitors 'were soe well liquor'd, that for that night they forgott quite the errand they came for', and Owain ap Gruffydd ap Nicholas was able to steal the king's commission. At the shire hall next morning, Gruffydd was attached, whereupon 'he humbly desir'd his lordship to procede against him in a faire and a legall way, and that his commission mought be publicklie read.' Finding it missing, 'Griffith ap Nicholas startes up in a furie, clapping his hatt upon his head, and looking about upon his sonnes and friendes; what says he, have we cozeners and cheaters come hither to abuse the kinge's majesty's power, and to disquiet his true harted subjects? Then turning about to the commissioners, he rappes out a greate oath, and sayes, ere the next day were at an end, he would hang them up all for traytours and impostors'. Whitney included, they were hurried off to prison and were only released on condition that they assumed Gruffydd's 'blew coate, and weare his cognizance' and admit their offences to the king. If true, this was indeed cavalier treatment of the Crown.

---

[50] P.R.O., Privy Seal Office, 1/9/478.

[51] *Cambrian Register*, i (1795), 59–61.

[52] W. Spurrel, *Carmarthen and its neighbourhood* (second edition, Carmarthen, 1879), 112; P.R.O., Min. Acc. 1168/1 m.1d.

[53] The commissioner is given as Lord Whitney. If the episode occurred about 1441, the person intended is probably Sir Robert Whitney, of Whitney in Herefordshire, who died on 12 March 1443. However, Mr. Melville has attributed the story to about 1454, placing Sir Robert's son, Eustace, who was never created a knight, at the head of the commission. H. Melville, *The Ancestry of John Whitney* (New York, 1896), 89–96; Roskell, *Commons in the Parliament of 1422*, 236–7. J. C. Wedgwood, *History of Parliament, Biographies of the Members of the Commons House, 1439–1509* (London, 1936), 943.

Such a humiliation would require a positive show of authority. In July 1442 a powerful commission, headed by Edmund Beaufort and Lord Audley, was appointed to combat a formidable array of offences in West Wales, whilst the propagandists of rebellion, poets relating 'Chronicles at Commortheas and other gaderings, etc., to the motion of the people', were to be arrested.[54] However, when the duke of Gloucester himself came to hold the sessions at Carmarthen in September 1442, he fined Einion ab Iankyn, Thomas' accomplice, a mere £10 for his offences and in later years he was regularly employed as a local official and a useful member of Gruffydd ap Nicholas' party.[55] Gruffydd ap David ap Thomas, on the other hand, seems to have been deserted by his patron and an exceptionally heavy fine of 1000 marks was imposed on him at the Carmarthen and Cardigan sessions.[56] His official career, moreover, was all but ended. Gruffydd failed to provide adequate sureties for the payment of this enormous fine and he was sent to the Fleet prison in London on 20 November 1442.[57] It was thought, however, that Carmarthen was a more suitable place for his confinement and the Council decided on 28 February 1443 that he should return there.[58] They still hesitated to surrender him from their grasp, but by 13 May the Council had been told that Sir William ap Thomas had taken security for the 1000 marks from Gruffydd ap David ap Thomas, and his release was ordered.[59] The next day, the keeper of the Fleet was directed to free him and two days later Gruffydd undertook to surrender himself at Carmarthen castle to be imprisoned until he found the 1000 marks.[60]

At the sessions of 1442 there were an extraordinarily large number of other men fined, who may have been implicated in the disorders of 1439. The fact that Gloucester was willing to forego the usual general fine for dissolving the sessions and instead allow them to run their full course in both counties, may indicate that the situation was critical.[61] In Carmarthenshire, for instance, over 30 people were fined, and although the fines were normally between £3 and £10, a few were very much larger.[62] What is significant in the Cardiganshire sessions, on the other hand, is not so much the number of people fined there, but rather the number of indicted persons who failed to turn up.[63] The sheriff, the officer

[54] *C.P.R., 1441–6*, 106; *Proc. P.C.*, v. 233.

[55] P.R.O., Min. Acc. 1168/3 m.10; above n.44.

[56] P.R.O., Min. Acc. 1168/3 m. 1; 1162/1 m.6.

[57] ibid., 1168/3 m.11; Exchequer, K.R., Memoranda Roll, 226, brevia directa baronibus, easter, m.7d.

[58] *Proc. P.C.*, v. 229.

[59] ibid., 272.

[60] P.R.O., Exchequer, K.R., Memoranda Roll, 226, brevia directa baronibus, easter, m.7d; *C.Cl.R., 1441–7*, 134. But in March 1444 the king was forced to make the entire community of Carmarthenshire and Cardiganshire act as security for the fine. P.R.O., Min. Acc. 1168/4 m.14d, 15.

[61] P.R.O., Min. Acc., 1168/3 m.1; 1162/1 m.6.

[62] Apart from Gruffydd ap David ap Thomas and his brother Rhys was fined 100 marks, Llywelyn ab John ap Gruffydd ap Traharn 50 marks and Owain ab Henry ap Thomas £20. P.R.O., Min. Acc. 1168/3 m. 1, 2d, 5d, 10, 10d, 11, 11d, 12.

[63] ibid., 1162/1 m.6d, 8d, 9, 10, 10d.

responsible for attachments and arrests, was performing his duties at this juncture by deputy, Thomas ap Gruffydd ap Nicholas.[64] Moreover, the constable of Aberystwyth castle, where a number of the already attached felons would be imprisoned awaiting trial, was Edmund Beaufort, another absentee governing by deputy, probably Thomas ap Gruffydd ap Nicholas.[65] In these circumstances, the unusual incidence of cases of suspected criminals failing to turn up at the sessions, and of escapes from custody, takes on a sinister aspect.[66]

The disorders of 1439 and the sessions of 1442 may be seen as a trial of strength between Gruffydd ap Nicholas and his faction on the one hand, and the rest of the official class of South Wales on the other. The success of the former is indicated by the dominance of his family in the 1440s and 1450s, and the achievement was cemented by the marriage of Thomas and Elizabeth, daughter of Sir John Gruffydd, a former constable of Aberystwyth castle and lord of Llangybi, Bettws Bledrws and Llanrhystyd in Cardiganshire, and of Abermarlais and Llansadwrn in Carmarthenshire.[67] If the great sessions under a man like Humphrey of Gloucester could not stem their rise, then the succeeding period, when the royal government had less and less time to devote to the principality and made no effort to replace baronial officials by efficient administrators, could not bring about their fall. The ambitions of the family continued to grow and on 14 March 1443 Gruffydd ap Nicholas and the abbot of Whitland were summoned before the Council 'under feyth et ligeance'.[68] The order was almost certainly connected with the activities of Gruffydd's son, Owain, against whom Maredudd Gogh, bailiff itinerant of Carmarthenshire in 1438–43, had presented 'bills of complaint' to the Council. On the same day, the chamberlain and deputy-justiciar of South Wales were commanded to arrest Owain and detain him in prison during the king's pleasure.[69] With Lord Audley and Gloucester, as chamberlain and justiciar, relying on Gruffydd ap Nicholas to perform their duties for them, this move could be nothing more than setting a father to catch a son who had his full support.

If Thomas was grasping power in Cardiganshire in 1439–42, and Owain causing the government some anxiety in Carmarthenshire in

---

[64] ibid., 1162/1 m.10d.

[65] ibid., 1306/7 m.5 (1447–8); 1224/1 m.5 (1452–3). Although this is somewhat later, Somerset had been constable since 9 December 1435 (*C.P.R., 1429–36*, 498) and there is no reason to doubt that Thomas secured the lieutenantship after 1439–40.

[66] On one occasion Sir James Ormond, the sheriff, and Thomas were even fined a token sum for allowing Gruffydd ap David Moel to escape from Cardigan castle; on another, Thomas was fined for not producing Maredudd ap

David ap Thomas at the Cardigan sessions. P.R.O., Min. Acc. 1162/1 m.10d.

[67] Meyrick, *Dwnn's Visitations*, i. 210; H. S. London, 'The Seal of Sir John Griffith of Wichnor and Burton Agnes', *The Transactions of the East Riding Antiquarian Society*, xxix (1949), 30–1. Sir John had extensive lands in England but came of the most influential family in Cardiganshire.

[68] *Proc. P.C.*, v. 244.

[69] ibid., 244–5.

the mid-1440s, the latter was similarly employed rather later in Pembroke-shire. In the early 1450s he was living at Tenby, sitting in the courts of justice with the mayor and bailiffs.[70] Furthermore, large numbers of armed men from Cardiganshire and Carmarthenshire were invading the county of Pembroke, robbing officials and tenants, capturing others and holding them to ransom 'in contempt of our auctorite and astate roial.'[71] The king directed the chamberlain and the justiciar to make public proclamation at the county courts and petty sessions, forbidding such depredations. It was a very strong command, betraying the government's anxiety over the situation in West Wales, and a sum of £1000 was named if they failed to take action, 'to be leveed of your godes and catells, landes and tenementes to oure use at every tyme that it shal mowe duely be proved that ye shewe your self remisse or negligent.' At Pembroke itself the receiver, John Perot, was instructed to proceed against the mayor and bailiffs of Tenby, who had ignored an earlier order to arrest Owain ap Gruffydd ap Nicholas. The franchises and liberties of the town were to be suspended and its officers appear before the Council. They themselves were once more ordered to attach Owain on pain of forfeiting 'all that ye may forfaite', and on the same day the sheriff of Pembroke was detailed to arrest him and bring him before the king 'in all hast possible'.[72] Apart from the issue of a commission of oyer and terminer in Carmarthenshire and Cardiganshire on 20 May 1451, which studiously excluded Gruffydd ap Nicholas as one of its members even in the guise of deputy-justiciar, no effective action was taken against him and his son.[73] The episode was apparently concluded on 30 September 1452, when Owain and Philip ap Rhys, parson of Carew in Pembrokeshire and probably involved in the disturbances, received pardon for a formidable array of offences which included insurrection and contravention of the statute against liveries.[74]

The factors which made possible the rise of the Dinefwr family would have gone unexploited without the personal qualities of Gruffydd ap Nicholas: a character strong enough to overcome any setback, and a temperament ruthless enough to sweep aside every restraint. He was indebted also to his forebears, who had made themselves respected and indispensable in the administration of Kidwelly and Carmarthenshire. Gruffydd's early experience of public office was within this familiar pattern, despite earlier efforts by English kings, most recently by Henry IV,

[70] P.R.O., Exchequer, T.R., Council and Privy Seal, 82 (15 July 1452).

[71] ibid. (another letter, dated the same day).

[72] P.R.O., Exchequer, T.R., Council and Privy Seal, 82 (two other letters of the same date).

[73] The commissioners were Lord Beauchamp (the justiciar of South Wales), Nicholas Ashton (a royal justice), Thomas fitzHenry (a lawyer) and Thomas Hedford. C.P.R., 1446–52, 446.

[74] C.P.R., 1452–61, 17–18.

to make office-holding the preserve of Englishmen.[75] Official position and influential patronage provided Gruffydd with excellent opportunities to augment his power in West Wales and to establish the control of his family over local government. Economically, too, trends were flowing in favour of such as Gruffydd ap Nicholas. The Black Death and Glyn Dŵr rebellion had quickened the tempo of changes already taking place in Welsh society, presenting opportunities for the wealthy to become wealthier, and for those with small land-holdings to enlarge and consolidate them by methods of escheat and sale which lay outside the old tribal tenurial system of divided inheritance held in trust for the entire kindred. An essentially private process, it is difficult to perceive, but Gruffydd ap Nicholas almost certainly benefited from it. More obvious was the number of leases of royal demesne lands, mills and wardships which he acquired and undoubtedly exploited. It was a process essential to the enterprising gentleman who aspired to a substantial estate in town and country, and provided a material foundation for his political power and the fortunes of better-documented successors in the sixteenth century. Judicious marriages to such as the Dwnns, Perots and Gruffydds were, moreover, a social achievement as well as an economic attraction.[76]

In the duchy of Lancaster and principality counties it was the royal authority which kept the operation of these forces within peaceful bounds. But in the feeble hands of Henry VI, the English monarchy was at its weakest. During his long minority the reflection of conciliar rivalries in the filling of important posts, and the consequent intrusion of baronial figures, left the way open for government by deputy, more often than not a Welshman. Later in the reign, magnate intrigues and approaching civil war were to divert attention elsewhere.[77]

[Royal government and governors in South Wales are fully examined in R.A. Griffiths, *The Principality of Wales in the Later Middle Ages*, vol. I: *South Wales, 1277-1536* (Cardiff, 1972).]

---

[75] *Rot. Parl.*, iii. 457, 508–9.

[76] *Dict. Welsh Biog.*, 313.

[77] It is hoped to deal with Gruffydd ap Nicholas' relations with the Crown during the late-Lancastrian period on another occasion. See below ch. 12.

Gruffydd ap Nicholas and the Fall of
the House of Lancaster

AT Carmarthen on New Year's day 1448, Owain ab Ieuan ap Philip accused Ieuan ap Gruffydd Gogh of felony. No ordinary trial followed, for the deputy-justiciar of South Wales, Gruffydd ap Nicholas, showed an unusual interest in the case. Ieuan's suspicions and Owain's bewilderment were intensified when the former saw his accuser taken into Gruffydd's house and maintained there in unaccustomed comfort for eight weeks, for three days of which he was entertained at Gruffydd's own table. When the day appointed for the settlement of the business arrived, Gruffydd produced white leather jackets and other clothing for them, and his men proceeded to decorate a place chosen for battle in the true style of the medieval joust. In the ensuing fracas Ieuan was slain and Owain's charges, therefore, were apparently justified, for although the procedure of the judicial duel was well-nigh obsolete in fifteenth-century England, recourse to it was still valid. What made the episode a travesty of even antiquated justice was the order by the deputy-justiciar that Owain be promptly beheaded. The head was sold to his friends for £40 and the bill for the preparations, amounting to 24s., was met out of the royal revenue. Gruffydd's contempt for justice, for the Crown, and for human sympathy was boundless, for the spectacle was nothing more than a morbid entertainment at the court of a powerful gentleman.[1] Indeed, Gruffydd ap Nicholas proved to be the most unscrupulous, the most ambitious, and eventually the most powerful of the king's subjects in West Wales, and it was he who for much of the late-Lancastrian period governed the area in the name of King Henry VI.

Born during the last decade of the fourteenth century, during the next fifty years he forged a career unequalled in the history of West Wales during the fifteenth century. Capitalizing on the benefits bestowed by a respected family well versed in the government of Kidwelly and Carmarthenshire, Gruffydd ap Nicholas made himself an indispensable agent of the Crown. Availing himself of the opportunities for material advancement open to royal administrators, he

I am indebted to Mr. T. B. Pugh for several valuable suggestions in the writing of this article.

[1] Public Record Office, Special Collections, Ministers' Accounts, 1306/7, m. 10; W. S. Holdsworth, *A History of English Law* (7th edition, London, 1956), I, 310; W. Blackstone, *Commentaries on the Laws of England* (4 vols., Oxford, 1773), III, 339–41.

also sought the patronage of two great magnates: Edmund Beaufort, count of Mortain and later duke of Somerset, who became steward of the duchy of Lancaster lordship of Kidwelly in 1433; and Humphrey, duke of Gloucester, who was justiciar of the royal counties in South Wales from 1440. The trust they and the Crown reposed in Gruffydd enabled him to create an imposing position for himself, and to defeat any who dared stand in his path. A ruthless giant among his contemporaries, he was a patriarch among his family, for two of his sons, Thomas and Owain, were willing instruments in the extension of his power into Cardiganshire and Pembrokeshire. Cardiganshire in 1439 was the scene of Thomas's challenge to the leaders of local society, and when disorder resulted he and his father refused to travel to Westminster to appear before the king's Council. At this stage, Gruffydd prefaced his defiance with plausible excuses, but when, as a later writer alleges, commissioners were sent to Carmarthen to investigate the situation, they received short shrift. Intimidated by a display of armed retainers, benumbed by judiciously plied liquor and flayed in open court by an indignant Gruffydd, they were arrested and sent back to London humiliated and wearing his livery. The government was hardly more successful with Owain ap Gruffydd ap Nicholas. If complaints about him in Carmarthenshire in 1443 led to his arrest (and this seems unlikely with his father acting as justiciar and chamberlain), his later activities in Pembrokeshire elicited no effective remedy before a full pardon in 1452.[2]

These years, up to about 1450, had shown Gruffydd ap Nicholas to be, if not contemptuous of royal authority, at least indifferent to the outraged reactions his activities provoked. The attitude which he adopted towards the monarchy was determined in the last resort by the degree of interference it exercised with his local prestige and power. If he proved a consistent champion of Henry VI in the days when the duke of York was thought to be fomenting rebellion, it was because he owed everything to the languid administration of Henry's later years.

Even the performance of his duties as a royal officer left much to be desired. Gruffydd's scant consideration for constitutional arrangements was remarked upon by John Leland a century later; Iscennen was 'a mere membre of Kidwelli lordship, but Syr Griffin Nicolas . . . did by poure sumwhat sever them to take justice at Cairmardine

[2] This first phase in Gruffydd ap Nicholas's career has been dealt with by Ralph Griffiths, 'Gruffydd ap Nicholas and the Rise of the House of Dinefwr', *The National Library of Wales Journal*, XIII, no. 3 (1964), 256–68. See above ch. 11.

and nat at Kidwelly'.[3] His disregard for the details of financial administration often produced complaints to the Council. On 12 March 1449, William Alberton, a clerk of the privy seal office, complained 'piteuousely' of his treatment at the deputy-chamberlain's hands; his £5 annuity was four years in arrears and neither he nor his brother in Bristol could persuade Gruffydd to disgorge 'in redy moneye'.[4] Owain Dwnn of Kidwelly, too, had cause to feel aggrieved. On 1 July 1448 he had stood as a pledge for the appearance of Hopkyn ap Rhys ap Hopkyn at the justiciar's tourn in Carmarthen castle on 27 February 1449. Owain, however, was discharged from his obligation, yet when Hopkyn did not appear Gruffydd was quick to detain him. It required a privy seal letter from the Council to obtain his release.[5]

When Gruffydd himself was involved, he could be downright obstructive. On 10 October 1452 the chamberlain, Lord Audley, was ordered to distrain upon the possessions of Gruffydd, Gruffydd ap David ap Thomas, and William ap John for £53 6s. 8d. which they owed as custodians of Cilgerran, Emlyn Is Cuch, and Duffryn Bryan.[6] Unfortunately for the Exchequer, the effective chamberlain was Gruffydd himself, and when the writ was returned it stated that their possessions were together worth only 40s. per annum. The barons were not to be deceived; they dismissed the return as false, and it was testified at the Exchequer that the goods and chattels of the three men in Carmarthenshire and Cardiganshire amounted to at least £40 and their lands to 100 marks more. Audley, a victim of his own deputy, was fined £5, and the barons, after speedy deliberation, decided to accept the 40s.[7] Even this small sum was better than nothing, for it is practically certain that where Gruffydd ap Nicholas was concerned nothing was what they could otherwise expect.

Yet, despite his self-seeking nature, there is no reason to doubt that Gruffydd was concerned to suppress lawlessness in others. In April 1448 he sent special messengers to the duke of Suffolk, at the head of the king's Council, warning him of attacks on the ships of English and Welsh merchants around the coasts of South Wales.[8] Some two years later, in May 1450, Maurice Boule was sent to the king and his Council specifically to assure them of the loyalty of

---

[3] L. T. Smith (ed.), *John Leland's Itinerary in Wales* (London, 1906), p. 60; D. Ll. Thomas, 'Iscennen and Golden Grove', *Transactions of the Honourable Society of Cymmrodorion*, 1940, pp. 116–17.
[4] P.R.O., Exchequer, T.R., Council and Privy Seal, 78/52. The annuity was granted on 10 February 1439, *Calendar of the Patent Rolls, 1436–41*, p. 238.
[5] P.R.O., Privy Seal Office, 1/18/947; Min. Acc. 1162/5 m. 8.
[6] P.R.O., Exchequer, L.T.R., Memoranda Roll, 226, communia, Michaelmas m.13d.
[7] Ibid. m. 3d.
[8] P.R.O., Min. Acc. 1306/7 m. 10.

West Wales; Gruffydd was awaiting the king's instructions and begged that they be sent under his signet so that there should be no mistaking that they were from the king himself.[9] It must have been some comfort to receive these assurances, for Suffolk had recently been impeached and murdered, whilst violence and local disorder were on the increase in several parts of England and were especially directed against the king's ministers.[10] A month later, Gruffydd was again in communication with the king at Kenilworth, asking that a commission of the peace be issued to the justiciar, the chamberlain, Sir John Scudamore, Sir Henry Wogan, and to himself and his son, Thomas. In particular, he again stressed the dangers to the ports and coasts of South Wales, and Gruffydd was given permission to issue the necessary orders under the seal of the Carmarthen Exchequer.[11] The lordships of Pembroke, Haverford, and Gower declined to obey these letters, claiming immunity as part of the Marches, but Gruffydd was swift to reply and a special directive under the great seal was obtained on 7 October 1450.[12] Meanwhile, in August, Richard, duke of York, had landed at Beaumaris and marched towards London. West Wales, through Gruffydd, made an immediate response; in September Gwilym ap John was sent to the king to enquire whether he wanted his subjects to join him immediately in view of York's appearance with an armed force. In a display of touching loyalty, Carmarthenshire, Cardiganshire, and Kidwelly made a grant of 300 marks to the king, and Gruffydd even went so far as to ask if Henry would prefer the cash be delivered to him personally rather than to the Exchequer;[13] to such a degree was the prevailing malady of Lancastrian government, the desperate cash needs of the royal Household, realized in West Wales.[14]

Thus, as quickly as the patronage of Gloucester had been snatched away by death in 1447, Gruffydd had whole-heartedly embraced that of the new justiciar of South Wales, Lord Beauchamp of Powick.[15] He had no qualms about abandoning the opposition to the duke of Suffolk when it had lost all power in West Wales, for a more promising association with the duke himself. He could cast off loyalty as dexterously as a deck-hand does a harbour-line. The spring of this solicitous behaviour towards the Crown, so out of character

[9] Ibid., 1224/4 m. 9.
[10] E. F. Jacob, *The Fifteenth Century, 1399–1485* (Oxford, 1961), pp. 491–8.
[11] P.R.O., Min. Acc. 1224/4 m. 9.
[12] Ibid.; *C.P.R., 1446–52*, p. 432.
[13] P.R.O., Min. Acc. 1224/4 m. 9.
[14] Parliament was showing intense interest in the royal Household and its finances in 1449–51, B. P. Wolffe, 'Acts of Resumption in the Lancastrian Parliaments, 1399–1456', *The English Historical Review*, LXXIII (1958), 596–608.
[15] G.E.C., *The Complete Peerage* (12 vols., London, 1910–59), II, 46–7.

in Gruffydd, may therefore not have lain entirely in a superficial devotion to the Crown. Moreover, in the parliament of 1449 the population of the royal shires and lordships in Wales, including those of the duchy of Lancaster, had complained about the taking of distress where no legitimate cause was shown; 'and in resistens therof ther is grete assembles of pepill, riotes, mayhemmys, and murdres doon and hadde . . .'. Punishment was impossible 'cause wherof the pepill of the seid parties dayly habundeth and encreseth in misgovernaunce'.[16] The petition seems to have been directed against local officials who were increasingly demanding 'cymorthau' or monetary aids from the local population, a practice long forbidden; punishment locally was difficult because of their powerful position. The ruthless exercise of authority by such as Gruffydd ap Nicholas in West Wales may well have prompted these outcries. At first the government was unwilling to take the drastic action against its own officers urged by the petitioners; they had asked that such men be proclaimed felons. However, in the next parliament, meeting later in 1449, the petition was again presented and the king gave way, agreeing to a trial period of five years.[17] This could amount to a serious curtailment of the activities of local governors bent on their own aggrandizement, and it may have induced Gruffydd to adopt an attitude more considerate of the government's feelings.

Yet, his grip did not slacken; indeed, through the agency of his son, Owain, it was extended into Pembrokeshire in the early 1450s.[18] The realization must soon have been forced upon the king and his advisers that reprimands could not but fail whilst the very disturbers of the peace held high office. Even the duke of York, who had granted his lordship of Narberth to Gruffydd ap Nicholas and the bishop of St. David's on 13 May 1449, probably as his feoffees, attempted to circumscribe Gruffydd's authority there on 15 May 1453 by substituting for the bishop a number of gentlemen, headed by two of his servants, Sir Walter Devereux and John Milewater.[19]

[16] *Rotuli Parliamentorum* (6 vols., Record Commission, 1767), V, 154–5.
[17] Ibid., V, 200.
[18] Above, p. 202.
[19] National Library of Wales, Slebech Papers, 341 (a later copy); *C.P.R., 1446–52*, pp. 234–5; ibid., *1452–61*, p. 71; Smith, *Leland's Itinerary*, p. 62. For the connection of Devereux and Milewater with York, see *C.P.R., 1452–61*, pp. 82, 586, 530, 547; J. C. Wedgwood, *History of Parliament, Biographies of the Members of the Commons House, 1439–1509* (London, 1936), pp. 271–2. The original transaction in 1449 appears to have been an outright grant of Narberth to Gruffydd and the bishop of St. David's, but the licence for the latter to transfer his interest to these gentlemen must have been granted at York's instance, even though his influence at this stage was at a low ebb (Jacob, op. cit., pp. 507–8). This would suggest that the grant had been made to Gruffydd and the bishop as feoffees of the duke, and although Gruffydd still regarded himself as lord of Narberth in 1460, the lordship was forfeited by the terms of York's attainder in 1459, which included lands held by feoffees to the use of the duke and his heirs. Below, p. 216; *Rot. Parl.*, V, 349; *C.P.R., 1452–61*, p. 585.

Independent of this move, but no less a blow to Gruffydd's local pre-
eminence, was the revival of the earldom of Pembroke for the king's
half-brother, Jasper Tudor. When the new creation was confirmed
in March 1453, Gruffydd ap Nicholas was compelled to surrender
custody of the lordships of Cilgerran, Emlyn Is Cuch, and Duffryn
Bryan to the new earl.[20] In West Wales these circumstances together
may have appeared as an attempt to muzzle a local politician who
had shown himself hostile to orderly government and, since 1450, to
the duke of York. Nevertheless, on 28 May 1453, Gruffydd was
presiding at the Carmarthenshire and Cardiganshire great sessions.[21]

Within a year, the duke of York, protector and defender of the
realm since 27 March 1454 while the king was incapable of governing
in person, was showing considerable initiative and energy in dealing
with the Percy–Neville and Devon–Bonville disputes in the north
and south-west of England, and his attitude towards West Wales
was hardly less forceful.[22] At this stage, York probably had the
support of the new earl of Pembroke, for, although Jasper's
sympathies had formerly been entirely with the king (and he received
some of the lands of York's attainted chamberlain, Sir William
Oldhall, on 25 March 1453) he may have come to favour the duke's
efforts to reform the government.[23] Therefore, on 25 May 1454, the
Council, including the bishops of Winchester, Ely, Norwich, and
Lincoln, and the duke of Norfolk, the earl of Salisbury, and Lord
Bourgchier, wrote directly to Gruffydd ap Nicholas, his two sons,
Thomas and Owain, and another relative, Rhydderch ap Rhys.[24]
They displayed grave disquiet and 'grete cause of displesir' because
of complaints that all four 'gretely greve oure subgettes and liege
men'. Their plan to re-emphasize the statutes of Henry IV was but
thinly veiled: 'we woll ye call to remebraunce it is youre duete to
confourme you to oure lawes and not be taking upon you the
contrarie therof to wronge oure liege men as it is surmised ye doo,

[20] *Rot. Parl.*, V, 253; *Calendar of the Fine Rolls, 1445–52*, p. 197; *Cambrian Register*, I
(1795), 58; J. M. Lloyd, 'The Rise and Fall of the House of Dinefwr, 1430–1530', University
of Wales (Cardiff), M.A. Thesis (1963), p. 16. Jasper was probably created earl of Pembroke
at the same time as his brother Edmund became earl of Richmond, on 23 November 1452.
H. T. Evans, *Wales and the Wars of the Roses* (Cambridge, 1915), p. 81 n. 4.
[21] P.R.O., Min. Acc. 1224/1 m. 1, 2.
[22] Jacob, op. cit., p. 510; N. H. Nicolas (ed.), *Proceedings and Ordinances of the Privy
Council of England* (7 vols., Record Commission, 1834–37), VI, 178, 189–91, 193–7.
[23] *C.P.R., 1452–61*, pp. 111–12. For his later association with York, see ibid., 143–4
(November 1453); *Proc. P. C.*, VI, 164–5 (December 1453), 167 (March 1454), 171 (April 1454);
J. Gairdner (ed.), *The Paston Letters* (4 vols., London, 1872–75 edition, reprinted 1901), I,
265–6 (January 1454).
[24] Rhydderch was said to be the son of Gruffydd's brother, but the relationship is otherwise unknown. P.R.O., Exchequer, T.R., Council and Privy Seal, 83/63, 64, 37. The Council
took similar action less than two months later, when the earls of Northumberland and
Salisbury were ordered to pacify the feuding Percies and Nevilles. *Proc. P. C.*, VI, 140–3,
147–51, 154–5.

charging you as straitly as we canne that ye in no wise occupie' any offices. Should this command be disregarded, they were ordered to appear before the Council at Westminster only twenty days after the letter had been delivered. The Council, however, had learnt from its experience with Gruffydd and his family in the past, and also wrote to the principal officers of the principality and to the local marcher lords: to Lord Audley, chamberlain of South Wales and lord of Cemaes and Llandovery; Sir John Beauchamp, justiciar of South Wales; the duke of Somerset, constable of Aberystwyth and Carmarthen castles and steward of Kidwelly; Sir Walter Scull, constable of Cardigan and Kidwelly castles and receiver of Kidwelly; the duke of Norfolk, lord of Gower; the bishop of St. David's; and the earl of Wiltshire, lord of Laugharne. 'Undre colour of th' offices that thay occupie undre you ayenst the fourme of a statut of oure aieul King Henry the iiiith', Gruffydd, Thomas, Owain, and Rhydderch had committed a number of crimes. 'As straitly as we can', the king ordered the addressees that 'ye withoute delay or tarieng', discharge them of 'al suche occupacions as thay or any of thaim stande depute unto you ayenst the said statute'. This was the severest action that could be taken, short of despatching an armed force to implement the orders.[25]

The situation was, in fact, absurd, and the efforts of the government at Westminster, in the long run, futile. Although Gruffydd ap Nicholas may have temporarily retired discreetly to the duke of Buckingham's lordship of Brecon in 1454, his control hardly faltered, and Rhydderch continued to enjoy several valuable Crown leases in the following years.[26] On 21 June 1454 both Gruffydd and Thomas ap Gruffydd ap Nicholas were still in power and even acknowledged as deputy-chamberlains of South Wales by the Council.[27] Moreover, their disregard for the law and the impartial administration of justice, continued unabated. According to his seventeenth-century biographer, it was about this time that Gruffydd

[25] It is of some interest to note that the three lay councillors who signed the directive were supporters of York, and that those to whom the reprimand was addressed were, apart from Norfolk, firm adherents of Henry VI. The document has been wrongly dated to 1453 in the P.R.O. file. Compare *Proc. P. C.*, VI, 181–2, 183–4, 186–8.
[26] A Gruffydd ap Nicholas, esquire, paid a fine in the financial year 1453–54 to obtain the legal protection of the lord of Brecon. Cardiff Free Library, Breconshire MS. 16, m. 7. Rhydderch was probably bailiff itinerant of Cantrefmawr in 1440–42 and assisted at the Cardiganshire great sessions on 26 June 1447; he leased the demesne lands at Gerardston, near Cardigan, in 1450, secured the profits of the constableships of the Cardiganshire commotes with Thomas ap Gruffydd ap Nicholas in the same year, and the Cardiganshire amobr fines from 1452, all of which he still held in 1457–58. P.R.O., Min. Acc. 1168/1 m. 9; /2 m. 9; 1306/7 m. 2; 1162/7 m. 7d, 4d; /8 m. 7d.
[27] P.R.O., Exchequer, T.R., Council and Privy Seal, 84/38. Thomas was also constituted one of the justices to hold the great sessions of Carmarthenshire in Lord Beauchamp's place on 17 July 1454. N.L.W., Badminton Manorial Records, 1561 m. 1, 10.

'did receave, maintaine and comfort' Philip ap Hywel, who had wrought considerable damage in the marcher lordship of Maelienydd. Both were found guilty at Shrewsbury before the justices of the peace, but some months passed before Gruffydd could be apprehended. On a visit to Hereford in August 1454, he was seized with 500 marks in his pocket, but 'while the officers were busie aboute his purse' Gruffydd was rescued by Sir John Scudamore, who had married his daughter, Maud.[28] Meanwhile, in 1452–53 Gruffydd ap Nicholas had spent £63 5*s.* 11*d.* on strengthening Carmarthen castle, the highest sum ever devoted to repairing a single royal building in the southern part of the principality since the Glyn Dŵr rebellion. It was indeed realized that the 'diverse and grete inordinate costes' had been primarily for Gruffydd's own benefit, to buttress his authority in the area and to make more comfortable a royal castle he had probably taken over as a residence. He had also 'purveied and ordeyned diverse ordinaunces as well artillarie as oder', and in June 1454 the royal auditors were instructed not to grant allowance for them without a special warrant.[29]

But Gruffydd had long reached the stage when he could risk the wrath of both protector and Council. The progress of the petitions and orders which flew back and forth between Carmarthen and London in the case of Gruffydd ap David ap Thomas illustrates the power of Gruffydd ap Nicholas on the one hand, and the inability of the central government to control the situation and its own officers on the other. Gruffydd ap David ap Thomas had been among the group of men who had assisted Thomas ap Gruffydd ap Nicholas to establish himself by force of arms in Cardiganshire in 1439; it may be that he was alienated by the failure of his patrons to rescue him in 1442 from the severe punishment that a 1,000 marks' fine involved.[30] His subsequent imprisonment in London and later at Carmarthen may well have turned Gruffydd ap Nicholas into his

---

[28] *Cambrian Register*, I (1795), 61–2. The story purports to be based on two authentic original records which have not been located. The first is described as an indictment laid before William Burley and Thomas Corbet, justices of the peace in Shropshire in the thirty-second year of Henry VI's reign. In fact, both were appointed to a commission of the peace there on 17 December 1453 and 1 March 1454, although the original indictment has not been located (*C.P.R., 1452–61*, pp. 675–6.) The second claimed to be an inquisition taken by Edmund de la Mare, escheator for Herefordshire, in the thirty-third year of the reign. He was indeed escheator there from December 1453 to November 1454 (P.R.O., List of Escheators for England (1932), 60), and his enrolled account reveals that 500 marks were seized from Gruffydd while he was in Hereford on 16 August 1454, because of certain felonies of which he had been indicted earlier in Shropshire (P.R.O., Exchequer, L.T.R., Escheators' Enrolled Accounts, 44, m. 69d). The arrest of a Philip ap Hywel ap Rhys, of Knucklas in the lordship of Maelienydd, was ordered early in 1454. Ibid., King's Bench, Plea Roll, 771, rex m. 23d.

[29] P.R.O., Exchequer, T.R., Council and Privy Seal, 84/38.

[30] Griffiths, *N.L.W. Journal*, XIII, 260–3. See above pp. 193–7.

'mortuell enemy'.[31] Whatever the cause of the estrangement, by July 1454 he and two of his servants were once again in prison at Carmarthen in the hands of Gruffydd ap Nicholas. He begged the Council that the justiciar and chamberlain (studiously omitting reference to their deputy) be ordered, under a bond of 2,000 marks, to free him and 'conducte of your seid oratour and his two servaunts out of tho parties where as the seid Gruffuth ap Nicholas hath any power or reule'. He was prevented from attending the Council himself to parade his grievances and reveal Gruffydd's crimes, but that body, headed by the duke of York and including the duke of Buckingham, the earl of Salisbury, Lord Bourgchier and the bishops of Winchester, Ely, and Lincoln, readily granted his petition on 24 July.[32]

Within a month, Gruffydd ap David ap Thomas was again complaining of the extortions of Gruffydd ap Nicholas, his sons, and Rhydderch ap Rhys by reason of their offices. He accused them of 'maliciously and untruely proposyn to make untrue recordis uppon the said Gruffydd ap David ap Thomas of grete sommes of goode which were his undoyng for ever'.[33] On this occasion, no order was sent to the justiciar and chamberlain, who in any case had long ago severed all effective connection with West Wales. Instead, the Exchequer auditors, William Weldon and William Welwyk, were instructed on 21 August to 'do noon otherwyse upon the saide matier but as right, reason and conscienne axen and requiren'.[34]

Almost a year passed without any further action in the matter. But then, in June 1455, Gruffydd ap David ap Thomas erupted once more with indignation at the forcible confiscation from him, more than a year previously, of certain letters under the privy seal which were intended to afford him redress.[35] Three brothers, Thomas, Rhys, and David ap Morgan (ap David Vaughan), had assaulted him in May 1454, stolen the letters and handed them over to Gruffydd ap Nicholas, who thereupon incarcerated him once more in Carmarthen

[31] P.R.O., Exchequer, T.R., Council and Privy Seal, 85/17. For another possible cause of friction, see Griffiths, *N.L.W. Journal*, XIII, 260. And see above p. 193.

[32] P.R.O., Exchequer, T.R., Council and Privy Seal, 85/17. This Council, of an undoubtedly Yorkist complexion, is strikingly similar to that of May 1454, except that York himself was now present, Norfolk had been replaced by the duke of Buckingham, and Bishop Lyhert of Norwich by the prior of the Hospital of St. John of Jerusalem in England (above, p. 206). Compare the Council members present on 20 July 1454. *Proc. P. C.*, VI, 208–9.

[33] P.R.O., Exchequer, T.R., Council and Privy Seal, 85/80.

[34] Ibid. Weldon and Welwyk were appointed auditors in the principality in South Wales by letters patent dated 2 July 1453. *C.P.R.*, *1452–61*, p. 92. See also T. B. Pugh, *The Marcher Lordships of South Wales, 1415–1536* (Cardiff, 1963), pp. 298–9.

[35] P.R.O., Exchequer, T.R., Council and Privy Seal, 86/6.

castle.[36] It was a symptom of the times that on this occasion Gruffydd ap David ap Thomas claimed that Gruffydd ap Nicholas had threatened him with far worse treatment, calling him a servant of the duke of York. Although this claim must be treated with some reserve, since the petition was addressed to a Council dominated by the duke, it is possible that the antipathy between Gruffydd ap Nicholas and Gruffydd ap David ap Thomas had brought the latter into close connection with York, whose championship of a reformed administration required that he put an end to lawlessness throughout the kingdom, an object thwarted by Gruffydd ap Nicholas in 1454.[37] Alternatively, with the king helpless in York's hands, to associate Gruffydd ap David ap Thomas with the duke may have been a simple ruse by a loyal Gruffydd ap Nicholas to justify the imprisonment of an enemy. The Council was not slow to oblige the prisoner, and on 6 June 1455 required Gruffydd ap Nicholas to free him and allow him to appear before them on 9 July following, 'therto answere to suche thinges as shal than be declared ayenst hym on oure behalf.'[38] Yet the tone of the letter is surprisingly conciliatory in view of the serious charges laid against Gruffydd ap Nicholas. Not only was Gruffydd ap David ap Thomas regarded as the offender who would have to answer to the Council, but the sanctions that ought to have been threatened against Gruffydd ap Nicholas if he failed to take the appropriate action, were absent, and he was merely required 'that ye lieve not this upon the faithe and liegeaunce that ye owe unto us'.[39] The key to the new attitude of York and his circle is to be found in the political situation in England and the changes that attended it in Wales.

When Gruffydd was forced to adopt an attitude to the growing antagonism that developed in the 1450s towards civil war, he was almost consistently a champion of Henry VI, the king whose feeble rule had allowed him so much personal power.[40] Despite the grant to him by the duke of York in May 1449 of the lordship of Narberth,

[36] Thomas had been among those fined at the Carmarthenshire sessions of 1442 and may have been implicated in the affair of 1439 on the side of Thomas ap Gruffydd ap Nicholas and his father (P.R.O., Min. Acc. 1168/3 m. 10). David was beadle of Caio in 1433–37 and bailiff itinerant of Cantrefmawr in 1442–43 (ibid., 1223/9 m. 1; 1167/5 m. 4; /8 m. 4; 1168/3 m. 9); Rhys was beadle of Mallaen in 1437–38 (ibid., 1167/6 m. 3d); Thomas was beadle of Mallaen in 1434–36 and 1443–44 (ibid., 1223/9 m. 1; 1167/5 m. 3d; 1168/4 m. 3d).

[37] P.R.O., Exchequer, T.R., Council and Privy Seal, 86/6. Henry VI was York's prisoner after the battle of St. Albans on 22 May 1455 (Jacob, op. cit., pp. 511–12). There is no other evidence that Gruffydd ap David ap Thomas was ever associated with the duke.

[38] P.R.O., Exchequer, T.R., Council and Privy Seal, 86/7. Gruffydd was apparently not allowed to appear before the Council on the required day. P.R.O., Ancient Petitions, 115/5703.

[39] P.R.O., Exchequer, T.R., Council and Privy Seal, 86/7.

[40] Lewis Glyn Cothi, the Carmarthenshire poet, twice emphasized his loyalty to the Crown. J. Jones and W. Davies, *The Poetical Works of Lewis Glyn Cothi* (Oxford, 1837), pp. 131–7.

twice in 1450 Gruffydd had hastened to assure the king of the loyalty of himself and West Wales, even offering an armed force to confront York, newly returned from Ireland.[41] Again, in 1453, he expressed concern to the Council about certain rumours regarding the estate and dignity of the king, and pledged once more the loyalty of his subjects in West Wales.[42] It was not until 1455, however, that Gruffydd was personally faced with the problem of supporting or opposing the duke of York. On 22 May, Edmund Beaufort, duke of Somerset, was killed at St. Albans, and Henry VI fell into the hands of his enemies. York, Warwick, and Bourgchier seized the highest offices of state, and in West Wales Somerset's place as constable of Aberystwyth and Carmarthen castles and walstottus (or steward) of Widigada and Elfed was quickly taken by the victorious duke himself on 2 June 1455.[43] At Kidwelly he was succeeded as steward of the lordship by Edward, son of Viscount Bourgchier, on 6 June; whereas Scull, another of York's supporters, had been receiver and constable of the castle there since 1445.[44]

By the summer of 1455, therefore, all the royal castles in West Wales were nominally in Yorkist hands. But it would require more than a parchment grant executed at Westminster to change the balance of power in the area. Despite the order of the Yorkist Council on 9 July 1455 to release Gruffydd ap David ap Thomas, he continued to languish in Carmarthen castle. Gruffydd ap Nicholas's control over the countryside was described by him in another petition, this time addressed to the Commons in Parliament in the winter of 1455–56.[45] It was an ideal occasion for the presentation of a petition for redress from one who, rightly or wrongly, was now regarded as the leader of York's faction in West Wales. In the middle of November, the Commons, apprehensive at the increasing disorder of the country, pressed the Lords to recognize York as protector once again, even though the speaker, Sir John Wenlock, was not yet committed to York's side.[46] Gruffydd ap Nicholas was accused of maintaining a reign of terror in 'robbyng, murderyng,

[41] *C.P.R., 1446–52*, pp. 234–5; P.R.O., Min. Acc. 1224/4 m. 9; above, pp. 203-4.
[42] P.R.O., Min. Acc. 1224/1 m. 8.
[43] *C.P.R., 1452–61*, p. 245. Sir Walter Scull, one of York's adherents, still retained Cardigan castle, in name at least. P.R.O., Min. Acc. 1224/2 m. 5.
[44] R. Somerville, *History of the Duchy of Lancaster* (London, 1953), I, 640–2.
[45] P.R.O., Ancient Petitions, 115/5703. The petition is undated, but the only convenient parliament for its presentation is that which met on 9 July 1455 and dissolved on 12 March 1456. Moreover, the reference to action to be taken by the coming 7 January makes it likely that the petition was presented in the second session, lasting from 13 December 1455 to 14 January 1456. F. M. Powicke and E. B. Fryde (eds.), *Handbook of British Chronology* (2nd edition, London, 1961), p. 532.
[46] J. S. Roskell, 'John, Lord Wenlock of Someries', *Bedfordshire Historical Record Society* XXXVIII (1958), 30–2; S. B. Chrimes and A. L. Brown (eds.), *Select Documents of English Constitutional History, 1307–1485* (London, 1961), pp. 305–9.

dispoilyng and distroiyng many of the kynges liege peple in those parties'. Moreover, the castles of Carmarthen, Cardigan, Aberystwyth, Kidwelly, and Carreg Cennen were said to be still in the hands of Gruffydd, his two sons, and Rhydderch ap Rhys, despite the recent change of constables.[47]

Gruffydd ap David ap Thomas felt confident of a sympathetic hearing from such an assembly, and demanded stern measures. If he were not released by 7 January 1456, then his captor should be deprived of all his offices; even if Gruffydd ap Nicholas submitted he should still give a £1,000 recognisance for his future good behaviour. Gruffydd, his sons, and accomplices were also to be ordered to appear before the king, and if they refused to come within three weeks then they should forfeit a further £2,000. The castles of Carmarthen and Aberystwyth, of course, were to be delivered to York or his deputies at once or at the latest by the end of February 1456. An extraordinarily severe sanction, approved by the king, was suggested against whoever attempted to retake the strongholds: he should 'stonde and be attaynted of high treson'.[48] The petition was accepted without modification, and the campaign against Gruffydd ap Nicholas continued.

In the lordship of Kidwelly, Gruffydd, as deputy-steward under the duke of Somerset, had raised soldiers to garrison Carreg Cennen and Kidwelly castles in the months of uncertainty in 1455, but after the Yorkist victory the auditors were warned not to approve the expenditure.[49] Furthermore, York's act of resumption of January and February 1456 was made the occasion to deprive him of the castle and demesnes of Dinefwr and to grant them to Sir William Herbert of Raglan as from Michaelmas 1456 for twenty years.[50] It is doubtful if these operations at a distance had any immediate effect at all on the situation in West Wales, and by the early months of 1456 the king and queen were reasserting themselves in the government.[51] Edmund Tudor, earl of Richmond and half-brother of Henry VI, was in South Wales by May 1456, and on 7 June

---

[47] In 1455 sums were spent by Gruffydd on the repair and garrisoning of Carreg Cennen and Kidwelly castles. J. M. Lewis, *Carreg Cennen Castle* (Ministry of Works, H.M.S.O., 1960), p. 5. In 1454–55 Thomas ap Gruffydd ap Nicholas was evidently in charge of Aberystwyth castle. N.L.W., Badminton Manorial Records, 1561, m. 5.

[48] P.R.O., Ancient Petitions, 115/5703.

[49] P.R.O., Duchy of Lancaster, Min. Acc. 574/9079 m. 3d, 5; /9080 m. 3, 4d; /9082 m. 4d.

[50] P.R.O., Min. Acc. 1168/8 m. 8. Herbert was one of York's tenants in the lordship of Usk and was to be one of Edward IV's closest advisers. G.E.C., *Complete Peerage*, X, 400–1.

[51] The only enduring achievement of York's protectorate was the securing of Calais for the earl of Warwick. G. L. Harriss, 'The Struggle for Calais: an Aspect of the Rivalry between Lancaster and York', *English Historical Review*, LXXV (1960), 30, 40–6.

John Bocking wrote to John Paston that he and 'Griffith Suoh (presumably Gruffydd ap Nicholas) are at werre gretely in Wales'.[52] Despite York's grant, Edmund took over Carmarthen castle and probably acted in Pembrokeshire as the representative of his brother Jasper.[53] In the lordship of Kidwelly the clash between the earl and Gruffydd threatened to disrupt the administration, for in the autumn the bailiffs of the town felt it necessary to send men to escort the duchy of Lancaster auditors with their books over the mountains from Monmouth.[54] It was probably the unwelcome presence of superior authority in the form of Edmund Tudor that roused the hostility of Gruffydd ap Nicholas, whose power had so recently been unchallenged.

The duke of York was determined to resist Edmund and prosecute his rightful claim to the constableships he had been granted. In August 1456 two of his more powerful tenants in the Marches, Sir William Herbert and Sir Walter Devereux, probably acting on his orders, set out for West Wales with a force of 2,000 men drawn mainly from Herefordshire and the adjacent Marches. Carmarthen castle was attacked and taken, and Edmund Tudor made prisoner. Cardigan, already in the hands of a constable sympathetic towards York, Sir Walter Scull of Holt in Worcestershire,[55] was by-passed as the force moved north to take Aberystwyth.[56] The subsequent action of Herbert and Devereux suggests that the justification for the attack was the grant of the castles to York in 1455. For now, in August 1456, they seized the archives in the two strongholds and confiscated the seal of the chamberlain of South Wales. They issued a commission to themselves and to Thomas Mymme of Weobley to hold the great sessions, and this they proceeded to do, despite the fact that already in the previous May Gruffydd ap Nicholas had presided over sessions at Carmarthen.[57] The pseudo-justices were later accused of releasing all who were indicted before them, but their point had been made; they had acted on York's behalf as legal representatives of the government in West Wales.

[52] Gairdner, *Paston Letters*, I, 392. Nevertheless, Gruffydd presided at the Carmarthenshire great sessions on 24 May. P.R.O., Min. Acc. 1168/8 m. 2.

[53] Evans, op. cit., pp. 90–1. Jasper at this time was in attendance on the king; in June 1456 he was at Sheen with 'noo more Lordis'. Gairdner, *Paston Letters*, I, 392.

[54] P.R.O., Duchy of Lancaster, Min. Acc. 574/9080 m. 1 ('tempore perturbacionis et surreccionis populi Wallenci inter comitem Richemond et Griffinum Nicolas').

[55] Wedgwood, *Biographies*, pp. 773–4. Scull had been constable of Cardigan castle since 14 September 1442; he became keeper of the Wardrobe and treasurer of the Household during the period of Yorkist domination in 1460–61.

[56] P.R.O., Ancient Indictments, King's Bench, 35/24 and 71 (two copies). I am grateful to Dr. R. L. Storey for drawing my attention to these documents.

[57] P.R.O., Ancient Indictments, King's Bench, 35/71; Min. Acc. 1168/8 m. 2. Mymme had been associated with Devereux on a commission in December 1453. *C.P.R.*, *1452–61*, p. 166.

In April 1457 the whole episode was reported in an inquisition taken at Hereford, and at the end of the month the king and queen themselves arrived at the town with the duke of Buckingham and the earl of Shrewsbury.[58] It was arranged that Herbert and his confederates should appear before the king and his Council at Leicester, where they would be pardoned in an effort to appease both sides. It was rumoured that many were falsely indicted and that the inhabitants of Hereford feared reprisals from Sir William Herbert 'and hys affinite'.[59] Nevertheless, Herbert and at least twenty-one others were granted their pardon on 7 June 1457, whilst two more had already received theirs in May.[60] It is unlikely that such a lightning attack from the Marches could prove of lasting value to York in West Wales. Indeed, it may have alienated Gruffydd ap Nicholas, who would almost certainly resent a further powerful encroachment upon his preserve, when throughout the summer and early autumn he was forced to suffer Edmund's presence. But it would have been foolish for Gruffydd to oppose himself to both Edmund and York's lieutenants at the same time, especially when all three were threshing about in West Wales. The capture of Edmund at Carmarthen in August, therefore, may have hustled him into making overtures to Sir William Herbert; but if so, they were soon terminated.[61] The expulsion of Gruffydd from Dinefwr and its granting to Herbert as from Michaelmas 1456, as well as the probable release of Edmund Tudor at about the same time, may well have driven Gruffydd to resolve his differences with the king's half-brother, who in any case was removed by death early in November.[62] Moreover, in the early autumn, with the royal government based at Coventry, Queen Margaret had embarked upon a campaign of her own to conciliate the gentry of the Midlands and Marches of Wales. Late in October she was travelling through the border counties, and on 26 October full pardon was granted to Gruffydd ap Nicholas and his sons, Thomas and Owain, for 'all treasons, insurrections, rebellions, misprisions, felonies, contempts and offences' committed before 8 September in the case of Gruffydd and Owain, and before

[58] The inquiry was held on 5 April, and on 1 May the royal party was reported, in a letter to John Paston, to be at Hereford. P.R.O., Ancient Indictments, King's Bench, 35/71 dorse; Gairdner, *Paston Letters*, I, 416–7.

[59] Paston's correspondent enclosed the names of those who were indicted, 'to see and laugh at theyr Wellsh names descended of old pedegris'. Gairdner, *Paston Letters*, I, 417.

[60] *C.P.R., 1452–61*, pp. 353, 357, 360. All but seven of those pardoned were mentioned in the indictment drawn up at Hereford, which incriminated fifty-seven by name and many others anonymously.

[61] Westminster Abbey MS. 5479ˣ dorse. Sir Henry Wogan had written to Herbert, his brother-in-law, 'that Gr. Nicolas might have the gode wille of Sir William Herbert yf he wold . . .'. The document is undated, but it would not seem to be out of place at this juncture. I am grateful to Mr. T. B. Pugh for drawing my attention to it.

[62] Evans, op. cit., p. 92; P.R.O., Min. Acc. 1168/8 m. 8.

29 August in that of Thomas, 'and the convictions and attaints thereof and any consequent outlawries'.[63]

Despite the death of Edmund Tudor at Pembroke in November 1456, York's bid for the support and control of West Wales failed. On 21 April 1457 he is recorded euphemistically as agreeing to surrender the constableships of Aberystwyth, Carmarthen, and Carreg Cennen to Jasper Tudor in return for £40 per annum.[64] Indeed, it was with his brother's removal that Jasper first began to display the interest in Wales which he retained throughout his life, often with unfortunate consequences for himself. Early in 1457 the countess of Richmond and her infant son (later to be King Henry VII) were installed in Pembroke castle, and Jasper himself strengthened Tenby to act as his headquarters in West Wales.[65] The following two years saw an uneasy balance of power maintained by both sides. Queen Margaret and the duke of York were each intriguing for support at home and abroad, while the duke was conceded a certain position in the government, with a predominance in the Council.[66] Gruffydd ap Nicholas and his sons were close associates of Jasper in these years, and on 1 March 1459 Thomas and Owain were appointed with the earl and his father, Owain Tudor, to arrest individuals in West Wales, including servants of John Dwnn, the principal supporter of York in the area.[67] At about the same time, the garrisons of Carreg Cennen and Kidwelly were strengthened on Jasper's orders, after a force of York's retainers, perhaps even led by the duke himself, had descended on the lordship.[68]

Jasper had become the commanding figure in Lancastrian Wales, on whom the king and queen relied for aid in that sector. He was undoubtedly a cornerstone of the Lancastrian position, particularly in West Wales where loyalty to the Crown was strong. The ageing Gruffydd ap Nicholas found himself outshone and outdistanced by the youthful energy and royal confidence enjoyed by Jasper Tudor. Although his sons were to be prominent in the Lancastrian cause, Gruffydd retreated into the background, the patriarchal figure in the evening of his life, reconciled to leaving the organization of the enterprise to younger, firmer hands. There is no definite record of

[63] Evans, op. cit., p. 96; *C.P.R., 1452–61*, p. 326. Thomas enjoyed the profits of the constableships of the Cardiganshire commotes from 1456 to 1461. P.R.O., Min. Acc. 1162/7 m. 1; /9 m. 1d.; /10 m. 1d.

[64] *C.P.R., 1452–61*, p. 340.

[65] Evans, op. cit., p. 96. Jasper had hitherto been a close companion of the king. Ibid., p. 92 and n. 1.

[66] Ibid., pp. 97–102; Jacob, op. cit., pp. 513–14.

[67] *C.P.R., 1452–61*, p. 494; Evans, op. cit., p. 95.

[68] P.R.O., Duchy of Lancaster, Min. Acc. 584/9249 m. 2 ('tempore insurreccionis Ricardi nuper ducis Eboraci et aliorum de comitiva sua').

his death, but it has been shown that the story of his participation and death in the battle of Mortimer's Cross on 2 February 1461 in the ranks of the earl of March, is a 'spurious tale' that 'gained currency in later years'.[69] In fact, Gruffydd ap Nicholas was probably dead when the battle was fought. Mr. H. T. Evans was unable to trace him beyond 1456, and the fact that he was omitted from the commission issued on 1 March 1459, which included his two sons, Owain and Thomas, led him to conclude that he had died in the meantime.[70] However, he was still alive and sufficiently active in 1456–57 to be mayor and escheator of the town of Carmarthen.[71] Indeed, after the death of Lord Audley at Blore Heath on 23 September 1459, his temporary successor as chamberlain, Prior Morgan of Carmarthen priory, was ordered to distrain on Gruffydd's lands for 3s. 4d. owing from the profits of resumption in West Wales in 1449–50. When the writ was returned to the Exchequer on 11 November 1459, Morgan reported that he had taken a horse worth 3s. 4d. from Gruffydd, who was evidently still alive. Moreover, throughout the record of the transaction on the memoranda roll, compiled sometime in 1460, Gruffydd is always referred to as living; the demisory 'nuper' would otherwise surely have been inserted.[72] One of the last acts in a crowded life of which posterity has record, was his grant, as lord of Narberth and Efelffre, of the castle and manor of Narberth and the lordship of Efelffre to his son Owain on 20 February 1460.[73] Gruffydd probably died soon afterwards, whilst his withdrawal from political and official activities can be explained by his age and Jasper's presence.

Gruffydd was three times married. The first marriage, to Mabli, daughter of Maredudd ap Henry Dwnn of Kidwelly and sister of Owain Dwnn, may account for the latter's association with Gruffydd in the retinue accompanying Gloucester to the Bury Parliament in 1447, and for his appearance as Gruffydd's deputy in February 1442 when he was sub-steward of Kidwelly.[74] The second marriage

---

[69] Evans, op. cit., p. 129; *Cambrian Register*, I (1795), 63. The story was included by the seventeenth-century biographer of Gruffydd, possibly to mask the unfortunate support his family gave to the losing side in 1461.

[70] Evans, op. cit., p. 130; *C.P.R., 1452–61*, p. 494.

[71] P.R.O., Min. Acc. 1168/8 m. 11. Moreover, on 26 August 1458 Gruffydd granted to Thomas Perot certain lands in the lordship of Llanstephan. P.R.O., Exchequer, K.R., Ancient Deeds, 10846.

[72] P.R.O., Exchequer, L.T.R., Memoranda Roll, 232, recorda, michaelmas, m. 5d. In 1458–59 Gruffydd was also approver of the demesne settlement of Maerdref in Iscennen. P.R.O., Duchy of Lancaster, Min. Acc. 574/9082 m. 5d.

[73] N.L.W., Slebech Papers 279 (wrongly attributed to 1451 in the N.L.W. calendar of the Slebech papers).

[74] Somerville, op. cit., p. 640; H. Ellis (ed.), *Original Letters illustrative of English History* (2nd series, London, 1827), I, 108–9. Mabli's sister, Gwalys, had married Gruffydd's uncle, Gwilym ap Philip ab Elidir. Meyrick, *Dwnn's Visitations*, I, 20, 210.

was to Margaret, third daughter of Sir Thomas Perot; to this union is conceivably due the association of John Perot with Gruffydd in farming Dinefwr from 1439.[75] His last marriage was with Jane, daughter of Iankyn ap Rhys ap David of Gilfach Wen, near Llandysul in Cardiganshire; Iankyn had been a royal officer in the county in the early decades of Henry VI's reign.[76] With three wives, only three surviving sons seem to have been born to Gruffydd: John, Owain, and Thomas. John lived a comparatively uneventful life, although he joined his father and John Perot in leasing Dinefwr between 1439 and 1456.[77] Owain was more like his father, acting as his *agent provocateur* in Pembrokeshire in the early 1450s, and in 1461–62 leading the occupying force of Lancastrian rebels in Carreg Cennen castle with his brother, Thomas.[78] It was through Thomas that the line of Gruffydd ap Nicholas passed to Sir Rhys ap Thomas and the ill-fated Sir Rhys ap Gruffydd.[79] During the late-Lancastrian period, Thomas maintained the position in Cardiganshire for which he and his father had fought hard in 1439, but on Gruffydd's death his attention was transferred to Carmarthenshire. He became farmer of Dinefwr in 1460–61, and after the accession of Edward IV garrisoned Carreg Cennen for the deposed Henry VI until Sir Richard Herbert arrived in 1462 with a powerful force of soldiers and engineers to raze it to the ground.[80] Henceforward, the Dinefwr family was temporarily eclipsed; Thomas was excluded from office in West Wales and by 1474 he was dead.[81]

There can be no doubt that Gruffydd ap Nicholas was the most powerful personality in West Wales in the mid-fifteenth century. 'Great as is his revenue in Wales, still greater are his possessions . . . he overflowed Dinevor . . . ere he grew to man's estate'.[82] He was related to the most influential families in West Wales, was *persona grata* with the ruling English officials in both duchy of Lancaster and principality lands, and by their indulgence or indifference had been able to build a family fortune and position that endured the changes of dynasty in 1461 and 1485. His patronage

[75] J. E. Lloyd and R. T. Jenkins (eds.), *The Dictionary of Welsh Biography* (The Honourable Society of Cymmrodorion, 1959), p. 313; P.R.O., Min. Acc. 1167/5 m. 8d; /8 m. 7.
[76] *Dict. Welsh Biog.*, p. 313. Iankyn was escheator of Cardiganshire from 1424 to 1435. P.R.O., Min. Acc. 1223/6 m. 2; 1161/7 m. 7; Griffiths, *N.L.W. Journal*, XIII, 261. Above p. 194.
[77] P.R.O., Min. Acc. 1167/8 m. 7.
[78] Ibid., 1224/6 m. 8; Griffiths, *N.L.W. Journal*, XIII, 263–4. See above p. 197.
[79] *Dict. Welsh Biog.*, pp. 840–1, 847.
[80] P.R.O., Min. Acc. 1169/1 m. 6d; 1224/6 m. 8.
[81] P.R.O., Min. Acc. 1169/8 m. 11.
[82] H. W. Lloyd, 'Sir Rhys ap Thomas and his family', *Archaeologia Cambrensis*, IV, ix (1878), 208–9, quoting Lewis Glyn Cothi's ode to Gruffydd ap Nicholas, for which see Jones and Davies, *Lewis Glyn Cothi*, pp. 131–7. Another poet even acclaimed him as 'Cystenin Caerfyrddin fawr', *Arch. Camb.*, IV, ix (1878), 203–5.

of the Eisteddfod held at Carmarthen—or Dinefwr itself—sometime
between 1451 and 1453, a landmark in the development of medieval
Welsh poetry and the organization of local cultural festivities,
assured him the immortal praise of the bardic fraternity.[83] He was
a man to be feared as the behaviour of Margaret Malefant shows, for
in her haste to escape him, she flew across South Wales and into the
arms of a man who was 'purposyng and ymagenyng to ravysshe ye
seide Margaret, and to have hure to hes wyf'; whilst his ruthless
cruelty is displayed in the duel he sponsored in 1448 at the government's expense.[84] Although the biography of Gruffydd contained in
the seventeenth-century history of his family must be approached
with caution, its estimate of his character bears the stamp of honesty:
he 'proved to be a man of a hott, firie, and cholerrick spiritt; one
whos counsells weare all "in turbido", and therefore naturallie
fitlie composed and framed for the times; verie wise he was, and
infinitlie subtile and craftie, ambitiouse beyond measure, of a busie
stirring braine . . .'.[85]

Like many another, Gruffydd ap Nicholas had taken full advantage
of a combination of factors which enabled men of lowly origins to
rise in the world of the fifteenth century.[86] His dominion in West
Wales was the more complete as royal government under Henry VI
grew feebler. The Crown's power over its local representatives
became even weaker when, in their search for greater revenue, the
Lancastrians devised a system whereby the great sessions of Carmarthenshire, Cardiganshire, and, later, Kidwelly were prematurely
dissolved in return for a substantial grant. When offenders could
expect to assuage the law with a cash payment, and when the royal
representative was frequently among the most notorious lawbreakers,
good government was bound to founder and royal control
disintegrate.[87]

---

[83] *Dict. Welsh Biog.*, p. 313; M. H. Jones, 'Carmarthen Eisteddfod, 1451', *The Transactions of the Carmarthenshire Antiquarian Society*, V (1909–10), 35, 37–8. For the eulogies of the poets, Evans, op. cit., pp. 4, 12 n. 1, 23 n. 2; *Arch. Camb.*, IV, ix (1878), 203–12; Jones and Davies, *Lewis Glyn Cothi*, pp. 131–7. Gruffydd seems to have been something of a poet himself. *Historical Manuscripts Commission, Report on Manuscripts in the Welsh Language* (2 vols., London, 1898–1910), I, 88, 96.

[84] *Rot. Parl.*, V, 14–15; above, p. 201.

[85] *Cambrian Register*, I (1795), 57. This biography, which is in fact a history of the Dinefwr family, was written in defence of the reputation of Sir Rhys ap Gruffydd, traitor to Henry VIII and great-great-grandson of Gruffydd ap Nicholas. Its author, writing about 1625, is thought to have been Sir Rhys's great-grandson, Henry Rice, but despite its partisan origins it is evident that in many respects the account of Gruffydd ap Nicholas's career is surprisingly accurate. W. Ll. Williams, 'A Welsh Insurrection', *Y Cymmrodor*, XVI (1902), 1–4; above, p. 206 and n. 20, and p. 208 and n. 28.

[86] Griffiths, *N.L.W. Journal*, XIII, 264–5. Above pp. 198–9.

[87] Pugh, *Welsh Marcher Lordships*, pp. 36–43.

Not only in West Wales was ineffectual government bringing the Lancastrians into ill repute. In East Anglia, although the Paston letters may have brought unfair publicity, the ineffectiveness of complaints and the general lawlessness are patent.[88] In the West Country, the feud between Lord Bonville and the earl of Devon was turning the area periodically into a private jousting-field, and after a decade and a half of abortive remedy Parliament made the duke of York protector in 1455–56 specifically to deal with the impasse.[89] In the north of England the Percies and Nevilles were at each other's throats in the 1450s, dangerously uninhibited by local agencies of law enforcement which they dominated.[90] Gruffydd ap Nicholas was, therefore, not alone in the contempt he showed for legal authority; his reported contemptuous treatment of the royal commissioners in 1441 is comparable with that of the subpoena-ed woman who 'reysyd upp her neghebors with wepyns drawen forto slee and mordre ye said bryngers of ye writte . . . and compellyd hem forto devour the same Writte . . . bothe Wex and parchement'.[91] His disregard even for the commands of the royal Council in 1454–55 was no isolated phenomenon, for the Reading parliament of 1453 had recently declared that commandments 'to appear before him (the king) in his Chancery, or before him and his Council . . . be, and many Times have been disobeyed'.[92] The fault lay ultimately with defective kingship, but as long as it bestowed unbridled power upon Gruffydd he would support Lancaster against York, more especially when the latter began to show signs of reasserting central control over local affairs. Surveying the confusion, Mr. McFarlane has concluded that 'One of the most obvious characteristics of this late medieval society was the opportunity which it offered to the ambitious with the ability to seize it'.[93] He might have had Gruffydd ap Nicholas in mind.

[The context of Gruffydd ap Nicholas's career in English politics and Welsh society is availabe in Ralph A. Griffiths, *The Reign of King Henry VI* (London, 1981); Ralph A. Griffiths and Roger S. Thomas, *The Making of the Tudor Dynasty* (Gloucester, 1985); and Glanmor Williams, *Recovery, Reorientation and Reformation: Wales, c. 1415-1642* (Oxford, 1987).]

[88] H. S. Bennett, *The Pastons and their England* (Cambridge, 1922), pp. 5–7, 16–26, 183–91.
[89] A. Abram, *Social England in the Fifteenth Century* (London, 1909), pp. 85–7; J. R. Lander, 'Henry VI and the Duke of York's Second Protectorate, 1455 to 1456', *The Bulletin of the John Rylands' Library*, XLIII (1960), 59–64; Roskell, *Commons in the Parliament of 1422*, pp. 154–5.
[90] Above p. 206 and n. 24, J. A. Giles, *Incerti Scriptoris Chronicon Angliae* (London, 1848), pp. 45–6; C. A. J. Armstrong, 'Politics and the battle of St. Albans, 1455', *The Bulletin of the Institute of Historical Research*, XXXIII (1960), 11, 29; Somerville, op. cit., pp. 226–7. For references to lawlessness in other parts of the country, Abram, op. cit., p. 219.
[91] Ibid., pp. 82–3; above p. 214.
[92] *Statutes of the Realm*, II (Record Commission, 1816), 361.
[93] K. B. McFarlane, 'Bastard Feudalism', *Bull. Inst. Hist. Res.*, XX (1945), 177.

13

A Breton Spy in London, 1425-29

There was a singular absence in fifteenth-century England of official, government-sponsored chronicles comparable with those produced at St. Denis in France or at the Burgundian court. Nor are there any examples of informed personal memoirs by distinguished English comtemporaries similar to those of Philippe de Commynes. As a result, most English chronicles are neither as full nor as well-informed as their continental counterparts. Although written in the capital for citizens of the city, London's chronicles contain material which is more akin to local news and ill-formed rumour than to duly authorised accounts based on unimpeachable sources or first-hand experience; they provide information that was of interest to ordinary folk rather than to politicians or great figures. One consequence of this is that an apparently innocuous story or minor item of reportage given by these chronicles may conceal matters of deeper significance or relationships of wider import than might otherwise appear to be the case.[1] The vividness and, at the same time, parochialism and incompleteness of such chronicle comments is well illustrated by the story of a Breton who was slain in a London street in 1429.

Several of the London chronicles extant today carry the essentials of this story. Their authors were primarily concerned to record the dramatic, superficial facts of the case which would interest the reading citizen, perhaps be known to him sketchily already, and deserved to be recorded for posterity. To the Londoners, the death of a foreigner guilty of theft and of the murder of a defenceless widow would appear as a satisfactory and satisfying conclusion to the incident at a period when anti-alien sentiments frequently ran high.[2] At least five surviving chronicles incorporate details of the story. The fullest account appears in a version of the *Brut* Chronicle which, although usually cast in a form different from that of a city chronicle, relies for most of its fifteenth-century information

---

[1] Denys Hay, 'History and Historians in France and England during the Fifteenth Century', *Bulletin of the Institute of Historical Research*, XXXV (1962), 111-27 (reprinted in idem, *Renaissance Essays* [London, 1988], ch. IV); C.L. Kingsford, *English Historical Literature in the Fifteenth Century* (Oxford, 1913), ch. IV.

[2] For a brief comment on anti-alien feeling in the second half of the century, see P.M. Kendall, *The Yorkist Age* (London, 1962), pp. 304-10.

on the newer tradition of London chronicle-writing; it was continued in London and probably acquired its information from the pool of chroniclers and scriveners established around St. Paul's Cathedral and elsewhere.[3] Compiled soon after 1434, its material is strictly contemporary with the incident of 1429.[4] Independent of this is the city chronicle known today as 'Gregory's Chronicle', which adds a few distinctive details about the incident to those provided by the *Brut*.[5] Two other London chronicles, written in mid-century, closely rely for their information about the story on the same source as the *Brut*; they therefore contribute nothing further to our understanding of the Breton's death.[6] If such chronicles are at all representative of the written news available for reading and consultation in London in the mid-fifteenth century, the main facts of the Breton's story were known to all.

According to this popular information, sometime between Easter (27 March) and Whitsun (15 May) 1429, a Breton thief was interrupted by a London widow as he was stealing from her house in Whitechapel. She had originally taken him into her house as an act of charity, but now he set on her, murdered her and fled for sanctuary to St. George's Church in Southwark, across London bridge. Eventually, the murderer took the Cross as a penance and agreed to abjure the realm. On his way through London to the coast in the custody of the parish constables, he passed near the scene of his crimes; as he did so, the women of the parish set on him, pelted him with dung and stoned him until he collapsed dead in the street. They showed him no mercy and no pity; not even the constables and others who were with them were able to stop the attack. Such were the events observable and recorded by the chroniclers or their informants.

If it were not for the enquiries officially conducted into the two deaths, of the widow and her murderer, posterity would know no more about the episode. But inquisitions *post mortem* were opened with some speed and information unknown to the chroniclers came to light as a result. The enquiries revealed details about motive and identity, about the attitude of Londoners to their city authorities and to aliens.

The widow's inquisition *post mortem* was held on 27 May 1429.[7] It

---

[3] Kingsford, *English Historical Literature*, ch. V; F.W.D. Brie (ed.), *The Brut, or the Chronicles of England*, Vol. II (Early English Text Soc., 1908), pp. 442-43.

[4] Another, later, version of the popular Brut, written in the second half of the century and printed by William Caxton in 1480, adds nothing to the earlier account: Brie, *The Brut*, II, 500; Kingsford, *English Historical Literature*, pp. 119-22.

[5] J. Gairdner (ed.), *Historical Collections of a London Citizen* (Camden Soc., 1876), pp. 163-64.

[6] C.L. Kingsford (ed.), *Chronicles of London* (Oxford, 1905), p. 132 (written after 1446); J.G. Nichols and E. Tyrrel (eds.), *A Chronicle of London* (London, 1827), p. 117 (written soon after 1442).

[7] Public Record Office, KB9/224 m.55. The murder took place a little later than the vague chronology of the chroniclers indicates (above).

transpired that she was Joan, the wife of a certain Thomas Wynkefeld, and that the murderer was her Breton servant, Ivo Caret. Aware of the comparative wealth of the lady after her husband's death, Ivo (so the enquiry maintained) tried to rob her soon after 12 o'clock during the night of 26-27 May 1429. Joan evidently surprised him and was hit on the head with a pestle, bludgeoned with a hatchet and her body dismembered with a large knife. The jurors reported to the Middlesex coroner next day that on 3 September 1425 and at other times since in Whitechapel, Ivo, his kinsman, Michael Caret, and others had acted as spies, eliciting information and secrets about relations between England and Brittany. It was probably these revelations that prompted the government on 1 June to request a report on Joan's death by the following day.[8]

Ivo's own inquisition *post mortem* on 4 June 1429 made available further details which the coroner was commanded on 8 June to report to the government within five days.[9] This second report showed that after arriving in London in 1425, Ivo had been in secret communication not only with Brittany, but also with France and Scotland, a threatening trinity which would arouse distrust and hostility in Londoners' minds. On his way under safe-conduct into exile, he was set upon by one of Joan Wynkefeld's relatives, Margaret Conys, a tapster who may have been acquainted with Ivo in the brewing industry,[10] and a large crowd of other women. The parish constables were pinned to the ground to prevent them intervening. Ivo was then taken by his captors to the moat beyond the royal highway so that there should be no direct affront to the king, and there he was stoned to death. Not surprisingly, the jurors reported that, apart from Margaret Conys, the identity of the women who had killed this wicked foreigner was unknown to them, and in any case they had since fled.

Apart from the sinister circumstances of Ivo Caret's residence in London, there were other features of this double murder of 1429 which explain why the entire portfolio of evidence was passed to the court of King's Bench. For one thing, Ivo was a subject of the duke of Brittany; for another, he was supposedly engaged in treasonable activity. Moreover, he had been murdered whilst leaving sanctuary of his own free will under safe-conduct and under the protection of the local constables. Hence, the day after the coroner of Middlesex sent in his inquisition on Ivo's death on 13 June, a further royal writ was despatched to the coroner of Surrey, within whose jurisdiction Ivo had sought sanctuary.[11] His full report was handed in at King's Bench on 20 June. It transpired that Ivo had lived in the Whitechapel parish of St. Mary Matfelon without Aldgate, and that

---

[8] Ibid., m.54.
[9] Ibid., 224 m.46-47.
[10] For Ivo's life as a brewer, see below p. 224.
[11] PRO, KB9/224 m.29-30.

he had joined the brewer's trade on settling in London. After breaking into Joan Wynkefeld's house and battering her to death, he had fled across the Thames to seek sanctuary in St. George's Church, Southwark. Among the goods he had stolen were some items of silver and gold worth 26s. 8d., and he had been aided by John Stafford, a neighbour from the same parish. In accordance with the privilege of sanctuary, it was arranged that he should leave St. George's on 3 June and abjure the realm, leaving through the assigned port of Orwell (Suffolk).

From all the information made available to it during the first three weeks of June, the court of King's Bench was able to satisfy itself that in the event practical justice had been done and only one end was left untied – his murderers were still at large. But then, as the jurors were perhaps indicating when they pleaded ignorance of their whereabouts, few Englishmen would want to hound Margaret Conys and her accomplices relentlessly to the bench of justice.

The episode provides a glimpse of the underworld of fifteenth-century London – its crime, its violence, the vulnerability of law enforcement officers to a vengeful community that was prepared to take matters into its own hands (and female hands at that). It shows, too, that when the course of foreign relations suggested it, international espionage was employed: spies moved freely in the capital and were able to insinuate themselves into crafts, trades and unsuspecting households, risking their safety in an anti-alien environment.

In the summer of 1424 Duke Jean V of Brittany began slithering away from his traditional English alliance, so that in January 1426 the English government announced 'open war' against Brittany and took precautions against Breton raids on the English coast. Putting Breton interests and independence to the fore, Duke Jean cautiously sought to establish friendly relations with Charles VII of France and Duke Philip of Burgundy. By October 1425 Jean was referring to Charles VII as 'his nearest'; a month earlier Ivo Caret had begun his spying activities in London.[12] Although Anglo-Breton relations had entered a more passive phase by 1429, this owed more to the chastening of Duke Jean than to a renewed burst of friendship, and Breton piracy still required vigilance on the southern coast of England.[13]

The Bretons had not been above negotiating with the Scots in order to hinder England's diplomacy and her war effort in France: in October 1427 an embassy led by John Steward, the constable of Scotland, journeyed from Brittany to his own country with the probable intention of discussing

[12] G.A. Knowlson, *Jean V, duc de Bretagne, et l'Angleterre* (Rennes, 1964), pp. 118-32; N.H. Nicolas (ed.), *Proceedings and Ordinances of the Privy Council of England* (7 vols., Record Commission, 1834-37), III, 181.

[13] Knowlson, *Jean V*, pp. 140-43; *Calendar of Patent Rolls, 1422-29*, p. 553.

a royal marriage and Scottish action against the English.[14] He would have found fertile ground for his intrigues. The hostility between England and Scotland, and the unruliness of the border between them were deep-seated and of long standing; the frustrations on the English side – not least as a result of a continued Scottish presence in French armies on the continent – were bitter in the later 1420s.[15] Ivo Caret's communications with Brittany, Scotland and France after 1425 take on considerable significance in these circumstances.

As far as they went, the London chronicles are notably accurate in their accounts of news and events in the city. But their contemporary or near-contemporary authors had limited horizons and restricted sources, which rarely extended to the administrative, financial, or judicial departments of government or to those employed in them. The underworld of informers was, by its very nature, closed to them; it would only be revealed fortuitously as a result of an occurrence such as Joan Wynkefeld's murder. It is just possible that the anglophobia of a London enquiry damned the dead Ivo to a career of spying in an attempt to mitigate the brutal vengeance wrought on him in an excess of misplaced female zeal. Whatever the precise facts, not even the city's law enforcement officers could prevent the fatal attack on Ivo Caret, the suspected Breton spy.

[14] Knowlson, *Jean V*, p. 138.

[15] R. Nicholson, *Scotland: The Later Middle Ages* (Edinburgh, 1974), pp. 246-52. Despite the release from England of the captive James I in 1424, the search for peace between England and Scotland continued without conclusion: *Calendar of Patent Rolls, 1422-29*, pp. 405-6; Nicolas, *Proceedings of the Privy Council*, III, 221.

14

William Wawe and his Gang, 1427

William Wawe is immortalized in some verses composed about 1440 by an anonymous author.[1] They were written in honour of Humphrey, duke of Gloucester, probably at the abbey of St. Albans:[2]

> Yf heretike ought kouthe pike him fro
> Yf Sharpe or Wawe hadde of the lawe a feste
> Yf right was fond in al this londe vnto
> Hit to gouerne he doon the sterne unto.

Most other contemporary comments about the early-fifteenth-century Hampshire criminal are meagre and uninformative, and as such they reflect the nature of fifteenth-century chronicle-writing. City chronicles written in London include superficial notices of striking events, news or rumour but these usually relate to great political matters or else occurrences of direct interest to the London citizens who read, commissioned or bought the completed chronicles. Less important happenings in other parts of the country which did not seem to the chroniclers to be of immediate relevance to the kingdom at large rarely rate a mention.[3]

It is remarkable, therefore, that a version of the popular *Brut* Chronicle, which draws most of its fifteenth-century material from strictly London sources, should give prominence to a thief like William Wawe, whose criminal activities did not impinge upon London at all.[4] Certainly, not one among the newer tradition of London chronicles makes any reference to him. On the other hand, a short chronicle composed by an anonymous author at St. Albans Abbey, the seat of distinguished chroniclers in the past, has survived, with a record in some detail of Wawe and his gang

---

[1] K.H. Vickers, *Humphrey, duke of Gloucester* (London, 1907), pp. 394-95.
[2] E.P. Hammond (ed.), *English Verse between Chaucer and Surrey* (repr. New York, 1969), p. 204.
[3] C.L. Kingsford, *English Historical Literature in the Fifteenth Century* (Oxford, 1913), ch. IV.
[4] F.W.D. Brie (ed.), *The Brut, or the Chronicles of England*, vol. II (Early English Text Soc., 1908), pp. 441-42, 568.

terrorizing parts of Hertfordshire and Buckinghamshire in the 1420s.[5]
Not only was this chronicle written in a locality which suffered directly
from Wawe's activities, but St. Albans was intimately concerned with
certain aspects of the affair; its chronicle therefore incorporates more
detail than any other about the nature of the gang's crimes.[6]

Of these two chronicles – the *Brut* and that produced at St. Albans – the
former's interest in Wawe is, not surprisingly, confined to his last
gruesome days spent in London: his appearance in the court of King's
Bench at Westminster as a thief and an outlaw in 1427, his sentence to
death, his transporting to Southwark and then, in a cart, standing and
bound for all to see, through the city streets to Tyburn, where he was
hanged on 3 July. Wawe's head was cut off and stuck, like many another,
on London Bridge. Such was a Londoner's contact with the thief, to be
faithfully reflected in the details available to a scrivener engaged in
writing a continuation of the *Brut* Chronicle in the city. He was able to
produce a public obituary notice of a criminal whose field of operations
had been some distance from the capital and beyond the ken and interest
of the chronicler and his expected readership. The only piece of
information unrelated to London which the chronicler provides is the
report that Wawe had been taken from sanctuary at Beaulieu Abbey
(Hampshire) as a prelude to being brought to London.[7]

The St. Albans Chronicle provides a much fuller account of Wawe's
career acquired at first hand, although it may not have been quite so well
informed about his London execution and dated it to 16 July.[8] It describes
something of the character of his gang, its activities and, therefore, of
William Wawe's place in early-fifteenth-century criminal society. Several
of the gang (so the chronicler noted) had been captured in the months
before Wawe's own arrest at Beaulieu. One was seized at Barnet in
Hertfordshire, not far to the south of St. Albans, round about 12 March
1427 and was imprisoned temporarily at the abbey while on his way to
London. Another was taken at Watton, in Hertfordshire, on 30 March; he
too was conveyed to St. Albans and then on to the house of William Flete,
a Hertfordshire gentleman who was well known at the abbey and had
recently been escheator of Hertfordshire and Essex, before being hanged
in London on 8 May.[9] It is not surprising that the St. Albans writer should
have carefully noted the fate of these accomplices of Wawe, for he
doubtless witnessed their sojourn at his abbey. On the other hand, he was
rather vague as to where Wawe himself was captured, probably because,

---

[5] H.T. Riley (ed.), *Annales Monasterii S. Albani Johanne Amundesham monacho* . . . (2 vols.,
Rolls Series, 1870-71), I, 11-12, 14, 17.
[6] For comment, see Kingsford, *English Historical Literature*, pp. 150-51.
[7] Brie, *The Brut*, II, 568.
[8] Riley, *Amundesham*, I, 12.
[9] Ibid., I, 22-23, 64; *Calendar of Patent Rolls, 1422-29*, pp. 385, 391.

unlike the other members of his gang, Wawe was not taken to London *via* St. Albans. The chronicler had evidently heard of a fracas at Sleaford in Lincolnshire and suggested that as the location; but he had also heard something about Wawe seeking sanctuary at Beaulieu, though the chronicler thought that this meant the small priory of Beaulieu in Bedfordshire and not the greater abbey in Hampshire. On this single matter – Wawe's capture – the local St. Albans writer was understandably imprecise. Of Wawe's crimes the chronicler was in no doubt, for a number of them were committed in the vicinity of St. Albans itself. Wawe appeared to him as a notorious robber of clerics, a despoiler of religious houses (for he had fallen upon Sopwell nunnery in Bedfordshire on 16 February 1427, and on the nuns of Burnham in Buckinghamshire on another occasion), and a plunderer of merchants. The gang's depredations remained clear in the chronicler's memory, for a few years later he recorded that one of Wawe's former associates, William Venables, was executed in London on 11 February 1430, and that another, Geoffrey Irish, a professional transcriber, died on 1 March 1431.[10] It was evidently a sizeable gang, by no means confined to ill-educated cut-throats, and stiffened with an Irish element. Wawe's alleged confessor, for example, was Robert, rector of Hedgerley, only four miles from the unfortunate Buckinghamshire priory of Burnham; he was examined before the Convocation of Canterbury in July 1428 as a suspected heretic, but despite an hour-long examination, during which Robert's replies were vague and scornful, nothing conclusive resulted.[11]

The Irish character of the Wawe gang appears more sharply in the official record of the legal proceedings taken against Wawe in April 1427.[12] At an enquiry held on the bishop of Winchester's estates at Hook at Overton (Hampshire) on 28 April 1427, it was stated that 'Wawe' was but a pseudonym, and that other names used by the criminal were 'Irish' and 'Barre'; he was said to have originated from Deane in Hampshire where his father, variously called Theobald Barre or John Ireland, was a hermit. Wawe, therefore, seems to have been one of that Irish community living in England which was noted for its lawlessness and regularly engaged in criminal activities in the early-fifteenth century. Parliament frequently took steps to deal with the Irish – even to the point in 1422 of ordering the deportation of those who had no visible means of support or occupation.[13]

Wawe's own criminal career was of long-standing, as the court of King's Bench realized when he was presented before it on 27 May 1427.

[10] Riley, *Amundesham*, I, 47, 61.

[11] E.F. Jacob (ed.), *The Register of Henry Chichele, Archbishop of Canterbury, 1414-1443* (4 vols., Oxford, 1938-47), II, 188.

[12] Public Record Office, KB9/222/2/50; KB27/664, *rex*, Easter, m.15.

[13] *Rotuli Parliamentorum* (6 vols., London, 1767), IV, 190-91, 254-55.

On 25 March 1419, when he was living at Northcott in Middlesex, he had stolen three horses at Finchley and was condemned as a common thief. He escaped from the Marshalsea prison in London and continued his criminal career as an outlaw during the next eight years.[14] By 1427 his reputation was that of a thief and highwayman, a despoiler of churches, a traitor, murderer, heretic and rebel. On 12 March the king's Council heard complaints about his attacks on the royal highway and his robbing of churches and nunneries in Bedfordshire and Buckinghamshire. A reward of £100 was offered for his capture, dead or alive, and no one was permitted to give him food, drink or lodging. During the two months before Wawe's eventual capture, his gang turned its attention to the Deane area of Hampshire, attacking and robbing clergy with the same ferocity they had exhibited further north. A servant of the war-captain, Sir John Radcliffe, was recruited to their ranks, and so too was a Worcestershire man, Richard Bykenel, who incidentally continued his outrages in Middlesex well after Wawe was apprehended. They were aided around Beaulieu by local lawbreakers for about a month in March 1427 and Wawe's father also gave them shelter.[15] It is this southern sector of the gang's activities which confirms that it was Beaulieu Abbey in Hampshire, rather than the Bedfordshire priory, which offered its leader eventual sanctuary.

Wawe was extracted from the abbey against his will, and this violation of sanctuary gave him hope that he might be able to regain his freedom by argument in the court of King's Bench.[16] The arresting officer was one of England's more prominent soldier-administrators, Sir John Radcliffe, who had been seneschal of Gascony since 1423 and was now in England preparing for an expedition to northern France in aid of the duke of Bedford; on 20 March 1427 he was commissioned to arrest Wawe and bring him before King Henry VI's Council.[17] The St. Albans chronicler correctly noted that Radcliffe was the captor, and he may have been chosen partly because one of his servants was in Wawe's gang; on 7 May 1427 he was paid expenses for travelling to Beaulieu.[18] Wawe was arraigned before Richard Wyot, the steward of Henry Beaufort, bishop of Winchester, at the bishop's court at Hook at Overton in Hampshire on 28 April. The offences with which he was indicted extended far beyond the felonies known to the St. Albans chronicler. A society fearful of the challenge of lollardy and all too eager to regard religious deviation as part

[14] PRO, KB27/664, *rex*, Easter, m.15; N.H. Nicolas (ed.), *Proceedings and Ordinances of the Privy Council of England* (7 vols., Record Commission, 1834-37), III, 256-59.

[15] PRO, KB9/222/2/50; 224 m.112, 120.

[16] PRO, KB27/664, *rex*, Easter, m.15.

[17] PRO, E403/678 m.20; F. Devon (ed.), *Issues of the Exchequer, Henry III to Henry VI* (Record Commission, 1837), pp. 398-99.

[18] Riley, *Amundesham*, I, 12; PRO, E403/681 m.1.

of a more general threat to society found it easy to accuse Wawe and his friends of heresy as well as treason and murder.[19] Actual evidence for his heretical beliefs is well-nigh non-existent.[20]

The indictment was passed on to the court of King's Bench at Westminster; meanwhile, Wawe fled to Beaulieu Abbey for sanctuary on 2 May. Sir John Radcliffe was directed to seize him there and hold him in custody, and this he did on 14 May. Wawe was transferred to the Tower of London pending trial.[21] The hearing at Westminster, which opened a fortnight later, revolved not around Wawe's criminal activities, for these had merited and incurred outlawry in Henry V's reign, but rather around the privilege of sanctuary and its alleged violation by Radcliffe.[22] The abbot of Beaulieu had already been instructed to produce verification of the liberties and franchises under which Wawe had been given shelter; he came to the court armed with charters dating from King John's reign in order to prove that his monastery, and one of its buildings, Gameshouse, in which Wawe took refuge from 2 to 14 May 1427, enjoyed rights of sanctuary. According to Wawe, Sir John Radcliffe had taken him out of Gameshouse by force, even though he had been listed in the register of sanctuarymen which Beaulieu, in common with other monasteries, kept up to date. But the Crown's attorney was determined not to lose Wawe now that the government was at last within an ace of securing him; he denied that Radcliffe had used force and that Gameshouse was a privileged refuge; he stressed rather that Wawe was a notorious and convicted thief with a well-known record and should therefore be denied privilege of sanctuary. This argument, and above all that of expediency, carried the day and William Wawe was duly hanged.

To judge by the poetic encomium of the duke of Gloucester, Humphrey was a vigorous hounder of heretics and lawbreakers, among whom William Wawe was prominent. He was protector and defender of the realm after his elder brother, the duke of Bedford, returned to France in March 1427, and he had a special devotion to St. Albans Abbey, in whose vaults his body was in due time interred.[23] He had already dealt swift justice to at least one of the Wawe gang in March 1427, and he was probably fully aware of the gang's activities after staying at the abbey and visiting Sopwell Priory the following month.[24] It is possible that now, in

[19] M. Aston, 'Lollardy and Sedition, 1381-1431', *Past and Present*, XVII (1960), 1-44 (reprinted in idem, *Lollards and Reformers* [London, 1984], pp. 1-48). For Richard Wyot, see G.L. Harriss, *Cardinal Beaufort* (Oxford, 1988), pp. 67, 72, 145, 150, 361.

[20] PRO, KB9/222/2/50; Devon, *Issues of the Exchequer*, pp. 398-99; Nicolas, *Proceedings of the Privy Council*, III, 268-69; *Calendar of Patent Rolls, 1422-29*, p. 422.

[21] Ibid.; PRO, KB27/664, *rex*, Easter, m.15.

[22] J. Bellamy, *Crime and Public Order in England in the Later Middle Ages* (London, 1973), pp. 106-14.

[23] Vickers, *Humphrey, duke of Gloucester, passim*.

[24] Ibid., p. 194.

April and May, he played an active part in ensuring Wawe's condemnation to death at Tyburn. It is noteworthy that in suppressing Wawe and his men, the duke and a servant of his bitterest political rival, Bishop Beaufort, worked successfully together.

The Wawe gang was a band of marauders drawn from southern England and active in at least two separate areas; perhaps driven from the vicinity of St. Albans, they moved southwards to Wawe's own home countryside. In their attacks on people and property, they exhibited the common inclinations of the thief and also the anti-clericalism (though hardly the heresy) of their day without the chivalry which might have discouraged them from descending on nunneries. It is ironic that Wawe saw his last slim chance of escaping death in championing the sanctuary rights of the religious orders he had desecrated. Part-Irish in its personnel, the gang represented a particularly lawless sector of the community which accordingly received harsh treatment from government and Parliament alike.

15

The Trial of Eleanor Cobham: An Episode in the Fall of Duke Humphrey of Gloucester

O N[1] three days in mid-November 1441 the streets of London witnessed the spectacle of the duchess of Gloucester, wife of King Henry VI's nearest relative and heir presumptive, walking penitently to church to atone for her sins. On Monday, 13 November the duchess went by water from Westminster to the Temple landing-stage ; alighting, she made her way bare-headed and on foot, dressed in black and led by two knights, from Temple Bar along Fleet Street to St. Paul's Cathedral, clutching a wax taper which was there offered at the high altar.[2] The poor woman returned to Charing Cross the same day and prepared herself for a second humiliating journey.[3] On Wednesday, 15 November she set off from Westminster to the Swan pier in Thames Street, and from there walked to St. Magnus's Corner, up Bridge Street to East Cheap, Grace Church, Leaden Hall Corner and on to Christ Church, Aldgate, where a second taper was humbly offered. Two days later, on Friday, 17 November, the third and final penitential progress was made : by water from Westminster to Queen Hithe, then by foot along Broad Street to Cheapside and up to St. Michael's, Cornhill, where yet another taper was offered before she returned once more to Westminster and the custody of the constable.[4]

It was an astonishing sight for Londoners ; the details of the duchess's delvings into witchcraft —and perhaps more—which were brought into the full glare of publicity at her trial, were the scandal of the age.[5] A somewhat similar event had occurred

[1] I am indebted to Dr. Margaret Sharp for reading, and commenting on, a draft of this article.

[2] F. W. D. Brie (ed.), *The Brut*, ii (1908), 481 ; J. S. Davies (ed.), *An English Chronicle from 1377 to 1461* (1856), p. 59 ; N. H. Nicolas and E. Tyrrell (eds.), *A Chronicle of London* (1827), p. 129 ; J. G. Nicholas (ed.), *Chronicle of the Grey Friars of London* (1852), p. 18.

[3] R. Flenley (ed.), *Six Town Chronicles* (1911), p. 115.

[4] *Brut*, ii. 481 ; *English Chronicle*, pp. 59-60 ; *Chronicle of London*, p. 129.

[5] Every fifteenth-century chronicle written in England mentions the episode. The fullest accounts are those of the two versions of the *Brut* : *Brut*, ii. 478-82,

within the memory of many living in 1441 : in 1419 the queen-dowager, Joan of Navarre, had been accused of treasonable witchcraft during the reign of her step-son, Henry V.[1] Unlike the duchess, however, Queen Joan was neither tried nor convicted, and her imprisonment was short and not without its comforts.[2] The events of 1441 had deeper layers of significance, for the duchess's husband, Humphrey of Gloucester, was at a critical stage in his later life ; ever claiming an exclusive authority in the king's Council, his opponents had become strong enough to contemplate his destruction. A wife's indiscretions could provide them with an opportunity.[3]

Duke Humphrey returned from his last foreign parade, to Calais, towards the end of August 1436 to a vote of thanks from the Commons in Parliament, and while Cardinal Beaufort was abroad at the peace conference of 1439, Humphrey had the king's ear and influenced his attitudes.[4] Eleanor shared her husband's glory in this Indian summer. The king's New Year's gifts to her

508-9, and *English Chronicle*, pp. 57-60 (whose chronology is very confused), both of which must be indebted to an eye-witness account. The London chroniclers naturally offer substantial coverage, especially *Chronicle of London*, pp. 128-30, and A. H. Thomas and I. D. Thornley (eds.), *The Great Chronicle of London* (1938), pp. 175-6 (compiled half a century later). Even chroniclers at work outside London give some details : J. A. Giles (ed.), *Incerti scriptoris chronicon Angliae de regnis . . . Henrici IV, Henrici V, et Henrici VI* (1848), possibly compiled at York ; and Trinity College, Dublin MS. 5.10, whose author does not seem to have moved to London until 1448. (For these chroniclers see M. V. Clarke and V. H. Galbraith, " The Deposition of Richard II ", in M. V. Clarke, *Fourteenth Century Studies* (1937), pp. 82-86 ; G. L. Harriss, " A Fifteenth-Century Chronicle at Trinity College, Dublin ", *Bulletin of the Institute of Historical Research*, xxxviii (1965), 212-18.) One or two ballad-writers voiced their opinion on the events of 1441 and the lessons commonly drawn from them : T. Wright (ed.), *Political Poems and Songs*, ii (1861), 205-8, and, for a fuller version of the same poem, R. H. Robbins (ed.), *Historical Poems of the XIVth and XVth Centuries* (1959), pp. 176-80.

[1] A. R. Myers, " The Captivity of a Royal Witch ", *Bulletin of the John Rylands Libarry*, xxiv (1940), 263-84 ; xxvi (1941-2), 82-100.

[2] Ibid. xxiv (1940), 272-7.

[3] The only modern accounts of the duchess of Gloucester's trial are those of J. H. Ramsay, *Lancaster and York*, ii (1892), 31-35, and K. H. Vickers, *Humphrey, Duke of Gloucester* (1907), pp. 269-80.

[4] For Humphrey's reception, see *Rotuli Parliamentorum*, iv. 502 ; for his influence during Beaufort's absence, see Richard Arnold, *The Customs of London* (2nd ed., 1811), p. 283, and Ramsay, op. cit. ii. 14.

in 1436 and 1437 were among the finest he gave on these occasions, and when Duke Humphrey made the arrangements for Queen Joan's funeral on 11 August 1439, Eleanor was a prominent mourner.[1] By 1441, however, Gloucester's influence was no longer so formidable ; it had been eroded by his opponents to the point of enforced retirement. Soon after the return of Cardinal Beaufort from the peace negotiations in October 1439, Gloucester, who held rigidly to a policy of no surrender in France, began to lose ground rapidly. By the end of February 1440 he was being elbowed out of the Council by the cardinal and the archbishop of York, John Kemp, and he attended few of its meetings during the two years after the summer of 1440.[2] If a further opportunity to discredit the duke arose (perhaps even to neutralize permanently his influence in the state), his opponents, led by Beaufort, would avail themselves of it. The duchess of Gloucester played into their hands.

Duke Humphrey's second wife, Eleanor Cobham, was unpopular from the moment they married. With his inherent rashness, in 1428 he had forsaken the wife, Jacqueline of Hainhault, whose marriage to an English duke in 1423 had so outraged the duke of Burgundy. To desert the noble duchess acquired at such cost and take up with one of her more lowly ladies-in-waiting caused adverse comment at the time. Nor was the new duchess able to endear herself to English opinion during the following decade and a half. Eleanor Cobham came of a knightly family of Kent, her father being Sir Reginald Cobham.[3] Evidently a strong-minded individual, her ambition matched even that of her husband, and perhaps without the inconstancy which allowed

[1] N. H. Nicolas (ed.), *Proceedings and Ordinances of the Privy Council of England*, v (1835), 62, 56 ; P.R.O., Exchequer, T.R., Council and Privy Seal, 57/96 ; 56/26.

[2] Arnold, *Customs of London*, pp. 279-86 ; *Proc. P.C.*, v, *passim*. Gloucester was present at the important Council meeting in June 1440 which made financial provision for the royal Household, and at two other meetings in the following November ; he was also summoned to a meeting at Easter 1441, but it is not known whether he attended (P.R.O., Exchequer, T.R., Council and Privy Seal, 63/76 ; 65 (9 and 19 November) ; 67/42 (20 March 1441)).

[3] Vickers, op. cit. pp. 164-6. 202-6 ; G.E.C., *The Complete Peerage*, iii (1913), 354.

Humphrey's designs to be blocked by determined adversaries. By contrast, Eleanor's marital achievement strengthened her determination to enhance the prestige and authority of herself and her husband. At the time of her disgrace, public opinion hated and distrusted her for her vaulting ambition and even extortion, which she was said by a northern writer to have displayed in despoiling the almsmen of the Hospital of St. John at Pontefract.[1] One chronicler noted how she flaunted her pride and her position by riding through the streets of London, glitteringly dressed and suitably escorted by men of noble birth.[2] Another echoed the sentiments of ballad-writers, who emphasized the moral behind the humiliation of unwonted ambition : Oh ! How the mighty have fallen ![3] The dominance of this self-willed woman was evident to all, and during the chancellorship of Bishop John Stafford (1432-41) a petition for redress was addressed by a York man to her alone as " the right high and fulle mighty Princesse and fulle gracious lady Duchesse of Gloucestre ".[4] It was Eleanor's ambition which inveigled her to destruction.

Eleanor Cobham's vulnerable point was her interest in witchcraft and necromancy ; when she combined this with political ambition, her indulgences were transformed by some into treason. The temporary disgrace of Queen Joan revealed the eager interest among the high-born in fifteenth-century England in the feasibility of predicting the future by communicating with the dead ; and Eleanor kept a number of dubious priests in her household, men who practised necromancy and witchcraft.[5] Both she and Duke Humphrey had been friendly with Queen Joan, the convicted royal witch, and, indeed,

---

[1] Giles, op. cit. part 4, p. 30.

[2] Ibid. ; see also C. L. Kingsford, *English Historical Literature in the Fifteenth Century* (1913), pp. 340-1, and *English Chronicle*, p. 60 (" whoos pride, fals couetise and lecherie were cause of her confusioun ").

[3] Giles, op. cit. part 4, p. 30 ; *Political Poems and Songs*, ii. 205-8 ; Robbins, op. cit. pp. 176-80.

[4] P.R.O., Ancient Correspondence, 57/97. Stafford became chancellor on 26 February 1432 (F. M. Powicke and E. B. Fryde (eds.), *Handbook of British Chronology* (2nd edn., 1961), p. 85).

[5] Below, pp. 238-9. For necromancy-scares earlier in the century, see Myers, BULLETIN, xxiv. 273-4.

Gloucester had extended his protection to Friar Randolph, the man who lay at the heart of the scandal of 1419.[1] Moreover, of the surviving books which Eleanor is known to have owned, one was a semi-medical, semi-astrological work translated from Arabic—just the kind of volume to be found in the library of a fifteenth-century noblewoman combining an interest in witchcraft and medical prediction.[2]

Eleanor's interest in witchcraft, therefore, seems attested, and she was even prepared to admit some of the charges against her later. The formal indictment supplied the details.[3] When it came to assessing her motives, the enquiry undertaken on the order of a Council from which her husband was being excluded may have resorted to fabrication in order to discredit the duchess even further and, by implication, the duke.[4] Yet, the allegations were not entirely fantastic, for Eleanor Cobham was undeniably ambitious. Certainly, no contemporary suggests that the trial of the duchess was engineered simply for political reasons by her husband's enemies ; that was something which Tudor writers contributed to fifteenth-century historiography.[5] Indeed, it is remarkable how poor a reputation Eleanor Cobham had among fifteenth-century chroniclers, in contrast to the glowing reports of Duke Humphrey which these predominantly Yorkist writers give. Her repugnant ambition or her dubious activities—or both—would have ensured that. Eleanor was said in 1441 to be anxious to discover when King Henry VI would die so that she should be queen ; it was, perhaps, no unnatural wish in the ambitious wife of the heir presumptive.[6] Eleanor's associates were accused of declaring that the lords of the Council ruled the young king and would be executed unless their behaviour

---

[1] Vickers, op. cit. p. 276 and n. 1 ; Myers, BULLETIN, xxiv. 264-5.

[2] Vickers, op. cit. p. 275. For Duke Humphrey's own treatise on astrology, see Ramsay, op. cit. ii. 32, n. 2.   [3] Below, p. 241.

[4] The surviving indictments of Eleanor and her associates are in P.R.O., King's Bench, Ancient Indictments, 72/1-6, 9, 11, 14.

[5] The Tudor writers, Robert Fabyan (*The New Chronicles of England and France*, ed. H. Ellis (1811), p. 614) and Edward Hall (*Chronicle* (1809), p. 202), were the first to suggest unequivocally that Eleanor's trial was the work of her husband's enemies.

[6] Eleanor's desire to be queen was still being stressed in 1447 as the cause of her misfortune (P.R.O., King's Bench, Plea Roll, 745 rex m. 22).

improved ; yet, the wife of a duke whose close kinship to the
king gave him a special claim to a position on a Council from
which he was increasingly barred, might well be hostile to
Cardinal Beaufort and the other councillors.   Moreover, it need
be no coincidence that her association with necromancers and
astrologers was said to have begun about April 1440, for at that
point Gloucester had recently been cast into the political wilder-
ness and was in process of being defeated on the issue of whether
the captive duke of Orleans should be released in order to promote
peace between England and France.[1]   Gloucester's enemies had
no need to manufacture the damning charges against Eleanor
Cobham : her dabblings in the occult provided material enough
and her unbridled ambition aroused deeper suspicion.   But a
vigorous public prosecution of the duchess would squeeze every
ounce of political capital out of the incident and thereby destroy
Gloucester, the man and the politician.

It was in the summer of 1441 that the play opened which was
to end in Eleanor being condemned for witchcraft and treason.
In the evening of 28 or 29 June Eleanor was cavorting in London
with her habitual insufferable pride, dining in Cheapside at the
King's Head, which had been originally built by Edward III
so that the royal family might have a vantage point from which to
view the city's pageants and festivities.   While at dinner, she
received a message that some of her associates and servants had
been accused.[2]   Master Roger Bolingbroke (or Bultingbroke), a
prominent Oxford priest who was a member of Duke Humphrey's
household and Eleanor's personal clerk, was one of them.[3]

---

[1] Arnold, op. cit. pp. 280-6 ; Ramsay, op. cit. ii. 24-25.

[2] Kingsford, *English Historical Literature*, pp. 340-1 (28 June), 156 ; Giles,
op. cit. p. 30 (28 or 29 June).

[3] J. Gairdner (ed.), *Historical Collections of a London Citizen* (1876), p. 183 ;
Great Chronicle, p. 422 ; *Brut*, ii. 478.   Bolingbroke is described as a gentleman
of London, a clerk and B.A. in the official indictment (P.R.O., King's Bench,
Ancient Indictment, 72/4).   For the suggestion that he was an author himself,
see Ramsay, op. cit. ii. 32, n. 2.   He was certainly principal of St. Andrew Hall,
Oxford, in September 1438 (A. B. Emden, *A Biographical Register of the University
of Oxford to 1500*, i (1957), 214-15).

Another was Master Thomas Southwell, canon of St. Stephen's Chapel in the palace of Westminster, rector of St. Stephen's, Walbrook, London, and vicar of Ruislip, Middlesex.[1] John Home (or Hunne) was a third, canon of both Hereford and St. Asaph, and Eleanor's chaplain, who had acted as secretary for both Duke Humphrey and herself.[2] Marjery Jurdane (or Jourdemain), of Eye (or Ebury) near Westminster, shared the accusation ; she had been charged with sorcery as long ago as 1432 and was described by one writer as an ancient pythoness.[3] They were all charged with conspiring to bring about the king's death : Roger through necromancy ; Thomas by celebrating mass unlawfully at the lodge in Hornsey Park, near London, with strange heretical accoutrements ; and Home for taking part with both.[4]

Southwell's imprisonment in the Tower was ordered on 10 July ; three days later, he was deprived of his canonry of St. Stephen's, Westminster, in favour of the king's almoner, John Delabere.[5] But Bolingbroke was the most prominent of the côterie. His revelations were evidently interesting enough to attract the attention of the king's Council by 12 July, for a valet of the Crown, Bartholomew Hallay, was instructed not to let Roger out of his sight and, together with several persons sent from Windsor to Westminster for the purpose, to present him before the Council.[6] Bolingbroke had probably incriminated

[1] Ibid. iii (1959). 1734-5 ; *Brut*, ii. 480 ; P.R.O., King's Bench, Ancient Indictment, 72/4.

[2] Ibid. 72/5, 6, 9 ; *Great Chronicle*, pp. 175, 422 ; *Brut*, ii. 508-9 ; Flenley, op. cit. p. 116, n. 1 ; J. Le Neve, *Fasti Ecclesiae Anglicanae, 1300-1541*, ii (1962), 37 ; xii (1967), 49 ; xi (1965), 44 ; P.R.O., Chancery Warrants, 1428/57-58 (where Home is described as a clerk or chaplain of London and Hereford, formerly secretary to Eleanor Cobham, and lately canon of St. Asaph Cathedral).

[3] *Great Chronicle*, pp. 175, 422 ; *Brut*, ii. 480 ; Giles, op. cit. part 4, p. 31 ; T. Rymer (ed.), *Foedera, conventiones, literae* . . . , iv (1740), 178.

[4] *English Chronicle*, p. 57 ; P.R.O., King's Bench, Ancient Indictments, 72/5, 6, 9. The fragmentary annals formerly attributed to William Worcester say that Eleanor herself was arrested on 28 June ; this is almost certainly untrue (J. Stevenson (ed.), *Letters and Papers illustrative of the Wars of the English in France*, ii. pt. 2 (1864), p. 763).

[5] P.R.O., Chancery Warrants, 730/6011 ; *Calendar of the Close Rolls, 1433-41*, p. 422.

[6] P.R.O., Exchequer, E.R., Issue Rolls, 742 (12 July 1441). The Exchequer was ordered to pay Hallay his expenses on this date.

the duchess of Gloucester, and the Council seems to have exploited her involvement. A week or so later, on Sunday, 23
July, the public recanting of Roger Bolingbroke was staged at St.
Paul's Cross.[1] During a sermon by Bishop Low of Rochester,
he was placed on a specially erected platform, surrounded by his
ludicrous instruments : a painted chair, on which he sat, with a
sword tipped with a copper image at each of its four corners,
images of wax and silver, and with Bolingbroke himself clasping a
sword in one hand and a sceptre in the other, while he wore a
surplice and a paper crown on his head. The sermon over,
Bolingbroke recanted. The spectacle was devised to mock the
heresy of his views and his indulgence in the magical arts. It
may have excited comment among the spectators that the entire
proceedings were enacted before a considerable section of
Henry VI's Council : Archbishop Chichele of Canterbury,
Cardinal Beaufort, Bishop Robert Gilbert of London, Bishop
William Aiscough of Salisbury, the earls of Huntingdon, Northumberland and Stafford, as well as before the mayor and aldor-
men, commoners and foreign residents of London. It was a
remarkable audience for a recantation, but if Bolingbroke had
incriminated the duchess of Gloucester, prominent members of
the Council might have been prepared to take the matter further.[2]
Indeed, the entire theatrical performance looks as if it had been
engineered to demonstrate to the populace the heinousness of the
offences and to prepare it for further revelations and prosecutions.

The arrest of her associates alarmed Eleanor Cobham, who
feared her own implication. After hearing of their arrest (or

[1] One chronicler says it was 22 July, another 25, but it was clearly a
Sunday, therefore the 23rd (Flenley, op. cit. p. 115; *Chronicle of London*,
p. 128; *Brut*, ii. 478; *English Chronicle*, p. 57). Vickers, op. cit. p. 270 n. 4,
prefers the previous week, 16 July, simply on the grounds of chronological convenience and in the face of the chroniclers' explicit statements. His dating of the
entire episode leaves much to be desired.

[2] *Brut*, ii. 478; *English Chronicle*, p. 57; Stow, *Annales or Generall Chronicle
of England* (1631), p. 381. Chichele, Beaufort, Huntingdon, Stafford and
Northumberland had been re-appointed to the king's Council in November 1437,
but it must be admitted that in February 1440 Gloucester had protested at
Huntingdon's exclusion from the Council by Beaufort and Kemp (S. B. Chrimes
and A. L. Brown (eds.). *Select Documents of English Constitutional History,
1307-1485* (1961), pp. 275-6 ; Arnold, op. cit. p. 280).

after Bolingbroke's recanting), she fled for sanctuary to Westminster Abbey.[1]   Her fears were well founded, and her husband
was in no position to save her from the consequences of her
indiscretions.   Cited to appear at St. Stephen's Chapel, Westminster, to answer charges of conspiring to bring about Henry
VI's death, Eleanor was examined on 24 July on twenty-eight
points of felony and treason.   Before Archbishop Chichele,
Cardinal Beaufort, Archbishop Kemp and the bishops of Salisbury,
London, and Bath and Wells (the chancellor), she strenuously
maintained her innocence and was allowed to return to sanctuary
in the Abbey.[2]

It was on Tuesday, 25 July that she appeared a second time
at St. Stephen's.   Her examination on that day was preceded by
that of Roger Bolingbroke, evidently brought from custody to
incriminate the duchess formally.   Moreover, the king's Council
examined Roger, who claimed that his various activities had been
at Eleanor's bidding in order to tell her fortune.   It was on the
basis of this statement that Eleanor appeared on this second
occasion, face to face with Bolingbroke ; she thereupon admitted
five of the twenty-eight charges.   Archbishop Chichele, with the
agreement of the young king, committed her to Leeds castle in
Kent in the custody of Sir John Steward, constable of the castle,
John Stanley, usher of the king's Chamber, and others of the
royal Household, until the king and Council should decree her
punishment.   Whether the suspicion of treason was justified or
not, the Council, headed by enemies of Gloucester such as
Beaufort and Kemp, was preparing to deal with the unfortunate
duchess.[3]

[1] *English Chronicle*, p. 57, prefers the latter.   The pseudo-William Worcester
gives the specific date of 19 July, but also mentions Eleanor's arrest as taking
place three weeks earlier ! (Stevenson, op. cit. ii, pt. 2, pp. 762-3).

[2] *Brut*, ii. 478-9, says 25 July, whereas *English Chronicle*, p. 58, says it was
Monday, 22 (*sic*, 24) July.   It was probably on the 24th, since judgement at her
second appearance was given on 25 July.   Below, p. 250.   Kemp was a close
political associate of Beaufort (Arnold, op. cit. pp. 280-6).

[3] *English Chronicle*, p. 58; *Brut*, ii. 479; *Calendar of the Patent Rolls, 1436-1441*,
p. 559; *1441-1446*, pp. 23, 40.   Steward was in receipt of a life-annuity of 40
marks, granted by Henry V, and had recently been a member of the king's Household as master of the horse ; he even attended a meeting of the Great Council in
April and May 1434 (P.R.O., Exchequer, E.R., Warrants for Issues, 58/49;

Next day, Wednesday, 26 July, the lay power took over prosecution of the case, with the ominous implication that it alone could impose the death penalty.   A commission was issued to enquire further in London into the alleged plot against the king. It included the mayor, aldermen and commoners of the city, but also the earls of Huntingdon, Northumberland and Stafford (the lay councillors who had taken part in the earlier investigation), the treasurer of England (Lord Cromwell), Lord Fanhope and Lord Hungerford, all of them members of the king's Council.[1]   A series of enquiries was made in London with Bolingbroke and Southwell as the principal defendants and Eleanor as an accessory ; all were indicted of sorcery, felony and treason.[2]   The jurors asserted that Bolingbroke, Southwell and Home, on various occasions after April 1440 in the parishes of St. Martin's in the Vintry, St. Bennet Hithe and St. Sepulchre, had used magical figures, vestments and instruments and invoked demons and evil spirits to anticipate when Henry VI should die ; Southwell, with a book of necromancers' oaths and experiments in hand, stood chanting protective masses. It was claimed that they had fashioned a figure of the king to work on, and were thereby able to calculate that he would die of melancholia at the end of May or early in June 1441.[3]   Eleanor was said to have encouraged them in all this and to have promised them gifts in return, while their belief in the king's impending demise was disseminated among the city population.[4]   It was further claimed that Eleanor, the wife of the heir presumptive, wished to be queen and was interested to discover when that eventuality

Proc. P.C., v. 119-20 ; iv. 212, 216).   For John Stanley see J. C. Wedgwood *History of Parliament, Biographies* (1936), pp. 797-9.

[1] *Proc. P.C.*, v. passim ; *English Chronicle*, p. 58, and Stow, *Annales*, p. 381, also add the earl of Suffolk and justices of both Benches.

[2] *English Chronicle*, p. 58 ; *Brut*, ii. 479 ; Flenley, op. cit. p. 115.

[3] P.R.O., King's Bench, Ancient Indictments, 72/1-6, 9, 11, 14. On 27 July, presumably before the enquiries could get under way, Southwell's moveable goods were granted to John Delabere, who had already occupied his canonry (P.R.O., Chancery Warrants, 1428/24 ; above, p. 239).

[4] One of those told this by Bolingbroke was John Solers, esquire of the Household (he had been sergeant of the king's tents and pavilions since April 1438) (P.R.O., King's Bench, Ancient Indictment, 72/11 ; Exchequer, E.R., Issue Rolls, 742 (29 May 1441) ; *C.P.R., 1436-1441*, p. 157).

would occur. The lords of the Council, few friends of Gloucester among them, had also received attention from Bolingbroke, who, it was said, had declared that they dominated the king and would be beheaded unless they changed their habits.[1] The witch of Eye had already given a woman's view, when she confessed that Eleanor had long employed her as a sorceress, primarily to concoct medicines and potions to induce Duke Humphrey to love and marry her.[2] The duchess's well known ambition and fascination with necromancy and witchcraft gave easy credence to these charges, especially after she herself admitted some of them to be true. But she incurred a great risk in indulging in them at all when Duke Humphrey was virtually powerless to protect her.

Condemned by an ecclesiastical tribunal and a secular enquiry, Eleanor did not yet give up hope of escaping punishment. She feigned sickness in order to remain in sanctuary and avoid being sent to Leeds castle, but her further plan to escape by water was foiled.[3] On 9 August 1441 Henry VI ordered her to appear again before Archbishop Chichele on 21 October, presumably to receive sentence, and cautioned anyone (and he may have had Gloucester and his friends in mind) against hindering the archbishop in the performance of his task, or attempting anything against Eleanor or her property in the meanwhile. Henry VI was evidently anxious to mingle firmness with consideration, as one ballad-writer remembered.[4] Two days later, the fallen duchess was handed over to Sir John Steward, John Stanley, Sir William Wolff and a group of Household servants. Indeed, members of the king's Household were to be given exclusive custody of Eleanor from this moment onwards, and it is

---

[1] This is not a dissimilar charge from that of Duke Humphrey himself, when in February 1440 he denounced the influence of Beaufort and Kemp over Henry VI, to the exclusion of himself and other deserving councillors like the duke of York and the earl of Huntingdon (Arnold, op. cit. pp. 280-2, 286).

[2] Not without considerable success ! Below, p. 245, n. 2 ; *English Chronicle*, pp. 58-59 ; Stow, *Annales*, p. 381.   [3] *English Chronicle*, p. 59.

[4] *Foedera*, v. 110 ; the entry in *C.P.R., 1436-1441*, p. 559, errs in giving 1 October as the date for her re-appearance. Speaking of Henry VI, Eleanor is made to say in one ballad : "That worthy prynce of high prudence
         Of my sorow hade gret petye "
(Ramsay, op. cit. ii. 33 n. 2 ; Wright, *Political Poems and Songs*, ii. 207).

worth remarking that the steward of the Household at this juncture was William de la Pole, earl of Suffolk and a political associate of Cardinal Beaufort.[1] While these men and their charge made their way to Leeds, scene of Queen Joan's detention in 1420-2, Eleanor's accomplices found themselves in the Tower of London.[2]

In the long summer interval, the Council presumably decided her fate. Sir John Steward was commissioned to hire carriages in preparation for Eleanor Cobham's return to Westminster, and on Thursday, 19 October he brought her from Leeds and put her in the care of the constable of England, prior to further examination.[3] It was Adam Moleyns, as clerk of the Council, who read the articles of sorcery, necromancy and treason to her in St. Stephen's Chapel a day or two after her return.[4] Archbishop Chichele declined to attend because of ill health, although the prospect of seeing the wife of his friend, Duke Humphrey, being so humiliated must have fortified his withdrawal. Instead, Eleanor stood before Bishop Gilbert of London, Bishop Aiscough of Salisbury, Bishop William Alnwick of Lincoln, Bishop Thomas Brouns of Norwich, and several

[1] Suffolk was steward of the Household until December 1446 (Powicke and Fryde, op. cit. p. 76). For Sir John Steward and John Stanley, see above, p. 241. Wolff had also attended the Great Council in April and May 1434 (*Proc. P.C.*, iv. 212).

[2] *Brut*, ii. 479-80 ; *Historical Collections of a London Citizen*, pp. 183-4 ; Myers, BULLETIN, xxiv. 265, 277-83. Henry Vavasour and Thomas Wesenham, esquires, and John Slithurst, William Nixon, John Becket, Stephen Coot, John Water and Piers Preston, yeomen of the Chamber, were among those assigned to take charge of the duchess of Gloucester. Wages were ordered for them on 25 July 1441 (P.R.O., Exchequer, E.R., Warrants for Issues, 57/304). Eleanor gave Sir John Steward a diamond ring while she was his captive, and John Stanley acquired the goods of Roger Bolingbroke on 22 November 1441 (Vickers, op. cit. p. 274 ; S. Bentley (ed.), *Excerpta Historica* (1833), p. 278 ; *C.P.R., 1441-1446*, p. 40).

[3] Ibid. p. 23 ; *Brut*, ii. 480. Meanwhile, Gloucester, as justiciar of South Wales, felt able to travel to Cardigan, where he held a meeting of the great sessions of the county on 5 October 1441 (P.R.O., Ministers' Accounts, 1161/10 m. 6).

[4] *English Chronicle*, p. 59, puts the date at Saturday, 21 October, whereas *Brut*, ii. 480, prefers 20 October. Moleyns was clerk of the Council from at least 1438, had himself become a councillor by November 1441, and was shortly to be identified with the Suffolk and Beaufort clique (Emden, op. cit. ii. 1289-91 ; *Proc. P.C.* v. 173 ; Powicke and Fryde, op. cit. p. 92).

doctors and masters of divinity ; as before, she admitted some of the charges but denied others.[1]   It was clearly an ecclesiastical sentence that had been decided upon, although the role which Moleyns played reflects the vital interest of the Council in the proceedings. For the moment, however, the hearing was adjourned over the weekend, to be resumed at St. Stephen's on Monday, 23 October. Bolingbroke, Southwell and the witch of Eye, with all their paraphernalia, were produced to face Eleanor. Once more, she denied many of the charges, but pitifully confessed that she had encouraged her friends in their activities in order to have a child by Gloucester.[2]   Nevertheless, they were all convicted and only punishment remained.[3]

Anticipating the dreadful death reserved for heretics and necromancers, Southwell died in the Tower on 26 October.[4] Next day, it was the turn of the witch of Eye ; after recanting, she was taken from the Tower, handed over to the sheriffs of London and burned at Smithfield.[5]   The same day, Eleanor Cobham formally abjured before the bishops the heresies her activities implied and was ready to receive her penance from Chichele or his commissioners on 9 November.[6]   Before that was done, however, one more blow was delivered at the wretched prisoner and Duke Humphrey, at the same time softening in small degree

[1] *English Chronicle*, p. 59 ; *Brut*, ii. 480 ; Vickers, op. cit. p. 275.   Chichele had been ailing since at least November or December 1439, and in April 1442 was to ask the Pope for permission to resign his see (E. F. Jacob, *Henry Chichele* (1967), pp. 109, 116).   Gilbert was well qualified to investigate matters bordering on heresy, for he had studied the errors in Wyclif's works in 1411 ; while Brouns had been one of Beaufort's companions on the peace mission of 1439, and Aiscough was the king's confessor by 1440-1 (Emden, op. cit. ii. 766-7 ; i. 281-2 ; idem, *A Biographical Register of the University of Cambridge to 1500* (1963), p. 28 ; P.R.O., Exchequer, K.R., Various Accounts, 409/6 fol. 16ᵛ).

[2] For their alleged illegitimate children, see Vickers, op. cit. p. 205.

[3] *English Chronicle*, p. 59 ; *Brut*, ii. 480 ; *Great Chronicle*, p. 176.

[4] *English Chronicle*, p. 59 ; *Brut*, ii. 480.   However convenient this was for the authorities, it was a nuisance for Robert Brutte, who had entrusted to Southwell, as a canon of St. Stephen's, a chest full of his estate records for safe keeping ; only in November 1443 did he succeed in regaining possession of the chest (P.R.O., Exchequer, E.R., Warrants for Issues, 59/105).

[5] *Brut*, ii. 480 ; *English Chronicle*, p. 59 ; *Great Chronicle*, p. 176 ; Giles, op. cit. part 4, p. 31 ; *Chronicle of London*, p. 129 ; Kingsford, *English Historical Literature*, p. 340.   [6] *English Chronicle*, p. 59.

the momentous nature of this attack upon his duchess.   On 6
November before a commission of bishops, headed even by the
sick and aged Chichele and Cardinal Beaufort, Eleanor was
solemnly divorced from the duke of Gloucester as a prelude to her
final punishment.[1]   Three days later, on 9 November, the
penance was pronounced at St. Stephen's by Archbishop Chichele
and his colleagues : Eleanor, with a burning taper in her hand, was
to proceed from Westminster to a London church on three
market days, when London's population would be swollen to its
maximum by visiting tradesmen and shoppers.[2]   This she did on
Monday, Wednesday and Friday, 13, 15 and 17 November.   If
she attracted great compassion from some of the onlookers on
each occasion, others were able to meditate on the greatness of the
fall of a very foolish and ambitious woman.[3]

There remained Bolingbroke and Home in the Tower of
London.[4]   Like Eleanor herself, Roger Bolingbroke had been in
the custody of a Household official, Bartholomew Hallay, valet of
the Crown, for much of the time since the beginning of July.[5]
On 18 November Roger appeared at Guildhall before the mayor,
the duke of Norfolk and several justices to hear his condemnation
by Sir John Hody, chief justice of King's Bench.   He was then
drawn from the Tower through the streets of London to Tyburn,

[1] *Brut*, ii. 480-81.   It was the same commission which had just convicted her,
including the bishops of London, Salisbury, Lincoln and Norwich, and certain
doctors and masters of divinity.   Above, pp. 244-5.   This is the only source
which mentions the divorce, but its precise dating encourages belief.   There is no
justification for Kingsford's suggestion (*English Historical Literature*, p. 93) that
Duke Humphrey " may not have been an altogether unwilling party to the proceedings ".   Indeed, for an indication of their crushing effect on him, see below,
p. 251, n. 3.
[2] *Brut*, ii. 481 ;   *English Chronicle*, pp. 59-60 ;   *Historical Collections of a
London Citizen*, p. 184.
[3] *English Chronicle*, pp. 59-60 ;   Giles, op. cit. part 4, pp. 30-31 ;   Wright,
op. cit. ii. 205-8.   For the penitential journeys, see above, p. 233. Citizens of
London were ordered to show Eleanor no respect, but they were not to molest her
either (R. R. Sharpe, *London and the Kingdom* (3 vols., 1894-5), i. 281).
[4] On 16 November the sheriffs of London were ordered to bring them from
the Tower to Guildhall two days later (*C.C.R., 1441-1447*, pp. 5-6).
[5] F. Devon, *Issues of the Exchequer, Henry III to Henry VI* (1837), pp. 441-2.
On 24 February 1442 Hallay was paid £10 for the expenses of himself, Bolingbroke
and two attendants for nine weeks.   See also p. 239.

where, protesting still his innocence of treason, he was hanged, disembowelled and quartered, his quarters being sent to several notoriously active centres of Lollardy and heresy : Oxford, Cambridge, Bristol and another town, according to one chronicler ; Oxford, Cambridge, York and Hereford, according to another. His head was left to grace London Bridge.[1] On the same day, John Home appeared at Guildhall, but fared much better ; he and a certain esquire, William Wodham, received charters of pardon.[2] With the principal actors despatched, there was no need to be vindictive towards those in supporting roles.

Condemned and penitent though she was, her associates dead or pardoned, Eleanor Cobham was not allowed the luxury of an honourable confinement like that accorded Queen Joan after 1419.[3] As a prisoner, she could still guarantee Duke Humphrey's good behaviour ; accordingly, elaborate measures were taken to ensure that she remained safely incarcerated for the rest of her life, in the custody of royal Household officials. On 19 January 1442 Henry VI himself wrote a letter under the signet from his manor of Sheen to the chancellor, Bishop Stafford, telling him of the decision to give Sir Thomas Stanley, controller of the Household, responsibility for the custody of the former duchess and her household in Cheshire. The chancellor was to order the sheriffs of the counties *en route* from Westminster to assist Stanley in a journey which was to be delayed by neither

---

[1] C. L. Kingsford (ed.), *Chronicles of London* (1905), p. 149 ; *Brut*, ii. 481, 509 ; *Great Chronicle*, p. 176 ; *English Chronicle*, p. 60 ; *Chronicle of London*, p. 130 ; Flenley, op. cit. p. 116. Hody was chief justice of King's Bench (*C.P.R.*, *1436-1441*, *passim*). For these centres of Lollardy see J. A. F. Thomson, *The Later Lollards, 1414-1520* (1965), chaps. II, III, and pp. 197, 211-19.

[2] Kingsford, *Chronicles of London*, p. 149 ; *Chronicle of London*, pp. 129-30 ; *Great Chronicle*, p. 176 ; Flenley, op. cit. p. 116 ; *Brut*, ii. 509. Pardon of all offences committed by, and judgements delivered against, Home before 14 November was granted on 17 November 1441 ; nine days later he was confirmed in the benefice of Worth Maltravers, in the diocese of Salisbury, and died in 1473, still canon of Hereford (P.R.O., Chancery Warrants, 1428/56-57 ; *C.P.R.*, *1441-1446*, p. 27 ; Le Neve, *Fasti*, xii. 49). Wodham's offences may not have been connected with Eleanor Cobham ; his final release from the Tower was ordered on 3 December (*C.P.R.*, *1441-1446*, p. 75 ; P.R.O., Chancery Warrants, 1368/24 (although not given, the year must be 1441).

[3] For the brief comfortable confinement of Queen Joan from 1419 to 1422, see Myers, BULL ET IN, xxiv. 265-70.

sickness on Eleanor's part nor the feigned illness of which she was known to be capable.[1] The Household servants, led by John Stanley, who were allowed 10*s*. a day for their prisoner and her tiny entourage of five attendants, relinquished their charge on 22 January, in preparation for the journey to Cheshire.[2] Two days later, Sir Thomas Stanley and his prisoners had made their way to the abbot of Westminster's manor of Neat, a short distance up river from Westminster, where they rested until the morning of the 26th.[3] Later that day, Eleanor left in a horse-drawn bier for Chester, where Stanley was to have 100 marks per annum to cover her expenses in detention, a beggarly sum compared with the household budget of Queen Joan during her short captivity.[4] A formal agreement for Eleanor Cobham's custody was drawn up at Chester on 10 February 1442 between John Stanley and the Household officials, on the one hand, and her new keeper, Sir Thomas Stanley, on the other ; Eleanor's 100 marks were pro-

[1] H. Ellis (ed.), _Original Letters illustrative of English History_, 2nd series (1827), i. 107. In fact, many of her household were immured in the Tower (Trinity College, Dublin MS. 5. 10, fol. 173ᵛ (a Latin Chronicle)). Until at least Christmas, she had been in the charge of Sir John Steward, John Stanley and Thomas Wesenham, esquires, Thomas Pulford and James Grisacre, valets of the Crown, John Wattes, valet of the Household, and John Martyn, groom of the Household (Devon, _Issues of the Exchequer_, p. 440). For an earlier feigned illness on Eleanor's part, see above, p. 243.

[2] Devon, _Issues_, p. 441 ; P.R.O., Exchequer, E.R., Warrants for Issues, 58/104, 110, 111 (with Wesenham described as a sergeant of the pantry, Pulford an usher of the Chamber, Grisacre a yeoman of the Chamber, and Wattes as a porter of the Household). The pseudo-William Worcester maintains that she was sent to " Let-poole " castle in Stanley's custody immediately after the penance, and a contemporary poem consigns her to " Lerpole ". But there is no reliable evidence that Eleanor was ever placed in Liverpool castle (Stevenson, op. cit. ii. pt. 2, p. 763 ; Robbins, op. cit. p. 179 (the version of the same poem in Wright, op. cit. ii. 208, omits this reference to " Lerpole ")).

[3] _Brut_, ii. 482. Apart from Sir Thomas Stanley, Ralph Lee, a Household servant, was paid £100 in February 1442 for his expenses in taking Eleanor to Chester (Devon, _Issues_, p. 441 ; P.R.O., Exchequer, E.R., Warrants for Issues, 58/108 (the order for payment, dated 23 January)).

[4] _Brut_, ii. 482 ; _English Chronicle_, p. 60 ; _Chronicle of London_, p. 130 ; Trinity College, Dublin MS. 5.10, fol. 173ᵛ. Queen Joan's total expenditure in the year March 1420-1 was about 1,000 marks, ten times that allowed to the former duchess of Gloucester (Myers, BULLETIN, xxiv. 271). For Sir Thomas Stanley, see J. S. Roskell, _The Knights of the Shire for the County Palatine of Lancaster, 1377-1460_ (Chetham Soc., xcvi (1937)), pp. 162-72; he was certainly controller of the Household and constable of Chester castle by April 1439 (_C.P.R., 1436-1441_, p. 286).

vided from the revenue of the mills and fisheries lying along the River Dee.[1]

The government was ever nervous of the former duchess's strict confinement while Duke Humphrey lived. On 26 October 1443 Stanley, as constable of Chester castle, was ordered to take her to Kenilworth, and elaborate arrangements were made for her protection on the way ; she and twelve attendants seem to have arrived there on 5 December, to be guarded by Lord Sudeley, chamberlain of the Household, constable of Kenilworth castle and newly-appointed treasurer of England.[2] The move may have been prompted by periodic rumours of plots to free Eleanor Cobham or murmurings against her initial imprisonment ; on 27 May 1443, for instance, a Kentish woman called Juliana Ridligo from Greenwich, where Gloucester owned a manor, demanded Eleanor's release to Duke Humphrey, and even reviled the king himself on Blackheath.[3] More distant confinement seemed advisable by 1446, possibly in response to such rumoured attempts to free her as those with which Gloucester's servants were charged in February 1447.[4] At any rate, in July 1446 Sir Thomas Stanley was again ordered to transfer her, this time to the Isle of Man, of which he was lord ; it was probably there that she died about 1457, ten years after her husband's death and long forgotten by all save one or two chroniclers.[5]

The trial had been the *cause célèbre* of the age. The sharp and

[1] P.R.O., Ministers' Accounts, 796/7 m.8d (1441-2) ; 796/8 m.7d (1442-3).

[2] *C.P.R., 1441-1446*, p. 206 ; Devon, *Issues*, pp. 447-8. Sudeley was the king's chamberlain from 1441 to 1446, constable of Kenilworth castle from 1433, and had recently succeeded Lord Cromwell as treasurer on 7 July 1443 (Powicke and Fryde, op. cit. p. 102 ; R. Somerville, *History of the Duchy of Lancaster*, i (1953), 560). Eleanor was evidently still to be kept under Household scrutiny, although Henry VI was prepared to send her a valuable, be-curtained canopy for her bed at Kenilworth (P.R.O., Exchequer, Various Accounts, 409/12, fol. 94 (1443-4, Household account)). I am grateful to Mr. Roger S. Thomas for the latter reference.

[3] The woman was pressed to death after a trial in King's Bench (*Brut*, ii. 483-4 ; Kingsford, *Chronicles of London*, p. 152). For the trial, see P.R.O., King's Bench, Plea Roll, 725 rex m.35d.

[4] P.R.O., King's Bench, Ancient Indictment, 255/2 ; Plea Roll, 745 rex m.22.

[5] Stanley became lord of Man in 1437 (Powicke and Fryde, op. cit. p. 63; *C.Cl.R., 1441-1447*, p. 233). Giles, op. cit. part 4, p. 31, is the only source to give an indication of the date of her death, at Flint castle in Stanley's custody. *Chronicle of London*, p. 130, maintains that she died at Chester castle, but *Brut*, ii. 482, 508,

acrimonious division among the king's advisers had brought Eleanor Cobham's foolish dabblings in witchcraft and necromancy close to heresy and treason.   Very probably full advantage was taken of her unpopularity and indiscretions to strike at Gloucester, for the public humiliation of his wife would also discredit the duke.   As a result, the Council took an interest in the incident from the beginning, and certain of its members were closely involved in her trial.   Beaufort and Kemp, Gloucester's most venomous opponents, appeared at the crucial stages, with the infirm Chichele pronouncing the formal condemnations.   The king was brought to agree to the action taken against his aunt : he underlined Chichele's committal of her to Leeds castle on 25 July 1441, and his own Household servants acted as custodians of both Eleanor and Bolingbroke from the outset.[1]

And yet, the long and confused story of the proceedings against Eleanor Cobham reflect a basic uncertainty of how a royal duke's consort, suspected of treason, should be tried and judged.   Her errors of faith could be corrected by a bench of bishops, but the treason they detected on 24-25 July was outside their competence.   Hence, a special enquiry by laymen was instituted next day in London ; but even then it was far from clear that Eleanor warranted a trial in King's Bench, and the principal defendants were therefore Bolingbroke and Southwell.   During a long adjournment, Eleanor languished in Leeds castle in the custody of personal servants of the king ; on her return to Westminster in October 1441, the king's constable was her temporary keeper, and she remained in the hands of Household officials until her death.   This may reflect a new approach to the case of the awkward duchess.   The customary penance was her eccles-

Flenley. op. cit. p. 102, and Kingsford, *Chronicles of London*, p. 149, say that she ended her days in the Isle of Man.   Vickers, op. cit. pp. 273-4, would place her death in Flint castle in 1459, but the Isle of Man seems preferable since there is no trace of a subsequent removal from there.   By special act of Parliament, on 3 March 1447, Eleanor was deprived of any claim to dowry after the recent death of Duke Humphrey, and she continued to be excluded from general pardons thereafter (*Rot. Parl.* v. 135 ; *C.P.R., 1447-1452*, pp. 11, 546).

[1] See above, pp. 239 ff.   Despite their chronological confusion, it is worth noticing that the annals of the pseudo-William Worcester attribute Eleanor's consignment to Leeds castle to the king's Council, and her final imprisonment to the king's own order (Stevenson, op. cit. ii. pt. 2, pp. 762-3.)

iastical punishment, but the perpetual imprisonment does not seem to have been imposed by any common law court. Either a prerogative court like that of the Household or Marshalsea was employed, or the problem of a peeress accused of treason defeated the Crown's legal advisers.[1] For the short term, Eleanor was safely locked away in Chester, Kenilworth or the Isle of Man ; but for the long term, the legal lacuna needed to be eliminated. When Parliament assembled at Westminster on 25 January 1442, Eleanor was on her way to Chester ; but for the future, the Commons petitioned that all doubt and ambiguity about the trial and judgement of peeresses for treason and felony be removed. It was accordingly resolved and made statutory that peeresses should be so judged by the judges and peers of the realm, just like English peers.[2]

So stands the trial of Eleanor Cobham. It has a timeless importance in the history of English law and the definition of the legal status of peeresses, if not of women generally. Its importance as a weapon with which to strike at Duke Humphrey of Gloucester is illustrated by the unusual care taken to ensure Eleanor's condemnation and her secure imprisonment in after years ; Gloucester's continued eclipse by the Beaufort faction testifies to its success.[3] When Duke Humphrey returned to the Council board towards the end of August 1442, he did so as a broken figure, whose exalted position supported but shallow power.[4]

[1] For the court of the Household or Marshalsea, held by the steward (in 1441 the earl of Suffolk) and marshal of the Household, see E. C. Lodge and G. A. Thornton (eds.), *English Constitutional Documents, 1307-1485* (1935), pp. 283-4. No record of a trial in King's Bench has been located on the relevant Plea Roll.

[2] Chrimes and Brown, op. cit. pp. 276-7, taken from *Rot. Parl.*, iv. 56. See also W. Holdsworth, *A History of English Law*, i (7th edn., 1956), 388, and F. Thompson, *Magna Carta* (1948), pp. 390-2. Apart from the reasons advanced by Professor Myers for the failure to bring Queen Joan to trial in 1419, uncertainty as to the proper procedure may also have played a part (Myers, BULLETIN, xxiv. 274-7).

[3] John Hardyng, writing within twenty years of Eleanor's trial, affirms the dispiritedness and disrepute into which Gloucester fell as a result of his wife's disgrace (H. Ellis (ed.), *The Chronicle of John Hardyng* (1812), p. 400).

[4] For Gloucester's last years, see Vickers, op. cit. pp. 280-94. One other result of Eleanor Cobham's trial was the appointment of a commission of doctors, notaries and clerks in October 1441 to enquire into the superstitious sect of necromancers and witches in England (Devon, *Issues*, p. 440 ; P.R.O., Exchequer, E.R., Warrants for Issues, 58/63).

[H.A. Kelly, 'English Kings and the Fear of Sorcery', *Mediaeval Studies*, XXXIX (1977), 206-38, subsequently went over some of the same ground. For the political background, now see Ralph A. Griffiths, *The Reign of King Henry VI* (London, 1981), and G.L. Harriss, *Cardinal Beaufort* (Oxford, 1988), ch. 16. Subsequently, evidence came to light which established that Eleanor Cobham died at Beaumaris Castle, in North Wales, on 7 July 1452, still in captivity: see below p. 275.]

16

The Winchester Session of the 1449 Parliament:
A Further Comment

SINCE THE DAYS of Bishop Stubbs, historians of the medieval English parliament and of the fifteenth century have lamented the serious lacunae which exist among the surviving sources for the study of this central institution of government and for the exploration of this much-misunderstood period. Consequently, the crumbs of evidence which have been located—albeit sometimes in the shape of later copies or transcripts —have been subjected to ultramicroscopic analysis and minutely detailed interpretation. This has certainly been the fate of those fragmentary materials relating to the parliament of 1449 which (aside from the formal parliament roll) have been publicized recently by several historians. These materials consist of (1) a list of members—both lords and commons—of the parliament whose first session opened at Westminster on February 12, 1449; (2) a memorandum of lords' attendance at the same session on March 20, 21, and 24, 1449, along with a report of an exchange of views among the lords on March 20; and (3) a list of lords thought to have been present at the third session of this parliament, held at Winchester between June 16 and July 16, 1449, together with a report of another exchange of views between some of the lords.[1]

These documents survive today as copies of the originals (or as copies of copies of the originals) written in the sixteenth or seventeenth century; but it is remarkable that of all Henry VI's parliaments, it is the assembly of 1449 alone to which all the surviving documents refer. This is undeni-

---

[1] For (1), R. Virgoe, "A List of the Members of the Parliament of February, 1449," *Bulletin of the Institute of Historical Research*, XXXIV (1961), 200-210 (with the document printed on pp. 206-210 from British Library, Cotton MS., Claudius C II, fols. 94-96); for (2), *English Historical Documents*, IV, *1327-1485*, ed. A. R. Myers (London, 1969), p. 469 (printed in modernized English from B.L., Lansdowne MS. 229); for (3), A. R. Myers, "A Parliamentary Debate of the Mid-fifteenth Century," *Bulletin of the John Rylands Library*, XXII (1938), 388-404 (with the list and report of the Winchester session printed on pp. 402-404 from B.L., Harleian MS. 6849, fol. 77, of which a facsimile appears facing p. 388); W. H. Dunham, Jr., "Notes from the Parliament at Winchester, 1449," *Speculum*, XVII (1942), 402-415 (with the same list and report printed on pp. 402-404). Myers has also reproduced the Harleian document in modernized English in *Eng. Hist. Docs.*, IV, 468-469. A. R. Myers, "A Parliamentary Debate of 1449," *Bulletin of the Institute of Historical Research*, LI (1978), 78-83, appeared too late for me to compare its conclusions with those expressed here. The documents there printed from B.L., Harleian MS. 78, fol. 1, and College of Arms MS. 2 H 13, fol. 390, enhance the significance of the earlier document printed below.

ably a curious fact, since the business of this parliament in no way singles it out for special interest by Tudor and Stuart observers. Dr. Virgoe's suggestion that "a corpus of the records of this Parliament existed, at least in fragmentary form, until late in the sixteenth century" is the best available explanation.[2] The discovery of another version of the report of the discussion at Winchester in 1449[3] enables the lines of this assembly to be drawn more firmly; and as a sixteenth-century copy, the document's survival reinforces Dr. Virgoe's explanation of the continued existence of these particular fragments.

Of the historical pieces relating to this parliament of 1449, one in particular has aroused discussion because of its complex structure and the political interest of its contents. The British Library's Harleian MS. 6849, fol. 77, with its list of spiritual and temporal lords who supposedly attended the Winchester session of June-July 1449, has been printed and analyzed by Professors A. R. Myers and W. H. Dunham, Jr. The manuscript was written by Sir William Dethick, Garter king-of-arms, probably between 1603 and 1612, and is in his own hand. On these matters, both historians are in agreement.[4] The discovery of a yet earlier version of this document, in Huntington MS. 202, enables some of the points of difference between Myers and Dunham to be examined further and certain other problems to be clarified. Thereby, historians' knowledge of this parliament and of its procedure may be taken two or three steps forward.

The Huntington document is contained in a small paper volume which appears to be a memoranda book of miscellaneous extracts assembled by Edward Stafford, duke of Buckingham (d. 1521), and by his only son and heir, Henry, Lord Stafford (d. 1563). Among these extracts are the names of noblemen abstracted from a variety of fifteenth-century English, Burgundian, and French chronicles, as well as items copied from parliament and patent rolls of the mid-fifteenth century. From references on folios 6^v, 7, and 8, it would seem that this volume was compiled during 1560-1562 and copied from books belonging to Duke Edward ("my Lordes Bookes").[5] Some time after 1562, it was sent to the Garter king-of-arms who, Lord Henry Stafford opined in his address, would be able to see that the entire volume had been collected as a result of his father's efforts and under his direction. Lord Stafford was naturally anxious to have it

---

[2]Virgoe, op. cit., p. 206. Compare, for the first parliament of Edward IV, *The Fane Fragment of the 1461 Lords' Journal*, ed. W. H. Dunham, Jr. (New Haven, 1935); for Henry VII's fourth, W. Jay, "List of Members of the Fourth Parliament of Henry VII, 1491-92," *B.I.H.R.*, III (1925-26), 175.

[3]Henry E. Huntington Library, California, HM 202, fols. 30^v-31^r.

[4]Myers, *B.J.R.L.*, XXII (1938), 389-390; Dunham, *Speculum*, XVII (1942), 402.

[5]Huntington MS. 202, fol. 8. For Duke Edward's interest in the preservation of records, see C. Rawcliffe, "A Tudor Nobleman as Archivist: The Papers of Edward, Third Duke of Buckingham," *Journal of the Society of Archivists*, V, No. 5 (1976), 294-300. Miss Rawcliffe does not mention Huntington MS. 202.

returned.[6] Thus, the reported discussion at the Winchester parliament of 1449 (Huntington MS. 202, fols. 30^v-31^r) is half a century earlier in date than the Harleian document and, indeed, purports to have been copied from a manuscript kept by Duke Edward, fifty years before 1560-1562— that is, within a half-century or so of the events it records. It therefore strengthens the confidence with which historians may approach the Winchester parliament via the Harleian and Huntington documents. It may even be that the Huntington document is more reliable than that originally printed by Myers and Dunham as far as those matters dealt with by both documents are concerned. But, likewise, each contains materials which the other does not, and hence the two documents supplement one another (as is indicated below).

The document in the Harleian MS was written by Sir William Dethick, Garter king-of-arms (1543-1612), and sent to his antiquary-friend, Sir Robert Cotton (1571-1631), probably sometime between 1603 and 1612. The sources from which Dethick produced his copy could not be established by either Myers or Dunham. The history of the volume compiled by Henry, Lord Stafford, may throw some light on this question. Henry Stafford's interest in historical documents and antiquarian pursuits is well known.[7] He was an able man, whose intelligence had been sharpened by an education at the Inns of Court. Later on he supervised the transcription of deeds relating to his own family and recorded the creations of members of the English nobility, a subject close to his heart and his family's fortunes after the attainder and execution of his father in 1521. He also demonstrated an interest in coats of arms and pedigrees, and a catalog of the library at Stafford Castle in 1556 included at least one chronicle of England and other realms which he, and perhaps his father, could have used in compiling the Huntington MS.[8] Moreover, Henry had been in contact with the Garter king-of-arms in 1558 about his own affairs, and hence Stafford's sending of a book of historical extracts to Dethick in the early 1560's need cause no surprise.[9] Between 1550 and 1584 Sir Gilbert Dethick, a Derbyshire gentleman, was Garter king-of-arms. He was succeeded in 1584 by his son William, the man who penned the Harleian MS, in which appears the report of the same 1449 discussion as that recorded in the Huntington MS, belonging to the Staffords. Perhaps Henry Stafford passed not only his and his father's compilation to Sir Gilbert to peruse in the early 1560's, but also

---

[6]Ibid., fol. 2^v.

[7]G.E.C., *The Complete Peerage* (London, 1910-59), XII, i, 184 and n. (f).

[8]Staffordshire Record Office, D(W) 1721/1/10, noted in *Historical Manuscripts Commission Report*, IV (1874), 325-326, 328. Another library catalog was compiled by Henry Stafford himself in 1565.

[9]Ibid., p. 326. It should also be noted that Lord Stafford was for a time keeper of the records in the Tower of London: Rawcliffe, op. cit., p. 297.

the version of the report of the Winchester parliament on which that item
in the Staffords' book was based. If so, it may never have been returned,
and therefore Sir Gilbert Dethick's son, Sir William, could have had to
hand a manuscript on which he in turn might base his own copy of the
Winchester discussion. The fact that the two surviving versions of this
discussion—in the Harleian (Dethick) MS and the Huntington (Stafford)
MS—are by no means identical may simply be a comment on the
selectivity of the two copyists.[10]

Both Myers and Dunham detected two or more clearly defined parts to
the document in the Harleian MS: a list (which may be called A) of
spiritual and temporal lords ostensibly attending the Winchester session
of the 1449 parliament; a report (B) of an exchange of views among
several lords, with a conclusion; and a note (C) that a letter from the
Aragonese mercenary in English employ in France, François de Surienne
(l'Arragonais), had been read before the lords in Parliament on the same
day the exchange of views had taken place. Myers is inclined to regard B
and C as part of the same report, although Dunham was less certain on
this point.[11] The Huntington document does not include either A or C,
and Dunham may therefore have been justified in hinting that C was not
originally part of the report of the discussion (B), but rather a separate
item relating to this parliament which was known to Sir William Dethick
(or his source). In addition, the Huntington document incorporates a
hitherto unknown statement, D, relating to the way in which the taxation
granted by the commons in this session should be spent. It seems likely,
therefore, that A, B, and C were, as Dunham sensed, separate items
which Dethick (or his source) amalgamated into one document; D was
unknown to him or ignored by him.

The report in B is the record of an exchange of views about how best to
raise armies to be sent to Normandy and Guienne ("howe goodd might
be had for the settinge furth of the armyes into normandy and guyen," in
the words of the Huntington document). D represents the final decision as
to how the commons' grant should be spent. B and D, therefore, may be
read as if they were an expression of the lords' views and the conclusion
eventually reached on the subject, and might be considered to follow one
another logically, as they appear in the Huntington document.[12] This
being so, the Huntington document is unlikely to be a faithful rendering
of some "journal" of the daily proceedings of the lords, but rather an ab-

[10]For Sir Gilbert Dethick, who was something of a scholar and presumably, therefore, interested
in Henry Stafford's books and documents, see *Dictionary of National Biography*, XIV, 418-419; A. R.
Wagner, *Heralds of England* (London, 1967), pp. 200-201.

[11]Myers, *B.J.R.L.*, XXII (1938), 392, 394-395; Dunham, *Speculum*, XVII (1942), 412, 414.

[12]During the course of the debate, the treasurer of England, Bishop Lumley of Carlisle,
recommended discussing the matter with the commons: below, p. 262.

straction from it of the record of two related events that occurred nearly a month apart. This need not preclude Myers' suggestion that the clerk of parliament in 1449, John Fawkes, kept a "diurnal" and compiled the original of these reports.[13] A, which is unique to the Harleian MS, may have been compiled by Dethick himself (or by an earlier Garter king-of-arms), as a note at its conclusion states ("Collected and noted per Garter"); but Myers and Dunham are inclined to allow it a fifteenth-century origin.[14] The Huntington document is of no help in solving this problem, apart from allowing the suggestion to be made above that Dethick's source derived from Lord Stafford. In other respects, however, it provides additional or confirmatory evidence to that previously known.

Both Myers and Dunham concluded that the Harleian document referred to the parliamentary session held at Winchester between June 16 and July 16, 1449. The content of the lords' discussion and the explicit reference in the list of lords to a parliament held at Winchester during Henry VI's reign removes all reasonable doubt on this matter. The Huntington document adds that the lords' discussion (B) took place in the parliament chamber at Winchester on June 19. The year can be no other than 1449, the only occasion when a parliament of Henry VI's was held in the city. If the Harleian document is reliable, the letter from François l'Arragonais (C) was read before the lords in parliament on that same day, June 19.[15]

Myers and Dunham disagreed about the forum in which the lords' discussion (B) took place. Myers concluded that, along with the list of lords(A) and the note about l'Arragonais's letter(C), the report referred to a discussion in Parliament itself. Dunham, on the other hand, was inclined to regard the discussion as taking place in the king's council or possibly in a committee of the "higher house."[16] The Huntington document supports Professor Myers' contention that the report (B) was indeed the record of a parliamentary discussion among the lords: it was held in the parliament chamber on June 19, three days after the session had begun. It is doubtful if a council or any other small body would have been

[13]Myers, *B.J.R.L.*, XXII (1938), 396. The commons' grant was not made until the last day of the session, July 16: below, p. **259.**

[14]Myers, op. cit., pp. 392, 394-395; Dunham, *Speculum,* XVII (1942), 414-415. Yet, apart from the presence in the list of lords of certain peers who are not known to have been summoned to this parliament, there is an apparent omission from the list which may keep alive the doubts about whether or not the list was put together later by Dethick. According to "John Benet's Chronicle," the duke of Buckingham attended this Winchester session: see "John Benet's Chronicle," ed. G. L. and M. A. Harriss, in *Camden Miscellany,* XXIV (1972), 195.

[15]De Surienne had written two letters to the duke of Suffolk, the king's closest adviser, sometime after May 25, 1449; one of these is likely to have been the letter read on June 19: Dunham, *Speculum,* XVII (1942), 409, n. 2.

[16]Myers, *B.J.R.L.*, XXII (1938), 396-397; Dunham, *Speculum,* XVII (1942), 409-415. Myers implicitly reiterated his preference for a parliamentary debate in *Eng. Hist. Docs.*, IV, 468-469.

noted as meeting there. On other recent occasions when councillors had met while Parliament was in being, they are not known to have sat together in the parliament chamber, although often in "the Council chamber of Parliament."[17] This, then, was no preparatory airing of views or formulation of tactics or plans in order to guide the proceedings of Parliament; this was a frank and open debate among the lords in Parliament itself.[18]

The occasion for the parliamentary discussion among the lords on June 19, 1449, has been well described by both Myers and Dunham: the critical stage which English fortunes had reached in France, particularly after the provocative seizure of the border Breton fortress of Fougères by François de Surienne on March 24. Thereafter, the armies of Charles VII resumed their offensive against the Lancastrians and successfully assaulted a number of towns and fortresses. The question of assembling men, money, and supplies for new expeditions to northern and southwestern France was therefore urgent when parliament met at Winchester on June 16. Nevertheless, the Huntington document adds or clarifies certain details of the discussion that took place three days later.

According to the Huntington document, the boldest and most constructive proposal made during the lords' discussion originated with William Booth, bishop of Chester (that is, bishop of Coventry and Lichfield). It involved nothing less than those who had lands in France devoting a year's revenue from their property to its defense, and those grantees and annuitants of Henry VI likewise assigning one year's income from their grants and annuities to help raise the proposed armies for France. The Harleian document ascribes these views to Adam Moleyns, bishop of Chichester and keeper of the privy seal, whom the Huntington document links instead with the bishop of Norwich in advocating impartial justice at home and sending to France half the archers raised in the English shires, along with the financial grant made available for the purpose. There are some grounds for believing that the Huntington document is the more accurate of the two and that the Harleian document has confounded the bishops of Chester and Chichester. In the first place, although both documents are later copies, the Huntington document is the earlier and in general has fewer inaccuracies or inexplicable readings.[19] Moreover, with

---

[17]Public Record Office, London, E 28/63/65, 67 (Dec. 1439 at Westminster); *Proceedings and Ordinances of the Privy Council of England,* ed. N. H. Nicolas (1834-37), V, 269, 273-279 (May 1443 at Westminster). Dunham himself, in *Speculum,* XVII (1942), 413 and n. 2, states, "Even in 'time of parliament,' the council sat in its own chamber."

[18]One might also note the formula used to introduce the matter for discussion: "The question is. . . ." This was employed both in the reported discussion at the first session of this parliament on Mar. 20 and in the report of June 19 (Myers, *Eng. Hist. Docs.,* IV, 469; below, p.261). It would have been the standard form employed by the clerk of Parliament.

[19]See the document printed below, and especially its notes, 3, 9, 10, 11, and 29.

regard to this particular statement, the Harleian document omits a crucial phrase and misreads another, so that the purport of the statement is impossible to divine confidently.[20] The Huntington document makes the meaning plain.

Then, too, it may be questioned whether the bishop of Chichester as keeper of the privy seal would have made such a radical proposal, which (at least in part) ran clean contrary to the government's policy at that juncture and, indeed, resembled some of the demands that were being vainly made by the commons against the inclinations of the king and his principal ministers, of whom Moleyns was one. The suggestion that the annual value of all grants and annuities should be devoted to the military emergency smacked of the calls for resumption which were being heard at this time. In fact, this very session of Parliament witnessed a forceful demand for resumption from the commons which the king and his ministers refused to concede, and hence the session dissolved with only a meager financial grant approved.[21] A year later, the first act of resumption passed through Parliament, though not for the specific purpose voiced by the bishop on June 19, 1449. Booth, on the other hand, would have felt no such constraints in making the proposal, even though he may still have been Queen Margaret's chancellor and would later be associated with the hated court faction that was castigated by the commons and others in 1450-1451.[22] There is no inherent implausibility in ascribing to him proposals in 1449 which were intended to relieve the military pressure in France and avoid a bitter clash with the commons in England. For the keeper of the privy seal to have voiced these particular suggestions publicly in Parliament might, on the other hand, seem unlikely. Finally, the views associated by the Huntington document with Adam Moleyns place him precisely beside Cardinal Kemp and the duke of Suffolk, as one might expect of a loyal servant and close associate of both men.

The proposals which Bishop Booth alone articulated sprang from two considerations. On the one hand, he expressed what may have been a growing feeling—certainly a natural one—in the country: namely, that those with estates in France should shoulder the main burden of their defense, and ought to do so by contributing one year's income from their overseas lands. The principle that lay behind this was by no means novel and had something in common with the government's own policy of urging landowners in Wales and Ireland to reside on their estates

---

[20]See Myers, *B.J.R.L.*, XXII (1938), 391, 400; *Eng. Hist. Docs.*, IV, 468. Dunham, however, did hint in *Speculum*, XVII (1942), 411 and n. 3, that perhaps landowners in Normandy were intended in the bishop's statement.

[21]*Six Town Chronicles*, ed. R. Flenley (Oxford, 1911), p. 125. For the resumption question, see B. P. Wolffe, *The Royal Demesne in English History* (London, 1971), pp. 112ff.

[22]A. C. Reeves, "William Booth, Bishop of Coventry and Lichfield (1447-52)," *Midland History*, III (1974-75), 11-29.

personally for their defense.[23] But the element of compulsion in appropriating a year's landed income would be painfully new. The companion proposal, that royal annuitants and grantees should surrender one year's income from their grants and annuities, reflected the growing clamor for resumption after more than a decade of inordinate generosity by Henry VI. Booth had not been a conspicuously favored recipient of the king's benevolence outside the sphere of ecclesiastical benefices, and perhaps he appreciated the danger of the times.[24] If so, no one else among the lords shared his fears or supported his proposals on June 19.

The other opinions expressed by the lords were more cautious in scope, and several of them did not deal directly with the problem of equipping new expeditions. The diversity of opinions produced a predictably feeble conclusion: that the usual methods of raising money and supplies should be adopted. This, presumably, is what was communicated to the commons in the hope that a grant would be made to supplement the meager half-tenth and -fifteenth conceded in the first session of this parliament. The fact that the commons' grant was not made until the very end of the parliament, almost a month after the lords' discussion and conclusion, may demonstrate how difficult it had become for the hard-pressed Lancastrian government to induce the commons to release yet more money for the French war. In fact, the modest additional half-tenth and -fifteenth that was eventually granted on July 16 was, the Huntington document suggests, specifically designed not to equip two new expeditions to France, but to defend Calais, pay its garrison, support the strategic fortress of Le Crotoy at the mouth of the Somme, keep the seas safe, and defend the Scottish border. No provision was made for the financing of an expedition to France; "defence of the realm" was evidently being interpreted more literally than had been common in the past. Moreover, all earlier grants and assignments out of this taxation were declared null and void by the commons.[25] The outcome of the military-financial discussions of lords and commons in June-July 1449 resulted in withdrawing the lines of defense to the coastline of France and the border with Scotland. All else, it might be presumed, was now considered futile.[26]

[See Appendix on next page for Huntington MS. 202]

---

[23]*Calendar of Close Rolls, 1441-47*, p. 255 (1444); Nicolas, *Privy Council*, V, 3 (1436); P.R.O., E 28/78/237 (1436-38).

[24]Adam Moleyns, on the other hand, had been comfortably endowed with grants in recent years: *Dict. Nat. Biog.*, XXXVIII, 131-133, with further evidence in *Calendar of the Patent Rolls, 1436-41*, passim and ibid., *1441-47*, passim.

[25]*Rotuli Parliamentorum* (London, 1767), V, 143-144. For the concern expressed in this parliament about the safety of Calais, see ibid., pp. 146-147. But cf. Myers, B.I.H.R., LI (1978), 81-82.

[26]Compare Prof. J. S. Roskell's appraisal of the commons' attitude in 1449 in his *The Commons and Their Speakers in English Parliaments, 1376-1523* (Manchester, 1965), p. 234.

Appendix: Huntington MS. 202

[fol. 30ᵛ]

.xix. die Junii in camerarie parliamenti apud Winton'.[1]

The[2] question was put furth howe goodd might be had for the settinge furth of the armyes into normandy and guyen.

The Lord Sturton thinketh that[3] ther wold be certein comyssioners of oyer and terminer to enquiere of murders and ryottes don[4] ageinst the peace and[4] also of lyveries and that every[5] shireve[6] certify therof.[7]

The Lord Sudeley and[4] the Lord Cromwell thynke that dewe Justis might be had and a goodd acord among the Lordes first.

The bisshop of Chester[8] thinketh .ii. weies to have gooddes. One[9] ys that all they that have lyvelod beyond the sea[10] geve the value[11] of a yere of thet lyvelod for defens of thes[12] land. And also that they that have grauntes and annyties of the king[13] gave a yeeres value of the same[14] to help furth the armyes in defens of[15] thes contrey.

The bisshops of Norwich and[4] Chichester[16] holden that Justis[17] mey be had without any diffidens,[18] and that half the[19] archiers shuld be sent furth with the grauntes that ben graunted for the defens of the[20] parties.

The bisshops of Baeth and[4] Wurceter be of the same opynyon.[21]

---

[1] In the Harleian MS the document begins thus:

Cardinalis		Dux Suff.
Archiepiscopus Cant.		
Episcopus Wynton.	Comes Warwic.	Prior St. Johnis de Jerulalem
		in Anglia.
Episcopus Caerlyle.	Comes Devon. In parliamento	
Episcopus Landeve.	Comes Wiltes. Apud Winton	
Episcopus Bathe	Comes Wigorni. H. vj..	Dominus Roos.
Episcopus Wygorni		Dominus Grey de Ruthin.
Episcopus Cicestriens.	ViceComes Beaumont.	
Episcopus Norwic.	ViceComes Burcher	
Episcopus Chester [inserted]		Dominus Groby
Episcopus Covent.		Dominus Mollyns
Episcopus Bangor.		Dominus Dudly
		Dominus Lysle
Abbas Westm.		Dominus Cromwell
Abbas Gloc.		Dominus Sudley
		Dominus Sturton
		Dominus Southwik

Collected and noted per Garter

[2] In Harl. this heading begins: "Question is how good might. . . ."

[3] "There" [sic] substituted in Harl.

[4] Word omitted in Harl.

[5] Word interlineated.

[6] "should" inserted in Harl.

[7] This opinion continues in Harl. thus: "certefie to the Commissioners All the names of knightes, Esquires and all other men of might within his shiere That they maye knowe whom they maye empannell suche as be sufficient."

The bisshops of Sarum and[4] Ely wold have presidentes seen of such like maters.[22]

[fol. 31[r]]

My[23] Lord threasorer thinketh that this diligense that the Lordes do for this matter[24] might be entreated of with the comons.

The bisshop[25] of Winton holdeth that yf dew Justis mey be had and them[26] to ordeyn[27] other of the shiere archiers.

My[23] L. Cardynall and my L. of Suff' holdeth[27] the same opynyon.

The conclusion of the[28] comynycation is to take the usuall waies[29] of graunt of goodd for the defens of the Land.[30]

And ther were assignmentes made to the threasorer and chamberlens of the checker of the furst money that shall growe of the half quinessm and half dissme in[5] thys parlament granted by the comons, to be paid in forme as followeth.

ffirst to be paid for wages to the Soldiers of Calleys	m[li.] [£1,000]
Also for victuall and artillery for the same town	m[li.] [£1,000]
Also for wages and artillery to the threasorer of Calleis	c[li.] [£100]
Also for the keping of the east march toward Scotland	m[li.] [£1,000]

---

[8]Apparently given as Chichester in Harl., though the entry is blurred.

[9]Misread as "And" in Harl.

[10]The previous three words are rendered as "bond them selfe for to" in Harl.

[11]The next three words are omitted in Harl.

[12]Rendered as "to defend that land" in Harl.

[13]"grant" inserted in Harl.

[14]Harl. extends this as "of the grant and annuyte before hand."

[15]Rendered as "for the deffence of" in Harl.

[16]Identified as "Chester" in Harl.

[17]"without difference" inserted in Harl.

[18]The previous three words omitted in Harl.

[19]"Shere" [sic] inserted in Harl.

[20]"those" substituted in Harl.

[21]The previous five words are rendered as "houlden after the same" in Harl.

Also for the keping of the west march
   toward Scotland $m^{li.}$ [£1,000]
Also for Rokesborough $v^c mk.$ [500 marks]
Also for Crotey $v^c mk.$ [500 marks]
for the keping of the sea $ii^m li.$ [£2,000]

[For the financial context of this parliament, see G.L. Harriss, 'Marmaduke Lumley and the Exchequer Crisis of 1446-9', in J.G. Rowe (ed.), *Aspects of Later Medieval Government and Society: Essays presented to J.R. Lander* (Toronto, 1986), pp. 143-78.]

---

[22]The opinion is rendered as "houlden that the presedentes that hathe ben in suche matters should be seen" in Harl.

[23]Rendered as "the" in Harl.

[24]Harl. continues thus: "bothe for Ordinance and for men to be sett forthe and for to se the wayes how good might be had for them to be sent forthe which should be layed before the Commons. And they to be entreated to Consider the great dillegence would put theyre handes to theyre good benevolence to see how good might be had to performe the purpose of sending forthe the sayd Armyes."

[25]Rendered as "the Lord" in Harl.

[26]"then" in Harl.

[27]"of" inserted in Harl.

[28]"this" in Harl.

[29]Word omitted in Harl.

[30]The following sentence follows in Harl.: "Item this daye was the Lettre that Sr Francis Le Arragonois sent to the Duk of Suffolk Red before the Lordes in the parliament the whiche was thought right notabley wrytten." The remainder of the document is omitted from Harl.

17

Richard of York and the Royal Household in Wales, 1449-1450

RICHARD, duke of York returned from Ireland in 1450 and landed at Beaumaris, the small fortified borough at the south-eastern tip of the island of Anglesey. Immediately on his arrival in Wales, attempts were made by King Henry VI's officers of the principality to prevent him disembarking and travelling unhindered to England. This was done ostensibly on instructions from the royal Household, for by that date the principality in north Wales had become a Household preserve.[1] Duke Richard therefore arrived in a part of the realm whose government was in the settled control of members of the king's Household. He can scarcely have been unaware of this, and for him to sail into its heart in 1450 was either foolhardy or worth the risk. In studying this confrontation in Wales, the historian is witnessing a provincial rehearsal of one of the acts in the drama which eventually led to the death of the duke of York and the deposition of the Lancastrian king in the 'Wars of the Roses'.

The meticulous author of the contemporary Latin chronicle known today as 'John Benet's Chronicle' gives the date of York's landing as about 8 September and, for an event which occurred at a great distance from the regular haunts of most contemporary chroniclers, this is as precise a date as we have any right to expect. York had, in fact, landed a few days earlier than this, for he had reached his castle at Denbigh on the mainland by 7 September.[2] The duke then made his way to his castle at Ludlow in Shropshire, presumably *via* those estates which, like Denbigh and Montgomery, he held in the Welsh Marches. He rode across midland England, and

---

[1] R. A. Griffiths, 'Patronage, Politics and the Principality of Wales, 1413–61', in H. Hearder and H. R. Loyn (eds.), *British Government and Administration: Studies Presented to S. B. Chrimes* (Cardiff, 1974), pp. 82–86. In May and June 1450 the principality in south Wales, under the leadership of the domineering esquire, Gruffydd ap Nicholas, sent to the king messages of loyalty, offers of money and requests for authority to defend the ports and coasts of south-west Wales; offers of help were renewed in September, when it was known that York had landed in the north. Public Record Office, Special Collections, Ministers' Accounts, 1224/4 m.9; R. A. Griffiths, 'Gruffydd ap Nicholas and the Fall of the House of Lancaster', *ante*, II, no. 3 (1965), 215–16. See above pp. 203–4.

[2] G. L. and M. A. Harriss, 'John Benet's Chronicle for the years 1400–1462', *Camden Miscellany*, XXIV (Camden Soc., 1972), 162–69, 202; J. T. Rosenthal, 'The Estates and Finances of Richard, Duke of York (1411–1460)', in W. M. Bowsky (ed.), *Studies in Medieval and Renaissance History*, II (1965), 198.

when he arrived at Stony Stratford in Buckinghamshire on
23 September, he was dressed in red velvet and was mounted on a
black horse and an Irish hobby; he lodged outside the town gate at
'The Red Lion'.[3] Further south, near St. Albans, the 'western men'
who had accompanied him from the Marches cut a poor figure, their
unruly behaviour causing apprehension in some quarters.[4] On the
27th (again according to the Latin chronicler) he reached London
and took his large force of about 5,000 armed men ostentatiously
through the city to the palace of Westminster.[5] King Henry VI had
only just returned from a judicial tour of Kent, where a commission
was enquiring into the unrest associated with John Cade's uprising
earlier in the summer.

What was particularly ominous about the meeting between king
and duke was the size of the latter's retinue. But in view of recent
unrest in England and the duke's declared intentions, this was
perhaps understandable.[6] We are unusually well informed about
what Duke Richard claimed were his intentions when he came to
Westminster in October 1450, for he presented two bills to King
Henry which were statements of both grievance and proposed
action.[7]

These bills were not the first communications that Richard had
sent to Henry since the landing at Beaumaris ('as I have wretyn to
your excellence here be fore', he reminded the king in the first bill).[8]
Immediately on his arrival in Wales, not only were attempts made by
the local royal officers to prevent him disembarking, but they also
tried to deny him supplies, lodging and 'othir thyng that myght torne

---

[3] 'John Piggot's Memoranda' in C. L. Kingsford, *English Historical Literature of the Fifteenth Century* (Oxford, 1913), p. 372.

[4] J. Gairdner (ed.), *The Paston Letters* (6 vols., London, 1904), II, 174–75.

[5] 'John Benet's Chronicle', p. 202. The annals formerly attributed to the fifteenth-century antiquary, William Worcestre, claim that he marched through London with 4,000 men on 30 September, but when it comes to dates and figures 'John Benet's Chronicle' is more reliable. J. Stevenson (ed.), *Letters and Papers illustrative of the Wars of the English in France* (2 vols. in 3, Rolls Series, 1861–64), II, ii, 769.

[6] Apart from the sources noted in no. 5 above, J. A. Giles (ed.), *Incerti scriptoris chronicon Angliae* (London, 1848), part 4, p. 42, comments on the large number of men York brought into the king's presence. It was also popularly rumoured in west Wales in September that he would shortly make his way to the king with an armed force: P.R.O., Min. Acc., 1224/4 m.9.

[7] These bills, and the king's replies to them, survive in several copies: *Paston Letters*, II, 174–78; Kingsford, *English Historical Literature*, pp. 358–60; *Historical Manuscripts Commission, Beverley Corporation Manuscripts* (London, 1900), pp. 32–35. See also, from the sixteenth century, John Stowe, *The Chronicles of England* (London, 1580), pp. 666–70; H. Ellis (ed.), *Holinshed's Chronicles* (6 vols., London, 1807–8, reprinting the 1587 edition), III, 230–33. See R. A. Griffiths, 'Duke Richard of York's intentions in 1450 and the origins of the Wars of the Roses', *Journal of Medieval History*, I (1975), 187–209. Below ch. 18.

[8] Beverley Corporation Archives, Town 'Chartulary', f. 36–37, printed in Griffiths, 'Duke Richard of York's intentions', p. 203. I am grateful to the Town Clerk of Beverley for providing me with a photograph of the relevant folios of the 'Chartulary'. Below, p. 300.

to my worship or ease'.[9] This formed the substance of a protest which may have been forwarded to the king while York was still in the Welsh Marches in mid-September.

The officers responsible were named by York as Henry Norris, Thomas Norris, William Bulkeley, Bartholomew Bolde and William Griffith, 'your officers of Northwalys'. Henry Norris, a Lancashire esquire, had served as deputy to the principal financial officer of the principality in north Wales, the chamberlain, since before May 1437. Ever since April 1439, the chamberlain had been Sir Thomas Stanley, controller of the king's Household, constable of Chester castle and, from 1443 to 1450, justiciar of north Wales and Chester jointly in survivorship with William de la Pole, duke of Suffolk; after the latter's assassination in May 1450, Stanley succeeded to these two offices in his own right.[10] Also waiting at Beaumaris harbour was Thomas Norris, presumably one of Henry's kinsmen; he had been appointed captain of the town of Beaumaris for life on 16 July 1439 with a small force of five soldiers under his command. Despite the act of Resumption passed in the Leicester Parliament of May 1450, Thomas did not lose his captaincy and, indeed, had received a renewal of the appointment as recently as 6 August.[11] William Bulkeley of Cheadle (in Cheshire) was a burgess of Beaumaris by 1450. Despite a substantial estate in Cheshire, his administrative career (or his marriage in the early 1440s to Elen, sister of another member of the reception party, William Griffith) laid the foundations of the prominent position his family came to occupy in the borough in later years. In 1444 the burgesses of Beaumaris petitioned Parliament on his behalf so that, at the age of twenty-six, he could escape the restrictions placed by law on those who married Welsh. As a result, on 16 August 1448 he was able to secure the post of serjeant-at-arms in north Wales for life; and before that date he had entered the king's service as one of his esquires.[12]

[9] Ibid.

[10] For Norris, see *Calendar of Close Rolls, 1436–41*, p. 120; P.R.O., Exchequer, T. R., Council and Privy Seal, 72/11; 73/67; Min. Acc. 1216/7 m.10; /8 m.10. For Stanley, see *Calendar of Patent Rolls, 1436–41*, p. 286, and a detailed biography in J. S. Roskell, *The Knights of the Shire for the County Palatine of Lancaster, 1377–1460* (Chetham Soc., new series, XCVI, 1937), pp. 162–72.

[11] *C.P.R., 1436–41*, p. 301; P.R.O., Min. Acc., 1216/8 m.5, 11. He is to be distinguished from the later M.P. for Wootton Bassett and Devizes (Wilts.), for whom see J. C. Wedgwood, *History of Parliament: Biographies of the Members of the Commons House, 1439–1509* (London, 1936), pp. 639–40.

[12] *C.P.R., 1446–52*, p. 129; D. C. Jones, 'The Bulkeleys of Beaumaris, 1440–1547', *Transactions of the Anglesey Antiquarian Society and Field Club*, 1961, pp. 1–20; G. Ormerod, *The History of the County Palatine and City of Chester* (3 vols., London, 1875–82), III, 624, 627. He is to be distinguished, sometimes with difficulty, from his namesake contemporary, William Bulkeley of Eaton (Cheshire), who served as deputy-justiciar of Chester under Humphrey, duke of Gloucester and the duke of Suffolk; he died in 1467. Ibid., III, 266–67, 269.

Little is known of Bartholomew Bolde, esquire, with the cardinal exception of the unique surviving rental of his property in and around the borough of Conway, not far from Beaumaris across the Menai Strait. Bolde was descended of a well known Lancashire family which had sent colonists to Conway after the conquest of north Wales by Edward I. He was a locally prominent burgess and a minor official in both Conway itself and the neighbouring commote of Arllechwedd Isaf (Caernarvonshire); between 1420 and 1453 he invested in property in this area with a shrewdness amply confirmed by the surviving rental. On 21 November 1441, Bartholomew and Ralph, Lord Sudeley, who was chief butler in Henry VI's Household, were granted for life in survivorship the captaincy of Conway town with a garrison of eight soldiers. He was therefore well placed to bar the duke of York's path in 1450, and as he made his way to Beaumaris he was in the company of colleagues and friends; indeed, his daughter and heiress, Alice, married William Bulkeley's eldest son.[13]

The only native-born Welshman in the group was Gwilym ap Gwilym ap Gruffydd (or, more commonly, William Griffith), who came from a local Caernarvonshire and Anglesey family. Later in the 1450s he would act as Sir Thomas Stanley's deputy as chamberlain of north Wales, whilst his mother was Joan, daughter of Sir William Stanley of Hooton (Cheshire). William's son and heir, also named William Griffith, would marry a grand-daughter of Sir Thomas Stanley himself. Although the elder William is not known to have occupied any official position of consequence in north Wales in 1450, he was already closely associated with the Stanleys and secured from the king in 1440 and 1443 letters of denizenship which freed him from the irksome disabilities imposed on Welshmen by Henry IV's Parliament. By 1450–51 he was an esquire of the king's Hall and Chamber.[14]

Those who tried to prevent Duke Richard from disembarking, therefore, had much in common besides their employment in north Wales: personal ties with one another and, outside the group, with Sir Thomas Stanley; a Cheshire or Lancashire identity which

---

[13] P.R.O., Min. Acc. 1216/7 m.6. By the time the rental was compiled in mid-century, Bolde's estate consisted of 600 acres of arable, 200 acres of meadow and 1,000 acres of pasture. See T. Jones Pierce, 'The *Gafael* in Bangor Manuscript 1939', *Transactions of the Hon. Society of Cymmrodorion*, 1942, pp. 158–88, reprinted in T. Jones Pierce, *Medieval Welsh Society*, ed. J. B. Smith (Cardiff, 1972), pp. 195–228; C. A. Gresham, 'The Bolde Rental (Bangor MS. 1939)', *Transactions of the Caernarvonshire Historical Society*, XXVI (1965), 31–49. After being deprived of the post of captain of Conway by the act of Resumption of 1451, Bolde and Sudeley secured a renewal of their grant on 20 April 1453: P.R.O., Min. Acc. 1217/1 m.3.

[14] Ibid., 1217/2 m.l; /3 m.l, 7; Exchequer, K.R., Various Accounts, 410/6 m.39*v;* *Dictionary of Welsh Biography down to 1940* (London, 1959), pp. 1124–25.

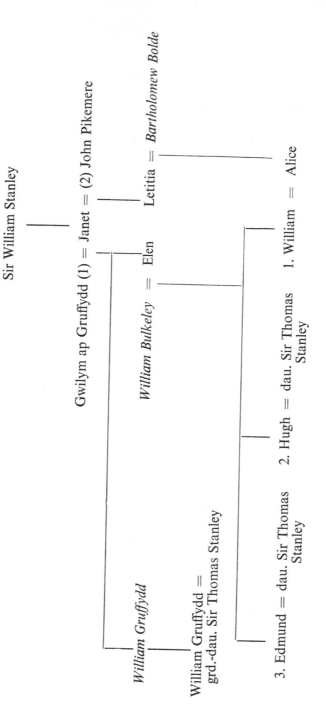

Sir William Stanley

Gwilym ap Gruffydd (1) = Janet = (2) John Pikemere

William Bulkeley = Elen

Letitia = *Bartholomew Bolde*

William Gruffydd

William Gruffydd =
grd.-dau. Sir Thomas Stanley

3. Edmund = dau. Sir Thomas
Stanley

2. Hugh = dau. Sir Thomas
Stanley

1. William = Alice

The names of those who tried to apprehend the duke of York are printed in italics.

Stanley shared; and more than a suspicion of that Household connection which Stanley, as controller and the duke of Suffolk's colleague, had helped to create in north Wales and Chester. The five men were merely one branch of a Household affinity which included Sir Ralph Botiller, steward of the Household and constable of Conway castle, Sir William Beauchamp, the king's carver and constable of Beaumaris castle, and John Stanley, an usher of the Chamber who was also constable of Caernarvon castle and sheriff of Anglesey.[15]

When York reached London towards the end of September 1450, he assembled a more comprehensive battery of complaints; they amount, in the first of York's surviving bills, to a manifesto of private grievances entirely concerned with attacks upon himself and his servants. Yet they illustrate, too, the apprehension with which King Henry and his Court viewed the duke's return and the crude use to which they put the royal Household in order to prevent his progress to Westminster. York maintained that while he was in Ireland he had been accused unjustly of treason, and that on his return not only had attempts been made by the royal officers in north Wales to bar his path, but efforts had been made by members of the king's Household to apprehend him and his principal councillors. Although he hastened to assure Henry VI of his loyalty, he was determined 'fully to pursewe to your highnesse for conclusion of thees maters', by pressing the king to make due enquiry and mete out justice accordingly.[16] Henry replied to York without delay 'to aese yow' of the things that had caused the duke such disquiet. He reassured him, promised to deal severely with anyone found guilty of falsely impugning the duke's loyalty, and implied that he would again communicate with him 'at oure more laisere'.[17]

In this first bill, Duke Richard expanded his earlier complaint, and much of the responsibility for prompting him to do so must rest with the king's own servants. Repeating his protest about the five officers, he added that Henry Norris, deputy-chamberlain of north Wales, had informed him that their intervention had been on the instructions of William Say, one of that élitist body of Household officials known as the ushers of the Chamber. Say's justification was ostensibly the belief that York was a traitor. Say had been a yeoman of the Crown, a king's serjeant and usher of the Chamber (of which

[15] Griffiths, 'Patronage, Politics and the Principality of Wales, 1413–61', pp. 82–86.
[16] Beverley Corporation Archives, Town 'Chartulary', f. 36–37; Griffiths, 'Duke Richard of York's intentions in 1450', p. 203. Below p. 300.
[17] Ibid., p. 204, from Beverley Corporation Archives, Town 'Chartulary', f.37–38. There is a sixteenth-century version in Stowe, op. cit., pp. 668–69.

Sir Thomas Stanley was controller and Sir Ralph Botiller steward)
since at least April 1443. More recently he had been sent on royal
business to Normandy in 1445 and had accompanied Henry's new
queen to England later in the same year. The personal trust reposed
in him by the king was further indicated by his appearance among
the feoffees of the duchy of Lancaster appointed to supervise the
implementation of Henry's will, and like that of many Household
officials his loyal service was rewarded by the inclusion of his name
among the list of those exempt from the 1450 act of Resumption.[18]

Indeed, Duke Richard claimed that the precautions taken to
apprehend him were widespread, with letters being sent to Chester,
Shrewsbury and elsewhere, as well as to Henry Norris. If true, the
communications represent the casting of a net that could be drawn
tight around two of the main land routes from the north Wales
coast into England, *via* York's marcher estates. Circumstantial and
other evidence supports the duke's allegations. John Talbot, Lord
Lisle, was said by York—and one chronicler bears him out—to have
been ordered to 'hearken upon me' from Holt castle, some eight
miles south of Chester in the marcher lordship of Bromfield and Yale;
the £16 which he was given by the king on 18 September was in fact
a reward for expenses he had incurred 'by our commandement . . .
in riding upon oure erthins unto the Duc of York'.[19] Henry Norris,
for his part, was officially instructed to ride throughout north Wales,
accompanied by other servants of Sir Thomas Stanley, in order to
discover all he could about the duke's arrival and report back to the
king.[20] Sir Thomas himself was said to have received a similar
commission to be vigilant in Cheshire, Thomas Pulford in the city
of Chester, William Elton at Worcester, William Broke at
Gloucester and Richard Belth at Beaumaris. All of them, claimed
York, were under strict orders not only to imprison him in Conway
castle, but also to seize and execute his chamberlain, Sir William
Oldhall, and to put two of his councillors, Sir Walter Devereux and
Sir Edmund Mulso, under lock and key during the king's pleasure.[21]
The very precision with which York made his accusations encourages
belief in them, and an examination of the group of political spies he
named, in company with those who confronted him at Beaumaris,

[18] *C.P.R., 1441–46*, p. 160; P.R.O., Exchequer, E.R., Warrants for Issues, 61/248; 62/143;
Rot.Parl., V, 165–66, 191. For his subsequent exemption from the 1455 act of Resumption,
see ibid., p.313.

[19] *Letters and Papers*, II, ii, 769; P.R.O., Exchequer, E.R., Warrants for Issues, 67/232.

[20] P.R.O., Min. Acc. 1216/8 m.10 (1449–50).

[21] Although the bill mentions only 'Pulforthe', 'Elton', 'Broke', and 'Richard Grome of
your Chambir', there can be no doubt that they are the persons identified above. For York's
councillors, see Rosenthal, op. cit., pp. 181, 190; Wedgwood, op. cit., pp. 271–72, 618.

makes the charges seem even more plausible. Of Sir Thomas Stanley, the duke of Suffolk's second-in-command in north Wales and Chester and, for some years, in the royal Household, little more needs to be said to link him centrally with these intrigues. Thomas Pulford had close connections with him, not only as a man of Cheshire stock, but also as a yeoman usher of the king's Chamber, escheator of Flint from January 1437, and custodian of the mills and fisheries along the River Dee; he even shared part of the Dee fishery with Stanley after September 1445.[22] Both William Elton and William Broke were yeomen of the Crown who were sufficiently trusted by the king to be sent on other missions at about this time.[23] Elton, moreover, was briefly constable of Kidwelly Castle (Carmarthenshire) in 1445, and as an usher of the Chamber he figured among the crop of Household exemptions from the 1450 act of Resumption.[24] Richard Belth was also a yeoman of the Crown and, as York himself informs us, a groom of King Henry's Chamber. He had been porter of Cardigan castle in south Wales since 26 September 1447, and although this grant was resumed by Parliament in 1450, he too was eventually confirmed in office.[25]

Apart from Lord Lisle, therefore, the prospective ambushers were all Household men, most of them serving in the king's own Chamber, where their superior as controller of the Household, Sir Thomas Stanley, was able to harness them in support of those of his 'connection' in the government of north Wales. But, as the payment to Lisle and the instruction to Henry Norris indicate, this was no private scheme of Stanley's. It was a plan devised in the royal Household and whose execution was reported to the king himself. Indeed, Henry was candid enough in his reply to York's first bill to make it clear that he was fully aware of these efforts to ascertain the duke's movements.[26] And they may have been more widespread than even York suspected, for on 18 and 19 September, just at the time

[22] For Stanley, see above p.267; for Pulford, *C.P.R.*, *1436–41*, pp. 39, 47; *Reports of the Deputy Keeper of the Public Records*, XXXVII (1876), pt. 2, pp. 602–3; B. P. Wolffe, *The Royal Demesne in English History* (London, 1971), p. 265 (where he was protected from the 1450 act of Resumption in his life-grant of Holywell manor in Rutland).

[23] For Elton's travels on the king's business in 1447 and to Normandy in 1449, see P.R.O., Exchequer, E.R., Warrants for Issues, 63/29; 66/77. He was one of those detailed by special order of the king to keep watch on York's chamberlain, Sir William Oldhall, in 1452 while the latter was in sanctuary: ibid., 68/100; 69/108. For Broke's custody at Windsor castle of men involved in 'certaine tresons' in 1450, see ibid., 67/189.

[24] R. Somerville, *History of the Duchy of Lancaster*, I (London, 1953), 641; *Rot.Parl.*, V, 192; *C.P.R.*, *1446–52*, p. 548. He was serjeant of the king's Hall and Chamber by 1450–51: ibid., p. 423; P.R.O., Exchequer, K.R., Various Accounts, 410/6 m.39v.

[25] For a biographical note on Belth, see R. A. Griffiths, *The Principality of Wales in the Later Middle Ages*, Vol. I: *South Wales, 1277–1536* (Cardiff, 1972), pp. 218–19.

[26] Beverley Corporation Archives, Town 'Chartulary', f.37–38; Griffiths, 'Duke Richard of York's intentions in 1450', p. 204. See below p. 301.

when Lord Lisle was being paid for his services, a reward of £10 was given to Lionel, Lord Welles and Richard Waller, 'upon oure erande unto the Duc of Yorke'. Their mission may have been identical with that of Lisle and the others, in whose company both Welles and Waller would feel at home. For Welles was a member of the royal Household by February 1438 and more recently had married the sister of Edmund Beaufort, duke of Somerset and York's bitter rival, while Waller in 1450 was a personal servant of the king.[27]

The reasons for Duke Richard's return to England and for the king's sharp reaction to his landing provide a many-sided comment on the deteriorating relations between the duke and the king's Court in the later 1440s. The explanation for the choice of Beaumaris as a landfall may, by contrast, be a simple one, though not without potential political significance. It was one of the ports of access to north Wales for shipping from Ireland, though by no means the most important of them. Moreover, it was the port from which York had sailed to Ireland in 1449.[28] But if the duke was anxious to reach his estates in the Welsh Marches in 1450, he could probably have followed a more direct route and (in view of the royal power in north Wales) a less dangerous one. It was the presence of a distinguished political prisoner in Beaumaris castle which may have attracted the duke's attention.

Eleanor Cobham, the widowed—though probably divorced—second wife of Duke Humphrey of Gloucester, the king's uncle, had been transferred to the fortress during 1449 and Richard may have encountered her on his visit later in the year. An insufferably ambitious woman, Eleanor had not been popular after her marriage to Humphrey, but in 1441 her trial for witchcraft and her humiliating penance in the streets of London engendered some sympathy, whilst the nostalgia with which her husband was regarded after his death was unmistakeable. The reputation of Duke Humphrey in the popular memory had sweetened with the passage of time, and during Cade's rebellion in 1450 the myth of the 'good Duke of Gloucester' was launched, three years after his death.[29] The rebels held York in an equally favourable light, and this alone was enough to make the government anxious for the security of the one person who could establish a yet more perilous link between the two dukes

---

[27] P.R.O., Exchequer, E.R., Warrants for Issues, 67/28, 29; G.E.C., *Complete Peerage* (12 vols., London, 1910–59), XII, part 2, pp. 443–44.
[28] On 28 June 1449, York rewarded John Malpas, a valet of his chamber, for riding as a messenger in his service; the warrant was dated at Beaumaris. British Museum, Egerton Charter 8785 m.2.
[29] *Historical Manuscripts Commission*, VIII (1881), appendix I, section 2, pp. 266–67.

—Eleanor Cobham. If Richard planned to seize her at Beaumaris and make capital of the posthumous reputation of her husband, it would indeed represent a subtle and far-sighted strategy. If he did cherish such an alliance, there is no sign that he attempted to abduct Eleanor in September 1450 or champion her cause in after years. Nevertheless, the nervousness of the king and the fears of his Household officials were not without justification on this score.

At her trial, nine years before, a sinister connotation had been placed on Eleanor's interest in astrology and magic; as a result, she and some of her associates were accused of treasonable conspiracy by members of the king's Council, who eagerly grasped the opportunity to besmirch the reputation not only of Eleanor but also of her husband Humphrey. Indeed, there are indications that her degradation was contrived by the Court, and members of the Household were given exclusive charge of her as she was chivvied from castle to castle in the following years. Eventually, she was placed in the custody of Sir Thomas Stanley on the Isle of Man, of which Stanley was lord.[30] In March 1449 it was decided to transfer her to Beaumaris, where the king's carver, Sir William Beauchamp, was constable of the castle under the overall authority of Stanley and the duke of Suffolk as joint-justiciars of north Wales.

The reason for what proved to be the final move in the sorry saga of Eleanor's progress from prison to prison in north-west England is not obviously apparent. It may be that the Household's grip which had closed on north Wales and Cheshire made Beaumaris a more secure place than Man, for although Stanley was lord of the Isle, he is not known ever to have visited it.[31] By contrast, he and his servants would find Beaumaris rather more accessible and easier to police, while at the same time Eleanor would remain reasonably beyond the resources of those who (as in 1447) were thought to be plotting her release. Equally, the Isle of Man was more exposed to naval attacks by the Scots, the Irish and even by the French. Shortly before 1450, hostile Scots, Bretons and others had even landed on the island of Anglesey itself and caused serious damage, and in 1448–49 the Scots were said to be committing depredations there daily. But it is likely that the Isle of Man suffered such attacks even

---

[30] R. A. Griffiths, 'The Trial of Eleanor Cobham: An Episode in the Fall of Duke Humphrey of Gloucester', *Bulletin of the John Rylands Library*, LI (1969), 381–99. (I was unaware of Eleanor's move to Beaumaris when that article was written.) Thomas Pulford, John Stanley and Ralph Legh, who were prominent in north Wales and Cheshire government, were among the Household officials put in charge of Eleanor in 1441–42: ibid., pp. 389, 391, 392 n.2, 396 and n.l, 3; Griffiths, 'Patronage, Politics and the Principality of Wales', pp. 81–84; above pp. 19, 21.

[31] R. H. Kinrig, *History of the Isle of Man* (Oxford, 1944), pp. 124–25.

more severely. As it was, Anglesey and Beaumaris castle were urgently reinforced in 1449 against both foreign invaders and Welsh dissidents.[32] These reinforcements (of eight soldiers, and then twelve and one priest) were needed that much more speedily once it was decided to transfer Eleanor Cobham to the island. On 10 March 1449 at Man castle, she was handed over by John Glegge, Sir Thomas Stanley's representative and janitor of Flint castle (where Stanley was constable), to William Bulkeley, the Cheshire esquire who was serjeant-at-arms in north Wales and lived at Beaumaris. Bulkeley was acting on behalf of Sir William Beauchamp, the constable of Beaumaris castle, whence she was taken forthwith with a great company.[33]

Eleanor died at Beaumaris on 7 July 1452 and was buried there (perhaps in the early-fourteenth-century parish church of St. Mary and St. Nicholas) at great cost to Sir William Beauchamp.[34] She was certainly alive and in residence in the castle when the duke of York sailed into the harbour, not a stone's throw away, in September 1450. It is hardly surprising that Henry VI and his Household servants should feel great anxiety for the former duchess's safe keeping at a time when disturbing rumours of Duke Richard's intentions were reaching the ears of the king.[35]

The circumstances of Richard, duke of York's landing in north Wales in 1450 reflect the role of the king's Household in the polity of late-Lancastrian England and in the sequence of events that brought England to the threshold of civil war. The fifteenth-century Household was vitally important to the Crown in the provinces of England. Thus, in the north-west and in Wales the Household affinity was well entrenched by 1450, enlisting local men and even

---

[32] P.R.O., Min. Acc. 1216/7 m.7.
[33] Glegge, another Cheshireman, continued to keep an eye on Eleanor at Beaumaris: *Deputy Keeper's Reports*, XXXVIII, part 2 (1876), p. 307; Ormerod, op. cit., II, 178. Beauchamp received 100 marks *per annum* to cover her expenses at Beaumaris, and the cost of the journey from Man amounted to £150 8s. 7d.: P.R.O., Min. Acc. 1216/7 m.10; /8 m.9, 12; 1217/1 m.11. For Bulkeley, see above p. 267.
[34] Beauchamp received 100 marks to defray the burial costs: P.R.O., Min. Acc. 1217/1 m.11; *An Inventory of the Ancient Monuments in Anglesey* (Royal Commission on Ancient and Historical Monuments in Wales and Monmouthshire, 1937), pp. 3–8. The only chronicler to suggest a date for Eleanor's death implied that it took place in 1457, and it was this reference that partly led C. L. Kingsford (*English Historical Literature*, p. 63) to conclude that the Latin Chronicle, *Incerti scriptoris chronicon Angliae* (Giles, op. cit., p. 31), was written after 1457. It can no longer be so used.
[35] Cf. Wolffe, *Royal Demesne*, p. 98 n.6: 'Had she lived and been allowed to receive her dower and jointure, she might have been a power in the land comparable to Jacquetta dowager duchess of Bedford.'

local affinities such as that which Sir Thomas Stanley commanded; but especially did it install more important personages in the government of Chester and north Wales so that the authority there of the Household could be strengthened. Such men 'divided their time between his [i.e. the king's] court and their own countries in a seasonal interchange which was not their least important function'.[36] Aside from its role in provincial government, the Household affinity had a special role in times of crisis, in matters of security, and occasionally in offensive operations. It was in this capacity that it was charged with the care of Eleanor Cobham after 1441 and with confronting the duke of York at Beaumaris and in the Marches in 1450.

[P.A. Johnson, *Duke Richard of York, 1411-1460* (Oxford, 1988), ch. 4, places these events in the general context of York's motives.]

[36] D. A. L. Morgan, 'The King's Affinity in the Polity of Yorkist England', *Transactions of the Royal Historical Society*, V series, XXIII (1973), 4–5, 20–21.

18

Duke Richard of York's Intentions in 1450 and the Origins of the Wars of the Roses

As with most civil wars, it is impossible to state categorically when the Wars of the Roses began. Some would unhesitatingly plump for 22 May 1455, when the supporters of King Henry VI and Richard, duke of York clashed at St. Albans, and the king's principal minister, Edmund Beaufort, duke of Somerset, was left for dead in the street and King Henry himself was taken into protective custody by Richard. But, at the risk of flirting with hindsight, others might prefer 1452, the year in which York made his first armed challenge to the king and his government, led by Somerset, at Dartford in Kent on 1 March, but was successfully disarmed by an act of deception. Or, alternatively, the year 1450 might seem more appropriate as marking the opening of the Wars, with, first, a parliamentary attack on the government's record at home and abroad; then, the assassination of King Henry's chief adviser, the duke of Suffolk, in May; a popular revolt in the south-east of the country in June and July; and – the final blow – the unauthorised appearance in England of a disgruntled duke of York later in the year. To understand the intentions of Duke Richard in 1450 is to help understand the state of English politics in that year and to appreciate the extent to which Richard's own role would need to be transformed before he could emerge as one of the leaders in the civil wars.

Richard, duke of York returned from Ireland, where he was King Henry VI's lieutenant, in September 1450. He landed at Beaumaris in Anglesey and made his way to Westminster *via* his own estates in the Welsh Marches. The duke had returned unannounced and when he reached his destination he was accompanied by a large retinue. Efforts were made to apprehend him by those members of the king's Household who had charge of the government of north Wales, but he gave them the slip and arrived at Westminster full of complaint.[1]

The confrontation between Duke Richard and his king represents the first overt attempt by the duke in the 1450s to remedy certain grievances about which he felt strongly. According to Professor Jacob, 'He came now as a reformer' and 'pressed upon him [i.e. Henry VI] certain reforms

---

[1] *Review*, VIII (1976), 14-25, and above ch. 17.

which the king declared his intention of submitting to a committee'.[2] Professor Storey believes that York submitted 'demands that the king's council should be reformed, that he should have a place on it, and that Edmund, duke of Somerset, should be dismissed, perhaps even put on trial for his conduct as lieutenant of France'.[3] However tangible such aims later became, there is room for considerable doubt that York publicised them in 1450 or had even formulated them precisely in his own mind at that stage.

Despite the ominous nature of the duke's arrival in the king's palace, it should not be regarded as an attempt to overawe or cajole the king. Henry VI received the duke in friendly humour and Richard appears to have responded with a degree of humility appropriate to a meeting with his sovereign. This was no confrontation of rivals; nor was it a meeting between an overmighty subject and a cowed or helpless monarch.[4] In two communications which the duke addressed to Henry at about this time, he assured the king of his loyalty and good intentions, and King Henry acknowledged as much in his replies, stating that Richard had shown him 'good humble obeisance' in both word and deed. The king had every opportunity to speak directly and truly on this matter, as he did on others, and there can be little doubt that he was conveying an accurate impression of the duke's demeanour.[5] Only in 1459, when the Parliament at Coventry was cataloguing episodes that would justify the attainder of York and his friends, was it stated with partisan fervour that the duke came 'with grete bobaunce and inordinate people, to youre Paleis of Westmynster unto youre presence, with grete multitude of people harneised and arraide in maner of werre, and there bette downe the speres and walles in youre Chambre, havyng no consideration to youre high presence, by the which myght be understond his disposition'.[6] Government propaganda was then distorting the manner of York's coming in the light of what had happened in England since 1450.

We are unusually well informed about what Duke Richard claimed were his intentions when he came to Westminster in October 1450; it may

[2] E.F. Jacob, *The Fifteenth Century, 1399-1485* (Oxford, 1961), p. 499; cf. K.B. McFarlane, 'The Lancastrian Kings, 1399-1461', in *Cambridge Medieval History*, VIII (Cambridge, 1936), 410.

[3] R.L. Storey, *The End of the House of Lancaster* (London, 1966; reprinted Gloucester, 1986), p. 93.

[4] J. Stevenson (ed.), *Letters and Papers illustrative of the wars of the English in France* (2 vols. in 3, Rolls Series, 1861-64), II, ii, 769; G.L. and M.A. Harriss (eds.), 'John Benet's Chronicle for the years 1400-1462', in *Camden Miscellany XXIV* (Camden Soc., 1972), p. 202; cf. M.E. Christie, *Henry VI* (London, 1922), p. 386.

[5] The communications, two from the duke and two replies from the king, are printed in the Appendix. Reference to them in the following pages is to the text printed there; for the quotation, see the Appendix, No. 2.

[6] *Rotuli Parliamentorum* (6 vols., London, 1767), V, 346.

even be that he fully intended that contemporaries, if not posterity, should be. Richard presented two bills to King Henry which were statements of both grievance and proposed action.[7] These, and the king's replies to them, have provided the basis for historians' judgements on Richard in 1450, but they deserve to be subjected anew to detailed analysis and interpretation. Several copies of the bills survive, and there is more than a suspicion that they were easily accessible in London at the time they were written – perhaps even circulated by the duke himself. Before 6 October 1450 a copy of the second bill had been acquired by William Wayte, a clerk in the service of William Yelverton, justice of King's Bench and no friend to the ruling faction at court, headed until recently by William de la Pole, duke of Suffolk; Wayte presumably obtained it when he 'was in my Lord of Yorks howse'. He sent it to John Paston and in a covering letter added that other 'copyes go abowte the cetye i now, for the love of God'.[8] One of them came into the hands of a London citizen who, shortly after May 1452, incorporated it in a collection of anti-court propaganda which Mr. Kingsford designated a 'Collection of a Yorkist Partisan'. Several contemporary chroniclers, particularly those writing in London, were also aware of what York had to say, especially in his second bill, and it is likely that they picked up their information from the versions that were available in circulation.[10] Copies of the two bills and of the royal replies even found their way into the 'Chartulary' of the town of Beverley in Yorkshire, whose lord was the archbishop of York. In October 1450 the archbishop was John Kemp, who, as chancellor of England since January 1450, is well nigh certain to have studied York's bills, if not helped to compose the king's answers.[11] John Stowe, the noted sixteenth-century antiquary and manuscript collector, also possessed all four documents. Stowe's father and grandfather were London citizens and he may have inherited the copies ('I finde them recorded') from them or one of their

[7] Each communication was referred to by Henry VI in his replies as a 'bill', and neither was in the form of a letter, omitting as they did both an opening address and a concluding dating clause.

[8] J. Gairdner (ed.), *The Paston Letters* (6 vols., London, 1904), II, 174-78. For Yelverton's concern for the proper administration of justice in Norfolk shortly afterwards, at the expense of Suffolk's associates, see ibid., II, 85-86, 90-91.

[9] C.L. Kingsford, *English Historical Literature of the Fifteenth Century* (Oxford, 1913), pp. 165, 358-60.

[10] For example, E. Tyrrel and N.H. Nicolas (eds.), *Chronicle of London, 1089-1483* (London, 1827), pp. 136-37; J.A. Giles (ed.), *Incerti Scriptoris Chronicon Angliae . . . de regnis Henrici IV, Henrici V, et Henrici VI* (London, 1848), p. 42.

[11] *Historical Manuscripts Commission, Beverley Corporation Manuscripts* (London, 1900), pp. 32-35. Immediately preceding the bills in Beverley's 'Chartulary' is another document which can be regarded as a 'state paper' of crucial concern to the chancellor: the agreement reached between the French and the city of Bordeaux on 12 June 1451 prior to the surrender of Bayonne and Bordeaux: ibid., p. 31. The 'Chartulary' was begun towards the end of the fourteenth century and the latest document in it is dated 1454: ibid., pp. 4-5.

acquaintances; at any rate, he incorporated them in his *Chronicles of England*, published in 1580, whence Abraham Fleming abstracted them for inclusion in the edition of Raphael Holinshed's *Chronicles* published in 1587.[12]

The duke of York's bills do not seem to have been presented to the king on the same occasion, for when Henry referred to the second one he spoke of 'your last bille last put up unto us'; nor were they necessarily handed to him personally, for he replied to the first bill after 'we have seen the billis [sic] late taken to us'.[13] But it is certain that Henry received them both while he was at Westminster (between 28 September and 8 October) and when Duke Richard was residing at the bishop of Salisbury's house in the city of London (until 9 October).[14] They had been presented to the king by the time that William Wayte got his hands on a copy of the second bill on or before 6 October. Both bills and replies, and the sequence of events of which they were a part, suggest that King Henry and Duke Richard were victims of the spoken and written accusation, of wild rumour and innuendo reminiscent of Renaissance Italy. It was Henry VI's enfeebled grip on government which allowed them to take on such a credible and semi-authoritative air that political stability was threatened and a dangerous confrontation precipitated between the king and his greatest subject.

The king's efforts to prevent the duke from landing in north Wales and to hinder his journey to Westminster are apparent from the complaints which Richard voiced in his first bill.[15] The reasons for Henry's sharp reaction to York's arrival are partly revealed in his reply to Duke Richard's first bill. If enquiry into his movements had turned to ambush, that was York's fault. It was the manner of his coming – suddenly, with no clear warning – that caused suspicion and the royal servants 'to do as thay

---

[12] J. Stowe, *The Chronicles of England* (London, 1580), pp. 666-70; H. Ellis (ed.), *Holinshed's Chronicles* (6 vols., reprinted London, 1808, from the 1587 ed.), III, 230-33. In copying from this edition of Stowe, Holinshed repeated a phrase from King Henry's answer to York's first bill which Stowe had earlier repeated in error (see the Appendix, No. 2). Holinshed introduced the documents with the abbreviated marginalia, 'Abr. Fl. ex I.S. pag. 666, 667 in Quart.'. Stowe's earlier *A summarie of Englyshe Chronicles*, published in 1565, does not contain the documents, and neither therefore does the 1577 edition of Holinshed's Chronicles. Stowe (and hence Holinshed) mistakenly associated the documents with the Dartford episode of 1452. I am grateful to Mrs. P. Selwyn of University College, Swansea, for elucidating the relationship between Stowe and Holinshed.

[13] See below.

[14] Christie, *Henry VI*, p. 386; 'John Benet's Chronicle', p. 203. Bishop Ayscough of Salisbury had been murdered on 29 June 1450, and Richard Beauchamp was not translated to the see until 14 August; the temporalities were restored to him on 1 October. It may be, therefore, that the house was considered temporarily suitable for the duke: E.B. Fryde, D.E. Greenway, S. Porter and I. Roy (eds.), *Handbook of British Chronology* (3rd ed., London, 1986), p. 271.

[15] Griffiths, *Welsh History Review*, VIII (1976), 14-25, and above ch. 17.

dide'. Moreover, Henry was predisposed to react sharply because of the 'moche straunge langage' which had been floating about the realm in recent months, especially in the uncertain atmosphere created by the assassination in January 1450 of Adam Moleyns, bishop of Chichester, keeper of the privy seal and, what is more to the point, the duke of Suffolk's closest associate in the governing faction about the king. Seditious bills and other hostile propaganda had been disseminated in London in recent weeks, and yet more threatening rumours were beginning to grip the authorities. For example, on 26 March 1450 an enquiry alleged that during the previous two months there had been treasonable discussions at Ipswich about the deposition of the king and the possibility of raising an army to put Richard of York instead on the throne.[16] Henry could even instance his own unnerving encounters with shipmen and others, who had attacked 'oure astate' and threatened him 'be your [that is, York's] sayeng', predicting the duke's return with thousands of men for illicit purposes. A number of people had expressed such sentiments to his face, and some of them had been executed or imprisoned for their temerity. Henry was not exaggerating his experiences over the past year, even if he over-reacted with credulous ease. It was small wonder that, as one Latin chronicler noted, he feared the duke's arrival and intended to resist him.[17]

Shipmen had been among the disgruntled soldiers and sailors who set upon Bishop Moleyns at Portsmouth. The final blow was said to have been delivered by Cuthbert Colville, a veteran soldier who had joined York's personal retinue in France in 1441; but Colville was no exclusive partisan of the duke, for he was also an esquire of the king's Household.[18] Later in the same year, Henry himself had first-hand contact with a shipman. As he made his way to Leicester for the Parliament that met there on 29 April 1450, he was confronted at Stony Stratford by John Harries, a shipman of Terrington (Yorkshire). Threshing the air with a flail, Harries declared darkly 'that the Duke of York then in Yreland shuld

---

[16] *Calendar of Close Rolls, 1447-54*, pp. 194-95; R. Virgoe, 'The Parliament of 1449-50' (unpublished University of London Ph.D. thesis, 1964), p. 198.

[17] Giles, op. cit., p. 42. A measure of the king's alarm early in 1450 is the grant (dated 9 February) to each groom and page of the Household of a bow and sheaf of arrows 'for the sauftye of oure persone', and the ban, ten days later, on the carrying of weapons in London and the south-east: Public Record Office, PSO 1/17/876; *Calendar of Close Rolls, 1447-54*, p. 182.

[18] C.L. Kingsford, 'An historical collection of the fifteenth century', *English Historical Review*, XXIX (1914), 514; Virgoe, thesis cited, pp. 192-95. John Stowe's version of King Henry's reply to York's first bill, in which the king is noted as referring to '*your* [that is, York's] disordinate and unlawfull slaying' of Bishop Moleyns, is a misreading of '*the* disordinate and unlafull sleyng'. It has misled historians to postulate a direct connection between the murder and the duke: for example, B. Wilkinson, *Constitutional History of England in the Fifteenth Century (1399-1485)* (London, 1964), pp. 89, 111 n.1. For shipmen's reputation among contemporaries for illegality, even for murder, see J. Mann, *Chaucer and Medieval Estates Satire* (Cambridge, 1973), p. 171.

in lyke manner fight with traytours at Leicester Parliament and so thrashe them downe as he had thrashed the clods of erthe in that towne'. On the commission of oyer and terminer nominated in Northamptonshire to investigate Harries's activities was Thomas Daniel, an esquire of the body and usher of the Chamber who came from Cheshire; he was chamberlain of the palatinate and one of Suffolk's most devoted lieutenants.[19] In the course of the enquiry, Daniel was said to have 'labored his [that is, Harries's] deathe with yomen of the crowne', and such pressure may have been in York's mind when he complained to the king that 'certeyn persones laboured instantly for to have endited me of Treson' before empanelled juries. This would not have been the first time that he considered himself to be the victim of character assassination, for some time in 1447-8 he believed that Bishop Moleyns, keeper of the privy seal, was contriving to build a case against him of embezzlement and gross dereliction of duty in Normandy, even to the extent of sending men to England to testify to these charges. York could be forgiven if in 1450 he was predisposed to distrust the activities of ministers and servants of the king.[20]

In the summer of 1450, John Cade's rebellion forged an even more obvious link with York in Ireland. Not only did the rebel leader adopt the name of John Mortimer, thereby implicitly claiming a blood relationship with the duke and enlisting his reputation in the commons' cause, but the rebel demands included one that the king should 'take abowte hym a nobill persone, the trewe blode of the Reame, that is to say the hye and myghty prince the Duke of Yorke, late exiled from our soueraigne lordes presens of the false traitour Duke of Southfolke and his affinite'.[21] According to their own lights, the intentions of the rebels were honourable and loyal enough, and they claimed that it was the king's entourage that was putting a sinister interpretation on their demands: 'they enforme the

[19] J.C. Wedgwood, *History of Parliament. Biographies of the Members of the Commons House, 1439-1509* (London, 1938), pp. 253-55; *Calendar of Patent Rolls, 1446-52*, p. 383; Kingsford, *English Historical Literature*, p. 371; J.S. Roskell, 'Sir William Oldhall, Speaker in the Parliament of 1450-51', *Nottingham Medieval Studies*, V (1961), 314 (reprinted in his *Parliament and Politics in Late Medieval England* [3 vols., London, 1981-83], II, 175-200). Daniel was exempt from the 1450 act of Resumption. For other instances of popular denunciations of the king, even to the point of allegedly plotting his death or overthrow, though without naming York specifically, see 'John Benet's Chronicle', p. 197 and n. 114; Kingsford, *English Historical Review*, XXIX (1914), 514-15; R. Flenley (ed.), *Six Town Chronicles* (London, 1911), p. 129; PRO, KB 9/73/1 et seq.; 122/7 (Chichester, August 1450); 122/28 (Brightling, in Sussex, July 1450); 133/39, 22 (Wiltshire, September 1450).

[20] Kingsford, *English Historical Literature*, p. 371; B.P. Wolffe, 'The Personal Rule of Henry VI, in S.B. Chrimes, C.D. Ross and R.A. Griffiths (eds.), *Fifteenth-Century England, 1399-1509* (Manchester, 1972), pp. 41-42.

[21] Kingsford, *English Historical Literature*, pp. 360-62. The *Brut* Chronicle (F.W.D. Brie [ed.], *The Brut, or the Chronicles of England*, II [Early English Text Soc., CXXXVI, 1908], 517) explicitly states that Cade called himself 'Mortymer, cosyn to ye duke of Yorke'.

kynge that the Comyns wolde ffurst destroye the Kynges ffreends and afteer hymeselfe, and thenne brynge in the Duke of Yorke to be Kynge'.[22] The intriguing possibility that York was personally involved in encouraging Cade's rebels has defied efforts at proof one way or the other. It is possible, as a later hostile jury claimed, that the duke's chamberlain, Sir William Oldhall, had taken Cade's part and proclaimed his leadership at Bury St. Edmunds, and that he encouraged the Kentishmen to join York *en masse* on the way from Ireland. But the circumstances of these accusations – by Oldhall's enemies in February 1453, when York was powerless to help his servant – undermine faith in their veracity, and still less reliance can be placed on the accusation, made at the same time, that on 6 March 1450 Oldhall had plotted to replace Henry VI with Duke Richard. Similar doubts may be cast on the claim of a commission of enquiry in 1452 that in the autumn of 1450 a group of local gentlemen were busy organising a rising in the city of Norwich in support of the duke of York, predicting that he would seize the Crown when he returned from Ireland.[23]

Such tittle-tattle of slender foundation was at the root of York's complaints in his first bill. He feared that he would be indicted of treason as a result of it, and that his descendants would be disinherited and his blood corrupted in law. His fears seemed all the more justified in view of the credulity of the king, the machinations of his courtiers, and the consequent seriousness with which threatening utterances by obscure individuals were evidently being treated.

York's contention that he had been wrongfully accused, and that commissions were being induced to indict him of treason, bore striking similarity to the rebels' description of how Humphrey, duke of Gloucester met his end three years earlier: 'enpechid of tresone by on ffalse traytour alone'. If York was apprehensive lest the treatment of the two dukes be made to accord even more closely, so that he, like Gloucester, might be 'so sone merderud, and nevur myzt come to onswere', his mind was hardly set at ease by the circumstances of his arrival in Wales and his confrontation with the Household officials.[24] York's claim that the intention was 'to have undo me, myn Issue, and corrupt my blode', would strike familiar

---

[22] *Historical Manuscripts Commission*, VIII (1881), 266-67.

[23] Storey, *End of the House of Lancaster*, pp. 79, 225. In his reply to York's first bill, Henry VI mentioned that one of those who had threatened him to his face was called 'Wastnesse'. It is just possible that he was referring to John Wasteneys, a Nottinghamshire man who represented the shire in the Parliament of 1450-51 which attacked the most prominent courtiers. York's companions in 1450, Mulso, Oldhall and Devereux, were all present in this Parliament; indeed, it was the only one in which Mulso and Oldhall sat: Wedgwood, *History of Parliament*, pp. 924, 271, 618, 647.

[24] *Historical Manuscripts Commission*, VIII (1881), 266-67; cf. Kingsford, *English Historical Literature*, pp. 360-62.

chords in those who heard it.

Moreover, the reputation of Duke Humphrey in the popular memory had so sweetened with the passage of time that within three years of his death a myth of the 'good Duke of Gloucester' was abroad.[25] For the names of York and Gloucester to be linked in such a favourable light by an articulate expression of popular opinion was enough to make the government anxious for the security of the one person who could forge a yet more perilous connection between them: Eleanor Cobham, the widow of Humphrey, duke of Gloucester. In September 1450, when York sailed into the port of Beaumaris, Eleanor was to be found incarcerated in the adjacent castle, a prisoner whose release might have considerable and unpredictable political repercussions.[26] All these apprehensions, some justified but others not, worked sedulously on the mind of the king and his advisers so that their suspicion of Duke Richard reached fearful proportions.

Duke Richard was no less disturbed by rumour, innuendo and wild accusation than Henry VI, although in his case they may have appeared more threatening after travelling the distance to Ireland. Richard, then, may have been just as much a victim as Henry VI of the undergrowth of rumour and hearsay that was thrusting him forward as the prospective reformer of England's ills in the supposititious tradition of Humphrey of Gloucester. Far from encouraging this thinking, particularly during Cade's rebellion, the duke may have been seriously embarrassed by it and afraid of the consequences if the king were to believe it. The first bill he put before Henry at Westminster certainly gives the impression that the return to England in 1450 was, at least in part, an attempt to vindicate himself, and his respectful behaviour in the king's presence reflects just that.

Aside from accusations, which unnerved the king and, probably, the duke, there were other matters that caused York disquiet. As he stated to Henry, he believed that efforts were being made to have him attainted – or worse – and some historians have implied that this was a prelude to undermining his claim to be Henry's heir presumptive.[27] It would, indeed, have been inconceivable for an attainted family to provide the heir to the English throne should Henry and his queen continue childless. York had some grounds for these fears, though they may have been based on no more authoritative source than the Commons' manifesto of complaint against the duke of Suffolk in 1450. It was stated in Parliament on 7 February that Suffolk's motive in securing the wardship of Margaret

[25] *Historical Manuscripts Commission*, VIII (1881), 266-67.

[26] R.A. Griffiths, 'The Trial of Eleanor Cobham: an Episode in the Fall of Duke Humphrey of Gloucester', *Bulletin of the John Rylands Library*, LI (1969), 381-99, reprinted above pp. 233-52; idem, *Welsh History Review*, VIII (1976), 14-25, and above pp. 265-76.

[27] Jacob, *Fifteenth Century*, p. 499; Storey, *End of the House of Lancaster*, p. 74.

Beaufort, only daughter and heiress of John, duke of Somerset (d. 1444), was not simply to enjoy custody of an important and wealthy heiress, but also eventually to marry her to his son, John de la Pole, 'presumyng and pretendyng her to be next enheritable to the Corone of this youre Reame, for lakke of issue of you Soverayne Lord'. This plan was supposedly formulated on 20 July 1447, although, as the Commons acknowledged, the marriage appears not to have taken place until the parliamentary session itself, between the date of Suffolk's arrest on 28 January 1450 and 7 February; both Margaret and John were then about seven years old. The Commons' charge was highly partisan, embedded in a catalogue of alleged iniquities committed by Suffolk; in any case, it was far from unusual for the guardian of a desirable heiress to contrive to marry her to one of his sons. Suffolk, in fact, freely admitted that he had had such an idea in mind, but he maintained that the prospective bride was the even more wealthy Anne Beauchamp, daughter and heiress of Henry, duke of Warwick (d. 1445) and Suffolk's ward since 1446; she, however, died in January 1449 at the age of five, before any marriage could take place.[28]

The only indication that Suffolk had such a sinister motive comes from the record of an enquiry held in London on 4 July 1450, at the height of Cade's revolt when the rebels were themselves in control of the city and overawed the commission to such effect that Lord Say, the king's chamberlain and treasurer of England, was condemned to death. It was recorded on this occasion that Suffolk, on the same 20 July 1447, had proposed to marry his son to Margaret and place them both on the throne as king and queen of England. If anything, this evidence is even more tainted than the Commons' formal assertions, from which it may have been entirely plagiarised.[29] In response to a petition on behalf of John and Margaret, a papal dispensation dated 18 August 1450 allowed them to remain married, despite their relationship in the fourth and fifth degrees.[30] If the match had such profound dynastic implications, surely this would have been the opportunity to have had them scotched, after Suffolk's death and with the fright of Cade's revolt fresh in the king's mind. But only in February 1453 were the couple in fact divorced and then for reasons that are unknown to us.[31]

If York feared for his position as heir presumptive to Henry VI in 1450, rumours of this sort may have been responsible. It is difficult to estimate how much real justification there was for such fears in the unstable situation of that year. Contemporary ideas about the rules of succession to

[28] *Rot. Parl.*, V, 177, 182; G.E. Cokayne, *The Complete Peerage*, ed. V. Gibbs et al. (12 vols. in 13, London, 1910-59), XII, i, 48, 447-48; XII, ii, 384.

[29] Storey, *End of the House of Lancaster*, p. 74.

[30] Margaret Beaufort and Henry VI shared the same great-grandfather, John of Gaunt.

[31] *Complete Peerage*, XII, i, 449-50; *Calendar of Papal Registers, 1447-55*, pp. 472-73; 'John Benet's Chronicle', p. 209. Although the end of the marriage was described as a divorce by contemporaries, it may in fact have been an annulment based on non-consummation.

the English throne were ill-formed and therefore it was possible to assert that the Beauforts, with Margaret as their most senior representative by birth, had an acceptable claim to provide Henry's heir, despite the illegitimacy of Margaret's grandfather, one of John of Gaunt's sons. On the female side, Henry had two half-brothers, Edmund and Jasper, the sons of his mother, Katherine of Valois, and the Welsh squire, Owen Tudor. It may not have been entirely fortuitous, in view of Henry's continuing childlessness, that when Margaret's wardship and marriage were available a second time after her divorce from John de la Pole, they were kept firmly in the royal family by being granted to Henry's half-brothers on 24 March 1453. By then, the threat from the duke of York loomed larger and the anxieties of 1450 may have acquired more solid form. As Professor Chrimes comments, 'Henry VI can scarcely have made it [the grant] without some expectation that the collateral lines would become entwined', and in 1485 it was indeed the son of Margaret and Edmund Tudor who succeeded to the English throne as King Henry VII.[32] But it is open to question whether these possibilities really justified the apprehension felt by York three years earlier, or whether Henry VI had yet conceived such a distrust for the duke that he could not tolerate the thought of him or one of his sons as his heir.

York did not detail these matters precisely in his bills to the king in October 1450. However, there can be no doubt that he deeply resented his treatment by Henry's government, his exclusion from the king's patronage and the king's counsels by such as Suffolk, and the likelihood that, after Suffolk's death, he would continue to be spurned in favour of Edmund Beaufort, duke of Somerset. It may have been this dismal prospect that converted important grievances into dynastic alarm a few years later, before the birth of the prince of Wales in October 1453 clarified the situation for a time.

Among these grievances were the large debts which York had incurred in the service of the house of Lancaster both by way of loans and as royal lieutenant in France and Ireland. According to Dr. Steel, during 1443 alone the duke lent as much as £12,333 6s. 8d. to the king and in so doing became his largest single creditor by far in the period 1442-52; the total loan of £26,000 which was ordered to be repaid in July 1446 was a stout prop of Lancastrian finance. Although efforts had been made almost immediately to give York some security for his loans (for example, some of the Crown jewels) and then to provide repayment by assignment, only

---

[32] S.B. Chrimes, *Lancastrians, Yorkists and Henry VII* (2nd ed., London, 1966), pp. 76-78; idem, *Henry VII* (London, 1972), p. 13. Edmund Beaufort, duke of Somerset, who, as a younger brother of Duke John (d. 1444), was Margaret's uncle, was not the 'nearest of kin to Henry VI' (cf. Jacob, *Fifteenth Century*, p. 499), although the senior surviving male of the Beaufort line; his claim to be the Lancastrian heir was therefore that much weaker in theory in a rather uncertain legal situation.

about half of the tallies he received on 21 February 1444 proved cashable.[33] The scale of York's loans is as noteworthy as the failure to repay them was serious for the duke, for his net income from land, his major resource, was of the order of £5,800 a year.[34] Moreover, Richard's years of service as lieutenant-general and governor of France and Normandy caused the Crown's indebtedness to grow even larger. The result was that when he was relieved of his command in June 1446, the Exchequer owed him £38,666 for the years 1443-45 alone, and in order to secure at least part of this enormous sum he had to forego £12,666 of it.[35] Even so, by the end of July 1446, more than £11,600 of the £14,000 worth of tallies that had been issued to him had not been cashed and had now to be replaced by an alternative supply. Dr. Steel has calculated that during the decade 1442-52 he received a bundle of 'bad' tallies amounting to the dangerously inflated sum of £21,008; nobody else was in an unfortunate position remotely comparable to York's.[36]

The duke's appointment to the lieutenancy of Ireland in July 1447 intensified his sorry financial plight. His complaints to the king on the subject were correspondingly forthright and repeated, and Henry made no attempt to deny their truth. York's dilemma even forced him to contemplate selling or mortgaging some of his English manors to a group of friends and servants in September 1449, 'to helpe hym to the charges and costes that he hath and shall at this tyme bore to do your highnesse service' in Ireland.[37] And although Henry gave ready permission for such transactions to take place, he was less forthcoming about paying the duke his salary. Sometime in the first half of 1450, York asserted that the king owed him, as lieutenant of Ireland alone, the sum of £3,133 6s. 8d., but he also listed a further £6,000 from annuities and other sources which had equally failed to materialise from the Exchequer. It is hardly surprising that the duke was able to claim that the constant borrowing and property deals to which he was forced to resort had impoverished him 'to [his] right greet hindering and grevous damage'. Fearful perhaps of what he might do to remedy his own situation, especially in the context of recent rumours involving the duke, Henry ordered the Exchequer on 17 May 1450 to

---

[33] A. Steel, *The Receipt of the Exchequer, 1377-1485* (Cambridge, 1954), pp. 220-22, 257; PRO, E404/62/224.

[34] Steel, *Receipt of the Exchequer*, pp. 220-22; K.B. McFarlane, *The Nobility of Later Medieval England* (Oxford, 1973), pp. 177-78.

[35] Storey, *End of the House of Lancaster*, p. 75; PRO, E404/62/188, 230.

[36] Steel, *Receipt of the Exchequer*, pp. 226-27, 258-59. Even so, one of the tallies issued on 20 July 1446 (for £100) was still uncashed in May 1449 and had to be returned to the Exchequer: PRO, E404/65/182. To take another example, a tally of £300 issued to York on 21 February 1444 was replaced in July 1445 and again in May 1449: PRO, E401/785 m. 15; 790 m. 20; 810 m. 7.

[37] PRO, E28/79/3.

settle its account with him without disputing the figures.[38] He appears also to have explored less direct methods of improving his financial position by seeking the sympathy of some of the king's councillors, for on 15 June he let his brother-in-law, the earl of Salisbury, know that unless his army in Ireland was paid, he might have to abandon his responsibilities there and return to England to live. Such representations do not seem to have led to any speedy transfer of funds from the king's Exchequer to the duke.[39] Four years later, he was still lamenting that he had been forced:

> to celle a grete substance of my lyvelood, to leye in plege all my grete Jowellys, and the most partie of my Plate not yet raquited, and therfor like to be loost and forfaited; and overe that, to endaungere me to all my Frendes, by chevisance of good of thaire love, for their accomplisshement of the service and charge, whiche at the seid desire I toke upon me in the saide Reaume of France, Duchie and Lond of Irlond, not faisible without notable good, for the which divers sommes of monneye bee to me due; for paiement wherof, many promisses have been to me made, not parfourmed.[40]

York's frustrating financial experiences contrast with the care taken by the government to honour its obligations to John and Edmund Beaufort. This difference in treatment helped to intensify the resentment which York already felt towards a family which he distrusted and a régime that discriminated against him. Whatever dynastic suspicions York may have harboured, there were more immediate factors causing hostility between him and the Beaufort brothers. Their careers had become entwined in France, where John Beaufort seems to have been promoted by Henry's government at the express expense of the duke of York. On 30 March 1443, Beaufort was appointed lieutenant and captain-general of France and Gascony for seven years while York was still serving a five-year term as lieutenant-general and governor of France and Normandy. York can be forgiven for not appreciating the subtly different titles of what was, in

---

[38] N.H. Nicolas (ed.), *Proceedings and Ordinances of the Privy Council of England* (7 vols., Record Commission, 1834-37), VI, 92-93; PRO, PS01/18/933. The Irish salary was fixed at £2,666 13s. 4d. for the first year of York's term as lieutenant and £1,333 6s. 8d. for each of the subsequent eight years. The Exchequer eventually delivered a first instalment of £1,333 6s. 8d. to York's cofferer more than one year late on 7 November 1448: PRO, E404/63/160; 65/59. Subsequent assignments of cash in February and December 1449 do not seem to have been honoured before the duke made his complaint in 1450: Nicolas, *Proceedings and Ordinances*, VI, 89-90; PRO, E404/65/104; 66/77. See also A.J. Otway-Ruthven, *A History of Medieval Ireland* (London, 1968), pp. 381-82.

[39] J.R. Lander, *The Wars of the Roses* (London, 1965), pp. 62-63; PRO, E403/815, 818. The most that can be said is that on 6 October 1450, by which time York had reached London, four tallies worth £113 3s. 0d. were given to him, authorised by a privy seal letter issued at about Easter, which may well have been that of 17 May.

[40] *Rot. Parl.*, V, 255.

effect, the supreme command in English France, and the lame explanation that Beaufort should exert his authority only where York was unable to do so. York felt a sense of injury – perhaps even of humiliation – which he angrily communicated to the government at home. Moreover, John Beaufort was created duke of Somerset at the same time, and provided with a larger army than York had at his disposal. The final rub was the preferential treatment Beaufort was given at the Exchequer, which found £25,000 for advance wages for his forces; York, on the other hand, was told to be patient, since England could not properly support reinforcements for both commanders.[41] Relations between the Beauforts and York deteriorated further when the question of York's successor as lieutenant-general arose in 1445-46. It was eventually decided to replace York by John Beaufort's brother Edmund, the new duke of Somerset, and to transfer York to Ireland, where he was appointed royal lieutenant for nine years.[42] The ingratitude of the Lancastrian government appears all the more galling when it is recalled that during the decade 1442-52, when York lent large sums of money to Henry and received a poor crop of assignments in return, Edmund Beaufort (admittedly a less wealthy man) advanced relatively minute sums to the king and received not one-tenth of York's total of so-called 'bad' tallies.[43] When Edmund failed to prevent the French advance into Normandy and himself surrendered the city of Rouen in October 1449, York's personal resentment merged in the tide of shame and disgust rising in England generally.

Duke Richard's return to England in September 1450 may, in its timing, have had a closer link with the activities of his rival, Somerset, than with the more widespread expressions of unrest of the previous ten months. Despite the rumours and predictions, York apparently made no effort to return to England during the year following his landing at Howth in Ireland on 6 July 1449[44] – not even during the parliamentary session

---

[41] Storey, *End of the House of Lancaster*, p. 72; Nicolas, *Proceedings and Ordinances*, V, 251-53, 259-61, 288-90.

[42] Storey, *End of the House of Lancaster*, pp. 73-74. Whether Suffolk or Henry VI himself was responsible for York's 'exile' has been the subject of discussion by Dr. Wolffe ('The personal rule of Henry VI', p. 41). 'John Benet's Chronicle', p. 195, maintains that it was the malicious advice of Suffolk that induced Henry to send him there, and the London author of 'Gregory's Chronicle' notes that he was 'exsylyde in to Irlonde for hys rebellyon, as thoo aboute the kynge informyde hym, fully ande falsely as hyt was aftyr warde i-knowe': J. Gairdner (ed.), *The Historical Collections of a Citizen of London* (Camden Soc., 1876), p. 189. But see Giles, op. cit., p. 35.

[43] Steel, *Receipt of the Exchequer*, pp. 258, 259. It should be said that York and Somerset both suffered from the 1450 act of Resumption, passed in Parliament while they were abroad. This may have quickened the resolve of both men to return to England later in the year: B.P. Wolffe, *The Royal Demesne in English History* (London, 1971), pp. 129-30.

[44] Otway-Ruthven, *Medieval Ireland*, p. 379. York sailed to Ireland from Beaumaris and, as he no doubt had learnt to expect, was required to foot about a third of the bill: PRO, E404/65/82; 66/116.

that saw the attack on Suffolk, or during the upheaval that in June precipitated Cade's revolt. It is more likely that news of Somerset's return to England on 1 August 1450 prompted York to set sail for Beaumaris a month later. By 15 August Somerset had joined the king's Council, thereby helping to fill the gap left by the removal of Suffolk; on 11 September he was appointed constable of England.[45]

We know next to nothing of York's means of communication with England during his absence in Ireland. But in his chamberlain, Sir William Oldhall, he had an ubiquitous news-vendor. Like Sir Edmund Mulso and others, Oldhall had probably accompanied York to Ireland early in July 1449, but he had evidently returned to England by the following year because in April 1450 he received a protection to set forth once again across St. George's Channel; he appears to have done so some time in the summer.[46] Henry VI, too, kept in contact with his Irish lieutenant, and in June 1450 he sent Lancaster king of arms on an errand to the duke.[47] Whatever the means employed, the duke probably soon learnt of Somerset's return. He was still at Trim on 26 August, but within a fortnight he was stepping ashore in Beaumaris harbour.[48]

Richard of York's intentions in 1450 can be ascertained not only by examining the motives which prompted his return from Ireland, but also by scrutinising his subsequent actions and their consequences. His reaction to the king's Household is significant. There was no certainty that the Household affinity which the duke of Suffolk had headed would survive intact the duke's death in May 1450, or that its coherence could be smoothly maintained by someone else. However steadfast Sir Thomas Stanley was in holding part at least of this group together in north Wales to bar York's path in September, some of the king's servants elsewhere were more faint-hearted – or else quicker to put their personal security before group loyalty. Either explanation may account for the fact that John Sutton, Lord Dudley, and Reginald Boulers, abbot of Gloucester and, from 14 August 1450, bishop of Hereford, rode to meet York at Ludlow; they did so, according to one chronicler, for their own safety.[49]

[45] Storey, *End of the House of Lancaster*, p. 75; *Complete Peerage*, XII, i, 51-52.

[46] W.G.H. Quigley and E.F.D. Roberts (eds.), *Registrum Johannis Mey* (Belfast, 1972), pp. 155-56; Roskell, 'Sir William Oldhall', pp. 98, 100; Wedgwood, *History of Parliament*, p. 618. Oldhall set foot in Ireland before 2 October 1449, but he was said in 1453 to have plotted King Henry's deposition in England on 6 March 1450.

[47] PRO, E404/66/184.

[48] Otway-Ruthven, *Medieval Ireland*, p. 383.

[49] 'John Benet's Chronicle', p. 202. Boulers had recently been attacked by his Gloucestershire tenants for his alleged role in the loss of the French territories: Kingsford, *English Historical Literature*, pp. 355-56. It may be significant that, unlike most Household officials and courtiers, Dudley was not confirmed in his grants cancelled by the 1451 act of Resumption: Wolffe, *The Royal Demesne*, pp. 282, 285.

The same motive is likely to have prompted Thomas, Lord Hoo, the former chancellor of Normandy whom Cade's rebels had ridiculed, to risk his life and hurry to meet York as he was on his way to London; near St. Albans Sir William Oldhall had to intervene to protect Hoo from 'the western men' who were accompanying the duke.[50] And what manoeuvres lay behind the cryptic comment made by John Paston's correspondent on 6 October that Oldhall and Lord Scales, the seneschal of Normandy who had helped to drive Cade's rebels out of London, 'ar friends become'? For Oldhall, as York's chamberlain, was evidently regarded as the intermediary through whom York's favour might be sought and, perhaps, even as the organiser of strategy for the duke in these turbulent months.[51] After Suffolk's demise, men like Dudley, Boulers and Hoo may have concluded that York was destined for greater prominence at court and a more central role in policy-making. Beaufort's emergence as the royal favourite *par excellence* was no foregone conclusion.

The same selfish fears may have been in the mind of William Tresham, who set out from his Northamptonshire home on 23 September to rendezvous with York. Nothing might have been heard of this journey if Tresham had not been waylaid and hacked to death. He was an experienced lawyer and royal official, M.P. for Northamptonshire on many occasions and speaker of the Commons on no less than four of them. Apart from a minor connection with Richard of York – acting as feoffee in one of his Rutland manors by February 1449 – Tresham's career owed everything to his employment in the royal Household and by the duchy of Lancaster.[52] Although speaker for the Commons when they launched their charges against Suffolk in the 1449-50 Parliament, he must be regarded as their spokesman on that occasion and not as the initiator or formulator of their accusations. After this experience, he continued to benefit from courtly favour and, like many a Household official, was exempt from the 1450 act of resumption. Thus, the most that can be said of his loyalties in September 1450 is that they were in a state of flux and that

---

[50] Gairdner, *Paston Letters*, II, 174-75; *Complete Peerage*, VI, 562-63. In a cordial meeting, Henry VI is himself reported as appealing to Oldhall to speak to York about the possibility of the duke offering his assistance to one of the king's esquires of the body, John Penycock, who had earlier been denounced by Cade's rebels: Gairdner, *Paston Letters*, II, 174; J.S. Roskell, *The Commons and their Speakers in English Parliaments, 1376-1523* (Manchester, 1965), p. 244.

[51] *Complete Peerage*, XI, 506; Gairdner, *Paston Letters*, II, 176, 179-80. Men were advised to 'cherse and wirchep well' Sir William Oldhall. Even the Norfolk bullies, Sir Thomas Tuddenham and John Heydon, were prepared to offer £2,000 to be well received, presumably by the duke of York. See also Roskell, *Commons and their Speakers*, pp. 244-45.

[52] J.S. Roskell, 'William Tresham of Sywell, Speaker for the Commons under Henry VI', *Northamptonshire Past and Present*, II (1957), 189-203 (reprinted in idem, *Parliament and Politics*, II, 137-52).

he himself, like Dudley and Boulers, was in an uncertain frame of mind.[53]
It was Tresham's wife, Isabella, who, in a petition to Parliament in 1450-
51 for action against her husband's assailants, claimed that he was riding
to meet with York in response to a letter from the duke; but this may have
been an embroidery of the truth with the object of enlisting the sympathy
of an avowedly anti-court assembly which included several of York's
servants among its members.[54] The suggestion that the perpetrators of the
crime thought that Tresham's intention to meet York would later be a
valid excuse for their action argues for a greater degree of foresight than
was probable in September 1450.[55] The attack on Tresham, his son
Thomas and their servants was hatched by a Rutland squire, Simon
Norwich, as a result of a long-standing quarrel; and those who actually
committed the murder had been in violent dispute with the Treshams
over property a month or so earlier, on 10-12 August.[56] As more than one
contemporary claimed, they may have been servants of Lord Grey of
Ruthin, a Northamptonshire landowner, but there is no sign that Grey
himself was privy to the incident or that it had any other political
significance.[57] A number of people were hastening to ingratiate
themselves with York at this juncture, and William Tresham may have
been one; indeed, he was deceived into informing his attackers of the route
he was about to take by a certain William Kyng, who also claimed to be
anxious to petition the duke.[58]

The disarray of the Household after the assassination of Suffolk and the
shock of Cade's revolt would therefore be apparent to York soon after he
reached England. His hostile reception in north Wales by some of its
members cannot have been a great surprise to him; the appearance of
Dudley and Boulers at Ludlow was much more significant, and it was this

[53] When Tresham was waylaid he was wearing the collar of the king's livery: *Rot. Parl.*,
V, 211-13. His son Thomas, who was wounded in the ambush, was another Household
servant who continued in favour after 1450: J.S. Roskell, 'Sir Thomas Tresham, Knight,
Speaker for the Commons under Henry VI', *Northamptonshire Past and Present*, II (1959),
313-23 (reprinted in idem, *Parliament and Politics*, II, 267-78).

[54] *Rot. Parl.*, V, 211-13. The pseudo-William Worcestre simply records that Tresham
was riding towards the duke: Stevenson, *Wars of the English in France*, II, ii, 769. Tresham
was never a member of York's Council, as R.L. Storey claimed (*End of the House of Lancaster*,
p. 80), and Professor Roskell had already expressed some unease on the question of his
connection with Duke Richard: 'William Tresham of Sywell', pp. 198-99, 201-3; 'Sir
Thomas Tresham, Knight', p. 315.

[55] Roskell, *Commons and their Speakers*, p. 240 n.2.

[56] PRO, KB9/94/1, especially no. 22.

[57] Stevenson, *Wars of the English in France*, II, ii, 769; Kingsford, *English Historical
Literature*, p. 372. Thomas Tresham, in fact, became a feoffee of Lord Grey (now earl of
Kent) in June 1470: Roskell, 'Sir Thomas Tresham, Knight', p.320. Among the murderers
were four Welshmen who may have come originally from Grey's Welsh estates to live in
Northamptonshire: R.I. Jack (ed.), *The Grey of Ruthin Valor* (Sydney, 1965), p. 74 n.4.

[58] *Rot. Parl.*, V, 211-13.

temporary confusion in the court circle that helped determine his course of action thereafter. The second bill which he presented to Henry VI at Westminster reflects his appreciation of the fluid political situation in September-October 1450 and the possibility open to him of taking advantage of it.

The second bill was quite different in tone and content from the first. As we have seen, it was composed slightly later – perhaps after the Duke had been able, with the special help of Sir William Oldhall, to estimate the strength of his opponents, gauge popular opinion and have consultations in London. On this occasion, Richard transformed himself from a private petitioner presenting personal complaints into a public spokesman for those who, by reason of the 'grett grutchyng and romer' in the realm, were seeking the reformation of justice and good government in England. In so doing, he took up the mantle of the Commons in the Parliament of 1449-50 and, indeed, of Cade's rebels during the summer of 1450. Insisting to the king that there was urgent need to improve the quality of judicial administration, he urged Henry to arrest without bail those indicted of treason, 'what astatte, degre, or condicion so ever thei be', and he offered his services in the punishment of the guilty. One of the London chroniclers interpreted his request as a desire to see justice dispensed and the law executed on all those about the king, as well as in the realm at large, who were known to be traitors, from the highest among them to the lowest. The disliked Household officials were his main quarry, and Justice Yelverton's servant reported to John Paston that York 'vesaged so the mater that alle the Kynges howshold was and is aferd ryght sore'.[59]

The counties of eastern and south-eastern England provided the most promising ground on which to pursue his quarry. On 1 August 1450, commissions of oyer and terminer had been nominated in Kent as a consequence of the disturbances that had exploded in Cade's revolt and were still continuing in a desultory fashion. By the time York arrived in London, a large number of indictments had been presented, many of them of Household servants whose suppression of Cade's forces had overstepped the frontiers of legality and had degenerated into oppression, theft and violence.[60] On 2 August a similar commission was appointed for Norfolk and Suffolk, and although it may not have begun its hearings when York rode into London, a protest movement was on foot in those

---

[59] C.L. Kingsford (ed.), *Chronicles of London* (Oxford, 1905), pp. 136-37; Gairdner, *Paston Letters*, II, 174. The belief of the pseudo-William Worcestre that York asked the king to call Parliament is probably mistaken; it would argue an extraordinary ignorance on York's part, for Parliament had already been summoned on 5 September, to meet on 6 November, and York himself had probably received a writ of summons: Stevenson, *Wars of the English in France*, II, ii, 769; Wedgwood, *History of Parliament*, pp. 145, 154.

[60] Virgoe, thesis cited, pp. 223-25, 232, 241-43. Among the indicted were the Household men, Lord Dudley, Thomas Daniel, Sir Thomas Stanley and William Stanley.

counties which was certain to lead to the indictment of further members of Henry's Household and of Suffolk's affinity. The sheriff of Norfolk and Suffolk was determined to punish oppression of the population with strict impartiality. Sir Thomas Tuddenham, one of Suffolk's cronies, and other 'extortioners' were the principal target, and John Paston's servant advised his master to organise a demonstration in Norwich against them so that York should be left in no doubt of their unpopularity. The presumption was that the duke would be a ready listener to 'sum fowle tales of hem, and sum hyddows noys and crey'. Thus, York's personal complaints could be merged with those of many of Henry's subjects in eastern England with such coincidence that John Paston was informed that the bill 'is meche after the Comouns desyre, and all is up on justice, and to putte all thos that ben indyted under arest with owte suerte or maynpryce, and to be tryed be lawe as lawe wyll'.[61] Whether this was the result of a genuine sense of identity and of obligation to provide a remedy on the part of the duke, or a dexterous manipulation of widespread popular opinion – or a combination of both – it is now impossible to be certain.

In any event, Duke Richard was energetic in his determination to exploit the situation and to nurture complaints against those who had formerly wielded power under Suffolk's patronage where they would be most keenly expressed. During mid-October he travelled hither and thither from Fotheringhay (in Northamptonshire) to places in East Anglia – to Pikenham in Norfolk, the city of Norwich (which was hysterical with anti-Suffolk sentiment), the famous shrine at Walsingham, and to Bury St. Edmunds, where York met the duke of Norfolk on 16 October to discuss the candidates they would jointly promote in the forthcoming parliamentary elections.[62] As K.B. McFarlane showed, York tried to enlist help to produce equally amenable M.P.s in Oxfordshire and Northamptonshire.

Attempts to influence elections to Parliament may not have been the only moves prompted by York's fear of losing the initiative he had gained by returning from Ireland. Soon after he visited Fotheringhay Castle in October, a plot was being discussed there round about 3 November (or so a later enquiry alleged) which involved Sir Edmund Mulso's elder brother, Thomas Mulso; Sir Edmund himself was steward of York's

---

[61] Gairdner, *Paston Letters*, II, 174, 175, 177; Storey, *End of the House of Lancaster*, pp. 55-57, 78, 217-25.

[62] Stevenson, *Wars of the English in France*, II, ii, 769; Roskell, 'Sir William Oldhall', p. 101; Gairdner, *Paston Letters*, II, 175, 179-82, 184-85. The duke of Norfolk had his own reasons for wishing to see some of the courtiers humbled: Storey, *End of the House of Lancaster*, p. 79.

[63] K.B. McFarlane, 'The Wars of the Roses', *Proceedings of the British Academy*, L (1964), 89-90.

estates at Fotheringhay and Grantham. The intention was apparently to depose the king by force.[64] Sir William Oldhall was accused of similar plottings there some days later, on 11 November, presumably during a short recess in the Parliament of which he was speaker for the Commons. Several servants of the duke of Norfolk were said to be associated with him, so the discussion at Bury St. Edmunds the previous month may have covered matters other than the parliamentary elections.[65] At Royston in Cambridgeshire, one of York's companions on his Irish sojourn, John Wykes of Newmarket (Cambridgeshire), was allegedly involved in machinations against the king, and other disturbances were said to have occurred at Grantham and Stamford (in Lincolnshire), and at Chelmsford in Essex about 11-12 November. These centres and some of those accused of plotting had close connections with the duke of York and his estates in the area. It is worth making the suggestion that these were demonstrations of strength in favour of York and organised, if not by himself, perhaps by his councillors in October and November 1450.[66] London itself was in a state of high tension on the eve of Parliament's assembly, with rival gangs roaming the streets and displaying now York's badge, now the king's.[67] But the possibility cannot be eliminated that relatively innocuous meetings were later interpreted by hostile enquiries as treasonable conventicles.

York's efforts in and outside London, in and outside Parliament, proved vain. It is not known precisely when King Henry replied to York's second bill. It may have been before York set off from London about 9 October; but it may equally have been while he was away in East Anglia. No amount of manoeuvring in the provinces would avail if Henry were to stand firm and deny him the essentials of what he demanded. This is precisely what the king did. Henry's second reply was more curt than the

---

[64] PRO, KB9/94/1/2; SC6/1115/6 m.1, 6. Thomas Mulso was M.P. for Northampton-shire in 1450-51, perhaps as a result of York's canvassing: Wedgwood, *History of Parliament*, pp. 618-19.

[65] PRO, KB9/94/5; Storey, *End of the House of Lancaster*, p. 79. Professor Roskell suggested ('Sir William Oldhall', p. 104 n.61) that the indictment is misdated and should refer to 1451, when similar disturbances were afoot. But it fits equally well the circumstances of 1450 and the date as given in the indictment is here preferred. For other risings for the same purpose in Hastings and Horsham (Sussex) on 5 and 23 October respectively, see PRO, KB9/122/7; /15.

[66] PRO, KB9/7/1/10; 65A/19, 36, 38, 41, 42; 26/1/28; *Calendar of Patent Rolls, 1446-52*, p. 227. Stephen Christmas of Staplehurst (Kent), who had a safe conduct in February 1449 to travel to Ireland, was indicted for rising against the king on 27 January 1451: R. Virgoe, 'Some Ancient Indictments in the King's Bench referring to Kent, 1450-52', in F.R.H. DuBoulay (ed.), *Kent Records: Documents illustrative of Medieval Kentish History* (Kent Archaeological Soc., 1946), p.246; *Calendar of Patent Rolls, 1461-67*, p. 380. I am indebted to Anne Marshall for drawing my attention to these indictments and their precise significance.

[67] Storey, *End of the House of Lancaster*, p. 80; Roskell, 'Sir William Oldhall', pp. 102-3.

first. He conceded that the duke's intentions might be honourable enough, but he skilfully checkmated him by announcing that he had decided to employ a 'sad and so substancial consaile' to which more powers and authority would be given than the Council had enjoyed hitherto since 1437.[68] Although it was envisaged that York should be a member of this Council, Henry rejected the idea (to which he was so attached under Suffolk's influence) that he should be advised by one man alone, and he declared his preference for the 'grettest and the leste, the riche and the power', who, 'in liberte, vertu, and effecte of your [sic] voices ben equal'. For this purpose, he stated that he was sending for the chancellor, Archbishop Kemp, and other lords of the Council to discuss the present situation and other matters. This announcement of the king's took the wind completely out of York's sails. As the Parliament of 1459 commented, York had been 'answered by You [that is, Henry VI] to his desires and demaundes, that it seemed to all youre true subjetts that the spirit of wisdom of God was in You and he went awey confused'.[69] One Latin writer accurately grasped the sense of Henry's reply when he wrote that the king gave York no thanks for his proposal to assist in action against disloyal subjects, and retorted that when such aid was needed, he, the king, would ask for it.[70] The same strength of will is apparent during the Parliament which met on 6 November 1450. The petition that twenty named members of the king's Household and court – including Lord Dudley, Thomas Daniel, Reginald Boulers, Thomas Pulford, John Penycock, Lord Hoo, Sir Thomas Stanley and John Stanley – should be dismissed and removed from the king's presence by 1 December was rejected in all essentials. Moreover, Household officials such as Sir Thomas Stanley, William Elton, Richard Belth, Thomas Pulford, William Say, Bartholomew Bolde and Thomas Norris were eventually reinstated in the grants they had had to surrender to the Exchequer in accordance with the act of Resumption, and on 4 July 1451 Sir Thomas Tuddenham was pardoned all but £200 of the substantial fine of £1,396 imposed on him by the commissioners in East Anglia.[71]

It would be a mistake to assume that Richard of York's intentions in 1450 were identical with, or as well formed as, those of 1452 or later in the Wars of the Roses. Nevertheless, they do amount to the first step towards

---

[68] For some slight indication that Henry did temporarily concede greater powers to his Council late in 1450, see Wolffe, *The Royal Demesne*, p. 131 n.28.

[69] *Rot. Parl.*, V, 346. Professor Storey (*End of the House of Lancaster*, p. 82) hazarded that Kemp was responsible for this skilful reply, and certainly his town of Beverley secured a copy of each communication between king and duke for inclusion in its 'Chartulary'.

[70] Giles, op. cit., p. 42.

[71] S.B. Chrimes and A.L. Brown (eds.), *Select Documents of English Constitutional History, 1307-1485* (London, 1961), p. 292; Storey, *End of the House of Lancaster*, p. 57.

making an appeal for support from at least a few of the English magnates
and a sector of what might be termed popular opinion. It is possible to
observe in 1450 the beginnings of that process whereby his own personal
grievances could be converted into a more general and coherent bid for
wider sympathy. On this occasion, the bid was confined to the counties of
eastern and south-eastern England. It is difficult, therefore, to endorse the
judgements of E.F. Jacob and R.L. Storey on the newly-returned duke
(above). Professor Wilkinson came closer to the reality when he
concluded that 'There is no clear trace of any general political views in the
correspondence between Richard of York and Henry VI. York's
discontent was personal . . .'[72] He was, above all, bent on defending his
honour in the face of attack, securing remedy of his financial grievances
after years of service to the house of Lancaster, and, perhaps, on
protecting the hereditary rights of his lineage.

That York took advantage of popular disenchantment with
Lancastrian rule need not bear witness to his own ability or percipience.
The events of 1450 show that both king and duke were victims of rumour
and misinformation; it was Henry's enfeebled grip on government which
allowed these to take on a credible and semi-authoritative air in an
unstable political environment. The duke's success in 1450 was strictly
limited: the firmness of Henry VI left him nonplussed and the
forthcoming Parliament was the only alternative open to him. If the duke
showed any adroitness at all in 1450 it was in modestly extending the
relevance of his appeal to the inhabitants of eastern and south-eastern
England, but even there he seems to have relied heavily on the skill of his
chamberlain, Sir William Oldhall. '. . . no one could have been better
suited by rank and fortune [than York] for the leadership of what was now
certainly the popular cause', but, as K.B. McFarlane felt it necessary to
add, 'time would disclose his want of judgement.'[73] Bertie Wilkinson's
verdict on the duke in 1450 is a just one:

> it would be folly to make a statesman out of this fifteenth-century worldling.
> Nevertheless, we may credit him with a political vision which *occasionally*
> transcended his personal ambition . . . It is possible, indeed, that his political
> aims broadened and developed in the years after 1447, and particularly *after
> 1450*.[74]

King Henry's reaction to York's arrival betrays his serious weakness as
a king: he was credulous, over-sensitive of threats, whether they came
from obscure shipmen or his lieutenant of Ireland, and unable to see
problems in due proportion (at least in 1450). These traits were

---

[72] Wilkinson, *Constitutional History*, p. 89.
[73] McFarlane in *Cambridge Medieval History*, VIII, 405.
[74] Wilkinson, *Constitutional History*, pp. 88-89 (my italics).

emphasised when his personal grip on government slackened and his régime suffered a severe shock in the first half of 1450. The opening of the year marked the high-point of the Lancastrian Household as an effective political instrument in the realm. Before the year was over, the position of the Household had been severely shaken. York's first clash with it may not have succeeded in reducing either its size or its political influence, but the encounter did ensure that more strenuous attempts would be made to do so in the future.

Some pre-conditions of civil war were present in England by the end of 1450, and the duke of York was beginning to emerge as the acknowledged leader of protest. The king himself drifted further from reality, even to the point of mental collapse in August 1453; while his government did little to repair its tarnished reputation in England or in France. Nevertheless, it was several years before Duke Richard's grievances were to be closely identified with those of articulate Englishmen as a whole (though there is no reason to doubt that they shared a common frustration in 1450), and his practical need for political support was not satisfied easily, as his ineffective demonstration at Dartford in 1452 indicated. But the events of 1450 had shown how both might be achieved in time. Further incompetent government by the house of Lancaster, an example of vigorous Yorkist administration during Richard's protectorate for the sick king (1454-55), and a significant shift of influential opinion towards the duke, enabled him to transfer his exasperation with the king and his advisers to the streets of St. Albans in May 1455. By then England had moved closer to open civil strife; the only missing element of importance was the dynastic one.

Appendix

Duke Richard of York's bills of 1450, with the king's replies

1. The duke of York's first bill[1]
(Stowe, *Chronicles of England*, pp. 666-68[S])

Please it your highnesse to conceive, that sith my departing out of this your Realm, by your commandement, and being in your service in your land of Ireland, I have bin informed that diverse language, hath bene sayde of me to your moste excellente estate whiche shoulde sounde to my dishonour and reproch, and charge of my person: howe be it that, I aye have bene, and ever will be, your true liegeman and servaunt: and if there be any man that wyll or dare say the contrarie, or charge me otherwise, I beseech your rightwisenesse to call him before your high presence, and I wyll declare me for my discharge as a true Knighte ought to do, and if I doe not, as I doubt not but I shall, I beseech you to punishe me as the poorest man of your lande: and if hee bee founde untrue in his suggestion and information, I beeseech you of your highnesse that he be punished after his desert, in example of all other.

(Beverley Corporation Archives, Town 'Chartulary', f.36-37[B].[2] The sixteenth-century version printed above continues in Stowe, *Chronicles of England*, pp. 666-68.)

Plese it unto your excellence for to knawe that as weel afor my departying out of this your Reame for to go into your land of Irland in your ful noble service and sethyn certayne persones have layn in wayte to herkyn up on me as Sir John Talbot knyght at the castell of Holte, Sir Thomas Stanlay knyght in Chesschire, Pulforthe of[3] Chestir, Elton of[3] Worcestre, Broke of[3] Glowcestre and Richard Grome of your Chambir at Beammerreys, whilke had in charge as I was[4] enformed for to take me and put me in the castell of Convay, and to strike of the hede of Sir William Oldhalle knyght, and to have put in prison Sir Walter[5] Devoreux and Sir Edmond Mulso[6] knyght withouten enlargisshyng unto the tyme your highnesse had appoynted there delyverance.

Item, at suche tyme as I proposid for to arreyved at your haven of Beammereys

---

[1] The Beverley 'Chartulary', f. 36, introduces this bill with the words 'Copy of the first bill unto the kyng fro the duke of York the yeer afore wretyn'.

[2] The copy of this bill in the 'Chartulary' omits the preceding paragraph. I am grateful to the Town Clerk of Beverley for allowing me to publish the relevant folios here. In printing the following documents, inconsequential differences between the versions have not been noted. As is clear from the following notes (S) is not derived from (B): although the former has some errors (for example, nos. 5, 6, 10, 16), it does not perpetuate others committed by (B) (for example, nos. 3, 15).

[3] at (S).

[4] interlineated in MS.

[5] William (*sic*) (S).

[6] Malso (*sic*) (S).

for to comyn unto your noble presence to declare me your trewe man and subiecte as my deute is, my landyng was stoppid and forbarred be Herry Norys,[7] Thomas Norys,[8] William Buklay,[9] William Gruffe[10] and Bartilmew Bolde,[11] your officers of Northwalys, that I schulde not land there, nor have vitaile, nor refreschyng for me and my fellischip, as I have wretyn to your excellence here be fore. So ferforth that Herry Norys,[7] depute to the chambirlayn of Northwalys, sayde unto me that he had in comaundement that I schulde in no wyse have landyng there, nor refreschyng[12] for man, hors, nor othir thyng that myght torne to my worschip or ease, puttyng the blame unto William Say, usscher of your chambir, sayeng and affermyng that I come ayenst your entent as your tratoure, as I am enformed. And more ovir certain lettres was wretyn,[13] made and delivered unto Chestir, Schrowsbery and to othir places for to lette myn entre into the same.

Item, above alle these[13] wronges and iniures above said and[13] doon unto me of malice withouten any cause, I beyng in your land of Ireland in your[14] service, certayn commyssions ware made and directed unto divers persones which for the execucion of the same sette in certayn placis and the iniures[15] enpaneld and charged, the which jures[16] certeyn persones laboured instantly forto have endited me of treson, to thentent to have undo me, myn issue and corrupt by blode, as it is opynly publisched. Besekyng your maieste rial of your righwisnesse to do examyn thees maters and thereuppon to do such justice in this behalve as the cause requireth, ffor myn entent is fully to persewe to your highnesse for conclusion of thees maters.

[7] Henrie Norres (S).
[8] Thomas Norres (S).
[9] Buckeley (S).
[10] Grust (*sic*) (S).
[11] Bartholmew Boulde (S).
[12] 'nor lodging' inserted in (S).
[13] omitted in (S).
[14] 'honourable' inserted in (S).
[15] Juries (S).
[16] iniuries (*sic*) (S).

2. *Henry VI's answer to the duke's first bill*[1]

(Beverley Corporation Archives, Town 'Chartulary', f.37-38 [B]. A sixteenth-century version is in Stowe, *Chronicles of England*, pp. 668-69 [S].)

Cosyn we have seen the billis[2] late taken to us[3] and have undirstande the good humble obeisance that in your self ye schewe unto us as wel in worde as dede. Wherefore oure entent is the more hastily to aese yow of suche thyngez as were contenyd in your saide bille. As how it be that at oure more laisere we myght answere you to your said bille, yit we late you wit that for the cause aforseide we will declare you now oure entent in this matere. Soth it is that a lang tyme[4] the pepill hath[5] yeven[6] upon yow moche straunge langage and in special anon eftir the [7] disordinate and unlafull sleyng of the Bischop of Chichestre,[8] divers and many of the untrue schypmen and othir sayden in[9] their maner wordys ayenst oure astate, makyng manasse unto oure persone be your sayeng, that you schuld be fechid home with many thousandis, and that ye schulde take upon you that that ye nothir aught nor as we doutenat ye wole not attempte, so far forth that it was sayde unto oure persone be divers and specialy we remembre of oon Wastnesse[10] which had suche wordis unto us. And also ther were divers of suche fals pepill that wentyn and had suche langage in divers of your[11] townes in oure londe, which be oure true[1 2 3] subiectes were takyn and deuly executid. Wherefor we sende to diverse of oure portis[13] and placis forto herkyn and take hede if any of suche maner[14] of commenyng were and if there had been for to have resisted it, but comyng in to oure land[15] as ye did oure entent was not that nor ye nor lesse of estat of you[16] subiectes or[17] servantes schulde have been[18] warned, but in goodly wise resayved. How it be that peraventure your sodayn comyng withouten certayn warnyng causid thaym[19] to do as thay dide consideryng the causes aforseid. And as touchyng to the enditement afor specified,[20] we thynke verily[21] there was non suche and if ye may treuly prove that any suche persones was there abowte, the mater schal be demenyd as the case requireth, so that ye schal knawe it is to oure gret displesure. Uppon this aesyng of your hert in alle suche maters we declare, repute and admitte you as oure trewe faithful subiecte and as oure weel bilovid[22] cosyn.

---

[1] In Beverley's 'Chartulary', the king's answers to York's two bills are amalgamated and headed 'The answer of the kying to the seid billes'. Once again (S) is not derived from (B).

[2] byll (*recte*) (S).

[3] that yee tooke us late (S).

[4] space in MS.; 'among' inserted in (S).

[5] 'been' deleted in MS., but inserted in (S).

[6] interlineated in MS., but omitted in (S).

[7] your (*sic*) (S). See p. 281, note 1 [18].

[8] Chester (S).

[9] MS. torn.

[10] Wasnes (S).

[11] our (S).

[12] omitted from (S).

[13] Courtes (*sic*) (S).

[14] interlineated in MS.

[15] 'our true subiecte' inserted in (S).

[16] our (S).

[17] 'none of youre' inserted in (S).

[18] 'letted nor' inserted in (S).

[19] oure servauntes (S).

[20] that yee spoke of (S).

[21] and holde or certaine that (S). The entire phrase from 'certayne warnyng' was inadvertently repeated in (S), and therefore by Holinshed in 1587 (see above pp. 279-80).

[22] our faythfull (S).

3. The duke of York's second bill[1]

(BL, Additional MS. 43,488 f. 7, printed in Gairdner, *Paston Letters*, II, 177-78, from Fenn, *Original Letters*, I, 64 [P]. Other mid-fifteenth-century versions are in Kingsford, *English Historical Literature* [K], and Beverley Corporation Archives, Town 'Chartulary', f. 36 [B]. A sixteenth-century version is printed in Stowe, *Chronicles of England*, pp. 669-70 [S].)

Please it your hyghnes tendirly to considere the grett grutchyng and romore[2] that is unnuversaly in this your reame of that justice is nouthe dewly ministrid[3] to suche as trespas and offende a yens your lawes and in special of them that ben endited of tresone and other beyng openly[4] noysed of the same. Wherfore[5] for gret inconveniens that have fallen and gretter is lyke to[6] fallen here after in your seid reame, whiche God defende, but if be your hyghnesse provysione covenable be med for dew reformacion and punyshment in this behalf. Wherefor I your humble[4] sugett and[7] lyge man Richard Duke of York, willyng as[8] effectually as I kan and desiryng suerte and prosperite of your most roiall person and welfare of this your noble reame, councel and advertyse your excellent for the conversacion[9] of good tranquillite and pesable rewle among alle trew[10] sogetts for to ordeyn and provyde that dew[11] justice be had a yenst alle suche that ben so endited or openly

[1] The Beverley 'Chartulary', f. 37, introduces its copy of the bill with 'The copy of the secunde bille'; (K) has 'This is the Copy of the bill that my Lorde York put unto the Kynge with other etc.'. (P), (B), (K) and (S) are sufficiently different from one another as to make it unlikely that any one of them was copied from any other. (K) has the largest number of peculiarities: see p. 299.

[2] greate murmur and grudging (S); grete gruchyng and murmur (B).

[3] maynteyned (K).

[4] omitted in (K).

[5] whereby (S), (K), (B).

[6] 'do and' inserted in (K).

[7] 'trew' inserted in (K), true (S), trewe (B).

[8] interlineated in MS.

[9] conservacion (K), (B).

[10] other (S).

[11] trew (K), true (S).

so noysed,[12] where inne[4] I offre[13] and wol put me in devoure[14] for to execute your comaundements in thes premises[15] of suche offenders[16] and redresse of the seid mysrewlers[17] to my myth and powere. And for the hasty execucion here of lyke it your hyghnes[18] to dresse your letteres of prevy sealle and writts to your officers and ministres to do take and areste alle soche persons so noysed or endited, of what astate, degre or condicion so ever thei be, and them to comytte to your toure of London or to othere your prisons, there to abyde with outen bayle or maymprice[19] on to the tyme that that (*sic*) thei be[20] utterly tryed and declared[21] after the cours of your lawe.

[12] named (S); 'with in your Realme' inserted in (K).
[13] 'myselfe' inserted in (S); me (B).
[14] put remedy for (K).
[15] 'for the punyssion' inserted in (K); for punyschyng (B); for the punishing (S).
[16] defendours (B).
[17] to redresse the same mysrules (B); misrules (S).
[18] excellens (K).
[19] in bayl withouten maynprice (B).
[20] 'therof' inserted in (K); there of (B).
[21] determined (S); determyned (B).

4. Henry VI's answer to the duke's second bill[1]

(Beverley Corporation Archives, Town 'Chartulary', f.38 [B]. A sixteenth-century version is in Stowe, *Chronicles of England*, p. 670 [S].)

Item,[2] as touchyng your last bille last put up unto us cosyn,[3] we undirstande weel that ye of your good hert consaile and advertise us to settyng up of iustice and to spede punyschyng of certayn persons endited or noysed, offeryng your service to be redy at oure commaundement in the same. Soth it is that[4] many gret causes moving us we have determenyd in oure oune[3] saule so stablish with sad and so[3] substancial consaile yevyng them more ample auctorite and power then evir we did afor this; in the which we have appoynted yow to be oon. But seth it is not accustumed nor expedient to take a conclusion or a conducte be avise or consaile of on persone be hym self, for which consideracion[6] is observid that in counsales[3]

[1] The Beverley 'Chartulary' amalgamated both answers of the king: see above p. 301. (S) is not derived from (B).
[2] Coosin (S).
[3] omitted in (S).
[4] 'for' inserted in (S).
[5] to 'S'.
[6] the conservation (*sic*) (S).

grettest and the leste,[7] the riche and the power, in liberte, vertu and effecte of your voices ben equale, we have therefore determynde with in oure self to sende for oure chanciller of Ingelond and for othir lordis of oure counsaile thay all to gedire[8] with in schort tyme riply to commyn thees and othire oure gret maters. In the which communicacion such conclusion with grace of god almyghty[3] sal be take as schal be to his plesure to the weel of us and oure land asweel in thes maters as in othire.

[7] beste (*sic*) (S).
[8] yea and al other, togither (S).

[There is further, more recent comment, and context, in R.A. Griffiths, *The Reign of King Henry VI* (London, 1981), and P.A. Johnson, *Duke Richard of York, 1411-1460* (Oxford, 1988).]

19

The King's Council and the First Protectorate of the Duke of York, 1450-1454*

HARVARD UNIVERSITY (Houghton Library) fMS Eng. 751 fos. 211ᵛ–214ᵛ, includes a record of three meetings of King Henry VI's council, held respectively on 30 November 1453, 5 December 1453, and 3 April 1454. Although this record, and indeed the entire Harvard volume, was written about the end of the fifteenth century, there is no reason to doubt that it is a faithful copy (apart from a few minor misreadings and incidental omissions) of what may justifiably be regarded as contemporary council minutes. These minutes are not otherwise known and together they have considerable administrative, political, and personal significance.

The bound manuscript volume is described in the Harvard University Library's catalogue as 'Parliamentary lists *etc.*'.[1] Its datable lists of individual summonses to parliament run from the twenty-eighth year of Edward I (1299–1300) to the beginning of the reign of Henry VII, and it is likely that the volume was compiled not long after the last datable entry, perhaps during the first decade of Henry VII's reign. But its contents are far more varied than the modern title of the volume suggests. They may more accurately be described as a genealogical collection relating to English baronies, with the summonses of parliamentary peers included as well as lists of attainders, peerage creations, and some drawings of noble seals (for example, the seal of Henry Holand, duke of Exeter). In such a collection, reports of discussions among the lords of Henry VI's council during 1453–4 would not be inappropriate. The deliberations and attendance-lists of the three council meetings, the signatures appended to the second minute, and the catalogue of opinions ascribed to the lords and other councillors in the third minute are sufficient explanation of the inclusion of all three minutes in a volume compiled by someone deeply interested in late-medieval baronies and the English peerage.

One virtue of these minutes is that they shed valuable light on the procedures of record keeping adopted by the king's council in the mid-fifteenth century. From the reign of Richard II, the recording of attendance at the king's council, and of business transacted there, became more systematic and more sophisticated than hitherto. In

---

* The documents below are reproduced with kind permission of The Houghton Library, Harvard University. I am grateful to Ms Melanie Wisner for facilitating my study of them and to Ms Lorraine Attreed for verifying a few points.

1. See also S. de Ricci, *Census of Medieval and Renaissance Manuscripts in the United States and Canada*, supplementary vol. ed. C. U. Faye and W. H. Bond (New York, 1962), p. 226.

addition to the brief reports of conciliar decisions written as endorsements on petitions and as occasional memoranda, rolls and journals of proceedings in the king's council appear to have been compiled at irregular intervals during the following century and a half, doubtless facilitated by the establishment, in or before 1377, of a permanent office of a paid clerk of the council.[1] Even so, there seems to have been no consistency in the form and structure of these more sophisticated records until the reign of Henry VIII; nor is there any certainty that all conciliar decisions – let alone the discussions that preceded them – were recorded, or that whatever records were made were consistently full and complete. According to Professor A. L. Brown, the inclinations of individual clerks of the council, rather than any established practice of their office, were the single most influential factor in determining the nature of conciliar record keeping during the fifteenth century.[2] John Prophete, the council's clerk during 1389–95, compiled a journal in 1392–3 which recorded some of the council's business; it seems to have been written up from a series of individual reports of council meetings, possibly from a draft journal which recorded such meetings (including those that were especially large and significant and known as great councils).[3] Yet there is no sign that Prophete's initiative (if indeed it was his) was continued by himself or his immediate successors as clerks of the council, though it is possible that common sense and the need to keep some record of council business dictated that it should be. Certainly, during the fourteen years between 1421 and 1435 when, significantly, Henry V was abroad (where he died in 1422) and his successor was so young that a council ruled for him, a 'Book of the Council' was compiled to record the transactions of the council – the dates of meetings, lists of those who were present, and some of the decisions taken.[4] Thereafter, during Henry VI's adult rule, evidence for a similarly formal and systematic record is lacking, though Henry Benet, a privy seal clerk who often acted for the clerk of the council during 1435–47, seems to have kept a detailed set of rough minutes of council meetings.[5]

1. See most recently A. L. Brown's two papers, *The Early History of the Clerkship of the Council* (Glasgow, 1969), pp. 4–7, and 'The King's Councillors in Fifteenth-century England', *Transactions of the Royal Historical Society*, 5th ser., xix (1969), 95–99. For the records of the Tudor council, see G. R. Elton, 'Why the History of the Early-Tudor Council remains unwritten', in his *Studies in Tudor and Stuart Politics and Government*, i (Cambridge, 1974), 308–38.

2. Brown, *Clerkship*, pp. 15 ff.

3. See J. F. Baldwin, *The King's Council in England during the Middle Ages* (Oxford, 1913), pp. 489–504, for this journal.

4. See N. H. Nicolas (ed.), *Proceedings and Ordinances of the Privy Council of England* (7 vols., Record Commission, 1834–7), vols ii–iv, for this 'book'.

5. These minutes are printed *ibid.* v–vi (1436–46). A cautionary note about the possible loss of other council minutes after 1446 is sounded by R. Virgoe, 'The Composition of the King's Council, 1437–61', *Bulletin of the Institute of Historical Research*, xliii (1970), 135–6.

The responsibilities that unexpectedly devolved on the lords of the king's council during Henry VI's illness in 1453–4 may have convinced the councillors and Thomas Kent, who had been the official clerk of the council since 1443, that a careful and formal record of meetings and decisions, even of discussions, should once again be preserved, as had been the case during the king's minority. On the second occasion (after the battle of St Albans on 22 May 1455) when Henry VI was unable to rule in person and Richard, duke of York was proclaimed protector and defender of the realm and chief councillor, a formal 'Book of the Council' was indeed kept. At a great council meeting at Westminster on 24 July 1455, sixty spiritual and temporal lords formally swore an oath in the king's presence to maintain their allegiance to Henry VI, to do nothing prejudicial to him or his crown, and to resist any who threatened to do so. This oath was enacted in parliament (and duly recorded on the parliament roll) and it was further ordered that it should 'be written and incorporat in the boke of the Counseill, there to remayne of record among other Actes and Ordenaunces'.[1] The council minute of 30 November 1453, newly discovered in the Harvard MS, records the swearing of a similar oath by forty-eight spiritual and temporal lords and five additional councillors, and according to the Harvard MS this and the two other minutes copied therein were among 'acts, appointments, and ordinances made and established in the council in the thirty-second year of Henry VI for the direction of the council and for the rule and governance of the realm and common weal'.[2] This does not prove that a 'Book of the Council' was being kept in 1453–4, but the explanatory heading does imply that a number of 'acts, appointments, and ordinances' relating to conciliar discussions during the crisis caused by the king's illness were brought together as a coherent record. Only three were copied into the Harvard MS, though others are known from different sources.[3] It may be suggested that conciliar deliberations during the months following the king's breakdown in health in August 1453 were formally recorded, presumably by Thomas Kent, though whether in the form of a 'book' is not known. It may be suggested further that those minutes which concerned the government of the realm during the king's incapacity were later abstracted to form an official record of the discussions on this subject. There were two occasions when this would be most likely to have been done: either soon after the establishment of the first protectorate of the duke of York on 3 April 1454, or in preparation for the

---

1. *Rotuli Parliamentorum*, v. 282–3.
2. *Infra* p. 315.
3. E.g., the assurance given to York by the Council on 21 November 1453, that he would no longer be prevented from having his own councillors about him, was enacted among 'thactes of the counsaill': *Calendar of Patent Rolls, 1452–1461*, pp. 143–4.

inauguration of York's second protectorate on 19 November 1455, when knowledge of what had taken place in 1453-4 would have provided guidance and a precedent.[1] Be that as it may, all one can say with certainty is that the compiler of the Harvard MS copied only three council minutes into his genealogical collection. As to the identity of this copyist and the explanation for his interest in these three minutes alone, nothing further can be said until the Harvard MS as a whole has been carefully studied and analysed.

Even more valuable is the light which these minutes shed on the nature of the political crisis of 1453-4. When Henry VI fell ill at the beginning of August 1453, the monarchy and the government of England were plunged into a constitutional and political crisis of the first magnitude. On occasions in the past, kings had been unable to shoulder their responsibilities in person, either as a result of absence or youth or because of the actions of some of their powerful subjects. But never had a medieval English king suffered such a crippling bout of mental and physical illness as Henry VI experienced between the summer of 1453 and Christmastide 1454. For about seventeen months he was quite incapable of ruling his kingdom. The main consequences of this illness and the means eventually devised to cope with them are well enough known.[2] But the confusion, uncertainty, and suspicion that divided opinion within the aristocracy, the government and the court have hitherto had to be inferred from isolated incidents and unofficial observations.[3] The minutes copied into the Harvard MS provide important and authoritative evidence of how the king's councillors and the spiritual and temporal peers reacted to the crisis; they even enable us to eavesdrop a vital discussion that took place within the council chamber itself.

Political disenchantment and popular unrest had reached such a pitch by 1450 that the king's chief minister, William de la Pole, duke of Suffolk, was murdered in May, John Cade led thousands of insurgents to London in June and July, and serious rioting took place in London during the following winter. Abroad, Normandy capitulated to French forces in 1449-50, and by mid-1453 the whole of Gascony had been overrun. It was an affront to many that the Lancastrian commander who surrendered Rouen and negotiated his own and his family's safe retreat from Normandy, Edmund Beaufort, duke of Somerset, took Suffolk's place as King Henry's closest confidant. And the king's cousin (and, in the eyes of many, his heir),

---

1. *Rot. Parl.* v. 242-4, 284-90, reprinted in S. B. Chrimes and A. L. Brown (eds.), *Select Documents of English Constitutional History, 1307-1485* (1961), pp. 299-302, 305-9. See J. S. Roskell, 'The Office and Dignity of Protector of England, with special reference to its origins', *ante*, lxviii (1953), 226-7.

2. The most recent studies are B. P. Wolffe, *Henry VI* (1981), ch. xiv, and R. A. Griffiths, *The Reign of King Henry VI* (1981), ch. xxiii.

3. *E.g.*, the newsletter sent to the duke of Norfolk on 19 January 1454: J. Gairdner (ed.), *The Paston Letters* (6 vols., 1904), ii. 295-9.

Richard, duke of York, felt himself unjustifiably ignored and unjustly victimized by the king and the court. These tensions, and the frustrations and recriminations that accompanied them, vitiated the efforts of the council and the aristocracy to deal with the implications of the king's illness, and in particular to devise an acceptable form of government for the realm whilst the king remained incapable. The first minute, of a meeting held on 30 November 1453 in the star chamber at Westminster, was that of a great council, to judge by the number present and the important declaration it issued. This declaration reflected the collective responsibility assumed by the lords to uphold the law and the king's authority, and it demonstrated the firm measures they were prepared to take at this time of grave uncertainty. The lords publicly and solemnly showed their resolve by swearing an oath individually 'on a booke'. Already, on 24 October, a number of councillors had acknowledged the undesirability of continuing to exclude the duke of York from important discussions, and they urged that he attend the great council that was imminent.[1] He accordingly arrived in London on 12 November and on the 21st was present at a great council that vindicated his right to have his own advisers about him.[2] At this meeting, the duke of Norfolk launched an outspoken attack on the duke of Somerset, who was consigned to the Tower two days later. With his removal, on 30 November the assembled great council could exhibit a striking unity and solidarity at a time when the authority of king and council seemed in jeopardy.

There was an unusually full attendance at this meeting, especially of bishops and senior peers (that is, of the rank of viscount and above). Senior officers of state and of the household were prominent among them: John Kempe, archbishop of Canterbury and chancellor; John Tiptoft, earl of Worcester and treasurer of England; Lord Sudeley, steward of the household, and Lord Cromwell, chamberlain of the household.[3] Of the senior peers who were absent, Somerset was in custody and the duke of Exeter was perhaps already contemplating his alliance with the Percy family which led to violent feuding with the Nevilles in Yorkshire some weeks later.[4] Probably for the same reason, the earls of Northumberland and Westmorland were absent; in any case, by February 1454 Westmorland was so ill that he was unable to attend parliament.[5] The king's half-brother, Edmund Tudor, earl of Richmond, was absent too, perhaps in west

1. Nicolas, *op. cit.* vi. 163–4.

2. G. L. and M. A. Harriss (eds.), 'John Benet's Chronicle for the years 1400–1462', in *Camden Miscellany*, xxiv (Camden Society, 4th ser., ix, 1972), 210; *supra*, **307, n. 3**; Griffiths, *Henry VI*, p. 721.

3. Thomas Liseux, keeper of the privy seal, and Lord Dudley, treasurer of the household, were not present.

4. R. A. Griffiths, 'Local Rivalries and National Politics: the Percies, the Nevilles and the Duke of Exeter, 1452–1455', **below pp. 338-40.**

5. Nicolas, *op. cit.* vi. 181–2. His illness was verified by the council itself.

Wales enforcing the king's authority in Carmarthenshire and Cardiganshire, and that of his brother Jasper as earl in Pembrokeshire, as he was to do later.[1] Only the absence of the thirty-six-year-old earl of Arundel is difficult to explain – but then during the next five or six years he showed some reluctance to commit himself to either side in the political quarrels, and caution may have dictated his attitude on this occasion too.[2] Two-thirds of the bishops were present on 30 November and took the oath; of those who were absent, four (the bishops of Exeter, Rochester, Llandaff, and St Asaph) were probably too ill to travel to Westminster for they certainly had good cause for not attending parliament a few months later.[3] As for Beauchamp of Salisbury, Carpenter of Worcester, and Pecock of Chichester, they were closely connected with the king and his household and may have felt disinclined for this reason to attend the Westminster meeting on 30 November.[4] Although there were eighteen of the lesser lay lords present, rather more (twenty-three) were absent – mostly because of illness or age, one may surmise. In fact, ten of the absentees were over fifty, of whom four were so ill by February 1454 that they were unable to attend parliament; two of the younger peers were similarly indisposed.[5] Of the remaining eleven absentees on 30 November, Lord St Amand was personally in attendance on Henry VI at Windsor during the latter's illness, and several others were most likely in the north, where they were either involved in the Percy–Neville conflict (Lords Egremont, Poynings, and Latimer among them) or, like Lord Roos, may have felt anxious about the effect of this violence on their estates.[6] Thus, on 30 November there was a substantial attendance of adult, available peers to swear to uphold the law and act collectively against 'any person whatsoever estat, degree or condycyon he be of' who flouted the king's and the council's authority. Confidants of the king and officials of his government sat beside York and Norfolk, the bitterest of Somerset's critics. There too were Salisbury and Cromwell, whose defence of their landed interests in Lincolnshire and Yorkshire against the Percies is likely to have drawn them towards York; whilst Warwick's quarrel with the duke of Somerset over lands in Glamorgan may already have led the earl to seek allies beyond the

---

1. R. S. Thomas, 'The political career, estates and "connection" of Jasper Tudor, earl of Pembroke and duke of Bedford (d. 1495)' (unpublished University of Wales [Swansea] PhD thesis, 1971), pp. 152, 157, 160–1.

2. Griffiths, *Henry VI*, pp. 692, 830–1. Arundel's sympathies probably lay with York.

3. Nicolas, *op. cit.* vi. 181–2 (which notes the bishops of Exeter and Rochester); J. S. Roskell, 'The problem of attendance of the lords in medieval parliaments', *B.I.H.R.* xxix (1956), 190 n. 3 (which mentions the bishops of Llandaff and St Asaph).

4. Griffiths, *Henry VI*, pp. 268, 346, 349–50, 849.

5. Nicolas, *op. cit.* vi. 181–2; Roskell, *B.I.H.R.* xxix (1956), 190, n. 3.

6. Griffiths, *Henry VI*, p. 759; *idem*, *Speculum*, xliii (1968), 604 ff. **Below 336 ff.**

king's court.[1] The oath, though sworn in general terms, was an expression of conciliar and aristocratic solidarity, in which the duke of York's position had been considerably strengthened.

The second minute in the Harvard MS records the proceedings at a great council held in the star chamber at Westminster five days later, on 5 December 1453. It reveals that, important though the declaration of 30 November had been, practical arrangements for the government of the realm in the short term needed to be established in view of the king's 'inffirmytey' and the impossibility that he, with his advisers, could take any decisions.[2] On 5 December, therefore, a smaller group (twenty-three in all) assembled and assumed responsibility for the 'pollytyque rule and gouernance of this land in all suche things as must of nessesseyte be entendyd unto'. This was a major practical step towards resolving the dilemma of how a personal monarchy was to be ruled by an incapable monarch. The step was taken as a matter of urgency to cope with the immediate crisis, for the lords present 'entend not nor wyll procede in other matters but in such as of veary nesestye must be entended unto vntill the tyeme there poure be more ample by awtoryty suffycyently declared'. Yet it is significant that an even smaller number of peers (fourteen) actually subscribed to the formal decision to place the king's powers in the hands of a council. The record of the meeting makes it evident that York and his associates had grasped the initiative and were determined to play the leading rôle while the king was ill. The bishops (eight of them, led by the chancellor, Archbishop Kempe) were prominent, but apart from the duke of Buckingham, the lay peers who subscribed to this ordinance were all closely connected with York: Norfolk, Warwick, Salisbury, and Lord Bourgchier, York's brother-in-law.[3] Those who were present at the discussion but did not subscribe their names to its decision included a group of peers whose loyalties bound them more closely to the king and his household: the king's half-brother, Jasper Tudor, earl of Pembroke, the earl of Worcester, treasurer of England, the earl of Wiltshire, a favourite at court, Lord Dudley, treasurer of the household, Lord Scales, one of the queen's counsellors, Lord Stourton, a former treasurer of the household who had been raised to the peerage in Suffolk's day, and even Lord Cromwell, chamberlain of the

---

1. *Ibid.* pp. 593–605; R. L. Storey, *The End of the House of Lancaster* (1966), pp. 135–7, 239–40.

2. This is the first known official acknowledgement of the seriousness of Henry's illness.

3. Apart from Norfolk, Thomas Ludlowe (d. 1459), abbot of Shrewsbury, was the only other signatory of the ordinance who was not recorded earlier as attending the meeting. Shrewsbury was a town close to York's Marcher estates and where he had considerable influence. See A. B. Emden, *A Biographical Register of the University of Oxford to A.D. 1500* (3 vols., Oxford, 1957–9), ii. 1172; J. C. Wedgwood, *History of Parliament, Register, 1439–1509* (1938), p. 189 (1453–4).

household.[1] York and his supporters had therefore achieved a measure of political ascendancy, though it was limited to the present emergency and was not greeted enthusiastically by several influential figures.

In the weeks that followed, Henry's queen, Margaret of Anjou, formulated her own demands for the regency of England as an alternative to a council.[2] It was doubtless the difficulty of reconciling these two widely differing options – a difficulty not unlike the dilemma facing politicians in 1422 – that delayed a settlement of the question of who should govern England during the king's incapacity. The arguments took place in a highly charged atmosphere and by 19 March 'a sadde and wyse counsaill' had still not been established.[3] The chancellor's promise of a 'good and comfortable answer' to the speaker's request that it should be was rendered worthless on 22 March when Archbishop Kempe died. Next day, a delegation of lords was sent to seek an audience of the king at Windsor. Amongst other things, they were instructed to discuss the appointment of a council, 'wherfor certaine Lordes and persones be named under the kynges correction, to take uppon theym the seid charge', and to seek Henry's endorsement of their appointment 'or whethir he will chaunge or sette asyde eny of theym'. As in 1422, the lords in parliament had rejected the idea of a regency and instead resolved to establish a council whose authority to govern would be fuller than that assumed by certain lords on 5 December. The failure to elicit any response from the king led directly two days later to York's nomination as protector and defender of the realm. His powers were the powers conferred on the king's uncles in 1422. Among the articles which the duke submitted next day to the lords in parliament was a request 'that suche Lordes Spirituel and Temporel, as be named and chosyn of the Kynges Counsaill take uppon theym so to bee, and also accept and admit the charge therof'. These lords were presumably those whose names had been presented to the king a few days earlier. It was now agreed that they 'that be named to be of the Kynges Counsaill, shuld have communication togedre, and to be advised therupon'.[4]

The third document in the Harvard MS records the discussion which these nominated councillors had at a meeting (probably a great council) in the star chamber on 3 April 1454. The new chancellor, Richard Neville, earl of Salisbury, who was also York's brother-in-

---

1. Griffiths, *Henry VI*, pp. 262, 422–3. Next day, the duke of York received a formal exemplification under the great seal of the assurance of 21 November that he should have his own advisers about him (*C.P.R., 1452–1461*, pp. 143–4; *supra* 309). On that same day, a warrant was signed by Archbishop Kempe, the duke of York, Viscount Bourgchier, Bishop Bourgchier of Ely, and also by the earls of Worcester and Pembroke (Virgoe, *B.I.H.R.* xliii (1970), 164–5).

2. Gairdner, *op. cit.* ii. 297.

3. *Rot. Parl.* v. 240–2.

4. *Ibid.* pp. 242–4, reprinted in Chrimes and Brown, *op. cit.* pp. 299–302.

law and one of his closest associates among the lords, invited them all to express their willingness to serve as councillors and to give the duke their support. The record of their answers not only provides a rare glimpse of what took place behind the closed doors of the council chamber, but enables the historian to overhear one of the most revealing discussions of the reign.[1] It demonstrates too how seriously this crisis was viewed and how strong were the misgivings of most of the nominated councillors about associating themselves with a new protectorate to which the queen was bitterly opposed. Not even those who subscribed to the council's assumption of temporary, extraordinary powers on 5 December were ready to give York full-hearted support and co-operation on 3 April. They took their cue from the entire body of lords in parliament, who on 28 March had formally recorded, after the example of 1422, that they had 'in semblable case of necessite be compelled and coarted so' to confer on York the authority of a protector.[2]

On 3 April there was an unmistakable reluctance on practically all sides, lay and clerical, to serve on the new council. So many pleaded that they were handicapped by illness that the naive might be pardoned for concluding that a serious epidemic was raging among the lay peers of the realm: Buckingham, Oxford, Cromwell, and even Norfolk, the scourge of the duke of Somerset some months earlier, adopted this course, and if Cromwell had some reason to plead great age, poor health and general debility (he died on 5 January 1456 at the age of about sixty-two), Norfolk's combination of bombast and excuse is likely to have aroused scorn and disdain in his listeners. On the episcopal side, the plea of pressing diocesan duties sat uncomfortably with a bench of bishops who had not always been conspicuous for their concern for their flocks and their sees during the past century and more. Yet four of them (the bishops of Worcester, Norwich, Lincoln, and Coventry and Lichfield), along with the prior of the Hospital of St John of Jerusalem, claimed to have such urgent duties elsewhere and associated themselves with Bishop Waynflete of Winchester's high-minded assertion that conscience would not allow him to devote his time continually to council matters in this difficult period, and with his proposal that a rota for episcopal attendance should be adopted. Other excuses ranged from youth and inexperience in the case of the twenty-five-year-old earl of Warwick (though he had been very ready to participate in the deliberations of 30 November), lack of experience in the case of Lord Scales (who was in his mid-fifties, had been a notable soldier in his day

1. One of the few comparable reports extant is Nicolas, *op. cit.* v. 223–4 (6 February 1443); a less full report of councillors' opinions is *ibid.* pp. 73–8 (18 November 1437). Salisbury had been appointed chancellor the day before, 2 April.

2. *Rot. Parl.* v. 24, reprinted in Chrimes and Brown, *op. cit.* p. 300.

and by 1453 was one of the queen's advisers), to poverty, which the Gascon dean of St Seurin equated with lack of wisdom. Viscount Beaumont had a more convincing objection which he unequivocally laid before his colleagues: he was the queen's man and he made it perfectly plain that he had no intention of compromising his loyalty to Margaret of Anjou.[1] Of those who were prepared to serve, few showed the sense of responsibility of the earl of Worcester, treasurer of England, or of Archbishop Booth of York; and none was as eager as Warwick to overcome the disability of youth. The earl of Shrewsbury and the bishops of Worcester, and Coventry and Lichfield were content eventually to place themselves at the disposal of their fellow lords, though they did so with resignation rather than with enthusiasm. Moreover, it required considerable argument and persuasion to induce a number of these lords to overcome their declared scruples, and it is likely that the pressure was exerted by York himself and the chancellor, Salisbury. All but John Carpenter, bishop of Worcester, ultimately consented to serve as councillors during the first protectorate.

The difficult and delicate nature of the situation at the beginning of April 1454, and the fact that the commons in parliament had persistently urged the appointment of a council, prompted several of the lords (notably the earl of Worcester, Lord Cromwell, and the prior of the Hospital of St John of Jerusalem) to urge that the commons be fully taken into the confidence of the new council and that proper financial provision be made for the councillors. The vastly experienced Cromwell also insisted that councillors should be guaranteed their safety in travelling to and from council meetings, so vivid was his memory of the attacks upon him by Suffolk's henchman, William Tailboys, in the late 1440s.[2] As for the two commoners at the meeting on 3 April, it was easier for Sir Thomas Stanley, controller of the household, and John Say, who had long been a household servant, to agree to serve as councillors, since it seems to have been accepted that the king's powers now resided in the lords; Stanley and Say merely fulfilled the rôle of messengers. When all is said and done, this was hardly the material from which an effective council was likely to be constructed. York and Salisbury did not even have the energetic support of those, like Norfolk, who had attacked Somerset the previous autumn. To advocate a protectorate when the king was adult and the queen so fiercely hostile created a

1. Less convincing was Beaumont's claim that he had far to travel; his seat may have been at Folkingham (Lincs), but he had felt able to join the king's council in 1439, and in May 1450 he was appointed chamberlain of England (Griffiths, *Henry VI*, pp. 279, 288).
2. R. Virgoe, 'William Tailboys and Lord Cromwell: crime and politics in Lancastrian England', *Bulletin of the John Rylands Library*, lv (1973), 459–82. One attack took place outside the star chamber itself on 28 November 1449.

new and dangerous dimension, one into which the English aristocracy was loath to enter. Indeed, within a fortnight of the meeting
on 3 April, the chancellor recruited several other lords to the council,
and particularly peers who were closely identified with King Henry
and his household. On 15–16 April Lords Sudeley, Dudley, and
Stourton agreed to serve and the compensatory presence of Thomas
Bourgchier, bishop of Ely, was small consolation for the duke of
York.[1] This, therefore, was no partisan Yorkist body signalling a
decisive victory by Duke Richard over the queen and the court
during the winter of 1453–4. Rather had a protectorate been
unenthusiastically established, partly to forestall a regency by the
queen; and the supporting council preserved a strong element of men
who had served Henry VI well before he became ill. The three
minutes copied into the Harvard MS provide important evidence of
the complex personal and political manoeuvres that preceded the
creation of this protectorate, including the significant limitations
which were imposed on the new protector and which eventually
enabled Henry VI to re-assert his authority peaceably after Christmas
1454.

1. Virgoe, *B.I.H.R.* xliii (1970), 149, 156; Nicolas, *op. cit.* vi. 174 (16 April).

Harvard University (The Houghton Library), fMS Eng. 751, fos. 211ᵛ–214ᵛ
fo. 211ᵛ
Acta, apunctuamenta et ordina[ciones][1] facta et stabilita in consilio
anno Henrici sexto tricesimo secundo pro directione consillii [*sic*] et
pro Regimine ac gubernacione Regni et republicae.

The .xxx. daye of November anno predicto in the ster chamber at
Wistmyster it was moved, opened, declared and also [agreed][2]
considered that divers and many comandements afor this tyeme have
bye the kings autoryte, advyse and ordinaunce of his counsell ben
directid and sent as well to Lords of this land as other persons the
wiche in no wyese have been obeyed nor entendid to full gret example
of disobeysaunce to other the kings subiets to the hurt also and
derogacyone of there riall eastate the awtoryte of hym and of his
counsell and shuld dayly cause gret inconvenyence to ensue without
remedye wes had in that behalfe. Ffor so muche hit was avysed,
apointed, assented and fullye concludid that every Lord spirituall and
temporall shuld be sworne on a book and assure by the faythe of his
bodye trowthe and aleageaunce that [he] [owghe][2] owethe to the
kinge that from this day fourthe yf any person whatsoever estat,
degree or condycyon he be of in any manner refuese or straine [*i.e.* ?
restrain] hym to obeye the comandement [or],[2] advyse or lawfull and

leafull ordinaunce to be made bye the king bye the advyese and autoryte of his counsell, in that case everyche of the Lords shall put him in his full devoure aswell by meane of his person as goods to the correcyon and ponyshment of hym that so disobeyethe and to compell and make hym effectually to applye and obey the [kings]² sayd commandment, advyse and ordenaunce and to bring hym affor the king and his counsell, nor sparing so to do for affeccyon, favor, nihenes of blod nor nother cause whatsoever hit be, the wiche advyese, apointment and ordenaunce the Lords names folowe promysed and swar on a booke everyche on [of]² his behalfe truly to observe and kepe in all things truely contened in the same.

fo. 212ʳ

These Lords tok the aforenamed othe³

The Lord cardinall
archebishopp of Canterbury
chauncelor
thearcbishope [*sic*] of York
the bishop of London
the bushope of Duresme
the bishope of Winchester
the bushop of Eley and Chester
the bushope of [London]²
Lyncolne
the bushope of Bathe
the bushope of Norwyche
the bushope of St Davyd
the bushop of Herfford
the bushope of Carelyle
the bishop of Banger
the deane of Saynt Severynes
the dueke of Yorke
the dueke of Norffolk
the dueke of Buckingham
Therle of⁴ Pembroke
therle of Stafford
therle of Warwyke
therle of Oxfford
therle of Salesbury
therle of Shrewysbery
therle of Devonshyre
therle of Worsyter
therle of Wyltshyre

The Viscount Beamount

the Viscount Bourchyer
the prior of Sancti Jones
The Lord Croumwell
the Lord Scales
the L. Ffauconbrig

the L. Gray Ruthyn
the L. Willowghby
the L. Sturtone
the L. FfizWarren
the L. Scrope of Bowlton
the L. fizHuhe
the L. Bechampe
the L. Sudley
the L. Berners
the L. Bonvyle
the L. Greystoke
the L. Gray Rumond
the L. Grey Wilton
the L. Saye
the L. Clynton
Sir Thomas Stanley
Sir Willyam Lucy
Sir Thomas Tyrrell
Sir Richard Haryngton
Jhon Say

fo. 212ᵛ

.v°. die Decembris anno .xxxii. Henrici sexti

In the sterred chamber at Wystmyster the Lord cardynall, tharchbyshope of Yorke, the bushops of London, Winchester,

Norwyche, Eley, Chester and Lyncolne, the dueks of York and Bukingham, therles of Pembrok, Warewyck, Salesbury, Worsyter [of][2] tresorer of englond, and Wiltshyre, the Viscount Bourchyer, the prior of St. Jones, the Lords Cromwell, Dudley, Scales and Sturtone, assembled in gret counsell as peres of the land, consyderinge that great and many maters wer dayly moved amongs them of gret weight and charge concerninge the [weale][5] of oure sayd souerne Lord the king, his lands and subiets, and that the kings inffirmytey of the wiche thes wer as sory as they cold be, suffered hym not to entend to the [publique][2] pollytyque rule and gouernance of this his land and to the observaunce and kepynge of his lawes as the nessecytye asketh and requyerethe. And also that good ne reason wold hit shuld stand without ruele and gouernaunce have advysed, conseulyd and apointed that they in estuinge imeparable inconvynyentees [that][5] shuld els now ensue wold entend to that, that shuld be to the pollytyque rule and gouernance of this land in all suche things as must of nessessyte be entendyd unto and by the whch yf the wer not forsene grete inconvenyence wer lyeke to ensue aswell in that that belongethe unto pollitique rule and gouernaunce thereof as to the observance and keping of the kyngs lawes makinge expres protestacion that only for the weale of the kynge and of his lands they tooke uppon them and entend not nor wyll procede in other matters but in such as of veary nesestye must be entended unto untill the tyeme there poure be more ample by awtoryty suffycyently declared.

Domini se subscribentes[6]

J. Cardinall	W. Norwich	R. York
W. Ebor' episc'	R. Co' et Lych'	H. Bukingham
T. London' episc'	J. Lyncolne	J. Norffolk
T. Eliensis episc'	T. abas Salop'	R. Warwik
		R. Salsbury
		Buchyer

fo. 213[r]

.iii°. die Aprilis anno .xxxii[do]. Henrici sexti

At Wistmyster in the starre chamber beinge there assembled the Lords suche as wernamed to be of the kyngs counsell, myelord therle of Saleburye chauncelor of englomd opened and shewed to the remnant of the Lords willinge they shuld call to remembrance that amongs other artycles conceved and mynystred bye the dueke of Yorke named to be protector and defendor of this land, it was declared he wold not take uppon hym the sayde name and charge bolomgine [sic] thereunto without that the Lords named to be of kings counsell wold semblablye take uppon them the name of counsalors and charg apertenynge [there][2] unto them. Fforsomuche my lord chauncellor willing the Lords shuld saye there entent in this behalffe, he demaunded ffirst the dueke of Norfolke whether hit was his wyll to take upone hym the sayd name and charge of counsalor, the wiche dueke of Northfolke answerynge sayde he was that person that wold wythall his hart doo all that was in hym that might be to the kings pleasure and the will of his Lords and subiets and wold not spare to do the servyse he could and to gyve attendaunce and assystance as he shuld and mowght do and so he wold without that inffirmytye with the wiche he is manye tyemes vexed wiche letted him so for to doo. The dueke of Bukingham in lykewyese declared hym selfe addinge he could not take uppon hym to attende dayly and contyneallye specyally for suche sicknes as he is at dyvers tymes vysyted with and that he may not at seche tyemes endure to ryede; with this also he made protestacyone that yf it so wes that hym thowght expedyent for suche causes as shuld move hym to be dicharged of the sayd occupacione of counsalor thate so be; morover he disirethe that for the tyeme he shall occupye he might have for his attendaunce accordinge to his eastate.

fo. 213^v

The [sayd]^2 Archebyshope of Yorke acording to the same sayd that he wold geve suche assistaunce as he could reasonbly doo. The bushope of Wynchester sayed his consyence wold not suffer hym contynualy to attend but as he might reasonablye he wold and was thowght hym that some of his bretherne the bushops shold [attend]^2 attend for one tyme and some for another. With this the bushope of Worsyter sayd he would be ruled as the Lords wold have hym. The bushope of Norwyche in lykes wyese sayd soo that he have lycens among other to attend to his ayre and to vyeset his diosses as hit aperteneth unto hym. The bushope of Lyncolne sayd the same addinge that in certayne tyemes of the yeire he mighte be spared as specially in Lent and Advent. The bushope of Chester sayd [he]^7 wold for his parte wold doo as other the Lords spyrytuall had sayd they wold doo. Therle of Warewyke sayd he [was]^5 yonge of age and yonger of discrecyon and wysdome so that he was unable to [attend]^5 that occupacyone. Notwithstanding he wold with right goodwyll doo that wiche was in his poure. Therl of Oxford the same as farr as his sikness would suffer hym with the wyche as he sayd he was many tyemes full sore vexed with. Therle of Shrewysbury would be ready to do his part [as]^5 other men dyd. Therle of Woryster moved hit was thowght to hym nessessarye and full expedient to all the Lords that shuld take uppon theme the sayd charge to have knolege of the execucyone of theire powre and to ffend meanes howe (suche]^2 [meanes howe]^8 suche charges as rest upon the kinge shuld nowe be borne. Also in which wes [*sic* ways] the Lords of the counsell shuld be contentyd of theire duety and as for hym selfe he wold be ready to doo suche servyse to the kinge as he could.

fo. 214^r

The Vyescount Bourchyer for diverse reasons and specyallye for he thowght hym selfe unable disired he might be excused but fynally he graunted he wold do as other with that he might be sene to aftyr his eastate as other aftyr theires. The pryor of Saynt Johannes leing for suche charge as he had with his ordere and relygyon bosowght he might be excused not withstandinge he assentyd to take it upon hym, movinge hit shuld be declared in the commene howse the eastate of the land and what charges rest uppon the kinge and that the Lords take this upone them for the welthe of the kinge and his land. Croumwell alleagynge the greate adge he is of, his inffyrmyte and feblenes dissired as he mighte bee excused as he thowght reasone wold it should so be and for asmuche as the remnant of the Lords wyllyd and prayed hym not to straunge hym to use his adge, experyence and wysdom for the commone welthe to his great lawde and meryt, he graunted to take hit uppon hym and do his part as far as his sayd adge, sicknes and feblenes would suffer hym, advysynge as it was moved beffore bye therle of Worsyter and the prior of St. Jhonnes that declaracyone shold be made to the commons willyng also that meanes shuld be found for the contentynge of the Lords of the counsell adding thereto that hit might be so provyded and ordayned for all suche as wer or should be of the kings counsell shold nowe com safe and surely thereto abyed and depart also thereffro in lykewyese. Scales layd for him selfe his uncunnynge and experyence and for many causes he was full unable as he sayde to [the]² so great a worke ffynally applyinge hym selfe to do as other, he sayd he wold not contyneally attend nor be accomptable for that he shuld [he shuld]⁸ receave for the sayd cause.

fo. 214ᵛ

The Viscounte Beamound remembryd that he was with the quene for the wiche he would not departe in takynge uppone hym this charge; he sayd also it was conteyned in thartycles of the counsell that every man shuld have full freedom to saye what he thowght in matters as of counsales, without any displeasure, indignacyon or wrothe of any other person for his sayinge the wyche he wold shuld be kept and observed; he sayd also he had far to come to the counsell and thereffor he wold take uppone hym not to come at al tymes but at suche tyemes as he godly might and sayd his povertye and lytle discresshyone constranethe hym to disire his excuse; not withstanding sythe the Lords willed hym he wold he wold performe theire wille and to do part with the other. Sir Thomas Stanley knight sayd he wyst well he was nemed to the charge only to do suche arrants as the Lords wold lay uppone hym and thereffore he wold as far as he cold do it with right good wyll. Jhon Say esquyre sayd the same. The deane of Saint Severnes thowghe he wes powre the wiche made a man to be reputed no gret wisdom yet he would doo suche servyce as he could with right good wyll.

1. MS slightly damaged.

2. Word deleted.

3. The following list of names was evidently an integral part of the record of the meeting of 30 November and was appended to it in holograph by the clerk who compiled it in the mid-fifteenth century; as such it was reproduced by the copyist who wrote the Harvard MS.

4. 'of' repeated.

5. This or a similar word omitted.

6. The following list of names was evidently appended to the record of the meeting of 5 December as a series of individual signatures.

7. Word interlineated.

8. These words repeated.

[For further comment and context, see P.A. Johnson, *Duke Richard of York, 1411-1460* (Oxford, 1988), ch. 6.]

20

Local Rivalries and National Politics: The Percies, the Nevilles and the Duke of Exeter, 1452-1454*

G. M. Trevelyan remarked that "the Wars of the Roses were to a large extent a quarrel between Welsh Marcher Lords, who were also great English nobles, closely related to the English throne."[1] It is true that most of the leading magnates in this dynastic struggle held one or more lordships in Wales, but it was not the political situation resulting from this which led to war in the 1450's. Rather was Wales a refuge and a reservoir of men and money for its lords, and it illustrated more graphically than most regions the chronic lawlessness and local autonomy which feeble royal rule could bring in the fifteenth century.[2] If, instead, Trevelyan had looked northwards, especially to Yorkshire, he might well have described the Wars of the Roses as in part a quarrel between great Yorkshire magnates who were also involved in the campaign to reform and ultimately displace Lancastrian government.

In the mid-fifteenth century, the three ridings of Yorkshire lay under the shadow of four of England's greatest landowners: the king, as duke of Lancaster, and the Percy family, headed by the earl of Northumberland, rubbed shoulders with their rivals, Duke Richard of York and the Neville earl of Salisbury.[3] The Percy manors between the Pennines and the North Sea were interposed between the main Salisbury estates in the north riding and those of the duke of York to

---

* I am indebted to Mr T. B. Pugh of the University of Southampton and Dr C. D. Ross of the University of Bristol for a number of valuable suggestions in the writing of this article.

[1] G. M. Trevelyan, *History of England* (3rd. edition, 1945), p. 259.

[2] For Wales in the fifteenth century, see H. T. Evans, *Wales and the Wars of the Roses* (1915), T. B. Pugh, *The Marcher Lordships of South Wales, 1415-1536* (1963), and Ralph A. Griffiths, "Gruffydd ap Nicholas and the Fall of the House of Lancaster," *The Welsh History Review*, ii, no. 3 , above ch. 12.

[3] R. Somerville, *History of the Duchy of Lancaster*, i (1953), 513–537; J. M. W. Bean, *The Estates of the Percy Family, 1416-1537* (1958), especially pp. 36–41, 44–48 for the relative value of the Yorkshire manors; Joel T. Rosenthal, "The Estates and Finances of Richard, Duke of York (1411-1460)," in W. M. Bowsky (ed.), *Studies in Medieval and Renaissance History*, ii (1965), especially pp. 150, 194 (these statistics can be challenged, but they provide a rough guide to relative values); G. M. Coles, "The Lordship of Middleham, especially in Yorkist and early Tudor Times" (unpublished University of Liverpool M. A. thesis, 1961), chs. 1, 2.

the south, where, moreover, the duke's estates lay close to those of the king himself.[4] The Yorkshire inheritances of these four politically-minded houses were such that neighbourly rivalries were inevitable and overt hostilities possible. The king and the duke of York seem to have rarely visited their Yorkshire estates, so that local feuds occurred most often between the Percies, the Nevilles and their associates.[5] The city of York provided a focus for these rivalries and became a prize coveted by the most powerful, for the leading Yorkshire families kept houses in the city as the natural centre of England east of the Pennines — economically, religiously, socially and, quite often, governmentally.[6] Moreover, York was surrounded by Percy manors, with Salisbury's estates at Stamford Bridge and Sheriff Hutton not far away. Thus, the two virtual battles between Percy and Neville in 1453 and 1454 were fought close to the city's walls, and its capture was one of the duke of Exeter's objectives when he intervened in northern politics.

*   *   *   *   *

The Percy-Neville dispute was a struggle of giants. The first Percy earl of Northumberland was created in 1377, the first Neville earl of Westmorland twenty years later. Both were great north country landowners in Yorkshire, the Lake District, and the northernmost shires of England, the one often used by the Crown as a counterweight to the influence of the other. Although rather earlier than the Nevilles in the field of advancement, the Percies forfeited their lead — and their estates — after deserting Henry IV in 1403; whereas Earl Ralph Neville of Westmorland enlarged his holdings and influence by foresight and fecundity before his death in 1425. It needed patient advocacy by Henry Percy, grandson of the first earl, between 1416, when the earldom of Northumberland was restored, and 1440 to recover most (but not all) of the lost possessions.[7] By the mid-fifteenth century, therefore, relations between Percy and Neville were poisoned by jealousy and resentment.

The Nevilles had their own troubles. Earl Ralph of Westmorland (d. 1425) was more prolific than his family's interests required. His elder son by his first wife predeceased him, and it was therefore his grandson, Ralph, who inherited the earldom of Westmorland; but the bulk of his properties descended to his second wife, Joan Beaufort. When Earl Ralph died in 1425, the new earl of Westmorland found himself heir to only part of the Neville estates. It was Joan, with remainder to her eldest son, Richard Neville, who secured the Yorkshire properties centred on Middleham, Wensleydale, Sheriff Hutton, and Cleveland,

---

[4] See the map in R. L. Storey, *The End of the House of Lancaster* (1966), p. 128.

[5] Duke Richard of York is not known to have visited England north of Fotheringay (Northants.) before 1454; he found his Welsh estates more palatable. Rosenthal, "Estates and Finances of Richard, Duke of York," in Bowsky, *Studies in Medieval and Renaissance History*, II (1965), 197–200.

[6] J. N. Bartlett, "The Expansion and Decline of York in the later Middle Ages," *The Economic History Review*, 2nd series, XII (1959–60), 17–20. The accounts of the Yorkshire estates of the Percies were audited at York in 1441–42 at least (E. J. Fisher, "Some Yorkshire Estates of the Percies, 1450–1650" (unpublished University of Leeds Ph.D. thesis, 1954), vol. I, ch. 2, p. 160).

[7] For the Percies, see Bean, *Estates of the Percy Family*, pp. 3–11, 69–79, 158–60, and G. E. C., *The Complete Peerage* (12 vols., 1910–59), X, 456–464, IX, 708–12; for the Nevilles, E. F. Jacob, *The Fifteenth Century* (1961), pp. 319–326, and *Complete Peerage*, IX, 497–503, XII, part 2, 544–547.

the lordship of Raby (Durham) and the Neville lands in Cumberland and Westmorland.[8] This Richard, recognised as earl of Salisbury in 1429, became the principal Neville beneficiary in counties where the Percies were also powerful landowners. Moreover, dissension between the earls of Salisbury and Westmorland was inevitable, and the settlement of 1443 did not remove the bitterness. As a result, Westmorland and his family gave no aid to Salisbury and his offspring in the Percy quarrel.[9]

The Percy-Neville rivalry was reflected in (and partly caused by) the interest which each showed in the wardenship of the east and west marches towards Scotland. By the mid-fifteenth century the wardenship of the east march was the preserve of the Percies in the person of Northumberland's son, Henry, Lord Poynings, warden from 1 April 1440. Similarly, the west march was in Neville custody: first, Earl Richard of Salisbury from 12 December 1443, and then, ten years later, he and his son, Earl Richard of Warwick, jointly.[10] Despite the hazard of holding office in a peculiarly disturbed part of the realm, neither family was willing to forego the possibility of power and profit offered, and neither would allow the other into its sphere. Moreover, each warden was enabled to raise a private force of retainers at the king's expense.[11] This system may have allowed Salisbury to retain for life Sir Walter Strickland and 290 men in September 1449; and Lord Poynings' retinue as warden must have swollen his father's body of retainers and supplemented those receiving black and red livery in 1453–54 from his brothers, Lord Egremont and Richard Percy.[12] By 1453 Northumberland had a considerable number of knights and esquires in his service. Those retained by Egremont and Richard Percy were humbler men, eventually condemned as illegally retained because they were "familiares servientes . . . non existant nec in servicio suo retenti nec in una lege neque in altera eruditi." [13] Many of these Percy retainers were prominent among those indicted for their part in the skirmishes with the Nevilles in the 1450's.

[8] Jacob, *Fifteenth Century*, pp. 320–321, 323; *Complete Peerage*, XII, part 2, 547–549; T. B. Pugh and C. D. Ross, "The English Baronage and the Income Tax of 1436," *Bulletin of the Institute of Historical Research*, XXVI (1953), 7–8; Coles, "Lordship of Middleham," ch. 2.

[9] A state of war virtually existed in 1430–39 between Westmorland and his sons on the one hand, and Joan Beaufort and her sons on the other. *Ibid.*, pp. 35–40; *Complete Peerage*, IX, 716, XII, part 2, 549–550; Storey, *End of the House of Lancaster*, pp. 109–115. For Westmorland's aloofness, see below, p. 335.

[10] R. L. Storey, "The Wardens of the Marches of England towards Scotland, 1377–1489," *The English Historical Review*, LXXII (1957), 593–615, especially 599, 602–607, 614. For the financial benefit derived by the Percies from the wardenship of the east march up to 1453, see Bean, *Estates of the Percy Family*, pp. 105–107.

[11] Storey, *Eng. Hist. Rev.*, LXXII (1957), 604, 607. The statutes of livery acknowledged that the wardens of the march had the privilege of maintaining private, liveried forces. *Rotuli Parliamentorum* (6 vols., 1767), v, 487, 634.

[12] *The Dictionary of National Biography* (63 vols., 1885–1900), XL, 280; Storey, *End of the House of Lancaster*, pp. 122–123; Bean, *Estates of the Percy Family*, pp. 92, 96–97; Public Record Office, King's Bench, Ancient Indictments, 148/10; 149/4/11, 4/12, 7/2, 8/4.

[13] *Ibid.*, 149/4/11. The statutes of Henry IV, as reiterated in 1429, were evidently invoked against them: "no Knight, nor other of less Estate should give any Livery of Cloths or Hats to other than to his Menials, and his Officers and Men learned in the one Law or the other." *Statutes of the Realm* (11 vols., 1810–28), II, 240–241.

The disturbances between Northumberland and Salisbury were not as intense before 1453 as they were later. Nevertheless, rumours of lawlessness wafted about the name of Northumberland, and in 1443 disturbances between him and Archbishop Kemp of York were attributed to certain letters written by the earl.[14] The haughty independence of the Percies was impressive. On 14 January 1453 a group of his tenants could apparently boast that no sheriff or other royal officer could make an arrest or execute an order within the Percy lordship of Topcliffe or any other of Northumberland's estates.[15] To emphasise the point, Thomas de la More, sheriff of Cumberland in 1452–53 and one of Salisbury's servants, reported at the end of his term that Egremont had long ago threatened to kill him; he told this to Salisbury so that king and Council could be informed.[16]

Despite this behaviour, there was no apparent victimisation of Northumberland and his family after the earl's rehabilitation in 1416. He himself (b. 1394) became constable of England in May 1450; his eldest son, Henry, created Lord Poynings in 1446, became warden of the east march but rarely participated in Court politics.[17] The second surviving son, Thomas, became Baron Egremont in November 1449 at the age of twenty-five; "Quarrelsome, violent and contemptuous of all authority, he possessed all the worst characteristics of a Percy for which his grandfather Hotspur is still a byword." He it was, together with his younger brothers, Ralph and Richard, who led the Percy clan in its feud with the Nevilles in the 1450's.[18] Northumberland's youngest son of all, William, followed the classic career for the youngest: the church. In 1436 he became prebendary of Riccall, in the diocese of York, when he was a mere boy; and he retained it until his transference to be prebendary of Driffield (also in York) in 1451; in August 1452 he became bishop of Carlisle.[19]

[14] N. H. Nicolas (ed.), *Proceedings and Ordinances of the Privy Council of England* (7 vols., 1834–37), v, 275; Sir John Salvin, of whom more later, was one of Northumberland's supporters (J. H. Ramsay, *Lancaster and York* (2 vols., 1892), II, 53 note 2). Earlier in 1443, Richard Aldburgh, the younger, who was to be one of Egremont's supporters in 1453–54, appeared at the York sessions accused of disseising one of the Nevilles in Swaledale; Aldburgh was accompanied by his father, the elder Richard, by William Aldburgh and three others (P. R. O., Justices Itinerant, 1/1544 m. 9, 9d; K. B., Anc. Indict., 149/4/27, 11/16). A number of men from the Percy manors of Tadcaster, Topcliffe, and Spofforth, who were later associated with Lord Egremont in 1453 and 1454, found themselves in prison in York castle by May 1447; they included Alexander Chatton of Topcliffe, who took Egremont's livery in 1453 (*Calendar of the Patent Rolls, 1446–52*, p. 41; below, p. 334).

[15] P. R. O., K. B., Anc. Ind., 149/11/24. The occasion was an attempt by three deputy-sheriffs of Yorkshire to arrest Oliver Stockdale, a yeoman from Thorpe Under Lees. The officers were brutally repelled by Stockdale and a gang of local inhabitants, 120-strong; the names of twenty-nine are recorded, of whom at least seven were later involved in more serious riots on behalf of the Percies. Below, p. 334).

[16] *Rot. Parl.*, VI, 63–64 (misdated to 1472); Storey, *End of the House of Lancaster*, p. 126. The Council did in fact consider Thomas de la More's complaints in July 1454 (P. R. O., Exchequer, T. R., Council and Privy Seal, 85/26, 27). It seems that the sheriff of Cumberland could not perform his duties in the Percy honor of Cockermouth. Storey, *End of the House of Lancaster*, pp. 106–123.

[17] *C. P. R., 1446–52*, p. 326; *Complete Peerage*, IX, 716–717.

[18] Storey, *End of the House of Lancaster*, p. 125; Ramsay, *Lancaster and York*, II, 163; *Rot. Parl.*, V, 194; Bean, *Estates of the Percy Family*, pp. 84 note 3, 98 note 1. Ralph Percy had custody of Dunstanburgh castle (Northumb.) as deputy-constable for life. Somerville, *Duchy of Lancaster*, I, 538.

[19] J. le Neve, *Fasti Ecclesiae Anglicanae, 1300–1541*; VI. *Northern Province* (1963), pp. 45, 76; F. M.

Salisbury (b. *c.* 1400) and his family had none of the handicaps of the Percies to overcome. The earl was a regular member of Henry VI's Council, and his territorial position in the north was buttressed by strategic offices in the duchy of Lancaster and on the Scottish border.[20] His eldest son, Richard, was diverted elsewhere after becoming earl of Warwick in right of his wife in July 1449. Two other sons, Thomas and John, were his representatives in the Percy-Neville quarrel: in August 1445 Thomas was associated with his father and elder brother in the stewardship of the Lancaster honors of Pontefract, Knaresborough, and Pickering, and it was his marriage in 1453 which precipitated the Percy conflict; he was knighted at Christmas 1449, together with his brother John, Salisbury's third son and steadfast champion.[21]

These two families occupied an impressive territorial and official position in Yorkshire and the north in the 1450's: each led by an earl in his fifties, still vigorous and with a career of achievement behind him; each with an eldest son whose interests were being diverted elsewhere; each with younger offspring ready to take up arms in their father's cause. In 1453 each family possessed manpower, leadership and a militant temperament; Eleanor Neville, Salisbury's sister and Northumberland's wife, was the only bond — a slim one — between the two.

* * * *

Their hostility attained a new bitterness in 1453. A conflict took place at Heworth, near York, on 24 August which deserves to be described as the first overt "battle" between the Percies and the Nevilles in the 1450's. The inflamed situation was probably caused by news of the impending marriage of Sir Thomas Neville to Maud Stanhope, widow of Robert, Lord Willoughby of Eresby (d. July 1452), and niece and co-heiress of Ralph, Lord Cromwell.[22] This particular match was obnoxious to the earl of Northumberland. Resentment at Neville aggrandisement was second nature to him, but it was heightened by the connection with Lord Cromwell. Cromwell's service to Henry VI had been rewarded with substantial estates, among them the two former Percy manors of Wressle (Yorkshire) and Burwell (Lincolnshire). Two-thirds of each were granted to Lord Cromwell for life in February 1438, together with reversion of the remainder; the grant was converted into one in fee simple in February 1440. Meanwhile, in 1439 Northumberland, seeking restitution of his family estates, clarified his

---

Powicke and E. B. Fryde (edd.), *Handbook of British Chronology* (1961), p. 213; Storey, *End of the House of Lancaster*, p. 126.

[20] *Complete Peerage*, XI, 395–398; Somerville, *Duchy of Lancaster*, I, 513; *Proc. P. C.*, VI, *passim*; Storey, *End of the House of Lancaster*, pp. 109–117. He was warden of the west march from 12 December 1443. Above, p. 323.

[21] Somerville, *Duchy of Lancaster*, I, 513; Storey, *End of the House of Lancaster*, pp. 116–17; *Complete Peerage*, IX, 717; J. Stevenson (ed.), *Letters and Papers illustrative of the Wars of the English in France* (2 vols., Rolls Series, 1861–64), II, part 2, 770. Salisbury's brother, Robert Neville, was bishop of Durham from 1438 to his death on 8 July 1457. Powicke and Fryde, *Handbook of British Chronology*, p. 221; *Dict. Nat. Biog.*, XL, 300–302.

[22] *Complete Peerage*, XII, part 2, 665–666. Royal licence for the marriage was issued on 1 May 1453. *C. P. R., 1452–61*, p. 64.

claim to some of them, including Wressle and Burwell.[23] Thus, in 1453 Northumberland claimed two manors, most of which were held by Cromwell, who was now sponsoring his heiress' marriage to Sir Thomas Neville.[24] At a time when the domestic and public concerns of the baronage revolved around marriages and enfeoffments, leases and bequests, Northumberland could justifiably feel aggrieved.[25]

In June 1453 Sir John Neville and Lord Egremont were the adversaries and Henry VI was repeatedly driven to command their presence, all excuses apart. The irresolute king's bark was futile and the government's control of the situation in Yorkshire feeble, for on 29 June Sir John is reported to have planned Egremont's capture on his way to Topcliffe. There, in Percy country, Neville was said to have roused the men of Topcliffe to ambush their lord's son, causing considerable disturbance in the process.[26] With royal commands freely ignored like this, Henry VI dissolved Parliament on 2 July 1453 so that he could make a tour of punishment and pacification through the distraught parts of his kingdom — among them undoubtedly Yorkshire.[27]

A frontal assault having failed, the government resorted to more oblique action; on 7 July it required Egremont to prepare himself and his men for military service in Gascony. This might be the surest means of removing one source of trouble, but not even the military emergency there inspired obedience in Egremont; he did not go abroad and the government was still faced with the problem of order in the north.[28] Having failed twice, it tried a third method: a commission of northern notables including Northumberland and Salisbury themselves. On 12 July 1453 the earls, Viscount Beaumont, and fourteen others received a commission of oyer and terminer to investigate all "felonies, trespasses, congregations, insurrections, confederacies, combinations, and liveries of badges, gowns, and caps" in the north riding. It was reissued a fortnight later, partly because of the seriousness of the situation, but also perhaps because the commissioners were not

[23] Bean, *Estates of the Percy Family*, pp. 8, 73–75. For Cromwell's wealth and estates before his death in January 1456, see K. B. McFarlane, "The Wars of the Roses," *The Proceedings of the British Academy*, L (1964), 97 note 1; Pugh and Ross, *Bull. Inst. Hist. Res.*, xxvi (1953), 6–7; and E. Price, "Ralph Lord Cromwell and his Household" (unpublished University of London M. A. thesis, 1948).

[24] Burwell, at least, was among the richest of Cromwell's possessions, worth £38.10s. 6d. in 1445–46. *Historical Manuscripts Commission: Report on the Manuscripts of Lord de l'Isle and Dudley* (1925), I, 209. For Cromwell's two heiresses, see *Complete Peerage*, III, 552–553; *C. P. R., 1452–61*, p. 275; *H. M. C., L'Isle and Dudley MSS*, I, 176–177.

[25] For earlier Yorkshire disorders stemming from land disputes, see Jacob, *Fifteenth Century*, pp. 328–329.

[26] *Proc. P. C.*, VI, 140–142; P. R. O., Exchequer, T. R., Council and Privy Seal, 83/32, 57; K. B., Anc. Indict., 149/8/5; Storey, *End of the House of Lancaster*, p. 129. The outcome is unknown but Egremont must have escaped.

[27] *Rot. Parl.*, v, 236.

[28] Storey, *End of the House of Lancaster*, p. 129; P. R. O., Exchequer, T. R., Council and Privy Seal, 83/7. Egremont does not appear among those in Gascony during the last months of English rule, or who were paid at this time for assisting the earl of Shrewsbury there. Lord Bonville was despatched to Gascony at about the same time, possibly to remove one element in the West Country disturbances. P. R. O., Exchequer, E. R., Issue Roll, 794; Warrants for Issues, 69/201–26.

very effective.[29] Although most of them were neither Percy nor Neville adherents, there was a handful of the latter to weight the investigations in their favour. Unlike Northumberland, Salisbury sat on the Council at this time and may have helped determine the composition of the commission.[30] Thus, Sir James Pickering was soon to be denounced as a prominent rioter with Ralph Neville; Sir Henry fitzHugh and his brother-in-law, Sir Henry Le Scrope of Bolton, fought for Neville against Percy later in the year and maintained their Neville affiliations thereafter; Robert Constable of Flamborough came of a family closely associated with Salisbury, and although Robert Danby was a royal justice, he seems to have been in the earl's service by 1458.[31] The Percies had no comparable representation. Such a partially partisan body would hardly carry conviction for peace, certainly not among the Percies.

Disturbances continued as widespread as ever. On 24 July Egremont's brother, Richard Percy of Cleatop, conducted an orgy of breaking and entering at Halton and Swinden (Yorkshire); he was accompanied by three Yorkshire supporters of the Percies: John Pudsay of Bolton in Craven, Richard Tempest of Stainforth, and John Caterall of Brayton in Craven.[32] Thereupon, the government was driven to a much more drastic expedient, amounting to a partial abdication of its power. On 27 July it laid the onus for ending the disturbances squarely upon the shoulders of Northumberland and Salisbury: they were instructed to keep their sons in order, and Egremont and Sir John Neville were again ordered to cease their activities in Yorkshire.[33] Furthermore, a new commission, headed by Sir William Lucy, was sent into the shire. It suffered from fewer of its predecessor's defects and should have stood a better chance of success: it was smaller, more compact and well blessed with legal experience. Sir William Lucy, from Northamptonshire, was a member of the king's Council; he had long military experience in France, knowledge of negotiations with the Scots, and seems to have revealed none of his later partisanship.[34] Of his colleagues, Peter Ardern had begun his legal training

---

[29] *C. P. R., 1452–61*, pp. 121–123. The other commissioners were Sir Henry fitzHugh, Sir Henry le Scrope, Peter Ardern, John Portyngton, Robert Danby, Sir Thomas Stanley, Sir Ralph Bigod, Sir James Pickering, Thomas Tresham, William Chedworth, Robert Tanfield, Robert Constable of Flamborough, Guy Rouclif, and Robert Drax.

[30] *Proc. P. C.*, vi, 143–144: P. R. O., Exchequer, T. R., Council and Privy Seal, 83/68.

[31] FitzHugh married Alice, daughter of the earl of Salisbury, and Le Scrope's mother was Margaret, daughter of Earl Ralph I of Westmorland (*Complete Peerage*, v, 428–429, xi, 542–543). Robert Constable may have been the man who was named by Salisbury in 1436 as trustee of his mother's inheritance should she die while he was abroad; another Robert was chancellor and receiver-general of the palatinate of Durham for Bishop Robert Neville (1438–57), and receiver of Pontefract, Pickering, and Tickhill for a time while Salisbury was steward and constable there (Coles, "Lordship of Middleham," pp. 122–123; Somerville, *Duchy of Lancaster*, i, 516). For Danby's connection with Salisbury, see J. Gairdner, ed., *The Paston Letters, 1422–1509* (4 vols., 1872–75), i, 421.

[32] P. R. O., K. B., Anc. Indict., 149/6/7; Bean, *Estates of the Percy Family*, p. 98 note 1; for two members of the Tempest family receiving annuities in Yorkshire from the earl of Northumberland in the first half of the fifteenth century, see *ibid.*, pp. 92 note 1, 195 note 3. For Pudsay and Caterall, see below, p. 332.

[33] *Proc. P. C.*, vi, 147–149; P. R. O., Exchequer, T. R., Council and Privy Seal, 83/24, 22.

[34] *C. P. R., 1452–61*, p. 122. Lucy was assigned £26.13s. 4d. to cover his expenses in travelling north-

in the duchy of Lancaster in 1438, graduating to become a justice of Common Pleas in 1448. The careers of John Portyngton and Robert Danby were similar, the former reaching the Common Bench in 1443, the latter more recently in June 1453.[35] It was also more realistic to extend the terms of reference of the new commission to include Northumberland, Cumberland, Westmorland, and Yorkshire generally.

The Lucy commission seemed the final, necessary word. On the day of its appointment, a number of prominent rioters were reprimanded and ordered to submit to it. Among them were Ralph Neville, esquire, four knights (Sir John Conyers, Sir James Pickering, Sir Ralph Randolf, and Sir Thomas Mountford) and three esquires (Richard Aske, Thomas Sewer, and John Alcombe). They were probably Neville's principal accomplices in the late troubles, for Conyers was one of Salisbury's retainers and Pickering, one of the recent commissioners, would soon be the duke of York's councillor.[36] Action against the Percy faction was taken on 10 August; nine were singled out as instigators of riots and ordered to obey Sir William Lucy. Headed by Sir Ralph and Richard Percy, they included knights and esquires who can be linked with the Percies.[37] Sir Henry Fenwick of Cockermouth (Cumberland) had been associated with Northumberland since at least 1444 and was his lieutenant of Cockermouth castle in 1453–54.[38] Sir William Martindale of Newton (Cumberland) was one of the earl's retainers in 1453–54 and his steward of Cockermouth.[39] John Swynburne, also of Cockermouth, was retained by Northumberland in 1453–54 for a £4 fee and acted as his receiver in Cumberland and bailiff of Allerdale in the same year.[40] William Lee of Cockermouth, Henry Belingham of Burneside (Westmorland), and Sir John Pennington of Muncaster (Cumberland) were in the earl's service by 1453–54; the remaining miscreant, Roland Kirkeby of Cockermouth, was also connected with the Percy family.[41]

---

wards to enquire into "certain great and riotous assemblies of people against our peace there now late made." P. R. O., Exchequer, E. R., Issue Roll, 794; Warrants for Issues, 69/214. For Lucy, see J. Wedgwood (ed.), *History of Parliament. Biographies of the members of the Commons House, 1439–1509* (1936), pp. 559–560, and below, p. 332.

[35] Somerville, *Duchy of Lancaster*, i, 425, 451, 469, 472; *C. P. R., 1452–61*, p. 85. Lucy's three companions had served on the earlier commission of 12 July 1453; Ardern was also chief baron of the Exchequer by Michaelmas 1452. Above, p. 327; P. R. O., Exchequer, E. R., Issue Roll, 792 (23 October).

[36] *Proc. P. C.*, vi, 149–151; P. R. O., Exchequer, T. R., Council and Privy Seal, 83/25, 23. For Pickering, see C. A. J. Armstrong, "Politics and the Battle of St. Albans, 1455." *Bull. Inst. Hist. Res.*, xxxiii (1960), 27, and Wedgwood, *History of Parliament, Biographies*, pp. 682–683; for Mountford, *ibid.*, pp. 603–604; and for Conyers, Coles, "Lordship of Middleham," appendix B.

[37] *Proc. P. C.*, vi, 154–155.

[38] Bean, *Estates of the Percy Family*, pp. 24, 96; below, p. 332. Fenwick was J. P. in Cumberland in 1453–54, and sheriff there in 1436–37 and 1458–59, though he probably died during his second term since his executors rendered his account.

[39] Bean, *Estates of the Percy Family*, pp. 96–97; below, p. 332. He was J. P. in Cumberland in 1434 and M. P. for the county in 1447. Wedgwood, *History of Parliament, Biographies*, p. 580.

[40] Bean, *Estates of the Percy Family*, pp. 96–97; below, p. 332.

[41] Bean, *Estates of the Percy Family*, pp. 96–97; below, p. 333. Lee was to be J. P. in Cumberland in 1459–61, M. P. for the county in 1459, and a knight about 1460–61. Wedgwood, *History of Parliament*,

These rivalries were encouraged by dissension within the city of York. Under the lax government of Henry VI, the citizens found it politic to court the friendship of neighbouring magnates: in the 1440's gifts were offered to the Percies, the earls of Salisbury and Shrewsbury, and to Lord Scrope; and by 1453 city representatives were waiting upon Salisbury, Lord Clifford, and Lord Greystoke. Moreover, rifts among the citizen-body could be exploited by the local aristocracy; the Percies were thereby able to rely upon a formidable body of citizens in 1453.[42] For all the legal experience of the commissioners and the boldness with which the government named those it considered responsible for the recent outrages, it was quickly apparent how pitifully inadequate these efforts were. The mental collapse of the king by August 1453 deepened the confusion, and the Percy-Neville dispute was able to escalate into open warfare

* * * * *

The occasion for the "battle" which was now to take place on 24 August 1453 was undoubtedly the wedding of Sir Thomas Neville and Maud Stanhope. This took place in mid-August at Lord Cromwell's Lincolnshire castle of Tattershall, and as the Neville party was returning northwards, Salisbury clashed with Egremont near York. The annalist at Whitby Abbey was well placed to report that "there arose . . . a great discorde betwixt him (Northumberland) and Richard, the Erle of Salisbery hys Wyfe's Brother, insomuch that many men of both partes were beten, slayne, and hurt." A large force led by Egremont and his brother, Richard Percy, attempted to assassinate Salisbury, his wife Alice, his son Sir Thomas Neville and his wife Maud (or Matilda), his other son, Sir John Neville, and those in the earl's retinue.[43] What better occasion than a wedding at which to destroy a large part of Salisbury's family?

The Nevilles seem to have been making for Sheriff Hutton, a dozen miles north of York, for it was not far from the east walls of the city, at Heworth, that the Percies ambushed them on Friday, 24 August. Whether Northumberland approved the plot is unknown; certainly, his two sons, Egremont and Richard Percy, carried it out. They concerted plans at York the previous day with some of the citizens, and forces may have been raised in other Yorkshire towns and villages.[44] On the 24th they lay in wait with a formidable force of armed sympathisers; the aim was the destruction of the entire Neville company.

Biographies, p. 532. For Pennington, see *ibid.*, p. 675; and for Kirkeby's later Percy sympathies, below, pp. 332-3.

[42] P. M. Tillott, ed., *The Victoria County History of England: The City of York* (1961), pp. 59, 28. Salisbury seems to have spent a good deal of time at Middleham in the 1440's and 1450's. Coles, "Lordship of Middleham," pp. 40–41.

[43] Stevenson, *Wars of the English in France*, ii, part 2, 770; Storey, *End of the House of Lancaster*, p. 130; *Cartularium Abbathiae de Whitby* (1879), ii, 694–695 (misdated to 1452); P. R. O., K. B., Anc. Indict., 148/8, 16, 17; 149/5/2, 6/8, 11/16; Plea Roll, 781 rex m. 28. Ramsay mistakenly identifies this "battle" with that of Stamford Bridge in the following year, and in this he is followed by Dr Holmes. Vickers, on the other hand, dates the "battle" of Stamford Bridge to August 1452. Ramsay, *Lancaster and York*, ii, 165–166; G. A. Holmes, *The Later Middle Ages* (1962), p. 218; K. H. Vickers, *England in the Later Middle Ages* (7th edition, 1950), p. 442.

[44] P. R. O., K. B., Anc. Indict., 148/8, 16; Storey, *End of the House of Lancaster*, pp. 130–131. Fifty-

The outcome of the "battle" is unknown, but cannot have been decisive.[45] Nor is it possible to estimate the strength of the Nevilles; only five members of the family are named, but their retinue must have been impressive. By contrast, the size and character of the Percy force are better documented, for in June 1454 it was the subject of a full-scale enquiry. Although this was headed by the duke of York, protector of England and Salisbury's friend, and the jurors presenting indictments against the Percies were not strictly impartial,[46] the substantial truth of its findings is corroborated elsewhere. Inevitably, in view of the political situation of 1454, York and his colleagues indicted the Percies; even so, the initiative had been theirs.

Of those accused of attacking the wedding party with Egremont and Richard Percy, 710 are named in indictments presented before Richard of York and his fellow commissioners of oyer and terminer at York in June 1454.[47] Each indictment produced on the Crown's behalf by a local jury was declared a "true bill," and the guilty were punished accordingly.[48] The accused were predominantly Yorkshiremen: 94% of them from the county and 15.3% from the city of York. This is hardly surprising, for the Percies held manors throughout all three ridings, as well as property in York itself, providing a network of communication and influence which would enable the Percy brothers to raise a force in their support. In the west riding all Northumberland's manors were represented, with twenty from Tadcaster, five from Healaugh, eight from Spofforth, six from Leathley, and five from Linton; in the north Topcliffe contributed twenty-one,[49] and Over and Nether Catton nine; and in the east riding Pocklington supplied seven. But the indicted were not exclusively from Percy estates: Scarborough raised twenty-eight, Doncaster seventeen, Hull sixteen, and Whitby thirteen. York, with its contingent of more than 100, was the main single source. Outside the shire, a handful of sympathisers came from Lincolnshire, Westmorland, and Lancashire; from Cumberland, a shire in which the Percies held even more manors than in Yorkshire, came thirty-eight of the indicted, thirty-five of them from Cockermouth, the principal Percy honor.

---

four of the conspirators were later named and many more may have been involved: all but two came from York itself, where the Percies owned a town house, Percy Inn; at least twenty-four were freemen of York. A. Raine, *Mediaeval York* (1955), pp. 108–109; *Register of the Free-men of the City of York*, I (1272–1558) (Surtees Society, xcvi, 1896), *passim*; P. R. O., K. B., Anc. Indict., 148/8, 16; 149/4/17.

[45] The "battle" is placed at Huntingdon, near York, in one of the indictments, but there can be no doubt that it is the same incident. *Ibid.*, 149/5/2. The encounter is briefly described by Storey, *End of the House of Lancaster*, pp. 130–131.

[46] For example, one of the juries was led by Sir Ralph Randolf, who was probably involved with the Nevilles in disturbances earlier in the year. Above, p. 328; P. R. O., K. B., Anc. Indict., 149/11/16d.

[47] For the list of men alleged to have been with the Percies, see P. R. O., K. B., Anc. Indict., 148/3, 8, 16; 149/4/17, 5/2, 11/16, 6/8; Plea Roll, 781 rex m. 28. A number of the names appear in more than one list; where this has been detected, the necessary adjustment in the total has been made.

[48] Of the 710 names listed, 446 were condemned to forfeiture, 144 to outlawry, nine were pardoned and one was dead by June 1454; 110 have no punishment recorded for them.

[49] Five of these, together with three others, had been involved in the scuffle with royal officers at Thorpe under Lees in January 1453, when they had declared that no royal officer could execute orders or make arrests on any of Northumberland's estates. Above, p. 324.

Coming predominantly from the Yorkshire plain and dales, about half of those named were described as yeomen, among them tenants of Percy manors prepared to support their lord even unto battle [50] Moreover, they may have shared Percy antipathy towards the Nevilles, their intermingled properties promoting rivalry and breeding enmity. Only nine were described as labourers, and vagabonds mustered a sole representative. Egremont's following, therefore, was alleged to be not a labouring or unemployed rabble, but a congregation primarily of tenant farmers. Its urban element was dominated by a group of York citizens more than a hundred strong, about a third of whom were either merchants or else involved in the cloth and leather trades. By the mid-fifteenth century these industries were in decline, with York's overseas commerce contracting, cloth-making suffering competition from the western dales, and the skinners encountering difficulties. By the 1450's the city's population had begun to fall and its citizens faced a chilly future.[51] Even without the ties of loyalty and interest which bound some to the Percies, the economic recession contributed to the potential violence in a large city. At least thirty of the indicted were freemen of York, for this was seemingly no rising of the urban proletariat, as some of the Flemish and Italian cities had experienced. John Gilliot was no *Ciompi*, but a mercer who secured his city's freedom in 1439, became a chamberlain of York in 1451, and mayor in 1463–64 and 1473–74 The forfeiture to which he was condemned for his part at Heworth did not adversely affect his standing in the community.[52] Similarly, William Snawsell, goldsmith, was made freeman of York in 1436 as the son of a freeman, became chamberlain in 1457–58, mayor ten years later, and sheriff in 1464–65; he, too, emerged unscathed from the events of August 1453.[53]

Outside the city, the shire as a whole was famed for its cloth, and could muster a body of industrial workers and artisans in the Percy cause. Twenty walkers (fullers) were condemned for their part in the "battle," along with fifteen weavers, seventeen tailors, two litsters (dyers), and five websters (weavers). Workers in leather and hides were also present: eight sadlers, two glovers, two shoemakers, and five souters (cobblers). The prominence of York and Scarborough as ports is indicated by the nine merchants and six chapmen or mariners associated with Egremont. Even three dissident Scots joined the fray.[54]

To convert such people into an effective ambushing force would need firm organisation. Northumberland's sons could provide a certain cohesion among Percy tenants; elsewhere, the customary leaders of local society, knights, esquires, gentlemen, and clergy, would be useful. Like John Burne of Bainton, they could assemble and marshal the several hundred individuals: excluding Egremont and

---

[50] Of the total of 710, 330 were described as yeomen and 44 as husbandmen.

[51] H. Heaton, *The Yorkshire Woollen and Worsted Industries* (1920), chs. 1, 2; Tillott, *City of York*, pp. 88–91; Bartlett, *Econ. Hist. Rev.*, 2nd series, XII (1959–60), 27–33.

[52] *Register of Freemen*, I, 152, 178, 187. He was a member of the gild of Corpus Christi, master of the Merchants' Company in 1459, 1460, and 1476 and died on 24 September 1484. *The Register of the Guild of Corpus Christi in the City of York* (Surtees Society, LVII [1871]), 55.

[53] *Register of Freemen*, I, 152, 178, 187; *List of Sheriffs*, p. 230; P. R. O., K. B., Anc. Indict., 148/8.

[54] One was called Jok Patenson! *Ibid.*, 149/6/8. It is interesting to note the presence of five scholars from York, all of whom had their possessions forfeited. *Ibid.*, 149/11/16.

his brother, six knights, thirty-two esquires, twenty-six gentlemen, and twenty-four clerks were present. They were the key to Percy effectiveness at Heworth. Many of the knights were in Northumberland's service: Sir John Pennington, from Cumberland, was probably his retainer;[55] whereas Sir John Salvin of North Duffield, Sir John Stapleton of Wighill, and Sir John Hothom from the Percy manor of Scorborough had been in receipt of fees from Northumberland since 1442 and were evidently still in his service in 1453.[56] Sir William Buckton seems to have engaged Salisbury in person at Heworth.[57] Finally, Sir William Lucy of Gainsborough (Lincolnshire) was also with the Percies, although only a couple of months previously he had been the king's commissioner in the north of England.[58] Such knights as these, most of them already in Percy service, could act as aides to Egremont and Richard Percy at Heworth.[59]

There were equally strong ties between the Percy family and some of the esquires and gentlemen. John Pudsay of Bolton in Craven, and John Caterall of Brayton in Craven had been involved with Richard Percy in earlier disturbances, and the latter would be retained by Egremont on 4 February 1454.[60] A third rioter with Richard Percy in July had been Richard Tempest of Stainforth in Craven, whose family was probably connected with the earls of Northumberland.[61] John Swynburne of Cockermouth had also displayed his Percy allegiance beforehand; and three members of the Belingham family, Richard of Cockermouth and both the elder and younger Robert of Burneside, were at Heworth, for a relative, Henry Belingham, was in receipt of Northumberland's annuity in Cumberland in 1453–54.[62] Nor did William Lee of Cockermouth's implication

---

[55] *Ibid.*, 149/11/16; Bean, *Estates of the Percy Family*, p. 96. For his later opposition to the earl of Salisbury, see below, p. 362. Thomas Pennington of Muncaster (Cumb.) was also at Heworth. P. R. O., K. B., Anc. Indict., 149/11/16.

[56] Bean, *Estates of the Percy Family*, pp. 92 note 1, 97; P. R. O., K. B., Anc. Indict., 149/11/16. For Salvin, see above, p. 324 and below, p. 335. Robert Stapleton of Beverley, gentleman, who was at Heworth, may have been Sir John Stapleton's kinsman. P. R. O., K. B., Anc. Indict., 149/6/8.

[57] The following note was inserted above his name: "contra comite Sarum in campo." *Ibid.*

[58] Above, p. 327; P. R. O., K. B., Anc. Indict., 149/5/2. His willingness to join the Percies may be attributed to his wife, Elizabeth, daughter of Sir Henry Percy of Athol; Lucy was to die in battle against the Yorkists. Wedgwood, *History of Parliament, Biographies*, pp. 559–560; below, p. 362.

[59] Salvin is noted as dead in the indictment, although this may be a confusion with his father (d. 1452), *C. P. R., 1452–61*, p. 7; P. R. O., K. B., Anc. Indict., 149/11/16; Bean, *Estates of the Percy Family*, p. 92 note 1. Stapleton died in 1455 and Hothom in 1460 (*Ibid.*). A few other knights had their names struck off the indictments, but their association with the Percies is clear: Sir Henry Fenwick of Cockermouth and Sir William Martindale of Newton (Cumb.). *Ibid.*, pp. 24, 96–97; P. R. O., K. B., Anc. Indict., 149/11/16; above, p. 328.

[60] P. R. O., K. B., Anc. Indict., 149/11/16, 6/7; 149/8/4; above, p. 327. No punishment was recorded for Pudsay, but his goods, worth 20s., were forfeited for felony in 1454–55; he received a pardon for treason and outlawry on 26 October 1457 (P. R. O., Exchequer, K. R., Escheators' Accounts, 60/7; *C. P. R., 1452–61*, p. 386). Caterall's experience at Heworth did not deter him from subsequent iniquities later in the year. Below, pp. 334-5.

[61] P. R. O., K. B., Anc. Indict., 149/11/16, 6/7. Nicholas Tempest was an indentured retainer of the first earl in 1404; Sir John Tempest received his annuity from the second earl in 1442–43 and probably continued to do so until his death in 1463 (Bean, *Estates of the Percy Family*, pp. 92 note 1, 95 note 3). For Richard's earlier rioting, see above, p. 327.

[62] P. R. O., K. B., Anc. Indict., 149/11/16, 6/8; Bean, *Estates of the Percy Family*, pp. 96–97. Swin-

prevent him from receiving a Percy annuity in the same year, and Thomas Fairfax of Selby may have been related to Guy Fairfax, granted a life-annuity of £10 in Yorkshire by Northumberland on 30 April 1451.[63] Finally, both Roland Kirkeby and Oliver Hudleston came from Cockermouth, the Percies' greatest honor, and Kirkeby at least had been involved in recent Percy lawlessness.[64] By contrast, some of the esquires cannot be as closely linked with Northumberland and his sons. John Portyngton, of Portington (Yorkshire), had recently been one of the king's commissioners in Yorkshire, so that his participation in the battle is as surprising as that of Sir William Lucy. Richard Methan, on the other hand, had a reputation for violence, for on 3 December 1449 he was pardoned for slaughtering a man at Snaith (Yorkshire).[65] But they all had in common a substantial social status as leaders of their communities, able to muster tenants, yeomen, and labourers in support of their favoured causes.

Clergy could be just as useful as the gentry; a parish priest could persuade his flock to follow his lead. Moreover, at least two incumbents of churches on Percy manors were listed as being at Heworth: Thomas Colvel, vicar of Topcliffe, and William Wodd, rector of Leathley. In addition, the vicars of Northcave, Middleton Tyas, Wadworth nigh Doncaster and Ilkley, and the rectors of St Wilfrid's (York), Bulmer, and Kilvington were also accused of engaging in activities ill suited to their cloth.[66] Even more Percy tenants could be dragooned by the two Percy officials who have been identified: Stephen Story, bailiff of Hunmanby, and John Hudson, bailiff of Seamer.[67]

The Percy affinity in the fifteenth century was not composed entirely of gentry.

---

burne may even have been the fourth earl's receiver in Northumberland in 1471–72 (*Percy Bailiffs' Rolls of the Fifteenth Century* [Surtees Society, cxxxiv (1921)], pp. 91–95). Richard Belingham was escheator of Cumberland and Westmorland in 1444–45, and M. P. for Cumberland in 1449–50; he received a pardon on 16 September 1455. Wedgwood, *History of Parliament, Biographies*, p. 63. For the later Lancastrian sympathies of a Robert Belingham, see below, p. 362.

[63] Bean, *Estates of the Percy Family*, pp. 92 note 2, 96; K. B., Anc. Indict., 149/6/8, 11/16. For Lee, see Wedgwood, *History of Parliament, Biographies*, p. 532. For Thomas Fairfax's later rebellious activities, see below, p. 349. There were a few esquires whose names were erased from the indictments, but who can be firmly linked with Northumberland: John Broughton of Broughton (Cumb.) and Henry Belingham of Burneside (West.) (Bean, *Estates of the Percy Family*, p. 96; P. R. O., K. B., Anc. Indict., 149/11/16). On the other hand, it is surprising to find Robert Constable of Flamborough among the indicted, for his family, if not he himself, was associated with Salisbury (*Ibid.*, 149/11/16; above, p. 327). It is interesting to note that when Egremont arranged an award between two disputing parties in 1452–53, he was associated with seven of those mentioned above: Sir Henry Fenwick, Sir John Pennington, Sir William Martindale, John Broughton, William Lee, Henry Belingham, and John Swinburne. *H. M. C., Twelfth Report* (1890), pp. 3–4.

[64] P. R. O., K. B., Anc. Indict., 149/11/16; above, p. 328.

[65] *Ibid.*, 149/5/2, 11/16, 6/8d; *C. P. R., 1446–52*, p. 304.

[66] P. R. O., K. B., Anc. Indict., 149/6/8 and dorse, 5/2, 11/16.

[67] *Ibid.*, 149/11/16; Bean, *Estates of the Percy Family*, pp. 76–77, 159. Both were condemned to forfeiture in June 1454. Peter Lounde, bailiff of Pocklington in the following year, was at Heworth (*Ibid.*, 149/11/16; below, p. 354). One might also include among Percy officials two men described as *receptor*: William Forsut of Ripon and Henry Raket of Husthwaite (P. R. O., K. B., Anc. Indict., 149/6/8). A former duchy of Lancaster official was also present: Richard Chymney of Allerston, who held office in the honor of Pickering from 1433 (*Ibid.*, 149/11/16; Somerville, *Duchy of Lancaster*, I, 536).

A few of the yeomen and artisans at Heworth were said to have been retained, albeit illegally, by Egremont. John Benet of Newbald, Robert Ashwell of North-allerton, and Thomas Guberthorne of Thirsk were given his red and black livery at Healaugh on 12 May 1453.[68] Three others from Topcliffe would receive his livery at York on 4 February following: Oliver Stockdale, who had caused trouble earlier in 1453, Thomas Mawer, and Alexander Chatton.[69] Quite often more than one member of a family left their fields or their looms to join Egremont: John Cowper of Wildon took with him his son William; John Eylemere of Westhall, in Whorldale, was accompanied by his two sons, John and William, all of whom ex-perienced forfeiture for their pains; and Robert Wilson from the Percy manor of Buckden was outlawed with his sons, John and Richard, when it was all over.[70]

* * * *

The Heworth incident was the most serious to date of a number of clashes be-tween Percy and Neville. It threw the citizens of York into a veritable paroxysm of alarm, and the civic authorities spent the ensuing weeks in vain attempts at mediation between Salisbury and the Percies.[71] The futility of their efforts was manifest to all, for the autumn of 1453 was punctured with renewed outbursts between the two families, each turning a deaf ear to royal reproofs and civic pleadings.

Many of those accused of accompanying Egremont and Richard Percy on 24 August evidently did not disperse. Richard himself, with John Caterall and Wil-liam Chamber of Gowkthorp, led them on a tour of pillage on behalf of Lord Egremont which took them to Gargrave church in Craven on 9 September. There, these "sons of the devil and heretics" entered the church and attacked Lawrence Caterall, bailiff of Staincliff wapentake, at his devotions. Lawrence fled to the vestibule of the church near the high altar, but Percy and his companions pursued him. They jumped onto the altar and almost on top of the vicar, who was saying mass and rushed to protect the host, at the same time begging his visitors in the name of God to cease their hooliganism. Having seized Lawrence, the insurgents left for Isel castle in the lordship of Cockermouth. From this castle, which be-longed to William Lee, one of Northumberland's dependents, Lawrence was taken to Cockermouth itself, where he was imprisoned until he ceased to be bailiff of Staincliff.[72] Lawrence's offence against the Percies is unknown.

[68] P. R. O., K. B., Anc. Indict., 149/7/2. Benet was subsequently condemned to forfeiture, the other two to outlawry.

[69] *Ibid.*, 149/8/4. Stockdale later received a pardon; Mawer and Chatton were declared outlaws, but pardoned on 1 March 1455. Above, p. 324; P. R. O., Chancery, Pardon Roll, 41 m. 8, 9.

[70] P. R. O., K. B., Anc. Indict., 149/11/16, 6/8. Two others who were involved at Heworth, John Estall and William Vessy, merchant, both of York, were to be among those accused in August 1460 of uttering falsehoods in order to arouse discord among the magnates of the realm; Vessy would also be involved with Egremont in further risings in 1454. *Ibid.*, 148/8; 149/11/16; *C. P. R., 1452–61*, p. 608; below, p. 343.

[71] Storey, *End of the House of Lancaster*, pp. 131–132.

[72] P. R. O., K. B., Anc. Indict., 149/4/25; Storey, *End of the House of Lancaster*, p. 131; J. F. Cur-wen, "Isel Hall," *Transactions of the Cumberland and Westmorland Archaeological and Antiquarian Society*, new series, XI (1911), 122–123. If Caterall can be identified with John Caterall of Wressle

John Caterall was prominent in another raid, led by Sir John Salvin, also a Percy retainer, on the house of William Hebdon, vicar of Aughton, on 25 September 1453. It was very much a Percy enterprise: twenty-three of the forty-one implicated can be linked with other Percy risings; nineteen were accused of having fought at Heworth, whilst thirteen would come out in support of Egremont in May 1454. The leaders, Sir John Salvin and John Caterall, were, needless to say, long in the service of Northumberland and his younger son; their careers show that they had little respect for law and order.[73] These two incidents indicate that whatever the outcome of the "battle" of Heworth, the Percies could still muster marauding bands of rioters and proceed unhindered by the king's officers.

The Nevilles behaved likewise, for on 24 September Sir John Neville broke into Northumberland's house at Catton in the north riding, breaking windows and shattering tiles. Sir John had made his point: Yorkshire was no uninterrupted Percy preserve and the Percies had not neutralised the Nevilles at Heworth.[74] In Cumberland, too, Northumberland and his brood had split opinion in the shire, for when the sheriff, Thomas de la More, sent his deputy and bailiffs to levy the royal revenue in 1453, they were attacked and wounded by Egremont's men in a manner reminiscent of Heworth and Gargrave.[75] Not even the Crown's representatives were immune to Percy outrages.

/ The government's response was hesitant and exhortatory, and at first it seemed relieved that the disturbances had not been worse. On 8 October 1453 Earl Ralph Neville of Westmorland, Bishop Robert Neville of Durham, and Archbishop William Booth of York were commended for refraining from assisting the Nevilles, but if the government had fully appreciated Neville family politics, it need have had no fear of the Westmorland branch making common cause with Salisbury and his sons.[76] Yet, the government did not confine itself to expressing thanks for small mercies. On the same 8 October letters tinged as much with sorrow as with anger were sent to Northumberland and Salisbury, exhorting them to remember their position as commissioners of the peace and members of the king's Council. They were reminded that Parliament, which was still in session, had warned lords to express their grievances in writing and not in blood; yet, the

---

(some distance from Brayton), such behaviour was habitual in him; the latter was one of the "robbers, ravishers extortioners, and oppressors" against whom a petition was presented in Parliament in 1459 (*Rot. Parl.*, v, 367–368). For the later Lancastrian activities of Caterall of Brayton, see below, p. 362.

[73] P. R. O., K. B., Anc. Indict., 149/12/24; above, p. 332. Salvin had been involved with Northumberland in a quarrel with the archbishop of York as long ago as 1443. Ramsay, *Lancaster and York*, ii, 53 note 2.

[74] P. R. O., K. B., Anc. Indict., 149/8/5.

[75] *Rot. Parl.*, vi, 63–64 (s.a. 1472); P. R. O., Exchequer, T. R., Council and Privy Seal, 85/26, 27; above, p. 324.

[76] *Proc. P. C.*, vi, 158–159; above, p. 323. Moreover, Earl Ralph II of Westmorland was married to Northumberland's sister, Elizabeth. Sir Charles Oman speculated that Westmorland's inactivity may have been due to chronic illness, but there is no evidence for this. C. Oman, *The History of England from the accession of Richard II to the death of Richard III, 1377–1485* (1906), p. 357; J. R. Lander, "Marriage and Politics in the Fifteenth Century: the Nevilles and the Wydevilles," *Bull. Inst. Hist. Res.*, xxxvi (1963), 122 and note 6, 123, 137.

letters concluded wearily, the earls continued to make the "grettest assemblee of our liegemen." Stronger language was directed at Egremont and Sir John Neville on the same busy day: they were reminded that they had been created barons in expectation of future service not rebellious rioting; gritting its teeth, the Council warned them both that if they did not desist, they would suffer forfeiture.[77]

Too often in these years royal admonitions had little force, but it could not be otherwise so long as the two earls countenanced the rape of each other and ignored royal commands. The king's peace mattered less to them than private gain, and at this juncture, in the early autumn of 1453, the government was at its weakest for many decades. Henry VI had become seriously ill by 10 August, but his queen and advisers tried to make light of the fact in order to continue ruling uninhibited by the vociferous duke of York. In such circumstances, no government could afford to take a severe line with magnates whose favour it needed or whose enmity it must avoid. Restraint, even to the point of weakness, was the inevitable order of the day, so that within a fortnight of the Council's letters, the round of disturbances began again.[78] At least fifty armed men were accused of assembling at Topcliffe on 17 October, probably under the aegis of one of the Percies, for several of those named can be identified with other Percy risings.[79] Others had close connections with Northumberland: William Bertram of Newcastle-upon-Tyne had served as the earl's retainer from December 1440, and between 1441 and 1450 received profitable grants and offices in his lordship of Prudhoe, not far from Newcastle.[80] Similarly, John Carlele, esquire, also of Newcastle, had been receiving a life-annuity from the Percies in Northumberland since 21 October 1443.[81] Indeed, Newcastle, where Northumberland had a house and property, provided the largest single contingent (twenty-strong) for this new outbreak; eighteen others came from Yorkshire, with the vicar of Great Driffield, a chaplain, and a preaching friar representing the warriors of God.[82] Once again, the Percies had apparently raised a force not of wandering, discontented jobless, but of respectable tenants, merchants, and artisans, able to provide their own weapons and transport.

The aim was to trigger off several risings as a prelude to more serious happenings three days later. Then, on 20 October 1453, the leaders of both sides converged on Topcliffe and Sandhutton in the north riding. For the first time in the current round of disturbances the earl of Warwick accompanied his father, to-

---

[77] *Proc. P. C.*, vi, 159–163; Storey, *End of the House of Lancaster*, pp. 131–132.

[78] Jacob, *Fifteenth Century*, p. 508; Ramsay, *Lancaster and York*, II, 166.

[79] P. R. O., K. B., Plea Roll, 778 rex m. 3d; Anc. Indict., 149/4/26. Edward Andreton of Tuxford (Notts.) and John Neel of Newcastle-upon-Tyne would be involved in the riots of May 1454, whilst Thomas Baxster of Beverley was outlawed for his role at Heworth. *Ibid.*, 149/6/8; below p. 351.

[80] Bean, *Estates of the Percy Family*, pp. 92, 97. Bertram was M. P. for Northumberland in 1435, 1449–50 and 1450–51. Wedgwood, *History of Parliament, Biographies*, pp. 71, 161; see also *C. P. R., 1446–52*, pp. 202, 446, 477, 592.

[81] Wedgwood, *History of Parliament, Biographies*, p. 157; Bean, *Estates of the Percy Family*, p. 92 n. 2; P. R. O., K. B., Anc. Indict. 149/4/26. He was a former mayor of Newcastle. *Extracts from the Records of the Merchant Adventurers of Newcastle-upon-Tyne* (Surtees Society, xciii, 1895), p. 82.

[82] P. R. O., K. B., Anc. Indict., 149/4/26.

gether with Sir Thomas and Sir John Neville. Also in the Neville party were Sir Henry fitzHugh and Sir Henry Le Scrope, both members of that partisan commission headed by Salisbury which had been appointed the previous July. Likewise, Henry, Lord Poynings for the first time joined his father and younger brothers, Egremont and Richard Percy; Sir Thomas Clifford of Skipton in Craven, a cousin of Northumberland's, was also with them.[83] Once again the result of the confrontation is unknown.

The impotence of the government, with the queen trying to exclude York from the counsels of the prostrate king, may have encouraged Percy and Neville to contemplate a decisive encounter, uninhibited by fear of royal reprisals. It would be premature to regard this as the beginning of the contest between York and Queen Margaret's advisers. Yet, it is possible that at this juncture, towards the end of October 1453, Salisbury and Warwick first decided to support York's attempts to reform the government and ensure his own position in it.[84] The continuing illness of Henry VI and the birth of Prince Edward on 13 October made it essential that more positive arrangements be made for the government of the realm. York demanded recognition of his position as a senior magnate, while Margaret and the duke of Somerset were equally determined to exclude him from the Council meeting in October to "sette rest and union betwixt the lords of this lande." It was probably pressure from some of the lords of the Council which ensured that on 24 October York should, after all, be invited to attend; among them were York's brother-in-law, the earl of Salisbury, Salisbury's son, the earl of Warwick, and Lord Cromwell; neither Northumberland nor Poynings was present.[85] Moreover, the alliance of York as a prominent Yorkshire landowner might well have been sought by the Nevilles in their increasingly serious encounters with the Percies. With Salisbury and Warwick facing Northumberland and Poynings, the growing identification of the former with York's cause would force the Percies into support of the queen and Somerset.

The uncertainty continued and in the opening weeks of 1454 magnates made their way to London well armed and prepared for a trial of strength.[86] In the north Poynings, Egremont, and Clifford, together with John, Viscount Beaumont, the queen's steward and, although Salisbury's brother-in-law, no friend of

[83] *Ibid.*, 149/11/3; Storey, *End of the House of Lancaster*, p. 132. Clifford was the son of Elizabeth, daughter of Northumberland's father, Henry Hotspur; his son John was listed as being with Egremont at Heworth. *Complete Peerage*, III, 293; *Dict. Nat. Biog.*, XI, 77–78; Storey, *End of the House of Lancaster*, p. 130.

[84] Warwick's quarrel with Somerset over the custody of lands in Glamorgan in the summer of 1453 may well have fortified Neville's resolve to break with the Court (Storey, *End of the House of Lancaster*, pp. 135–136, 239–240). Dr Storey dates the alliance between York and the Nevilles to the autumn of 1453 and Professor Wilkinson to the ensuing winter, but Mr Armstrong is content to wait until April. Storey, *End of the House of Lancaster*, p. 137; B. Wilkinson, *Constitutional History of England in the Fifteenth Century, 1399–1485* (1964), p. 95 and note 5; Armstrong, *Bull. Inst. Hist. Res.*, XXXIII (1960), 11.

[85] Ramsay, *Lancaster and York*, II, 167; Vickers, *Later Middle Ages*, p. 440; *C.P.R., 1452–61*, pp. 143–144; *Proc. P. C.*, VI, 163–164.

[86] Gairdner, *Paston Letters*, I, 264; Ramsay, *Lancaster and York*, II, 168–169.

York's, were reported to be "maken all the puissance they kan and may to come hider with theym" to London. On the other side, Salisbury was expected with a large number of knights and esquires, whilst Warwick was in York's company and expected in London on 25 January.[87] Apart from Northumberland, the principals who had assembled their forces on 20 October were streaming to London, mutual hostilities unabated. Then they had apparently been playing for local stakes; now they were competing for the government of England itself. If the Nevilles could number York among their friends, the Percies acquired a powerful ally at about the same time.

* * * *

On 19 January 1454 it was reported in a news-letter that Henry Holand, duke of Exeter, and Lord Egremont had recently "ben sworne togider" at Tuxford (Lincolnshire).[88] Thus opened a new phase in the Percy-Neville conflict. Like the Percies, Exeter had cause to distrust Lord Cromwell. Towards the end of 1443 John Cornwall, Lord Fanhope, died, and on 14 February following his Bedford-shire manors, including Ampthill, were granted to a group of Lord Cromwell's feoffees.[89] The transaction gave rise to a dispute between Exeter on the one hand, and Cromwell and Edmund, Lord Grey of Ruthin on the other. Within months of Fanhope's death, Cromwell had secured the Bedfordshire properties "against Exeter," with Lord Grey witnessing the arrangement.[90]

The descent of Ampthill and the other Bedfordshire manors is as complicated as fifteenth-century devices for the transference of land can make it. The manors of Ampthill, Millbrook, and Grange by Millbrook, held in chief of the Crown, were finally quitclaimed to Lord Fanhope and his heirs on 28 October 1440 by Elizabeth, co-heiress of the St Amand property of which they formed part.[91] Fan-hope died on 10 or 11 December 1443 without heirs, but possibly in anticipation of his impending demise, he had recently transferred his estates to feoffees.[92] They, on 14 February 1444, surrendered their rights to another group of men acting for Ralph, Lord Cromwell; Grey of Ruthin witnessed the deed.[93] The transfer had been Fanhope's wish, in gratitude for the "love, friendship and

---

[87] Gairdner, *Paston Letters*, I, 264–266. Lord Egremont distributed livery to eight men at York on 4 February 1454, most of them veterans of Heworth. P. R. O., K. B., Anc. Indict., 149/8/4, 11/16; 148/16. For Beaumont, see Jacob, *Fifteenth Century*, p. 481 and *Complete Peerage*, II, 63.

[88] Gairdner, *Paston Letters*, I, 264. Tuxford was described as being "beside" Doncaster, although it is about twenty miles further south.

[89] *C.Cl.R., 1441–47*, pp. 218–219, 222–223. The final quitclaim of the manors to Cromwell's feoffees is dated 23 May 1444.

[90] Trinity College, Dublin MS E. 5.10 f. 186.

[91] *C.Cl.R., 1435–41*, pp. 431–432; *Complete Peerage*, XI, 300–301.

[92] P. R. O., Chancery, Inquisitions Post Mortem, 139/114/21 no. 4. Although done without royal licence, the Crown acquiesced in the transaction shortly after Fanhope's death, on 28 January 1444, in return for an ameliorative fine of 20 marks. Fanhope also held other Bedfordshire manors, but not as tenant-in-chief. At his death the net value of his entire Bedfordshire property was £65 per annum, Ampthill being the most valuable manor at £30 per annum.

[93] *C.Cl.R., 1441–47*, pp. 218–219, 222–223; R. I. Jack, *The Grey of Ruthin Valor* (1965), pp. 34–35. A slightly different account of the transaction is given by Roskell, *Speakers in English Parliaments*, p. 238, note 1.

kindness" shown him by Cromwell, and he had arranged that his feoffees should give Cromwell first option to purchase the manors for £1,000. They showed some reluctance to fulfil their master's wish, but Cromwell secured the manors in mid-February 1444 after petitioning the chancellor.[94]

If Cromwell held the Fanhope lands in Bedfordshire "against Exeter," he did so with a claim well grounded in legal practice and better documented than that of Exeter. In 1444, at the age of thirteen, the duke's youth made it difficult for him to pursue his claim; by 1452, however, he was ready to do so. His claim to Ampthill and the other Bedfordshire manors presumably derived, albeit tenuously, from the fact that his grandmother, Elizabeth of Lancaster, widow of the duke of Exeter (d.1400), was the wife of Lord Fanhope when she died in 1425.[95] After Fanhope had died without heirs, Elizabeth's grandson may have tried to capitalise on this relationship in 1452. If Exeter felt himself aggrieved by Cromwell, Lord Grey of Ruthin felt equally misused by Exeter. Both Grey and Exeter were grandsons of Elizabeth of Lancaster, for Grey was the son of her daughter, Constance; each of them could, therefore, claim an obscure connection with the late Lord Fanhope.[96] After Fanhope's death, however, Grey witnessed Cromwell's enfeoffment of the Bedfordshire manors; when Exeter began to cause trouble in 1452–53, Grey rallied to Cromwell against his cousin.[97]

In the first flush of manhood, Exeter launched himself into the campaign to recover the manors, especially Ampthill, initiating "actions, suits, plaints, trespasses, debates and demands" against Cromwell in 1452. The result was a commission of arbitration to include the bishop of Ely, the prior of the Hospital of St John, Lord Sudeley, and two justices (including the chief justice) of Common Pleas. On 15 July 1452 Exeter and Cromwell each entered into a recognisance of 6,000 marks to abide by the decision of the arbitrators on the question of legal title to the manors, provided the decision were given by 11 November following.[98]

[94] P. R. O., Chancery, Early Chancery Proceedings, 1/13/134. An account of this complicated transaction is given by R. I. Jack, "The Lords Grey of Ruthin, 1325 to 1490" (unpublished University of London Ph.D. thesis, 1961), pp. 359–360. Cromwell was one of Lord Fanhope's executors. P. R. O., Chancery, Warrants, 1546/50.

[95] Trinity College, Dublin MS E. 5.10 f. 186; G. L. Harriss, "A Fifteenth-Century Chronicle at Trinity College, Dublin," *Bull. Inst. Hist. Res.*, xxxviii (1965), 216; *Complete Peerage*, v, 253–254. Exeter was born on 27 June 1430 and had livery of his father's estates in July 1450. Powicke and Fryde, *Handbook of British Chronology*, p. 433.

[96] *Complete Peerage*, v, 253–254, vii, 164–165. The Greys had difficulties with Fanhope while he was alive. I. S. Leadam and J. F. Baldwin (edd.), *Select Cases Before the King's Council, 1247–1482* (Selden Society, 1918), pp. cxi–cxiv, 104–107.

[97] Having supported Cromwell's acquisition of the Bedfordshire properties and thereby renounced his own claim, Grey may have resented Exeter's presentation of his claim. Thus, Leyland's confused report that the king gave to Exeter some of the lands claimed by Grey would be an oversimplification; Leland also suggested that Ampthill reached Fanhope through the dowager-duchess of Exeter. L. T. Smith (ed.), *The Itinerary of John Leland* (3 vols., 1907), i, 103; *Complete Peerage*, vii, 164 n. (j).

[98] *C.Cl.R., 1447–54*, p. 360. In 1452 Exeter seems to have employed a number of dubious legal devices to support his claim, persuading two groups of feoffees, one acting for the St. Amands and the other for Fanhope, to convey their rights in the property to Exeter; but it is doubtful if they had any rights to convey. William Page (ed.), *The Victoria History of the County of Bedford*, iii (1912), 272 (this account of the manor of Ampthill is unsatisfactory).

It seems likely that their award (if any) was in Cromwell's favour, based on the enfeoffment of February 1444, for the dispute comes to the surface again in 1453 when Exeter threw Cromwell out of Ampthill, only to find himself being prosecuted at Westminster in a plea of novel disseisin. Exeter now maintained that Cromwell had granted him the manor, at first on a four-year lease and later in perpetuity. This Cromwell disputed. Both parties, with Grey supporting Cromwell, attended with armed men to overawe the court. Whereupon, on 4 July 1453 the king ordered the arrest of the three magnates: Exeter was installed in Windsor castle, Cromwell in Wallingford, and Grey in Pevensey.[99] They were released within a week, Cromwell to secure the protection of a great magnate house by marrying his niece to Sir Thomas Neville, and Exeter, who seems to have secured Ampthill temporarily, to contemplate over the next six months an alliance with the enemies of Cromwell and the Nevilles.[100]

It is also possible that a dispute between Exeter and one of the Westmorland Nevilles played a minor role in preparing the duke for the Percy alliance. Both Exeter and Sir John Neville, Westmorland's brother and second husband of Exeter's half-sister, were trying to get their hands on jewels left by Exeter's father (d.1447) to his widow, the Dowager-duchess Anne. But this is unlikely to have been a decisive factor inducing Exeter to enter the Percy-Neville feud, if only because the Westmorland Nevilles gave little support to their Salisbury cousins in the 1450's.[101] These private dissensions were soon to be engulfed by more public events at Westminster.

The governmental crisis had not been resolved when Parliament reassembled on 14 February 1454. It is true that the duke of York was empowered the previous day to open Parliament as the king's lieutenant, but the first weeks of the session proceeded by manoeuvre and countermanoeuvre by Yorkist sympathisers and the queen's supporters.[102] The struggle for power by Duke Richard in this Parliament may be reflected in the progress of Lord Cromwell's petition for "surety of peace" against the duke of Exeter, now in league with the Percies. The petition was presented before York and the lords on 9 March and read twice that day;

[99] *Les Reports del cases en ley, que furent argues en le temps de le Roy Henry VI* (2 vols., 1679), I, 8–9 (I am grateful to Mr J. G. Reid for providing this reference); Trinity College, Dublin MS E.5.10 f. 186. Dr Harriss's account differs slightly from that offered here. Harriss, *Bull. Inst. Hist. Res.*, XXXVIII (1965), 216.

[100] Cromwell's accusation of trespass against Exeter was still pending in the Michaelmas term of 1453. It occasioned considerable uproar locally "because the lord of Exeter is a great and prepotent prince in that county" (presumably Bedfordshire)! *Les Reports del cases . . . en le temps de le Roy Henry VI*, I, 9; M. Hastings, *The Court of Common Pleas in Fifteenth Century England* (1947), pp. 222–223. Cromwell continued to be troubled by Exeter, for on 9 March 1454 he petitioned Parliament for "surety of peace" against the duke. Below, p. 341.

[101] Indeed, in 1460–61 Sir John Neville was a firm Lancastrian, unlike his Salisbury relatives. He agreed to end his designs on the dowager-duchess's jewels on 22 February 1456; Exeter may have continued his efforts. *Complete Peerage*, v, 212–215, IX, 504; *C.Cl.R., 1454–61*, pp. 142–143.

[102] The councillors who granted the commission to York were potentially favourable to him: Salisbury, Warwick, Cromwell, Greystoke, Grey of Ruthin, and fitzHugh were there, but Northumberland, Poynings, and Exeter were not. J. F. Baldwin, *The King's Council during the Middle Ages* (1913), p. 197 and note 3.

but the "great pains" which Cromwell urged be inflicted on Exeter were such that some were reluctant to approve the petition, and it was postponed for a few days. It was only on 20 March that consent was given, and two days later the petition was passed on to the Commons.[103]

But the tide had seemed to be flowing in York's favour for some weeks. Immediately the session began, the lords upheld York's imprisonment of Speaker Thorpe, despite frenzied objections from the Commons.[104] Moreover, although the king's baby son, Edward, was created prince of Wales and earl of Chester on 15 March, thereby formally acknowledging his position as heir to the throne, York could see triumph in sight. The death of Chancellor Kemp on 22 March, and the report on the king's continued ill health three days later, finally precipitated the proclamation of York as protector and defender of the realm on 27 March. Salisbury became the new chancellor five days later.[105] Symptomatic of this growing ascendency of York and the Nevilles was the renewed action taken against the Percies. Shortly after the session opened, letters were sent to Lord Egremont requiring his appearance before the Council on 3 March; but they were never delivered because Egremont avoided his usual residences to evade the summons.[106] When Egremont did not put in an appearance, more determined measures were demanded in Parliament. A petition was presented which catalogued the riots, forcible entries, judicial maintenance, and terrorising which Egremont and his brother, Richard, had committed before the session began. Letters under the great and privy seals commanding their presence before king and Council (and there were many examples in 1453) had been ignored, and even the recent communications had had no effect. The petition was fully granted and involved elaborate procedures for one last attempt to force the Percies to wait upon the chancellor at the risk of forfeiture and outlawry.

Later in the session, possibly after York had become protector on 27 March, a more general attempt was made to reassert the government's authority in the provinces. An act imposed forfeiture on all who ignored royal orders to appear before the Council — an act which would take effect from 1 May 1454.[107] To this session and York's initiative may also belong another statute which denounced wardens of the east and west marches towards Scotland who illegally extended their powers of attachment from Northumberland, Cumberland, and Westmorland into Yorkshire, "sumtyme for thaire singuler lucre, and sumtyme for malice."[108] The parliamentary session which opened in the midst of faction, thus

---

[103] *Rot. Parl.*, v., 264.

[104] Furthermore, the new speaker, Sir Thomas Charlton, was related to Salisbury's wife and acted as the earl's feoffee in 1458. Roskell, *Speakers in English Parliaments*, pp. 253–256.

[105] *Ibid.*, p. 256; Ramsay, *Lancaster and York*, II, 169–172; Storey, *End of the House of Lancaster*, pp. 139–140. Moreover, the impeachment of York's ally at Dartford in 1452, the earl of Devon, was unsuccessful on 14 March.

[106] *Rot. Parl.*, v, 394–396. For the dating of this petition, see below.

[107] *Rot. Parl.*, v, 266–267. This act is more likely to have been passed in this session than in either of those of 1453, since it was to come into operation on 1 May 1454 and be proclaimed by the sheriffs before 24 June 1454. Ct. *Dict. Nat. Biog.*, XIV, 280.

[108] *Rot. Parl.*, v, 267 (this statute is adjacent to the one above).

showed a notable determination to come to grips with the problem of the provinces and the disintegration of royal authority. Once it became apparent that York was gaining the upper hand, culminating in his appointment as protector, the reforming measures gathered momentum. Although personal rivalry and political hatred lay behind many of these, York and his associates (including Salisbury and Warwick) displayed a firmness and resolution altogether lacking in English government since the minority of Henry VI.

The ending of Parliament just before Easter (21 April 1454) enabled York to supplement the statutory and conciliar measures of the past two months with more practical steps. Regardless of events at Westminster, little had been accomplished to remedy the disorder in the north.[109] Indeed, the signs that York and the Nevilles were gradually winning the day may have prompted some anti-Percy reprisals. On 26 March Sir Thomas Neville of Brancepeth (Durham), Westmorland's brother, seems to have indulged in an unusual display of cousinly affection towards Salisbury and his sons. He was accused of organising a gang of at least twenty-four who broke into the house at Egton in Eskdale of Sir John Salvin, Northumberland's annuitant and a prominent member of Egremont's ambushing party in 1453; the walls of the house were pulled down and possessions worth £80 carried off.[110]

With Parliament no longer in session, it was the protector's responsibility to come to grips with the problem of the north, and the need for public order must have bulked large in York's mind. He may also have been concerned about his valuable Yorkshire estates, whilst his chancellor, Salisbury, was a party to the disputes and could contemplate revenge now that he had the opportunity. In any case, by the beginning of May rumours had reached Westminster of renewed insurrection in Yorkshire. Accordingly, on 10 May letters were sent to the earl of Northumberland much stronger in tone than those which the queen's government had dared issue in the previous October. It was pointed out to him in no uncertain terms that his son, Egremont, had ignored the earlier orders of 1453, and that the situation resulting from his *contretemps* with Salisbury had only been saved by Westmorland, the archbishop of York and the bishop of Durham. Responsibility for the conflict was laid squarely on Egremont's shoulders, but Northumberland was peremptorily ordered to appear before the Council by 12 June. At the same time, Lord Poynings and Sir Ralph Percy were commanded to appear by 2 June and Lord de Roos on 27 May.[111] Similarly firm action was taken against Exeter after his provocative meeting with Egremont in January. As from 3 April he was superseded as admiral of England by commissioners headed by Salisbury, who agreed to serve for three years as keepers of the sea in return for

---

[109] Moreover, in the West Country two of the earl of Devon's sons were responsible for disturbances at Exeter in April 1454. J. R. Lander, "Henry VI and the duke of York's second protectorate, 1455 to 1456," *The Bulletin of the John Ryland's Library*, XLIII (1960–61), 60.

[110] P.R.O., K.B., Anc. Indict., 149/10/10. For Salvin, see above, p. 332. Sir Thomas Neville of Brancepeth fought against Edward IV in 1461 and was attainted. *Rot. Parl.*, v, 478.

[111] *Proc. P. C.*, vi, 178–179; P.R.O., Exchequer, T.R., Council and Privy Seal, 84/19. For de Roos's anti-Yorkist sympathies, see below, p. 356.

2,000 marks.[112] If Exeter had any lingering doubts about opposing the regime of York and Salisbury, this poaching on his official preserve dispelled them. With reports in the air of a rising led by Exeter and the Percies, the duke was summoned to the Council much more urgently than Northumberland; he had to be there by 16 May at the latest.[113] Now that York and Salisbury had the opportunity, any contemplated insurrection would be nipped in the bud and Exeter and the Percies humbled at one fell swoop.

* * * *

Well might the government take these precautions, for Exeter and Percy were about to declare open war in the north in May 1454. A small group of York citizens were accused of breaking into Salisbury's town house on the 6th and attacking one of his tenants, John Skipwith. Five of the seven citizens named were freemen of York, and all but one had been involved with Egremont at Heworth.[114] Moreover, on the 10th, the day on which his father and brothers were summoned to Westminster, Egremont rode to Spofforth to rendezvous, according to the later indictments, with armed men from York who had been terrorising the citizens.[115] It smacked of a concerted rising, for on the same day Thomas Fairfax of Selby and John Martin of Cawood, both of whom had apparently fought at Heworth, brought further contingents to Spofforth to assist Egremont.[116]

Eventually, on 14 May, Egremont was joined by Exeter at York with a rebel force; they held illicit meetings to increase their strength, believing that some of the citizens supported them. The mayor, Thomas Nelson, and the recorder, Guy Roucliff, evidently resisted; but under duress in the minster they submitted to the insurgents.[117] As they were led to the north gate at Bootham Bar, both men were further ill-treated — to within an ace of death, it was later claimed. The entire

[112] P.R.O., Exchequer, E. R., Issue Roll, 799 (25 May 1454); Warrants for Issues, 70/1/68–69. The members of the commission were the earls of Salisbury, Oxford, Shrewsbury, Worcester, and Wiltshire, Lords fitzWarren and Stourton, and Sir Robert de Vere.

[113] P.R.O., Exchequer, T.R., Council and Privy Seal, 84/13; *Proc. P. C.*, VI, 180–181. On the same day, 10 May, the Council concerned itself with a similar dispute in Derbyshire, between the Longfords and Blounts. Storey, *End of the House of Lancaster*, pp. 152–153.

[114] P.R.O., K.B., Anc. Indict., 148/7; *Freemen of York, passim*; Storey, *End of the House of Lancaster*, p. 142. Skipwith had his own house in York ransacked by the same men a week later. P.R.O., K.B., Anc. Indict., 148/13.

[115] *Ibid.*, 148/11. Five of the eleven involved were freemen of York: the same number had been with Egremont at Heworth. *Ibid.*, 149/11/16; *Freemen of York, passim*.

[116] P.R.O., K.B., Anc. Indict., 149/11/12. For Fairfax and Martin, see *ibid.*, 149/11/16, 6/8, and above, p. 333.

[117] On 11 November 1453 Nelson was attacked at Tadcaster by William Barton, a yeoman who had been with Egremont at Heworth and accompanied Exeter in May 1454, P.R.O., K.B., Anc. Indict., 148/6; 149/6/8, 9/8. Nelson (1415–83) was a freeman of York in 1432, chamberlain in 1441–42 and mayor twice, in 1453–54 and 1464–65; in 1447–48 he was sheriff of York and M.P. for the city in the Parliament of 1453. He became a prosperous York merchant and owned a number of country properties. *Freemen of York*, pp. 147, 159, 173, 184; *List of Sheriffs*, p. 230; *Return of M.P.'s*, I, 349; Tillott, *City of York*, pp. 105, 112; Wedgwood, *History of Parliament, Biographies*, p. 625. Roucliff was J.P. in the east riding in 1453–58, and served on the commission of oyer and terminer in the north riding on 25 July 1453. *C.P.R., 1452–61*, pp. 682, 123.

city was in uproar as the scent of revolution spread through its narrow streets and "shambles."[118] Anarchy and destruction did not stop at the city walls, for during the next few days many of Egremont's former associates of 1453 joined in the renewed disturbances against the Nevilles and their adherents at Spofforth, Topcliffe and the surrounding countryside.[119] Nor did the county boundary limit Exeter's activities, for he was now writing seditious letters to Lord Greystoke and the people of Lancashire and Cheshire in an attempt to raise them too — not without success, for Lancashire men rallied to him and the duke may even have visited the palatinate to lead them.[120]

The government took alarm at this turn of events. Now that Parliament was no longer in session, York as protector could himself travel to Yorkshire. Meanwhile, on 16 May Sir Thomas Stanley, the duchy of Lancaster's receiver in Lancashire and Cheshire, and Sir Thomas Harrington, another duchy servant and one of Salisbury's retainers, were ordered to prevent people from joining Exeter and Egremont, especially from Lancashire. Stanley did his work well, ejecting Exeter from the shire, scattering his supporters, and holding Lancaster castle against seizure "by subtil menes and straunge imagination." But it was on Yorkshire that the duke of York concentrated most of his energies.[121] He was on his way north by 16 May, accompanied by Lord Cromwell, who must have been especially eager to come to grips with Exeter. On about the 19th the party arrived at York, and Exeter and Egremont promptly fled.[122] The visit proved of great expense to the city and shire, but at least it was the most resolute action taken to date.[123]

Exeter had too much at stake to give in so easily, for his rising was more than a spontaneous outburst prompted by personal resentment. According to the indictments of June 1454, he had far more ambitious aims and had allied with the Percies as the best means of achieving them; they were revealed on 21 May at Spofforth and elsewhere in Yorkshire.[124] The risings which had been occurring in

[118] P.R.O., K.B., Anc. Indict., 148/15; Storey, *End of the House of Lancaster*, p. 144. For a map of mediaeval York, see Raine, *Mediaeval York*, end plan.

[119] These rioters were identified with some of those who fought at Heworth and were indicted simultaneously for both risings in June 1454; they numbered 376. P.R.O., K.B., Anc. Indict., 149/6/8.

[120] *Proc. P. C.*, VI, 189–190; Somerville, *Duchy of Lancaster*, I, 226–227.

[121] *Proc. P. C.*, VI, 130–131 (misdated to 1453); P.R.O., Exchequer, T.R., Council and Privy Seal, 84/15; Somerville, *Duchy of Lancaster*, I, 226–227, 494. Despite his earlier antipathy towards York, Stanley may have disliked the queen and Exeter by 1454; this would explain his appointment as the king's chamberlain by the Yorkist government after the battle of St Albans in 1455. Wedgwood, *History of Parliament, Biographies*, p. 800. For Harrington, who died in 1460 in the Yorkist interest, see Coles, "Lordship of Middleham," p. 277; Wedgwood, *History of Parliament, Biographies*, pp. 426–427; Somerville, *Duchy of Lancaster*, I, 499–500.

[122] York had left Westminster by 16 May. P.R.O., Exchequer, T. R., Council and Privy Seal, 83/60, 21; Ramsay, *Lancaster and York*, II, 176–177; Trinity College, Dublin MS E.5.10 f. 187; A. H. Thomas and I. D. Thornley, ed., *The Great Chronicle of London* (1938), p. 187; C. L. Kingsford, ed., *Chronicles of London* (1905), p. 164; J. A. Giles, ed., *Incerti scriptoris chronicon Angliae de regnis Henrici IV, Henrici V, et Henrici VI* (1848), part 4, 45.

[123] *C.Cl.R., 1454–61*, p. 13.

[124] The following account of Exeter's rising is based upon the indictments laid before York and his fellow commissioners in June 1454. P.R.O., K.B., Anc. Indict., 149/4/27, 5/3, 9/8; Plea Roll, 778 rex m.3d.

several parts of Yorkshire since 10 May were probably part of Exeter's design. The Percy manor of Spofforth was its nerve centre, from which the insurrectionists radiated into other parts of the shire. At last, about 21 May, feverish meetings of fully-armed men took place beneath standards other than those of the king. They were, in fact, those of the duke of Exeter, who was accused of voicing a claim to rule at least part of England in the name of Henry VI.

Exeter and his supporters were later condemned for planning the death of the hapless king, but this may have been exaggeration to make conviction certain. When it was affirmed that Exeter considered assuming the government of the realm, it may have been a comment on the duke's belief that he, rather than York, should be protector of England during the king's incapacity. This may have been his central grievance.[125] When it was also reported that Exeter claimed to be duke of Lancaster in place of Henry VI, similar distortion may have occurred. For if Exeter could show to the northern populace that on hereditary grounds he had a claim to the protectorship, it might justify resorting to arms against York as the usurper of his rightful position. After all, Exeter was not appealing to lawyers, heralds, or others well versed in the intricacies of royal lineages; and in any case, had not the southern rebels in 1450 asked the king to bring into his entourage not only York but also Exeter?[126]

Exeter had a superficial claim to present to the people of the north, especially Lancashire. Unlike York, whose family connections were closer to the Plantagenet than the Lancastrian line, Exeter was firmly wedded to the revolution of 1399. If someone were required to exercise temporarily Henry VI's power, then the children of John of Gaunt and his first wife would provide the closest relatives of the royal house. Henry IV's two brothers had died young, but his two sisters had descendants living in 1454: the elder, Philippa, was represented by her grandson, King Alfonso of Portugal, and Elizabeth by her grandson, Henry Holand, duke of Exeter. In 1454, therefore, the latter was one of the two closest kinsmen of the invalid king. Gaunt had fathered other male children, but they were born illegitimately of Katherine Swynford, ultimately Gaunt's third wife, and were therefore related to the royal family only by half-blood. In any case, in 1454 their sole male descendant was Edmund Beaufort, duke of Somerset, the very person whose dominance at Court it was York's intention to destroy and Exeter need not have been an admirer of either Somerset or the queen.[127] On this hereditary basis, Exeter could claim with some justice the protectorship in place of the duke of York — the Portuguese king was obviously unsuited to exercise royal authority in England.

Those who wished to uphold Exeter's claim had thereby some justification. Exeter was reported to have welcomed any who would swear allegiance to him, promising in return relief from any tenths and fifteenths which might be imposed

---

[125] Despite the fact that York was Exeter's father-in-law, the latter having married Anne, York's eldest daughter, before 30 July 1447. *C.P.R., 1446–52*, p. 86; *Complete Peerage*, v, 212–215.

[126] And the dukes of Norfolk and Buckingham. Wilkinson, *Constitutional History*, p. 84. For a more literal interpretation of the charges against Exeter, see Storey, *End of the House of Lancaster*, pp. 144–146.

[127] See the accompanying table.

THE DUKE OF EXETER AND THE HOUSE OF LANCASTER

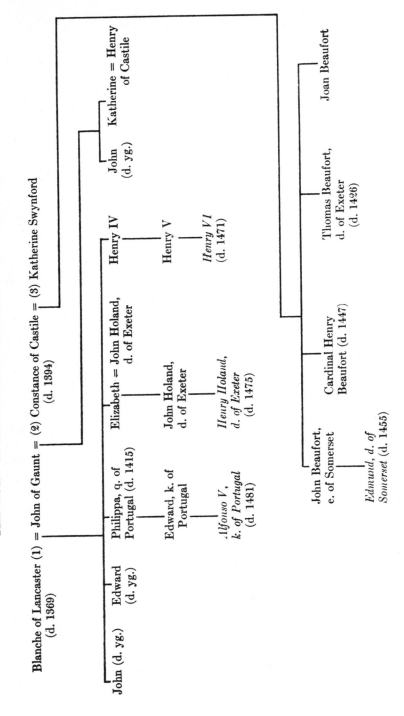

Blanche of Lancaster (1) = John of Gaunt = (2) Constance of Castile = (3) Katherine Swynford
(d. 1369)   (d. 1394)

John (d. yg.)

Edward (d. yg.)

Philippa, q. of Portugal (d. 1415)

Edward, k. of Portugal

Alfonso V, *k. of Portugal* (d. 1481)

Elizabeth = John Holand, d. of Exeter

John Holand, d. of Exeter

Henry Holand, d. of Exeter (d. 1475)

Henry IV

Henry V

Henry VI (d. 1471)

Katherine = Henry of Castile

John (d. yg.)

John Beaufort, e. of Somerset

Edmund, d. of Somerset (d. 1455)

Cardinal Henry Beaufort (d. 1447)

Thomas Beaufort, d. of Exeter (d. 1426)

Joan Beaufort

— it was easy to grant away taxes which an aspiring protector did not yet enjoy. To seal the bargain, Exeter would present the duchy of Lancaster's red and white livery to those willing to become his adherents: "Take here the duc of Lancastre's lyverey." From the government's point of view, the loyalty of subjects to their king was being lured away and abandoned. Exeter's suggested bid for the protectorship seemed hardly short of rebellion, and made all the more dangerous by its absorption of the Percy feud with the Nevilles. Well might one of the Pastons' correspondents exclaim of Exeter shortly afterwards: "God send hym gode councell hereafter."[128]

The soundness of the accusations against Exeter is borne out by activity in the king's Council early in June. On the 3rd the Council expressed displeasure at Exeter's presumption in usurping royal authority; at the language he had used at certain assemblies of the king's subjects; at the standards which had broken over these meetings; and at the duke's attempts to raise Lancashire and Cheshire in sympathy, areas dominated by the estates of the duchy of Lancaster. A few days later the Council again referred to Exeter's assumption of royal power and his unauthorised declarations to the citizens of York and Hull, presumably intended to rouse them in his support.[129] In all this, Exeter was not denounced as a rebel or a traitor; his actions evidently fell short of that and may, therefore, have been those of an erstwhile protector. The indictments taken in June sound suspiciously like exaggeration, especially if they were compiled by the Council itself after time for manufacture and imagination had passed.[130]

On 21 May Exeter, Egremont, and their adherents returned to York, where they demanded the keys of the city from Thomas Nelson, now recovered from his savage treatment a few days earlier. They even began negotiations at Topcliffe and Spofforth for assistance from King James of Scotland. Possibly at Exeter's instigation, the Scots had recently broken the four-year truce concluded in May 1453, and on 18 May 1454 complaints were expressed at Edinburgh of the violations committed by Scotsmen.[131] The government sent Garter king-of-arms with a letter to King James, but on 23 May he was intercepted at Spofforth by men from Berwick, Hartlepool, Cockermouth, and Yorkshire, evidently in the service of Exeter and Egremont.[132] In Yorkshire the riots continued, and Exeter and the Percies seem to have overrun much of the shire. At Wetherby on 28 May, Egremont brought the disturbances home to the inhabitants, whilst bands of rebels radiated from Spofforth to other towns and villages in Yorkshire, including Skip-

[128] Gairdner, *Paston Letters*, I, 290.

[129] *Proc. P.C.*, VI, 189–190, 195–197.

[130] For the view that the Council dictated the charges in the indictments, see Storey, *End of the House of Lancaster*, p. 145.

[131] Ramsay, *Lancaster and York*, II, 196 note 5; P.R.O., Exchequer, T.R., Council and Privy Seal, 84/27.

[132] Nine of these are known by name, among them at least four Yorkshiremen who were associated with Egremont at Heworth; one had recently been with Exeter at Spofforth and elsewhere on 21 May, whilst another, John Martin of Cawood (Yorks.), was accused of assembling men for the duke's rising since 10 May. P.R.O., K.B., Anc. Indict., 149/8/2, 11/16, 6/8, 4/27, 9/8d, 11/12.

ton.[133] On the same day the greatest *coup* of all was planned: the assassination of the duke of York and the other commissioners who had accompanied him from Westminster. The duke had presumably been bottled up in York since his arrival ten days earlier; he was now to be lured out and murdered. Robert Maulever, an esquire from Woodeshome (Yorkshire), was to be singled out as responsible for the project, and the deed was to be done at his own village; he wrote to various prominent men in the northern shires for support, but the plot evidently failed.[134]

Of those who were assembled by Exeter, Egremont, and Richard Percy in May 1454, the names of about 222 are known, but many more were involved. For a cause which was wider than that of the Percy feud, the known personnel was less heavily based on Yorkshire than that of the Heworth incident. Nevertheless, about 70% of those identified came from the shire, the city and the Percy manors of Topcliffe, Tadcaster, and Leconfield providing a solid corpus of men; the Percy honor of Cockermouth produced a contingent of twelve. Exeter himself was accompanied by his two bastard brothers, William and Robert Holand, together with thirty others from Bedfordshire, all but four of them from Ampthill, the manor Exeter had disputed with Lord Cromwell.[135] Moreover, Exeter's appeals to Lancashire did not go unheeded, for thirteen men of the county travelled to Yorkshire to take part in the insurrection.[136]

As at the "battle" of Heworth, it was not a force of vagabonds. Its backbone was the English yeoman, with a leaven of gentlemen and esquires to give it leadership and organisation. Apart from Exeter, his two brothers and two Percy allies, two knights were present: Sir John Salvin of North Driffield, who must have been notorious by this stage for his Percy affiliations and riotous propensities; and Sir Thomas Kirkby of Millbrook (Bedfordshire), presumably one of Exeter's retainers from the Fanhope manor.[137] The sixteen esquires included many hardened Percy dependents, even retainers: Henry, Robert and Richard Belingham from the honor of Cockermouth; John Swynburn, Oliver Hudleston, and Roland Kirkeby, also of Cockermouth.[138] From Yorkshire came John Pudsay of Bolton in Craven, and John Caterall of Brayton in Craven.[139] The gentlemen were more numerous (twenty-three in number), and again many can be associ-

---

[133] *Ibid.*, 149/6/3. Those accompanying Egremont included Robert Tipplyng of Spofforth and William Cure of Thorp Underwood, both apparently Heworth veterans. *Ibid.*, 149/11/16, 6/8d.

[134] *Ibid.*, 149/9/7.

[135] William Holand was retained to serve the king in Gascony in the summer of 1453. P.R.O., Exchequer, E.R., Issue Roll, 794 (30 July, 4 August). For his later Lancastrian activities, see below, p. 362. There were also two men from Millbrook and one from Flitwick, two of the Fanhope manors claimed by Exeter. Above, p. 338.

[136] At least 45% of those named were associated with earlier Percy enterprises: ninety-three of them at Heworth; six at the Topcliffe disturbances of October 1453; and one, John Stokton of Beverley, receiving Egremont's livery. P.R.O., K.B., Anc. Indict. 149/4/12; above, pp. 331-36.

[137] P.R.O., K.B., Anc. Indict, 149/5/3. For Salvin's punishment, see below.

[138] *Ibid.*, 149/11/16, 6/8, 4/27; above, pp. 332-33. Henry Belingham served as J.P. in Westmorland and a number of other shires, but not beyond 4 June 1454 when presumably his complicity in the Percy risings was discovered at the York sessions. *C.P.R., 1452–61*, pp. 680 and *passim*. For his later favour with the government of Henry VI, see below, p. 362.

[139] P.R.O., K.B., Anc. Indict., 149/5/3, 11/16; above, p. 332.

ated with Exeter or the Percies: some came from Ampthill with Exeter; others from Yorkshire had shown their Percy allegiance at Heworth and elsewhere, men like John Lyllyng of York, Thomas Frost of Fetherstone, and Thomas Fairfax of Selby.[140]

Ecclesiastical leadership was provided by a small group of beneficed clergy and chaplains, a few of whom had ministered to the indicted of Heworth: William White, vicar of Ilkley, was one, and others were John Danby, vicar of Middleton Tyas, and Thomas Dawne, rector of Bulmer; Exeter brought his own chaplain, John Boswell, from Ampthill. Thomas Pynchebek, bailiff of the Percy manor of Spofforth, the principal centre of the rising, was inevitably there.[141] From the city of York came at least nine freemen, almost all of them indicted for being involved at Heworth. With hardly an exception, the artisans of the cloth industry who figure in the lists came from Yorkshire: tailors, souters, walkers, and litsters. Those from outside the shire, brought either by the Percies from Cockermouth or by Exeter from Bedfordshire and further south, were yeomen tenants from their manors, or men of more gentle birth who may have been their liveried retainers.[142]

The entire Exeter plan was one of the most ambitious *coups* conceived against the government since the days of Henry V. It need not have been a plot against the dynasty, but rather against York as protector. As such it would require all the nerve and strength of Duke Richard and the Nevilles to weather the attack. York was already on the spot, but it was not until the beginning of June that official condemnation of Exeter and his works came from the Council, presumably under the guidance of Salisbury, Warwick, and York's other friends. On 3 June the riots in York were deplored, the presumption of Exeter denounced, and the treatment of Garter king-of-arms condemned. Exeter and his associates were optimistically summoned to appear before the king and Council on 25 June.[143]

Meanwhile, it was essential to prevent large sections of opinion in Yorkshire and adjacent shires from succumbing to the blandishments of Exeter and the Percies. The abbot of the Carmelite house at Hulne (Northumberland), who had given support to Egremont and his rebels and publicised their "strange proclamations," was asked to desist and instead to help restore peace in the area. On

---

[140] P.R.O., K.B., Anc. Indict., 149/11/16, 5/3, 4/27, 9/8, 6/8, 5/3d; above, p. 333. One was William Ashe of Ampthill, for whose later connection with Exeter see below.

[141] P.R.O., K.B., Anc. Indict., 149/5/3 and dorse, 6/8d., 4/27, 11/16, 6/8. Although Dawne is described simply as a clerk in the 1454 list, he appears as rector in the previous year. Above, p. 333. Danby was instituted as vicar of Middleton Tyas on 29 March 1451. A. H. Thompson, "The Register of the Archdeacons of Richmond, 1442–1477," *The Yorkshire Archaeological Journal*, xxx (1930–31), 73.

[142] John Stokton, yeoman, was retained by Egremont at Beverley (*Ibid.*, 149/4/27; 4/12; above, p. 348). Nine grooms were also indicted, two of the cellar and four of the chamber, but it is by no means clear whose grooms they were. The majority came from Leconfield, the Percy manor in Yorkshire, so that they may have been Northumberland's household officers. It is just possible that they were Yorkshiremen from the king's household who disliked the ascendancy of the duke of York and were willing to support Exeter. A solitary Welshman, Ieuan ap Gruffydd Gam ap Meurig, was present, far from home and now resident at Cockermouth. *Ibid.*, 149/5/3 and dorse.

[143] *Proc. P.C.*, vi, 189–190, 190–191; P.R.O., Exchequer, T.R., Council and Privy Seal, 84/41; above, p. 347.

the same day, 5 June, Thomas, Lord Clifford and the sheriff of Westmorland were given similar orders; Clifford needed a reminder, for his sympathies were with the Percies and his allegiance to death was to the Lancastrians rather than the Yorkists. On the other hand, grateful thanks were expressed to the citizens of York and Hull for withstanding Exeter's attacks and refusing to be seduced by his unauthorised proclamations. Indeed, the Council noted with satisfaction that both towns had received Duke Richard well; certainly, the citizens of York had no reason to sympathise with Exeter's claims after the cavalier treatment of their mayor and recorder.[144]

Although Richard had been in Yorkshire since about 19 May, it was not until the second week in June that he was able to take the offensive. Then, on the eighth, it was reported in London that he was established near York with a great force and was likely to remain there for about a fortnight.[145] In fact, he stayed even longer, for by 15 June it was possible to begin hearing accusations in York castle against the rioters; once they had started, the indicting juries went on with enthusiasm over the Trinity week-end until 26 June. For this business of indicting and punishing, York was joined by several magnates and justices. When the sessions opened on 15 June, Warwick was there with Lord Greystoke, two justices (Richard Bingham and Ralph Pole) and the mayor of York, Thomas Nelson. After the weekend, other lords arrived, so that by 22 June the earl of Shrewsbury, Lord Clifford, and Sir Henry fitzHugh were also sitting in the castle; Nelson withdrew, possibly because of his intimate involvement in some of the incidents reported.[146]

These sessions were a grand stock-taking of all the iniquities committed primarily by the Percies in Yorkshire since the summer of 1453; the charges receive general confirmation from other sources. Hundreds of the indicted were condemned to forfeiture; far less were outlawed and few pardoned. The actual implementation of these punishments depended on the effectiveness of the local law enforcement agencies. The massive job of bringing the condemned to book was the duty of the sheriff of Yorkshire, but his subordinates must have found it especially difficult to arrest or seize possessions where large masses of people were involved.[147] Risk could often over-ride duty.

The punishment of less than half of those indicted for activities in May 1454 is recorded in the lists available. The commissioners were more lenient with these than with the alleged participants at Heworth, possibly because they did not wish to create by severity a hardened core of anti-Yorkist feeling in the north; when the object was simply the destruction of a local rival, as in 1453, there was less fear of more serious repercussions. Certainly, the leaders of the rising, Exeter,

---

[144] *Ibid.*, 84/37; *Proc. P.C.*, vi, 193–97; above, p. 343 and below, pp. 361-2.

[145] Gairdner, *Paston Letters*, i, 290.

[146] P.R.O., K.B., Anc. Indict., 148/8d, 16d (15 June); 149/7/2 (22 June); Plea Roll, 781 rex m. 28 (25 June). See Storey, *End of the House of Lancaster*, pp. 145–146, 253, for the conjecture that the charges were assembled at Westminister and that all the York jurors were required to do was to list those involved.

[147] Compare the difficulties facing the sheriffs' officers who tried to arrest Oliver Stockdale and seize his possessions in January 1453. Above, p. 324.

Egremont, and Richard Percy were not apprehended at this time, but fell into York's hands later in 1454; indeed, twenty-two were eventually granted charters of pardon, including Egremont.[148] At least one of the rioters, William Occliff of Ampthill, fled to Scotland about 25 June to escape punishment.[149] Nevertheless, an example was made of selected individuals. Edward Andreton of Tuxford (Nottinghamshire), where the fateful meeting had taken place between Exeter and Egremont, eventually appeared in the court of King's Bench in Michaelmas term, 1455; he was accused of being involved in the riots at Topcliffe on 21 October 1453 and of supporting Exeter and Egremont in May 1454. Brought to London by the sheriff of York, he was produced in court in October, but presented a royal pardon covering all offences committed by him before 9 July 1455; on the strength of this and six pledges, he was released.[150] Robert Cropwell of Cockermouth was also transferred to Westminster, accused of taking part in the battle of Heworth and in the rising of May 1454.[151] On 1 July 1456 he was brought to London, only to display a pardon granted on 1 November 1455 of offences committed before the previous 9 July. But on this occasion the attorney-general interjected that Cropwell was of evil notoriety and was indicted before the keepers of the peace at York for treasons committed since 9 July; he was therefore detained in prison pending further investigations.[152] Robert Thomkynson, a yeoman from the Percy manor of Healaugh, was the third to be committed to King's Bench, in Michaelmas term, 1456.[153]

The sessions of June 1454 tried to delineate the scale of the Percy risings in Yorkshire since 1453. A subordinate commission was issued to York and Warwick on 2 June to investigate offences in Newcastle-upon-Tyne, which had supplied men for Northumberland at the confrontation with the Nevilles at Topcliffe in October 1453. Lancashire was dealt with at the end of the month after a further outburst near Bolton, during which the insurgents urged Egremont to join them; Sir Thomas Stanley again dispersed the rioters.[154] This remedial activity was the first step in the total defeat of the Percies, both as local rivals of the Nevilles and

---

[148] P.R.O., K.B., Anc. Indict., 149/4/27. A few had their possessions seized for felonies by the escheator of Yorkshire in 1454 and 1455: John Pudsay of Bolton in Craven, John Caterall of Brayton in Craven, and Thomas Guberthorne of Thirsk, who had been at Heworth; Robert Tipplyng of Spofforth, John Danby, vicar of Middleton Tyas, and Thomas Dawne, rector of Bulmer, who had supported Egremont and Exeter in 1453–54; and Roger Leconfield, rector of Donnington, who had supported Exeter in 1454. P.R.O., Exchequer, K.R., Escheators' Accounts, 60/6, 7; K.B., Anc. Indict., 149/11 /16, 5/3d, 4/2, 7; above, pp. 348-9.

[149] P.R.O., K.B., Anc. Indict., 149/9/8d.

[150] *Ibid.*, 149/4/26, 4/27; Plea Roll, 778 rex m.3d. This was the general pardon issued on 31 July 1455. See below, p. 357.

[151] He and fifteen others had attacked Thomas Laton at his manor of Dalmare (Cumb.) on 24 December 1452, taking him prisoner, chivvying him from castle to castle and shire to shire, until he was set free six months later. *C.Cl.R., 1447–54*, pp. 470, 467–468.

[152] The result of the case is unknown. P.R.O., K.B., Plea Roll, 781 rex m.28, 7.

[153] P.R.O., K.B., Anc. Indict., 149/5/3. Some miscreants were pursued at law well into the reign of Edward IV. Storey, *End of the House of Lancaster*, p. 148; P.R.O., King's Bench, Controlment Roll, 89 m. 2-6.

[154] *C.P.R., 1452–61*, p. 177; Somerville, *Duchy of Lancaster*, I, 226–227; above, p. 336.

as Exeter's allies in his bid for control of the government. For the moment the leaders, Exeter, Egremont, and Richard Percy, were still at large. Their capture during the remaining months of 1454 implied disaster for their cause, and the final *coup de grace* was delivered at St Albans on 22 May 1455.[155]

* * * * *

Duke Richard of York was back in London on 8 July 1454, and it was there, on 23 July, that Exeter fell into his hands.[156] Duke Henry had travelled secretly to Westminster early in June to escape York's wrath, now that his enterprise had collapsed, or to try a bolder hand and strike the government at its centre now that York was in the north.[157] He ignored orders to appear before king and Council, and sought sanctuary in Westminster Abbey; together with his bastard brother Robert, they were escorted out by York, much to the distress of the abbot and his monks.[158] Taken first to York's own household, Exeter was quickly transferred out of the city to Pontefract, one of the duchy of Lancaster castles whose constable was Salisbury. Three knights, Sir Brian Stapleton, Sir John Melton, and Sir Thomas Rempston, were assigned as his keepers on 24 July.[159] Exeter was imprisoned because of his recent activities in Yorkshire, and party politics dictated his treatment.[160] Later in the year, he was further penalised; on 30 November feoffees of Lord Grey of Ruthin were granted Ampthill and the other Fanhope manors.[161]

[155] As protector York was less successful, despite his initiative, in re-establishing central control over events in West Wales, where Gruffydd ap Nicholas was able to ignore the verbal assaults of the Council in May and June 1454 (Griffiths, *Welsh History Review*, ii, no. 3 [1965], 218–221). Nor were the Council's attempts to pacify Derbyshire and the West Country any more successful in these months. Storey, *End of the House of Lancaster*, pp. 153–154, 166. See above pp. 206-9.

[156] York was not at the Council meeting on 5 July, but was there three days later. P.R.O., Exchequer, T.R., Council and Privy Seal, 85/35, 12. He was certainly expected back in London on 8 July. Gairdner, *Paston Letters*, i, 293.

[157] On 8 June it was reported in London that "the Duc of Exeter ys here coverdtlye." Gairdner, *Paston Letters*, i, 290.

[158] Trinity College, Dublin MS E. 5.10 f. 187; P.R.O., Exchequer, T.R., Council and Privy Seal, 84/111; Chancery, Warrants, 769/9980; *Proc. P.C.*, vi, 214–219; Somerville, *Duchy of Lancaster*, i, 227; Thomas and Thornley, *Great Chronicle of London*, p. 187; Kingsford, *Chronicles of London*, p. 164; Edward Hall, *The Union of the two Noble and Illustrious Families of Lancaster and York*, ed. Henry Ellis (1809), pp. 233–234; Gairdner, *Paston Letters*, i, 290; Ramsay, *Lancaster and York*, ii, 177; John Stowe, *Annales of England* (3rd edition, 1605), p. 400; Storey, *End of the House of Lancaster*, p. 147. Both Hall and Stowe mistakenly date the imprisonment to York's second protectorate.

[159] P.R.O., Chancery, Warrants, 769/9980; Trinity College, Dublin MS E. 5. 10 f. 187; Gairdner, *Paston Letters*, i, 290; Thomas and Thornley, *Great Chronicle of London*, p. 187; Kingsford, *Chronicles of London*, p. 164; Somerville, *Duchy of Lancaster*, i, 515; *Proc. P. C.*, vi, 218. Stapleton, a Yorkshire and Lincolnshire landowner, was married to Rempston's daughter; he is described by Wedgwood as a "Lancastrian" on insufficient evidence. Melton, also a Yorkshire landowner, was named as feoffee in York's will. Wedgwood, *History of Parliament, Biographies*, pp. 804, 584.

[160] P.R.O., Chancery, Warrants, 769/9980. J. J. Bagley (*Margaret of Anjou* (n..d), p. 76), followed by E. F. Jacob (*Fifteenth Century*, p. 510), seems to regard the arrest of Exeter as the result of disturbances in the west of England, where admittedly he did have estates; but there is no indication that he was involved with the earl of Devon. *Complete Peerage*, v, 214 n. (a).; Lander, *Bull. J. Ryland's Lib.*, xliii (1960–61), 60–65.

[161] Jack, *Grey of Ruthin Valor*, pp. 35, 105. The price of 6,500 marks had been fully paid by 12 October 1473.

With Exeter inside Pontefract, York's regime could afford to be lenient towards the lesser rioters. On the very day when Exeter was seized, York and the other justices in Yorkshire were instructed to stop until 20 April 1455 all process against Northumberland and some of his men and to suspend all judgements already made against them; the sheriff of the county was to stop executing judgements given and the escheator to suspend seizing property and goods declared forfeit. An especially full Council was summoned next day to meet on 21 October, and special writs were sent to thirteen lords who had hitherto not appeared at conciliar meetings for some time. They were now summoned to a meeting of reconciliation at which full attendance was required: Lords Greystoke, Poynings, Clifford, and de Roos were among those from the north who received letters.[162]

Meanwhile, York spent some time in Yorkshire with the Nevilles, keeping an eye on Exeter at Pontefract and on the Percies generally, for the shire was still in the throes of party warfare. He had evidently returned northwards by the beginning of August, and was certainly at York on the 3rd; towards the end of the month he was probably a guest at Salisbury's castle of Middleham.[163] Vigilance was clearly still needed, and on 22 September the sheriff of Yorkshire and the city officials were commissioned to arrest and imprison all those guilty of unlawful assemblies.[164] Well might the government display its ragged nerves at this time. From 15 September to 14 October 1454 Lord Egremont, Richard Percy, and Lord Poynings were garrisoning the Percy manor of Spofforth, "for the safekeeping and defence of the township and lordship at the time of the quarrel between the lord (Northumberland or Poynings) and the earl of Salisbury."[165] Moreover, Exeter's arrest had not completely calmed the stir he had caused in Lancashire by his ambitious declarations. At the very end of September it was necessary to order several prominent commissioners, led by the earls of Westmorland and Shrewsbury, and including four of the Nevilles, to raise a force of Yorkshiremen to suppress Lancashire rebels who were plundering neighbouring shires and plotting the destruction of York's government.[166]

Indeed, the autumn of 1454 experienced a recrudescence of Percy violence against the Nevilles. A second "battle" was fought between the two families at Stamford Bridge, the Salisbury manor a few miles east of York. Several contemporary chronicles report the fighting, but historians for more than half a century have been lured into confusion by a Tudor writer. Under the year 1453 (*recte*

[162] P.R.O., Exchequer, T.R., Council and Privy Seal, 84/63; *Proc. P.C.*, VI, 214–217.

[163] P.R.O., K.B., Plea Roll, 778 rex m. 3d; Storey, *End of the House of Lancaster*, pp. 147–148; Harriss, "The Struggle for Calais: an Aspect of the Rivalry between Lancaster and York," *Eng. Hist. Rev.*, LXXV (1960), 37.

[164] *C.P.R., 1452–61*, p. 219; Storey, *End of the House of Lancaster*, p. 148.

[165] Fisher, "Some Yorkshire Estates of the Percies, 1450–1650," vol. I, ch. 2, p. 35, quoting Petworth MS, Min. Acc., D. 9.6. The party's expenses for this month amounted to £30. 14s. 2d.

[166] *C.P.R., 1452–61*, pp. 219–220. The Nevilles were Sir Thomas (of Middleham), his brother John, Sir Thomas (of Brancepeth), and Robert Neville, esquire. Many of the others were associated with the Neville family, including Lord Greystoke, Sir Henry fitzHugh, Sir James Strangeways, Sir John and Christopher Conyers, Sir James Pickering, and Richard Aske. Coles, "Lordship of Middleham," pp. 122–129, 274–276, appendix B; *C.Cl.R., 1422–29*, p. 281; *Rot. Parl.*, V, 349; *C.P.R., 1452–61*, p. 561; above, pp. 327–28.

1454), the Whitby annals record a "battle" at Stamford Bridge between two Neville brothers and two Percy brothers; the treason and flight of Peter Lound ("Piers of Lounde") enabled the Nevilles to emerge victorious with the two Percies captured and despatched to a London prison.[167] The Latin chronicle, which displays knowledge of northern events, includes a similar account produced, perhaps, at St Leonard's Hospital in York: at an encounter in 1454 Egremont led the Percy faction against Sir Thomas and Sir John Neville, sons of the earl of Salisbury. Again, the Neville victory is attributed to the flight of Peter Lound, bailiff of the Percy manor of Pocklington, taking 200 of Egremont's retinue with him; as Lound left the field, Egremont and Richard Percy were captured and taken to Salisbury's castle at Middleham. The only novel piece of information in this account is the site of the "battle," Castleton Bridge, but no Castleton is known near Stamford Bridge and the details of the "battle" hardly leave room for doubt that both accounts refer to the same "battle."[168] Slight confirmation of Stamford Bridge as its site comes from another Latin chronicle, which states that Egremont was captured near York on 31 October 1454 by Sir Thomas Neville, and that shortly afterwards Richard Percy, too, was taken, while hundreds were killed and many wounded.[169]

Minor details are provided by other writers, all of whom confirm that a Percy-Neville fracas took place about the beginning of November 1454, leading to the capture of the Percies. Middleham castle, Salisbury's seat, was an obvious place to which to take the Percy brothers immediately after the battle, but they were then handed over to the duke of York, taken to London and put in Newgate jail.[170] On 4 November, before the journey to London, they were arraigned at York before the justices of oyer and terminer, led by Richard Bingham and Ralph Pole. There they were condemned in large sums of money to various members of the Neville family: 8,000 marks to Salisbury; 5,000 marks to his wife, Alice; 1,000 marks to his son, Sir Thomas Neville; 2,000 marks to Sir Thomas and his wife, Maud; and 800 marks to Salisbury's other son, Sir John Neville. It was a total fine of 16,800 marks, representing in monetary terms a grand reckoning of offences committed by the Percies against the Nevilles over the past two years.[171]

---

[167] *Whitby Cartulary*, II, 694–695. For Lound's earlier association with Egremont, see above, p. 333.

[168] Giles, *Chronicon Angliae*, part 4, 45–46. For the authorship of this chronicle, see M. V. Clarke and V. H. Galbraith, "The Deposition of Richard II," in M. V. Clarke, *Fourteenth Century Studies* (1937), pp. 82–85.

[169] Trinity College, Dublin MS E. 5. 10 f. 187. Moreover, Pocklington, of which Peter Lound was bailiff, lies a few miles south of Stamford Bridge. The only Castleton which has been suggested as the site of the "battle" lies in Eskdale, nowhere near York. Ramsay, *Lancaster and York*, II, 207; *Complete Peerage*, IX, 89 and n. (b).

[170] One chronicle mentions that two Nevilles were responsible for the capture, which is dated 1 November 1454 instead of the following day, and that many were slain. R. Flenley, ed., *Six Town Chronicles* (1911), p. 158. Two more contemporaries confirm that the imprisonment in Newgate took place in November 1454. F. W. D. Brie, ed., *The Brut or the Chronicle of England* (2 vols., Early English Text Society, 1906–08), II, 523–24; Flenley, *Six Town Chronicles*, pp. 143, 109.

[171] H. T. Riley, ed., *Registrum Abbatiae Johannis Whethamstede*, I (Rolls Series, 1872), 303–304. Various other writers mention the fine, though they vary as to its amount, e.g., 18,000 marks (Giles, *Chronicon Angliae*, part 4, 46), or 17,000 marks (J. Gairdner, ed., *Three Fifteenth-Century Chronicles*

York had achieved a measure of the power he desired when he became protector of England in March 1454. At Stamford Bridge in November his Neville collaborators partly realised their dream, albeit a more local one: two of Northumberland's sons had been captured and were now in prison. The Neville success must have strengthened York's position, if only because it put an end in Yorkshire at least to that state of grave disorder whose remedy had been the protector's *raison d'être*. But it represented less a national political gain for the York-Neville axis, than a blow at the Percies' local power in the north.

The confusion surrounding the "battle" of Stamford Bridge originated with Robert Fabyan (d. 1513). The entire episode of Egremont's capture and imprisonment, culminating in his dramatic escape with three accomplices, was attributed in his chronicle to the year in which John Steward and Ralph Verney were sheriffs of London, 1456–57. Events occurring between 1454 and 1456 were telescoped into one year, and Sir James Ramsay followed suit.[172] Although the sheriffs were in office from October 1456 to October 1457, Ramsay assumed that 1457 was the *annus omnium*.[173] Committing himself to a "battle" in 1457, "in the north country atwene the lorde Egremonde and the sonnes of the erle of Salesbury and dyuerse men maymed and slayen atwene theym," Ramsay sought a suitable candidate. He discovered the "battle" of Castleton Bridge, dated by the Latin chronicler to 1454 and during which Egremont was captured. This seemed identical with Fabyan's account, and Ramsay concluded that the contemporary chronicler had confused the "battle" of Castleton with the earlier one at Stamford Bridge, whereas it was really another "great fray" which, Fabyan indicated, took place in 1457. His second error lay in failing to distinguish between the "battles" of Heworth (1453) and Stamford Bridge (1454). Since the Latin *Annales* mentioned a clash following the wedding of 1453 and the Whitby chronicle reported (mistakenly) a "battle" at Stamford Bridge in 1453, Ramsay assumed them to be one and the same. Instead of a sequence of two "battles," at Heworth on 24 August 1453 and Stamford on 31 October or 1 November 1454, he produced a "battle" at Stamford Bridge in August 1453 and one at Castleton in 1457.

Ramsay's authority was fatal.[174] The acceptance of this version by Charles Oman in 1906 and Kenneth Vickers in 1913 converted it into an orthodoxy, although the latter placed the "battle" of Stamford Bridge in August 1452. *The Complete Peerage* deepened the confusion by transfering Stamford Bridge to 1456 and allowing the two Percies to be captured on this occasion; Castleton retained

---

(Camden Series, 1880), p. 149). See also Brie, *The Brut*, I, 523–524. The York sessions of 4 November 1454 indicted a number of men who were presumably in the company of the Percy brothers. P.R.O., King's Bench, Controlment Roll, 87 m. 6, 6d.

[172] Robert Fabyan, *Newe Chronicles of England and France*, ed., Henry Ellis (1811), p. 632. Fabyan's account seems to be based primarily on the English *Brut*, which is rather vague in dating the incident and also compresses the events of 1454–56 into one year. Brie, *The Brut*, I, 523–524.

[173] Ramsay, *Lancaster and York*, II, 207. Ramsay even hazarded July 1457 as the month of the "battle" and placed Castleton six and one half miles south-east of Guisborough, near Eskdale.

[174] Professor Tait, in *The Dictionary of National Biography*, XL, 265–266, arrived at a similar conclusion two years later in 1894, repeating Fabyan's version.

its position in the following year, with the location of the "battle" plausibly transported to Eskdale in the north riding.[175] More recent writers have not improved the situation: although K. B. McFarlane, V. H. H. Green, and E. F. Jacob mention none of the "battles" specifically, G. A. Holmes misdates Stamford to August 1453 and Bertie Wilkinson continues to ascribe Castleton to 1457.[176]

During the winter of 1454–55 the political tide began to run against York, and it must have been increasingly obvious that he could not maintain his hold over the government for very much longer. Once it were lost, the magnates he had kept in confinement would be released. Henry VI recovered from his illness at the very end of 1454, and on 7 February 1455 Somerset was formally released from the captivity to which York had assigned him. At the request of some magnates, Henry proceeded to free other detainees under guarantee of making amends for their debts and illegal activities.[177] The intention of releasing magnates like Somerset and Exeter, one chronicler suggests, lay behind the resignation of Salisbury as chancellor on 7 March. But it probably provided no more than the occasion for it; he could never hope to remain chancellor once York's dominance was ended, and Somerset's release in February signalised just that.[178]

Exeter was one of the freed magnates. On 13 March 1455 Henry VI ordered his new chancellor to release him from Pontefract castle; he may have anticipated resistance from the constable (Salisbury) because failure to carry out the order involved forfeiture of 10,000 marks. Both Exeter and the cause of his imprisonment, which, with York bereft of power, could now be described as a consequence of "sinistre enformacion made upon him by certain persones not wele disposed," were to be produced at Court by Sir Humphrey Stafford.[179] Indeed, York's fall may have forestalled further action against Exeter. On 3 February, just before Somerset's release, Exeter was ordered to be removed from Pontefract to Wallingford castle by 11 February. But Exeter was still at Pontefract when he was

---

[175] Oman, *History of England, 1377–1485*, p. 376; Vickers, *Later Middle Ages*, pp. 442, 449; *Complete Peerage*, IX, 89 and n. (b). The printers of Vickers's book may have been responsible for assigning Stamford Bridge to 1452!

[176] K. B. McFarlane, "The Lancastrian Kings, 1399–1461," in *Cambridge Mediaeval History*, VIII (1936); Green, *Later Plantagenets*; Jacob, *Fifteenth Century*; Holmes, *Later Middle Ages*, pp. 218, 248; Wilkinson, *Constitutional History*, p. 101 and note 4. Bagley, *Margaret of Anjou*, p. 87, implies that the Percy-Neville quarrel broke out with renewed vigour in the winter of 1457–58. Recently Dr Storey has dated both "battles" accurately, though placing Stamford Bridge on 31 October 1454; he does not mention Castleton Bridge. *End of the House of Lancaster*, pp. 130–131, 148–149.

[177] Giles, *Chronicon Angliae*, part 4, 47; Armstrong, *Bull. Inst. Hist. Res.*, XXXIII (1960), 8–10. Lord de Roos, one of Northumberland's friends, went bail for his step-father, Somerset, on his release and in March 1455 was associated with the duke in negotiations with the Calais garrison. *Ibid.*, p. 8; Harriss, *Eng. Hist. Rev.*, LXXV (1960), 39; above, p. 342.

[178] Dr. Storey suggests that Salisbury's resignation was forced by the political changes which brought Northumberland, his son (the bishop of Carlisle) and Lord Clifford into the king's circle of advisers at this juncture. *End of the House of Lancaster*, p. 160.

[179] P.R.O., Chancery, Warrants, 769/9980, 9994; *C.Cl.R., 1454–61*, p. 13. Stafford, the duke of Buckingham's son and heir, was ordered on 18 March to receive Exeter, and on the following day the constable was requested to hand him over. A number of Percy adherents received pardons for unspecified offences in February and March 1455. P.R.O., Chancery, Pardon Roll, 41, *passim*.

freed in March: the transfer may have been overtaken by events at Court, resulting in the neutralisation of York's authority.[180]

Exeter's movements after his release are uncertain. Although freed by the king and a bitter enemy of York and the Nevilles, he was not at the king's side at the battle of St Albans on 22 May 1455, when York tried to recapture his influence over Henry VI. His absence cannot have been due to lack of sympathy with the king and his new advisers, for on the eve of battle Exeter's poursuivant was used by Henry and Somerset to negotiate with York and the Nevilles. When the latter received royal ultimata from the hands of such an envoy, they might well have felt that the Yorkshire feuds of recent years were colouring the attitudes of the king and Somerset.[181] The battle ended with York once more in the saddle and Henry VI firmly under his and the Nevilles' control. Northumberland lay dead on the field; Exeter was soon to fall into York's hands, if he had not already done so; and Egremont and his brother were locked away in Newgate. The duke, when apprehended, would naturally be returned to a strong castle; indeed, by 21 June he was languishing in Wallingford, when the earl of Worcester, who had recently been ordered to take charge of him there, was unable to do so because the duchess of Suffolk was constable of Wallingford and undertook responsibility for Exeter's safe keeping.[182] If York had failed to transfer Exeter to Wallingford during his earlier period of power, he could do so at pleasure after St Albans.[183]

York could afford to be magnanimous towards the rank and file of the Percy-Exeter adherents of 1453–55. On 31 July 1455 a general amnesty was declared in Parliament for all crimes and offences committed against the Crown before 9 July, and individual pardons followed.[184] Pieces of parchment, however, could not repair the damage sustained by Yorkshire. Dislocation of urban life must have been severe on occasion in York itself and in other towns and villages preyed upon for man-power by the warring parties. Indeed, the flames of the past two years left smouldering embers, for further commissions holding sessions were active in Yorkshire and Durham during the first half of 1455, and on 11 March 1457 Henry VI drew the attention of the civic authorities at York to the

---

[180] P.R.O., Exchequer, T.R., Council and Privy Seal, 86/39; *Proc. P.C.*, VI, 234. Dr Storey suggests another, equally hypothetical, explanation of Exeter's movements. *End of the House of Lancaster*, p. 253 note 17.

[181] Armstrong, *Bull. Inst. Hist. Res.*, XXXIII (1960), 30, 38. This is overlooked by Dr Storey (*End of the House of Lancaster*, p. 147), who assumes that Exeter was transferred to Wallingford shortly after his removal from Pontefract.

[182] Giles, *Chronicon Angliae*, part 4, 46; *Proc. P.C.*, VI, 245–246. He could not be installed in the obvious citadel, the Tower of London, for Exeter had been appointed constable on 28 February 1447 jointly with his father in survivorship. *Complete Peerage*, v, 212–15; *C.P.R., 1446–52*, p. 32; *Proc. P.C.*, VI, 245–246.

[183] At this juncture the Council was making further efforts to come to grips with the lawlessness caused in West Wales by Gruffydd ap Nicholas, who imprisoned a fellow Welshman ostensibly because he was one of York's servants. Griffiths, *Welsh Hist. Rev.*, II, no. 3 (1965), above, pp. 209-11.

[184] Ramsay, *Lancaster and York*, II, 187; *Rot. Parl.*, v, 283–284; P.R.O., K.B., Plea Roll, 778, rex m. 3d, 28; above, p. 351. Pardons granted in August 1455 to some of the leaders were either not made effective (e.g., Egremont's) or were delayed (e.g., Exeter's). Storey, *End of the House of Lancaster*, p. 148; below, p. 359.

"gret riottes and assembles of oure peple. . . made and committed within oure citee of York, by the which gret slaughters, murders of oure peple, and other mischeves were like to ensue that we ne wolde."[185] Later on in the Wars of the Roses, it was to be commented that "for their treuth unto ther souverain Lord, such as abode in York was robbed, spolid. . . and soo extremely empouverished that few of them was ever after of power to diffend themselves."[186] Moreover, the considerable bodies of yeomen and husbandmen from Percy manors up and down the shire removed the guiding hand from everyday agricultural activity. The temporary effect on production and rents must have been just as apparent as it was on Crown revenue; by the autumn of 1455, the finances of the shire were in confusion. On 5 December 1455 the recent sheriff, Sir John Saville, reported that he was unable to collect the usual revenue because of the disturbances, the cost of the duke of York's commission, and the cost of executing its orders and keeping men under arms to safeguard the area against perennial Scots raids.[187]

To add to Yorkshire's misery, the winter of 1455–56 may have witnessed a resurgence of Percy lawlessness. An undated petition complained that Northumberland had occupied several castles, including Wressle, persistently refusing to deliver them to Salisbury and even allowing his servants to murder the king's messenger, John Drayton. The seizure of Cromwell's manor of Wressle by the Percies might have been expected after the marriage of Cromwell's heiress to a Neville in August 1453, and it may have taken place before the manor was granted to Egremont in 1458.[188] The petition was presented to the Commons in Parliament and Northumberland was ordered to appear by the following 20 January, so that a winter session is indicated; between 1456 and 1458 this could only be the session lasting from 12 November to 13 December 1455, during which York became protector for the second time to deal with the chronically disturbed parts of the realm.[189]

The duke's success in fulfilling his brief was limited: in Yorkshire, as in Wales and the West of England, petitions to and threats from Westminster achieved

[185] P.R.O., Exchequer, E. R., Warrants for Issues, 70/2/92; 71/1/41; King's Bench, Controlment Roll, 89 m. 4d, 6; *York Memoranda Book*, II (Surtees Society, cxxv, 1915), pp. 200–201.

[186] Heaton, *Yorkshire Woollen and Worsted Industries*, p. 47.

[187] Saville was forced to seek pardon for those sums he was unable to collect for the Exchequer. P.R.O., Exchequer, T.R., Council and Privy Seal, 87.

[188] P.R.O., Chancery, Parliamentary and Council Proceedings, 32/8. After Cromwell's death Northumberland may have feared that the castle would fall into Neville hands as a result of the marriage.

[189] Powicke and Fryde, *Handbook of British Chronology*, p. 532; Lander, *Bull. J. Ryland's Lib.*, XLIII (1960–61), 46–69. A similar petition was probably presented in the same session against Gruffydd ap Nicholas, who had shown himself hostile towards York in West Wales (Griffiths, *Welsh Hist. Rev.*, II, no. 3 (1965), 223–224). The session lasted from 12 November to 13 December 1455, and not from 13 December 1455 to 14 January 1456, as stated there. An alternative occasion for the presentation of the petition against Northumberland is the parliamentary session lasting from 7 October to 1 December 1460, when the Yorkists were in power. It may postdate Cromwell's death in January 1456, for it was not he, its owner, but Salisbury who was to resume possession of it. Egremont had held Wressle for life only, and at his death at Northampton on 10 July 1460 it should have reverted to the Crown; Northumberland may have seized it instead. The figure XXXIX appears at the bottom of the document, possibly referring to 39 Henry VI (1460–61).

little at a distance, and in any case the protectorate did not long survive the beginning of 1456.[190] Furthermore, Exeter seems to have been released from captivity by the time that Parliament reassembled on 14 January 1456, for he then came to an agreement with the king: he entered into a recognisance of £2,000 to appear in Chancery on the forthcoming 3 November, or earlier if summoned, unless he were legitimately prevented from doing so by illness or imprisonment.[191] Then, later in the year, Egremont was once more at large, after escaping from Newgate on the night of 13 November.[192] The year 1455 had seen the victory of York and the Nevilles centrally and in Yorkshire, but the following months witnessed the partial erosion of their achievement.

* * * * *

Nevertheless, Exeter and the Percies did not have the capacity to take up the struggle anew; in any case, after 1456 there was less reason to plan an assault on York, whose political power was being gradually eroded. Exeter himself showed signs of unintelligence and some of his actions were frankly irresponsible. In February 1456 he was continuing to worry his step-mother about her share of his father's jewels, and Sir John Neville, Westmorland's brother, agreed to assume any obligation as a result of actions brought against her by the duke.[193] Then, on 5 November he, Somerset, and the earl of Shrewbury tried to ambush Warwick on his way to London.[194] His bitterness intensified when, towards the end of 1457, after a blundering pursuit of French privateers, he was relieved of the admiralship of England and replaced by Warwick ("to his grete displesir").[195] Finally, in the last days of January 1458, Exeter offended the king. He came to Westminster Hall in the very presence of Henry VI and enticed a Gray's Inn lawyer called Gyrkham away to the Tower (of which the duke was constable) and there retained him as his own servant.[196] Such treatment of one who seems to have been a legal officer of the Crown was hardly circumspect, and it roused the

[190] Dr. Harriss claims that the only achievement of York's second protectorate was the securing of Calais for the earl of Warwick. Harriss, *Eng. Hist. Rev.*, LXXV (1960), 30, 40–46.

[191] *C.Cl.R., 1454–61*, p. 109. His sureties included the duke of Buckingham, the earl of Oxford, Sir John Bourgchier, Lord Berners and Thomas, Lord Grey of Rugemont. The chronicle edited by Giles, (*Chronicon Angliae*, part 4, 47) seems to have confused the release of Exeter in 1455 and 1456, but this need not invalidate the fact that he was freed twice. Storey, *End of the House of Lancaster*, p. 253 note 17.

[192] Storey, *End of the House of Lancaster*, p. 149. Dr. Storey may be mistaken in thinking that Richard Percy also escaped, for on 14 May 1457 the duke of Exeter, the countess of Northumberland, Richard Belingham, and a number of others entered a £16,000 recognisance that he should remain in Newgate. *C.Cl.R., 1454–61*, p. 223.

[193] *C.Cl.R., 1454–61*, pp. 142–143; above, p. 340. Exeter at last secured the estates held in dower by his step-mother on 9 June 1458 after her death. *Complete Peerage*, v, 212–215.

[194] Flenley, *Six Town Chronicles*, p. 144; Wilkinson, *Constitutional History*, p. 100 note 3.

[195] Ramsay, *Lancaster and York*, ii, 202; *Complete Peerage*, v, 212–215.

[196] Trinity College, Dublin MS E. 5. 10 f. 193. The episode is also related, with unlikely embellishments, in a newsletter to the French king from the Burgundian court, to which Sir John Wenlock was an envoy. According to this, Exeter's action caused the ending of Parliament before the usual time, but no Parliament met between March 1456 and November 1459. Stevenson, *Wars of the English in France*, i, 367–368.

ire of the royal justices; within a year, Duke Henry found himself again in prison, this time in Berkhamstead castle.[197] His lack of tact, responsibility, and intelligence tended to isolate him politically, and this may account for his absence from the grand reconciliation of March 1458.

A settlement of the recent troubles had been achieved by the battle of St Albans. After a brief, partial resurgence of the defeated, in 1458 the king sought to arrange a general pacification, and the agreement of 23 March was reached between the leading magnates. York concluded a recognisance with the king of £10,000 for his past rebellions against, *inter alia*, the dowager-countess of Northumberland and her son, the earl, Lord Clifford, Lord Egremont, and Richard Percy, rebellions which must refer to his support of the Nevilles in their quarrel. Salisbury and Warwick did the same at 12,000 marks each, the former on behalf of his two sons, Thomas and John, who had spearheaded the Neville retaliation against the Percies in 1453–54. On the other side, both the earl and dowager-countess of Northumberland concluded a recognisance of 12,000 marks for all offences against York, Warwick, Salisbury, Sir Thomas, and Sir John Neville; whilst Clifford and Egremont each pledged themselves in 10,000 marks to the same group of magnates, and Ralph and Richard Percy in 2,000 marks each.[198] The atmosphere of reconciliation was conveyed to the populace of London by the theatrical "love-day" which followed on 25 March.[199] It was further agreed that Salisbury and his two sons should release Egremont from the bond of 16,800 marks by which he had been obligated in November 1454 to maintain the peace. His escape from Newgate had violated this pledge, but Salisbury and his sons now renounced any intention of taking action against the two sheriffs of London who were ultimately responsible for Egremont's custody. Instead, on 15 June 1458 Egremont obligated himself to Salisbury in 4,000 marks, payable if he failed to keep the peace towards the earl and his family during the next ten years. The March award also released from their obligations all those knights, esquires, and others, whether tenants or servants of the Percies, who had been obligated to York or the Nevilles to keep the peace.[200] The slate was wiped clean.

The violent history of the years since 1453 involving the Percies, the Nevilles, and the Duke of Exeter seemed to be closed. An epilogue of conciliation was added on 10 June 1458 when Egremont was granted the Yorkshire manor of Wressle, which had played such an unwitting role in precipitating the "battle" of Heworth.[201] Egremont himself promised to leave England, and a fortnight

---

[197] *C.Cl.R.*, *1454–61*, pp. 318–319, 350. Exeter was ordered to remain in Berkhamstead on 8 February 1459.

[198] *Ibid.*, pp. 292–293. The recognisance of May 1457, by which a number of people, led by Exeter, were made responsible for Richard Percy's continuance in prison, was cancelled on 24 March 1458 (*C.Cl.R.*, *1454–61*, p. 223). Ramsay implied that the agreements were prompted in part by the battle of Castleton in 1457, but this cannot now be upheld. Ramsay, *Lancaster and York*, II, 207–208.

[199] Ramsay, *Lancaster and York*, II, 209.

[200] H. T. Riley, ed., *Registrum Johannis de Whethamstede* (2 vols., Roll Series, 1872), I, 303–305; *C.Cl.R.*, *1454–61*, p. 306.

[201] *Complete Peerage*, v, 33–35; *C.P.R.*, *1452–61*, p. 428.

later the king gave him permission to go on pilgrimage.[202] But the general settlement, so painstakingly and pathetically effected by Henry VI, was a classic instance of "papering over the cracks." The hatreds of five years could not be erased so easily, nor the alliance of interests forgotten so quickly; when hostilities resumed in 1459, many on both sides found that their allegiances had been formed several years before on the plain of York.

* * * *

The Percy-Neville dispute was unusually crucial in the passage of events towards the outbreak of war. When it entered its most violent phase in 1453, it was still a northern feud between two rival houses whose history over the previous three-quarters of a century had made mutual hostility a way of life. But between the summer of 1453 and May 1455 their private disagreement was absorbed into the wider struggle for national, public objectives. The pitifully feeble government of Henry VI was starkly revealed by the political license of the north and by similar events in Wales and the West Country; although York was doubtless impelled by personal ambition to press his political claims, he may be fairly credited with a concern for better government. Out of his landed interest in Yorkshire, his family relationship with the Nevilles, and the latter's willingness to break with the Court was forged a political alliance in the winter of 1453–54 which could forward York's aims and assist the Nevilles in their quarrel with the Percies. But personal, territorial grievances and public, political resentments were not a monopoly of Duke Richard, for at this very time Exeter, too, may have been swayed by them. His bitter quarrel with Cromwell and his jealousy of York's achievement of political power propelled him towards an alliance with the Percies. By the spring of 1454 Exeter and the Percies were ranged against York and the Nevilles, and the Yorkshire feuds of past generations had fused into the newer struggle to reform or control Lancastrian kingship.

It is remarkable how rigid remained some of the allegiances contracted in the private violence of 1453–54 and earlier. At St Albans in May 1455 it is not surprising to find in the king's entourage Northumberland, Lord Clifford, Lord de Roos, and Sir William Lucy.[203] Moreover, Sir Ralph Percy was immediately denounced by the Yorkists as one of those primarily responsible for the battle, and Sir John Stapleton, another Percy adherent, died on 27 May 1455, possibly as a result of the battle five days before.[204] The loyalties of some magnates lasted

---

[202] *Ibid.*, p. 428. The connection between Egremont and Exeter survived these years, for on 10 April 1460 Egremont engineered the arrest, by a warrant under Exeter's seal as admiral of England, of a Scarborough merchant who claimed to have been an adherent of the earl of Salisbury. The merchant, John Robynson, was detained in Egremont's castle of Wressle for six weeks until he agreed to pay £50. P.R.O., Early Chancery Proceedings, 1/27/250.

[203] Armstrong, *Bull. Inst. His. Res.*, xxxiii (1960), 65 and note 3. William Percy, bishop of Carlisle and Northumberland's son, was the only bishop at St Albans, and he fled after the defeat of the royalists. *Ibid.*, pp. 21, 48.

[204] *Ibid.*, p. 57; P.R.O., Exchequer, Escheators' Accounts, 60/7; above, p. 332. Richard Belingham, another Percy sympathiser, was pardoned on 16 September 1455, possibly for his royalist activities. Wedgwood, *History of Parliament, Biographies*, p. 63.

even longer. Viscount Beaumont, who had been associated with the Percies in the winter of 1453–54, was in the forefront of those urging the king to proscribe the Yorkist lords after Ludford Bridge in November 1459, and he was rewarded for his services against York, Salisbury, and Warwick on 19 December.[205] He fell at Northampton in July 1460 on the royal side, together with Lord Egremont, the most tenacious of the Percy brood, and Sir William Lucy, who was struck down by servants of John Stafford who "lovyd that knyght ys wyffe and hatyd hym, and a-non causyd hys dethe."[206] In the same year, on 23 May, Sir John Penning-ton, long a Percy retainer, was granted that part of the Cumberland lordship of Egremont which Salisbury had forfeited after Ludford Bridge; he was pardoned as a Lancastrian in 1462.[207] A month later, during the last weeks of Lancastrian rule, Richard Aldburgh was placed on the commission of peace for the north riding for the first time; his allegiance to the Percies had evidently stood the test of time.[208]

The confusing events of the next eighteen months enveloped other north countrymen previously identified with the Percy house. On 24 August 1460 a commission, which included York, Salisbury, and Warwick, was ordered to arrest a number of Yorkshiremen who had uttered "falsehoods to arouse discords among the magnates of the realm." They included two Percy supporters, John Estall and William Vessy, merchant, both of York; whilst John Caterall, a gentleman of Selby, may have been none other than the troublesome Percy re-tainer from Brayton in Craven.[209] At Wakefield in December 1460, when York met his death, a number of Northumberland's Yorkshire adherents were present: Sir Henry Belingham, John Caterall of Brayton, Thomas Frysell of York, John Smothing of York, as well as the earl himself.[210] Indeed, Sir Henry Belingham, Robert Belingham, and John Smothing also took part in the battle of Towton in March 1461 with Northumberland, Clifford, and de Roos; unlike the earl, Sir Henry lived to encourage Queen Margaret and Prince Edward to join the Scots in an attack on Carlisle and himself to take part in the defence of Harlech in 1468.[211] In 1462 William Lee displayed his firm adherence to the house of Lan-caster through his Percy connection: on 5 February he was pardoned by Edward

---

[205] J. R. Lander, *The Wars of the Roses* (1965), p. 96; *C.P.R., 1452–61*, p. 533; above, p. 337.

[206] Wilkinson, *Constitutional History*, pp. 105–106; J. Gairdner, ed., *Historical Collections of a London Citizen* (Camden Series, 1876), p. 207; Stevenson, *Wars of the English in France*, II, part 2, 773.

[207] *C.P.R., 1452–61*, p. 587; Wedgwood, *History of Parliament, Biographies*, p. 675. In December 1459 he was placed on the Cumberland commission to resist the Yorkist lords. *C.P.R., 1452–61*, p. 560.

[208] *Ibid.*, p. 683 (25 June 1460); above, p. 324.

[209] *C.P.R., 1452–61*, p. 608; P.R.O., K.B., Anc. Indict., 149/11/16, 9/8; above, p. 334.

[210] They were all attainted for their part in the battle. *Rot. Parl.*, v, 477; above, p. 332.

[211] *Rot. Parl.*, v, 477–478; J. R. Lander, "Attainder and Forfeiture, 1453–1509," *The Historical Journal*, IV, no. 2 (1961), 125 and note 33. The duke of Exeter and his illegitimate brother, William, also fought for the king at Towton (*Rot. Parl.* v, 477–478). Another who fought and died in the battle was John Carlele of Newcastle, a Percy annuitant since 1443 (Wedgwood, *History of Parliament, Biographies*, p. 157; above, p. 336).

IV but almost immediately had a price of £100 placed on his head; before the month was out he had been captured and was executed on St David's day.[212]

Close blood relationships in the disputes of the 1450's proved as hard a cement as the bond between lord and retainer. Northumberland's cause was ably prosecuted by his sons, especially Egremont; Sir Thomas and Sir John Neville bore the brunt of Neville defence on behalf of their father, and Exeter was followed by his two bastard brothers. Marriage relationships were more tenuous: they could bind York closer to Salisbury, but another of the latter's sisters was married to Northumberland (d.1455). Moreover, Neville disunity enabled Earl Ralph of Westmorland (d.1484) to marry Henry Hotspur's daughter, and his brother, John, Lord Neville to die for Lancaster in 1461.

It is a mistake to conclude that feuds such as that between Percy and Neville could cause the Wars of the Roses. The Wars were not simply "the outcome of an escalation of private feuds," and it is unlikely that "the decision to take up arms in the spring of 1455 may have proceeded from them (the Nevilles), for having on their hands the feud with Thomas Percy Lord Egremont they may have thought that the time to strike was before the recently liberated Exeter could lend them further aid."[213] Nevertheless, one or two contemporaries regarded the feud as a crucial element in this very complex conflict. The Latin annalist declared unequivocally that the "battle" of Heworth in August 1453 was the beginning of the ensuing struggle: *initium fuit maximorum dolorum in Anglia.*[214] Moreover, immediately after St Albans in May 1455, when the victorious Yorkists sought a suitable culprit on whom to fasten blame for a "battle" in which the king had been wounded, they lighted at first upon Sir Ralph Percy, Northumberland's younger son, and Lord Clifford, both members of the Percy faction in the north.[215] Several weeks later, a quarrel blew up between Cromwell and Warwick over responsibility for the "battle"; Cromwell tried to excuse himself of all connection with it, but Warwick swore to the king that it was Cromwell who was the "begynner of all that journey at Seynt Albones."[216] This might seem strange indeed in view of the fact that Cromwell arrived at St Albans when the battle was practically over,[217] but if Warwick, who could draw upon intimate knowledge of the Percy-Neville dispute, was referring to Cromwell's part in the territorial jealousies of the Percies, Nevilles and Exeter in 1453–54, then Cromwell might well assume some responsibility for later events. His loyalty to the Lancastrians, to whom he owed so much, and his more recent affiliations with York and the Nevilles may have made him delay his arrival in the streets of St Albans.

---

[212] Wedgwood, *History of Parliament, Biographies*, p. 532.

[213] Storey, *End of the House of Lancaster*, p. 27; Armstrong, *Bull. Inst. Hist. Res.*, xxxiii (1960), 11.

[214] Stevenson, *Wars of the English in France*, ii, part 2, 770.

[215] Armstrong, *Bull. Inst. Hist. Res.*, xxxiii (1960), 57. Short of Northumberland himself, the other most suitable candidates would have been Egremont and Richard Percy, but they were in prison during the battle.

[216] Gairdner, *Paston Letters*, i, 345; Armstrong, *Bull. Inst. Hist. Res.*, xxxiii (1960), 58–59.

[217] *Ibid.*, p. 18; Gairdner, *Paston Letters*, iii, 30.

It distorts the picture of mid-fifteenth-century England to distinguish too sharply between violent outbreaks such as those in Yorkshire, Wales, the West Country, and East Anglia and the battles which took place from 1455 onwards involving the person of the king himself. It was the disintegration of public order, of which the former were the most glaring symptom, which made the latter inevitable. It was, equally, the personal enmities displayed in local violence which frequently determined the alignment of the warring parties, bringing magnates and gentlemen alongside Henry VI or Duke Richard in 1455 and later. St Albans was the first battle of the mid-fifteenth century in which the king himself was involved, but it did not mark the beginning of the Wars of the Roses: the credentials of Heworth, Stamford Bridge, and the struggle for the city of York merit scrutiny.

[Particular aspects of Lord Cromwell's position in the 1450s are illuminated by Rhoda L. Friedrichs, 'Ralph, Lord Cromwell and the politics of fifteenth-century England', *Nottingham Medieval Studies*, XXXII (1988), 1-21, and S.J. Payling, 'The Ampthill Dispute: a study in aristocratic lawlessness and the breakdown of Lancastrian Government', *English Historical Rev.*, CIV (1989), 881-907. A.J. Pollard, 'The Northern Retainers of Richard Nevill, Earl of Salisbury', *Northern History*, XI (1976), 52-69, is revealing of the Neville retinue, if a few years later. And B.P. Wolffe, *Henry VI* (London, 1981), Ralph A. Griffiths, *The Reign of King Henry VI* (London, 1981), and P.A. Johnson, *Duke Richard of York, 1411-1460* (Oxford, 1988), provide valuable context from differing standpoints.]

21

The Hazards of Civil War: The Mountford Family and the Wars of the Roses

Kin, property and civil commotion were elements central to the fortunes of every magnate house in mid-15th-century England and of not a few gentry families too. Kinship ties, with their concords and disagreements, were frequently at the heart of the social and political attitudes of the nobility in this period, as the Nevilles demonstrated by their divisions and the Herberts and Wydevilles by their solidarity. Property lay at the root of wealth, reputation and influence which none could afford to relinquish, and it was 'just as likely to divide families as to unite them'. In relation to the mid-15th-century, Professor Lander has concluded that 'Inheritance, jointure and other settlement disputes were at this time the most fertile source of long-embittered quarrels'.[1] The wranglings among the descendants of Ralph, earl of Westmorland (d.1425), as well as a multitude of other disputes, make this self-evident. Civil strife could draw kinsmen together as nothing else could in the protection of their friends, relatives, influence and possessions, as anyone who encountered the Herbert-Vaughan axis in south-east Wales could testify; equally, it could place at opposite poles relatives who were already antagonistic towards one another for other reasons (including quarrels over property).

The Mountfords of Warwickshire,[2] a gentry family which had links with several magnate lines, exemplify the importance of these factors during the late-Lancastrian and Yorkist periods. The five documents printed below make comprehensible some of the crucial stages in the family's fortunes during a period of rapid dynastic change and bitter aristocratic rivalries in Warwickshire and elsewhere; at the same time they hold an incidental interest for the student of parliamentary business in Edward IV's reign.[3] They were probably all at one time among the archives of the Mountford family, and certainly the two which Sir William Dugdale published in 1656

1. J.R. Lander, 'Marriage and Politics in the Fifteenth Century: the Nevilles and the Wydevilles', in *Crown and Nobility, 1450–1509* (London, 1976), 97 (originally published in *Bulletin of the Institute of Historical Research*, XXXV (1963)), for the two quotations.
2. The spelling 'Mountford' is here preferred, although contemporaries also used 'Mountfort'; they did not refer to the family as 'Montfort', as later commentators have done.
3. Birmingham Public Library, A 590–92; W. Dugdale, *The Antiquities of Warwickshire*, 2nd. edn. (2 vols., London 1730), II, 1010–11. M.C. Carpenter, 'Political Society in Warwickshire, c.1401–72' (unpublished University of Cambridge Ph.D. thesis, 1976), provides a detailed, sophisticated study of aristocratic affinities in the county.

were still in the possession of Simon Mountford of Staffordshire at that time.

Since before 1399, the Mountfords of Coleshill (Warwickshire) had served the house of Lancaster with conspicuous fidelity. Sir Baldwin Mountford died in Spain in 1386 whence he had travelled with John of Gaunt to press the latter's claim to the throne of Castile.[4] His eldest surviving son and heir, William Mountford, who had been born the previous year, took at least as notable a part in the military enterprises of the Lancastrian kings, usually in the company of Richard Beauchamp, earl of Warwick and the most prominent of Warwickshire landowners; William, in fact, was related to the earl, acted as his feoffee and served as an executor of his widow, Isabelle. After his return from France in 1422, he played an active part in local politics and administration as a Beauchamp client, and was eventually knighted for his loyal and constant service. He came from a substantial family, and his mother in particular was well-connected, being a daughter of John, Lord Clinton. William enhanced his Warwickshire position by marrying Margaret, the daughter and heiress of Sir John Pecche of Hampton-in-Arden. It was a successful saga, if unexceptional in its essentials; but it made of William by 1436 the wealthiest landowner in Warwickshire below the ranks of the barons.[5] Two of his most valuable properties were the manors of Coleshill and Ilmington.

By comparison, little is known of William's son Baldwin, except that he married Anne, daughter and ultimate heiress (after the death of her brother) of Robert Blanchmains, and shared in a modest part of his father's estate during Sir William's lifetime.[6] In Warwickshire he maintained the family's tradition of service by become a life-annuitant of Richard Neville, now earl of Warwick and the husband of the Beauchamp heiress, by January 1451.[7] The frequent assumption that Sir Baldwin II died in 1458 is evidently mistaken, as the evidence of the petitions below demonstrates; in fact, a writ *diem clausit extremum* was not issued following his death until 10 February 1475.[8] Yet the way in which the petitions below record the fight to protect the landed rights of Sir Baldwin's son, Simon, with (it seems) the passive assent and participation of Sir Baldwin himself, might reflect some incapacity on the part of the father or a

4. J.S. Roskell, *The Commons in the Parliament of 1422* (Manchester, 1954), 204–5 (a biographical note on Sir William Mountford). For a pedigree of the family, see Dugdale, *Antiquities*, II, 1007–8.

5. Roskell, *Commons*, 204–5; J.C. Wedgwood, *History of Parliament: Biographies of the Members of the Commons House, 1439–1509* (London, 1936), 604. Dr. Carpenter, thesis cited, appendix, 103, 110, provides further indications of Sir William's Beauchamp connection and his Crown service.

6. Wedgwood, *Biographies*, 603; Roskell, *Commons*, 204–5. Baldwin resided at Hampton-in-Arden. According to Dr. Carpenter (thesis cited, appendix, 122), he was married to Joan, sister of Sir Richard Vernon of Derbyshire, perhaps as his second wife.

7. *Ibid.*, appendix, 112.

8. *Calendar of Fine Rolls, 1471–85*, 83. See Wedgwood, *Biographies*, 603, for the erroneous date of his death.

disinclination to become engaged in bitter property disputes.[9] In June 1454, eighteen months after he had succeeded his father, Baldwin conveyed his rights in Ilmington to Simon and Richard Neville, earl of Warwick, the countess of Warwick and several others; two years after that, he contemplated transferring his claim to the manor of Coleshill to Simon as well (though this transaction was never, in fact, completed). Sir Baldwin may, indeed, have been preoccupied with other matters, for he decided to enter holy orders about 1460-61.[10]

Sir William Mountford sired another son, this time by his second wife. This son, Edmund, extended the tradition of Lancastrian service which had marked the family to date.[11] By July 1444 he had become one of the king's esquires and ten years later a server in the royal Household. A few years after that, he is encountered as King Henry VI's carver, a position he still occupied at the time of Henry's deposition in March 1461. Edmund's more local service in the midlands was consonant with family expectations and his own social position: he represented Warwickshire in the parliaments of 1447 and (at Coventry, where the duke of York and his collaborators were attainted) of 1459; by August 1459 he had been knighted. His steadfast loyalty to King Henry extended even to battle at Towton on 29 March 1461, as a result of which he was attainted by Edward IV and fled in the company of the deposed king and his queen, Margaret of Anjou.[12]

This was a common enough family story among gentry whom the Lancastrians patronised in war and peace. Even the firm attachment of Sir Edmund to his king after 1461 was shown by others. Less common were the tensions which arose in the Mountford family during the later years of King Henry's reign — tensions which embraced the principal Warwickshire magnates and their affinities, and exacerbated the personal and political rivalries that marred the closing decade of the reign.[13] Sir William Mountford had married twice, on the second occasion about 1420 a Breton lady, Jane (or Joan) Alderwich.[14] This second marriage in the event released a

9. Below 377-81.

10. *Calendar of Close Rolls, 1456–61*, 429, 186; Dugdale, *Antiquities*, II, 1011.

11. Wedgwood, *Biographies*, 602–3, with additional details in R.S. Thomas, 'The Political Career, Estates and "Connection" of Jasper Tudor, Earl of Pembroke and Duke of Bedford (d.1495)' (unpublished University of Wales Ph.D. thesis, 1971), 269; and T.B. Pugh (ed.), *The Marcher Lordships of South Wales, 1415–1536* (Cardiff, 1963), 295.

12. In 1459, when the Yorkist lords were assembling at Ludlow to confront the king, Henry VI was staying at Coleshill, Sir Edmund's manor: J.S. Davies (ed.), *An English Chronicle* (Camden Society, 1856), 80.

13. Some features of this family quarrel have been dealt with by Dugdale, *Antiquities*, II, 1010–12; and recently by Carpenter, thesis cited, and C. Rawcliffe, *The Staffords, Earls of Stafford and Dukes of Buckingham, 1394–1521* (Cambridge, 1978), 79–80.

14. After her husband's death in December 1452, she secured her position in England as an alien by taking out letters of denizenship on 22 January 1453: *Calendar of Patent Rolls, 1452–61*, 49. She also acquired the Mountfort manor of Ramenham (Berkshire) as dower: C.Rawcliffe, 'The Staffords, Earls of Stafford and Dukes of Buckingham, 1394–

fountain of resentment on the part of the eldest son of the first of William's marriages, Sir Baldwin II, against the son of the second, Sir Edmund. Before William's death in 1452, Jane and her son Edmund had induced him to enfeoff the Warwickshire manors of Coleshill and Ilmington to himself and his second wife jointly and to the heirs of their bodies, the first of whom was Edmund. This involved disinheriting the children of the first marriage, most notably Sir Baldwin Mountford and his son Simon. It was later claimed that on several occasions Sir William had tried to secure parliamentary approval of this re-arrangement of the Mountford inheritance, apparently without success, although Sir William's action was quite legal in common law. When Sir William died, Jane and Edmund were executors of his will, and they took steps to buttress further the mother's jointure and the son's inheritance: they enfeoffed two influential magnates in the king's favour with the manors, presumably to the use of Jane, Edmund and the latter's heirs. These magnates, Humphrey Stafford, duke of Buckingham, to whom the Mountfords were distantly related, and James Ormond, earl of Wiltshire, provided necessary protection by their reputation and influence nationally and as influential Warwickshire landowners. Should Edmund have no heirs, then the inheritance would revert to Buckingham himself and to his descendants. They embarked on a series of law suits in order to make Edmund's claims to the properties water-tight, while the interests of Edmund had been made more secure by the nomination of Buckingham to head the commission appointed in December 1452 to establish what estates Sir William had left and who was his heir.[15] The prominence of these magnates at King Henry's court, it was later maintained, enabled them to override the claims of Sir Baldwin II and his son Simon.[16] Although the latter were retained by Richard Neville, earl of Warwick, an equally prominent local magnate – Baldwin by January 1451 and his son by 1456–57 – Warwick was far from being the dominant figure in the shire his father-in-law had been; rather did this involvement of two powerful affinities in the Mountford family quarrel deepen the political and social divisions in the county at

1521' (unpublished University of Sheffield Ph.D. thesis, 1974), 332 n.112, based on Westminster Abbey MSS. 4532, 4542, 4555. Jane appears to have been previously married to one of the Brokesbys of Sewalby (Leicestershire), and her descendant, William, son and heir of Henry Brokesby, quitclaimed his right to Ramenham on 20 November 1478: *Calendar of Ancient Deeds*, VI, 209; Carpenter, thesis cited, appendix, 122; Westminster Abbey MSS. 4540, 4543.

15. *C.P.R., 1452–61*, 58; Dugdale, *Antiquities*, II, 1010. For Sir William's executors, see Lambeth Palace Library, Register of John Kemp, f.302, in which none of his older children is mentioned. It seems likely that Sir Edmund was also able to establish himself as the ultimate heir of his grandmother's family, the Clintons, after Sir William Mountford's death: *C.P.R., 1452–61*, 592.

16. Below 377. As a widow after 1452, Jane Mountford may have been a ward of the duke of Buckingham: *C.C.R., 1468–76*, 367.

large.[17]   Such diversions of property away from the common law heirs to other relatives were more likely than not to cause friction. Similar manoeuvres in another family, that of the Nevilles themselves, had produced private war and bitter argument somewhat earlier in the reign.[18]   Indeed, it is possible that his own and his father's successful experience at that time prompted Warwick to take as much initiative in espousing Baldwin's cause, at a time when the earl was anxious to recreate the Warwickshire affinity of his Beauchamp father-in-law in the face of competition from Buckingham and Wiltshire, as did Baldwin Mountford in seeking the earl's favour.

Sir William Mountford's decision to advance the interests of his younger son Edmund could not fail to cause consternation and resentment among members of the older branch of the Mountfords, who could be relied upon to avail themselves of any opportunity to recover what they regarded as their rightful inheritance. Such an opportunity presented itself during the increasing polarisation of political attitudes in late-Lancastrian England.   The death of Sir William Mountford on 6 December 1452 put into effect his dispositions in favour of his wife and younger son, and it precipitated a demonstration of resentment by Baldwin Mountford and his son, Simon, which was initially conducted in the courts but by the beginning of 1454 had degenerated into violence.   By the end of July, Baldwin was in possession of both Ilmington and Coleshill.[19]   This turn of events aggravated the already tense relations between, on the one hand, Warwick, his father Salisbury and their kinsman, Richard, duke of York, and, on the other, Buckingham, Wiltshire and their confederate, Edmund, duke of Somerset. During the autumn of 1453, similar, though more significant, disputes in other parts of the realm -- particularly in Yorkshire and Glamorgan -- were hardening the opposing political attitudes of these two groups of powerful magnates and their affinities.[20]   Moreover, in the following spring of 1454, Baldwin's Neville patrons achieved greater power in the realm during the protectorate of the duke of York and the illness of the distracted king.   The course of the Warwickshire quarrel among the Mountfords was henceforward largely determined by these wider considerations.

First, however, the common device of arbitration was employed to settle the family quarrel and remove a potential cause of serious disorder in the midlands.   At some point after April 1454, but

---

17. Carpenter, thesis cited, 148, 152, 170; appendix, 112. Baldwin may have become Warwick's annuitant in January 1451 precisely because his father was contemplating disinheriting him with Buckingham's assistance: *ibid.*, 198 n.5.

18. Lander, *Crown and Nobility*, 97–98, 111, 112.

19. Carpenter, thesis cited, 206–11.

20. R.A. Griffiths, 'Local Rivalries and National Politics: the Percies, the Nevilles and the Duke of Exeter, 1452–1455', *Speculum*, XLIII (1968), 589–632, and especially 605 and n.84. See above ch. 20, and especially 337 and n. 84.

prior to 1458, a group of highly influential lords acceptable to both parties — Archbishop Thomas Bourgchier of Canterbury, the duke of York, the earls of Salisbury and Worcester, and Viscount Bourgchier — undertook to arbitrate.[21]   Perhaps the most likely occasion for this panel's nomination arose when Richard, duke of York governed England as protector of the realm in 1454. The duke had been made protector on 27 March, Salisbury became chancellor of England on 2 April, Worcester had been treasurer since 1452, and Bourgchier was provided to the see of Canterbury after the death of Archbishop Kemp on 22 March 1454. The two Bourgchiers were half-brothers of Edmund Mountford's patron, the duke of Buckingham, while Salisbury was the father of Richard Neville, earl of Warwick, with whom Sir Baldwin Mountford was currently connected.[22]   Furthermore, an enfeoffment concluded by Sir Baldwin on 26 July 1454 was never in fact implemented, possibly because the arbitration had supervened.[23]   The decision of the arbiters was designed to satisfy the demands of both sides by dividing the Mountford property between them. Coleshill was awarded to the duke of Buckingham as Edmund's feoffee, whereas Baldwin's claim to Ilmington was confirmed.[24]   Simon Mountford undertook to act peaceably towards his uncle Edmund and his grandmother Joan, and he concluded a bond worth £1,000 with Buckingham to this end. The protector's personal role in this attempt to bring peace to the Warwickshire countryside may be regarded as one further example of his serious endeavour to pacify England during his months of power.[25]   Yet, the enfeebled authority of Lancastrian government by the mid-1450s and the irresponsibility of lordly maintenance are demonstrated by the ease with which these arrangements were violently upset, despite the weighty reputation of the magnates who made them. Within a few years, Buckingham himself had violated the arbitration's terms in the interests of his protégé, Edmund Mountford.

Sir Edmund Mountford was a personal servant of Henry VI and among his feoffees were two of the most powerful Lancastrian

---

21. Dugdale noted the arbitration; he is the only source to do so and probably obtained his information on this, as on other matters, from the Mountford family archives: *Antiquities*, II, 1010.

22. Below n.26.

23. *C.C.R., 1454–61*, 186. Dugdale, *Antiquities*, II, 1010, suggested that the arbitration took place after Baldwin had been threatened in order to induce him to surrender his claims to Edmund Mountford and his feoffees. This may be so, although it is unlikely to be a reference to the capture of Baldwin and his son Simon by the duke of Buckingham which probably occurred later. Dr. Carpenter (thesis cited, 212) favours the period 21 June 1454 – October 1456 for the arbitration, although Rawcliffe, thesis cited, 332-3, adopts Dugdale's chronology.

24. On 30 June 1454 Sir Baldwin quitclaimed his rights in Ramenham manor to Buckingham, Wiltshire and Buckingham's eldest son, presumably as feoffees for Sir Edmund Mountford and possibly as part of the arbitration arrangement. Jane Mountford had already made a similar grant in favour of her son on 31 May. Westminster Abbey MSS. 4538, 4541.

25. Griffiths, *Speculum*, XLIII (1968), 609–10. Above 341-42.

magnates, Buckingham and Wiltshire. Simon Mountford (his father appears to be a retiring figure in the late-1450s) was far less closely connected with the Lancastrian régime and by 1456—57 was, like Sir Baldwin, in the service of Richard Neville, earl of Warwick, who, apart from being at odds with Buckingham and Wiltshire in Warwickshire, was one of the few major figures at that time strongly opposed to the government of Henry VI.[26] It is even likely that this link with Warwick was exploited by Simon in order to acquire influential patronage as a protection against his kinsman, Edmund, who could rely on the support of the king himself. Such demonstrations of personal allegiance were being made at this time by other men, including Warwick himself in the Neville-Percy dispute in Yorkshire and in south Wales. In Simon Mountford's case, membership of a magnate affinity brought little immediate benefit, if only because Warwick spent most of the last four years of Henry VI's reign, from October 1456, outside the realm in Calais.[27] Simon accordingly found himself in captivity at Gloucester Castle after efforts by Buckingham, Wiltshire and Edmund Mountford had failed to induce him to surrender his claim to Coleshill and Ilmington like his less stubborn father, Sir Baldwin II.[28] But by November 1458, he too had given way, after resisting the blandishments of Edmund and his high-born allies for almost two years longer than his own father.[29] Of such material were political and personal attitudes formed in the mid-15th century. The dispute may ultimately have inclined Simon to the Yorkist side when noblemen could no longer avoid the crucial political decision in 1460—61 if they wished to protect their possessions or, in a new reign, regain what they had lost. This latter prospect opened before Simon Mountford after 4 March 1461.

The accession of Edward IV had important consequences for the Mountford family, and for the fortunes of Sir Edmund and Simon

26. Roskell, *Commons*, 205. Sir Baldwin had been in touch with Warwick, the son-in-law of his father's patron, as early as 1451, and in July 1454 he had planned to engage Warwick, the earl of March (later King Edward IV) and Jasper, earl of Pembroke as his residual legatees at Coleshill. In December 1456 there were rumours that Sir Baldwin was about to enlist the services of Warwick as a feoffee to use: *C.C.R., 1454—61*, 186, 429. As late as October 1470, when Warwick had put Edward IV to flight and placed Henry VI on the throne once more, the earl could still describe Sir Simon Mountford as his 'right trusty and well-beloved friend' whose interests he cared for: *Historical Manuscripts Commission*, XI (1887), part iii, 113.

27. Carpenter, thesis cited, 214—15.

28. By 11 December 1456, after he had been imprisoned for a fortnight at Coventry and then in Buckingham's own castle at Maxstoke, Sir Baldwin was induced to grant Ilmington to Edmund and to enfeoff Buckingham, Wiltshire and others with Coleshill: below 379; *C.C.R., 1454—61*, 185—86, 365. Other manors were similarly enfeoffed shortly afterwards: Kingshurst, Kingsford and Ullenhall (Warwickshire) and Ramenham (Berkshire): *ibid.*, 364.

29. *Ibid.*, 429. Simon was already immured in Gloucester castle in February and July 1457: Carpenter, thesis cited, 215. On 1 March 1459 he quitclaimed the family's Berkshire manor of Ramenham to Sir Edmund: Westminster Abbey MSS. 4537, 4544.

in particular.   Sir Baldwin II and his son later claimed that shortly
before Edmund retreated northwards with the defeated Queen
Margaret in 1461, he had been 'moved in conscience' to restore the
Warwickshire manors to the original heir at common law, Simon
Mountford, with the full agreement of his father, Sir Baldwin, who
was still alive.[30]   Such twinges of conscience were perhaps possible
in the 15th century.   Alternatively, Sir Edmund may genuinely
have feared for the ultimate fate of the Mountford inheritance if he
did not arrange for the manors to revert to his step-brother's line
now that he, a bachelor, was going into exile; they might otherwise
fall into the hands of the new Yorkist king and be granted to one of
his devoted followers.   A whit more likely is the proposition that
Sir Edmund's conscience did duty as a respectable justification for
the request by Sir Baldwin II and his son that the two estates should
be restored to them after the attainder of Edmund in the parliament
of November 1461.[31]   Whatever the reason, it was claimed by Sir
Baldwin and his son that Edmund had re-enfeoffed Simon with the
manors with Baldwin's assent, and had induced several of his original
feoffees (of whom Buckingham and his son were now conveniently
dead) to do the same.[32]   This re-enfeoffment probably took place
sometime after the Yorkist lords seized power following the battle
of Northampton on 10 July 1460 (when Buckingham was slain).
Sir Baldwin took the precaution of enfeoffing Edward, earl of
March (later King Edward IV) and the earl of Warwick with the
two manors on his and his son's behalf, before Simon was allowed
to take possession of the two manors shortly afterwards.   So sharp
had the political and personal differences within the Mountford
family become.[33]

   In the circumstances, it is scarcely surprising that Simon Mountford proved Yorkist in his sympathies after 1461; hence the petition
presented by himself and his father to the Commons in Edward IV's
first parliament.   This asked that all enfeoffments devised by Jane
and Edmund after Sir William Mountford's death in 1452 should be
declared null and void, except that made by Sir Edmund himself
in favour of Simon on the eve of his flight to the north.   There is no
sign of this petition on the extant parliament rolls of Edward IV's
reign, but it was almost certainly successful.   It survives in engrossed
form in an official court hand of the early years of Edward IV's
reign — presumably dating from the first available parliament, that
of November 1461.[34]   Indeed, it seems likely that this very petition
was the basis of a proviso attached to the act of attainder which,

   30. *C.P.R., 1461–67*, 51.
   31. Below 377-8). For the attainder, see *Rotuli Parliamentorum*, VI, 476 *et seq.*
   32. Buckingham had been killed at Northampton on 10 July 1460; his son was
already dead, and Wiltshire was executed soon after the battle of Towton (29 March 1461).
   33. *C.P.R., 1461–67*, 51.
   34. The petition is likely to have been presented at the earliest opportunity, namely,
in the first parliament of the reign (4 November 1461–6 May 1462). It was not presented
at Henry VI's parliament of the Readeption (1470–71), and is hardly likely to have been

inter alia, attainted Sir Edmund Mountford in November 1461. This proviso admittedly does not appear on the printed parliament roll, but a copy of it was still among the Mountford family archives in the 17th century and was used by Dugdale.[35]

Sir Simon Mountford, it is true, was involved in a personal dispute with one of Warwick's retainers from 1462 which resulted in treasonable activity in the summer of 1465 in association with his own father-in-law, Sir Richard Verney; but on 25 November 1466 he was fully pardoned and thereafter served regularly as a J.P. and commissioner in Warwickshire. In November 1469 he entered the service of William, Lord Hastings, Edward IV's chamberlain and friend, at a critical moment for the Yorkist monarchy's survival; but with the readeption of Henry VI, he was removed from the justices' bench, as were many other good Yorkist gentlemen.[36]

Simon and his father had cause to be apprehensive of the return of King Henry VI on 3 October 1470. Sir Baldwin was now an elderly gentleman-turned-priest ('in my last dayes', he described himself early in 1471), but Simon, for all his links with Warwick the Kingmaker, might be much more vulnerable as a retainer of Lord Hastings. Moreover, it was evidently anticipated that Sir Edmund Mountford would return to England and take advantage of the recent turn of events to lay claim to the Mountford inheritance he had forfeited in 1461. Therefore, at Hampton-in-Arden (Warws.) on 10 January 1471, Sir Baldwin declared in detail his own and his son's just claims to Coleshill, Ilmington, Ramenham and all other Mountford properties. He publicly affirmed what had been made clear to parliament in 1461, namely, that he and Simon had surrendered their hereditary rights only under the weight of Buckingham's threats and compulsion, 'which in thoo days had byn too hevy and too importable for me or my seid son to have boren'.[37] He now appealed 'To all true Cristen pepull' (with a special eye, it may be conjectured, on the Warwickshire gentry) for support in maintaining his title to the manors as duly entailed to him and his heirs, even though Sir Edmund seems still to have had the relevant

---

submitted in the 1472–75 parliament which probably saw Sir Edmund's attainder reversed (below 377-8). The parliament of 1467–68 met rather soon after the accusations of treason against Sir Simon in 1465–66 (for which, see above). This leaves the parliaments of 1461–62 and 1463–65; a preference for the earlier one is reasonable, especially in view of the phrase in (I).

35. Below 379. Dugdale was mistaken (*Antiquities*, II, 1010–11) in believing that this proviso was attached to an act of attainder passed against the late duke of Buckingham, who was never attainted. Apart from the indications of its intention, the proviso can be dated to 1461 by incidental internal evidence: Henry VI was no longer king (he had been replaced on 4 March 1461) but Simon Mountford had not yet been knighted (which had happened by 1462). Wedgwood, *Biographies*, 603.

36. *Ibid.*; Carpenter, thesis cited, 232–42; W.H. Dunham, *Lord Hastings' Indentured Retainers, 1461–1483* (New Haven, 1955), 40, 48–49, 124–25. It should be noted that Simon retained Warwick's favour even during the readeption of Henry VI: above n.26.

37. Below 379-81. Baldwin was about sixty years of age in 1471: Dugdale, *Antiquities*, II, 1010. Edmund was certainly in England by March 1471: below n.41.

deeds in his possession.[38]   Should Edmund's attainder be reversed
by the restored régime of Henry VI in 1471, Baldwin was determined
to ensure that the Mountford inheritance would remain with his own
heirs by virtue of prior entailments which the attainder of 1461
had simply reinforced.   In the event, the declaration at Hampton-
in-Arden proved unnecessary.   Henry VI was soon dethroned once
again, on 11 April 1471, before his parliament could undo the work
of its predecessor of 1461.   For a further period, therefore, Sir
Simon Mountford remained in possession of Coleshill and Ilmington.
After 1471 his local administrative service proceeded uninterruptedly
during the remainder of the Yorkist period, whilst in 1475 he accompanied the king on his expedition to France.   He even reconciled
himself to the new Tudor régime until, in 1495, he was arrested for
complicity in the Perkin Warbeck rebellion and beheaded.[39]

Simon's fall may not have been unconnected with Sir Edmund
Mountford, for whom the reign of Henry VII was a hey-day.
Edmund had followed Henry VI and Queen Margaret into exile
after Towton, and thereafter took part in Lancastrian raids from
Scotland into northern England; he travelled with Margaret to Tours
in June 1462 for the sealing of her treaty with Louis XI, and he
sailed with her small court to Sluys in August 1463. After escaping
from the skirmish at Hexham in 1464, he became a political refugee
at the château of Margaret's father at St. Mighiel in Bar.[40]

It has been generally thought that Sir Edmund did not return to
England until Henry Tudor landed in Pembrokeshire in 1485, but
more recent work has revealed that he was back in the realm and
evidently leading the life of a loyal gentleman by 1475.[41]   What
has hitherto remained concealed is when he reconciled himself to
Edward IV and how he achieved it.   It is well known that the king
was frequently ready to receive erstwhile Lancastrians into his
favour, not least after the final collapse of their cause in 1471
with the death of Prince Edward and the capture of the Lancastrian
queen.[42]   It was probably at that point that Sir Edmund Mountford
felt it wise to reach an accommodation with King Edward.   The
parliament of 1472–75 (and probably its earlier sessions) saw a
number of the attainders of 1461 reversed, although the extant
parliament roll does not record that of Sir Edmund Mountford.   A
number of his companions in Henry VI's Household and, later, in

---

38. These are presumably the records noted in Edmund's possession in *C.C.R., 1468–
76*, 367–68.

39. Wedgwood, *Biographies*, 603.

40. See the source mentioned above n.11, and C.L. Scofield, *The Life and Reign of
Edward the Fourth* (2 vols., London, 1923), I, 186, 252, 301, 368.

41. This was established by Pugh, *Marcher Lordships*, 295. Edmund took advantage
of Henry VI's readeption and had returned to Westminster by March 1471; he may even
have stayed in England and taken his chances with the restored Edward IV: *C.C.R., 1468–
76*, 178. See Wedgwood, *Biographies*, 602–3, and Roskell, *Commons*, 205, for the erroneous belief that he landed with Henry Tudor.

42. C.D. Ross, *Edward IV* (London, 1974), 64–68, 183–84.

exile availed themselves of the king's generosity, including Sir William Grimsby, Sir Richard Tunstall and Dr. John Morton. Sir Edmund probably did so too by means of the petition printed below.[43] His petition to the king expressed contrition for the treason he had committed and pledged his loyalty for the future; these sentiments were a prelude to a plea for forgiveness and the reversal of his attainder. Only when that was conceded could Sir Edmund return to England and enjoy his properties. The petition elicited a favourable response, as did those of his fellow Lancastrian partisans enrolled on the parliament roll. The price was a high one: Sir Edmund was required to acknowledge the position of Sir Simon Mountford, who had occupied Coleshill and Ilmington since 1461; his continued enjoyment of these properties was safeguarded, as were the rights of his heirs to inherit them.[44] This latter constraint on Sir Edmund's restoration to legal favour was less irksome than might be supposed, for he had apparently never married and therefore had no legitimate heirs of his body. Far less welcome was the provision that no one who had benefited from his forfeited properties since 1461 should be proceeded against in any way in the event of Sir Edmund's restoration. These were important limitations, but necessary ones if social peace were to be preserved and loyal Yorkist supporters not alienated. What Edmund regained, therefore, was not the two Warwickshire manors that had caused the family squabble (they remained with Sir Simon Mountford), but the Berkshire lands of his father, which he seems to have re-acquired by June 1478, when Sir Edmund nominated a fresh group of feoffees to replace those (now mostly dead) of the 1450s.[45] Sir Simon was not quite so easily placated, for before 1482 he had attempted to dispossess the occupants of Ramenham manor. An arbitration award soon afterwards re-established peace between uncle and nephew, in all probability leaving this manor in Sir Edmund's hands.[46]

This precaution taken, Edmund could resume his public career in England. He did so by joining the household of the grandson of the duke of Buckingham who had acted as his feoffee in the 1450s. Henry, duke of Buckingham was employing him as steward of his Household by 1475 and in the following year sent him to the Stafford lordship of Newport as an itinerant justice.[47] He survived

43. *Rot. Parl.*, VI, 16–23, 24–33, 43–48; Ross, *Edward IV*, 184; below 381–2. For Grimsby and Tunstall, see Wedgwood, *Biographies*, 400–1, 882–83.
44. Sir Simon held both Coleshill and Ilmington at the time of his execution in 1495: *C.P.R., 1494–1509*, 65, 73.
45. Westminster Abbey MS. 4551. Simon was described as of Coleshill in April 1488 (*C.C.R., 1485–1500*, 84), and when Edmund died in 1494 he held lands at Henley-on-Thames in Oxfordshire (*C.F.R., 1485–1509*, 198; Wedgwood, *Biographies*, 602–3). These latter were in addition to the Berkshire estates of his father William (*C.F.R., 1452–61*, 2).
46. Westminster Abbey MSS. 4554, 4546, 4542, 4531. Although the arbitration (referred to in *ibid.*, 4545, which is a bond of Sir Edmund's in £500 that he would abide by the award) is undated, the assignment of the manor to Sir Edmund's feoffees on 10 August 1482 is likely to have been its outcome.
47. Pugh, *Marcher Lordships*, 295.

Buckingham's rebellion against Richard III in 1483, securing a general pardon from the king on 18 November 1484. He remained in Stafford service after the accession of Henry VII, in whose first parliament in 1485—86 the reversal of the 1461 attainder was reiterated (although no mention was then made of Edward IV's reversal).[48]　Right from the beginning of the first Tudor's reign, Sir Edmund may be observed acting as steward of the lordship of Thornbury for Katherine Stafford and her second husband, the new king's uncle, Jasper Tudor, duke of Bedford. As such, he played on active part in the administration of his adopted countryside, Gloucestershire and south-east Wales, in the service of Duke Jasper, who continued the patronage extended to him by the Staffords.　Before Edmund's death early in 1494, he had become the duke's chamberlain.[49]

This striking come-back, to a position at the time of his death which was just as influential as the one he had occupied in 1460, was a direct consequence of the political tergiversations of the 'Wars of the Roses'.　Likewise, Sir Simon Mountford, who had been cajoled into surrendering important claims in the late-1450s, after a period of Yorkist service was brought to the point of rebellion in 1495; again, the dynastic revolutions had been largely responsible. Battles and executions were by no means the only hazard facing the gentlemen who had strong magnate connections and positive political attitudes in the mid-15th century. Nor were these attitudes solely — or even primarily — formed by events at Westminster; they were born of the interaction of personal concerns and ambitions with wider opportunities and connections.　Had Sir Edmund Mountford not been sponsored by King Henry and some of his ministers, it is doubtful if Sir Simon Mountford would have sought the patronage of Warwick and others or espoused the cause of Edward IV so eagerly.　Such was the essence of civil strife, as the study of the 'anarchy' of King Stephen's reign has already demonstrated.[50]

The efforts of these two men to seek redress and pardon from King Edward throws an additional shaft of light on the business conducted in his parliaments.　Neither of the two parliamentary petitions printed below is likely to have been the original available to (but ignored by) the clerk who compiled the parliament roll, if only because no comment or answer appears on them. They are more likely to be contemporary copies made at Westminster for retention in the Mountford family archives. The first petition is addressed to the Commons; the second is addressed to the king for presentation first to the Lords. The last document amounts to

　　48.　*Rot. Parl.*, VI, 278—79.
　　49.　Wedgwood, *Biographies*, 602—3; Thomas, thesis cited, 269.
　　50.　R.H.C. Davis, 'What happened in Stephen's reign, 1135—54', *History*, XLIX (1964), 9—11.

an amendment to the second petition after it had been approved, and its length explains its existence as a separate document rather than as a comment incorporated in the petition itself.[51] These Mountford petitions modestly extend the source-material available for the study of 15th-century parliaments and demonstrate the nature of the parliament rolls as an imperfect record of what took place during the sessions.

51. H.L. Gray, *The Influence of the Commons on Early Legislation* (Harvard, 1932), 11, 49–54.

DOCUMENTS

I.   Birmingham Public Library, A.590.

To the full discrete Comeyns in this present parliament assembled. Sheweth unto your grete Wysdoms Baldewyn Mountfort knyght and Symond his sone knyght. For asmyche as where Willyam Mountford knyght fader to the same Baldewyn was seased of the manors of Colshull and Ilmyndon with thappurtenaunces withinne the shire of Warrewyk and of thavouson of the church of Ilmyndon aforeseid to him and to his heires of his body begoten, as by severall gyftes by fynes and dedes therof made redy to be shewyd more openly appereth, which Willyam after the deth of Margret moder of the seid Baldewyn toke to wife one Jahane and had issue by hir one Edmond Mountfort kerver to Henry late in dede and not in right kynge of Ingland the sixth. And the seid Willyam at the laboures and desire of the seid Jahan and Edmond entendyng by alle his power to enherite the same Edmond in the seid manors discontynued his seid astate of the same maners and by fyne toke astate of theym to him and to the seid Jahan and to the heires of theire bodies begoten, which astate so had by discontynuaunce the seid Willyam in dyvers parliamentes laboured to have hadde auctorised, approved and affermed to the fynall disheritson of the seid Baldewyn and his heires. And also the same Jahane and Edmond after the deth of the seid Willyam, of the seid maners of Colshulle and Ilmyndon enfeoffed Humfrey late Duke of Bokyngham and James late Eorle of Wiltshire and dyvers other persones to the seid Baldewyn unknowen and theruppon by myght and favour of the seid pretensed kynge the same late Duke and Eorle sewyd dyvers accions of forsible entre and trespas agenst the seid Baldewyn and Symond and arted

theyme to plete suche matiers as to the seid late Duke, Eorle and
Edmond liked, and theym tried agenst the seid Baldewyn and
Symond, and afterward theire seid triall affermed by an atteynt and
also compelled the seid Baldewyn utterly to relece his right of the
seid manors to the seid late Duke and Eorle and also kepped the
seyd Symond in prison longe tyme be cause he wold not relece in
like wise and now a little before the goyng of the seid Edmond
Mountfort into the North with the seid pretensed kynge the same
Edmond moved in conscience of his seid laboures agenst the seid
Baldewyn and Symond of the seid manors with thappurtenaunces
by thassent of the seid Baldewyn enfeoffed the seid Symond of the
seid manors with thappurtenaunces to have to him and to his heires
and theruppon utterly renouncyd his pretence and clayme in theyme
and required the feoffees of the seid manors to relece theire right
in the seid manors to the seid Symond and his heires dyvers of which
feoffees sithen soo have done. Wherfore that it[1] wold like you to
pray the kynge oure liege lord by thassent of the lordes spirituels
and temporell in this present parlyament assembled and by auctorite
of the same to ordeyne, establisse and enacte that almaner feoffe-
mentes, grauntes, astates, releces and confirmacions made by the
seid Johane and Edmond or any of theyme to eny other persone
or persones, thenne to the seid Symond of the seid manors or eny of
theyme or eny parcell of theyme sythen the deth of the seid Willyam
Mountford. And also that almaner triels and rekeverees in the name
of the seid late Duke, Eorle and Edmond or eny of theyme by eny
other persone or persones to the use of the seid Edmond touching
the seid manors or eny of theyme or eny parcell of theyme hadde
be utterly voyde and of none effect. And that the same Symond
and his heires considered the feoffement made unto him of the seid
manors with thappurtenaunces by the seid Edmond by thassent and
agrement of the seid Baldewyn may have, kepe, enioye and reteyne
the forseid manors and avouson aforeseid with the appurtenaunces
and everyche of theyme and every parcell of theyme as to the seid
Baldewyn from the seid William Mountfort in case he hadde dyed
seased of the same manors and avouson with thappurtenaunces and
no discontynuaunce therof hadde be made of eny suche astate as
shuld have descendyd accordying to his iuste and trewe title of
theyme discharged of almaner charges and execucions hadde, made
and done by eny persone or persones sith the dethe of the seyd
Willyam Mountfort ayell to the seyd Symond.

---

[1] Interlineated.

II. W. Dugdale, *The Antiquities of Warwickshire*, 2nd. edn. (2 vols., London, 1730), II, 1010–11, from the archives of Simon Mountford of Bescot (Staffs.) in 1656.

. . . . Foresien alwey that this Act of atteynder in noo wise hurt nor prejudice the right, title, nor possession of Symond Mountfort esquire of, in, nor for the Mannours of Colshull and Ilmyndon in the Shire of Warrewyk, and the Manor of Rampnam in Berkshire, and the advouson of the Churches of the same Manors, with their appurtenances, parcells, and members; nor any of them, nor any parcell of them: nor the right, title, or possession of eny persone or persones having joynt estate in the said Manors or eny of them with the seide Simond; nor the right, title, nor possession of any persone or persones having estate in the seid Manors, or any of them, to the use of Baldewyn Mountfort Knight, fader of the seide Simond, nor eny of them, nor their heirs nor assignes, nor eny of the heires of the seide Baldewin or Simond; which Manors bin entailled on the heirs of the body of the seide Baldewyn begotten, as openly appeareth by evidens thereof redy to be shewed; for the disheryting of which Baldewyn and Symond of the seide Manors, Edmond Mountfort Kt. Karver to Henry the vi[th] late K. of England, in dede and not of right, by the favour and might of the seide late soo King, Humphrey late D. of Buck. and James late Earl of Wilteshire, be full unconsciensly moynes long time laboured, as opunly is known to many of the estates and worshipfull peopul of this Royalme, to the utterst empoverishing of the same Baldewyn and Simond.

III. Dugdale, *Antiquities*, II, 1011, from the archives of Simon Mountford of Bescot (Staffs.) in 1656.

To all true Cristen pepull to whom this present writinge shall come, Baldewyn Mountfort Kt. and Prest, sendeth greting, etc. Know ye me the foreseyd Baldewyn being in my good heele and good mynd, the day of the making hereof, at Hampton in Arderne, to say, testifye, and report for trouthe, there being present the Priour of Maxstoke, with many other, that all such Obligations, Recoveres, Relees, or other writings which y made to Humfrey late D. of Buck., Humfrey late Lord of Stafford, and James late Erle of Wiltes. or to Sir Edm. Mountfort my brother, or eny of them, for or of the Manours of Coleshull, Ilmyndon, Rampnam, or eny other parcell of my livelode, which was late Sir Will. Mountfort's my fader's, hit was done by compulcion of the seid Duke, and for fere of my deth, and of my son Sir Simond's: for in trouth the seid Duke keped me in Coventre .xiiii. deyes, and aftir had me to the Castel of Maxstoke, and there kept me. And my son Sir Symond was put in the Castell of Gloucester, and we coude never be delivered out, till we agreed to certain Articles written in a Bill anexid to this my writinge; which Articles were send bi the seid Duke and Edmond, under the Seale of the said Edmond, to my seid son, when he was in prison in the seid Castel of Gloucester, rehersyng that we should suffer Recoveres to be had ayeyne us, such as the late Duke, Earl of Stafford, and Earl of Wiltshire, or Edm. Mountfort, by the advice of their Councell cowde or would devise for their profet; and also to relece all our right, which we had in the seid Mannors, to the same Duke, and other above rehersed, and to do other things, as hit appeareth more plainly in the seid Bill; or els my seid son should never have comen out of Prison, nor y should not have abidden in my Country, but to have had and to have stonden in the indignacion of the Lordship of the seid Duke, and other Lords above rehirsed, which in thoo deys had byn too hevy and too importable for me or my seid son to have boren.

By the which Recoveres, Relece, and Obligations, so had and made by compulcion, the seid Edmund my brother would disherit me and mine yssue for ever, contrarie to right and consciens, God knoweth: For in trouth, where the seid Duke seid, that and if eny man would sey and prove, that eny of the seid Manors were entailled to me the seid Sir Baldwyn, eyther by Dede or by Fyne, he wold not be about to disherit me, nor myne heires for M.l. [£1,000] and my Lady of Buckingham affirmed, and seys the same since the deth of my seid Lord, late her husband: all that notwithstanding, the seid Edmond my brother, at the time of the seid Releces or Obligations made, or eny Recoveres had ayeyne me of the seid Manors, had in his kepinge all the evidences concerning the seid Manors, and he sware himself, and caused me to swere, and my brother the Parson, and Robert, before the seid Duke, that we saw never Dede of yntaile of the said Manors nor Fyne, whereby they should be entayled; where, that, indeed, the seid Sir Edmund was forsworn, and caused me and my Brether to be forsworn; for he had at that time divers Dedes and Fynes in his kepyng, whereby the seid Manors were and are yntailed, which byn now redy to shew.

Wherefore I the seid Sir Baudwyn, in my last deyes, requier and charge yow that be presente at the making hereof, that ye informe, in that ye may, my seid Lady of Buckingham, and my yonge Lord of Buck. and all other Gentilmen and good men of this Countrey, that the seid Manors bin entaylled to me both by Dede and by Fyne; which Dedes and Fynes I shew you here at this time, to the intent that my Children may have their livelode according to the taille, and as right and good consciens will, so that they be no disherit by the hiding of the seid Dedes and Fynes, and the colour and craft of my seid Brother Sir Edmond, being about to hurt, not onely his own soul, but the soules of the seid good Lord, late D. of Buck. and H. late Lord of Stafford his son, and James late Earle of Wiltes. with many other good and well disposid persons, labourers in the same mater, not understanding what they did, God knoweth. In witnes, etc. I have set my Seale and signe manuell at Hampton aboveseid, the Thursday next before S. Hillarie's dey .xlix[th]. H. 6. and of the taking ayene of his royall power the first yeere.

IV.   Birmingham Public Library, A. 591.

To the Kyng oure liege Lorde

Mekely besecheth youre highnesse in the mooste humble wise youre true liegeman Edmond Mountford knyght otherwise called Edmond Mountfort knyght. The whiche Edmond is and during his lyfe shalbe to yowe Souverain Lorde true and feithfull subiecte and liege man. Howe be it that the seid Edmond is nat of power ne may do youre highnesse soo goode service as his hert and wille wolde. For so muche as by force of an acte made in youre parliament holden at Westmynster the iiij[the] day of Novembre, the first yere of youre mooste noble Regne, hit was ordeigned that the same Edmond by the name of Edmond Mountfort knyght shuld stand and be convict of high treson. And by force of the same acte the same Edmond to forfaite to youre highnesse all castels, maners, landes, lordeshippes, tenementes, rentes, servises, fees, advowsons, hereditamentes and possessions with their appurtenaunces, whiche the same Edmond had of estate of enheritaunce or eny other persoone to his use had the iiij[the] day of Marche the first yere of your mooste noble regne or into the whiche the same Edmond or eny other persoone or personnes feoffes to the use of the same Edmond had the said iiij[the] day of Marche lawfull cause of entree within England, Irland, Wales or Caleis or in the marches thereof as in the said acte more pleynly it is conteigned. That it may pleas youre highnesse to consider the premisses and that youre suppliant is nowe sory and repentant of that he hath offend ayenst your royal estate and that he from this day forward entendeth and shalbe to the uttermest of his power your feithfull, true and humble subiect and liegeman. And theruppon of your mooste habundant grace by the advise and assent of the lordes spirituell and temporell and the communes in this present parliament assembled and by auctoritee of the same. To ordeyne, establisshe and enacte that the saide acte and all actes made in the saide parliament holden at Westm' the said iiij[the] day of Novembre ayenst the said Edmond by what name or names he be called or named in the same acte or actes be voide and of no force ner effect ayenst the same Edmond nor his heyres nor ayenst the feoffees to his use nor by reason of eny of the premisses, and that the same Edmond and his heyres by the same auctoritee have, possede, enherite, clayme and enjoye alle castels, maners, landes, lordeshippes, tenementes, rentes, services, fees, advousons, hereditamentes and possessions in lyke maner and fourme as the same Edmond and his heires shuld have doon or had if the same acte or actes never had bene maade ayenst hym. And that the same acte or actes be in no wise preiudice ne hurte unto the same Edmond ne to his heires of and in the premisses or eny of theym. And also to ordeyn by the same auctoritee that the same Edmond and his heyres shold have, holde, possede, clayme, enherite and enjoye all castels, maners, landes, lordeshippes, tenementes, rentes, services, fees, advousons, possessions and hereditamentes with theire appurtenaunces, whiche cam or aught to have comen to your handes by reason of the seid acte or actes made ayenst the seid Edmond or into the whiche the same Edmond or eny other feoffee to his use at the tyme of the seid acte or actes made, had laufull cause of entree, and into theym aswell uppon youre possession Souverain lorde as uppon the possession of every other persoone to entre withoute suyng of theyme or eny of theym oute of youre handes by peticion, liveree or otherwise, and theym to have, holde, enherite and enjoye in lyke maner and fourme as the same Edmond and his heires shold have had or doon if the seid acte or actes never had bene made ayenst the same Edmond, saving to Symond Mountfort knyght and his heires suche accion, right, title and laufull interesse as he therin had the saide iiij[the] day of Marche or eny tyme sithen aswel by your lettres patentes as otherwise. Saving also to every other persoone of your liege people and eche of theym suche right, title and lawfull interesse as they or eny of theym therein had the same iiij[the] day of Marche or eny tyme sithen. And that it be ordeyned by the same auctoritee that no persoone ner persoones whiche have before the first day of this present parliament and after the said iiij[the] day of Marche taken eny issuees or proffites of eny of the landes, tenementes or other of the premisses be therof enpeched ne chargeable to the said Edmond ner his heires ne to eny other feoffee or feoffees to the use of the same Edmond by wey of accion or otherwise. Provided alway that noo persoone ner persoones atteynted ner their heires have, take or enjoye eny avauntage, benefice or profit by this present acte but oonly the said Edmond and his heires, and the feoffees to the use of the same Edmond for and in the premisses oonly, which the same feoffees had to the use of the same Edmond and the said iiij[the] day of Marche or eny tyme sithen. And your said suppliaunt shal ever prey to god for the preservacion of youre royall estate.

V.   Birmingham Public Library, A. 592.

Hit be ordeyned by the seid auctorite that neither this acte nor any other acte or ordinaunce made or to be made for the seid Edmond Mountfort knyght[1] in this present parliament in any wise extend ne be not preiudiciall to Symon Mountfort knyght, his heirez nor any feoffeez to his use into or for any manorz, londes, tenementes, rents, servicez, possessions and enheritauncez or any parcell of theym, wherof the seid Symon or any other persone or persones to his use were seised or possessed in any wise the seid iiij[th] day of Marche the foreseyd first yere or any tyme sithen.

---

[1] Interlineated.

[A few supporting details are in Ian Rowney, 'Government and Patronage in the fifteenth century: Staffordshire, 1439-59', *Midland History*, VIII (1983), 49-69.]

Index

25
30 — 1